HEILONGJIANG
70-71

Helong

Jiang

JILIN
66-67

INNER MONGOLIA) AUTONOMOUS REGION

LIAONING
62-63

NER MONGOLIA) AUTONOMOUS REGION
58-59

He (Yellow R.)

BEIJING
MUN.
36-37

TIANJIN MUN.
42-43

Bo Hai

HEBEI
48-49

SHANXI
54-55

Huang He (Yellow R.)

SHANDONG
102-103

Yellow Sea

AANXI
156-157

HENAN
106-107

Jinghang Yunhe (Grand Canal)

JIANGSU
80-81

ANHUI
90-91

SHANGHAI MUN.
74-75

G MUN.

HUBEI
110-111

Chang Jiang (Yangtze R.)

Chang Jiang (Yangtze R.)

133

ZHEJIANG
84-85

East China Sea

JIANGXI
98-99

HUNAN
114-115

Chihwei Yu

Tiaoyu Tao

FUJIAN
94-95

Taiwan Haixia

TAIWAN
186-187

Taiwan Tao

XI ZHUANG
MOUS REGION
24-125

GUANGDONG
118-119

Xi Jiang

HONG KONG SAR
176-177

MACAU SAR
182-183

Dongsha Qundao

South China Sea

HAINAN
128-129

Hainan Dao

South China Sea Islands

GUANGXI ZHUANG
AUTONOMOUS REGION
124-125

GUANGDONG
118-119

FUJIAN
94-95

TAIWAN

Taiwan Tao

HONG KONG SAR
176-177

MACAU SAR
182-183

Dongsha Qundao

HAINAN
28-129

Hainan Dao

Xisha Qundao

Zhongsha Qundao

South China Sea

Nansha Qundao

Zengmu Ansha

ATLAS OF CHINA

 SINOMAPS PRESS

图书在版编目（CIP）数据

中国地图集＝Atlas of China／杜秀荣主编．－北京：

中国地图出版社，2006.7

ISBN 978－7－5031－4178－2

Ⅰ.中... Ⅱ.杜... Ⅲ.地图集－中国 Ⅳ.K992

中国版本图书馆CIP数据核字（2006）第045714号

ATLAS OF CHINA

Published and distributed by SinoMaps Press

(3 Baizhifang Xijie, Beijing, 100054 China)

210 x 297　18 Printed sheets

1st Edition, 1st Impression　Jan. 2007

ISBN 978-7-5031-4178-2/K · 2456　Impression 00001-10000

GS (2006)369　Price: RMB160.00

The national boundaries of China in this Atlas are drawn after the 1:4M
Relief Map of the People's Republic of China, published by SinoMaps Press in 1989

Printed in the People's Republic of China

CONTENTS

Pages		Scale
2-3	Satellite Image	1 : 16 000 000
4-5	Geographical Location	1 : 100 000 000
6-7	Administrative Divisions	1 : 20 000 000
8-9	Ethnic Groups	1 : 16 000 000
10-11	Population	1 : 16 000 000
12-13	Relief	1 : 16 000 000
14-15	Climate（Ⅰ）	
	Annual average Temperature	1 : 20 000 000
	Average Temperature,Jan.,Apr.,Jul.,Oct.	1 : 40 000 000
16-17	Climate（Ⅱ）	
	Annual Precipitation	1 : 20 000 000
	Precipitation, Jan.,Apr.,Jul.,Oct.	1 : 40 000 000
18-19	River System	1 : 16 000 000
20-21	Land Cover	1 : 16 000 000
22-23	Mineral Resources	1 : 16 000 000
24-25	Environmental Protection	1 : 16 000 000
26-27	Communications（Ⅰ）	1 : 16 000 000
28-29	Communications（Ⅱ）	1 : 16 000 000
30-31	Tourist Resources	1 : 16 000 000
32-33	Bo Hai,Yellow Sea & East China Sea	1 : 7 000 000
34-35	South China Sea	1 : 7 000 000
36-37	Beijing Municipality	1 : 700 000
38-39	Downtown Beijing	
40-41	Beijing	
42-43	Tianjin Municipality	1 : 520 000
44-45	Downtown Tianjin	
46-47	Tianjin & Tanggu	
48-49	Hebei Province	1 : 2 100 000
50-51	Shijiazhuang	
52-53	Bo Hai Coastal Region	1 : 2 000 000
54-55	Shanxi Province	1 : 1 800 000
56-57	Taiyuan	
58-59	Nei Mongol (Inner Mongolia) Autonomous Region	1 : 6 500 000
60-61	Hohhot	
62-63	Liaoning Province	1 : 2 100 000
64-65	Shenyang	
66-67	Jilin Province	1 : 2 400 000
68-69	Changchun	
70-71	Heilongjiang Province	1 : 3 800 000
72-73	Harbin	
74-75	Shanghai Municipality	1 : 520 000
76-77	Downtown Shanghai	
78-79	Shanghai	
80-81	Jiangsu Province	1 : 1 800 000
82-83	Nanjing	
84-85	Zhejiang Province	1 : 1 800 000
86-87	Hangzhou	
88-89	Changjiang (Yangtze R.) Delta	1 : 1 100 000
90-91	Anhui Province	1 : 1 800 000
92-93	Hefei	

94-95	Fujian Province	1 : 1 800 000
96-97	Fuzhou	
98-99	Jiangxi Province	1 : 1 800 000
100-101	Nanchang	
102-103	Shandong Province	1 : 1 800 000
104-105	Jinan	
106-107	Henan Province	1 : 2 100 000
108-109	Zhengzhou	
110-111	Hubei Province	1 : 2 100 000
112-113	Wuhan	
114-115	Hunan Province	1 : 2 100 000
116-117	Changsha	
118-119	Guangdong Province	1 : 2 400 000
120-121	Guangzhou	
122-123	Zhujiang Delta	1 : 950 000
124-125	Guangxi Zhuang Autonomous Region	1 : 2 400 000
126-127	Nanning	
128-129	Hainan Province	1 : 1 000 000
130-131	Haikou	
132-133	Chongqing Municipality	1 : 1 800 000
134-135	Downtown Chongqing	
136-137	Chongqing	
138-139	Sichuan Province	1 : 3 500 000
140-141	Chengdu	
142-143	Chengdu-Chongqing Region	1 : 1 100 000
144-145	Guizhou Province	1 : 2 100 000
146-147	Guiyang	
148-149	Yunnan Province	1 : 3 500 000
150-151	Kunming	
152-153	Xizang (Tibet) Autonomous Region	1 : 5 000 000
154-155	Lhasa	
156-157	Shaanxi Province	1 : 2 400 000
158-159	Xi'an	
160-161	Gansu Province	1 : 4 000 000
162-163	Lanzhou	
164-165	Qinghai Province	1 : 3 500 000
166-167	Xining	
168-169	Ningxia Hui Autonomous Region	1 : 1 200 000
170-171	Yinchuan	
172-173	Xinjiang Uygur Autonomous Region	1 : 6 500 000
174-175	Ürümqi	
176-177	Hong Kong SAR	1 : 200 000
178-179	Northern Hong Kong Island	
180-181	Hong Kong Island · Kowloon	
182-183	Macau SAR	1 : 31 000
184-185	Macau Peninsula	
186-187	Taiwan Province	1 : 1 800 000
188-189	Taipei	
190-283	Index	

LEGEND

GENERAL MAP

◎ **BEIJING** — Capital

⊙ Taiyuan — Province-level administrative center

○ Dandong — Other city

◎ Seoul — Foreign capital

PROVINCIAL MAP

SETTLEMENT

★ **BEIJING** — Capital

▣ **TAIYUAN** — Province-level administrative center

◎ Datong — Prefecture-level administrative center

— Jishou — Administrative center of autonomous prefectures, prefectures and leagues

Shaoshan
⊙ Daxing Qu
Wutai — County-level administrative center (Major city outside China)

○ Yangliuqing — Town,village

◎ **SEOUL** — Foreign capital

COMMUNICATIONS

Under construction
——————— Railway

Under construction
——————— Expressway

—[107]— National road and serial number

——————— Provincial road

——————— Other road

708nm
(1311km) — Shipping route and mileage,nm(km)

✈ — Airport

⚓ — Port

BOUNDARIES

Undefined International boundary
——————— National boundary

——————— Boundary of province, autonomous region and municipality

— — — — Boundary of special adminstrative region

– – – – – Regional boundary

·············· Military demarcation line

HYDROGRAPHY

— Coastline

— Perennial river, waterfall

— Seasonal river, dry river

— Underground river

— Reservoir,dam

Salt   Freshwater — Lake

— Seasonal lake

·············· Canal

——————— Irrigation canal

⚲ ⚲ — Spring,hot spring

○ — Well

TOPOGRAPHY & OTHERS

— Desert

— Gravel desert

— Wind-eroded unaka (monadnock) yardang

— Coral reefs

— Swamp,salt swamp

— Salt field

○ — Karst cave

⚬ — Volcano

1440 ▲ Song Shan — Peak and elevation(m)

✕ — Pass

⌐⌐⌐⌐ — Great Wall

☊ — World Heritage

⊗ — Key national scenic area

✴ — National nature reserve

⚘ — National forest park

☯ — National geological park

CITY MAP

— Street and block

Under construction
—□— Railway,station

Under construction
——————— Subway

Under construction
——————— Electromagnetic railway

Under construction
——————— Expressway

Under construction
——————— Main street,ring road

•————• Cable car

··········· City wall

— — — — District boundary

— Park,green belt

★ — Provincial government

★ — Municipal government

★ — District government

⬥ — Government office

☿ — Hotel,restaurant

◉ — Shop

🏫 — School

◇ — Hospital

○ — Bank

❶ — Insurance agent

✉ — Post office

▱ — Tel. office

✦ — Museum

▣ — Theatre

⬭ — Stadium,gymnasium

✿ — Factory

⊟ — Bus station

⊕ — Airport

⚓ — Port

☆ — Place of interest

• — Others

OCEAN

Ellesmere I.
North Magnetic Pole
(2001)
Queen Elizabeth Is.
E180°W 150°
268

Banks I.
Victoria I.
Pt. Barrow
Beaufort Sea

G r e e n l a n d

Baffin Bay
Baffin I.
Davis Str.

West Siberian Sea
Chukchi Sea
Chukchi Pen.
Kol.
Kamchatskiy
Bering Sea
Vulkan Klyuchevskaya Sopka
4750
Aleutian Is.
Aleutian Trench
Gulf of Alaska
Mt. McKinley
Alaska Range
Alaska Pen.
Rocky Mts.

Great Slave
Great Bear

Arctic Circle
K. Farvel
60°
4316

Hudson Bay

NORTH AMERICA
Labrador Pen.
Labrador Plat.
Ottawa
I. of Newfoundland

Northwest Pacific Basin
Northeast Pacific Basin
6691

Vancouver I.
Mt. Rainier
San Francisco
Great Plains
Appalachian Mts.
Mississippi Plain
Washington
Superior
Michigan
Huron
5778
Arqui dos Açores
Bermuda Is.
North American Basin
Sargasso Sea
30°

Hawaiian Is.
Midway Is.
Oahu
Honolulu
Hawaii
Mauna Loa
4170
5270

Pen. de la Baja
California
Altiplanicie
Mexicana
Ciudad de México
1023
G. of Mexico
Bahama Is.
Cuba
Greater Antilles
Tropic of Cancer
Mid America Trench
Caribbean Sea

West Mariana Basin
Marshall Is.
5631
Central Pacific Basin
7600

Gilbert Is.
5195
Solomon Is.
Tuvalu Is.
Phoenix Is.
Line Is.
Is. des Tuamotu
Is. de la Société
Cook Is.
8868
Arch. de Colón
(Galápagos Is.)
Quito
Equator 0°

PACIFIC OCEAN

Amazon Basin
Llano Orinoco
Guiana Highlands
C. Branco

OCEANIA
Coral Sea
New Caledonia I.
Samoa Is.
Fiji Is.
Tonga Trench
5304
Fiji Sea
Norfolk I.
1088
North I.
Wellington
Mt. Cook
3764
South I.
Chatham Is.
6018
Auckland Is.
Tasman Sea
Lord Howe Rise
Macquarie I.

Peru Basin
6601
Chile
Lima
New Illampu
6421
SOUTH AMERICA
Planalto do Brasil
Brasília

I. de Pascua
East Pacific Rise
4786

Co. Aconcagua
6960
Buenos Aires
Pampas
Tropic of Capricorn
Vol. Llullaillaco
6723
30°
638

Southwest Pacific Basin
5110

Patagonia
Rio Paraná
Is. Malvinas
(Falkland Is.)
I. Grande de
Tierra del Fuego
C. de Hornos
South Georgia
Argentine Basin

Pacific-Antarctic Ridge
Southeast Pacific Basin
4786
8265

Extr. de Magallanes
Drake Passage
South Shetland Is.
Scotia Sea
60°
Antarctic Circle

Ross Sea
Ross I.
Roosevelt I.
E180°W
150
120
90
Marie Byrd Land
Amundsen Sea
Bellingshausen Sea
Antarctic Pen.
Larsen Ice Shelf
Weddell Sea

ANTARCTICA
Ross Ice Shelf
West Antarctica
Ellsworth Land
Ronne Ice Shelf

Symbol	Description
⊛ Beijing	Capital
○ Shanghai	Major city
⊢·⊣	Continental boundary
4786	Depth of sea

Scale 1:100 000 000

0   1000   2000   3000   4000   5000 km

PACIFIC

JAPAN

R.O.KOREA

D.P.R.KOREA

Sea of Japan

Yellow Sea

East China Sea

RYUKYU Is.

TAIWAN

Taipei

Dongsha Qundao

HEILONGJIANG

JILIN

LIAONING

NEI MONGOL (INNER MONGOLIA) ZIZHIQU (Aut.Reg.)

R U S S I A

M O N G O L I A

KAZAKHSTAN

KYRGYZSTAN

UZBEKISTAN

TAJIKISTAN

AFGHANISTAN

PAKISTAN

KASHMIR

INDIA

NEPAL

BHUTAN

BANGLADESH

MYANMAR

XINJIANG UYGUR ZIZHIQU (Aut.Reg.)

XIZANG (TIBET) ZIZHIQU (Aut.Reg.)

QINGHAI

GANSU

NINGXIA HUIZU ZIZHIQU (Aut.Reg.)

SHAANXI

SHANXI

HEBEI

BEIJING

SHANDONG

HENAN

JIANGSU

ANHUI

SHANGHAI SHI

ZHEJIANG

HUBEI

CHONGQING SHI

SICHUAN

GUIZHOU

YUNNAN

HUNAN

JIANGXI

FUJIAN

GUANGDONG

GUANGXI ZHUANGZU ZIZHIQU (Aut.Reg.)

HONG KONG SAR

MACAU SAR

PEOPLE'S REPUBLIC OF CHINA

Beijing

Ulaanbaatar

Astana

Bishkek

Tashkent

New Delhi

Kathmandu

Thimbu

Dhaka

Seoul

Pyongyang

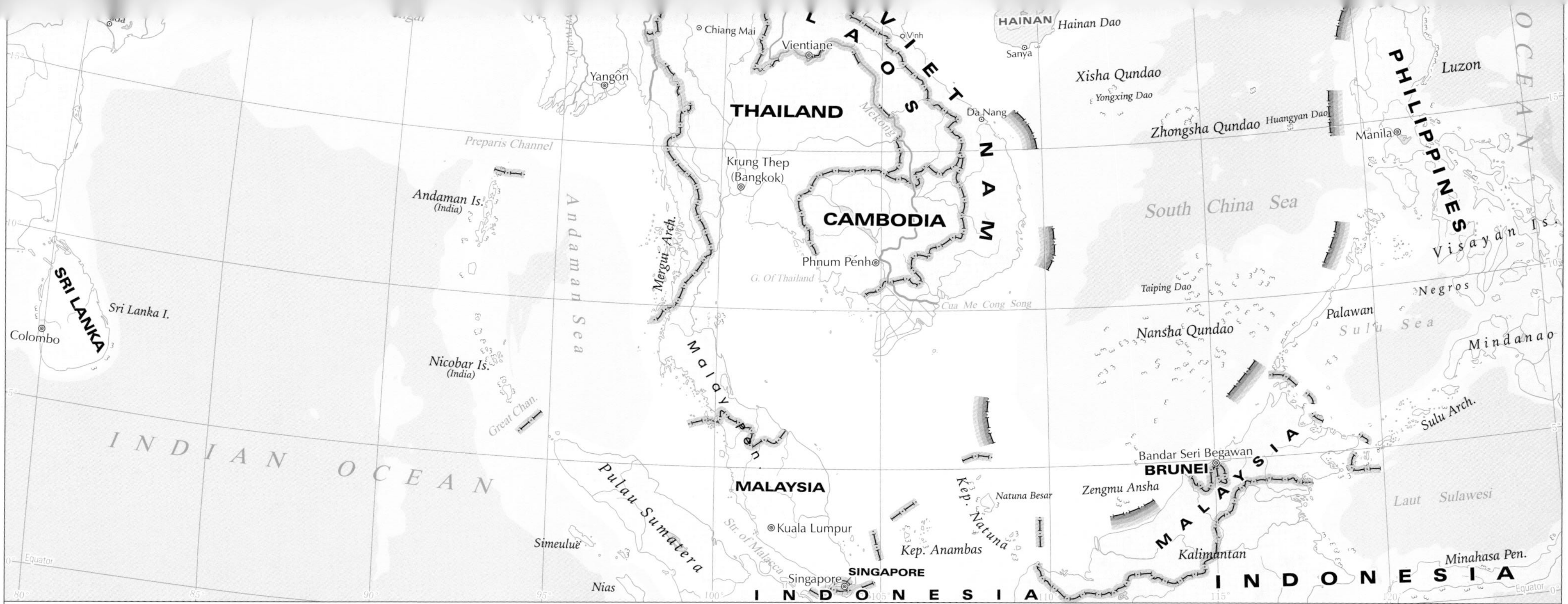

Statistics of Administrative Divisions (Data up to Oct. 31, 2006)

Province-level totals: Mun. 4 · Province 23 · Aut. Reg. 5 · SAR 2

Province-level division	City	Aut. Prefecture	Prefecture	League	District	City	County	Aut. County	Banner	Aut. Banner	Special District	Forest District
	\<Prefecture-level\>				\<County-level\>							
Beijing M.					16		2					
Tianjin M.					15		3					
Hebei Prov.	11				36	22	108	6				
Shanxi Prov.	11				23	11	85					
Nei Mongol Aut. Reg.	9			3	21	11	17		49	3		
Liaoning Prov.	14				56	17	19	8				
Jilin Prov.	8	1			20	20	17	3				
Heilongjiang Prov.	12		1		64	18	45	1				
Shanghai M.					18		1					
Jiangsu Prov.	13				54	27	25					
Zhejiang Prov.	11				32	22	35	1				
Anhui Prov.	17				44	5	56					
Fujian Prov.	9				26	14	45					
Jiangxi Prov.	11				19	10	70					
Shandong Prov.	17				49	31	60					
Henan Prov.	17				50	21	88					
Hubei Prov.	12	1			38	24	37	2				1
Hunan Prov.	13	1			34	16	65	7				
Guangdong Prov.	21				54	23	41	3				
Guangxi Zhuang Aut. Reg.	14				34	7	56	12				
Hainan Prov.	2				4	6	4	6				
Chongqing M.					19	4	17	4				
Sichuan Prov.	18	3			43	14	120	4				
Guizhou Prov.	4	3	2		10	9	56	11			2	
Yunnan Prov.	8	8			12	9	79	29				
Xizang Aut. Reg.	1		6		1	1	71					
Shaanxi Prov.	10				24	3	80					
Gansu Prov.	12	2			17	4	58	7				
Qinghai Prov.	1	6	1		4	2	30	7				
Ningxia Hui Aut. Reg.	5				8	2	11					
Xinjiang Uygur Aut. Reg.	2	5	7		11	20	62	6				
Hong Kong SAR												
Macau SAR												
Taiwan Prov.	Data not available											
Total	283	30	17	3	856	369	1464	117	49	3	2	1
	333				2862							

LEGEND

Symbol	Description
★	Capital
◎	Province-level administrative centre
◎	Prefecture-level city administrative centre (Major city outside China)
○	County-level administrative centre (City or town outside China)
◎	Foreign capital

Scale 1:20 000 000 — 0 200 400 600 800 1000 km

Population of ethnic minorities

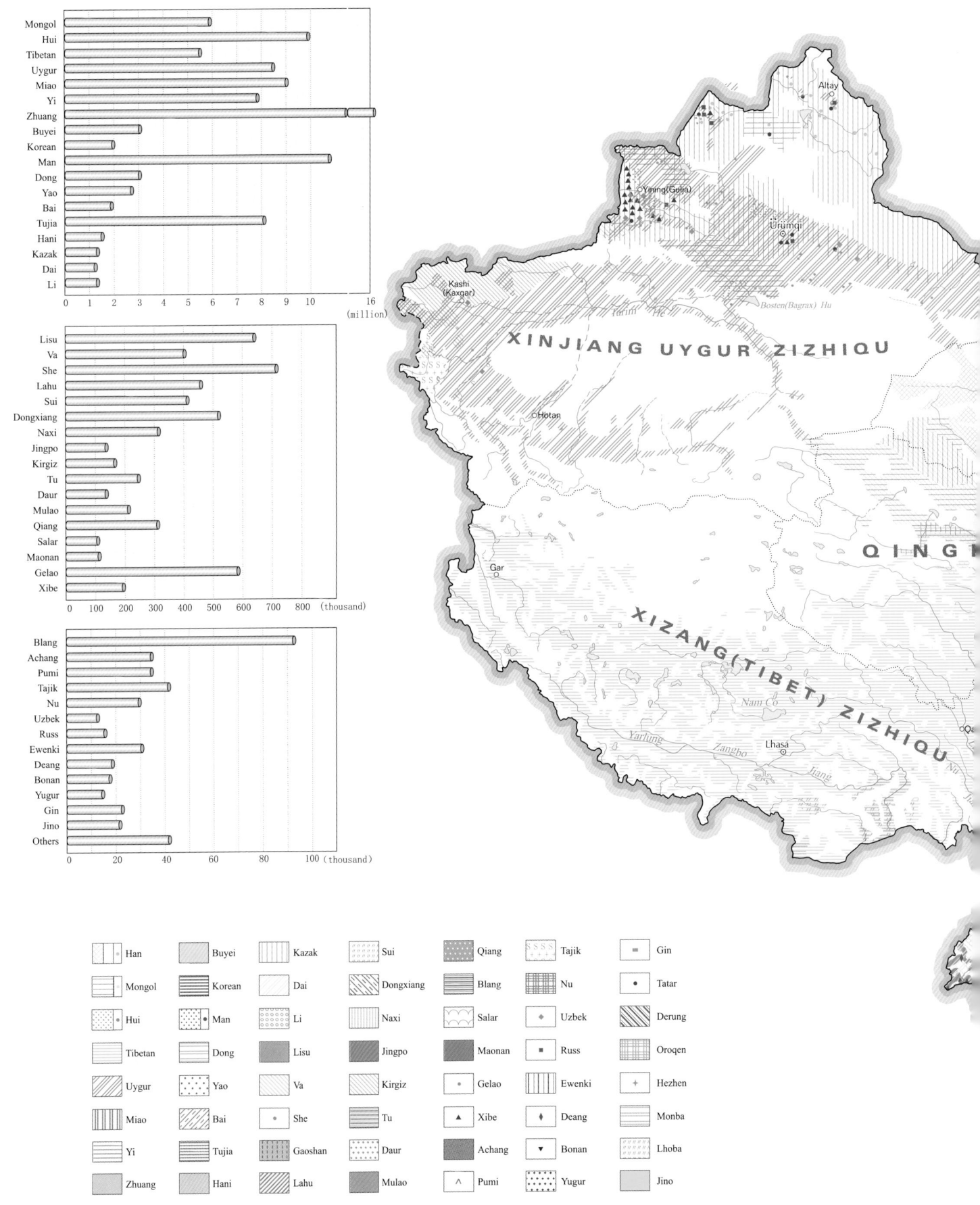

Ethnic composition

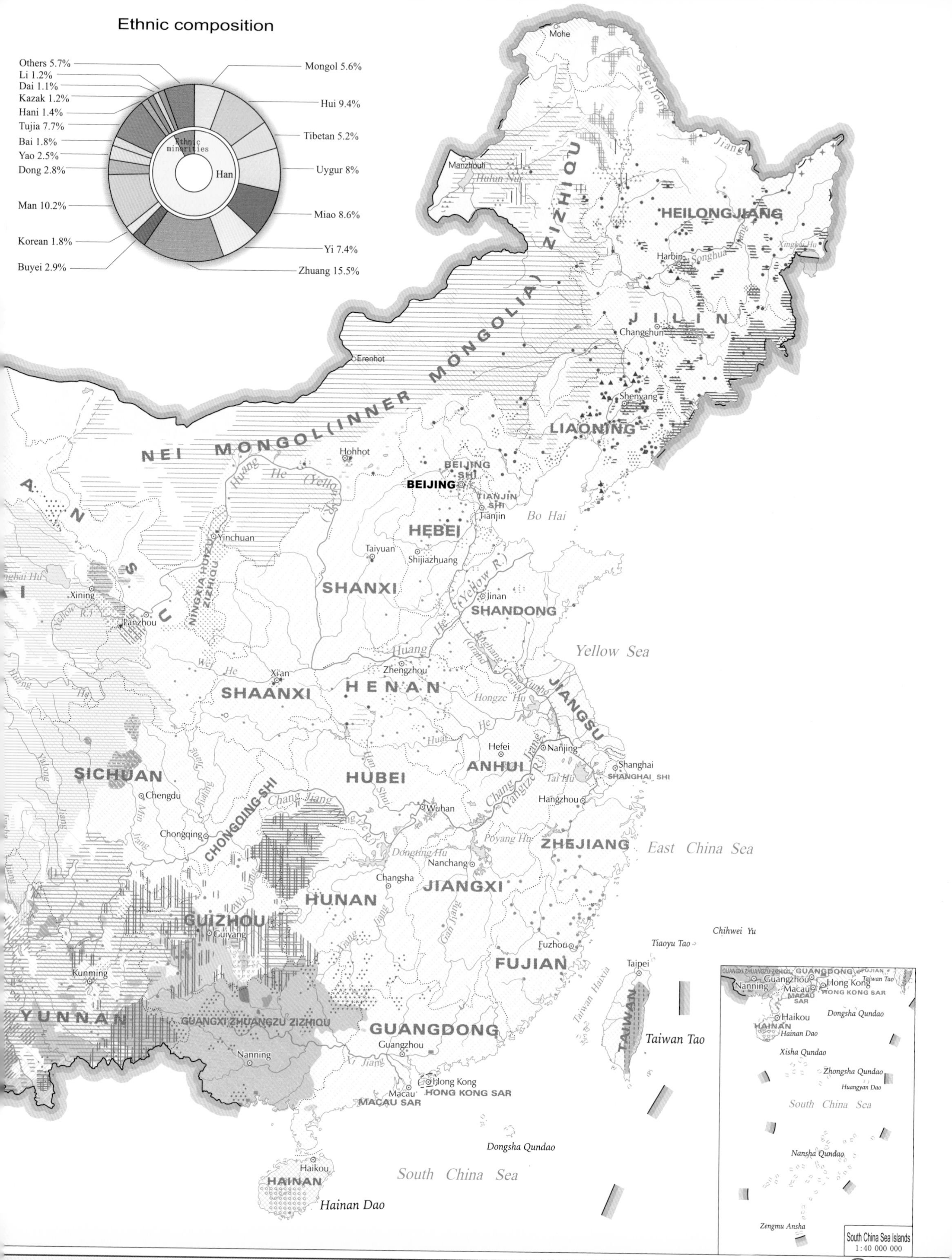

Others 5.7%
Li 1.2%
Dai 1.1%
Kazak 1.2%
Hani 1.4%
Tujia 7.7%
Bai 1.8%
Yao 2.5%
Dong 2.8%

Man 10.2%

Korean 1.8%

Buyei 2.9%

Mongol 5.6%

Hui 9.4%

Tibetan 5.2%

Uygur 8%

Miao 8.6%

Yi 7.4%

Zhuang 15.5%

Ethnic minorities

Han

Mohe

Heilong

HEILONGJIANG

Jiang

Manzhouli

Hulun Nur

Xingkai Hu

Harbin

Songhua

NEI MONGOL (INNER MONGOLIA) ZIZHIQU

JILIN

Changchun

Erenhot

Shenyang

LIAONING

Hohhot

BEIJING SHI

BEIJING

TIANJIN SHI

Bo Hai

Yinchuan

Huang He (Yellow)

Tianjin

HEBEI

NINGXIA HUIZU ZIZHIQU

GANSU

Taiyuan

Shijiazhuang

Xining

SHANXI

Jinan

Xining

Qohow R.

SHANDONG

Lanzhou

Huang He (Yellow R.)

Yellow Sea

Huang He

Xi'an

Zhengzhou

JIANGSU

SHAANXI

HENAN

Hongze Hu

Huang

He

Hefei

Nanjing

Huai

SICHUAN

CHONGQING SHI

HUBEI

ANHUI

Shanghai

Chengdu

Chang Jiang

Wuhan

Han Shui

Chang (Yangtze R.)

Tai Hu

SHANGHAI SHI

Chongqing

Hangzhou

Min Jiang

Poyang Hu

ZHEJIANG

East China Sea

Dongting Hu

Nanchang

Changsha

JIANGXI

Yalong

HUNAN

GUIZHOU

Guiyang

Gan Jiang

FUJIAN

Chihwei Yu

Tiaoyu Tao

Kunming

Fuzhou

Taipei

YUNNAN

GUANGXI ZHUANGZU ZIZHIQU

Xi Jiang

GUANGDONG

Taiwan Haixia

TAIWAN

Taiwan Tao

Nanning

Guangzhou

Taiwan Tao

GUANGXI ZHUANGZU ZIZHIQU

GUANGDONG

FUJIAN

Hong Kong

Nanning

Guangzhou

MACAU SAR

HONG KONG SAR

HAINAN

Haikou

Hainan Dao

Dongsha Qundao

Hong Kong

HONG KONG SAR

Macau

MACAU SAR

Xisha Qundao

Zhongsha Qundao

Huangyan Dao

South China Sea

Dongsha Qundao

HAINAN

Haikou

South China Sea

Nansha Qundao

Hainan Dao

Zengmu Ansha

South China Sea Islands
1:40 000 000

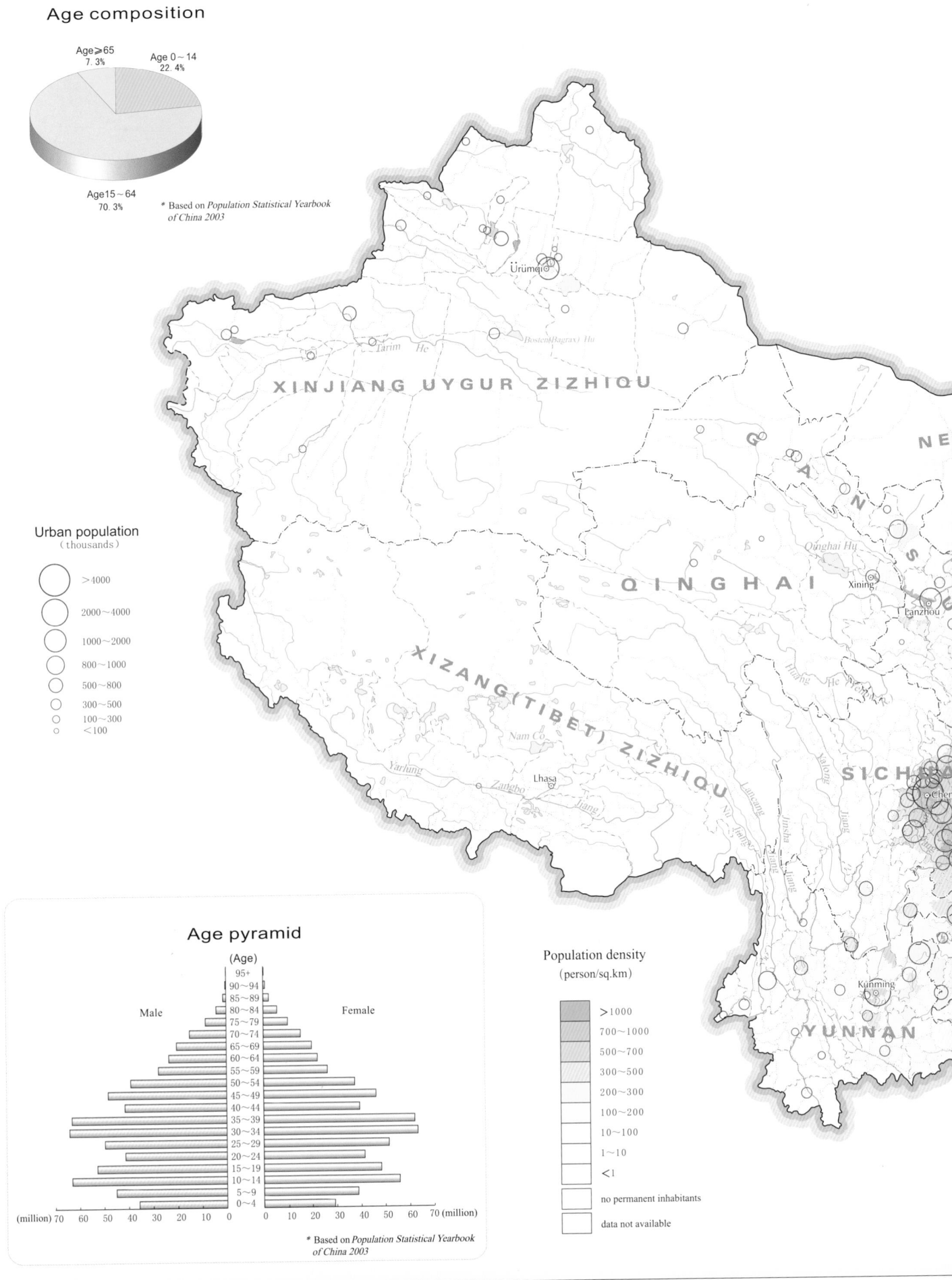

Age composition

Age≥65
7.3%

Age 0~14
22.4%

Age15~64
70.3%

* Based on *Population Statistical Yearbook of China 2003*

Urban population
（thousands）

>4000

2000~4000

1000~2000

800~1000

500~800

300~500

100~300

<100

Population density
(person/sq.km)

>1000

700~1000

500~700

300~500

200~300

100~200

10~100

1~10

<1

no permanent inhabitants

data not available

Age pyramid

(Age)

95+
90~94
85~89
80~84
75~79
70~74
65~69
60~64
55~59
50~54
45~49
40~44
35~39
30~34
25~29
20~24
15~19
10~14
5~9
0~4

Male

Female

(million) 70 60 50 40 30 20 10 0   0 10 20 30 40 50 60 70 (million)

* Based on *Population Statistical Yearbook of China 2003*

XINJIANG UYGUR ZIZHIQU

Ürümqi

Tarim He

Bosten(Bagrax) Hu

QINGHAI

Qinghai Hu

Xining

Lanzhou

XIZANG(TIBET) ZIZHIQU

Nam Co

Yarlung

Zangbo

Lhasa

Jiang

Nu Jiang

Lancang

Jinsha Jiang

Yalong Jiang

Huang He

SICHUAN

Cheng

Kunming

YUNNAN

NEI

G A N S U

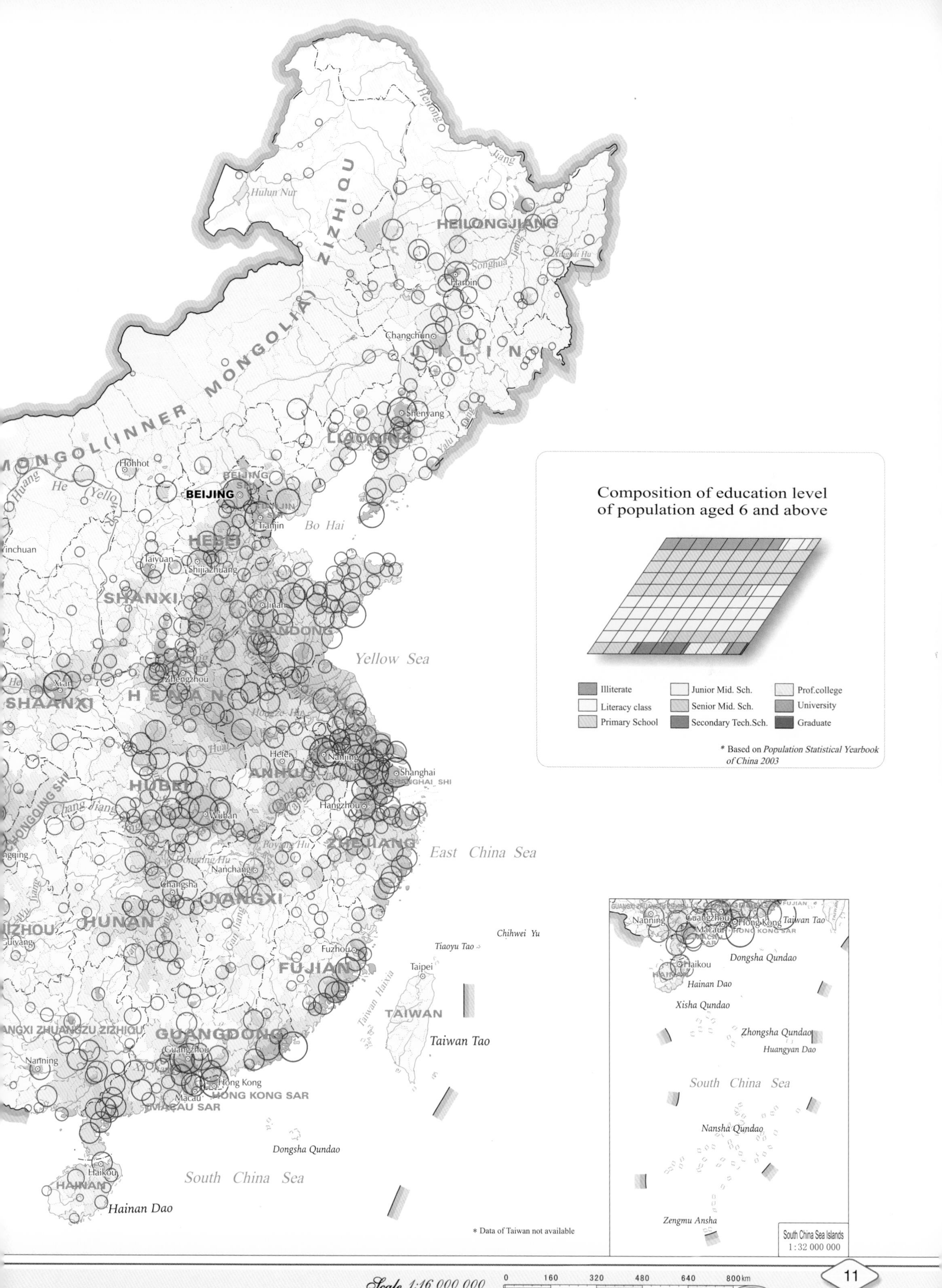

HEILONGJIANG

Hulun Nur

ZIZHIQU

Heilong

Jiang

Songhua

Harbin

Changchun

JILIN

Shenyang

MONGOL (INNER MONGOLIA)

Hohhot

LIAONING

Yalu

MONGOL (INNER MONGOLIA)

BEIJING

BEIJING

TIANJIN

Tianjin

Bo Hai

Huang

He

Yellow

HEBEI

Taiyuan

Shijiazhuang

inchuan

SHANXI

Jinan

SHANDONG

Yellow Sea

He

Xian

ZhengzhouHENAN

SHAANXI

Huang He

CHONGQING SHI

HUBEI

Hefei

Nanjing

ANHUI

Shanghai

Chang Jiang

Wuhan

Hangzhou

SHANGHAI SHI

ngqing

Poyang Hu

Dongting Hu

ZHEJIANG

East China Sea

Changsha

Nanchang

JIANGXI

IZHOU

HUNAN

Chihwei Yu

uyang

Tiaoyu Tao

FUJIAN

Fuzhou

Taipei

ANGXI ZHUANGZU ZIZHIQU

GUANGDONG

Taiwan Haixia

TAIWAN

Taiwan Tao

Nanning

Guangzhou

Hong Kong

HONG KONG SAR

Macau

MACAU SAR

Dongsha Qundao

Haikou

HAINAN

South China Sea

Hainan Dao

* Data of Taiwan not available

Composition of education level of population aged 6 and above

Illiterate	Junior Mid. Sch.	Prof.college
Literacy class	Senior Mid. Sch.	University
Primary School	Secondary Tech.Sch.	Graduate

* Based on *Population Statistical Yearbook of China 2003*

GUANGXI ZHUANGZU   FUJIAN

Nanning

Guangzhou   Hong Kong Taiwan Tao

Macau   HONG KONG SAR

MACAU SAR

Haikou   Dongsha Qundao

HAINAN

Hainan Dao

Xisha Qundao

Zhongsha Qundao

Huangyan Dao

South China Sea

Nansha Qundao

Zengmu Ansha

South China Sea Islands
1 : 32 000 000

Altitude Table 6000 5000 4000 3000 2000 1000 500 200 50 0 100 300 500 750 1000 1500 2000 2500 3000 4000 5000 6000 7000m

Major Mountains

Name	Main Peak	Altitude(m)
Himalayas	Qomolangma Feng	8 844.43
Karakorum Shan	Qogir Feng	8 611
Kunlun Shan	Kongur Shan	7 649
Daxue Shan	Gongga Shan	7 556
Hengduan Shan	Yulong Xueshan	5 596
Tian Shan	Tomür Feng	7 443
Nyainqêntanglha Shan	Nyainqêntanglha Feng	7 162
Gangdisê Shan	Loinbo Kangri	7 095
Tanggula Shan	Gêladaindong Feng	6 621
Hoh Xil Shan	Kangzhag Ri	6 305
Qilian Shan	Qilian Shan	5 547
Bayan Har Shan	Nyainboyuzê Feng	5 369
Altay Shan	Youyi Feng	4 374
Taiwan Shan	Yu Shan	3 952
Qin Ling	Taibai Shan	3 767
Taihang Shan	Xiaowutai Shan	2 882
Yin Shan	Koh Baxig	2 364
Wuyi Shan	Huanggang Shan	2 157
Nan Ling	Mao'er Shan	2 141
Da Hinggan Ling	Huanggang Liang	2 029

Major Plains

Name	Area (sq km)	Altitude (m)
Dongbei Pingyuan	350 000	<200
Huabei Pingyuan	300 000	<100
Changjiang Zhongxiayou Pingyuan	200 000	< 50
Zhujiang Sanjiaozhou	11 000	< 20

Major Plateaus

Name	Area (sq km)	Altitude (m)
Qingzang Gaoyuan	2 500 000	3000~5000
Nei Mongol Gaoyuan	700 000	1000~1500
Yungui Gaoyuan	500 000	1000~2000
Huangtu Gaoyuan	500 000	800~2000

Major Basins

Name	Area (sq km)	Altitude (m)
Tarim Pendi	560 000	778~1300
Junggar Pendi	380 000	500~1000
Qaidam Pendi	255 000	2600~3000
Sichuan Pendi	200 000	300~700

South China Sea Islands
1 : 32 000 000

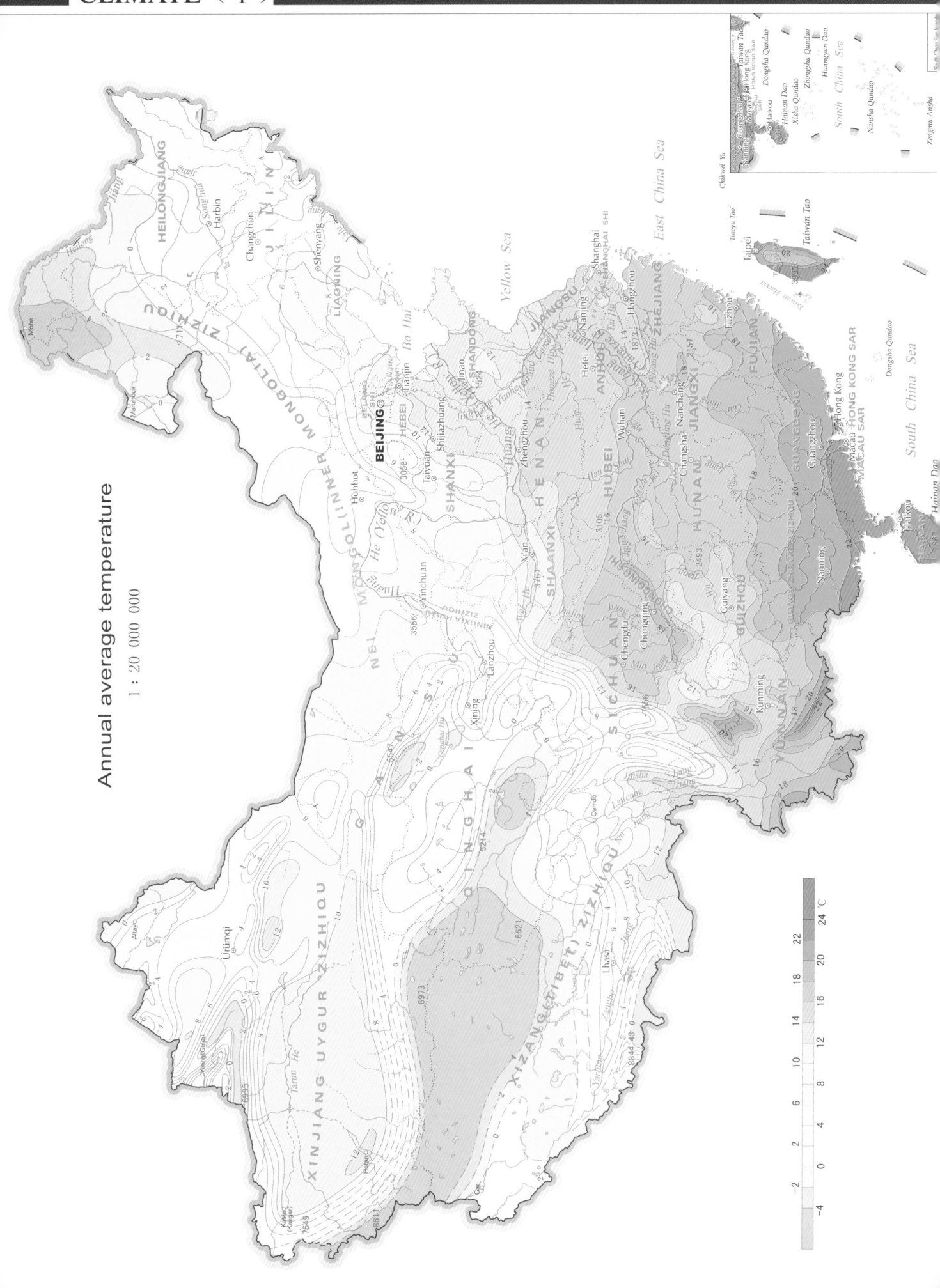

Annual average temperature

1 : 20 000 000

Average temperature, April

1 : 40 000 000

Average temperature, October

1 : 40 000 000

Average temperature, January

1 : 40 000 000

Average temperature, July

1 : 40 000 000

Annual Precipitation

1 : 20 000 000

South China Sea Islands

Dongsha Qundao
Hainan Dao
Xisha Qundao
Zhongsha Qundao
Huangyan Dao
South China Sea
Nansha Qundao
Zengmu Ansha

Chiwei Yu
Taiwan Tao
Tiaoyu Tao
Taipei
Taiwan Haixia

East China Sea

Yellow Sea

Bo Hai

South China Sea

Hainan Dao

HEILONGJIANG
Heilong Jiang
Songhua Jiang
Harbin
JILIN
Changchun
Shenyang
LIAONING
NEI MONGOL (INNER MONGOLIA) ZIZHIQU
Mohe
Manzhouli
Hohhot
Yinchuan
NINGXIA HUIZU ZIZHIQU
Lanzhou
GANSU
Xining
Qinghai Hu
QINGHAI
Golmud
XIZANG (TIBET) ZIZHIQU
Lhasa
Zangbo
Yarlung
Gar
Hotan
Tarim He
XINJIANG UYGUR ZIZHIQU
Ürümqi
Aksu
Yongingtoulai
Kashi (Kangar)

BEIJING
TIANJIN
HEBEI
Shijiazhuang
Taiyuan
SHANXI
Huang He (Yellow R.)
Jinan
SHANDONG
Zhengzhou
HENAN
Xian
SHAANXI
Wei He
Jialing Jiang
Chengdu
SICHUAN
Chongqing
Yunnan
Kunming
GUIZHOU
Guiyang
GUANGXI ZHUANGZU ZIZHIQU
Nanning
Min Jiang
Jinsha Jiang
Lancang Jiang

Shanghai Shi
Shanghai
JIANGSU
Nanjing
ANHUI
Hefei
Yangtze (Chang Jiang)
Wuhan
HUBEI
Changsha
HUNAN
JIANGXI
Nanchang
Hangzhou
ZHEJIANG
FUJIAN
Fuzhou
GUANGDONG
Guangzhou
Hong Kong
HONG KONG SAR
Macau
MACAU SAR
Haikou

25 50 75 150 300 600 1000 1200 1400 1600 1800 2000 2500 3000 4000 mm

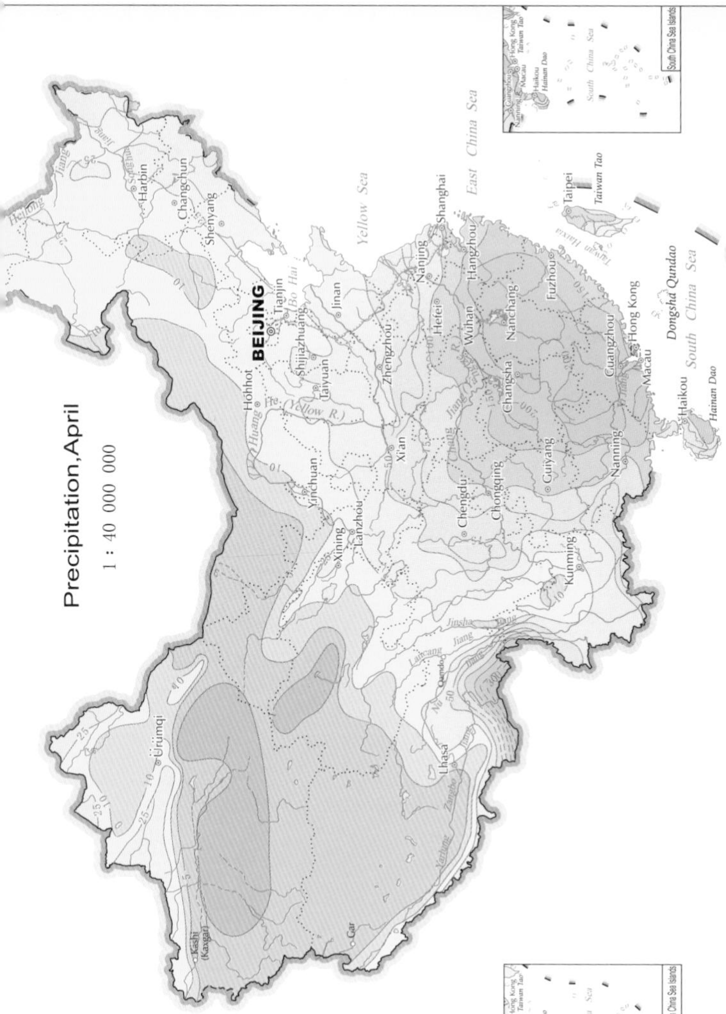

Precipitation, April

1 : 40 000 000

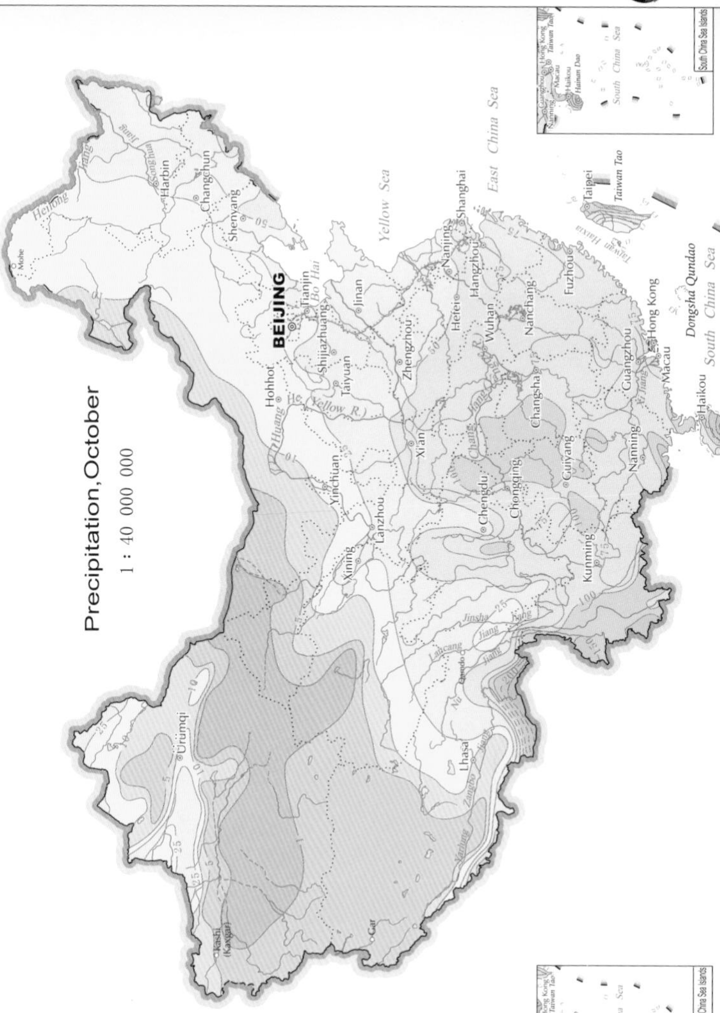

Precipitation, October

1 : 40 000 000

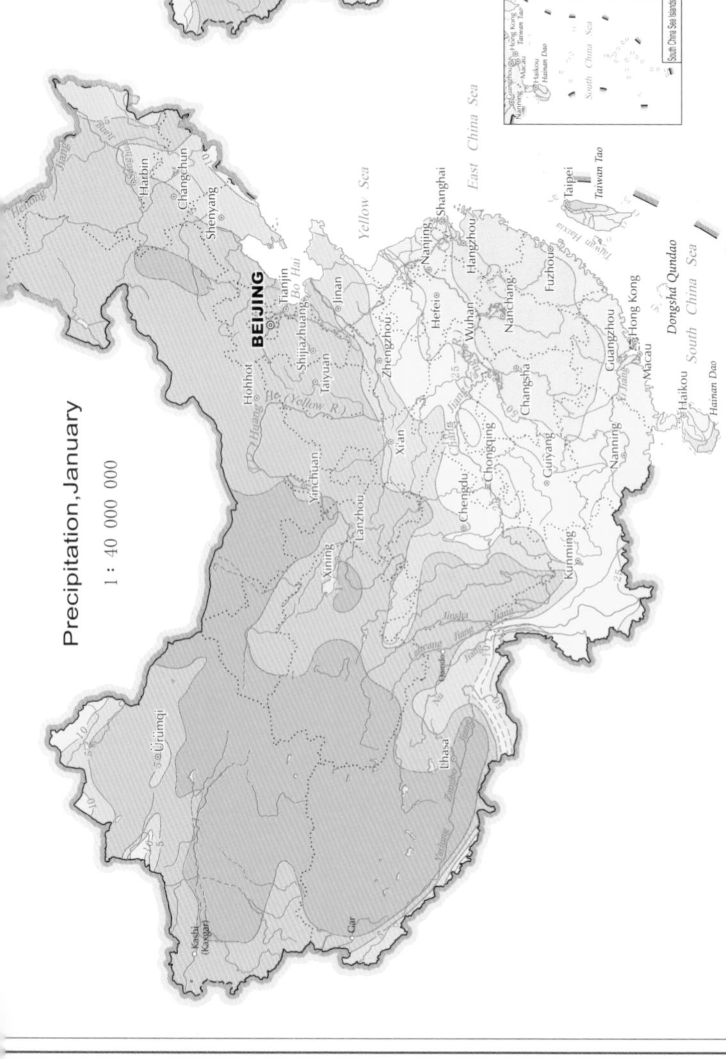

Precipitation, January

1 : 40 000 000

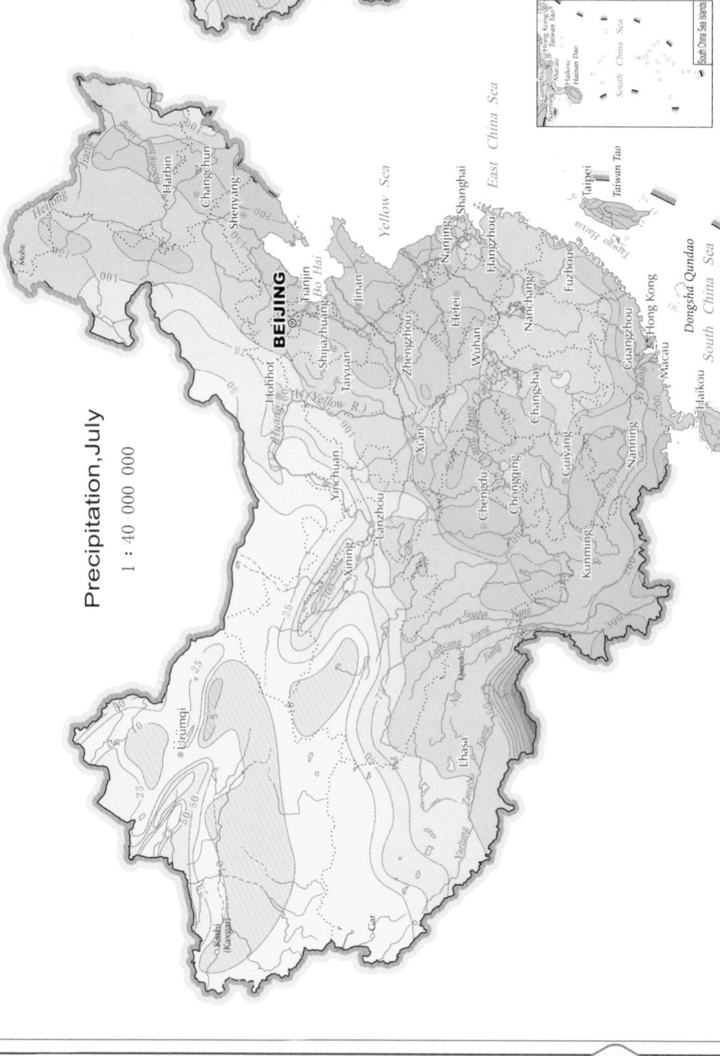

Precipitation, July

1 : 40 000 000

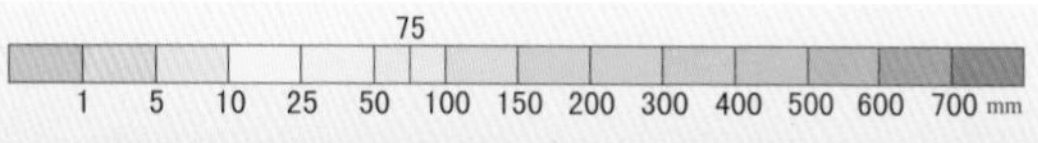

75

1   5   10   25   50   100 150 200 300 400 500 600 700 mm

TOSHKENT

BISHKEK

ULAANBAATAR

ISLĀMĀBĀD

NEW DELHI

KATHMANDU

THIMBU

HA NOI

VIENTIANE

Oz. Balkhash

Ertysh

Oz. Zaysan

Yenisey

Oka

Selenge Moron

Ozero Hovsgol Nuur

Urumqi

Kashi (Kaxgar)

Hami (Kumul)

Lop Nur

Lanzhou

Xining

Qinghai Hu

Chengdu

Chongqing

Yibin

Kunming

Guiyang

Hanoi

4374 Youyi Feng

Bogda Feng 5445

Altun Shan 5798

8611 Qogir Feng

Qomolangma Feng 8844.43

Gongga Shan 7556

Tropic of Cancer

Brahmaputra

Ganges

Mekong

Rivers and lakes labels:

Ertix, Altay, He, Urungur Hu, Urungur He, Ebinur Hu, Manas He, Ili He, Tekes He, Toxkan He, Kaxgar He, Yarkant He, Tarim He, Karakax He, Hotan, Keriya He, Qarqan He, Konqi He, Bosten (Bagrax) Hu, Aydingkol Hu, Kaidu-Karaxahari He, Korla, Shule, Ruo Shui, Gaxun Nur, Beida He, Hei He, Har Hu, Dabsan Hu, Qaidam, Golmud He, Caka Yanhu, Huang Shui, Huang He, Longyangxia Shuiku, Liujiaxia Shuiku, Hongyashan Shuiku, Qingtongxia Shuiku, Yellow R., Bayan Har Shan 5266, Geladandong Feng, Migriggyangzham Co, Za'gya Zangbo, Nag Qu, Nam Co, Siling Co, Gyaring Co, Zhari Namco, Ngangla Ringco, Tangra Yumco, Mapam Yumco, Langa Co, Maquan He (Damqog Zangbo), Sengge Zangbo, Langqen Zangbo, Nyang Zangbo, Yarlung Zangbo, Zangbo Jiang, Yamzho Yumco, Lhasa He, Lhasa, Qamdo, Nu Jiang (Salween), Lancang Jiang (Mekong), Jinsha Jiang, Yalong Jiang, Dadu He, Min Jiang, Tuo Jiang, Jialing Jiang, Wu Jiang, Dian Chi, Er Hai, Fuxian Hu, Nanpan Jiang, Beipan Jiang, Hongshui He, You Jiang, Zuo Jiang, Yuan Jiang, Gejiu, Panzhihua, Ertan Shuiku, Huangguoshu Pubu, Bangong Co, Aqqikkol Hu, Hoh Xil Hu, Ulan Ul Hu, Dogai Coring, Aksayqin Hu, Yushu, Quemar He, Tongtian He, Za Qu, Narin Gol, Yenisey

Numbers on map: 17, 18, 19, 20, 21, 22, 23, 28, 29, 30, 31, 32, 33, 34, 35

Legend

Perennial river, perennial lake

Seasonal river, seasonal lake
Dry course, dry lake

Underground river

Reservoir, canal

Fresh-water lake, salt lake

Snow cover, glacier

Spring

Swamp

- - - - - South-to-North water diversion route

Exterior drainage

Pacific Ocean drainage basins

1   Heilong Jiang
2   Suifen He
3   Tumen Jiang
4   Yalu Jiang
5   Liaodong Pen. rivers
6   Liao He
7   Hebei & W.Liaoning coastal rivers
8   Luan He
9   Hai He
10   Huang He
11   Shandong Pen. rivers
12   Huai He
13   Chang Jiang
14   Southeast coastal rivers
15   Zhu Jiang
16   Hainan-Leizhou Pen.-SE Guangxi rivers
17   Yuan Jiang-Song Hong
18   Lancang Jiang-Mekong

Indian Ocean drainage basins

19   Nu Jiang-Thanlwin
20   Dulong Jiang-Ayeyarwady
21   Yarlung Zangbo-Ganges
22   Sengge Zangbo-Indus

Arctic Ocean drainage basins

23   Ertix

Interior drainage

24   Wuyur He
25   Baicheng
26   Nei Mongol
27   Ordos
28   Hexi Corridor-Alxa
29   Qaidam
30   Junggar
31   Ili He
32   Tarim
33   Qiangtang Plateau
34   South Xizang
35   Upper Chang Jiang

———— Interior/exterior drainage boundary

- - - - - Drainage basin boundary

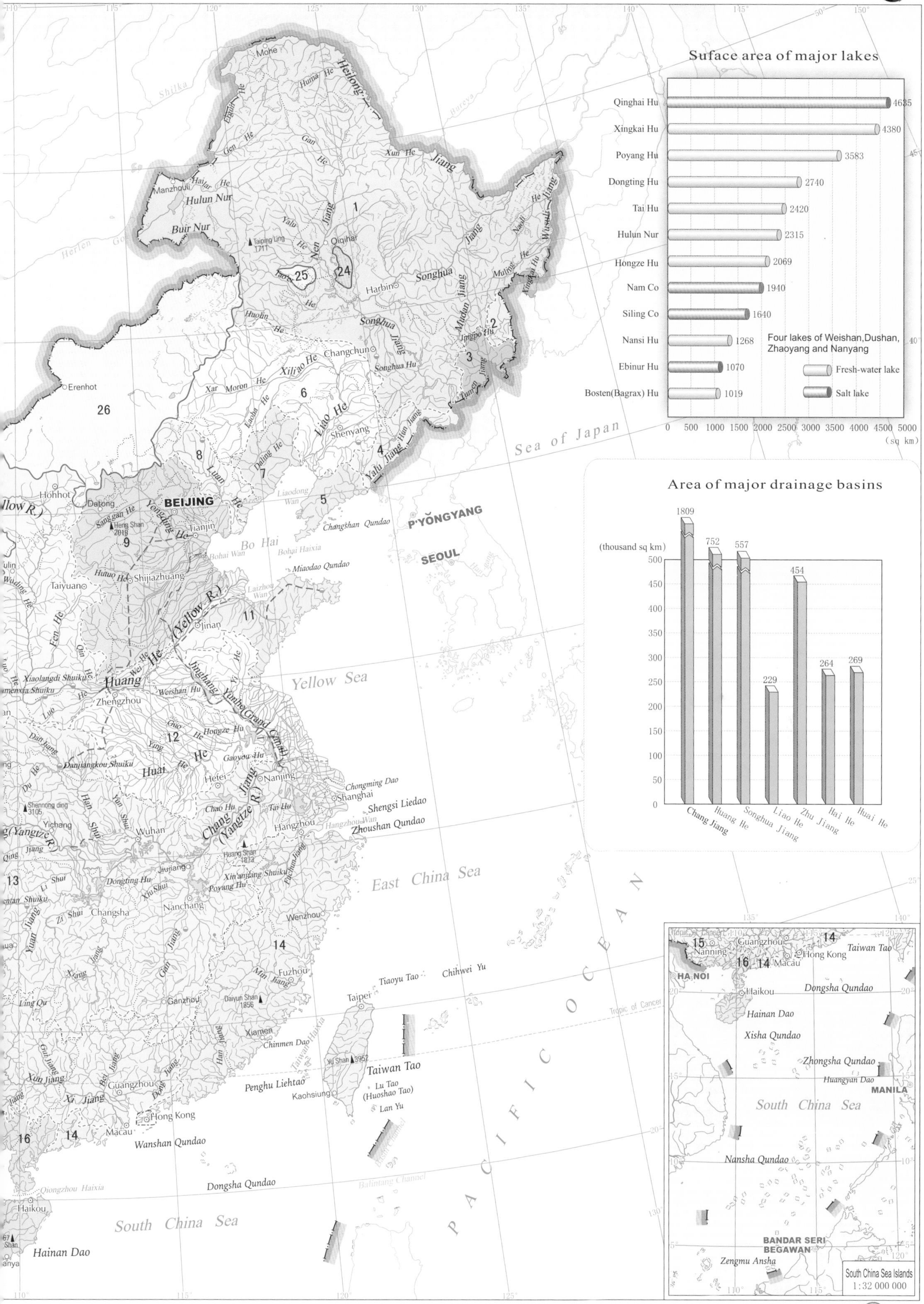

Suface area of major lakes

Lake	Area (sq km)
Qinghai Hu	4635
Xingkai Hu	4380
Poyang Hu	3583
Dongting Hu	2740
Tai Hu	2420
Hulun Nur	2315
Hongze Hu	2069
Nam Co	1940
Siling Co	1640
Nansi Hu	1268
Ebinur Hu	1070
Bosten(Bagrax) Hu	1019

Four lakes of Weishan, Dushan, Zhaoyang and Nanyang

Fresh-water lake
Salt lake

0 500 1000 1500 2000 2500 3000 3500 4000 4500 5000
(sq km)

Area of major drainage basins

(thousand sq km)

1809 752 557   454
500
450
400
350
300   264   269
250   229
200
150
100
50
0
Chang Jiang Huang He Songhua Jiang Liao He Zhu Jiang Hai Jiang Huai He

Map labels

Mohe
Shilka
Huma He
Heilong Jiang
Manzhouli
Hailar He
Gen He
Xun He
Gan He
Hulun Nur
Buir Nur
Taiping Ling 1711
Yalu He
Nen Jiang
Qiqihar
Bureya
Amur
1
Songhua Jiang
He
He Jiang
Ussuri
Herlen Gol
25 24
Harbin
Songhua
Mudan Jiang
Muling He
Xingkai Hu
Hailin
Jingpo Hu
2
Erenhot
Huolin He
Changchun
Songhua Hu
Tumen Jiang
3
26
Xar Moron He
Xiliao He
Liaohe He
6
Liao He
Shenyang
4
Yalu Jiang
Hohhot
Datong
8
Daling He
7
Luan He
5
Liaodong Wan
Sang'gan He
Heng Shan 2016
9
Yongding He
BEIJING
Tianjin
Bo Hai
Changshan Qundao
Bohai Haixia
P'YǑNGYANG
Sea of Japan
Taiyuan
Hutuo He
Shijiazhuang
Miaodao Qundao
SEOUL
Fen He
Qin
He
11
Jinan
Laizhou Wan
Yellow (Yellow R.)
Yellow Sea
Yiallow R)
Xiaolangdi Shuiku
Sanmenxia Shuiku
Huang He
Weishan Hu
Jinghang (Grand) Canal
Luo
Zhengzhou
Yun He
Guo He
Korea
Jing
Yi He
Hongze Hu
Dan Jiang
12
Huai He
Gaoyou Hu
Danjiangkou Shuiku
Du
Huai
Hefei
Han Shui
Yuan
Yin
Chao Hu
Nanjing
Chongming Dao
Shennong ding 3105
Shanghai
Shengsi Liedao
Yichang
Wuhan
Chang Jiang (Yangtze R.)
Tai Hu
(Yangtze R.)
Hangzhou
Zhoushan Qundao
Hangzhou Wan
13
Qing Jiang
Li Shui
Dongting Hu
Jiujiang
Huang Shan 1873
Xiu Shui
Xin'anjiang Shuiku
Zi Shui
Changsha
Poyang Hu
Nanchang
East China Sea
Yuan Jiang
Xiang Jiang
Gan Jiang
Wenzhou
14
Min Jiang
Fuzhou
Xiang
Gui Jiang
Ganzhou
Daiyun Shan 1856
Tiaoyu Tao
Chihwei Yu
Xun Jiang
Guangzhou
Xiamen
Chinmen Dao
Taipei
Taiwan Haixia
Tropic of Cancer
Xi Jiang
Bei Jiang
Macau
Hong Kong
Penghu Liehtao
Kaohsiung
Yu Shan 3952
Taiwan Tao
Lu Tao (Huoshao Tao)
Lan Yu
16
14
Wanshan Qundao
Qiongzhou Haixia
Dongsha Qundao
Bashi Channel
PACIFIC OCEAN
Haikou
Qiongshan
South China Sea
Hainan Dao

South China Sea Islands inset

15 Guangzhou 14
Nanning Hong Kong Taiwan Tao
16 14 Macau
HA NOI Haikou
Dongsha Qundao
Hainan Dao
Xisha Qundao
Zhongsha Qundao
Huangyan Dao
MANILA
South China Sea
Nansha Qundao
BANDAR SERI BEGAWAN
Zengmu Ansha

South China Sea Islands
1 : 32 000 000

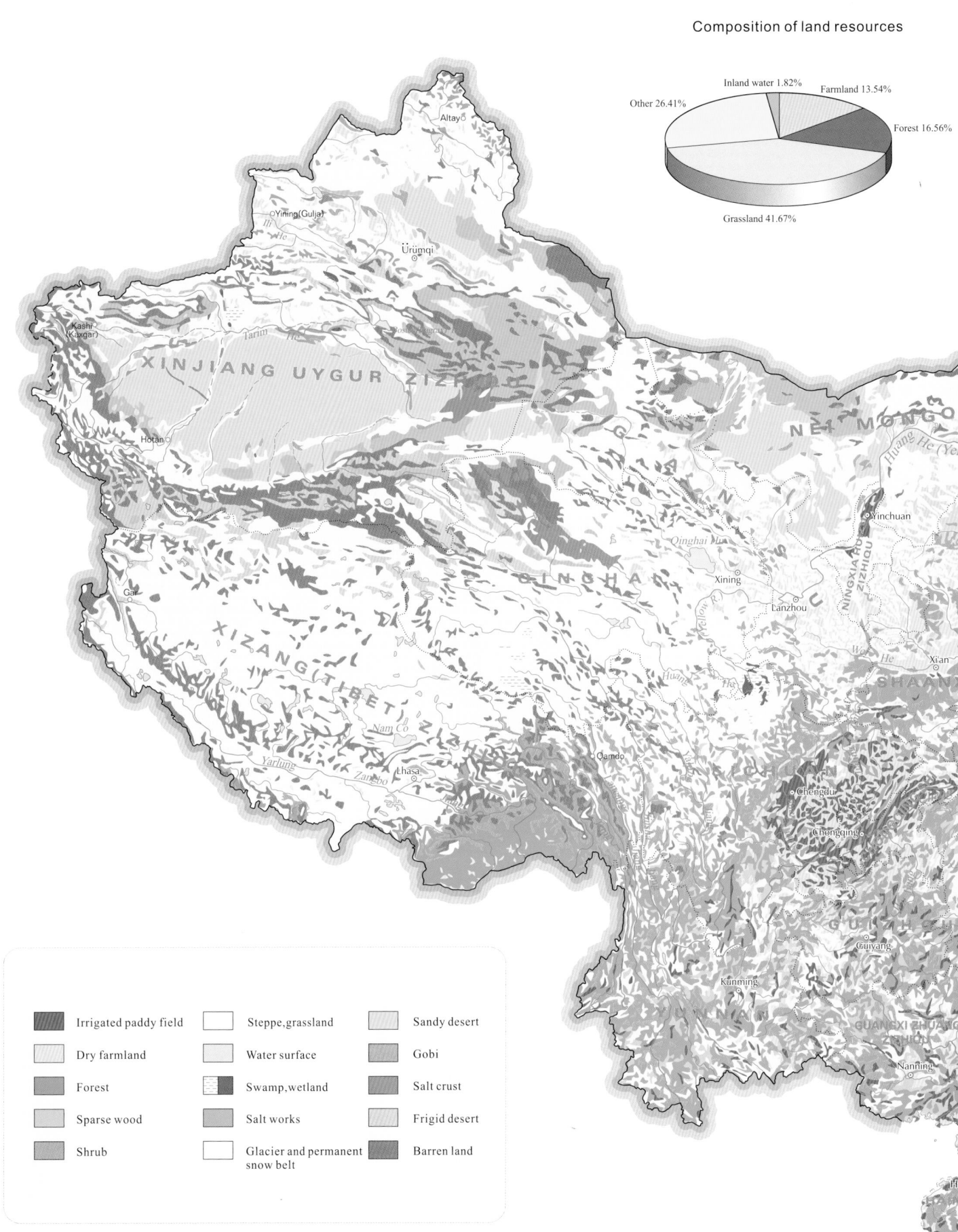

Composition of land resources

Inland water 1.82%   Farmland 13.54%

Other 26.41%

Forest 16.56%

Grassland 41.67%

Irrigated paddy field	Steppe,grassland	Sandy desert
Dry farmland	Water surface	Gobi
Forest	Swamp,wetland	Salt crust
Sparse wood	Salt works	Frigid desert
Shrub	Glacier and permanent snow belt	Barren land

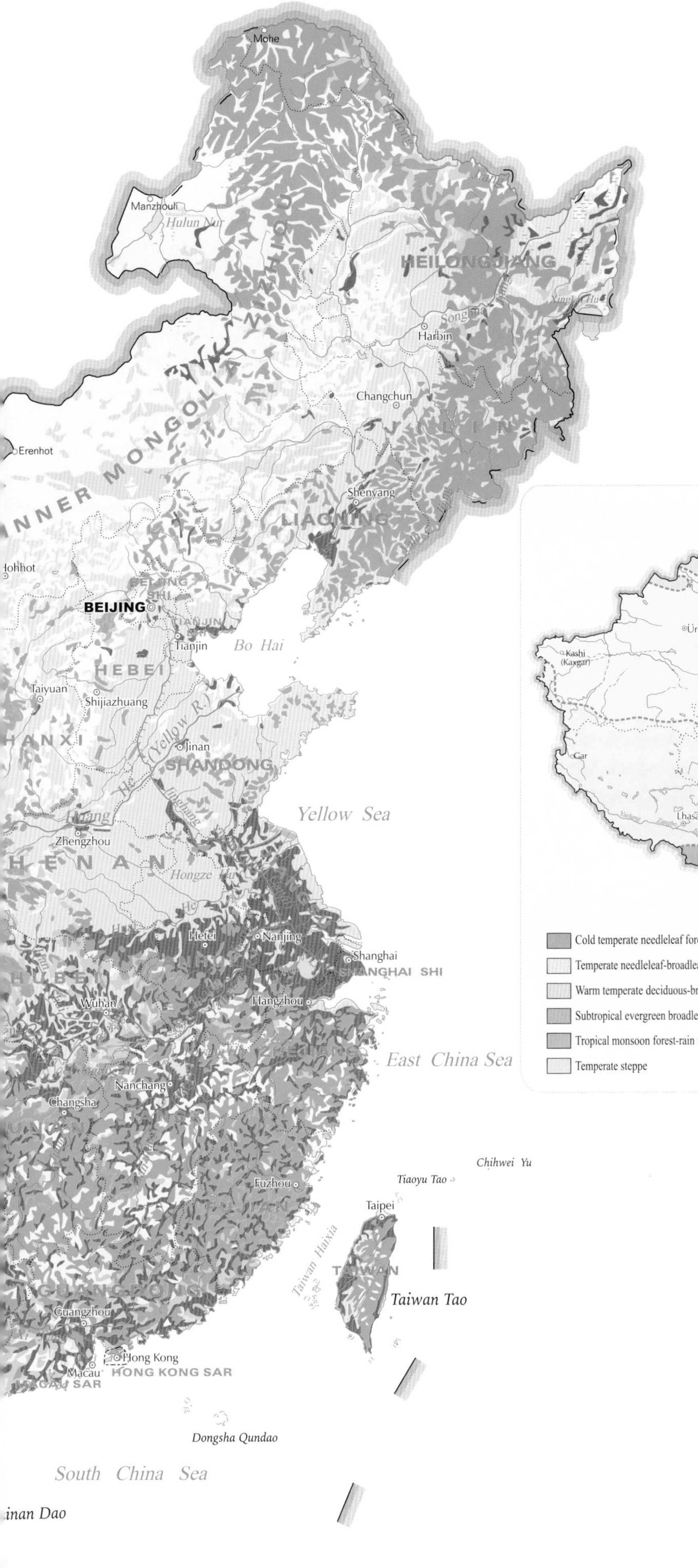

Mohe

Manzhouli
Hulun Nur

HEILONGJIANG

Songhua Jiang · *Xingkai Hu*

Harbin

Changchun

Erenhot

INNER MONGOLIA

LIAONING

Shenyang

Hohhot

BEIJING

Tianjin · *Bo Hai*

HEBEI

Taiyuan · Shijiazhuang

SHANXI

Yellow R.

He (Yellow R.)

Jinan · **SHANDONG**

Yellow Sea

Zhengzhou

HENAN

Hongze

He

Hefei · Nanjing

Wuhan · Shanghai

SHANGHAI SHI

HUBEI

Hangzhou

East China Sea

Changsha · Nanchang

Fuzhou

Guangzhou

Hong Kong
Macau
MACAU SAR · **HONG KONG SAR**

Hainan Dao

South China Sea

Dongsha Qundao

Chihwei Yu

Tiaoyu Tao

Taipei

Taiwan Haixia

TAIWAN

Taiwan Tao

Vegetation zones

1 : 50 000 000

Mohe

Ürümqi

Kashi (Kaxgar)

Harbin
Changchun
Shenyang

Hohhot
BEIJING
Tianjin
Shijiazhuang
Yinchuan
Taiyuan
Jinan

Xining
Lanzhou
Zhengzhou
Yellow Sea

Gar

Xi'an
Hefei · Nanjing
Chengdu · Wuhan · Shanghai
Hangzhou · *East China Sea*

Chongqing
Changsha · Nanchang

Lhasa · Qamdo

Kunming · Guiyang · Fuzhou
Taipei
Taiwan Tao

Nanning
Guangzhou · Hong Kong
Macau
Haikou
South China Sea
Dongsha Qundao
Hainan Dao

■ Cold temperate needleleaf forest	
□ Temperate needleleaf-broadleaf mixed forest	
▨ Warm temperate deciduous-broadleaf forest	
▨ Subtropical evergreen broadleaf forest	
▨ Tropical monsoon forest-rain forest	□ Temperate desert
□ Temperate steppe	□ Qinghai-Xizang Plateau alpine vegetation

Nanning · Guangzhou · Hong Kong
Macau · **HONG KONG SAR**
Taiwan Tao

Haikou
Hainan Dao

Dongsha Qundao

Xisha Qundao

Zhongsha Qundao

Huangyan Dao

South China Sea

Nansha Qundao

Zengmu Ansha

South China Sea Islands
1 : 32 000 000

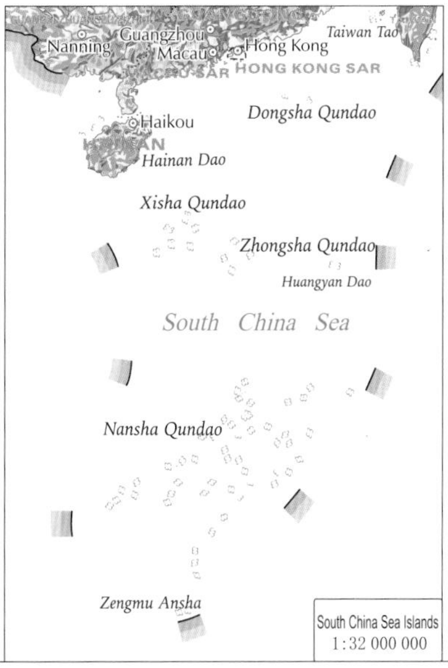

Dongsha Qundao

South China Sea

Hainan Dao

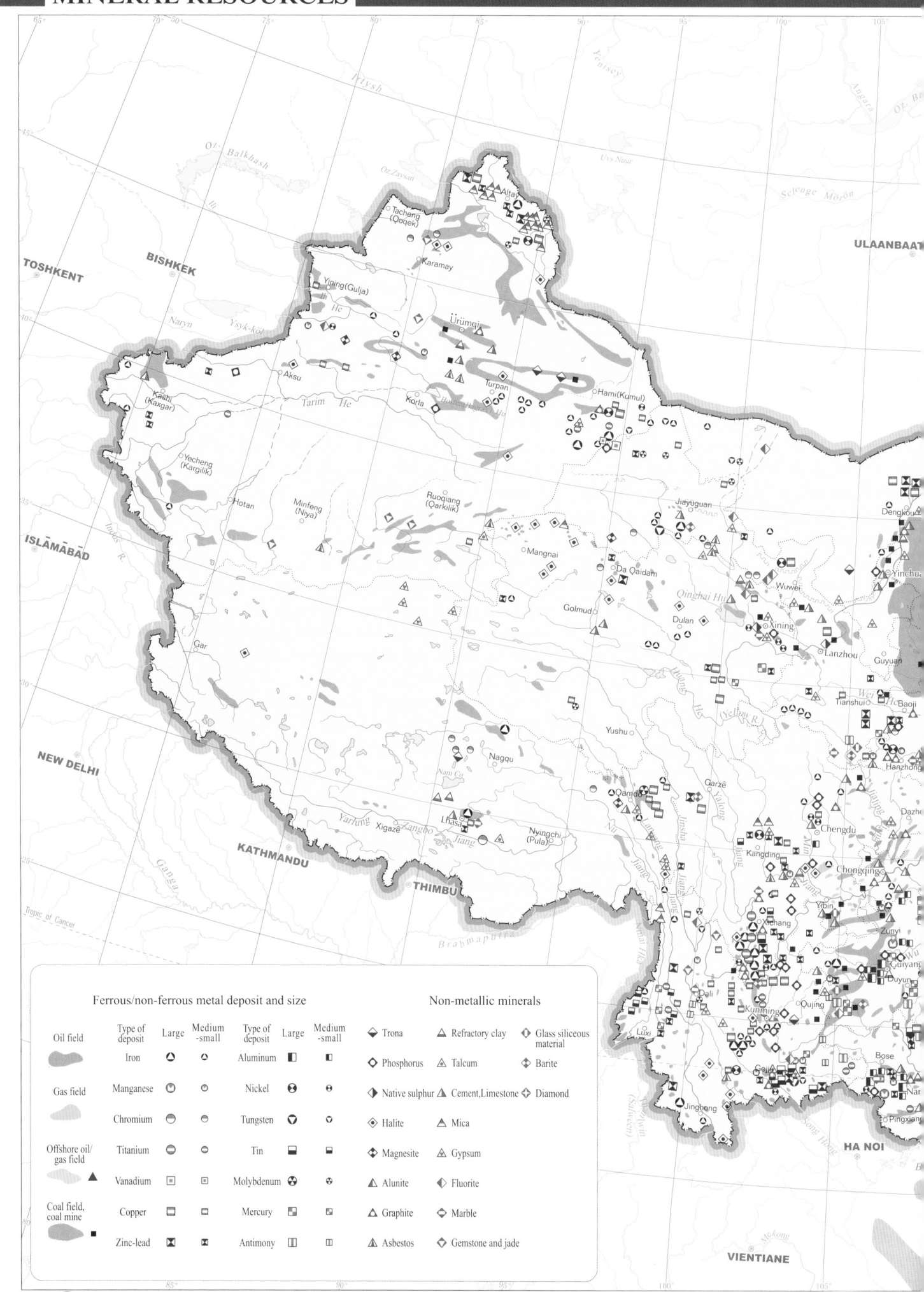

Ferrous/non-ferrous metal deposit and size

	Type of deposit	Large	Medium-small	Type of deposit	Large	Medium-small
Oil field	Iron			Aluminum		
Gas field	Manganese			Nickel		
	Chromium			Tungsten		
Offshore oil/ gas field	Titanium			Tin		
	Vanadium			Molybdenum		
Coal field, coal mine	Copper			Mercury		
	Zinc-lead			Antimony		

Non-metallic minerals

Trona	Refractory clay	Glass siliceous material	
Phosphorus	Talcum	Barite	
Native sulphur	Cement, Limestone	Diamond	
Halite	Mica		
Magnesite	Gypsum		
Alunite	Fluorite		
Graphite	Marble		
Asbestos	Gemstone and jade		

Mohe

Shilka

Heilong

Jiang

Heihe

Nenjiang

Bei'an

Manzhouli

Hulun Buir

Hulun Nur

Herlen Gol

Jiamusi

Qiqihar

Ulanhot

Baicheng

Harbin

Songhua

Mudanjiang

Sea of Japan

Xilinhot

Changchun

Jilin

Yanji

Erenhot

Tongliao

Siping

Chifeng

Shenyang

Tonghua

Ullan Qab

Zhangjiakou

Chengde

Jinzhou

Dandong

Tongchoson-man

Hohhot

Datong

Baotou

BEIJING

Tianjin

Dalian

Bo Hai

Sochoson-man

P'YŎNGYANG

SEOUL

Baoding

Bohai Haixia

Yalu Jiang

Huang He

Shijiazhuang

Dezhou

Huanghe Kou

Taiyuan

Yellow River

Jinan

Qingdao

Jiaozhou Wan

Changzhi

Houma

Zhengzhou

Xuzhou

Yellow Sea

Xuchang

Fuyang

Hongze Hu

Nanyang

Hefei

Huai He

Xiangfan

Nanjing

Han Shui

Shanghai

Changjiang Kou

Yichang

Wuhan

Shengsi Liedao

Hangzhou

Zhoushan Qundao

Dongting Hu

Ningbo

Poyang Hu

East China Sea

Changde

Nanchang

Changsha

Zhuzhou

Wenzhou

Huaihua

Nanping

Chihwei Yu

Nanchang

Fuzhou

Tiaoyu Tao

Guilin

Taipei

Tropic of Cancer

Ganzhou

Xiamen

P A C I F I C   O C E A N

Liuzhou

Wuzhou

Guangzhou

Shantou

Penghu Liehtao

Taiwan Tao

Kaohsiung

Taitung

Lan Yu

Hong Kong

Macau

Wanshan Qundao

Zhanjiang Gang

Dongsha Qundao

Qiongzhou Haixia

Haikou

Sanya

S o u t h   C h i n a   S e a

Hainan Dao

Deposit of major minerals
(100 million tonne)

24.2	2.0169×10¹²m³	3317.6	213.6	40.5	1862.1
Oil	Gas	Coal	Iron	Phos-phorous	Salt

Nanning

Guangzhou

Taiwan Tao

HA NOI

Macau

Hong Kong

Haikou

Dongsha Qundao

Hainan Dao

Xisha Qundao

Zhongsha Qundao

Huangyan Dao

MANILA

South   China   Sea

Nansha Qundao

BANDAR SERI BEGAWAN

Zengmu Ansha

South China Sea Islands
1 : 32 000 000

Kanas
Altay

Ganjiahu Sacsaoul

Yining(Gulja)
He
He
West Tianshan Mountain
Ürümqi
Bogd
Tomür Peak
Bayanbulag
Kashi
(Kaxgar)
Tarim He
Bosten (Bagrax)Hu
Lop Nur Wild Camel

Ejin Populus Diversifolia
Anxi Extremely-arid Desert
Dunhuang Yardang
Dunhuang Xihu L.
Hotan

Toli-Shule
Mt.Qilian
Liangucheng
Mt.
Youhulu
Yinc
Mt.Altun
Shapo
Urt Moron
Qinghai L.
Lian Chen
Mt.
Qinghai Hu
Xining
Mt.Xingleng
Gar
Gyaring L.Ngoring L.
Xunhuamengda
Lanzhou
Liujiaxia Dinosaur
Qumar R.
A'nyêmaqên
Gahai-Zaica
Hoh Xili
Mt.Lianhua
Qangtang
Longbao
Zoigê Wetlands
The Sources of Three Rivers
Hoang He Yellow R.
Jiuzhai Valley
Baishui R.
Jiaqu
Huanglong
Siling Co
Wanglang
Tangji
Mt.Longmen
Nam Co
Bioherm
Yarlung
Qamdo
Chagên Sumdo
Mt.Siguniang
Wolong
Longxi-Hongkou
Black-Headed Gull in the Valley
of Middle Yarlung Zangbo R.
Lhasa
Zangbo
Yi'ong
Yarlung Zangbo Canyon
Yunnan Golden Monkey in Markam
Hailuo Valley
Baishui R.
Chengdu
Jiang
Qomolangma Peak
Mêdog
Mt.Gongga
Fengtongzhai
Mt.Jin
Yading
Dadu R.Valley
Zigong Dinosaur
Chongo
Ciba Gully
Nanhe R. Mabian Dafengding
Changning Bamboo
Maigu Dafengding
Fubao Bamboo Sea
Baima Snow Mountain
Upper Changjiang R.Rare Fish
Chishu
Nujiang R.
Dashanbao Black-Headed Gull
Caohai L.
Mt. Yaoshan
Mt.Cangshan & Erhai
Sutie
Gui
Mt.Gaoligong
Yushe
Guizhou Dragon
Tengchong Volcanoes
Kunming
Mt.Wuliang
Mt.Maotian
Stone Forest
Mt.Ailao
Chengjiang Fauna Paleontology
Nangun R.
Mt.Wenshan
Mt.Dawei
Mt.Huanglian
Jinping Watershed
Naban R.Basin
Xishuangbanna

▲ World Biosphere Reserve

✳ National Nature Reserve

✳ National Marine Nature Reserve

⏺ National Geological Park

*Data of Hong Kong，Macau and Taiwan are not Available

Scale 1:16 000 000

| 0 | 160 | 320 | 480 | 640 | 800 km |

South China Sea Islands
1 : 32 000 000

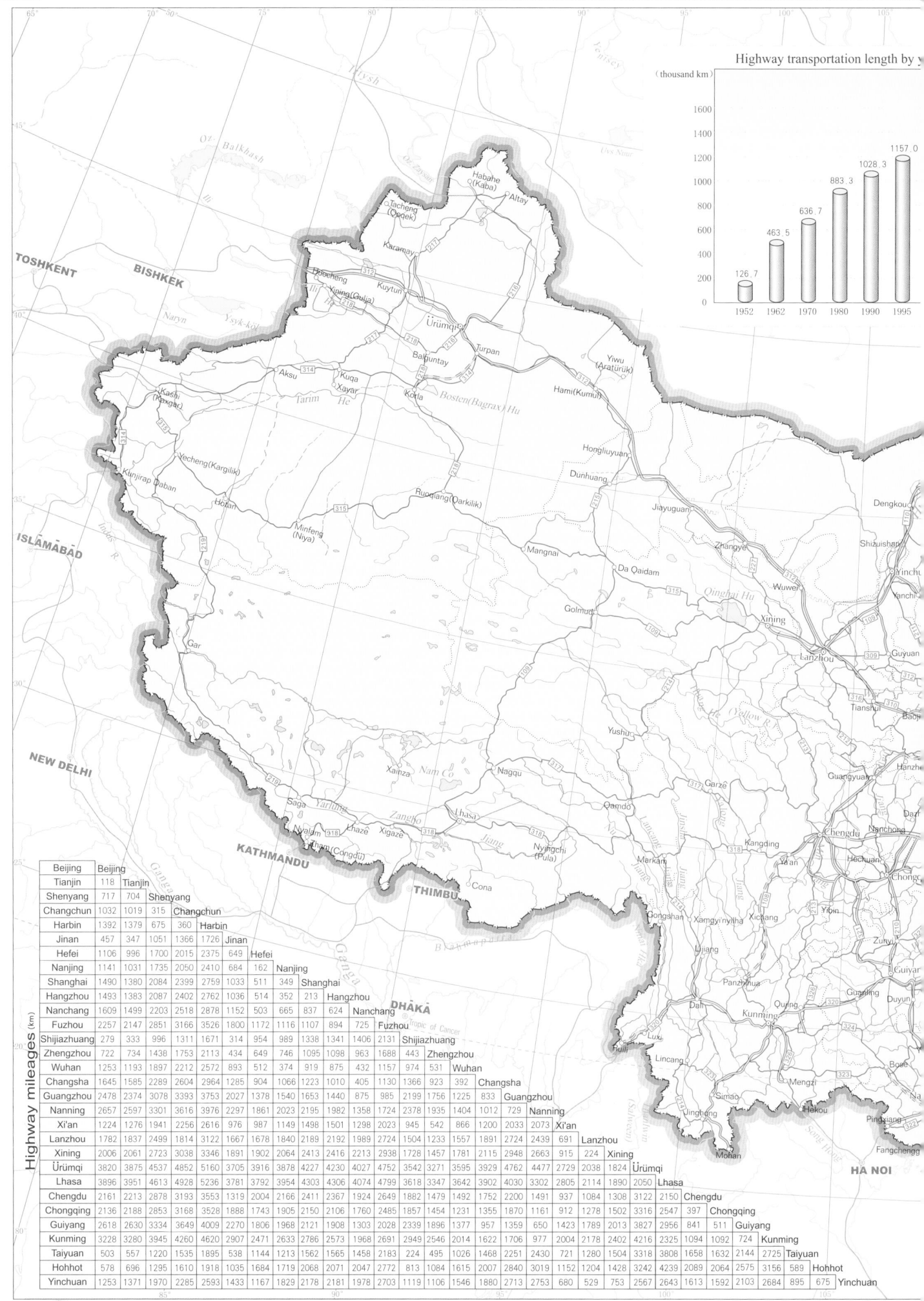

Highway transportation length by year

（thousand km）

Year	1952	1962	1970	1980	1990	1995
Length	126.7	463.5	636.7	883.3	1028.3	1157.0

Highway mileages (km)

	Beijing	Tianjin	Shenyang	Changchun	Harbin	Jinan	Hefei	Nanjing	Shanghai	Hangzhou	Nanchang	Fuzhou	Shijiazhuang	Zhengzhou	Wuhan	Changsha	Guangzhou	Nanning	Xi'an	Lanzhou	Xining	Ürümqi	Lhasa	Chengdu	Chongqing	Guiyang	Kunming	Taiyuan	Hohhot	Yinchuan
Beijing	Beijing																													
Tianjin	118	Tianjin																												
Shenyang	717	704	Shenyang																											
Changchun	1032	1019	315	Changchun																										
Harbin	1392	1379	675	360	Harbin																									
Jinan	457	347	1051	1366	1726	Jinan																								
Hefei	1106	996	1700	2015	2375	649	Hefei																							
Nanjing	1141	1031	1735	2050	2410	684	162	Nanjing																						
Shanghai	1490	1380	2084	2399	2759	1033	511	349	Shanghai																					
Hangzhou	1493	1383	2087	2402	2762	1036	514	352	213	Hangzhou																				
Nanchang	1609	1499	2203	2518	2878	1152	503	665	837	624	Nanchang																			
Fuzhou	2257	2147	2851	3166	3526	1800	1172	1116	1107	894	725	Fuzhou																		
Shijiazhuang	279	333	996	1311	1671	314	954	989	1338	1341	1406	2131	Shijiazhuang																	
Zhengzhou	722	734	1438	1753	2113	434	649	746	1095	1098	963	1688	443	Zhengzhou																
Wuhan	1253	1193	1897	2212	2572	893	512	374	919	875	432	1157	974	531	Wuhan															
Changsha	1645	1585	2289	2604	2964	1285	904	1066	1223	1010	405	1130	1366	923	392	Changsha														
Guangzhou	2478	2374	3078	3393	3753	2027	1378	1540	1653	1440	875	985	2199	1756	1225	833	Guangzhou													
Nanning	2657	2597	3301	3616	3976	2297	1861	2023	2195	1982	1358	1724	2378	1935	1404	1012	729	Nanning												
Xi'an	1224	1276	1941	2256	2616	976	987	1149	1498	1501	1298	2023	945	542	866	1200	2033	2073	Xi'an											
Lanzhou	1782	1837	2499	2814	3122	1667	1678	1840	2192	2192	1989	2724	1504	1233	1557	1891	2724	2439	691	Lanzhou										
Xining	2006	2061	2723	3038	3346	1891	1902	2064	2413	2416	2213	2938	1728	1457	1781	2115	2948	2663	915	224	Xining									
Ürümqi	3820	3875	4537	4852	5160	3705	3916	3878	4227	4230	4027	4752	3542	3271	3595	3929	4762	4477	2729	2038	1824	Ürümqi								
Lhasa	3896	3951	4613	4928	5236	3781	3792	3954	4303	4306	4074	4799	3618	3347	3642	3902	4030	3302	2805	2114	1890	2050	Lhasa							
Chengdu	2161	2213	2878	3193	3553	1319	2004	2166	2411	2367	1924	2649	1882	1479	1492	1752	2200	1491	937	1084	1308	3122	2150	Chengdu						
Chongqing	2136	2188	2853	3168	3528	1888	1743	1905	2150	2106	1760	2485	1857	1454	1231	1355	1502	912	1278	1502	3316	2547	397	511	Chongqing					
Guiyang	2618	2630	3334	3649	4009	2270	1806	1968	2121	1908	1303	2028	2339	1896	1377	957	1359	650	1423	1789	2013	3827	2956	841	511	Guiyang				
Kunming	3228	3280	3945	4260	4620	2907	2471	2633	2786	2573	1968	2691	2949	2546	2014	1622	1706	977	2004	2178	2402	4216	2325	1094	1092	724	Kunming			
Taiyuan	503	557	1220	1535	1895	538	1144	1213	1562	1565	1458	2183	224	495	1026	1468	2251	2430	721	1280	1504	3318	3808	1658	1632	2144	2725	Taiyuan		
Hohhot	578	696	1295	1610	1918	1035	1684	1719	2068	2071	2047	2772	813	1084	1615	2007	2840	3019	1152	1204	1428	3242	4239	2089	2064	2575	3156	589	Hohhot	
Yinchuan	1253	1371	1970	2285	2593	1433	1167	1829	2178	2181	1978	2703	1119	1106	1546	1880	2713	2753	680	529	753	2567	2643	1613	1592	2103	2684	895	675	Yinchuan

Numbering of national road

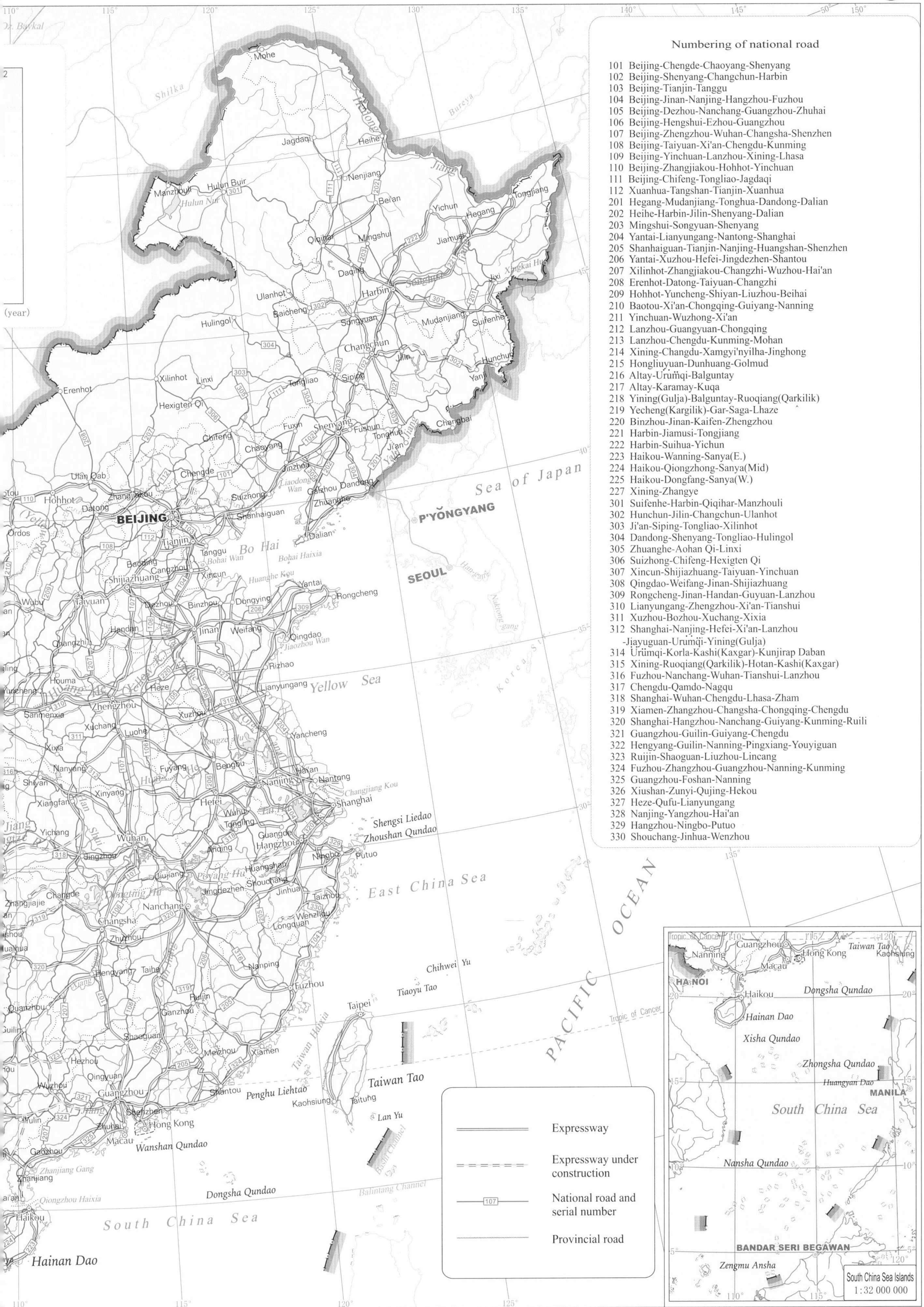

101 Beijing-Chengde-Chaoyang-Shenyang
102 Beijing-Shenyang-Changchun-Harbin
103 Beijing-Tianjin-Tanggu
104 Beijing-Jinan-Nanjing-Hangzhou-Fuzhou
105 Beijing-Dezhou-Nanchang-Guangzhou-Zhuhai
106 Beijing-Hengshui-Ezhou-Guangzhou
107 Beijing-Zhengzhou-Wuhan-Changsha-Shenzhen
108 Beijing-Taiyuan-Xi'an-Chengdu-Kunming
109 Beijing-Yinchuan-Lanzhou-Xining-Lhasa
110 Beijing-Zhangjiakou-Hohhot-Yinchuan
111 Beijing-Chifeng-Tongliao-Jagdaqi
112 Xuanhua-Tangshan-Tianjin-Xuanhua
201 Hegang-Mudanjiang-Tonghua-Dandong-Dalian
202 Heihe-Harbin-Jilin-Shenyang-Dalian
203 Mingshui-Songyuan-Shenyang
204 Yantai-Lianyungang-Nantong-Shanghai
205 Shanhaiguan-Tianjin-Nanjing-Huangshan-Shenzhen
206 Yantai-Xuzhou-Hefei-Jingdezhen-Shantou
207 Xilinhot-Zhangjiakou-Changzhi-Wuzhou-Hai'an
208 Erenhot-Datong-Taiyuan-Changzhi
209 Hohhot-Yuncheng-Shiyan-Liuzhou-Beihai
210 Baotou-Xi'an-Chongqing-Guiyang-Nanning
211 Yinchuan-Wuzhong-Xi'an
212 Lanzhou-Guangyuan-Chongqing
213 Lanzhou-Chengdu-Kunming-Mohan
214 Xining-Changdu-Xamgyi'nyilha-Jinghong
215 Hongliuyuan-Dunhuang-Golmud
216 Altay-Urumqi-Balguntay
217 Altay-Karamay-Kuqa
218 Yining(Gulja)-Balguntay-Ruoqiang(Qarkilik)
219 Yecheng(Kargilik)-Gar-Saga-Lhaze
220 Binzhou-Jinan-Kaifen-Zhengzhou
221 Harbin-Jiamusi-Tongjiang
222 Harbin-Suihua-Yichun
223 Haikou-Wanning-Sanya(E.)
224 Haikou-Qiongzhong-Sanya(Mid)
225 Haikou-Dongfang-Sanya(W.)
227 Xining-Zhangye
301 Suifenhe-Harbin-Qiqihar-Manzhouli
302 Hunchun-Jilin-Changchun-Ulanhot
303 Ji'an-Siping-Tongliao-Xilinhot
304 Dandong-Shenyang-Tongliao-Hulingol
305 Zhuanghe-Aohan Qi-Linxi
306 Suizhong-Chifeng-Hexigten Qi
307 Xincun-Shijiazhuang-Taiyuan-Yinchuan
308 Qingdao-Weifang-Jinan-Shijiazhuang
309 Rongcheng-Jinan-Handan-Guyuan-Lanzhou
310 Lianyungang-Zhengzhou-Xi'an-Tianshui
311 Xuzhou-Bozhou-Xuchang-Xixia
312 Shanghai-Nanjing-Hefei-Xi'an-Lanzhou
    -Jiayuguan-Urumqi-Yining(Gulja)
314 Urumqi-Korla-Kashi(Kaxgar)-Kunjirap Daban
315 Xining-Ruoqiang(Qarkilik)-Hotan-Kashi(Kaxgar)
316 Fuzhou-Nanchang-Wuhan-Tianshui-Lanzhou
317 Chengdu-Qamdo-Nagqu
318 Shanghai-Wuhan-Chengdu-Lhasa-Zham
319 Xiamen-Zhangzhou-Changsha-Chongqing-Chengdu
320 Shanghai-Hangzhou-Nanchang-Guiyang-Kunming-Ruili
321 Guangzhou-Guilin-Guiyang-Chengdu
322 Hengyang-Guilin-Nanning-Pingxiang-Youyiguan
323 Ruijin-Shaoguan-Liuzhou-Lincang
324 Fuzhou-Zhangzhou-Guangzhou-Nanning-Kunming
325 Guangzhou-Foshan-Nanning
326 Xiushan-Zunyi-Qujing-Hekou
327 Heze-Qufu-Lianyungang
328 Nanjing-Yangzhou-Hai'an
329 Hangzhou-Ningbo-Putuo
330 Shouchang-Jinhua-Wenzhou

Legend:
——————— Expressway
= = = = = Expressway under construction
〔107〕 National road and serial number
——————— Provincial road

South China Sea Islands
1:32 000 000

Scale 1:16 000 000
0 160 320 480 640 800 km

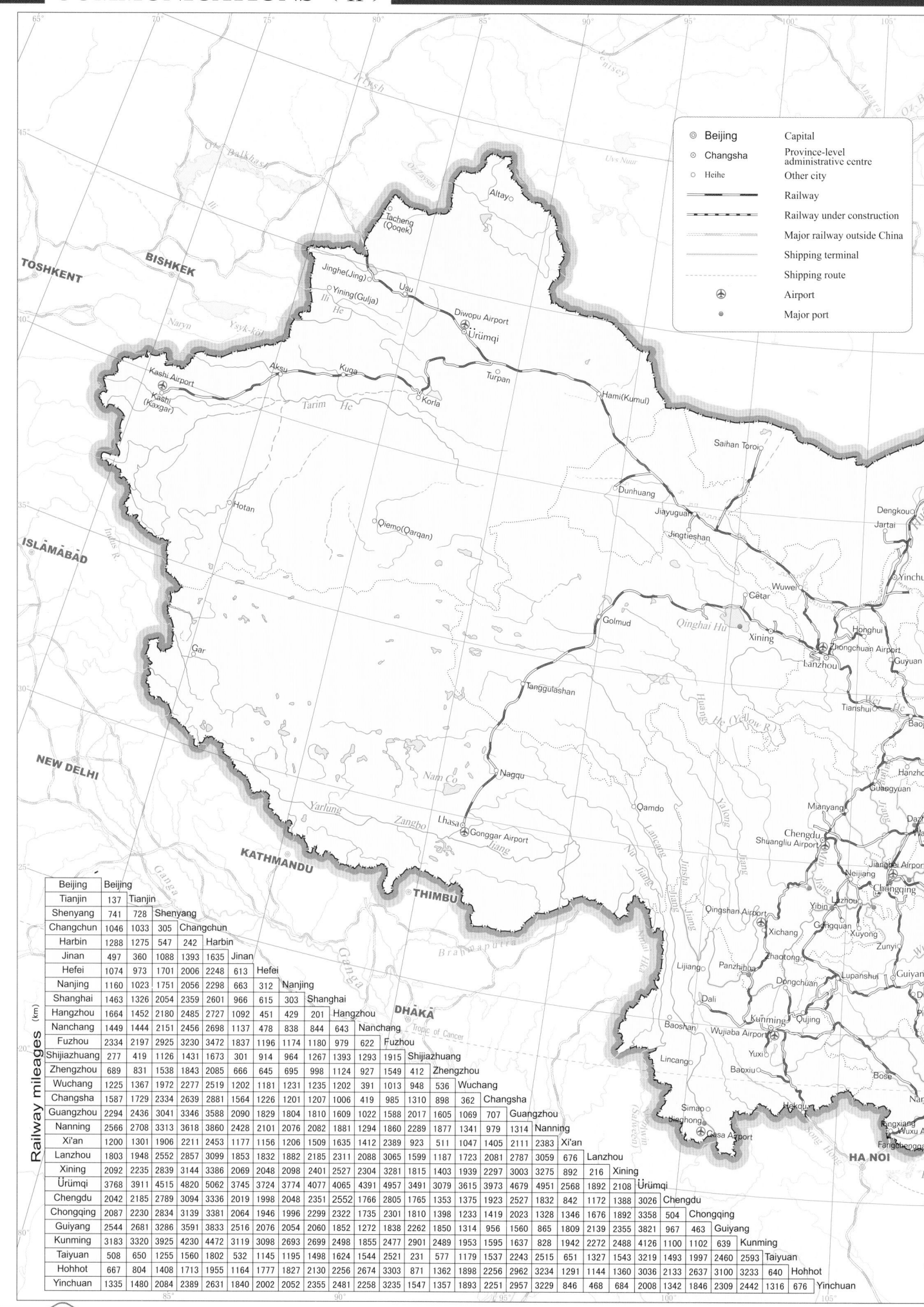

Legend:

◎ Beijing	Capital
◉ Changsha	Province-level administrative centre
○ Heihe	Other city
Railway	Railway
Railway under construction	Railway under construction
Major railway outside China	Major railway outside China
Shipping terminal	Shipping terminal
Shipping route	Shipping route
✈	Airport
•	Major port

Railway mileages (km)

	Beijing	Tianjin	Shenyang	Changchun	Harbin	Jinan	Hefei	Nanjing	Shanghai	Hangzhou	Nanchang	Fuzhou	Shijiazhuang	Zhengzhou	Wuchang	Changsha	Guangzhou	Nanning	Xi'an	Lanzhou	Xining	Ürümqi	Chengdu	Chongqing	Guiyang	Kunming	Taiyuan	Hohhot	Yinchuan
Beijing	Beijing																												
Tianjin	137	Tianjin																											
Shenyang	741	728	Shenyang																										
Changchun	1046	1033	305	Changchun																									
Harbin	1288	1275	547	242	Harbin																								
Jinan	497	360	1088	1393	1635	Jinan																							
Hefei	1074	973	1701	2006	2248	613	Hefei																						
Nanjing	1160	1023	1751	2056	2298	663	312	Nanjing																					
Shanghai	1463	1326	2054	2359	2601	966	615	303	Shanghai																				
Hangzhou	1664	1452	2180	2485	2727	1092	451	429	201	Hangzhou																			
Nanchang	1449	1444	2151	2456	2698	1137	478	838	844	643	Nanchang																		
Fuzhou	2334	2197	2925	3230	3472	1837	1196	1174	1180	979	622	Fuzhou																	
Shijiazhuang	277	419	1126	1431	1673	301	914	964	1267	1393	1293	1915	Shijiazhuang																
Zhengzhou	689	831	1538	1843	2085	666	645	695	998	1124	927	1549	412	Zhengzhou															
Wuchang	1225	1367	1972	2277	2519	1202	1181	1231	1235	1202	391	1013	948	536	Wuchang														
Changsha	1587	1729	2334	2639	2881	1564	1226	1201	1207	1006	419	985	1310	898	362	Changsha													
Guangzhou	2294	2436	3041	3346	3588	2090	1829	1804	1810	1609	1022	1588	2017	1605	1069	707	Guangzhou												
Nanning	2566	2708	3313	3618	3860	2428	2101	2076	2082	1881	1294	1860	2289	1877	1341	979	1314	Nanning											
Xi'an	1200	1301	1906	2211	2453	1177	1156	1206	1509	1635	1412	2389	923	511	1047	1405	2111	2383	Xi'an										
Lanzhou	1803	1948	2552	2857	3099	1853	1832	1882	2185	2311	2088	3065	1599	1187	1723	2081	2787	3059	676	Lanzhou									
Xining	2092	2235	2839	3144	3386	2069	2048	2098	2401	2527	2304	3281	1815	1403	1939	2297	3003	3275	892	216	Xining								
Ürümqi	3768	3911	4515	4820	5062	3745	3724	3774	4077	4065	4391	4957	3491	3079	3615	3973	4679	4951	2568	1892	2108	Ürümqi							
Chengdu	2042	2185	2789	3094	3336	2019	1998	2048	2351	2552	1766	2805	1765	1353	1375	1923	2527	1832	842	1172	1388	3026	Chengdu						
Chongqing	2087	2230	2834	3139	3381	2064	1946	1996	2299	2322	1735	2301	1810	1398	1233	1419	2023	1328	1346	1676	1892	3358	504	Chongqing					
Guiyang	2544	2681	3286	3591	3833	2516	2076	2054	2060	1852	1272	1838	2262	1850	1314	956	1560	865	1809	2139	2355	3821	967	463	Guiyang				
Kunming	3183	3320	3925	4230	4472	3119	3098	2693	2699	2498	1855	2477	2901	2489	1953	1595	1637	828	1942	2272	2488	4126	1100	1102	639	Kunming			
Taiyuan	508	650	1255	1560	1802	532	1145	1195	1498	1624	1544	2521	231	577	1179	1537	2243	2515	651	1327	1543	3219	1493	1997	2460	2593	Taiyuan		
Hohhot	667	804	1408	1713	1955	1164	1777	1827	2130	2256	2674	3303	871	1362	1898	2256	2962	3234	1291	1144	1360	3036	2133	2637	3100	3233	640	Hohhot	
Yinchuan	1335	1480	2084	2389	2631	1840	2002	2052	2355	2481	2258	3235	1547	1357	1893	2251	2957	3229	846	468	684	2008	1342	1846	2309	2442	1316	676	Yinchuan

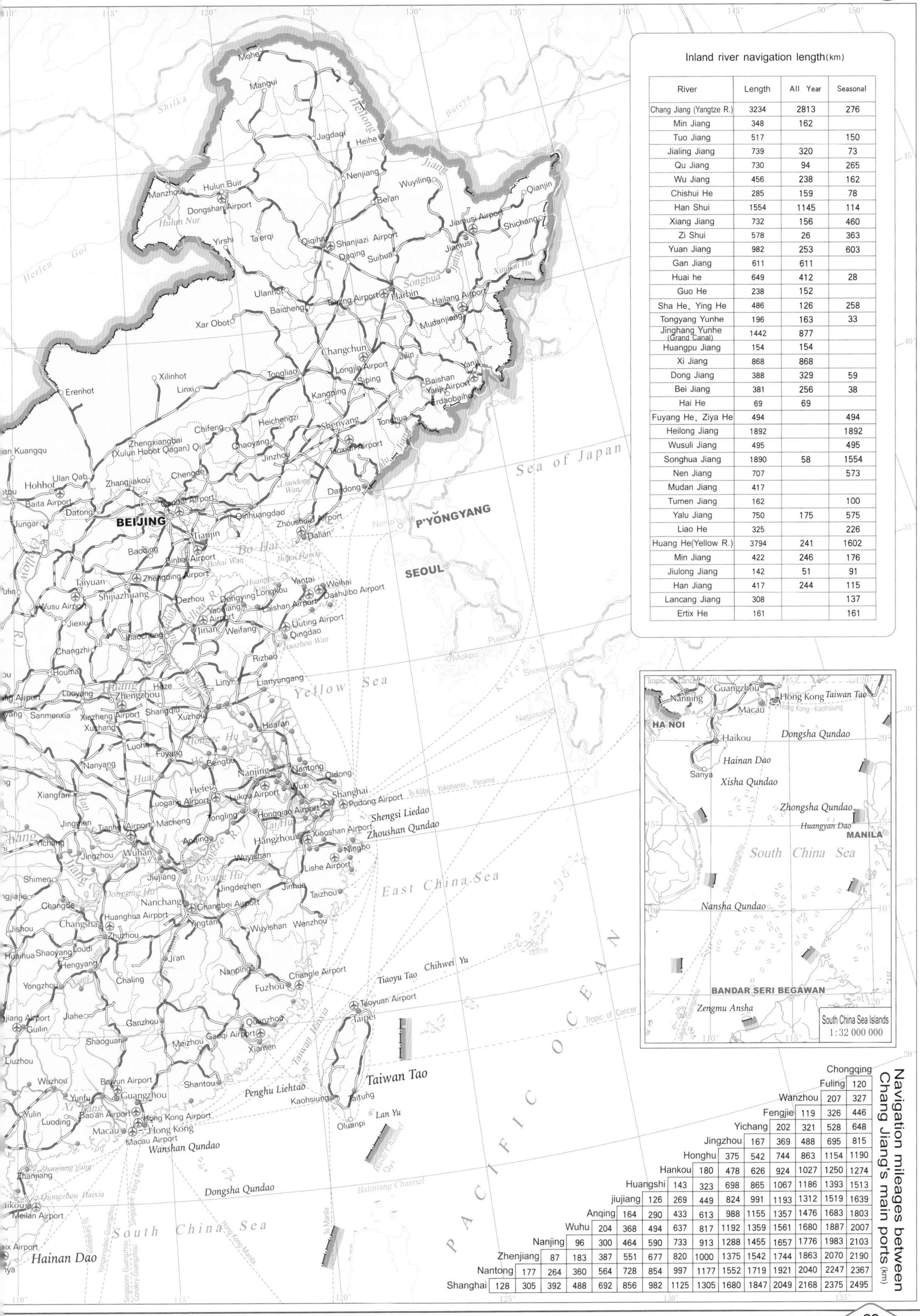

Inland river navigation length(km)

River	Length	All Year	Seasonal
Chang Jiang (Yangtze R.)	3234	2813	276
Min Jiang	348	162	
Tuo Jiang	517		150
Jialing Jiang	739	320	73
Qu Jiang	730	94	265
Wu Jiang	456	238	162
Chishui He	285	159	78
Han Shui	1554	1145	114
Xiang Jiang	732	156	460
Zi Shui	578	26	363
Yuan Jiang	982	253	603
Gan Jiang	611	611	
Huai he	649	412	28
Guo He	238	152	
Sha He、Ying He	486	126	258
Tongyang Yunhe	196	163	33
Jinghang Yunhe (Grand Canal)	1442	877	
Huangpu Jiang	154	154	
Xi Jiang	868	868	
Dong Jiang	388	329	59
Bei Jiang	381	256	38
Hai He	69	69	
Fuyang He、Ziya He	494		494
Heilong Jiang	1892		1892
Wusuli Jiang	495		495
Songhua Jiang	1890	58	1554
Nen Jiang	707		573
Mudan Jiang	417		
Tumen Jiang	162		100
Yalu Jiang	750	175	575
Liao He	325		226
Huang He(Yellow R.)	3794	241	1602
Min Jiang	422	246	176
Jiulong Jiang	142	51	91
Han Jiang	417	244	115
Lancang Jiang	308		137
Ertix He	161		161

South China Sea Islands
1 : 32 000 000

Navigation mileages between Chang Jiang's main ports (km)

	Chongqing	Fuling	Wanzhou	Fengjie	Yichang	Jingzhou	Honghu	Hankou	Huangshi	jiujiang	Anqing	Wuhu	Nanjing	Zhenjiang	Nantong	Shanghai
Fuling	120															
Wanzhou	207	327														
Fengjie	119	326	446													
Yichang	202	321	528	648												
Jingzhou	167	369	488	695	815											
Honghu	375	542	744	863	1154	1190										
Hankou	180	478	626	924	1027	1250	1274									
Huangshi	143	323	698	865	1067	1186	1393	1513								
jiujiang	126	269	449	824	991	1193	1312	1519	1639							
Anqing	164	290	433	613	988	1155	1357	1476	1683	1803						
Wuhu	204	368	494	637	817	1192	1359	1561	1680	1887	2007					
Nanjing	96	300	464	590	733	913	1288	1455	1657	1776	1983	2103				
Zhenjiang	87	183	387	551	677	820	1000	1375	1542	1744	1863	2070	2190			
Nantong	177	264	360	564	728	854	997	1177	1552	1719	1921	2040	2247	2367		
Shanghai	128	305	392	488	692	856	982	1125	1305	1680	1847	2049	2168	2375	2495	

Scale 1:16 000 000

0 160 320 480 640 800 km

TOURIST RESOURCES

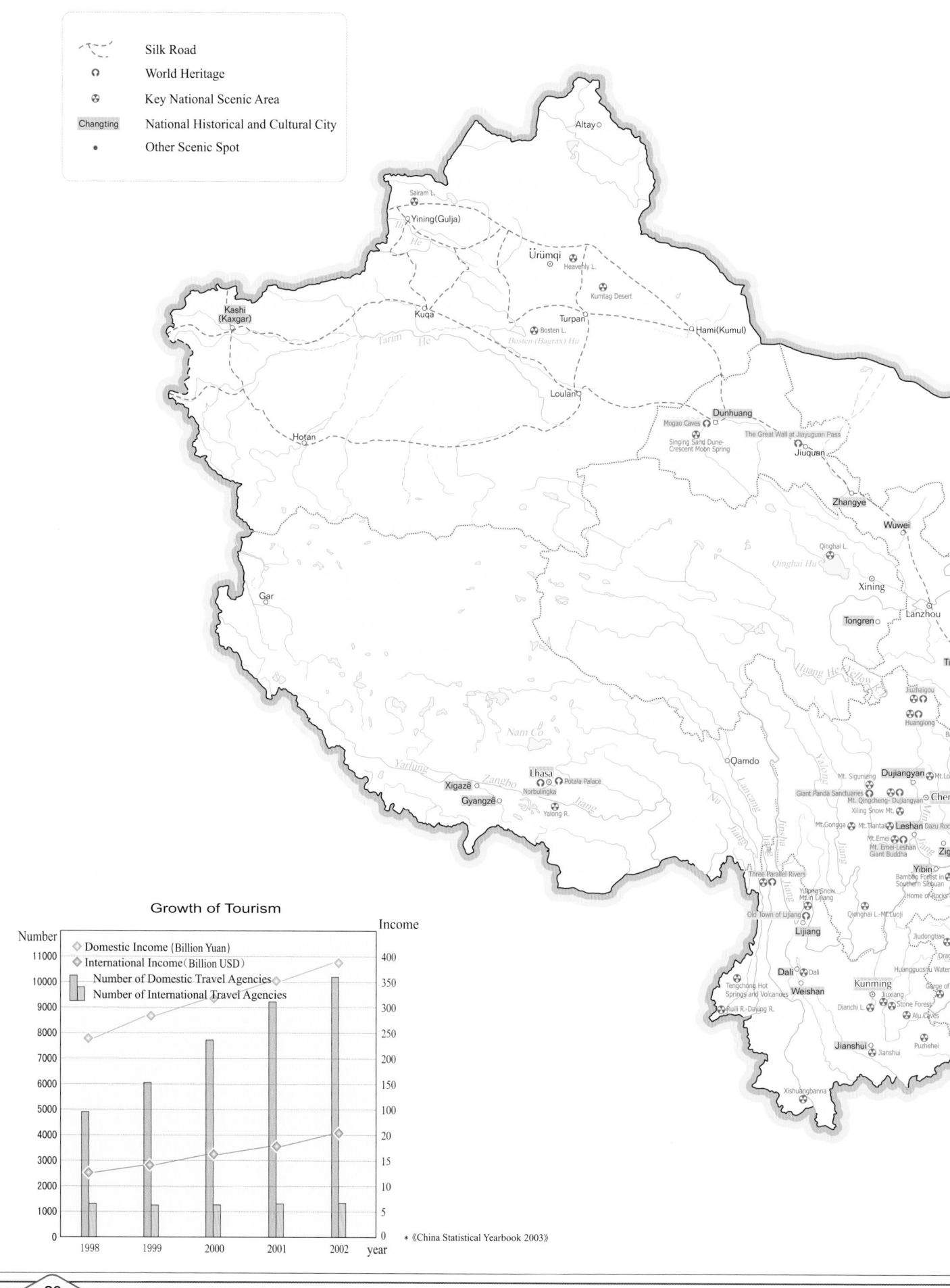

Legend
- ⌢ Silk Road
- ∩ World Heritage
- ☢ Key National Scenic Area
- Changting National Historical and Cultural City
- • Other Scenic Spot

Growth of Tourism

- ◇ Domestic Income (Billion Yuan)
- ◇ International Income (Billion USD)
- ▯ Number of Domestic Travel Agencies
- ▯ Number of International Travel Agencies

*《China Statistical Yearbook 2003》

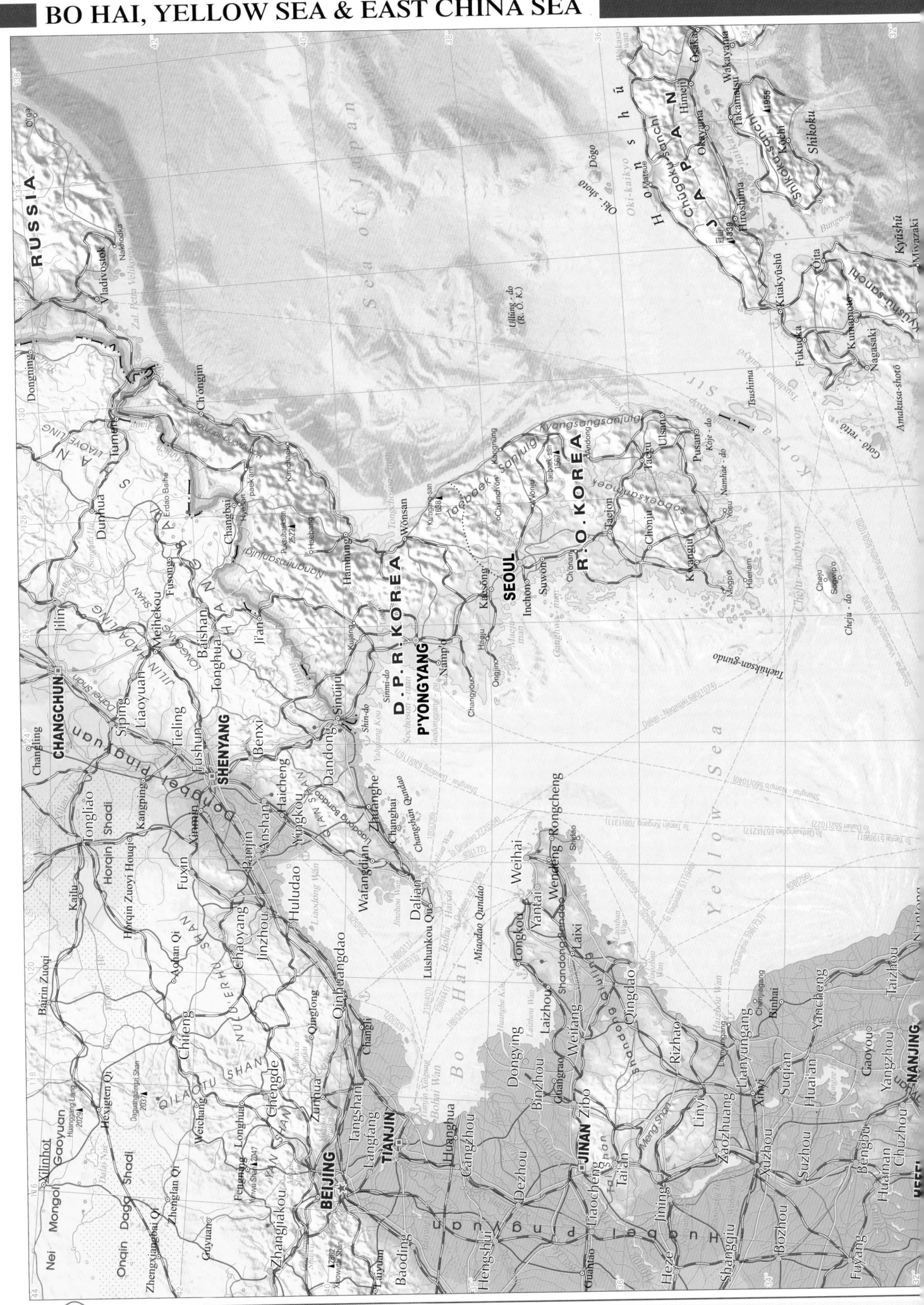

P A C I F I C   O C E A N

Kita - Daitō - guntō

Daitō-shotō

Oki - Daitō - jima

Makurazaki

Ōsumi - shotō

Tanega - shima

Yaku - shima

Tokara - rettō

Ō - shima

Amami - shotō

(Amami - Ō-shima)

Tokuno - shima

Okinoerabu - jima

R y ū k y ū - r e t t ō

Iheya - jima

Okinawa - jima

Okinawa - shotō

Kume - jima

Miyako - jima

Miyako - rettō

Ishigaki - jima

Sakishima - shotō

Iriomote - jima

Yaeyama - rettō

Chuhwei Yu

Yonaguni - jima

Huangwei Yu

E a s t   C h i n a   S e a

Tiaoyu Yu

Pengchia Yu

Chongming Dao

Zhoushan Dao

Shengsi Liedao

Changjiang Kou

Zhoushan Qundao

Zhousha Dao

Jiushan Liedao

Beilun Qu

Yushan Liedao

SHANGHAI

Suzhou

Jiaxing

Ningbo

Zhoushan

Taizhou

Wenzhou

Keelung

Taoyuan

Hualien

TAIPEI

Taiwan

Tao

HANGZHOU

Huzhou

Shaoxing

Hsinchu

TIANMU SHAN

Huili shan

Kuocang shan

Fuding

Hsueh Shan
3884

C H U N G Y A N G   S H A N

Taichung

Lu Tao

Jiaxing

Jiande

Jinhua

Lishui

Jianou

Ningde

Matsu Liehtao

Haitan Dao

Chia-i

Yu Shan
3997

Taitung

Lan Yu
(Hungshao Tao)

Jingdezhen

Huangshan

Shangrao

XIANXIA LING

Wuyishan

Shaowu

Yongan

FUZHOU

Nanri Dao

Chimmen Tao
Chinmen Gong

Penghu Tao

Kaohsiung

Fengkang

Oluanpi

Chihsing Yen

Ithbayat I.

Batan Is.

Batan I.

PHILIPPINES

Balintang Is.

Balintang I.

Babuyan I.

Nanchang

Jiujiang

Tongling

Anqing

Yingtan

Nancheng

Sanming

Nanping

Longyan

Zhangzhou

Quanzhou

Putian

Penghu Liehtao

Taiwan Qiantan

Chaozhou

Shantou

Dongsha Qundao

Dongsha Dao

Changting

Yunxiao

Xiamen

S o u t h   C h i n a   S e a

NANCHANG

S E N I

MANILA

Luzon

West Luzon Trough

Hsueh Shan 3884

CHUNGYANG SHAN

Taoyuan

Haitan Dao

Nami Dao

Putian

Quanzhou

Xiamen

Chinmen Tao

Zhangzhou

Longyan

Meizhou

Shanghang

Rujin

Ganzhou

Chenzhou

Kinfeng

Wuzhi Feng

NAN LING

Shaoguan

Lianzhou

Lianping

Heyuan

Longchuan

Chaozhou

Shantou

Shanwei

Taichung

Taiwan Tao

Chia-i

Tainan

Kaohsiung

Penghu Liehtao

Dongshan Dao

Nanpeng Liedao

Ouanpio

Chiseng Yen

Beiwei Tan

Dongsha Dao

Dongsha Qundao

Nanwei Tan

Xianfa Ansha

Huangyan Dao

Biwei Ansha

Wuyong Ansha

Zhongnan Ansha

Zhongsha Qundao

Mexi Ansha

Huaxia Ansha

Bofu Ansha

Yongxing Dao

Dong Dao

Xuande Qundao

Songtao Tan

Xisha Qundao

Shanhu Qundao

Huaguang Jiao

Zhongjian Dao

Bei jiao

Yongle Qundao

Da Nang

Kontum

Pleiku

V I E T N A M

L A O S

THAILAND

Ubon Ratchathani

Chăm Khsant

Savannakhet

Pakse

Seno

HONG KONG

Shenzhen

Dongguan

GUANGZHOU

Foshan

Zhongshan

Zhuhai

MACAU

Wushan Qundao

Chuanshan Qundao

Yangjiang

Hailing Dao

Qingyuan

Zhaoqing

Yunfu

Xinyi

Datian Ding 1703

Maoming

Zhanjiang

Suixi

HAIKOU

Wenchang

Boao

Qionghai

Wanning

Hainan Dao

Dazhou Dao

Qizhou Liedao

Leizhou Bandao

Leizhou

Xuwen

Lingao

Danzhou

Changjiang

Dongfang Ling

Ledong

Muzhishan Shan

Wuzhi Shan 1867

Sanya

Yulin

Qizhou

P E O P L E ' S   R E P U B L I C   O F   C H I N A

NAN LING

YUNKAI DASHAN

YUNWU SHAN

LIANHUA SHAN

Guilin

Liuzhou

DAYAO SHAN

Shengtang Shan 1979

Guigang

Laibin

Lingshan

Wuzhou

Cenxi

Yulin

Guiping

Hepu

Beihai

Weizhou Dao

Qinzhou

Fangchenggang

Dongxing

NANNING

Fusui

Chongzuo

Pingxiang

Baise

Tianyang

Debao

Jingxi

Fuing

DAMING SHAN 1760

HANAN DASHAN

Beibu Gulf

Dao Bach Long Vi

Dao Cat Ba

Hai Phong

Nam Dinh

HA NOI

Thanh Hoa

Vinh

Cha Tinh

Dong Ha

Dong Hoi

Quang Ngai

Bong Son

Nang Linh 2598

Dushan

Luodian

Wangmo

Ceheng

Nandan

Hechi

Heshan

Pingguo

Quijing

Yunnan Gaoyuan

Luliang

Xingyi

Yanshan

Tranlin

Hekou

Lao Cai

Yen Bai

Viet Tri

Son La

Dien Bien Phu

34

PHILIPPINE

Mindoro
San Jose
Busuanga
Culion
El Nido
Calamian Grp.
Dumaran
Puerto Princesa
Tubbataha Reefs
Palawan

San Miguel Is.
Panguturan Grp.
Balimbing
Tawitawi Grp.
Sibutu
Sambit

Sandakan
Balabac
Banggi
Kuamut
Tawauo
Sebatik

Balabac Strait
Kudat
Kota Kinabalu
Banau

Liyue Tan
Zong Tan
Nanfang Qiantan
Xianbin Jiao

Shuangzi Qunjiao
Nanzi Dao
Xiyue Dao
Feixin Dao
Wufang Jiao
Banyue Jiao
Siling Jiao

Zhongye Qunjiao
Zhubi Jiao
Daoming Qunjiao
Taiping Dao
Zhenghe Qunjiao
Meiji Jiao
Dongmen Jiao
Xiante Jiao
Nanhua Jiao
Anduu Tan

Jiuzhang Qunjiao
Chigua Jiao
Bai Jiao
Huangzu Jiao

Yongshu Jiao
Huayang Jiao
Huangla Jiao

Yinqing Qunjiao
Ruji Jiao
Pengbobao
Nantong Jiao
Beikang Ansha

Namwei Tan
Lizhun Tan
Guangya Tan
Wan'an Tan

Gunung Kinabalu
4101
2160

BANDAR SERI BEGAWAN
BRUNEI
Kuala Belait
Niaho
Zengmu Ansha
Nankang Ansha
Bintulu

Gunung Menyapa
2000

Pulau Kalimantan
Longnawano
Longnawano

Sibu
Sibuti
Kuching
Tanjung Datu

Tuy Hoa
Nha Trang
Da Lat
Phan Thiet
Phan Rang
Dao Phu Quy
Vung Tau

Buon Me Thuoc
Loc Ninh
T.P. Ho Chi Minh

PHNUM PÉNH
Kampong Cham
Takev
Chau Doc
Can Tho
Bac Lieu
Ca Mau
Mui Ca Mau
Con Dao

Kep. Natuna
Natuna Besar
Laut
Subi
Serasan
Selat Serasan

Kep. Tambelan

Kep. Anambas

Benua
Bintan

INDONESIA

MALAYSIA

YAN SHAN

YAN SHAN

Chao He

Bai He

Miyun Shuiku

Huairou Qu

Miyun

Luanping

Fengning

Chicheng

Xinglong

Yanqing

Huailai

Altitude Table

0 50 100 200 300 500 750 1000 1500 2000 2500 3000 m

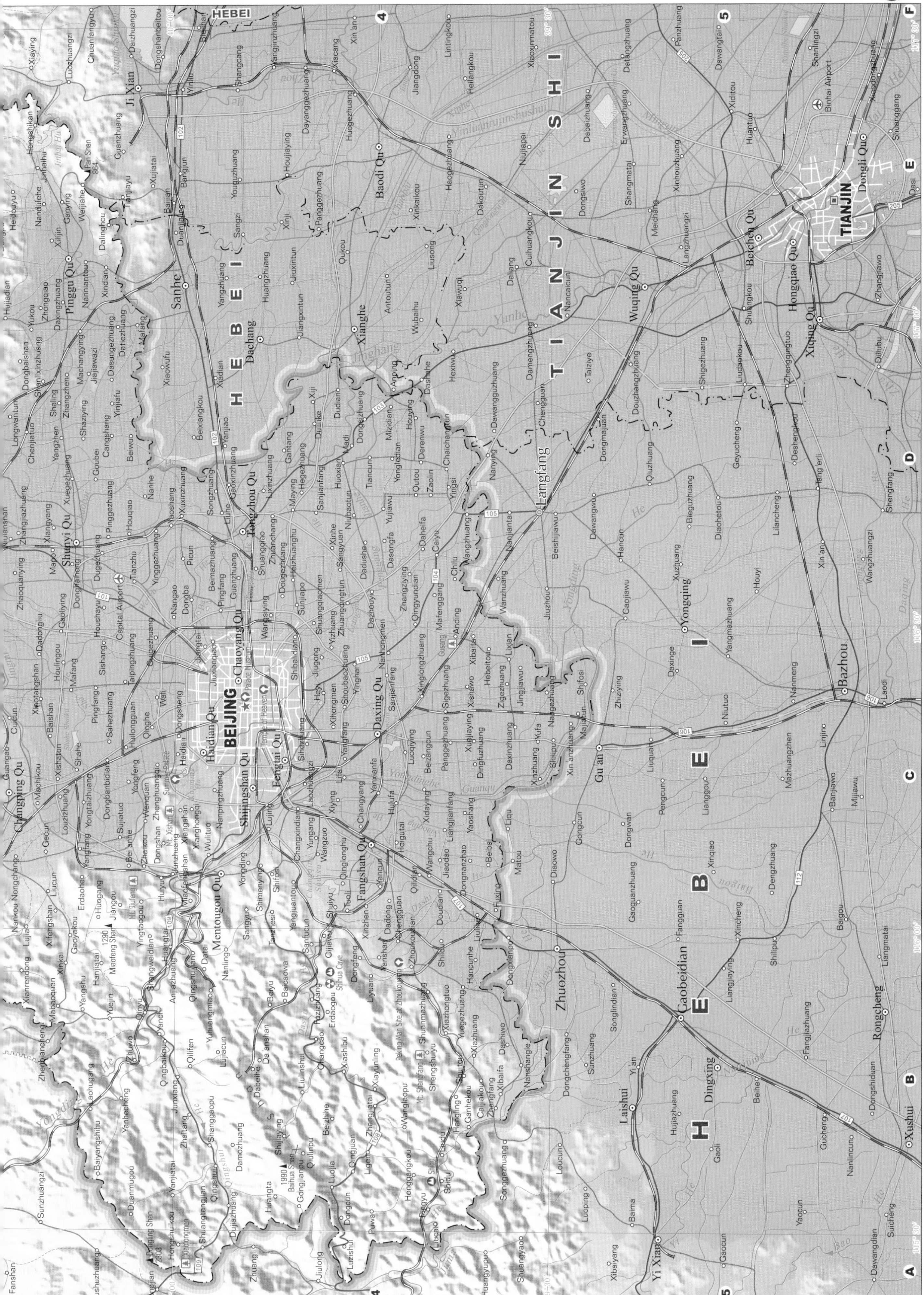

Scale 1:700 000 0 7 14 21 28 35 km

Beijing Municipality

Beijing, the capital of People's Republic of China, is abbreviated as"Jing". Located in the north of Huabei Pingyuan (Pln.), this municipality directly under the central government is the center of China's politics, culture and international exchange.

The earliest primitive men known as Peking Men lived in Zhoukoudian Area 700,000 years ago. The city of Beijing, which has a history of more than 3,000 years,now covers an area of 16,800 square kilometers, and with a population of 11.54 million, including such ethnic groups as Han, Man, Hui and Mongol.

■ **Geographical Features**

Topography With Miaofeng Shan to the west and Jundu Shan to the north, Beijing's terrain gradually descends from the northwest to the southeast, where there is the alluvial plain sloping to Bo Hai (Sea). Yongding He (R.), Chaobai He, Bei Yunhe, Juma He and Wenyu He are major rivers flowing through this area, of which Yongding He is the largest. Miyun Shuiku (Res.), the largest reservoir of Beijing, is built near the source of Chaobai He. There are 30 lakes or so across this region, including the famous Kunming Hu (L) and Yuyuan Tan (Pool).

Climate Typical temperate semi-humid continental monsoon climate rules the area, which brings distinctive seasonal difference to Beijing. Hot, rainy summers and cold, dry winters are joined by short springs and autumns in between. Annual rainfall in this area is between 500～700mm. The average annual temperature is 10～12℃ , with an average temperature of -10～-5℃ in January and 22～26℃ in July.

■ **Natural Resources**

About 60 mineral resources have been found in this area, among which 40 are proved reserves, including such nonferrous metals as gold, bronze, silver and zinc; as well as nonmetal minerals like silica, refractory clay, dolomite and limestone. Jingxi Coal Mine is one of the most important anthracite mines in China. Beijing's forest cover rate is around 18.93%.

■ **Agriculture**

Beijing has built non-staple food production bases in its own outskirts to satisfy the urban demand for vegetables, meat, milk and eggs. The outer suburbs mainly cultivate grain and oil crops as well as fruits. Country folk

culture tourism is also developed in these areas. The region not only harvests crops like wheat, corn, beans, cotton and the like, but also is well known for its prolific production of pear, apricot, peach, apple, grape and other temperate fruits.

■ **Industry**

Traditional industries like machinery, chemical industry, textile and printing are now giving way to fast developing technology-intensive industries like electronics, biochemistry and new materials, thus forming a diversified modern industrial system, with electronic products, textiles, handicrafts and Chinese medicines as its chief export products. Beijing now has become one of China's largest import and export terminals as well as one of its largest consumption markets.

■ **Transportation**

Railway As one of China's most important railway hub, Beijing is the starting point of several arterial railways such as Beijing-Kowloon, Beijing-Shanghai, Beijing-Guangzhou and Beijing-Harbin. With these railways, Beijing is not only connected with most of the major cities within China, but also with neighboring countries like D.P.R. Korea, Mongolia and Russia.

Highway Six express highways and dozens of national highways connect Beijing with the rest of China, providing the capital with extremely convenient traffic system.

Airways Beijing serves as the hub of China's national airways. With over 100 national and international flight courses connecting the city with most major cities in China and dozens of countries all over the world, Beijing Capital International Airport is now among the busiest

airports in Asia.

■ **Places of Interest**

As one of China's eight ancient capitals, Beijing boasts numerous cultural and historical relics, many of which have been included in the World Heritage List by UNESCO, e.g. Palace Museum, the Great Wall, Summer Palace, Temple of Heaven, the Ming Tombs and the Peking Man Site at Zhoukoudian. Located in the center of Beijing is Tian'anmen Square, the largest of its kind in the world, around which many famous buildings can be found, including Tian'anmen Rostrum (the Gate of Heavenly Peace), Monument to the People's Heroes, Chairman Mao's Memorial Hall, Great Hall of the People, and Chinese National Museum. Palace Museum was the royal palace for Ming

Summer Palace

and Qing Dynasties. This typical ancient Chinese style architectural complex has nearly 10,000 rooms, and is now the world largest and most complete remains of ancient royal palaces. The Summer Palace, which consists of Wanshou Hill, Long Corridor and Kunming Lake, was built to the northwest of Beijing city. It served as a summer reserve for the imperial family of Qing dynasty, and is now China's best preserved royal garden. By its side is Yuanmingyuan, which was another royal garden for Qing dynasty. It used to be called "Garden of Gardens" because of its architectural wonders and numerous valuables on display there. However, this famous garden was destroyed by the Anglo-French Allied Force and the Allied Force of Eight Powers, and is now only a park of Yuanmingyuan

Ruins.

Temple of Heaven is situated in downtown area. It was the place where the emperors of Ming and Qing dynasties worshipped heaven and prayed for good harvest. It is now famous for the Hall of Prayer for Good Harvest, the Circular Mound Altar, the Imperial Vault of Heaven, Echo Wall, Three Sound Stone and other famous sights.

The Ming Tombs lies in the northwest mountainous area, consisting of tombs for 13 Ming emperors, of which Dingling Tomb is the Largest. The Great Wall is an architectural wonder of ancient fortress. Other famous tourist attractions in this region are Yonghegong Lamasery, Beihai Park, Lugou Bridge (Marco Polo Bridge) and Fragrant Hills

Park.

■ Local Products

Beijing is known for its production of cloisonné, jade ware and carved lacquerware, local trade of silks and embroidery, inscriptions on bronze and stone ware, antiques and precious stone all enjoy long history. Beijing Roast Duck is a world known treat, while various kinds of local dim sum are very delicious. Tong Ren Tang is well known throughout the world for producing traditional Chinese medicinal herbs and traditional Chinese medicines.

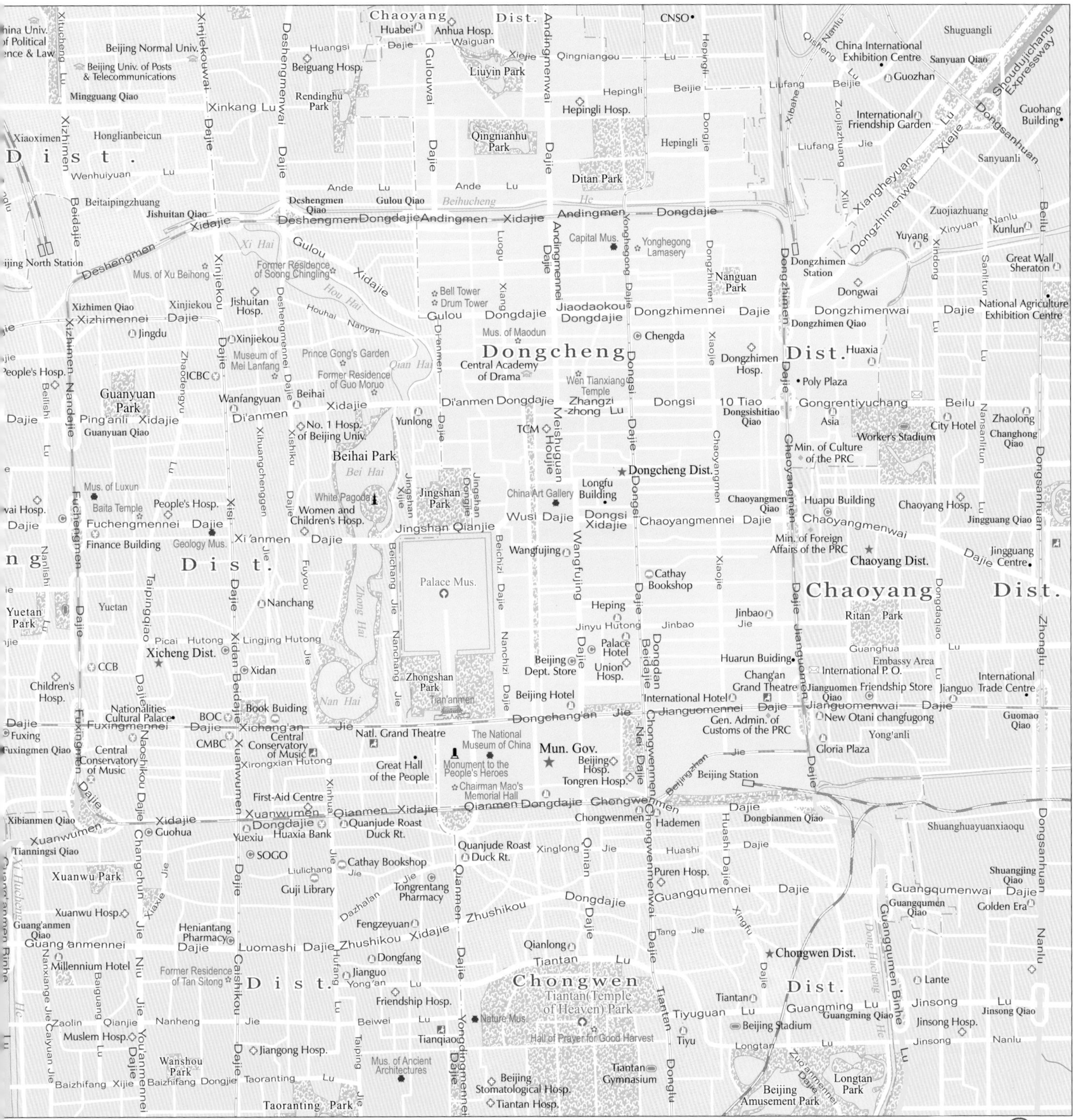

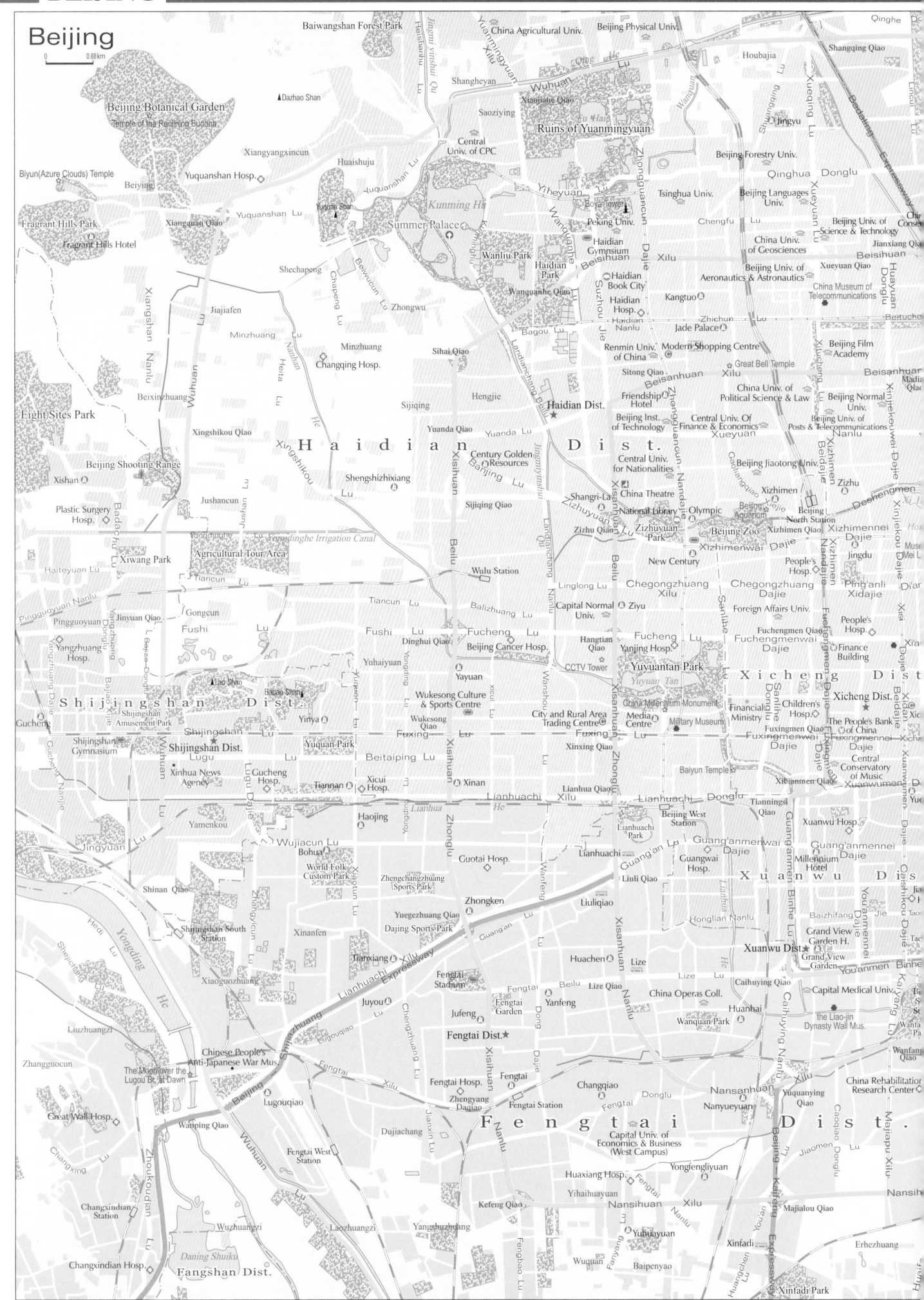

Beijing

0   0.88km

Baiwangshan Forest Park
China Agricultural Univ.   Beijing Physical Univ.
Qinghe
Houbajia
Shangqing Qiao

Beijing Botanical Garden
Temple of the Reclining Buddha
Dazhao Shan
Xiangyangxincun
Shangheyan
Xianjiahe Qiao
Ruins of Yuanmingyuan
Jingyu

Central Univ. of CPC
Huaishuju
Beijing Forestry Univ.

Biyun(Azure Clouds) Temple
Beijing
Yuquanshan Hosp.
Yuquan Shan
Kunming Hu
Yiheyuan
Qinghua Donglu
Tsinghua Univ.
Beijing Languages Univ.

Fragrant Hills Park
Fragrant Hills Hotel
Shechapeng
Summer Palace
Boya Tower
Peking Univ.
Chengfu Lu
Beijing Univ. of Science & Technology

Wanliu Park
Haidian Gymnsium
China Univ. of Geosciences
Jianxiang Qiao
Beisihuan

Xiangquan Qiao
Haidian Park
Beijing Univ. of Aeronautics & Astronautics
Xueyuan Qiao

Xiangguan Qiao
Wanquanhe Qiao
Haidian Book City
Kangtuo
China Museum of Telecommunications

Jiajiafen
Minzhuang
Haidian Hosp.
Zhichun Lu
Jade Palace
Beituche

Minzhuang
Sihai Qiao
Bagou
Haidian Nanlu
Beijing Film Academy

Changqing Hosp.
Renmin Univ. of China
Modern Shopping Centre

Beixinzhuang
Sitong Qiao
Great Bell Temple
Beisanhuan

Eight Sites Park
Sijiqing
Hengjie
Haidian Dist.
Friendship Hotel
China Univ. of Political Science & Law
Beijing Normal Univ.
Madia Qiao

Xingshikou Qiao
Yuanda Qiao
Beijing Inst. of Technology
Central Univ. Of Finance & Economics
Beijing Univ. of Posts & Telecommunications

Beijing Shooting Range
Xishan
Xingshikou Lu
Shengshizhixiang
H a i d i a n   D i s t.
Central Univ. for Nationalities
Xueyuan
Nanlu

Plastic Surgery Hosp.
Jushancun
Sijiqing Qiao
Shangri-La Hotel
China Theatre
Beijing Jiaotong Univ.
Zizhu

Yongdinghe Irrigation Canal
Zizhuyuan Lu
National Library
Olympic
Beijing Aquarium
Beijing North Station
Xizhimen
Deshengmen

Xiwang Park
Agricultural Tour Area
Tiancun
Zizhu Qiao
Zizhuyuan Park
Beijing Zoo
Xizhimen Qiao
Xizhimennei

Haiteyuan Lu
Wulu Station
New Century
People's Hosp.
Jingdu

Pingguoyuan Nanlu
Tiancun Lu
Linglong Lu
Chegongzhuang Xilu
Chegongzhuang Dajie
Ping'anli Xidajie

Yangzhuang Hosp.
Gongcun
Fushi
Balizhuang Lu
Capital Normal Univ.
Ziyu
Foreign Affairs Univ.
People's Hosp.

Yinyuan Qiao
Fushi Lu
Fucheng Lu
Fucheng Lu
Fuchengmenwai Dajie
Finance Building

Lao Shan
Dinghui Qiao
Beijing Cancer Hosp.
Hangtian
Yanjing Hotel
Fuchengmen Qiao

Babao Shan
Yuhaiyuan
CCTV Tower
China Millennium Monument
Yuyuantan Park

S h i j i n g s h a n   D i s t.
Yinya
Yayuan
Wukesong Culture & Sports Centre
Media Centre
Financial Ministry
Xicheng Dist.

Gucheng
Wukesong Qiao
City and Rural Area Trading Centre
Military Museum
The People's Bank of China

Shijingshan Amusement Park
Fuxing Lu
Xinxing Qiao
Fuxingmen Qiao
Fuxingmenwai Dajie
Fuxingmen Dajie

Shijingshan Gymnasium
Shijingshan Dist.
Lugu
Yuquan Park
Beitaiping Lu
Baiyun Temple
Central Conservatory of Music

Xinhua News Agency
Gucheng Hosp.
Xicui Hosp.
Xinan
Lianhua Qiao
Xibinmen Qiao
Xuanwumen

Jingyuan
Tiannan
Lianhuachi Xilu
Beijing West Station
Tianningsi Qiao

Yamenkou
Haojing
Lianhua He
Lianhuachi Park
Guang'anmenwai Dajie
Xuanwu Hosp.

Shinan Qiao
Bohua
Wujiacun Lu
Guotai Hosp.
Lianhuachi
Guangwai Hosp.
Guang'anmennei Dajie
Millennium Hotel

World Folk Custom Park
Zhengchangzhuang Sports Park
Zhongken
Liuli Qiao
X u a n w u   D i s.

Shijingshan South Station
Yuegezhuang Qiao
Liuliqiao
Honglian Nanlu
Grand View Garden H.

Xinanfen
Dajing Sports Park
Guang'an
Huachen
Lize
China Operas Coll.
Xuanwu Dist.
Grand View Garden

Tianxiang
Fengtai Stadium
Lize Qiao
Caihuying Qiao
Capital Medical Univ.

Juyou
Fengtai Garden
Yanfeng
China Operas Coll.
Huanhai
the Liao-Jin Dynasty Wall Mus.

Chinese People's Anti-Japanese War Mus.
Jufeng
Fengtai Dist.
Wanquan Park

The Moon over the Lugou Br. at Dawn
Lugouqiao
Fengtai Hosp.
Fengtai
Changqiao
Nansanhuan
Yuquanying Qiao
China Rehabilitation Research Center

Great Wall Hosp.
Zhengyang Daqiao
Fengtai Station
Dongfu
Nanyueyuan

Zhangguocun
Wanping Qiao
Dujiachang
F e n g t a i   D i s t.
Jiaomen

Changxing
Fengtai West Station
Capital Univ. of Economics & Business (West Campus)
Yongfengliyuan
Majiapu Xilu

Changxindian Station
Wuzhuangzi
Laozhuangzi
Yangshuzhuang
Huaxiang Hosp.
Nansihuan

Daning Shuiku
Changxindian Hosp.
Fangshan Dist.
Yihaihuayuan
Nansihuan
Xilu
Yuhuayuan
Xinfadi

Wuquan
Baipenyao
Huangtudian
Xinfadi Park
Erhezhuang

Hongshankou D

Zunhua

HEBEI

Tangshan

Fengnan Qu

Huanggezhuang

Yutian

Baodi Qu

Chengguan

Pinggu Qu

BEIJING SHI

Shunyi Qu

Sanhe

Dachang

Xianghe

Tongzhou Qu

HEBEI

Langfang

Altitude Table

20	0	20	50	100	200	300	500	750	1000	1500 m

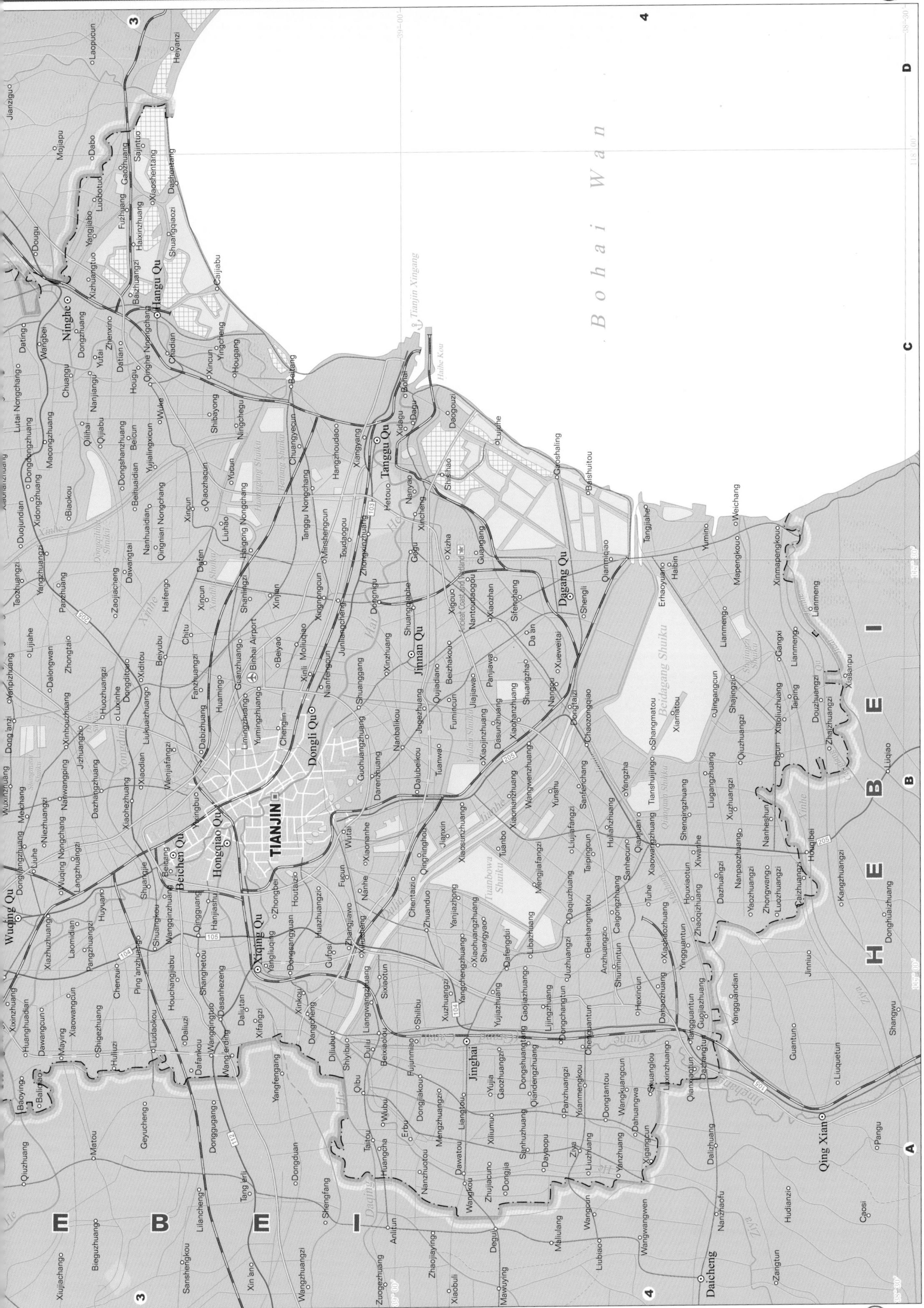

B o h a i   W a n

Tianjin Xingang

Hai He

Haihe Kou

HEBEI

TIANJIN

Hangu Qu
Ninghe
Tanggu Qu
Jinnan Qu
Dagang Qu
Dongli Qu
Hongqiao Qu
Beichen Qu
Xiqing Qu
Wuqing Qu
Jinghai
Qing Xian
Daicheng

HEBEI

Scale 1:520 000

0   5.2   10.4   15.6   20.8   26.0 Km

Tianjin Municipality

Tianjin is abbreviated as "Jin". Located on the northeast of Huabei Pingyuan (Pln.), along the lower reach of Hai He, Tianjin covers an area of over 11,000 square kilometers, and has a population of 9.32 million, including such ethnic groups as Han, Hui, Man, Mongol, and Korean.

■ Geographical Features

Topography Tianjin's terrain descends from northwest to southeast. Alluvial plain with a height between 2～5 meters takes up most part of the municipality. Hai He (R.), Ziya Xinhe, Yongding Xinhe, Chaobai He, and Ji Yunhe are major rivers flowing through the area, of which Hai He is the largest. Most shallow lakes on the low land have been built into reservoirs, among which Beidagang Shuiku is the largest. Other reservoirs include Yuqiao Shuiku, Dongqilihai Shuiku, and Tuanbowa Shuiku.

Climate Warm temperate semi-humid continental monsoon climate rules the area, which brings distinctive seasonal difference to Tianjin. Hot, rainy summers and cold, dry winters are joined by short springs and autumns in between. Annual rainfall in this area is between 550～680mm. The average annual temperature is around 12℃, with an average temperature of -6～-4℃ in January and 26℃ in July.

■ Natural Resources

Over 20 minerals have been found in this area, including oil, coal, natural gas, manganese, gold, tungsten, copper, aluminium, and marble, of which the reserves of oil and sea salt are of primary importance. Dagang Oilfield is well known in China, while Changlu is the largest sea salt production base in the country.

Diverting water from Luan He to Tianjin was a major irrigation work completed in 1980s, which satisfied the demand for fresh water in this region. The area has rich groundwater resources and terrestrial water resources, but water in this area contains too much minerals and is suitable mainly for industry, heat supply and medical use.

Tianjin's forest cover rate is around 7.47%, mostly white wax, Chinese scholar tree, Chinese toon, poplar, willow, and paulownia. Salt and alkali-resisting plants are mainly planted along the coast line, while reed, calamus, water chestnut, and lotus grow around lake area. Pine trees, cypress and fruits are mainly planted in mountainous areas in the north.

■ Agriculture

Suburban agriculture is developed around Tianjin. Vegetables, meat, eggs and dairy products are produced along Hai He and in outskirts of the city, while wheat, rice, corn and other grain crops are planted on farther plains. As one of the major northern production areas of rice, Tianjin also yield chestnut, walnut, haw, peanut, cotton, hemp, apple, pear, peach, Chinese dates, grape, persimmon and other fruits. Fresh water crab, carp and clam are raised along Hai He, while hairtail, yellow-fin tuna, prawn and shellfish are found in the offshore area.

■ Industry

Tianjin has traditionally been an important center of commerce and export in north China. It has been the cradle of China's modern industry, the center of textile industry, and is now an important industrial base. Industries here mainly include metallurgy, chemicals, ship building, electronics, instruments manufacturing, light industry, paper making, wool and clothes making, as well as pharmacy and food production, of which the production of ocean-chemicals and petro-chemicals are most well known. Oil and natural gas production in Dagang and Bo Hai (sea) are of primary importance to China, while the development of Tanggu Special Economic Zone attracts world attention.

■ Transportation

Railway Two main stems of Beijing–Shanghai and Beijing–Harbin railways meet in Tianjin, while Tianjin–Bazhou railway is connected with Beijing–Kowloon trunk line, making Tianjin a transportation hub in north China.

Highway Every county and town in this area is connected to those several national highways running through Tianjin. Three express highways including Beijing–Tianjin–Tanggu, Beijing–Shanghai and Beijing–Shenyang are in use.

Airway Binhai International Airport is the largest air cargo terminal in north China, with nearly 30 flight courses to Beijing, Shanghai, Hong Kong and other major cities in China as well as to Japan.

Waterway As an export oriented international sea port, Tianjin port is the largest sea port in north China, and possesses the largest container dock in the country. Over 20 ocean routes connect Tianjin with over 170 countries and regions throughout the world.

■ Places of Interest

As a National Historical and Cultural city for Tourism, Tianjin has rich cultural relics. Mt. Panshan, the natural division between Beijing and Tianjin, is located to the northwest of Jixian County. There are many ancient temples built on this scenic mountain. Dule Temple on the north of Jixian was built over 1000 years ago in Tang Dynasty. The standing statue of the Guanyin Bodhisattva in this temple is the largest of its kind found in China. The Great Wall at Huangyaguan exhibits astounding architectural intricacy of a fortress. Dagukou Fort Barbette on the Hai He estuary was built in late Ming Dynasty. It witnessed the heroic Chinese resistance against invasions. The 415-meter tall Tianjin Radio & TV Tower stands in the southwest of the city. It is the second highest tower in Asia and the fourth highest in the world. Other tourist attractions are: Tianhou Temple, Confucian Temple, Street of Ancient Culture and the Memorial Hall of Zhou Enlai.

■ Local Products

Rice, red bean, dried Chinese cabbage, garlic, chestnut and persimmon are well known agricultural products of Tianjin, together with prawn, crab and whitebait raised along coastline. Steamed stuffed bun, fried dough twist and deep-fried cake are three most renowned local flavours. New-year painting, coloured clay sculpture and kite are traditional local handicrafts.

Sculpture in Tianjin

Downtown Tianjin

Tianjin

Altitude Table

50 20 0 50 100 200 300 500 750 1000 1500 2000 2500 3000 m

Scale 1:2 100 000

0   21   42   63   84   105 Km

Hebei Province

With Shijiazhuang as its capital, Hebei Province, which is abbreviated as "Ji", is located on the north of Huabei Pingyuan (Pln.), bordering on Bo Hai (sea). It covers an area of over 190,000 square kilometers, and has a population of 67.82 million, including such ethnic groups as Han, Man, Hui, Mongol, Zhuang and Korean.

Eight Outlying Temples, Chengde

■ Geographical Features

Topography With Bashang Gaoyuan (Plt.), Yan Shan (Mt.) and Taihang Shan on the northwest, north and west at altitude between 500~1000 meters, Hebei's terrain descends from northwest to southeast, intersected by basins and low hills. The extended alluvial plain of Huang He (Yellow R.), Hai He and Luan He on the southeast is lower than 50 meters in altitude. Hai He and Luan He are two major rivers in this province. Five branches of Hai He, Chaobai He, Yongding He, Ziya He, Daqing He and Wei He all run through Hebei. There are few lakes in this region, the largest being Baiyang Dian. However, dozens of large and medium size reservoirs had been built, including Guanting and Gangnan.

Climate Warm temperate semi-humid and semi-arid continental monsoon climate rules the area, which brings about distinctive seasonal difference. Annual rainfall in this area is between 400~750mm. The average annual temperature is between 3~15℃ , with an average temperature in January between -16~ -3℃, while in July between 20~27℃.

■ Natural Resources

By now over 120 kinds of minerals have been found in Hebei, among which the reserves of minerals like marble, limestone, iron, coke and oil are among China's top ten. These rich reserves provide advantageous condition for the development of steel, building material and chemical industries. Huabei Oilfield, Kailuan Coal Mine, Handan Iron Mine are well known throughout China.

Hebei's forest cover rate is around 18.08%. There are more than 530 species of wild animals and over 3,000 species of plants and over 200 species of marine lives living in this region, making it one of the most important production bases of aquatic products in north China.

■ Agriculture

As a major agricultural province in China, and one of China's most important production areas of wheat, Hebei's production of grain, cotton and oil leads in China. The system of triple harvest in two years is practiced in most parts of the province. Wheat, corn, millet, broomcorn, beans, cotton, peanut, oil plants, beet, hemp and tobacco are planted in this region, while apple, pear, peach, Chinese dates, grape and haw are major fruits grown in this province. Vegetable planting and animal husbandry are also well developed in Hebei, with horses and sheep as the most important stocks. Qinhuangdao is the center of sea fishery, while Baiyang Dian (L.) is the most important base of freshwater fishery.

■ Industry

Traditionally known as an important base of coal, steel and textile industries, Hebei has now build up a well proportioned industrial system framed by coal mining, metallurgy, building material, chemicals, machinery, electronics, petroleum, light industry and pharmacy. The outputs of clean coal, raw coal, raw oil, electricity, steel, raw iron, building porcelain, flat glass, yarn, cloth, printing and dying, clothes, film and paper all take the lead in China.

■ Transportation

Railway Eight main stems, namely Beijing–Guangzhou, Beijing–Kowloon, Beijing–Shanghai, Beijing–Baotou, Beijing–Harbin, Beijing–Chengde, Beijing–Yuanpin and Beijing–Tongliao railways run through Hebei, and are joined by several branch lines like Datong–Qinhuangdao, and Shijiazhuang-Taiyuan railways.

Highway Nearly 20 national highways run through the province, which is more than those in any other provinces. Express highways like Beijing-Zhuhai,Beijing-Shijiazhuang,Beijing-Shenyang,Beijing-Shanghai,Shijiazhuang-Taiyuan and Xuanhua-Datong all pass through

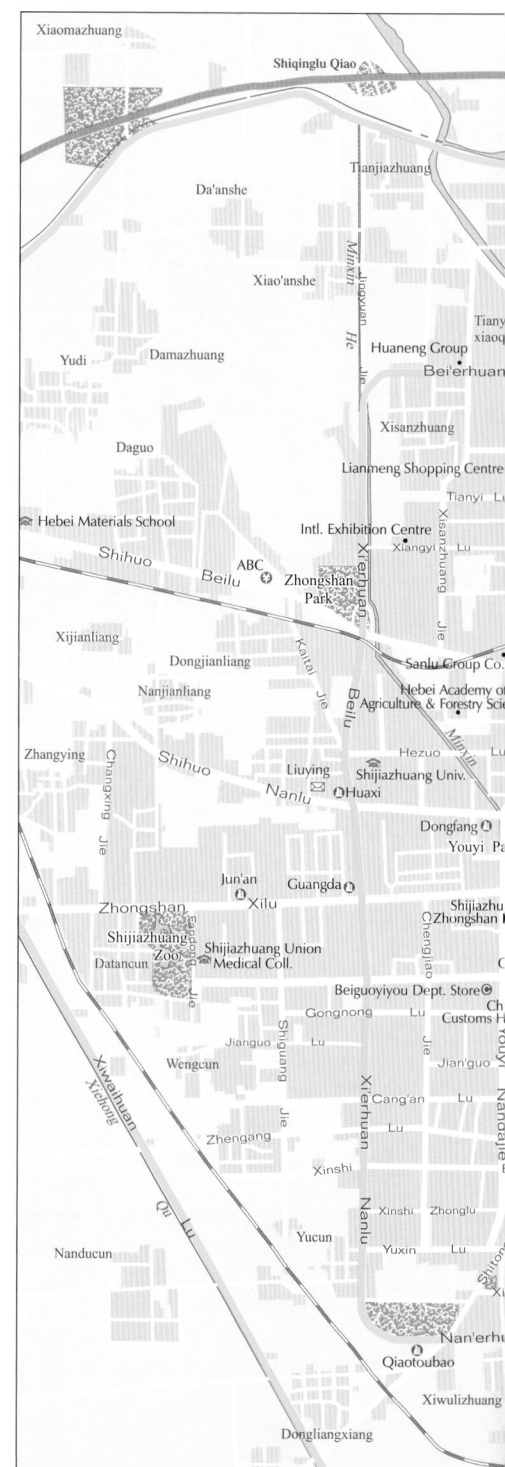

Hebei.

Airway Shijiazhuang Airport is an international air harbor. Flight courses from Shijiazhuang can reach Beijing, Shanghai, Guangzhou and over 20 other cities in China as well as destinations in CIS.

Waterway Hebei has a convenient ocean transportation system. Qinhuangdao, Huanghua, and Jingtang are major export sea ports, of which Qinhuangdao is the second largest export sea port in China, with an annual throughput close to a hundred million tons.

■ Places of Interest

Hebei has rich tourism resources. Chengde mountain resort and its outlying temples as well as the imperial tombs of Qing Dynasty are listed as World Heritage Sites by UNESCO. Chengde mountain resort was the provisional imperial palace of Qing dynasty and is now the world largest of its kind. Its outlying temples are a group of grand ancient buildings exhibiting characteristics of Han, Man and Tibetan architectural styles. The imperial tombs of Qing dynasty are located in Zunhua and Yi Xian (Co.). Qinhuangdao-Beidaihe is a wellknown seaside summer resort in north China. Shanhaiguan Pass in this region is the starting point of the Great Wall, known as "the First Pass in the World". Zhaozhou Bridge in Zhao Xian (Co.) is the earliest arc bridge exists in China. Other tourist attractions are Longxing Temple, Luxian Temple, Xiangtangshan Grottoes and Baiyang Dian (L.).

■ Local Products

Pear, grape, peach, Chinese dates and almond are famous local fruits, while mushroom, Chinese prickly ash, herbs and Chinese wolfberry are well known local agricultural products. Ceramics, wood carving, snuff bottle, paper-cutting, new-year picture, shell carving, and reed weaving are traditional local handicrafts. Unique local acrobatics, martial arts and tai-chi are world famous folk customs.

HEBEI

NEI MONGOL (INNER MONGOLIA) ZIZHIQU

Jianping

Kulongshan · Xuanjiangying · Tangtougou · Heilihe · Dengshang · The Source of Seahe R. · Guangtou Shan · Xiaochengzi · Gongyingzi

Fengyuandian · 2292 · Nantianmen Shan · 1465 · Lanqi · Longhua · Sanjia · Cangzi · Liuxi · Huangtuliangzi · Yushulinzizo · Lingyuan

Huapi Ling 2129 · Dushikou · Donghou Ding · Wudaoying · Xiguanying · Fengshan · Taipingzhuang · Hanmaying · Gaoshe · Chagou · Wudaohe · Shatuozio · Taitoushan · Wafangdian · Karqin Zuoyi

Qingsanying · Sandaochuan · 112 · Tucheng · Nanguan · Hongqi · Bofuonuo · Jingoutunp · Chengde Mountain Resort and its outlying temples · Guozhangzi · Tandaohe · Hekanzi · Lamadong · Laodazhangzi · Youzhangzi

Maying · Baicao · Tanghe · Heishanzui · Humaying · Luanping · Shuangluan Qu · Changshanying · Fuyingzi · Chengde · Bajia · Longxumen · Daqing Shan 1224 · Yangmadiar · Gejia

Chicheng · Yunzhou · Dongwankou · Yangmuzhazio · 1776 · Maozhen Shan · Dongmao · Changshaoying · Mayingzi · Anjiang · Xinzhangzi · Shangguangcheng · Shangpu · Dangba · Sandaohezi · Songlingzi · Pingfangzi · Jianchang

Longguan · Sanchakou · Yangtian · Diao'e · Houcheng · Tangbekouo · Siyingzi · Bakeshying · Liangjianfang · Dayingzi · Dezhangzio · Wangbaoyingzi · Gongshanzuio · Neishan

Zhaochuan · Pangjiabu · 2241 · Dahaituo Shan · Liubinbu · Liulimiao · Fengjiayu · Xinchengzi · 2116 · Wuling Shan · Xiatiazi · Kuangqu · Kuancheng · Du Shan 1846 · Dongdadi · Qinglong · Fenghuangshan · Wangjiadian · Fanji

Duanjiabu · Yongning · Sihai · Yunmeng Shan 1414 · Taishitun · Bulaotun · Shangshidong · Dashuiquan · Moguyi · Nianziyu · Dongdadi · Mutoudeng · Daqing Shan 1224

Cundu · Yanqing · Beixinbu · Madaoyu · Yanxi · Miyun · Dachengzi · Xinglong · Nantianmen · Banbishan · Sandaohe · Guanyang · Maquanzi · Qinglong · Gebetou · Zushan · Gaolin

Huailai · Beixinzhuang · Donghuayuan · Changdian · Huairou Qu · Gualanyu · Gushanzi · Xiaochang · Donghuangyu · Caonian · Guanchang · Yong'anbu

Guanting Shuiku · Changping Qu · Beixiaoying · Yukou · Kaoshanji · Xiaoying · Jinchangyu · Yanheying · The Great Wall at Shanhaiguan Pass · Shanhaiguan

BEIJING SHI · Shunyi Qu · Huilongguan · Pinggu Qu · Zhangzhen · Dongling · Zunhua · Donghuangyu · Jianchangying · Daxinzhuang · Changli

Zheitango · 2303 · Dongling Shan · Jinfeng Peak · Capital Airport · Gaolou · Sanhe · Xujiatai · Ji Xian · Shimen · Qianxi · Dongjiuzhai · Xinji · Caiyuan · Qian'an · Taiying · Haigang · Shanhaiguan

Qingshui · Miaofengshan · Summer Palace · **BEIJING** · Tongzhou Qu · **HEBEI** · Dachang · Liangjiadian · Fengrun Qu · Huoshiying · Wangguanying · Lulong · Chapeng · Yuguan · Qinhuangda

1990 · Baihua Shan · Hebei · Doudian · Daxing Qu · Xianghe · Baodi Qu · Yahongqiao · Kaiping Qu · Yejituo · Funing · Daihe

Sanpo · Fangshan Qu · Majuqiao · Xijio · Niubutun · Xiacang · Linnancang · Shijiwo · Lunan Qu · Guye Qu · Changning · Nijing · Qinhuangdao-Beidaihe · Beidaihe Qu

Xiayunling · Changgou · Andingo · Caiyu · Liusong · Lintingkou · Xinjuntun · Tangshan · Bachigang · Golden Coast

Zhuozhou · Songgezhuang · Gu'an · Jiuzhou · Dakoutun · Daxinzhuang · Fengnan Qu · Daodi · Luannan · Golden · Silver Beach

Yi Xian · Baima · Songlindian · Caoqiawu · Dongmaquan · Huangzhuang · Tangfeng · Daxinzhuang · Panggezhuang · Tangjiahe

Laishui · Gaobeidian · Xinlizhuang · Lixian · Dongmaquan · Wuqing Qu · Datangzhuang · Wanglanzhuang · Baigezhuang · Matouying · Leting

Dingxing · Liuzhuo · Liangjiaying · Longhuzhuang · **TIANJIN SHI** · Ninghe · Binhai · Luzan · Ruhe · Luanhe Kou

Zhangjiazhuang · Sizhuang · Bazhou · Xin'an · Beichen Qu · Hangu Qu · Heiyanzi · Tanghai · Tangjiahe

Xushui · Rongcheng · Baigou · Mijiawu · Dongduan · **TIANJIN** · Tanggu Qu · Nanbu · Shijiutuo · Yuetuo

Cuizhuang · Xiong Xian · Tanli · Xiqing Qu · Dongli Qu · Ancient Coastal Wetland · Getuo · Dongkengtuo

Anzhou · Anxin · Degui · Jinghai · Jingjin Qu · Tanggu · Tianjin Xingang · Yaotuo

Baoding · Wen'an · Jinghai · Tuanbo · Dagang Qu · Caofeidian

Qingyuan · Baiyang Dian · Wangcun · Chenguantun · Qianmiaqiao

Luzhuang · Longhua · Renqiu · Liangzhao · Liuhe · Xiaowangzhuang · Mapengkou · **Bohai Wan** · **B o**

Gaoyang · Yilunbao · Daicheng · Zangtun · Zhongwang · Nanpaihe

Dabaichi · Xiyan · Xinzhongyi · Shucheng · Qing Xian · Qijiawu · Luqiao

Minghua · Chuiyang · Litano · Xinxing · Xingji · Guanzhuang · Litianmu

Li Xian · Suning · Hejian · Liangjiacun · Hancun · Guxian · Daguanting · Huanghua

HEBEI · Anping · Raoyang · Xian Xian · Huaizhen · Changguo · Yang'erzhuang · Xincun

Tangfeng · Wangtongyue · Sunzhuang · Qiqiao · Jiucheng · Dongfeng Gang

Chenshi · Wuqiang · Jieguan · Haocun · Jiaohe · Fengjiakou · Xindian · Haixing · Dongfenggang

Shenzhou · Qiaojiatun · Fuzhen · Nanpi · Wumaying · Wangshu · Dashan · Mashanzi

Wuyi · Qianmatou · Xiaoqiaotou · Cuijiamiao · Hanzhuang · Zhaizi · Qiantong · Qingyun · Liubu · Chezhen · Xinhu · Xianhe

Hengshui · Fucheng · Lianzhen · Longwangli · Hujia · Xixiaowango · Shejiaxiang · Lijia · Xiahe · Tingluo · Hekou Qu · Gudao

Jing Xian · Daliu · Dingwang · Leling · Changlia · Wudi · Zhanhua · Chenzhuang · Huanghekou · Huanghe Estuary · Huanghe Kou

Jizhou · Wangchang · Yuji · Ningjin · Chaihudian · Liupowu · Yangxin · Liguo · Huanghe Delta · Laohuanghe Kou

Zaoqiang · Qinglan · Beiliuzhi · Baodian · Hualou · Wangji · Liuzhong · Dansi · Lijin · Kenli

Zhoucun · Xintun · Eytun · Wuqiao · Zhangxiqiao · Zhengdan · Xiaosang · Binbei · Dongying Qu · Shengli

Daying · Gucheng · Huangheya · Ling Xian · Zizhen · Yinxiang · Xindjan · Huji · Binzhou · Longfu · Yong'an · **Dongying** · **Laizhou Wan** · Sanshand

Dezhou · Santang · Linzi · Shanghe · Zhaojia · Qinghe · Xiaoyingo · Zhaodian · Chenyuan · Diaolongzuio · Zhuyc

Wucheng · Laocheng · Linpan · Fangzi · Linyi · Yangzhuangpu · Renfeng · Huaguan · Dingzhuang · Changbei Gang · Yangkou · Zhuc

Qinghe · Suliuzhuang · Shilou · Yingzi · Liangjia · Qudi · Gaoqing · Boxing · Guangrao · Wopu · Dajiawa · Xiaying · Qingxiang · Laizh

Xiajin · Zhangzhuang · Liannan · Jiyang · Xinzhen · Huantai · Gaocheng · Zhaihao · Zhenzheng · Madian · Qingzhou · Shahe

Linqing · Songlin · Xiangzhaozhuang · Gaotang · Huihe · Yaoqiang Airport · Weiqian · Sunzhen · Taizi · Yingli · Chahe · Yangzi · Shouguang · Changyi · Weizi · Pir

Kangzhuang · Jiangdian · Shitun · Xinjio · Diaozhen · Cuizhai · Mt. Heban · **SHANDO** · Zhangqiu · Zhoucun · Linzi Qu · **Zibo** · Daotian · Yuhe · Hanting Qu · Tongl

Bachalu · Nanzhen · Daqiao · Tangwang · Zaoyuan · **Zhangqiu** · Huitun · Linzi Qu · Tanfang · Dazesha · Tush

Altitude Table 200 50 20 0 50 100 200 300 500 750 1000 1500 2000 2500m

Bo Hai Coastal Region

Geographically, Bo Hai Coastal Region refers to the area along the coastline of Bo Hai, and part of Yellow Sea, a connecting zone of Northeast China, North China and East China in the shape of "C". But Bo Hai Coastal Economic Zone refers to the extensive area along the coastline of Bo Hai, and Yellow Sea, including Beijing, Tianjin, as well as coastal area in Liaoning province, Hebei Province and Shandong province. Generally the name refers to its economic reference.

Rich resources of oil, natural gas, molybdenum, lead, zinc, aluminium, manganese and gold have been found in this region. Liaohe, Dagang, Huabei and Shengli are important oil production bases in China. Prospect for oil in Bo Hai Wan is making rapid progress lately, promising great potentials. Coal mines in Kailuan, Jiaobei and Jingxi as well as iron mines in Jidong, Anshan and Qian'an are known for their rich reserves. Three out of four major sea salt processing bases of China are located in this area, producing over 50% of China's total salt output.

Bo Hai Coastal Region plays an important role in China's agriculture. Liaoning, Hebei and Shandong are major agricultural provinces in China. Wheat, rice, corn, soybean and cotton produced in Huabei Pingyuan (Pln.) and Liaohe Pingyuan are bounteous, so are peanut, tussor silk, apple, chestnut, pear, Chinese dates, walnut and grape produced in Liaodong, Jiaodong and Liaoxi hilly areas. Prolific aquatic products are yielded along Bo Hai coastline, with Dalian and Qingdao as two major ocean aquaculture bases.

This region is the most concentrated region of industries and cities in China. Centered round Beijing and Tianjin, most major northern cities are densely distributed around this area, forming an export-oriented multifunctional city complex eminent in politics, economy and education, and characterized by enormous science and technological strength. Beijing in particular, hosts a lot of world famous higher education institutions and research institutions.

As a production base of heavy industry and chemical industry, Bo Hai Coastal Region plays an important role in China's oil, metallurgy, electronics, building material, textile, and chemical industries. Shoudu Steel Plant in Beijing, Yanshan Petro -Chemical Plant, Anshan Steel Plant in Liaoning, heavy machinery and precision machines produced in Shenyang, textile in Shijiazhuang, as well as electronics and automobiles produced in Beijing and Tianjin are well known throughout China.

This region boasts a convenient transportation system composed by railway, highway, airway, ocean and offshore transport, as well as tube conveyance. There are over 40 seaports in this area, connecting with over 160 countries and regions all over the world by ocean routes, among which ports in Dandong, Dalian, Yingkou, Jinzhou, Qinhuangdao, Tianjin, Yantai and Qingdao are the most important. Dozens of main stems run across this region, including: Beijing–Shanghai, Beijing–Guangzhou, Beijing–Harbin, Beijing–Baotou, Beijing–Kowloon, Datong–Qinhuangdao and Qingdao–Jinan railways. It also has over 50 flight courses as well as over 20 navigable rivers, including: Liao He (R.), Hai He and Huang He. Express highways like Beijing–Shenyang, Shenyang–Dalian, Beijing–Tianjin–Tanggu, Jinan–Qingdao and Qingdao–Yantai connect this region with other parts of China efficiently.

Three most prominent cultural relics in this region are: the Great Wall as well as the imperial palace in Beijing and tombs of Ming and Qing Dynasties, Chengde Mountain Resort and its Outlying Temples in Hebei, as well as Temple, Cemetery and Mansion of Confucius in Qufu, all of which have been listed in the World Heritage List by UNESCO. Coastal cities like Dandong, Dalian, Qinhuangdao, Yantai, Weihai and Qingdao are renowned summer resorts.

Scale 1:2 000 000

0 20 40 60 80 100km

NEI MONGOL (INNER MONGOLIA) ZI-ZHIQU

DA QING SHAN

Yellow R.

Huang He

Mu Us Shadi

Zhangjiakou

HOHHOT

Baotou

TAIYUAN

SHIJIAZHUANG

Datong

Xinzhou

Shuozhou

Yulin

Shenmu

Ordos

Altitude Table

0 50 100 200 300 500 750 1000 1500 2000 2500 3000 4000m

Scale 1:1 800 000

0 18 36 54 72 90 km

Shanxi Province

With Taiyuan as its capital, Shanxi Province, which is abbreviated as "Jin", is located in north China, west to Taihang Shan. It covers an area of over 150,000 square kilometers, and has a population of 32.68 million, including such ethnic groups as Han, Hui, Man, Mongol, Miao, and Korean.

■ Geographical Features

Topography With Taihang Shan, Heng Shan and Wutai Shan to the east and Lüliang Shan and Huangtu Gaoyuan (Plt.) to the west, Shanxi's terrain descends from both sides towards the middle, where Jinzhong Pendi (Bsn.) lies. Thick layers of loess cover most part of the province's land surface. Fen He (R.), Qing He and Sushui He are branches of Huang He (Yellow R.), while Sanggan He, Hutuo He and Qingzhang He are branches of Hai He, of which Fen He is the largest river in the province. Xie Chi, also called Yan Chi, an ancient inland salt lake, is the largest lake in the province.

Climate Temperate semi-humid and semi-arid continental monsoon climate rules the area, which brings about distinctive seasonal difference to Shanxi. Hot, rainy summers and cold, dry winters are joined by windy springs and short autumns in between. Annual rainfall in this area is between 400~600mm. The average annual temperature is between 4~14℃ ,with an average temperature between -16~-2℃ in January and between 19~28℃ in July.

■ Natural Resources

As a major production base of energy in China, Shanxi has discovered over 120 kinds of minerals in reserve, of which the reserves of minerals like coal, bauxite, refractory clay, gallium and zeolite are the largest in China. Known as "the land of coal", Shanxi ranks the first in China in the total reserve, output and cross-province transfer volume of coal.

There are over 1000 rivers in the province, but 60% of these rivers are in the east and west mountainous areas, and most of them are seasonal. Shanxi is generally in want of water resources.

A great variety of life forms exist in Shanxi. There are over 400 species of land creatures in this area, of which 30 are rare creatures under national protection, like red-crown crane, pheasant, and sika deer. Over 2,700 species of plants grow in this area, including dozens of rare plants under national protection, and over 30 kinds of medicinal herbs, as well as over 100 species of grazing. Forest cover rate is 11.27% mainly found in Luliang Shan and Zhongtiao Shan, mostly of pine trees, firs, poplar, birch and Chinese scholar tree.

■ Agriculture

As a traditional agricultural region, Shanxi carries out the practice of three harvests in two years. Major crops include: wheat, millet, corn, broomcorn, potato, soybean, cotton, peanut, tobacco, benne and beet. Wheat and cotton are mainly planted south to Yanmen Pass, while millet, barley and beet are planted in the north. Animal husbandry is mainly developed on northwest highland, cows, sheep, donkey, mule and horses are raised here, and the province produces quality strains of cow.

■ Industry

Known as the "land of Coal", Shanxi is very well developed in coal industry, with Datong, Ningwu, Xishan, Huoxi, Hedong and Qinshui as major coal fields. The profit of coal export takes up 3/5 of Shanxi's total foreign currency income. Taiyuan is a well-known production base of alloy steel, heavy machine and coal chemicals.

■ Transportation

Railway Railways like Datong-Huashan, Shijiazhuang-Taiyuan, Taiyuan-Xinxiang, Handan-Changzhi, Datong-Qinhuangdao and other major trunk lines are connected with national artery railways like: Beijing-Baotou, Beijing-Guangzhou and Lanzhou-Lianyungang, forming an extremely convenient railway network reaching every major city and major northern sea ports in China.

Highway Centered round Taiyuan, Datong, Changzhi, Linfen and Houma, a complete highway network composed by national highways and provincial highways has been completed. Datong-Yuncheng is connected with Xi'an on the west, and Beijing-Zhangjiakou and Beijing-Shijiazhuang on the east, thus becoming part of Beijing-Tianjin-Tanggu and Beijing-Zhuhai network.

Airway Wusu Airport in Taiyuan provide flight courses to Beijing, Shanghai, Guangzhou and 20 other major cities in China.

■ Places of Interest

As one of the cradles of Chinese culture, Shanxi has rich historical and cultural relics. Mt. Wutai, one of the four sacred Buddhist mountains in China, is located to the northeast of Wutai County. Mt. Hengshan is located in Hunyuan County. As one of the five sacred mountains in China, Mt. Hengshan, the sacred place of Taoists known for its spectacular rocks, clouds and springs, is esteemed as Bei Yue (North Mountain). Hukou Waterfall on the northwest of Jixian County is the second largest waterfall in China. Ancient City of Pingyao and Yungang Grottoes have been included in theWorld Heritage List by UNESCO. Ancient City of Pingyao is the best preserved remains of an ancient city. Its city wall was first built in 1370. Yungang Grottoes to the northwest of Datong has a history of over 1,500 years. It is one of China's four famous art grottoes and is well known for its vivid imagery and perfect sculpting skill. Jinci Temple, a wooden architectural complex built over 900 years ago in Song Dynasty, is to the southwest of Taiyuan. Yongle Temple in Ruicheng County is a typical Taoist architecture of Yuan Dynasty. The wooden pagoda in Yingxian County is the highest, oldest and the best preserved wooden pagoda in China. Other tourist attractions include Mt. Lishan and Pangquan Valley National Nature Reserves.

■ Local Products

Fen Chiew (liquor) enjoys traditional renown. Mature vinegar made in Shanxi is of first class quality. Chinese dates, pear, grape, walnut, glutinous millet, persimmon, day lily and Chinese prickly ash are famous local agricultural products. Local flavours like hotpot, beef, noodle, pancake and fried millet cake are liked by many. Scissors, artistic porcelain and iron pan are traditional local handicrafts.

Yungang Grottoes

Taiyuan

0   0.69 km

ICBC
Xiwang
Fenxi
Jinqiao   Xijie
Jinqiao Dongjie
Datong Lu
Xincun
TISCO
Hengshan Lu
Zaogou
Wohushan
Nanwa
Dongshan

Ruicheng
Heping   Beilu
Xi   Ganqu
Fen
Fen   Ganqu
Dong   Lu
Zhangzitoucun
Dongshan Expressway

Sanjicun Station
Sanji
Sanjicun
Bei Paihong   Qu
Haida
Limin
Taiyuan North Station
Jiancaoping Jie
Taigang Hosp.
Wohushan Park
Dongjianhe
Ershimuwan Niutuo
Niutuocun
Gonglu

Xiaoshihecun
Shigao   Jie
Dongshexiang
Jie
Shengli   Jie
Xiaodongshe
Xiaodongliu
Heping   Beilu
Xinghua   Jie
Dadongliu
Xijie
Chengjiacun
Wanbailin
Shuguang Hosp.
Taiyuan Forest Park

Jiefang Lu
Jian'an Hosp.
Huamai
Jianlong Jie
Xiaozaogou
Taiyuan Liberation Memorial Hall

Shengli   Dongjie
PICC
Beilu
Shengli   Betsha He
Beida
Bayi Building
Jianshe
Jiefang   Wuyi Lu
Taiyuan East Station
Shanxi Cancer Hosp.
Jianziwan

angzhuang
Taiyuan Univ. of Science and Technology
Taiyuan West Station
Nanshe
Xinghua Xiaoqu
Yongleyuan Xiaoqu
Zijinghua
Yifen
Binhe Sports Centre
Shengli Bridge
Bayi Park
Longtan Park
Taiyuan Central Hosp.
Taiyuan Univ.
Xiaodongmen Jie
Jiefang
Sanqiao
Hanxiguan
Hanximen Jie
Dept. Building
Children's Hosp.
Tielu Hosp.
Yingchun
Jie
Dadongguan
Taihang
Jie

Finance Building
Fuxi
Binhe
Prov. Gov.
Fudong
Shanxi Theatre
Taiyuan People's Hosp.
Chongshan Temple
Wulongkou
Wulongkou
Beilu
Donghuayuan Xiaoqu
Songzhuang

Mun. Gov.
Xinhua Bookstore
Children's Park
Wuyi Building
Yingze
Shanxi Mus.
Taiyuan Station
Shuangtang
Shenjian
Chaoyang

Yuhe   Jie
Huayu
Dongjie
Yuhe He
Caishen
Xiayuan
Yingze
Xidajie
Youth Park
Yingze Bridge
Tianlong Building
Tangming
Yingze
Dajie
Hubin
BOC
Sanjin International Educational Hotel
Shanxi Xinhua Bookstore
Wuyi
Songzhuang

Xiaojingyu
Sanyi
Xiaojingyu
Houwang
Qianfeng
PICC
International Building
Shanxi
Kangle Jie
Shanxi Medical Univ.
Bingzhou
Shanxi People's Hosp.
Shuangta
Shuangtasi
Shuangta (Twin Pagoda) Temple
Martyrs' Cemetery of Shuangta

Guanghua   Jie
Jiuyuansha
Nanneihuan
Shanxi TCM Coll.
Fangzhi
Shuangta Nanlu
Xijie
Taiyuan No. 6 Hosp.
Shanxi Univ. of Finance & Economics
Jinwu
Jie
Guojiafeng

Dajingyu
Xizhan
Nanneihuan Bridge
Taiyuan Business Store
Nanneihuan
Lantian
Changzhi
Wangcun Nanjie   Eryingpan Jie Dicun
Honglou
Dongtaibao
Shanxi Tuberculosis Hosp.

Martyrs' Cemetery
Niejiashan
Shanxi Exhibition Hall
Xiaowangcun
Pingyang
Qinxian
Shanxi Stadium
Huaming
Beijie
Nanlu
Sanyingpan

Yijing   Jie
Taiyuan Univ. of Technology
Heping   Nanlu
Changfeng
Taiyuan Children's Sports Sch.
Meet All
Nanlu
Longbao
Qianjiafen

Yiying Jie
Nantun
Ganqu
Xinjinci
Yangjiabao
Xuefu
Haitang Building
Shuixian
Shanxi Univ.
Huangjiafen
Xutan
Dongjie

Taiyuan Pharmaceutical Factory
Shentanggou
Huagong
Paihong   Qu
Damacun
Nanwaihuan   Lu
Beiying   Xijie
Shanxi Tax Sch.
Shanxi Univ. of Finance & Economics
Taiyu
Shanxi Academy of Agricultural Science & Technology

Nanyancun
Jiujinci
Wujiabao
Nanwaihuan Lu
Jinyang   Jie
Jinyang Jie
Beiying Station
Beiyingcun

Jinshengzhen
Jinyang Hu
Xiaomacun
Xiwucun
Shanxi Meteorological Sch.
Datong-Yuncheng Gonglu
Dawucun
Taiyuan Normal Univ.

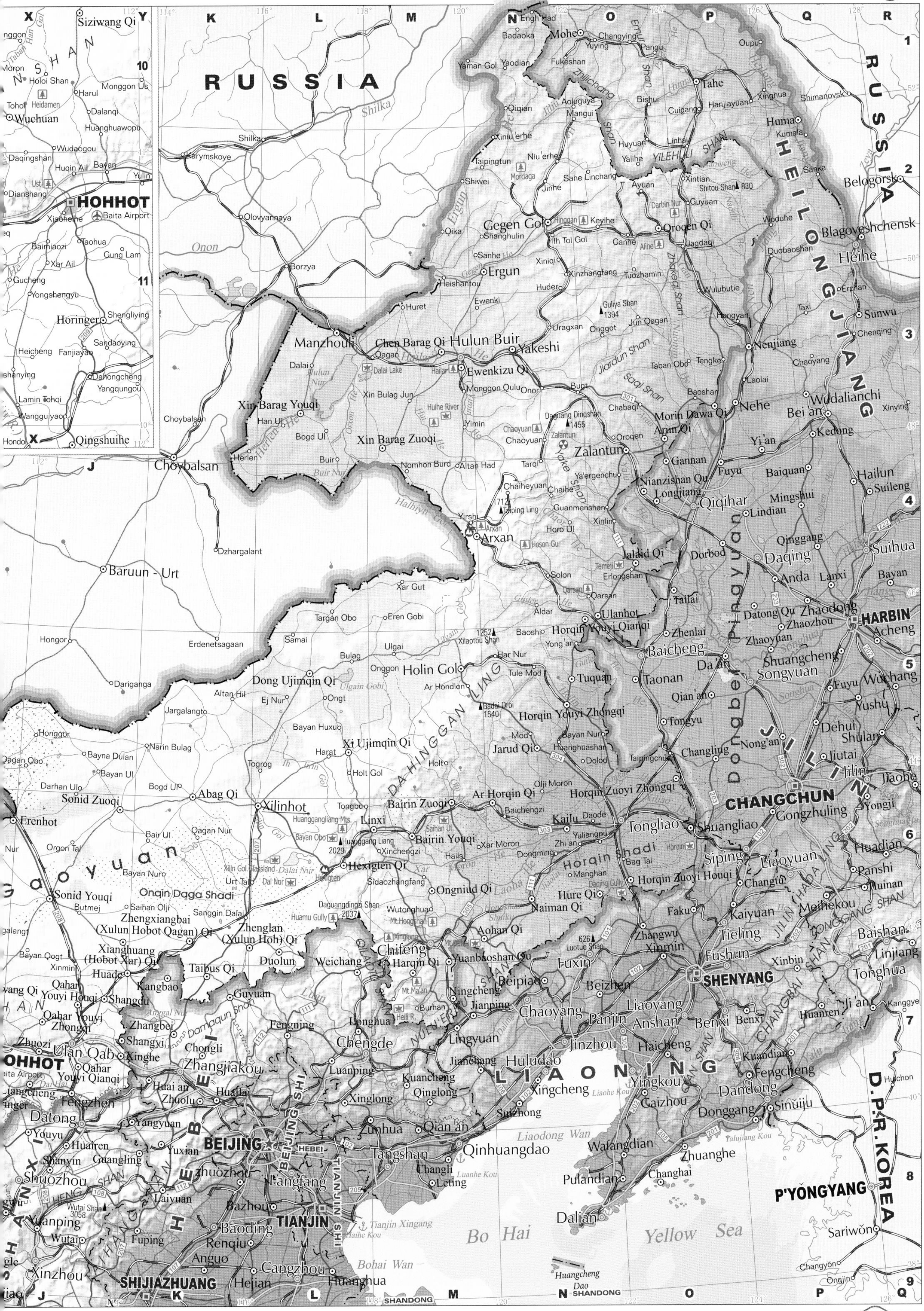

Nei Mongol (Inner Mongolia) Autonomous Region

With Hohhot as its capital, Nei Mongol (Inner Mongolia) Autonomous Region, which is abbreviated as "Nei Mongol", is located on the north border of China. It covers an area of over 1.1 million square kilometers, and has a population of 23.50 million, including such ethnic groups as Han, Mongol, Man, Hui, Daur, Ewenki and Korean, among which Mongols take up 70% of its population.

■ Geographical Features

Topography Nei Mongol forms the greater part of the Inner Mongolia Gaoyuan (Plt.), with an elevation of above 1,000 meters. The Da Hinggan Ling (Mts.), Yin Shan (Mt.) and Helan Shan stretch along its border. Extensive grassland is on the east of the region, while most of the west part is occupied by Tengger, Badain Jaran, Ulan Buh, Hobq and Mu Us deserts. Plains like Hetao Pingyuan, Nenjiang Pingyuan, Xiliaohe Pingyuan, Tumochuan Pingyuan are distributed along Huang He (Yellow R.), or at the foot of Yin Shan. Very few rivers are found in this region other than Huang He, which is the largest passing river in Nei Mongol. Most other rivers here are seasonal inland rivers. Numerous lakes like Hulun Nur, Buir Nur, Ulanshai Nur, and Dalai Nur, are found in this region, most of which are salt lakes in dry areas except Hulun Nur, which is the largest fresh water lake in Nei Mongol.

Climate Temperate arid and semi-arid continental climate rules here, bringing about sharp difference between winter and summer as well as between different localities. Summer here is cool and pleasant, while winter is long and cold. Annual rainfall in this area is between 50～450mm. The average annual temperature here is between -1～10℃, with an average temperature in January between -26～-10℃, while in July between 18～24℃.

■ Natural Resources

Rich reserves of diversified minerals were found in Nei Mongol. By now over 120 kinds of minerals have been found here, among which the reserves of minerals like rare earth, niobium, natural alkali, coal and 50 others are among China's top ten. Reserves of rare earth found in this region take up 90% of China's total. Coal reserves are particularly rich. Nonferrous metals found here include: ferrous sulfide, limestone, mica, silicon sand, quartz, gypsum, graphite, lake salt, Glauber's salt, marble and over 20 other different kinds.

Nei Mongol's forest cover rate is around 12.73%, mostly pine trees, birch and willows in Da Hinggan Ling area. As the largest natural pasturing area in China, the region has a total grassland area of 87 million hectares.

There are nearly 120 species of land vertebrates, over 360 species of birds and over 2,000 species of wildings living in this area, of which over 600 are herbs of medical value.

As the annual sunshine time here is between 2,600～3,400 hours, Nei Mongol has rich solar energy resources second only to Qingzang Gaoyuan. The region also has rich wind energy resources, and over 70% of its pastures are suitable for wind power generation.

■ Agriculture

As Nei Mongol occupies a long and narrow area from west to east, there is a great regional difference in its agricultural development, with farming in the south and pasturing in the north. Wheat, corn, potato, buckwheat, raw buckwheat, soybean and benne are planted on fertile soils of Hetao-Tumochuan Pingyuan and Xiliaohe-Nenjiang Pingyuan. Sheep, goat, cow, horse and camel are bred in pastures like Hulun Buir, Xilin Gol and Urad. The number of livestock raised here as well as the output of wool, cashmere and camel hair produced here are all ranked as China's No. 1. Sanhe Horses, Sanhe Oxen and fine wool sheep are all raised in Nei Mongol.

■ Industry

As a major production base of steel and coal in China, Nei Mongol has four of China's major open cut coal mines: Yiminhe Open-Air Mine, Huolinhe Open-Air Mine, Yuanbaoshan Open-Air Mine and Jungar Open-Air Mine.

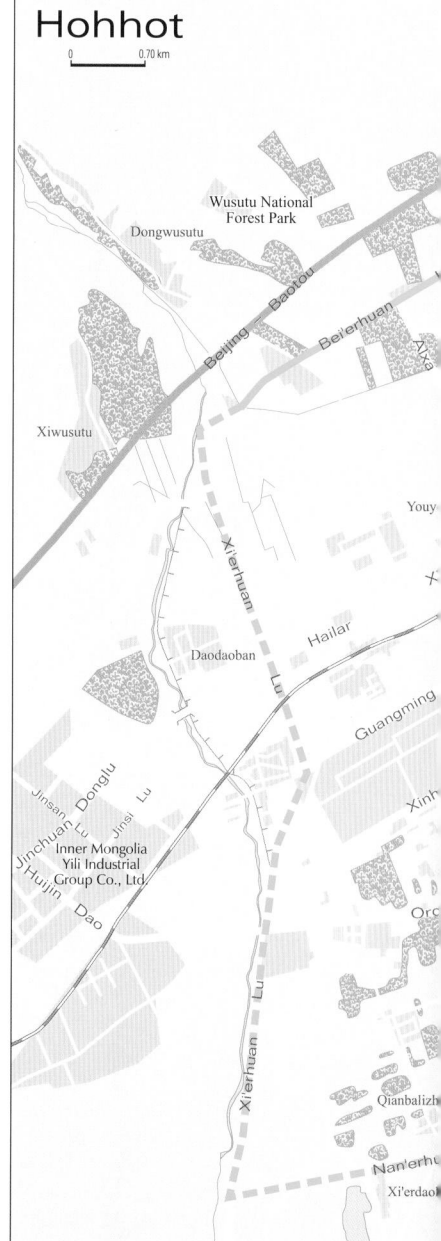

Hulun Buir Grassland

Coalmining, power engineering, metallurgy, machinery, forest and livestock products processing are major industries in this region. Food and beverage production, textile, paper making are also developed here. Forest machinery and dairy products of this region play important roles in China.

■ Transportation

Railway Three main stems including Beijing–Baotou, Baotou–Lanzhou and Beijing–Tongliao railways run through the region, and are supported by provincial railways like Jining–Tongliao, Jining–Erenhot and Baotou–Shenmu railways.

Highway National highways joined with railways provide a transportation network reaching every city and town in this region. The express highway between Hohhot and Baotou has been put into use.

Airway Centered round Hohhot, flights can

reach Baotou, Chifeng, Hulun Buir and Xilinhot as well as Beijing, Shanghai and 20 other major cities in China.

■ Places of Interest

Pasture scenery and unique ethnic culture are two major characteristics of Nei Mongol's tourism. Located in the northern border of the region, Da Hinggan Ling boast abundant resources of forest, river, diversified animals and wonderful natural sceneries. It is the largest primitive forest in China. The tomb of Genghis Khan is located at Ejin Horo Qi (B.), covering a total area of 50,000 square meters. The tomb of Princess Wang Zhaojun is located on the southern outskirts of Hohhot. Wang Zhaojun is regarded as the symbol of national unity, and her tomb is a monument to national unity. 70 kilometers from the city of Baotou, Wudangzhao is the largest and best preserved monastery in Nei Mongol. It was built during

the reign of Emperor Kangxi of the Qing Dynasty, after the model of Potala Palace in Tibet. Xiangshawan is to the south of Baotou. Sliding down from the sand hill, one can hear the sound of automobile and aircraft engines, a natural phenomenon that can not be explained. Other tourist attractions are: Five Pagodas Monastery, Dazhao Monastery, Mt. Arxan Hot Spring, Hulun Nur, Xiritala Grassland Scenic Spot, and Xilamuren Grassland Scenic Spot.

■ Local Products

As an important pasture in China, Nei Mongol produces various high quality leathers and wool products including thick caddice, carpet, camel's fine hair, cashmere and lamb skin. Saddles, Mongolian boots, and colourful stones are traditional local products. Local flavours like roast lamb, cream, dairy tofu, kumiss and liquor have distinctive taste.

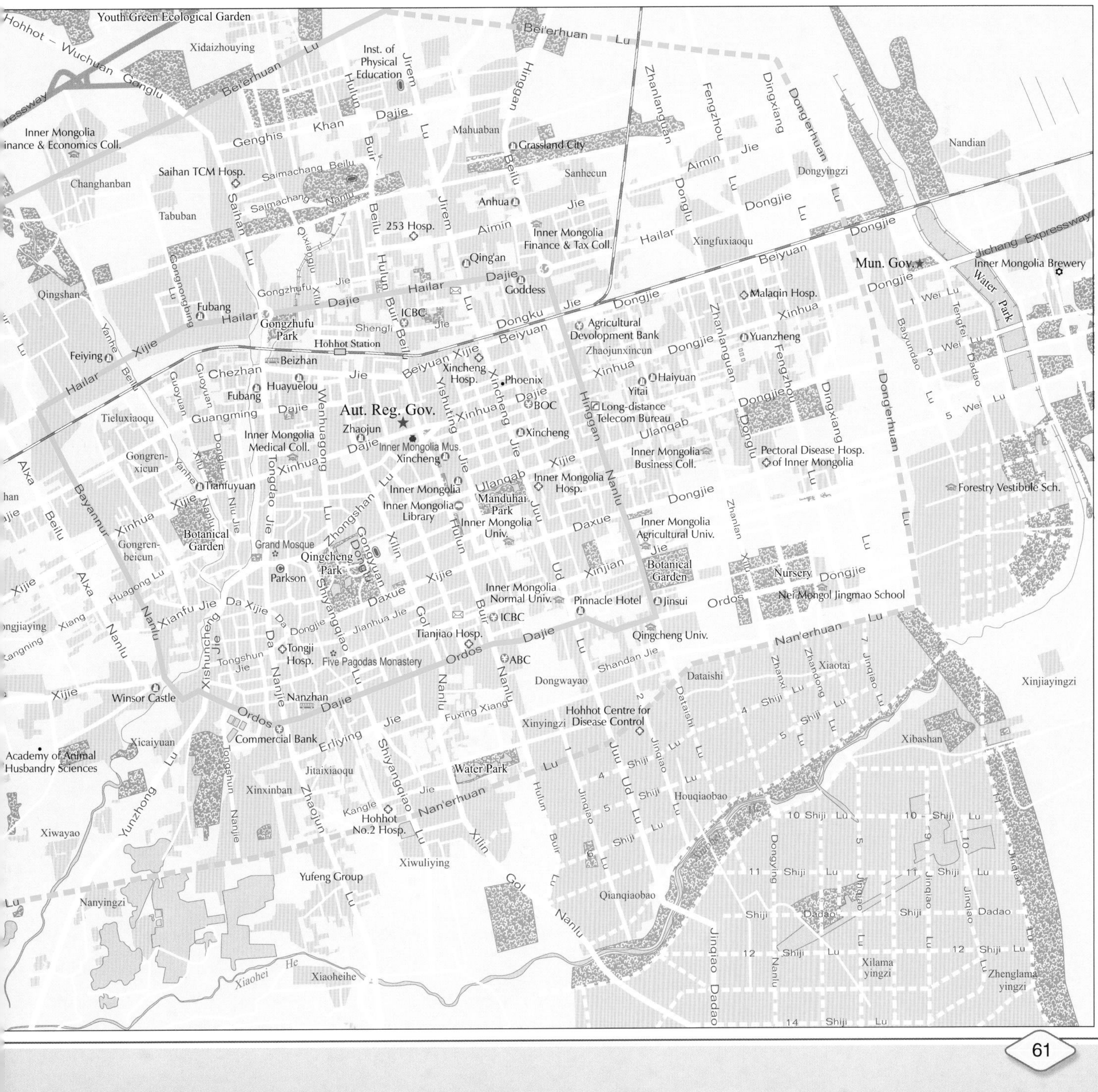

NEI MONGOL (INNER MONGOLIA) ZIZHIQU

Horqin Shadi

Hexigten Qi

Bairin Youqi · Bor Us · Ih Nur · Xar Moron He · Ping'an · Beixing · Yutiangpu · Dongliao

Shuangjingdian · Xiachang · Xar Moron · Xin Sum · Desheng · Dongxing

Wufendi · Bulen · Hails · Bayan Tohoi · Baixingtu · Narin · Qulut

Tianshenghao · Toufendi · Sidaozhangfang · Bayan Tohoi · Gurbanhua · Manghan

Zhirui · Guangdegong · Ongniud Qi · Axihan · Yutiangdao · Changsheng · Naiman Qi · Tarximod · Xiayangxumu · Sanjiazi · Hure Qi

Yangshugoumen · Udin Hua · Guras · Xinwopu · Liujiazi · Qogtoi · Ping an · Naringol · Mantar

Daguangdingzi Shan 2037 · Dujiadian · Hartohoi · Haxat · Yilongyongo · Ping an · Bayanhua

Jiangjiadian · Daliufen · *Hongshan Shuiku* · Mongli Gol · Xarholoi · Ping andi · Tayingzi

Xinbo · Jianchang · Sidaowanzi · Manihano · Niugutu · Hohon Gol · Fuxingdi · Jiumiao · Wuhuanchi

Damiao · Chutoulang · Wanbaoshan · Haladaokou · Aohan Qi · Fengshou · Qinglongshan · Bugt · Beita · Yusi · Dawujiazi

Guojiawan · Laofu · Honghuagou · Chifeng · Shaoguoyingzi · Taijiying · Beisijiao · Xinqiu Qu

Qipanshan · Yangjiawan · Reshui · Beiershijiazi · Xindi · Machango · Jinchanggouliang · Longtan · Quanyuyong · Dongguanying · Wangfu · Fuxin

Weichang · Niujiayingzi · Yuanbaoshan Qu · Heishui · Yichenggong · Huizhou · Gushanzi · Mt.Dahei · Dasanjia · Sanbao · Zhizhushan · Fosi · Mt.Haitang · Xinlit · Furongo

Harqin Qi · Wangyefu · Xiaochengzi · Taipingzhuang · Zhangjiayingzi · Xizi · Qingsongling · Harqin · Daqing Shan 1153 · Daban · Tohoit · Mayouying · Xinmin

Yaozhan · Andangou · Wangyadian · Baishan · Zhuluke · Damiao · Bianzhangzi · Har Nur · Chaoyang · Shangyuan · Sanbaoying · Gaotaizi · Beipiao · Qinghemen Qu · Baichangmen · Bada

Baihugou · Tangsanying · Banchui Shan 1807 · Songgon Gu · Ningcheng · Sanjia · Qingfengzhan · Yangshuwan · Shi ertuo · Chaoyang · Mt.Fenghuang · Batuying · Changheying · Hongjiangzi · Yamat · Heishan

Maojingba · Heilihe · Dianzi · Shahai · Zhongsanjia · Lianhe · Liulongtai · Qianyang · Yixian · Zhong'an · Luotuopu · Guangning

Longhua · Liangjia · Huangtuliangzi · Jianping · Xiaochengzi · Gongyingzi · Mutouchengzi · Nanshuangmiao · Qidaoling · Dizangsi · Liulongou · Zhangjiapu · Santaizi · Tianshiuo · Wujia

Hanmaying · Zhongguan · Lingbei · Ganzhao · Beisijiazi · Ershijiazi · Songlingmen · Danian · Yuji · Shishan · Yangjuanzi · Gaos

HEBEI · Sangou · Lingyuan · Xinglongzhuang · Yangjiaogou · Yangshan · Yaoling · Cuiyan · Linghai · Dongguo · Shixin · Pan

Luanping · Pingquan · Siguanyingzi · Dongjiadian · Shangzhi · Nanhuangmiao · Dahongtuo Shan 900 · Zhonghua · Xinxing · Pan

Shuangluan Qu · Chengde · Wafangdian · Harqin Zuoyi · Wafangzi · Gangyaoling · Nianniangong · Yanjia · Shuangtai Estuary · Dawa

Shangbancheng · Shanggu · Sanshijiazi · Songlingzi · Pingfangzi · Caochang · Niangniangmiao · Liujiazi · Shanshenmiao · Qiaojia · Qiaonan · Niangniangong · Xingsheng · Dayou · Zhaoquanhe · Gaojiao

BEIJING SHI · Chengde · Qianjin · Sanjiazio · Linglongta · Xiaodeyingzi · Dahongtuo Shan · Gangtun · Tasheng · Tianqiao · Dalinghe Kou · Erjiegou · Rongxing

Wuling Shan 2116 · Dangba · Dao'erdeng · Jianchang · Gongshanzui · Heishanke · Yangshuwan · Jiumen · Baita · Tasheng · Sirepu · Longgang Qu · *Jinzhou Wan* · *Liaohe Kou*

Kuancheng · Tangdaohe · Foyedong · Wangbaoyingzi · Lamadong · Sandaogou · Hongyazi · Xingcheng · Mt.Shoushan · *Dalinghe Kou*

Yingshouyingzi · Moguyu · Laodazhangzi · Yaolougou · Toudaoyingzi · Datun · Bajiazi · Nandashan · Caozhuang · Xingcheng Seashore · Juhuadao · *Juhua Dao* · Ying

Xinglong · Qinglong · Dongdadi · Daqing Shan 1224 · Gejia · Yangshuwan · Wangfei · Haibin

BEIJING SHI · Saheqiao · Xiaoyingzi · Dawutan · Liuzigou · Huangjia · Gaotaipu · Suizhong · *Liaodong Wan*

Zunhua · Buzidian · Zushang · Jiabeiyan · Fanjia · Qianwei · Huangdi · Tashantun · Bayuquan Qu

Jixian · Qianxi · Dacuozhuang · Yong anpu · Wangfengtai · Wanghu · Xiongyue · Jiulongdi

Dongjiuzhai · Shimenzhai · Xidianzi · Liguano

Yangjinzhuang · Yutian · Qian an · Huoshiying · Taiying · Shanhaiguan Qu · Wanjia · Yongning · Wanjialin

Fengrun Qu · Shaheyi · Lulong · Yuguan · Qinhuangdao · LIAODO

Daxinzhuang · Kaiping Qu · Luan Xian · Fuming · Beidaihe Qu · Donggang · Tuoshan · Yaridian

Lunan Qu · Anshan · Xinji · Changli · Fuzhoucheng · Delishi

TIANJIN SHI · Tangshan · Luannan · Tingliuhe · *Fuzhou Wan* · Xianyuwang · Wafangdian · Wav

Fengnan Qu · Luannan · Jianggezhuang · *Changxing Dao* · Changxingdao · Lidian · Datia

Ninghe · Jianzigu · Hugezhuang · Leting · *Luanhe Kou* · Bachageu · Pao'ai · Dengtun

Hangu Qu · Binhai · Tanghai · Xietun · Paotai · Fuzhouwan · Puland

Tanggu Qu · Yuetuo · *Hulushan Wan* · Jiaoliudao · *Xizhong Dao* · Pulandian Wan · Liangjiadian · Xingsh

Tangu Qu · Nanpu · Hatuo · Yaotuo · Dongkengtuo · Shijiutuo · *Ximayi Dao* · Daweijiao · Chengshantou Seashore · Daweijiao · Dengsheng

Shanggulin · Caofeidian · Snake Island-Mt.laotie · *Zhu Dao* · *Jinzhou Wan* · Jinzhou Qu · Xingang

Bohai Wan · She Dao · Haimaotuo · Zhoushuizizi Qu · Dalian Airport · Dalian · Sanshan Dao

HEBEI · *Bo Hai* · Tieshan · Lushunkou · Dalian Seashore · Lüshun · Jinshi Beach

Lüshunkou Qu · Jinshi

Altitude Table

200 50 20 0 50 100 200 300 500 750 1000 1500 2000 2500m

SHANDONG

Bohai Haixia · Yuan

F G H I J K

Shuangliao Gongzhuling Shanhejieo Shuanghe Nanlou Shan 1404 Changshan Songhua Hu

1

Ul Har Ereg Aduqin Waqban Yushutai Yitong Yantongshan Guanma Jinsha Erdaodianzi Huashulinzi

Jargalang Fujia Sanjiangkou Guojiadian Dagushan Yingchengzi Mingcheng Yushuqiazi Erdaodianzi

Haisgai Haliut Hotono Qijiazi Laosiping Bamiancheng Dawa Siping Shijiapu Xiaogushan Chaoyangshan Shahei huadian Hongshilazi

Qorin Zuoyi Houqi Qarso Dongga Shuangmiaozi Baiyu Pinggang Dexing Dongliao Liaoyuan Huangheo Baoshan Shidaohe Baishin

Changsheng Sanduo Xiaochengzi Baoli Simiancheng Quantou Lianhua Xifeng Anmin Anshu Daxing Dongfeng Huinan Na erhongo

Arxan Sihecheng Beisibu Dashazi Jinjia Changtu Taoran Gaojiadian Houshio Huinan Jingshan

Zhanggutai Erliusoukou Dongsheng Haoguantun Liangzhongqiao Chengping Zhenxin Meihekou Shengshuo Longquan Jingyu Sandaohu

Dade Houxinqiu Xiguantun Tongjiangkou Liuocheng Fangmu Helongo Xiaosiping Shancheng Jinchuan Fusong

Xinglongshan Baojiatun Faku Daqing Qinghe Qu Songshanpu Bakeshu Linfeng Yingchang Liuhe Jiangjiadian Liangshuihezi Jiangyuan Qu Wangou

Weizigou Sijiazi Kaiyuan Shijianfang Zhonggu Lijiatai Tukouzi Caosto Ankou Gushanzi Xinglin Xianrenjiao

Yujiawopu Diaobingshan Shangfeidi Chai Hongtumiao Houshi Gounaidian Liunan Jiangyuan

Zhoutzou Yemaotai Dagujiazi Kaoshan Morihong Shan 1013 Ying'emen Yangshuwai

Yaopu Tieling Cuizhenpu Dadianzi Zhenziling Shuiku Honghe Gully Qingyuan Dabeicha Baishan

Liangshan Taotun Baidizhai Hongtoushan Nankouqian Dashuhe Wandianzi Sipengo Erdaojiang Qu

Xinmin Dalama Gongzhutun Shifosio Hada Sanjianlin Shangliahe Shihua Dingzi 1090 Beisiping Tonghua Linjiang

Xinglongpu Yinjia Shenbei Xin Qu Wangbin Mantang Majuanzi Muqi Yongling Wangqingmen Tougao Yayuan

Yuhong Qu Fushun Dahuolang Shuiku Xiaodong Hou'an Mt. Houshi Yushuo Xiangshuihez Renao Shibu

SHENYANG Shiwen Xiahe Xinbin Hongmiaozi Daquanyuan Kasan

Taoxian Airport Hailang Qinghecheng Sanweishi Pingdingshan Huajianzi Yezhugou Cuaimozi

Sujiatun Qu Shahepu Waitoushan Gaoguan Weiziyu Muyuzi Dasiping Laotudingzi Beidianzi

Liaozhong Hongtou Dahenan Liubezi Shiqiaozi Guanyinge Shuiku Huanren Yahe

Dengta Shahu Dongfeng Benxi Water Tianshifu Balidianzi Siping

Liaoyang Takzi Benxi Lanheyu Huabo Shan 1336 Ji'an

Hongwei Qu Hanling 1294 Jiucai Dingzi Tianqiao Valley Shajianzi Kanggye

Anshan Gongchangling Qu Nanfen Qu Caohezhang Baishilazi Niumaowu Liangshuib Wiwon

Qianshan Qu Xiadahe Lianshanguano Saima Guanshui 1270 Sifangdingzi Budayuan Xialuhe Hunjiang

Haicheng Bahui Kaofental Hei Shan 1181 Caohekou Aiyang Dachuantun Taipingshao Zhenjiango

Dashiqiao Mafeng Jidongyu Taziling Qingchengzi Simenzi Daxing Qingyishan Kuandian Daxicha Koin

Bali Jiewen Muniu Sanjiazi Shimiaozi Lujiahe Shicheng Maodianzi

Gaizhou Chagou Huanghuadiano Dafangshen Tanggou Jiguanshano Dapu Yangmuchuan Changdiano Sakchu

Yinglco Zhoujia Panling Suzigou Chaoyang Fengcheng Baogan Dongtang Hwapung-ri

Damiaogou Hadabei Shihuiyao Dayingzi Baiqi Bianmen Fangshancheng Mt. Fenghuang Gulouo

Xiuyan Wolongquan Qianyingo Yangjiapu Shazhai Yulongo Husham Taegwang

Buyun Shan 1130 Sanjiashan Longtan Linggou Shaozihe Lanqi Dandong Sinuiju Kusong Huichon

Guiyunhua Ronghuashan Xinnongo Mt.Dagu Majjadian Langtou Yomju

Taipingling Huashan Xuling Wulu Donggang Seashore Wetland in Yalu R. Estuary Sonch'on

Guangmingshan Chengshan Shaling Nanjian Dalu Dao Yalujiang Kou Taegwang

Zhuanghe Dazheng Xiaolu Dao D.P.R. KOREA

Changhai Haixia Shicheng Dao Wangjiadao Ka-do Sukchon Yangdok

Dachangshan Dao Wumang Dao Sinmi-do Sunch'on

Dawangjia Dao Taehwa-do P'yongsong

Changshan Qundao Dongdalian Dao Haiyang Dao Sochoson - man

Zhangzi Dao Waichangshan Dao P'YONGYANG Songho Sinp'yong

Yellow Sea Onch'on Taedonggang-gu Hwangju

Nampo

Liaoning Province

With Shenyang as its capital, Liaoning Province, which is abbreviated as "Liao", is located in the south of Northeast China, facing the Yellow Sea and Bo Hai (sea) on the south. Covering an area of over 150 000 square kilometers, it has a population of 41.62 million, including such ethnic groups as Han, Man, Mongol, Hui, Korean, and Xibe. The population of Man and Xibe in this province is the largest in China.

■ Geographical Features

Topography Liaoning's topography is characterized by the central Liaohe Pingyuan (Pln.) (lower than 50 meters in altitude) sandwiched in between mountains and hills less than 500 meters above sea level on the east and west sides, such as Qian Shan (Mt.), Longgang Shan, Nulu'erhu Shan, Song Ling (Mt.) and Yiwulü Shan. Liaodong Bandao (Pen.) on the south thrusts between the Liaodong Wan (G.) and the Yellow Sea with a serpentine coastline characterized by numerous ports and gulfs. There are over 500 islands distributed along the coastline. Liao He (R.), Yalu Jiang (Sino-Korean boundary river), Daling He, Xiaoling He, Hun He, Taizi He and Raoyang He are major rivers in this region, of which Liao He is the largest.

Climate North temperate semi-humid and moist continental monsoon climate rules the area, bringing about distinctive seasonal difference. Annual rainfall in this area is between 500～1, 000mm. The average annual temperature here is -6～11℃, with an average temperature in January between -15～-5℃, while in July around 24℃.

■ Natural Resources

By now over 110 kinds of minerals were found in Liaoning, among which the reserves of minerals like iron, boron, magnesite, diamond, steatite, jade and several others are ranked as China's No. 1. The reserves of oil, natural gas, coal, sulfur, halite, manganese nodule, and placer are found on the continental shelf. Liaohe Oilfield is the third largest oilfield with natural gas in China. The reserves of oil and natural gas found here take up 15% and 10% respectively of China's total.

Liaoning's forest cover rate is around 30.95%. Rich living marine resources have been found in this province. There are over 520 species of offshore aquatic resources, including over 100 species of fish and great varieties of shellfish and algae, of which over 80 species are of economic value.

■ Agriculture

As a major production region of cotton and peanuts in northeast China, Liaoning's agriculture is quite well developed. Main crops are: broomcorn, corn, soybean, millet, sweet potato, potato, cotton, peanut, tobacco, tussor, and beet. The hilly area of east Liaoning is the main production area of tussor. Apple and peach produced in Dalian and Yingkou are well known. Pig, horse and cow are raised in the province, of which Tieling horse is of the best strain. Aquiculture is developed along the coastal area. Liaodong Wan and Haiyang Dao (I.) are two major fisheries. The output of prawn produced here leads in China.

■ Industry

With an industrial history of nearly a century, Liaoning is a major industrial base in China. Petro-chemical industry, metallurgy, electronics, machinery building material production, coal mining, power generation, textile and pharmacy are developed in Liaoning, among which the first four are pillar industries of this province. Many local industrial products play important roles in China's economy, including: steel, iron, rolled steel, soda ash, caustic soda, crude oil, natural gas, raw coal, machine tool, metallurgical equipment, mining equipment, transformer, and automobile. Shenyang, together with Beijing, Tianjin and Shanghai, are known as China's four centers of machine building industry.

■ Transportation

Railway Trunk lines like Beijing-Harbin, Shenyang-Jilin, Shenyang-Dandong,

Shenyang-Shanhaiguan, Shenyang-Dalian and Jinzhou-Chengde run through the province, connecting every county in the region.

Highway Centered round Shenyang, national highways and provincial highways connect every city, county, and major railway stations in this region. Express highways like Beijing-Shenyang, Shenyang-Dalian, Shenyang-Dandong and Shenyang-Fushun have further improved highway transportation system in Liaoning.

Airway Airports in Shenyang and Dalian offer flights to over 100 major cities in China as well as international destinations in Japan, Russia, and R.D Korea.

Waterway Dalian is a world renowned seaport

Shenyang Imperial Palace

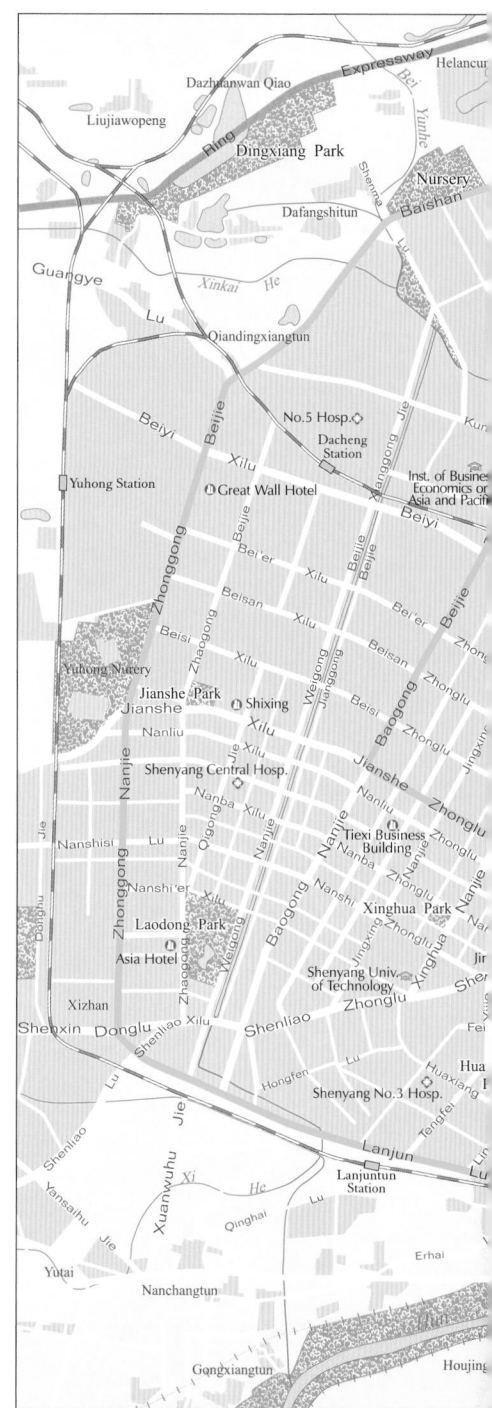

and a major import and export seaport in northeast China. Dalian, together with Yingkou, Dandong, Jinzhou and Huludao, are connected with over 140 international seaports by ocean routes.

■ Places of Interest

Liaoning has rich historical and cultural relics as well as beautiful natural scenery. Mt. Qianshan, a scenic mountain with 999 peaks, is located to the southeast of Anshan city. Many hotsprings were found along Yalu River where there are rich resources of propagation. Xianren Cave, Mt. Laotudingzi, Mt. Yiwulu, and other national nature reserves are also located in this area. Shedao Island near Lushunkou is a world renowned scenic spot. The Benxi Water Cave, a

limestone cave formed some five million years ago, is located in Benxi County, this rare physiography in north China is the longest limestone cave in Asia. Xingcheng Seashore runs for 14 kilometers long. This smooth beach covered with soft sands is an ideal summer reserve. The Jinshi Beach National Holiday Resort in Dalian is famed as a museum of geographical structure with many naturally-formed strange shapes of rocks. Other major attractions in Dalian include: Tiger Beach, Bangchui Island, Mt. Laotie, historical sites of war field in Sino-Japan and Japan-Russia Wars, and several wonderful bathing beaches. Shenyang Imperial palace and three tombs of Qing Emperors and the Capital cities and Tombs of the Ancient Koguryo Kingdom are

included in the World Heritage List by UNESCO. Other tourist attractions are: cliff painting in Liaoyang, Mt. Jinniu in Yingkou, Leifeng Memorial in Fushun and monuments of Liaoshen Campaign in Jinzhou.

■ Local Products

Apple, pear, peach are well known local fruits. Tussor silk produced in Dandong is a kind of famed costuming. Liaoning is also a major production area of "three treasures of Northeast China,"- ginseng, mink, and pilose antler. Shell carving, jade carving, agate carving, clean coal carving, glass wares and amber craftwork are traditional local handicrafts.

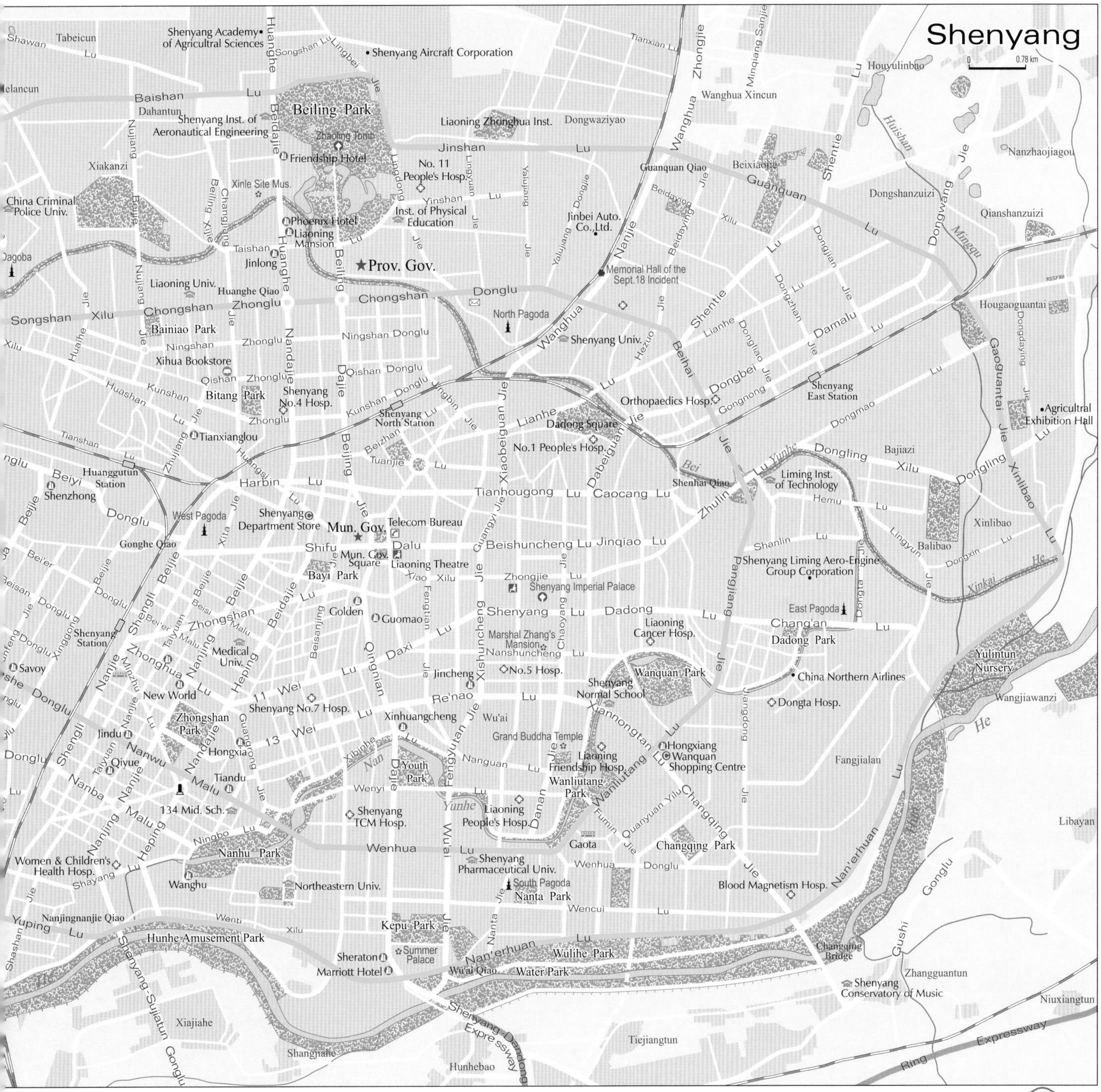

A 1 B C D E F

Oborjalag Guller Gol Qarsan Eregt Tailai Bayan Qagan Honggang Qu Anda Pingshan Linjiang
Shumugou Guller Gol Baomen Guler Gol Temeji Gang Ger Dandai Xinglongquanzi Shengping Songzhan Lanxi
Laotou Shan 1392 Ulanhot Dongping Hantu Wukeshuo Melmeg Talinhiag Datong Qu Zhaodong
Hørqin Youyi Qianqi Hure Dongsheng Lingdai Yinghua Xilt Melmeg Xiao'ertun Yaoxin Xingcheng Sifang
Barun Jirem Yong'an Najin Ping'an Zhenlai Heiyupao Chatai Yanjiang Gulong Daxing Yongle Fengle Wuzhan Zhaozhou
Tule Mod Liuhu Wanbao Wafang Zhennan Qingshan Shengli Honggangzi Yuellangpao Taiyangsheng Zhaozhou Sizhan Taiping Airport
Hondlon Shyiquan Jubao Yongmao Saghe Laifu Zhangjiadian Maoxing Fenghua Sanzhan
Tuquan Daiqin Tal Jun Tabin Jiaoliuheo Taodong Linhai Taohe Xuexin Sheli Lianjiazi Da'an Changchunling Wanlong Shuangche
Hoh Qel Datong Deshun Daba Chagan Xinping'an Da'an Changshan Sanyi Shiqiao Dalinzi
Barun Dorol Xin'aili Anding Erlong Wushengtang Shibahujao Xidawa Boduo Dawa Sanjingzi Gongpengzi Hong
Jarud Gahair Budun Hua Xianghai Shuanggang Bamian Longzhao Tianzijing Maoduzhuang Ningjiang Qu Erlongshan Dalinzi Caijiagou
Ih Bey Golin Baixing Xi Ail Jubaoshan Shizui Yuzi Menggutun Songyuan Qian Gorlos Xinwanfang Fuyu Xinchengju
Mod Bayan Nur Hongxing Daozi Qagan Hua Linzi Rangzi Chongxin Xinlio Zengsheng Xinzhan Xiyuan
Qabagt Huanghuashan Linsheng Xinglongshan Qijingzio Tongyu Shihuadao Caizi Zanzi Tingzijing Dashan Baodian Xiaochengzi Kaoshang Dafangshen Yush
Dolod Tuanjie Xinfa Sugongtuo Tongjiadian Suozi Yanzi Shenjingzi Hongquan Chengzijie Chaoyang
Jarud Hoyor Sihetun Zanyuo Ulan Hua Bianzhao Sanshihao Qian'an Changlong Yangshulic Halahai Gaojiadian Tiantai Mishule
Zili Machang Beizheng Ulan Od Ulan Tug Ciziging Dong Haxatu Sanshengyu Wanshun Xiaofangshen Xinnongo Weizigou Jiutai
Bor Ondor Dalji Taipingchuan Santuan Jiti Fulongquano Sanqingshan Datulong Sanbao Buhai Dagingzi Qitamu
Hua Huxu Yolin Mod Xifengku Bashiba Longfeng Gudian Guangming Taipingshan Bajilet Lijiadian Hepingo Erdaoji
Horqin Zuoyi Zhongqi Daxing Changling Qianqihao Haiqing Huangjin Zhucheng Xinglong Chenzijie
Xibe Hua Bulangin Jo Songjiaygo Qianihao Dongling Yongjiu Longwang Helong Huajia Jiutai
Xiaojieji Hua Tugan Baixingt Xidai Xiangyang Fuxian Bolichengzi Yulin Shuangchengpu Lanjiao Shitoukemen Zuojiao Gudianzi Ji
Junchang Qianjiadian Daode Xiliao Xinglong Wohu Shuanglong Huaide Qinjiatun Donghu Fengman
Xugin Kailu Maolin Bolishan Maochengzi Shangshutai Heshan Longjia Airport Fanjiatun Bonhe Taiping
Ping an Yuliangpu Tongliao Hongqi Shuangshan Bawu Fufeng Guanting Wancang
Baixingto Narin Har Ereg Budun Hargano Wangben Iujiaguazi Gujiazi Xiaochengzi Liufangzi Heilinzio Badahu-Jingyue L Xiyingcheng Yong
Yamenyingzi Manghan Hhar Us Shuanghao Linhai Yushutuo Shengli Caijia Nanwaizi Kaoshan Leshan Shuangyang Qu Xintingxiang Dachat
Qogtoio Iihtal Jargalangt Qars Baishan Guojiadian Ma'anshan Diaoshuihu Tongjia Shanhejie Xiyang
Oulut Lamadian Shijiapu Xiaogushan Xiwei Yingchengzi Xichang Mingcheng Guanba Yong
Horqin Zuoyi Houqi Haisgai Hoton Bamianchengzi Lishu Yeheo Quantai Jinzhou Heyuan Yuqingtun Yimao
Hure Qi Liujiazi Sanlazi Baoli Shamen Shilingzi Xi'an Qu Shihe Chaoyangshan Guodayuan Panshi
Shuiquan Naringol Fengjiao Houxinqiu Changsheng Beisijiazi Laocheng Donghao Huanghedi Kinghua Baoshan Mt.Guanmalianhu
Hohon Gol Hartao Laocheng Siping Liaoyuan Erlongshan Yizuoying
Jiumiao Zhangwu Faku Diaobingshan Kaiyuan Xifeng Daxing Dongfeng Sanhe Hailong Huinan
Yusi Luotuo Shan 626 Dagutazi Zhonggu Bakeshu Yingchang Fangmu Xiaosiping Yangzishao Shansonggang Shi
Fuxin Zidutai Paozio Dengshibazi Tieling Kaoshantun Shangfeidi Shancheng Hongmei Liuhe Luotongshan Jinch
Xinlitun Gongzhutuno Shenbei Xin Qu Jiangjiajie Sanxian Shijiadian Liangshi
Xiaotazi Badaohao Hengdaohezi Morihong Shan 1013 Xiangyang Ankou Tuoyanling Gangou
Shangyuan Wanghai Shan 866 Heishan Jinwutaizi Damintun Xinmin Fushun Nankouqian Lanshan Jinchanggou Sipeng Erdaojiang Qu Baishan
Yi Xian Beizhen Gaoshanzi Manduhu Suntun Qu Taoxian Airport Hou'an Xinbin Qinyuan Fujiang Tonghua Dongla
Liulongtai Jinzhou Linghai Dongguo Panshan Liaozhong Dengta Waltoushan Muqi Shituai Dingzi 1090 Sankeyushu Dadufu Qinghe
Gaoqiao Panjin Gaosheng Tai an Liaoyang Benxi Benxi Weiziyu Majiazi Huanren Shajiazi
Liaodong Wan Huangshatuo Liaoyang Taibai Shenwo Shui Jiuca Dingzi 1254 Sifang Dingzi 1270 Numelou Ji'an
Yingkou Haicheng Anshan Nanfen Qu Saimao Lantou Dingzi Guanshuih Hunjiang Wiwon

Altitude Table
4000 3000 2000 1000 200 50 20 0 50 100 200 300 500 750 1000 1500 2000 2500 3000m

HEILONGJIANG

RUSSIA

D. P. R. KOREA

Sea of Japan

Zal. Petra Velikogo

Vladivostok

Ussuriysk

Artem

Tavrichenko

Baoqing

Qitaihe

Boli

Mishan

Jixi

Jidong

Suifenhe

Dongning

Mudanjiang

Hailin

Ning'an

Wangqing

Hunchun

Tumen

Yanji

Longjing

Helong

Unggi

Ch'ŏngjin

Kyongsŏng

Myongch'on

Kilchu

Hyesan

Changbai

Baishan

Fusong

Dunhua

Jiaohe

Wuchang

Shangzhi

Acheng

HARBIN

Bin Xian

Bayan

Mulan

Tonghe

Fangzheng

Yilan

Huanan

Yilan

Linkou

Muling

Lishu Qu

Daqingshan

ZHANGGUANGCAI LING

CHANGBAI SHAN

LAOYE LING

MUDAN LING

WEIHU LING

HAOLING LING

TAIPING LING

Changbaishan Tianchi

Mt. Changbai
Changbai 2744

Jingpo Hu

Xingkai Hu

Tuman-gang-gu

Scale 1:2 400 000   0 24 48 72 96 120km

Jilin Province

With Changchun as its capital, Jilin Province, which is abbreviated as "Ji", is located in the central part of Northeast China. Covering an area of over 180,000 square kilometers, it has a population of 26.59 million, including such ethnic groups as Han, Korean, Man, Mongol, Hui, and Xibe.

■ Geographical Features

Topography Jilin is high in the southeast and low in the northwest. Mountains and hills are mainly in the northeast part, while in the midwest lie two plains—Songnen Pingyuan and Liaohe Pingyuan—divided by Songhua Jiang (R.) and Liao He (R.). Here there are small basins, including the Yanji, Hunjiang and Dunhua. The northwestern part of the province is a section of pasture. There are many rivers in this region, including Songhua Jiang, Yalu Jiang (Sino-Korean boundary river), Tumen Jiang (Sino-Korean boundary river), Mudan Jiang, Suifen He and Hun Jiang. Tian Chi (L.), Songhua Hu (L.), Yueliang Pao, Dabs Nur (L.) and Qagan Nur are major lakes among many.

Climate North temperate semi-humid and semi-arid continental monsoon climate rules the area, bringing distinctive seasonal difference. Summer here is short and warm, while winter is long and cold. Annual rainfall in this area is between 400~800mm. The average annual temperature here is between -3~7℃, with an average temperature in January around -18℃, while in July between 20~23℃.

■ Natural Resources

By now over 140 kinds of minerals have been found in Jilin, among which the reserves of minerals like oil shale, Iceland spar, diatomite, floatstone, cinder, dolomite, basalt, andesite marble and several others are abundant.

There are many rivers flowing through this province, of which over 16 rivers have drainage areas larger than 50 square kilometers. Numerous lakes are found in this region, among which nearly 1,400 lakes are larger than 6 hectares, adding up to a total acreage of 1,650 square meters.

Extensive marshes of diversified type inhabited by a great variety of life forms have been found in Jilin.

As a major forest area in China, Jilin's forest cover rate is around 37.43%, mostly pine trees, birches and poplars of dozens of different types. There are over 440 species of land animals and over 3,890 species of wildings living in this province.

Hot springs containing rich minerals found in Changbai Shan (Mt.) are the major geothermal resources of Jilin.

■ Agriculture

Jilin is a major production region of commodity grain and soybean in China. Major crops here are: corn, soybean, rice, broomcorn, millet, wheat, potato, beet, sunflower, tobacco as well as vegetables, fruits, oil plants, hemp and medicinal herbs. As a major forest area in China, Changbai Shan is a supply center of wood, raw material for paper making and Chinese medicinal herbs. Sheep, cow are raised in Baicheng, a major pasture in the province. Songhua Jiang, Nen Jiang, Songhua Hu and Yueliang Pao are major fisheries.

■ Industry

As the power supply hub in northeast China, Jilin's industries mainly consist of auto manufacturing, petro-chemical industry, power generation, forest machinery production, paper making, textile and pharmacy. Local industrial products like automobiles, passenger train, tractors, ferroalloy, charcoal products, wood, plywood, machine-made paper, and wine are well known in China. China FAW Group Corporation, Tonghua Winery, Fengman Hydropower Station are renowned local enterprises.

■ Transportation

Railway Railways like Beijing–Harbin, Shenyang–Jilin, Siping–Meihekou, Changchun–Tumen, Changchun–Baicheng and Siping–Qiqihar run across the province and take on 2/3 of its total freight volume.

Highway Centered round Changchun, Jilin, Siping, Tonghua, Baicheng and Yanji, national highways together with provincial highways connect every city and county in the province. Express highways like Changchun–Jilin, Changchun–Siping, Changchun–Harbin and Changchun–Shenyang have been put into use.

Airway Changchun Airport provide flights to Beijing, Shanghai and other major cities in China as well as international destinations in R.O. Korea and Russia.

Waterway Nen Jiang, Songhua Jiang, Tumen Jiang and Yalu Jiang are navigable from April to November. Jilin, Da'an and Linjiang are major river ports.

■ Places of Interest

Jilin has abundant tourism resources, most of which are along the route of Changchun–Jilin–Songhua Jiang–Changbai Shan. Changbai Shan, a national nature reserve, is located in the southeast of Jilin province. Known for its vertical change in natural scenery and primitive ecosystem, this area is listed as a Biosphere Reserve by UNESCO. Tian Chi, a legendary lake on a volcano crater, is located among its mountain range. Songhua Lake is the largest artificial lake in China. Jingyue Pool scenic area is to the southeast of Changchun. It is composed of an enchanting pool and the exhibition hall of "Manchuguo", the Japanese

Tian Chi (Heavenly Lake) of Mount Changbai

imperialism's puppet state. Xianghai Marsh is the habitat of red-crown cranes. It is a national natural reserve and is listed in Databook of World Major Marshes. Rime in Jilin is one of China's four major natural sights. It usually occurs from late November to next March and April, making the city a crystal fairy land. Capital Cities and Tombs of the Ancient Koguryo Kingdom in Ji'an are included in the World Heritage List by UNESCO. Other tourist attractions are: the ancient city of Huanglong Fu, Yehe and the pogoda of Liao Dynasty.

■ Local Products

Jilin is a world-renowned producer of the "three treasures of Northeast China", – ginseng, mink, and pilose antler (Ginseng in Fusong and pilous antler in Huinan are of best quality). The province is also well known for the production of glossy ganoderma, elevated gastrodis, and other precious traditional Chinese medicinal herbs as well as rare mushrooms, agaric, honey, pear, wood frog oil and wild grape. Wine produced in this province are liked by many. Embroidery, birch bark painting, artistic walking stick, and iron wares are traditional local handicrafts.

Changchun

RUSSIA

NEI MONGOL (INNER MONGOLIA) ZIZHIQU

DA HINGGAN LING

XIAO HINGGAN LING

YILEHULI SHAN

Khabarovsk
Birobidzhan
Svobodnyy
Belogorsk
Blagoveshchensk
Zavitinsk
Heihe
Sunwu
Xunke
Jiayin
Tangwanghe Qu
Wuyiling Qu
Xinqing Qu
Bei'an
Wudalianchi
Nehe
Nenjiang
Morin Dawa Qi
Oroqen
Mohe
Tahe
Huma
Huzhong

Altitude Table
4000 3000 2000 1000 200 50 0 50 100 200 300 500 750 1000 1500 2000 2500 3000m

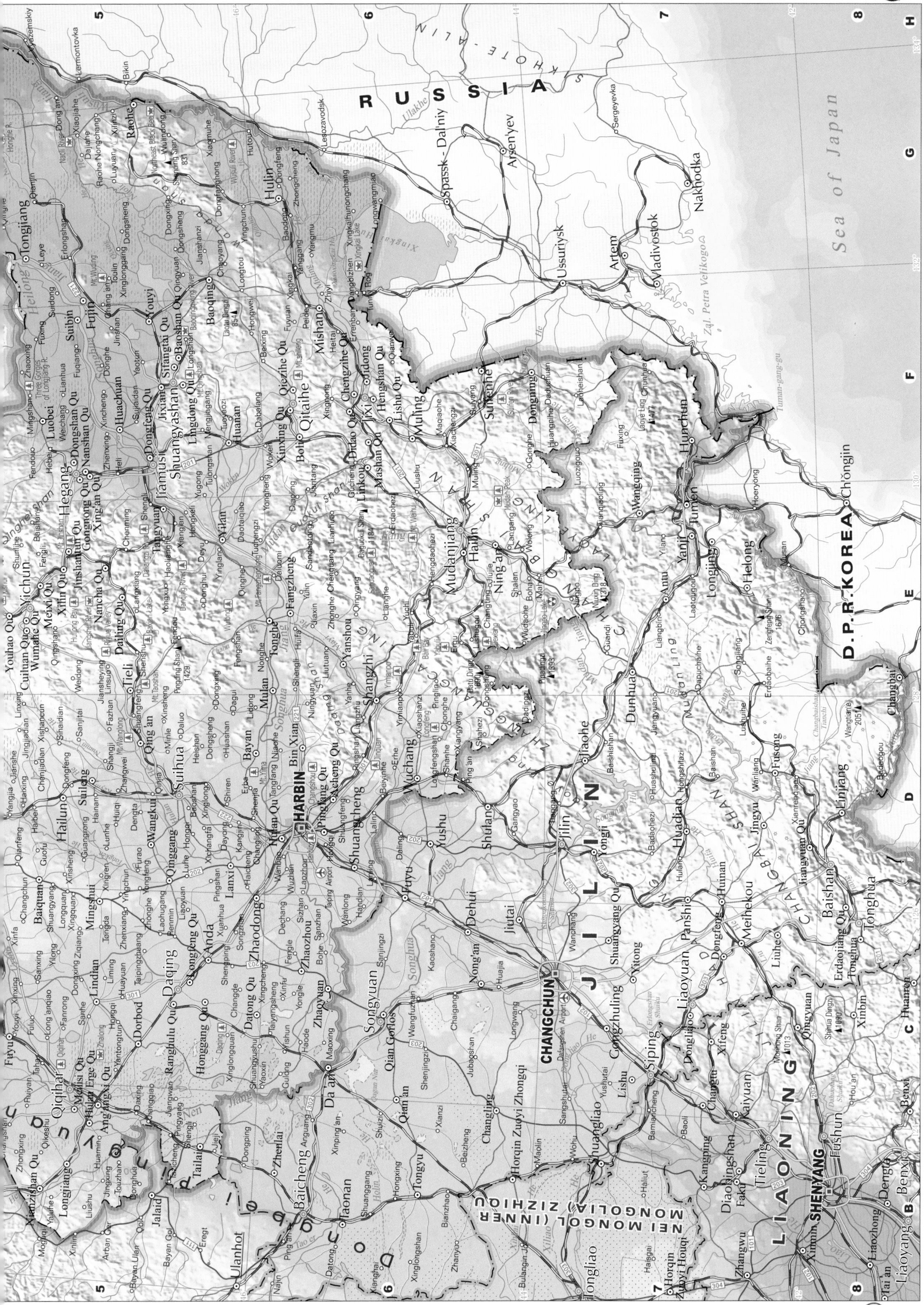

Scale 1:3 800 000

0   38   76   114   152   190km

Heilongjiang Province

With Harbin as its capital, Heilongjiang Province, which is abbreviated as "Hei", is located along the northeast border of China. Covering an area of over 460,000 square kilometers, it is a province on the utmost north and east of China with the highest latitude. The province has a population of 37.24 million, including such ethnic groups as Han, Man, Korean, Mongol, Hui, Daur, Xibe, Hezhen and Oroqen.

■ Geographical Features

Topography Heilongjiang is high in the northwest and low in the southeast, with mountains and plains each average 50% of its total area. The Xiao Hinggan Ling with an elevation of above 800 meters slants across the province in the middle. The alluvial plain of the Songhua Jiang and Nen Jiang lies to the west, while the low lying Sanjiang Plain made by silt deposits of the Heilong Jiang, Songhua Jiang and Wusuli Jiang lies to the east. Other major mountains are: Da Hiaggan Ling (Mts.), Zhangguangcai Ling, Laoye Ling and Wanda Shan. There are five large river systems in this region: Heilong Jiang, Songhua Jiang, Wusuli Jiang, Nen Jiang and Suifen He. Large lakes include Xingkai Hu, Jingbo Hu, Wuda Lianchi and Lianhuan Hu.

Climate Mild and cold temperate semi-humid continental climate rules the area. Summer here is short and rainy, while winter is long and cold. Annual rainfall in this area is between 400～700mm. The average annual temperature here is between -2～3℃, with an average temperature in January between -30～-18℃, while in July between 18～22℃. The coldest temperature ever recorded being -52.3℃ (Mohe), Heilongjiang is the coldest province in China.

■ Natural Resources

By now over 130 kinds of minerals were found in Heilongjiang, among which the reserves of minerals like oil, graphite, coal, gold, feldspar, pozzolana, quartz, and dozens of others are ranked among China's top ten. The province also has rich resources of minerals like copper, lead, zinc, and tungsten.

The total flow of Heilongjiang province is the largest among those three provinces in northeast China, with over 1,900 rivers having drainage areas larger than 50 square kilometers. Extensive primitive forest can be found in this province. Its forest cover rate is around 38.72%, mostly pine trees, willows and Chinese catalpa. Numerous wild animals and plants live in this province, including rare animals like northeast tiger, red-crowned crane, lynx, red deer, otter and reindeer as well as economic plants like agaric, mushroom, hedgehog hydnum, pine nut, and wild grape.

■ Agriculture

As a major production base of commodity grain and livestock, Heilongjiang's output and export volume of soybean are ranked as China's No. 1. Major crops here include: soybean, corn, wheat, rice, millet, potato, flax, sunflower, beet and tobacco. Da Hinggan Ling has a world renowned Korean pine forest and is an important wood producing area in China. Nenjiang Pingyuan (Pln.) is a high grade pasture where animal husbandry is well developed. The number of dairy cows raised here and the milk produced here all ranked China's No. 1. Sheep, dairy goat and pig are also breed in this region. Songhua Jiang is a major fishery, while abundant salmon and sturgeon are found in Heilong Jiang and Wusuli Jiang.

■ Industry

Heilongjiang is an important industrial base of China. It has well developed energy, machinery, chemical production, food processing, paper making, sugar-making, textile, and rubber industries. Productions of oil, wood, large size power generator, metallurgical equipment, freight train, mini cars, heavy machine tool, veneer and fiberboard all lead in China. Daqing Oilfield is one of those supreme oilfields in the world. Supreme coal mines are built in Hegang, Jixi, Shuangyashan and Qitaihe.

■ Transportation

Railway Main stems like Beijing–Harbin, Harbin–Manzhouli, Harbin–Suifenhe, Harbin–Jiamusi, Siping–Qiqihar, Qiqihar–Bei'an, Fuyu–Xilin and Linkou–Dongfanghong railways connect 2/3 of the cities and counties in the province, of which the railway from Suifenhe to Manzhouli via Harbin is the continental bridge connecting Asia with Europe.

Highway Highway network in the province extends in all directions. Suifenhe–Manzhouli, Harbin–Jiamusi express highways have been put into use.

Airway Harbin is an international air terminal in northeast China. Flight courses from Harbin can reach Beijing, Shanghai and over 30 other cities in China as well as destinations in Japan, Russia and R.O. Korea.

Waterway Songhua Jiang is the major inland navigation course. Most parts of Heilong Jiang, Nen Jiang and Wusuli Jiang are navigable.

■ Places of Interest

Located in the northeastern part of China, Heilongjiang Province boasts rich tourist resources due to its extraordinary geographical feature and climate conditions. Harbin, Yabuli and Hailin are renowned sites for snow activities endowed with favourable natural conditions and complete facilities. Jingpo Lake is the largest alpine barrier lake in China. It was formed about 10,000 years ago when the Mudan Jiang was blocked by the lava from volcanic eruptions. Zhalong, the well known "homeland of red-crown cranes", is situated to the southwest of Qiqihar. A vast marshland sprinkled with shallow lakes, the Zhalong Nature Reserve is the first nature reserve established in China for the protection of birds. Located in the southwestern part of Heihe city, the Wudalianchi Lake Scenic Area is another well-known national nature reserve. In this area 14 cones marked the sites of dormant volcanoes. With a perfect preservation of the original geographical conditions, it is acclaimed as the "Museum of Volcanoes". The Site of Longquan and the Upper Capital of Bohai Kingdom are cultural relics worth visiting. There are also a variety of special interest tours catering for tourists, such as the ice and snow tour, the forest tour, the summer resort tour, and the border town tour.

■ Local Products

Forest products like ginseng, pilose antler, Chinese magnoliavine, and other traditional Chinese medicinal herbs as well as edible wild herbs like agaric, mushroom, and day lily together with salmon and sturgeon in Heilong Jiang and Wusuli Jiang are renowned local specialties. Jade carving, ivory carving, silver table wares and antler painting are traditional local handicrafts. Local flavours like Oroqen roast mutton cubes are liked by many.

Snowfield Scenery

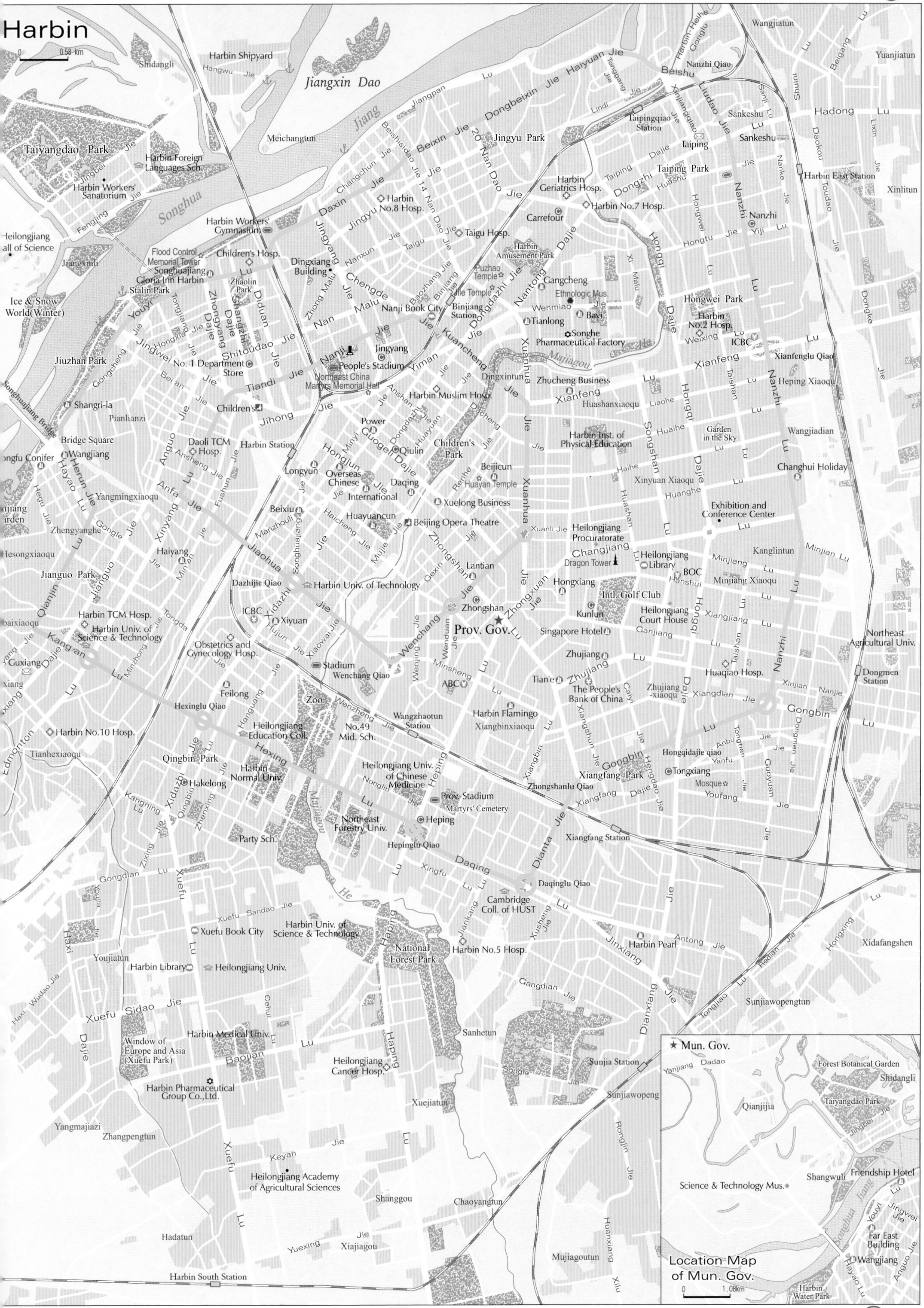

Harbin

0.58 km

Jiangxin Dao

Songhua Jiang

Taiyangdao Park
Harbin Shipyard
Shidangli
Hangwu Jie
Meichangtun

Harbin Foreign Languages Sch.
Harbin Workers' Sanatorium
Heilongjiang Hall of Science
Jiangxin
Ice & Snow World (Winter)

Beishisidao Jie
Beixin Jie
Dongbeixin Jie
Haiyuan Jie
Jingyu Park
Nanzhi Qiao
Beishu
Taipingqiao Station
Taiping
Taiping Park
Hadong Lu
Yuanjiatun
Harbin East Station
Xinlitun

Harbin Workers' Gymnasium
Children's Hosp.
Flood Control Memorial Tower
Songhuajiang
Gloria Inn Harbin
Stalin Park
Zhaolin Park
Dingxiang Building
Harbin No.8 Hosp.
Taigu Hosp.
Harbin Geriatrics Hosp.
Harbin No.7 Hosp.
Carrefour
Harbin Amusement Park
Puzhao Temple
Wenmiao
Gangcheng
Ethnologic Mus.
Bayi
Tianlong
Songhe Pharmaceutical Factory
Hongwei Park
Harbin No.2 Hosp.
Weixing
ICBC

Nanji Book City
Binjiang Station
Zhucheng Business
Xianfeng
Huashanxiaoqu
Xianfenglu Qiao
Heping Xiaoqu
Wangjiadian

People's Stadium
Northeast China Martyrs Memorial Hall
Harbin Muslim Hosp.
Dingxintun
Harbin Inst. of Physical Education
Garden in the Sky
Changhui Holiday

Jiuzhan Park
Shangri-la
Pianlianzi
Bridge Square
Wangjiang
Daoli TCM Hosp.
Harbin Station
Children's Park
Huayan Temple
Beijicun
Xinyuan Xiaoqu
Exhibition and Conference Center

Longyun
Overseas Chinese International
Daqing
Xuelong Business
Beijing Opera Theatre
Heilongjiang Procuratorate
Changjiang
Dragon Tower
Heilongjiang Library
BOC
Minjiang
Kanglintun
Minjian Lu

Dazhijie Qiao
Harbin Univ. of Technology
ICBC
Xiyuan
Zhongshan
Prov. Gov.
Kunlun
Singapore Hotel
Intl. Golf Club
Heilongjiang Court House

Obstetrics and Gynecology Hosp.
Stadium
Wenchang Qiao
ABC
Zhujiang
Tian'e
The People's Bank of China
Northeast Agricultural Univ.
Dongmen Station

Harbin No.10 Hosp.
Feilong
Hexinglu Qiao
Zoo
Wangzhaotun Station
No.49 Mid. Sch.
Harbin Flamingo
Xiangbinxiaoqu
Hongqidajie qiao
Tongxiang
Gongbin Lu

Qingbin Park
Harbin Normal Univ.
Hakelong
Heilongjiang Education Coll.
Heilongjiang Univ. of Chinese Medicine
Xiangfang Park
Mosque
Youfang

Northeast Forestry Univ.
Prov. Stadium
Martyrs' Cemetery
Heping
Hepinglu Qiao
Zhongshanlu Qiao
Xiangfang Station

Party Sch.
Daqing
Xingfu
Daqinglu Qiao
Xiangfang

Xuefu Book City
Harbin Univ. of Science & Technology
Cambridge Coll. of HUST
Harbin Pearl
Xidafangshen

Harbin Library
Heilongjiang Univ.
National Forest Park
Harbin No.5 Hosp.
Gangdian Jie
Sunjiawopengtun

Window of Europe and Asia (Xuefu Park)
Harbin Medical Univ.
Heilongjiang Cancer Hosp.
Sunjia Station
Sunjiawopeng

Harbin Pharmaceutical Group Co.,Ltd.
Yangmajiazi
Zhangpengtun
Xuejiatun
Shanggou
Chaoyangtun

Heilongjiang Academy of Agricultural Sciences
Hadatun
Yuexing
Xiajiagou
Mujiagoutun

Harbin South Station

Location Map of Mun. Gov.

Mun. Gov.
Yanjiang Dadao
Forest Botanical Garden
Shidangli
Taiyangdao Park
Qianjijia
Qianjia
Shangwuli
Friendship Hotel
Science & Technology Mus.
Far East Building
Wangjiang
Harbin Water Park
Songhua Jiang

1.08km

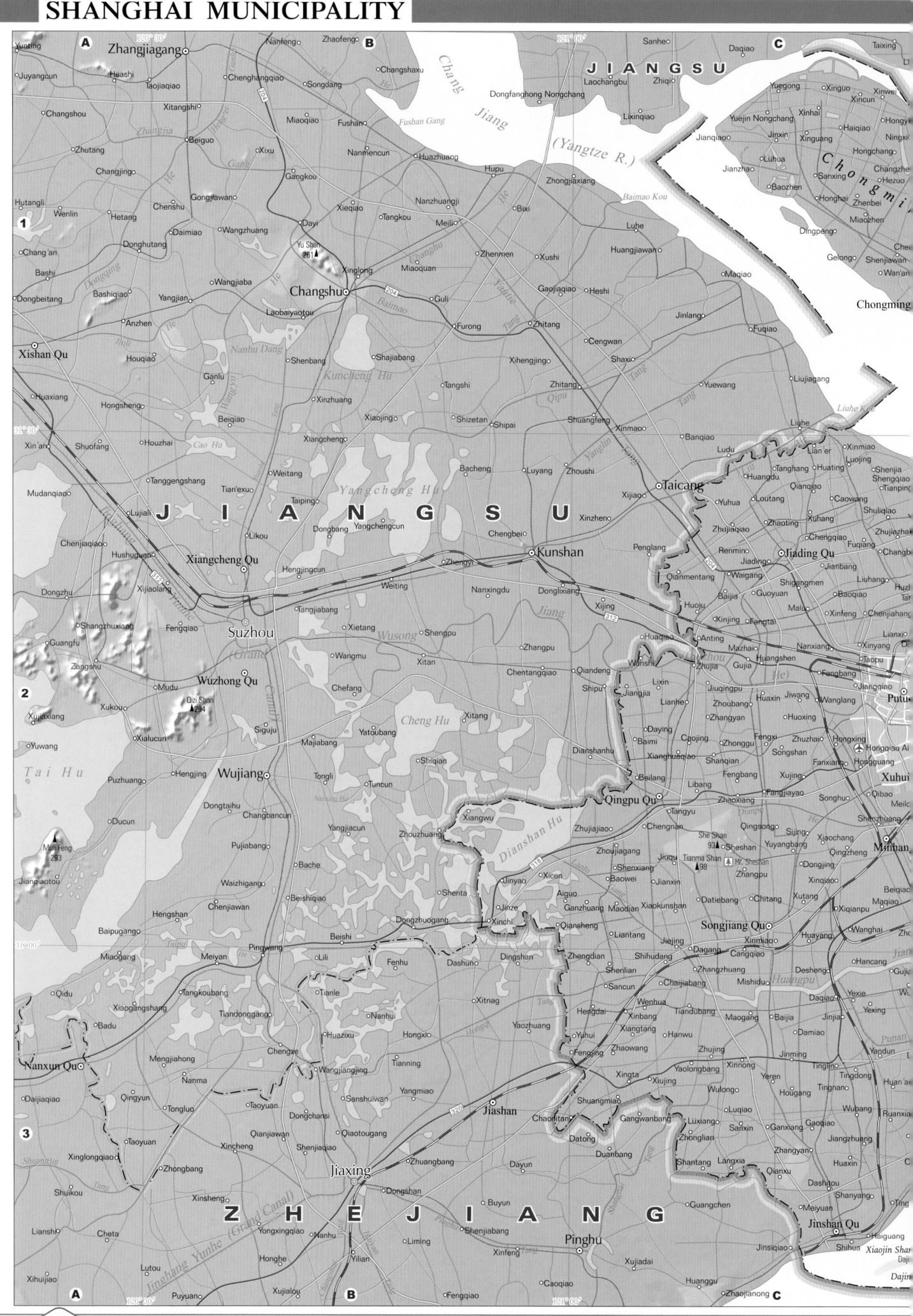

Altitude Table

| 50 | 20 | 0 | 20 | 50 | 100 | 200 | 300 | 500m |

121°30'
122°00' E
122°30'

D Xiangyang

Xinyi
Jiulong
Gongyicun
Xianao
Puji
Xingang

Xienao

J I A N G S U
Beixin
Minzhu
Songba

Qidong
Xinyao

Xingken

Huifeng

Huiping
Daxing
Tongkang

Xinglong Sha Hegun

Xinchang

Yiqing
Yinyang

Dongfanghong

Dongping
Gongyi

Dongfang

Changgong
Qianjiangyi
Pingdong

Qianjin Nongchang

Panlong
Xinmin

Jianshe
Xinjian
Shuhe
Yangbei
Beigang

D a o Gangyan
Hexing
Qixi
Yingbei

Xinhe
Dongxin
Jianzhong
Yangbin
Younan
Yongbei

Shuxin
Yonglong

Jiangbiano
Panghuang
Zhongxing
Chenjia

Sanyu
Qixiao
Dengta

Zhaxi

Tieta

Xinqiao

Y e l l o w   S e a

C h a n g j i a n g   K o u

1

31°30'

She Shan

Baoshan Qu
Wusong Kou
Youzixu
Baoshen
Panshio
Changxing
Qianwei

Paotaibang
Hongxing
D a o
Wusong
Lingqiao
Changxing

Songnan
Zhoujiabang
Xingango
Weibao
Fumin
Xiexingxu

Gaoqiao
Yuansha
Hengsha
Hengsha Dao

Lijiazhai
Gaodong
Fengle

Yincun
Yangyuan
Gulu
Xingsheng

Donggou
Nuli
Caolu

Yangpu Qu
Jinqiao
Zhangqiao
Limin

Zhabei Qu
Sanqiao
Wanggang

Heqing

ANGHAI
Pudong Xinqu
Callu

Zhangjiang
Chuansha
Hualu

Beicao
Cunqiao
Hongqiao
Xinlong

Yangsi
Hehe
Jiangzhen

Chenjingiao
Hengmiau
Zhaohang
Liutuan
Dengzheno

Kangqiao

Waxie
Liuzao
Pudong Airport

Zhixin
Hengqiao
Zhuanqiao
Zhuqiao

Minjian
Tiqiao
Donghai
Chaoyang Nongchang

Pujiang
Shenzhuang
Tanzhi
Yancang

Tangkou
Shabei
Sanzao
Chaozha

Yongxin
Xiasha
Xinqiao
Nanhui Qu
Huidong

Xianjin
Guoyuan
Huinan
Laogang

Yingwu
Luhui
Hangtou
Xuanqiao
Huanglu
Chaobin

Nandu
Jinhui
Tairi
Zhong'an
Wangting
Sandun
Gujiazhai

Yimin

Datuan
Wanxiang
Lubei

Nanhang
Fenshuidun
Shuyuan

Caojiazhai
Haichao
Heisanzao

Hanggian
Touqiao
Haiguan
Machang

Fengxian Qu
Qingcun
Situan
Tongqiao
Shinan

Zhuqiao
Fengcheng
Nichengo

Tangwai
Nongzhan
Donghai

Gonggeng
Ping an
Huijiao
Luchaogang

Daoyuan
Xingmiao
Qingshan
Qingfeng

Shiqiao
Liaobin
Qingyun
Lin'an

Tuolin
Haiwan
Shanghai Gulf

Xingsi

Fengjin
Zhujia

2

31°00'

E a s t   C h i n a   S e a

D a j i   Y a n g

Daji Shan

3

Jinji Shan

Donghai Bridge

Qingcun

Qiqu   Liedao
Xiaoyang Shan

Xiaoji Shan

Shengsi
Sijiao Shan

Maji Shan

Hangzhou   Wan
D
122°00'
E
Xugong Dao *Shengsi Liedao*

121°30'

Shanghai Municipality

Shanghai is abbreviated as "Hu". Located in the middle of China's east coastal area, it covers an area of over 5, 800 square kilometers, and has a population of 13.42 million, including such ethnic groups as Han, Hui, and Man.

■ Geographical Features

Topography Lying at the coastal area of the alluvial plain of Changjiang Delta, Shanghai is a flat piece of land low in altitude that descends slightly from west to east, intersected only by a few secluded hills. Huangpu Jiang (R.), Wusong Jiang and Dianshan Hu (L.) are among the many rivers and lakes in this area. Major islands are Chongming Dao, Changxing Dao and Hengsha Dao, of which Chongming Dao is the third largest island in China, smaller only to Taiwan Dao and Hainan Dao.

Climate Northern subtropical maritime monsoon climate brings to Shanghai adequate sunshine, plenty of rainfall and distinctive seasonal difference. Annual rainfall in this region is above 1, 100mm. The average annual temperature is around 16℃, with an average temperature in January around 3℃, while in July around 28℃.

■ Natural Resources

Numerous rivers and lakes as well as the sea nearby provide Shanghai with rich aquatic products. Its forest cover rate is around 3.66%.

■ Agriculture

Rice, wheat, cotton, rape, vegetables and fruits are main crops in this region. Pig and dairy cow are raised in suburban areas. The cultivation of bees, silkworms, medicinal herbs and spices are becoming more and more popular. Aquatic culture is developed along rivers and coastal area. Cotton fields are mainly found along the coastal area.

■ Industry

Shanghai has been a center of textile industry traditionally. In recent years, it has become one of China's largest industrial bases advancing new technology in areas like metallurgy, petro-chemical, machinery, ship building, automobile, electronics, space technology, computer, optical cable, laser, bioengineering, pharmaceutical technology and other hi-tech industries. With its strong industrial background and advanced technology, Shanghai's industries generally lead in China, particularly in the production of steel, finished steel products, automobile, electricity generator, integrate circuit, plastics,

chemical fibre, woolen cloth, family gadgets and durable consumer goods.

As a cosmopolitan and the largest center of commerce and finance in China, Shanghai is China's No. 1 in import and export volumes, and its total retail volume is larger than any of the other three municipalities directly under the central government. The production of clothes, woolen cloth, leather shoes, cosmetics, toys, bullion jewelry, traditional handicrafts and foods in Shanghai are diversified and well known. With Pudong as the renowned special economic zone, Shanghai has been developing steadily in finance, and has opened branch banks in London, Paris, New York, Singapore and Hong Kong, and is playing a more and more important role in international financial conduct.

■ Transportation

Railway Beijing–Shanghai and Shanghai–Hangzhou railways run through Shanghai, and are joined by several special railways.

Highway National highways connect Shanghai with Yantai, Urumqi, Chengdu, Lhasa and other cities. Yangpu Bridge and Nanpu Bridge are important hinges on the inner ring route, which is an important expressway assisted by the viaduct from north to south. Three express highways of Shanghai–Jiaxing, Shanghai–Nanjing, and Shanghai–Hangzhou connect Shanghai with its neighbours conveniently.

Pudong Scenery

Airway As an important aviation center and one of the three largest international air terminals in China, Shanghai has two airports of Hongqiao and Pudong, which provide international flight courses to over 70 cities in over 20 countries and regions throughout the world, as well as domestic flight courses to all major cities in every part of China, including Hong Kong and Macau.

Waterway Shanghai port is China's largest port and an important international transfer port in West Pacific Area. With 60 berths capable of harboring freights with a tonnage over ten thousand, and dozens of regular international

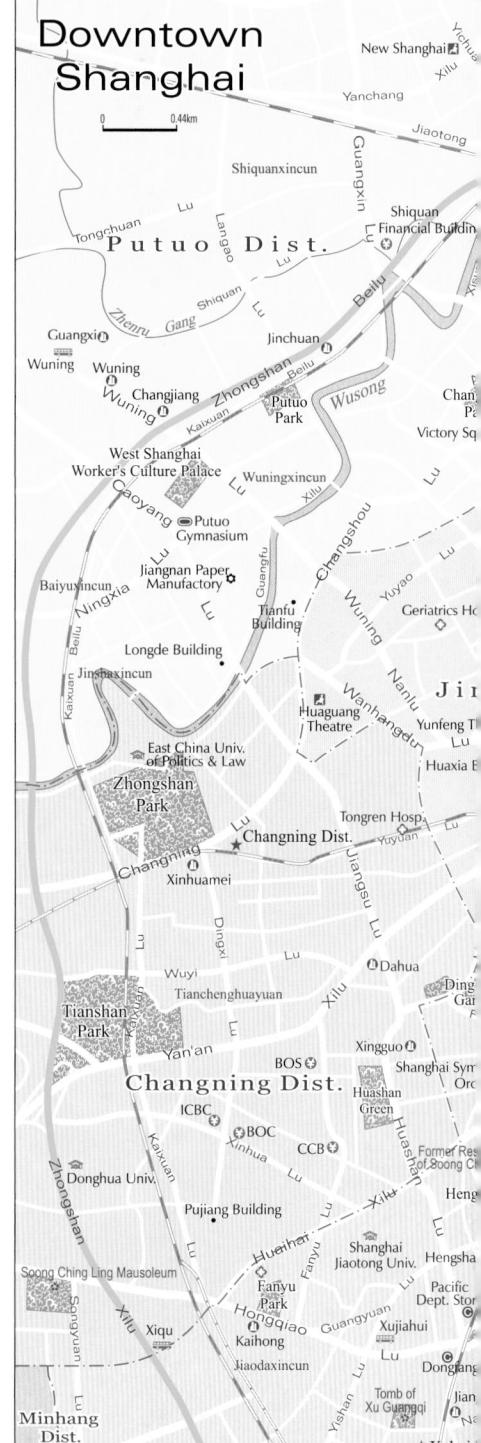

container's sea route, Shanghai port is the third largest in the world, next only to Rotterdam and Singapore. It also provides domestic freight routes to all major ports along the coast and river routes to Chongqing and other ports along Chang Jiang (Yangtze R.).

■ Places of Interest

Shanghai still preserves relics and unique gardens from Tang Dynasty onward. Yuyuan Garden in Huangpu District was built in 1559 and exhibits typical architectural and artistic traits of Ming and Qing Dynasties. Guyi Garden in Jiading District is characterized by its extensive use of bamboos. Jade Buddha Temple in Putuo District hold two jade Buddhist statues brought from Myanmar in 1882. Oriental Pearl TV Tower stands by Huangpu Jiang. It is the highest tower in Asia and the second highest in the world. Waitan refers to an area 4,000 meters long along the west bank of Huangpu Jiang, diversified styles of architectures from both Europe and Asia can be found there. Other major tourist attractions include Dianshan Lake, Shanghai Museum, and many residences of famous historical figures.

■ Local Products

As a traditional industrial and commercial city, Shanghai is well known for its production of jewelry, jade carving, artificial flower, costumes, clothes, woolen cloth, silk, tie, leather shoes, cosmetics, toys, furniture and various stationeries. Dim sum and candies produced in Shanghai enjoy great renown in China.

Shanghai

Changxing Dao

Chongming County

Jiang (Yangtze R.)

Chang Jiang

Changzheng

Miaojie Gang

Gonglu

Panshi-Yunsha

Jianxin Shi

Shisha Shisha

Lu

Shisha

Zhouhai Lu

2 Huandong Dadao

Yangyuanxincun

Gonglu

Shen

Lu

Intl. Trade Building

ICBC

Yinglun

Jinhai

Lu

Gaohang

Yanggao Beilu

Zhouqiaoxincun

Huagaoxincun

Dongli

Wulan

Baota Nunnery

Zhouhai Lu

Yanggao

Yanggao Lu

Hangjin Lu

Puxing Lu

Pudong

Dongjing Lu

Hudongxincun

Wuxing

Waigaoqiaogangqu

Gangcheng Lu

1 Huandong Dadao

Shiyouxincun Gaoqiao Park

Shanghai No.7 Hosp.

Hangjin

Pudong Beilu

Dongtang Lu

Pudong Dadao

Gongga Gang

Gangcheng

Shanglianxincun

Dongtang

Jiang

Zhonghua Shipyard

Liping Lu

Shanghai Univ. of Electric Power

Suitang Gang

Gongqing Forest Park

Jungong Lu

Yangpu Science & Technology Mus.

Shanghai Univ.

Ningguo Lu

Jiangdong

Gaosan Gang

Baoton Lu

Xiangyinxincun

Longchang

Yangpu

Huangxing Park

Jiangdong

Guopu

Huangpu Jiang

Nenjiang Lu

Zhongyuan Lu → Yingkou

Kailuxincun Gongnongxincun

Shijie Lu

Yinhang

Huangxing Lu

Yangpu Dist.

Heping

Jiangpu

Xinjiangwancheng

Shanghai Inst. of Physical Education

Jiangwan Stadium

Zhengli

Lantian

Tongji Univ.

Xinhua Hosp.

Dalian

Hongyang

Shanghai Univ.

Guoding Lu

Fudan Univ.

Xuchang

Lu

Jiangpu Lu

Shanghai Univ. of Finance & Economics

Hendan

Yunguangxincun

Zhongshan Beilu

Shanghai Intl. Studies Univ.

Liping

Sanju Building

Songhu Lu

Yixianxincun

Songtangxincun

Yingao Xilu

Qiaohong Apartment

Liangchengxincun

Wenshui Donglu

Guangzhong Lu

Pengjiang Hosp.

Hongkou Dist.

Shanghai Univ.

Luxun Park

Luxun Memorial Hall

TCM Hosp.

Nanlu

Tang Lu

Sitangxincun

Baode

Beijiao Station

Pengpuxincun

Xinlu

Guangyue Lu

Xiuyu

Qiujiang

Jiangyang Lu

Changjiang

Gonghe

Zunyi Hosp.

Sanquan

Pengpuxincun

Shuidian Lu

Guangzhong Park

Wenshui Wenshui

Zhabei Dist.

Chengjiao

Shuidian

Baoshan Dist.

Tieli

Tieshan Lu

Hulan

Dongjiao Jing

Changzhong

Wanrongxincun

Hutai

Hutai

Yongxiexiaoqu

Lu

Memorial Hall of Songhu Anti-Japanese War

Baogang Linjiang Park

Baoshan

Baoshan Martyrs' Cemetery

Baoshanxincun

Mudanjiang

Xiayuan Building

Navy Mus. of Shanghai

Wusong

Wusong Dock

Wusong Central Hosp.

Changjiang Lu

Wusong Customs House

Friendship Park

Tongji Lu

Jiangyang

Baoyang

Beisi

Tang

Shuichang

Beilu

Taihe

Baoshan Shipyard

Jiangyang

Yuebao

Fuyang

Yangheng Yangheng

Gongfuxincun

Renhe Hosp.

Wanxin Trade Plaza

Gongkangxincun

Dachang Qiao

Hutai

Dahua

Tao Xingzhi's Memorial Hall

Huating

Da Pu

Zhebei

Shanghai

Weiwu

Weisan

Lu

Baoshan Iron & Steel Co.,Ltd.

Yuepu Park

Yunchuan Lu

Yunchuan Lu

Fujin

Bao'an

Meigang

Gonglu

Gucun Hosp.

Tianxinhuayuan

Yangzao

Bang

Yunzao

Tianhexincheng

Huanbei

Tang Qiao

Hutai

Tao

Shanghai Univ.

Shangda

Nanda

Taopu Station

Xincun

Shanghai

Yangjiaqiao

Expressway

Shanghai Phamaceutical Factory

Hujia Qiao

Liyangdao

Putuo Dist.

Huangshi Huangxin

2 Huanxi

Nanhu

Tianshan

Nanhu

Tongji Univ.

Taopu

Qilianshan

Fengxiang

A20 Dadao

2 Huanxi Lu

Gonglu

Jiexin

Zhenchen

Gulang

Liuyangdao

Weiwu

Baolixincun

Jixian

Shitai

Luodong Lu

Panjing

Pan Jing He

Liandi

Jixian

Luonanxincun

Hutai Lu

Chenju

Jinqiuhuayuan

Chentai

Chenguang

Jiading Dist.

Lianyang

Lianyang

Gongxi

Chenjiahang

A20

Gonglu

Liuhang

Di Pu

Jing

Yangshuang

0 1 2km

SHANDONG

Zhaoyang Hu, Tengzhou, Xinzhuang, Linyi, Hellin, Longhe, Ganma, Zhudu, Pulianji, Chengwu, Yutai, Yucheng, Mushi, Shizhong Qu, Luozhuang Qu, Linshu, Cao Xian, Huancheng, Longgu, Huankou, Weishan, Zaozhuang, Cangshan, Diantou, Huandun, Durjshan, Longhe, Yandianlou, Guocun, Shan Xian, Zhaozhuang, Zhuzhai, Haozhui, Yicheng Qu, Xiangcheng, Quyang, Donghai, Zhangwan, Nanlji, Huangguang, Caitang, Wanggou, Feng Xian, Pei Xian, Shagou, Nigou, Lanling, Changcheng, Zhouzhuang, Tai'erzhuang Qu, Tiefuo, Gangshang, Hongzhuang, Quyang, Fangshan

HENAN

Shangqiu, Yucheng, Chezhan, Dangshan, Huangkou, Zhangji, Hekou, Liangzhai, Jing'an, Wuduan, Hanzhang, Chefushan, Guanhu, Suyangshan, Ahu, Anfeng, Gaoxu, Gua, Suiyang Qu, Yanji, Zhangjia, Zhengji, Dapeng, Xuzhou, Maocun, Tashan, Zhaodun, Caoqiao, Xinyi, Tangdian, Hudong, Sangxu, Xiwei, Wuji, Duji, Xiayi, Jiyang, Bei Zhen, Zhangzhuangzhai, Xiao Xian, Tongshan, Sanbao, Zhangji, Fangcun, Yizhuang, Zhancheng, Xinhe, Gupi, Huangdun, Wanglou, Gaoliu, Tongyang, Hanshan, Yanji, Zhaxia, Longmiao, Mengxing, Mangdang Shan 156

Anliu, Wuma, Peigiao, Suixi, Tiefo, Jiagou, Zhihe, Wangjia, Wangji, Liangji, Zhaohe, Yaoji, Yugou, Taoyuan, Suining, Shaji, Sankeshu, Daxing, Chuangcheng, Wangji, Qianji, Liangc, Shuyang, Bozhou, Yongcheng, Suixi, Fuli, Huigu, Xinbian, Fengmiao, Damiao, Liji, Dazhuang, Guanshan, Qiuji, Luowei, Cangji, Siyang, Lian, Luyi, Shibali, Guantango, Maqiao, Baisha, Linhuan, Hancun, Xi'erpu, Suzhou, Dadian, Louzhuang, Lingbi, Huangwan, Weiji, Pingshan, Xiaoliang, Meihua, Jieji, Xinyuan, Huaiyin Qu, Huai, Nanfeng, Zhaoqiao, Shatu, Shigong, Banpudian, Si Xian, Dunji, Chemen, Yaogou, Shangtang, Gaodu, Nanchenji, Wudun, Chuzho, Lixing, Gucheng, Guoyang, Linhu, Chudiano, Xiyang, Wugou, Longwangmiao, Yong Zhen, Guzhen, Caogou, Wuqiao, Chenweio, Sihong, Longji, Bancheng, Zhaoji, Heping, Jian

Erlang, Zhangcun, Jiangji, Banqiao, Licang, Feihe, Huaiyuan, Daxin, Xiaoxi, Tianganghu, Shuanggou, Baoji, Laozishan, Guantan, Jiangba, Renhe, Luliang, Santa, Ruji, Mengcheng, Shuangjian, Xiangqiao, Feihe, Heliu, Yuanji, Dongliuji, Wuhe, Changhuai, Liuxiang, Fengshan, Guanzhen, Tiefo, Huaihe, Xuyi, Maba, Dailou, Jinhu, Taihe, Zhongtuan, Sanyi, Kantuan, Macheng, Bengbu, Qiaotou, Nushanhu, Heqiao, Gusango, Huanghuatang, Tongcheng, Min

Fuyang, Zhengwu, Chahua, Xinzhangjio, Dingji, Tangji, Xiquan, Wudian, Fengyang, Zongpu, Mingguang, Jianxi, Qiuji, Guiwu, Jiupu, Wangdian, Ping'an, Wansho

Liushipu, Xieqiao, Panji Qu, Liufu, Banqiao, Daishan, Zhangbaling, Zhuzhen, Maji, Xieji

Funan, Huanggang, Nanzhao, Jiangkou, Jiangdianzi, Fengtai, Huainan, Yongkang, Chihe, Zilaiqiao, Lai'an, Shiguan, Guanfangji, Tianchang, Caoji, Bangang, Yanghu, Bagongshan Qu, Xiejiaji Qu, 340 Langwo Shan, Lianpu, Dingyuan, Yaopu, Wuyi, Luhe Qu, Hengliang, Qingsh, Yizheng

Wangliu, Xuji, Xindiano, Shou Xian, Cao'an, Changfeng, Zhangqiao, Zhouganen, Shuikou, Daying, Xinji, Yizheng, Huoqiu, Jianshe, Wabu, Zhuxiang, Zagjia, Jiangji, Jiepaiji, Gucheng, Dachang, Qixia Qu, Xiashu, Gushi, Hekou, Mengji, Ca'an, Yanliu, Wushan, Luoji, Yangdian, 394 Longwang Jian, Quanjiao, Pukou, Nanjing, Tangshan, Shifo, Changji, Huayuan, Liangyuan, Langanji, Guhe, Shiyang, Qiaolin, Xingdian, 448, Jiangning Qu, Xing

Guolutan, Liji, Sanyuan, Dongqiao, Gaoliu, Shushan, Feidong, Zhegao, Xifeng, Hanshan, He Xian, Wujiang, Dongshangling, Sanc, Wumiaoji, Yej, Yaolimiao, Xuji, Lu'an, Sanshilipu, Dabai, Hefei, Xishanyi, Huaji, Xianzong, Wugang, Taoyu, Lukou Airport, Tianwang, Jingantar, 1584, Jiangdian, Jinzhai, Dushan, Fenlukou, Shannan, Feixi, Qiaotouji, Zhongmiao, Taoxi, Fengle, Fuyuan, Baiqiao, Shenxiang, Ma'anshan, Lishu, Qingshan, Zhangdian, Jiehe, Shucheng, Chaohu, Dongguan, Daqiao, Xinfeng, Shar, Banzhuyuan, Wuxian, Longhe, Changgang, Shucha, Ketan, Lujiang, Wuwei, Tangnan, Gaochun, Wujiadian, Yanzihe, Shanqi, Shushan, Liudu, Nicha, Hengshan, Huangchi, Yangjiang, Yax, Jinjiapu, 1729 Tiantangzhai, Baimiache, Tiantangzhai, Taiyang, Baima Jian 1774, Tongcheng, Tangwan, Yijin, Luohe, Kushang, Zhongcang, Huangmi, Xihe, Zhengcun, Lan, Yuexi, Chashui, Zhubu, Fangang, Sanguan Shan 674, Tonglin, Shizishan Qu, Nanjing, Hanting, Xuancheng

HENAN

ANHUI

HUBEI

Altitude Table   100 50 20 0 20 50 100 200 300 500 750 1000 1500 2000m

SHANDONG   Ping Dao
              (Pingshan Dao)
E   F   G   H   I

Dashan Dao
(Danian Shan)
Cheniu Shan

Haizhou Wan

Qinshan Dao
Linhong
Kou   Dongxi Liandao
Lianyun Qu   Lianyungang
       Gaogongdao
       Banqiao
Yuntai Shan

Xuwei
Tongxing   Yanweigang
Xiache
Yangji
Yibei   Wudui
             Nanhe
Xiangshui   Dayou   Binhuai
Guannan   Xiaojian   Chantao   Batan
Xidun   Xinji   Gongzhuang   Binhai   Zhendong   Biandan Gang
        Huangwei   Linhai
Tangji   Tianchang   Baodun
Huangying   Zhenghong
Guoshu   Siming
Funing   Shizhuang   Fuyu   Sheyang   *Sheyanghe Kou*
Lupu   Xingou   Haihe   Huangshagang
Suzuo   Xuji   Banhu   Goudun   Xingqiao
Fuxing   Yilin   Gaozuo   Gangdong   Yangma   Xinyanggang Kou
        Yangji   Zhongzhuang   Shanggang   Shengfangqiang
Boli   Liujun   Xinxing   Panwan   Nongchang
Jianhu   Zhoufen   Teyong   Doulonggang Kou
Caodian   Shuisi   Yancheng   Fangqiang   Sanlong
Baoying   Guangyanghu   Peiliu   *Yancheng   Magou
Yanhe   Beilonggang   Beijiang   Xinfeng   Yandou Qu
        Liubao   Dagang   Biancang   Wanggang
Sishui   Shagou   Dazou   Dafeng   Yuhua
Jieshou   Zhoufen   Diaoyu   Liuzhuang   Xituan   Tongshang
        Linze   Chengdongshi   Daying   Xiaohai
        Hengjing   Changrong   Caoyan   Shenzao   Caomiao   Chuandong Gang
Xinghua   Mapeng   Daduo   Daiyao   Daqiao   *Dafeng David's Deer
Gaoyou   Situ   Ganduo   Zhuhong   Sanzao   Xujiadun
Guoji   Bagiao   Chenbao   Zhangguo   Caopie
Gaoxu   Zhouzhuang   Tainan   Nanshenzao
Zhenwu   Wubao   Qintong   Anfeng   Sancang
Guocun   Shaobo   Xinjie   Jianggang
Yiling   Jiangyan   Qiuhu   Tangyang
Hailing Qu   Zhangdian   Dagong   Laobagang
Jiangdu   Taizhou   Yazhou   Hai'an   Libao   Jiaoxie
Yangzhou   Yuanzhu   Guxi   Chaiwan   Hekou   Huanggang   Changsha
Hongqiao   Gaogang Qu   Banjing   Rugao   Shuangdian   Chahe   Rudong
Liuwei   Yangzhong   Fenjie   Motou   Linzi   Shigang   Caobu   Bingfang
Zhenjiang   Taixing   Nansha   Xiayuan   Liuqiao   Beixingqiao   Chuanyao Gang
Dantu Qu   Huangqu   Jishi   Shizhuang   Pingchao   Tongzhou   Sanyu   Haiyan
Baitu   Xiaohe   Zhangqiao   Xilai   Changjiang   Huolong   Baochang   Dayanggang Kou
Danyang   Qiwei   Deji   Nantong   Sijia   Zhaomin   Haozhigang Kou
Quanzhou   Lingkou   Nansha   Daxin   Sanxing   Zhangzhishan   Hezuo   Dongyuan
Yanling   Luoxi   Weitang   Shengang   Haimen   Linjiang   Nanyang
Zhixin   Jiangyin   Huaxicun   Zhanjiagang   Sanhe   Huifeng   Qidong   Donghai
Changzhou   Boyu   Miaoqiao   Xinhai   Yinyang
Jintan   Wujin Qu   Luqiao   Haiyu   *Chongming Dao*
Zhulin   Qishuyan Qu   Fenghuang   Meili   Dongzhang   Chongming
Huishan Qu   Zhujiang   Guizhuang   Yu'an
Shuibei   Qianhuang   Yu Shan   Mt. Yushan   Changshu   Heshi   Liuhe
Huangli   Hui Shan   261   Heshi   Shuangfeng   Changxing Dao
Zhaiqiao   Mt. Huishan   328   Xishan Qu   Ganlu   Houzhai   Youziwei
Liyang   Guanlin   Houzhai   Taicang   Hengsha
Xushe   Heqiao   Yangting   Taiping   Baoshan Qu   Hengsha Dao
Yixing   Zhoutie   Taihu Lake   Xiangcheng Qu   Jiading Qu   She Shan
        Masha   Wutangmen   Kunshan
        Maji Shan   Zhenhu   Zhangyi   Zhangpu
Tianmuhu   Xiang   Classical Gardens of Suzhou   Zhangpu   Shipu   **SHANGHAI**
Daibu   Mt.-Shanghai   Pudong Xinqu
Zhangzhu   Dingshu   Dongwu   Xukou   Wuzhong Qu   Tongli   Dianshanhu   Qingpu Qu   **SHANGHAI SHI**
Hengjian   Taihu   Fudong   Puzhuang   Qingpu Qu   Zhuqiao
Xinhang   Jiapu   Piaomiao Feng   Wujiang   Zhouzhuang   Minhang Qu   Nanhui Qu
Qiucun   Xiaoxi   336   Moli Feng   293   Shenxiang   Hangtou
Changxing   Xidongting Shan   Xishan   Wanping   Luxu   Shihudang   Songjiang Qu
Qiuqiao   **ZHEJIANG**   Dongdongting Shan   Moxgang   Pingwang   Fengxian Qu   Luchaogang
Guangde   Huzhou   Qidu   Shengze   **ZHEJIANG**   Xingta   Fengxian Qu
ZHEJIANG   Bashan   Tingli   Donghai Bridge   **ZHEJIANG**
E   F   G   H

Y e l l o w
S e a

Chang Jiang (Yangtze R.)
Chongming Dao
Changjiang Kou

Jiangsu Province

With Nanjing as its capital, Jiangsu Province, which is abbreviated as "Su", is located in East China, along the lower reaches of Chang Jiang (Yangtze River) and Huai He (R.). It covers an area of over 100,000 square kilometers, and has a population of 71.64 million, including such ethnic groups as Han, Hui, Miao, Tujia, Mongol, Man and Dong.

■ Geographical Features

Topography Changjiang Delta, Jianghuai Pingyuan (Pln.), Huanghuai Pingyuan and Binhai Pingyuan make up an extensive flat area with an altitude lower than 50 meters, which take up most part of Jiangsu. Chang Jiang, Huai He, Yi He, Shu He, Qinhuai He, Xinshu He, and two canals are major rivers in Jiangsu, while Tai Hu, Hongze Hu, and Gaoyou Hu are major lakes in this region.

Climate Divided by Subei Guangai Zongqu, the north part of Jiangsu is ruled by warm semi-humid monsoon climate, while the south enjoys subtropical humid monsoon climate. On the whole, this region enjoys mild temperature and adequate rainfall. Annual rainfall in this province is between 800 ~ 1,200 mm. The average annual temperature is between 13 ~ 16℃, with an average temperature in January between -1 ~ 3℃, while in July between 27 ~ 28℃.

■ Natural Resources

By now over 100 kinds of minerals have been found in Jiangsu, of which the reserves of 30 kinds are among China's top ten. The salt mine in Huaiyin is one of China's largest. Other minerals include: coal, oil, gas, halite, sulfur, phosphor, crystal, diamond, kaolin, copper, iron, lead, zinc, strontium, manganese and so on.

Extensive river system provides the province with a rich water resource of 27.5 billion cubic meters.

Jiangsu's forest cover rate is around 4.51%, mostly bamboos, firs, pine trees, and fruit trees, among which over 500 species are of medical value.

Jiangsu also has abundant aquatic resources, with Lusi, Haizhouwan as major fishing grounds, the province raise over 140 species of fresh water fish, over 30 species of shrimps and over 40 species of crabs.

■ Agriculture

As a major agricultural province in China, Jiangsu plays an important role in China's production of grain, cotton, oil, silk and fresh water fish. Main grain crops here are: rice, wheat, broomcorn, corn and sweet potato. Main cash crops here include: cotton, oil and mulberry. Tai Hu drainage area is well known for its prolific production of rice and silk.

Cotton is mainly produced along rivers and coastal area. Pig and sheep are raised here, and the province produce first class strains of pig, chicken, sheep and duck. Aquaculture along the coastal area is quite well developed. Fish, prawn, jelly fish, snail, clam, crab, and turtle are bred here, among which the production of whitebait, saury and crab is most famous.

■ Industry

Textile industry developed very early in this region. Electro-mechanics, petro-chemicals, building material and food production as well as other light industries are also developed in this region. Machines, automobiles, and various industrial artifacts are popular in domestic and international markets.

Township enterprises are quite well developed in this province. The well known South Jiangsu Model of developing township enterprises is particularly eminent. Most township enterprises here are involved in the production of textile, electronics, new material, precision machinery, fine chemicals and telecommunication equipments.

■ Transportation

Railway Centered round Nanjing and Xuzhou, four main stems including Beijing–Shanghai, Lanzhou–Lianyungang and Nanjing–Tongling railways all run through Jiangsu.

Highway Every city and county is connected by national highway or provincial highway. Four express highways have been in use: Shanghai–Nanjing, Nanjing–Hefei, Nanjing–Nantong and Nanjing–Lianyungang.

Airway Airports in Nanjing and other major cities provide flight courses to every major city in China.

Waterway Chang Jiang runs through Jiangsu from east to west, while Jinghang Yunhe (Grand Canal) runs from north to south, providing the province with a convenient water transportation system. Nanjing, Nantong and Zhenjiang are important river ports. Among them, Nanjing is the largest river port. Lianyungang is a renowned sea port.

■ Places of Interest

With a long history behind, Jiangsu has rich cultural relics, and is most famous for its architecture of Chinese ancient private gardens. Taihu Lake lies in the south of Changjiang Delta, its spectacular natural scenery and rich historical remains attract large numbers of tourists. Classical Gardens of Suzhou and Xiaoling Tomb of Ming Dynasty have been included in the World Heritage List by UNESCO. Suzhou, a city with 2,000 years of history, lies at the bank of Taihu Lake. Classical gardens in Suzhou are exemplary combination of architecture, plantation, carvings and paintings. Yangzhou, an old city lying in the south of Subei Plain, has been well known traditionally for its assembling of literati. Rich cultural and historical relics can also be found in the ancient capital Nanjing, like the Mausoleum of Sun Yat-sen, Zhonghuamen Gate and Xuanwu Lake.

■ Local Products

Embroidery produced in Jiangsu is one of China's four most famous embroidery styles. Silks produced in Nanjing have traditionally been used for the royal family. Other traditional local handicrafts include: Jade cravings in Yangzhou, Clay figures made in Wuxi, and potteries made in Yixing, all of which are well known throughout the world. Green tea produced around Tai Hu area is the best of its kind. Local flavours like ham, dried meat floss, preserved duck, and specially cooked pork and fish are liked by many. Jiangsu also produces quality liquor and vinegar.

Classical Gardens of Suzhou

Nanjing

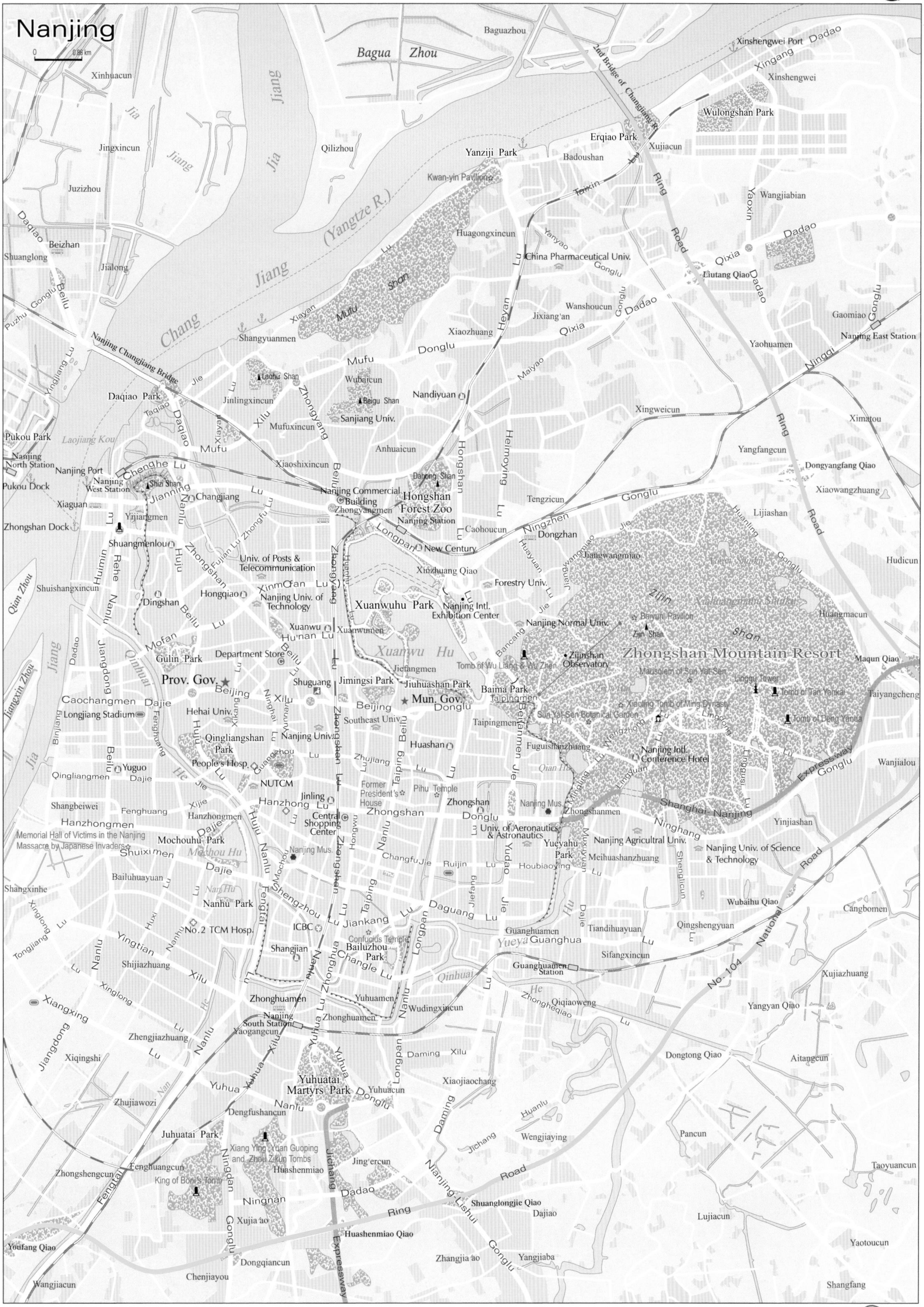

Altitude Table

200	50	20	0	50	100	200	300	500	750	1000	1500	2000	2500 m

Suzhou
Zhangpu
Zhang...
Dianshanhu
jiang
Qingpu Qu
F SHANGHAI
Hengsha Dao
G
H
I
1
Minhang Qu
Zhoupu
Zhuqiao
SHANGHAI SHI
Nanhui Qu
Dingshan
Songjiang Qu
Hangtou
Xitang
Fengjing
Wangjiangjing
Jiashan
Tinglin
Siluan
Daji Yang
Huimin
Fengxian Qu
Luchaogang
Xindai
Zhongdai
Jiaxing
Quantang
Donghai Bridge
Zhelin
Daji Shan
Huaniao Shan
Dapan Shan
Nanhu
Fengqiao
Jinshan Qu
Tanhu Shan
Shengsi
Ma'an Liedao
Hai Jiao
Puyuan
Wangdian
Mt. Jiulong
Xiaoyang
Shengsi Islands
Gouqi Dao
Shengshan
Haining
Xincang
Qinshan
Qiqu Shan
Dayang
Dahuanglong
feng
Haiyan
Liedao
Shengsi Liedao
Huangwan
Dabai Shan
Dayang Shan
2
Wangpan Shan
Xiaoqu Shan
Huangze Yang
Qushan
Huangze Shan
Langgangshan Liedao
g
Hangzhou
Daqu Shan
Siping
Sanxing Shan
Dayu Shan
Zhoushan Qundao
Wan
Daiqu Yang
Dongsha
Chongshou
Xinzha
Qijiebamei
Xihuo Shan
Dachangtu Shan
Changhe
Fuhai
Donghuo Shan
Dongsha
Daishan
Changtu
Zhongjieshan Liedao
Cixi
Daishan Dao
Miaozihu Dao
Liangxiongdi
Xietang
Simen
Ditang
Changbai Dao
Daxizhai Dao
Huangxing Dao
Shangyu
Mazhu
Qiaotou
Shiqiao
Mamu
Xiushan
Sijiemei Dao
Dongyuan
Yuyao
Zhangting
Longshan
Ligang
Xiushan Dao
Dongfu Shan
Shangpu
Lianghui
Cicheng
Huibie Yang
Cezi Dao
Cengang
Ximatou
Zhoushan Dao
Huangda Yang
Lianghui
Helou
Jintang
Zhoushan
Zhanmao
Mt. Putuo
Shengzhou
Fenghui
Dingzhai
Zhenhai Qu
Beilun Qu
Wangjia
Putuo Shan
Gulai
Mt. Xuedou
Dongqiao
Daxie
Changkeng
Putuo Qu
Siming Shan
Ningbo
Wuxiang
Baifeng
Zhujiajian
Chongren
Beizhang
Dongqianhu
Dongwu
Meishan
Qitou Yang
Zhujia Jian
Xinchang
Dayan
Zhangxi
Jiangkou
Sanshan
Taohua
Bamao
Xikou
Xiwu
Tangxi
Zhanqi
Taohua Dao
Qiaoying
Jiqi
Huangbiao
Tubi
Xiazhi Dao
Meiyu Yang
Cangyan
Qiangjiao
Xizhou
Juexi
Liuheng Dao
Bijia Shan
Qiaotouhu
Chunhu
Fenghua
Chayuan
Mopan Yang
Meilin
Qiucun
Huangtan
Sizhoutou
Dongchen
Lishuangfeng
Ninghai
Huchen
Xinqiao
Damu Yang
Mt. Tiantai
Huishan
Changjie
Shipu
Guanchuan'ao
Jiushan Liedao
Sanzhou
Qiantong
Minggang
Nanjiu Shan
Pingqiao
Sangzhou
Tiantai
Liu'ao
Hepu
Tantou Shan
Jietou
Nanping
Hengdu
Gaotang
Sanmen
Niutou Shan
Longxi
Tanling
Sanmen Wan
Huangtang
Lingjing
Datang
Hua'ao Dao
Baishuiyang
Dongcheng
Lipu
Xianju
Huaqiao
Yanchi
Genglou
Linhai
Taozhu
Dongyang
Que'er'ao
Maotou Yang
Yushan Liedao
Bulu
Kuocang Shan
Duqiao
Zhuxi
Shuiyang
Chuannan
Dongji Liedao
East China Sea
Dongji Shan
Toumen Shan
Huangyan Qu
Toutuo
Taizhou
Taizhou Wan
Yijiangshan Dao
Ningxi
Luqiao Qu
Huanglang
Shangdachen Dao
Maoshe
Zeguo
Jinqing
Huangjiao Shan
Taizhou Liedao
Fushan
Zhiren
Xiadachen Dao
Huangnan
Fuxio
Daxi
Xiyutou
Dajing
Wenling
Ruoheng
Yijigu Shan
Hesheng
Songmen
Longgang
Wugen
Niushan Dao
Aihuang
Shamen
Doumen
Honggiao
Shitang
Aiwan Wan
Sigu
Chengbei
Nanyue
Chumen
Yongjia
Yuhuan
Yueqing
Chenyu
Kanmen
Pishan Dao
Wengyang
Yuhuan Dao
Dalu Shan
Wenzhou
Huanghua
Damen
Luxi Dao
ai Qu
Longwan
Wenzhou Wan
Damen Dao
Zhuangyuan'ao
Longwan Qu
Niyu Shan
Dongtou
Baotian
Dongtou Dao
Dongtou Liedao
Shangwang
Tongpan Shan
Dongtou Yang
gyang
Beilong Shan
Xiwan
Chitou Dao
Beiji Shan
Dabei Liedao
Beijishan Liedao
Nanji Islands
Yanting
Nanji Shan
yu
Nanjishan Liedao
anshan Dao
an Dao
Lieyan
Qixing Dao
F
G
H

Zhejiang Province

With Hangzhou as its capital, Zhejiang Province, which is abbreviated as "Zhe", is located in the coastal area of southeast China, south to Tai Hu (L.). It covers an area of over 100,000 square kilometers, and has a population of 45.52 million, including such ethnic groups as Han, She, Tujia, Miao, Buyei, Hui, Zhuang, Dong, Li and Man.

■ Geographical Features

Topography Zhejiang's terrain gradually descends from southwest to northeast with low hills taking up most part of its total area. Major hills are Xianxia Ling, Yandang Shan, Kuocang Shan, Tiantai Shan, Tianmu Shan, and Huiji Shan, most of which are 200~1,000m in altitude. Basins and plains like Hangjiahu Pingyuan (Pln.), Ningshao Pingyuan, Wenzhou Pingyuan and Jinqu Pendi (Bsn.) all lie in the mid-east part of the province, making this area an important agriculture zone. Rivers and lakes are everywhere to be found in this province. Qiantang Jiang is the largest river in the province, whose open-up estuary produces world famous Qiantangjiang Tide. Xi Hu, Dong Hu, Nan Hu and Dongqian Hu are four major lakes in Zhejiang. A sinuous coast line provides the province with many favourable bays like: Hangzhou Wan, Xiangshan Wan, Sanmen Wan, Taizhou Wan, Wenzhou Wan and Yueqing Wan. Zhejiang has more islands along its coast than any other province in China. Zhoushan Dao is the fourth largest island in China.

Climate Subtropical humid monsoon climate rules the area, which brings about adequate sunshine and plenty of rainfall. Annual rainfall in this area is between 1,200~1,500mm. The average annual temperature here is between 15~19℃, with an average temperature in January between 3~8℃, while in July around 28℃.

■ Natural Resources

By now over 100 kinds of minerals have been found in Zhejiang, among which over 70 are non-metal minerals. The reserves of minerals like bone coal, alunite, pyrophyllite, fluorite, and diatomite are ranked among China's top three, while the reserves for silver, zinc, vanadium and cadmium are among China's top ten.

Abundant rainfall brings to the province a total water resource of nearly 9.4 billion cubic meters.

Zhejiang's forest cover rate is around 50.80%, mostly firs, pine trees, bamboos, tea-oil tree, tung tree, Chinese tallow tree and fruit trees.

Zhejiang has rich aquaculture resources. Hangjiahu area is one of China's three major production bases of fresh water fish, while Zhoushan fishing ground is the largest seawater fishery in China.

■ Agriculture

Agriculture in Zhejiang is highly commercialized. Zhebei Pingyuan is traditionally a renowned land of abundance and produces large amount of jute and silk pods. Main grain crops are rice, corn, wheat and sweet potato, while jute, cotton, rape, and mulberry trees are its major cash crops. 90% of counties in Zhejiang produce tea, and the total tea output of this province is the largest in China. Chicken, duck, fish, sheep and pig are raised here, and the province produces some first class strains of pig, chicken and sheep. Zhoushan and Shengsi fisheries produce rich amount of yellow-fin tuna, hairtail, cuttle fish, carps, shellfish and seaweeds.

■ Industry

Zhejiang has diversified industrial system including metallurgy, machinery, textile, food production as well as production of chemicals and building materials. The province is particularly known for the production of precision equipment, silk, linen and cotton textile, canned food, processed aquatic products, tea, liquor and paper.

■ Transportation

Railway With Hangzhou as the hinge, two main stems of Hangzhou-Ningbo and Jinhua-Wenzhou railways as well as two double-track railways of Shanghai-Hangzhou and Hangzhou-Zhuzhou run through Zhejiang.

Highway Centered round Hangzhou, extensive national highway or provincial highway system connect every city and county in the province. Three express highways have been in use, including: Hangzhou-Jinhua-Quzhou, Jinhua-Lishui-Wenzhou, and Ningbo-Taizhou-Wenzhou.

Airway Airports in Hangzhou, Ningbo and other places provide over 100 flight courses to domestic and international destinations.

Waterway Five major ports Ningbo, Zhoushan, Zhapu, Haimen and Wenzhou provide freights to over 70 countries and regions throughout the world. Regular ships to America and Japan are also available.

■ Places of Interest

With beautiful natural scenery and rich cultural relics, Zhejiang is one of China's most prosperous tourist destinations. West Lake (Xi Hu), which lies to the west of Hangzhou, is traditionally well known for its spectacular natural scenery and rich cultural relics around. Mt. Yandang is located in Yueqing City. It is one of China's ten most famous scenic mountains. Mt. Putuo is actually a small island of Zhoushan Qundao (Is.). It is one of the four sacred Buddhist mountains in China with many famous temples built on it. Shengsi Is. lies to the north of Zhoushan Qundao. It is composed of 380 islands covering an area of 67 square kilometers and providing unique archipelago scenery. Tianyi Ge is the oldest tower storing a large collection of books found in China. Other scenic spots include Mt. Mogan and Qiandao Lake.

■ Local Products

Zhejiang is traditionally well known for its production of silk, embroidery, lace, wood carving, stone carving, shell carving, scissors, umbrella and various quality porcelain products. The province also produces first grade green tea and some of China's most famous medicinal herbs. Zhejiang cuisine is one of the eight most famous cuisines in China. Ham, rice wine, rice dumpling and other local flavours are liked by many.

Xi Hu (West Lake)

Hangzhou

0   0.84 km

ANHUI

JIANGSU

ANHUI

ZHEJIANG

NANJING

Zhenjiang

Yangzhou

Jiangdu

Rugao

Taixing

Jingjiang

Jiangyin

Zhangjiagang

Changshu

Xishan Qu Wuxi

Suzhou

Wuzhong Qu

Wujiang

Jurong

Danyang

Jintan

Changzhou

Wujin Qu Qishuyan Qu

Huishan Qu

Xiangcheng Qu

Lishui

Liyang

Yixing

Tai Hu

Xidongting Shan

Dongdongting Shan

Gaochun

Langxi

Changxing

Nanxun Qu

Xuancheng

Guangde

Huzhou

Jiaxing

Ningguo

Anji

Mogan Shan
719

Deqing

Tongxiang

Yuhang Qu

HANGZHOU

Lin'an

Fuyang

Xiaoshan Qu

Binjiang Qu

Shaoxing

Shaoxing

Altitude Table

50 20 0 20 50 100 200 300 500 750 1000 1500m

Changjiang (Yangtze R.) Delta

The extensive area around Shanghai, Nanjing and Hangzhou is referred to as Changjiang Delta. This delta plain is located in the middle of China's coast line, and is the estuary of China's largest river Chang Jiang (Yangtze River). This area borders on Shanghai, Jiangsu and Zhejiang, covering an area of 50,000 square kilometers.

As part of Changjiang Zhongxiayou Pingyuan (Pln.), Changjiang Delta is flat and low in altitude. Rivers and lakes are everywhere to be found here. Major rivers are Chang Jiang, Qiantang Jiang, Fuchun Jiang, and Huangpu Jiang, while Tai Hu, Dianshan Hu, and Yangcheng Hu are major lakes. There are many islands outside Hangzhou Wan (Bay). Chongming Dao is the major island at Changjiang Estuary.

Subtropical humid monsoon climate rules the area, which brings about mild temperature and distinctive seasonal difference. Annual rainfall in this area is above 1,000mm. The average temperature in January is above 0℃, while in July around 28℃.

Endowed with favorable climate and fertile soil, this area is traditionally known as the land of abundance. In modern times, intensive agriculture has guaranteed a prolific harvest of rice in this area. Tai Hu drainage area is an important production base of sheep and silk pods. With three well known fisheries including Zhoushan Fishery, Lusi Fishery and Changjiangkou Fishry around, this area boasts prosperous aquaculture.

Changjiang Delta is the largest industrial base in China and has a long industrial history. Textile, silk, food, electronics, instruments, steel, machinery, shipbuilding, chemicals, metallurgy as well as many other industries are developed in this area. It is most well known for steel, ship and automobiles made in Shanghai; electronics and electro-appliances made in Nanjing; and silks and clothes made in Suzhou and Hangzhou.

Bordering on Yellow Sea and East China Sea, and situated on the estuary of Chang Jiang, this area has a convenient water transportation system that extends in all directions. Ports like Shanghai, Ningbo, Zhoushan and Zhenjiang have freights to over 300 ports in 160 countries and regions throughout the world, forming a modern transportation network.

As a traditional tourist destination, Changjiang Delta is particularly famous for its waterside scenery and classical gardens. Cities like Shanghai, Yangzhou, Suzhou, Zhenjiang, Hangzhou, Changshu and Ningbo are listed as national historical and cultural cities for tourism and tourists' best choices. Important tourist attractions in this area include: the Oriental Pearl TV Tower, Sheshan National Forest Park, West Lake, Taihu Lake, Zhuozheng Garden and Mt. Putuo, among which Classical Gardens of Suzhou has been included in the World Heritage List by UNESCO.

Scale 1:1 100 000 0 11 22 33 44 55km

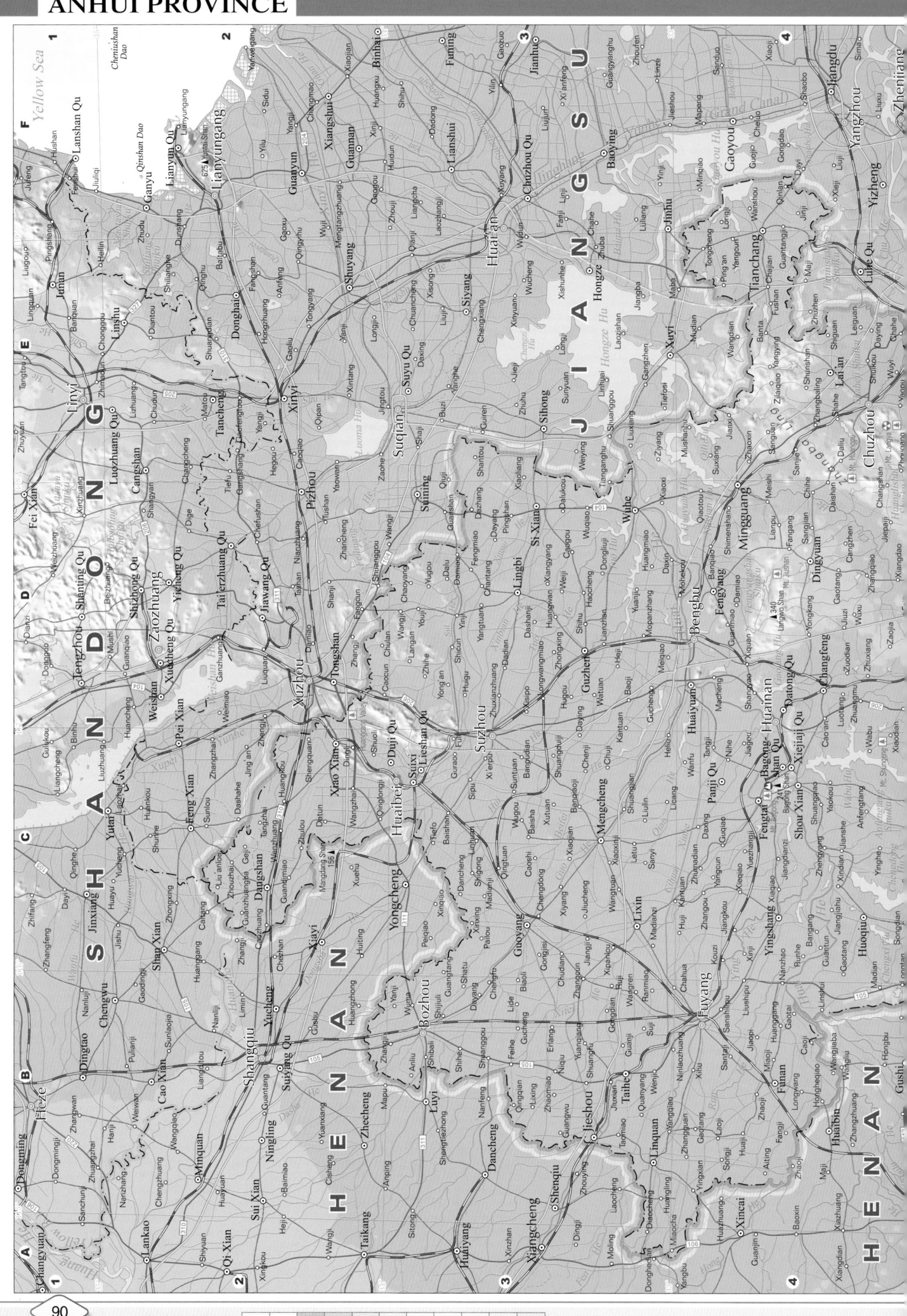

Altitude Table

50 20 0 50 100 200 300 500 750 1000 1500 2000m

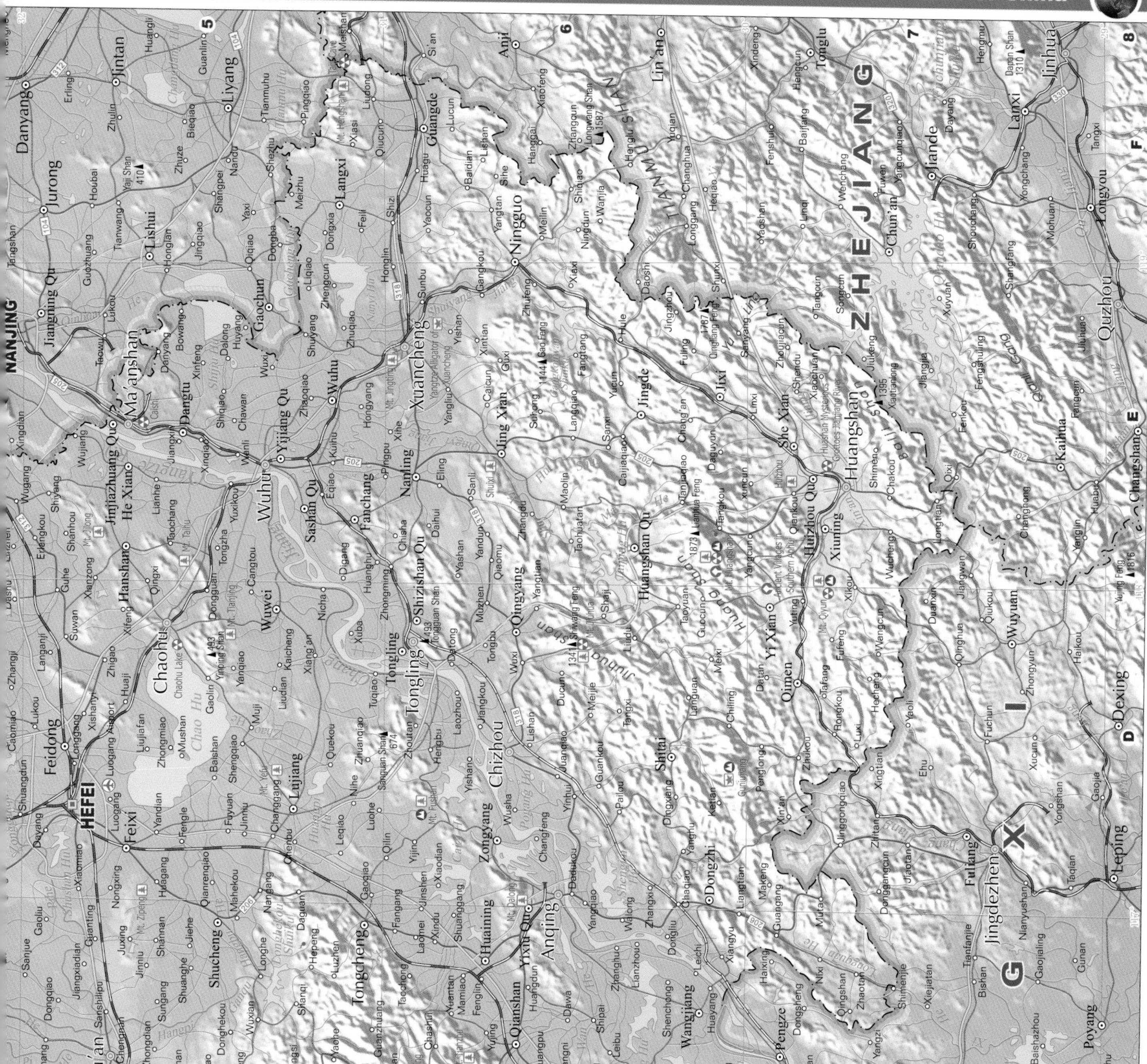

Scale 1:1 800 000

0 18 36 54 72 90 km

Anhui Province

With Hefei as its capital, Anhui Province, which is abbreviated as "Wan", is located on the northwest of East China, along Chang Jiang (Yangtze River). It covers an area of over 130,000 square kilometers, and has a population of 64.1 million, including such ethnic groups as Han, Hui, Mongol, Man, Miao, Yi, Zhuang and Buyei.

■ Geographical Features

Topography Anhui's terrain gradually descends from southwest to northeast, with mountains and hills taking up 2/3 of its total area. Major mountains in this province are Dabie Shan, Huang Shan and Jiuhua Shan; major hills are Jianghuai Hills and South Anhui Low Hills; while major plains are Huaihe Pingyuan and Wanzhong Pingyuan. Rivers in Anhui make up three major water systems: Chang Jiang, Huai He and Xin'an Jiang. Among them Huai He is the demarcation line between south China and north China. There are also plenty of lakes in this area, including Chao Hu, Longgan Hu and Daguan Hu.

Climate Anhui lies in a transitional zone between warm temperate and subtropical climate, thus enjoys a typical monsoon climate characterized by mild temperature, medium rainfall and clear distinction of four seasons. But climate differs a great deal in different areas: the area north to Huai He is ruled by warm temperate semi-humid monsoon climate, while the south is ruled by subtropical humid monsoon climate. The average annual temperature is between 14~17℃ , with an average temperature in January between -1~2℃ north of Huai He and 0~3℃ south of Huai He, while in July between 27~28℃ in the north and above 28℃ in the south. The average annual rainfall in the province is 750~1, 700mm.

■ Natural Resources

Rich mineral deposits of a large variety have been found in Anhui province. By now over 130 kinds of minerals have been found, among which the reserves of minerals like coal, iron, copper, sulfur, alunite, and magnetite are among China's top ten. Coke production along Huai He is so prosperous as to make the area the largest coke base in the province.

Anhui's forest cover rate is around 22.95%, mostly firs, mare's-tails, loblollies, bamboos, tung trees and oaks take up the most part. There are nearly 510 species of wild animals and over 2,000 species of plants living in this area, including such rare animals under national protection as Chinese alligators, white-flag dolphins and leopards, as well as around 1, 150 species of Chinese medicinal herbs, providing

the province with an incomparable biological environment. Alongside all these, the region is also rich in geothermal resources, and is known for some sanitaria with hot springs.

■ Agriculture

Anhui is one of China'a major agricultural bases and grain yielding provinces. Wheat, potatoes and other grain crops are grown in the area north of Huai He, while rice and wheat are grown south of Huai He. As a major tea producing province, Anhui is also rich in the production of cotton, rapeseeds, pods and jute. Cow, pig, sheep and fowls are raised in rural area, while freshwater fishery in this province is also prosperous.

■ Industry

As a production base of coal and steel, Anhui's industrial system is mainly supported by heavy industries like coal, metallurgy, chemical and machinery production, while household appliances, electronics, textiles and articles for daily use are also produced locally. The place is famous for Ma'anshan's steel, Tongling's copper and coals produced along Huai He. The production of refrigerator, washing machine and alcohol are leader of their kinds in China.

■ Transportation

Railways National railways like Beijing-Shanghai, Beijing-Kowloon and Lanzhou-Lianyungang are joined by provincial railways like Bengbu-Wuhu, Fuyang-Huainan, Hefei-Konglong and Wuhu-Guixi.

Highway Centered round major cities like Hefei, Lu'an, Bengbu, Fuyang and Wuhu, national highway system runs across the whole province, and is accelerated by express highways like Hefei-Nanjing, Hefei-Guangde and Hefei-Tongling.

Airway Luogang Airport provides flight courses connecting the province with over 30 major cities in China.

Waterway Chang Jiang provides a major waterway in the province, while its many branches and Huai He are all navigable. Wuhu, Ma'anshan, Tongling, Anqing and Yuxikou are major river ports.

■ Places of Interest

Anhui boasts numerous places of interest, of which Mt. Huangshan and Ancient Villages in Southern Anhui have been included in the World Heritage List by UNESCO. Mt. Huangshan lies north to Huangshan City and is famous for its spectacular natural scenery, particularly its gorgeous pines, mountain rocks, clouds and hot springs. Ancient villages lie around the foot of Mt. Huangshan. Mt. Jiuhua, one of China's four sacred Buddhist mountains, lies in Qingyang County. Over 90 temples holding over 6,800 Buddhist statues were built there and over 700

high monks live there. On Mt. Tianzhu, which lies in Qianshan County, you can find the thousand-year-old Buddhist temple Sanzu Si as well as the natural wonder Feilai Feng (Rock from Heaven). Mt. Langya has always been favoured by poets and writers; Mt. Qiyun is one of China's Four Sacred Taoist Mountains; while Mt. Sikong is "the first mountain of China's Chan Sect". Alongside wonderful natural scenery, the province is also rich in cultural relics as it is a major site of remains from Three Kingdoms (220-280AD).

■ Local Products

Anhui has been most famous in producing traditional four treasures of the study-writing brush, ink stick, ink slab and paper. Paper cutting and wood carvings are traditional handicrafts of the province. Tea produced in this region is of very high quality, while fruits like pears, pomegranates and grapes are well known. Local alcohol is liked by many, while Anhui cuisine is one of the eight most famous cuisines in China.

Mount Huangshan

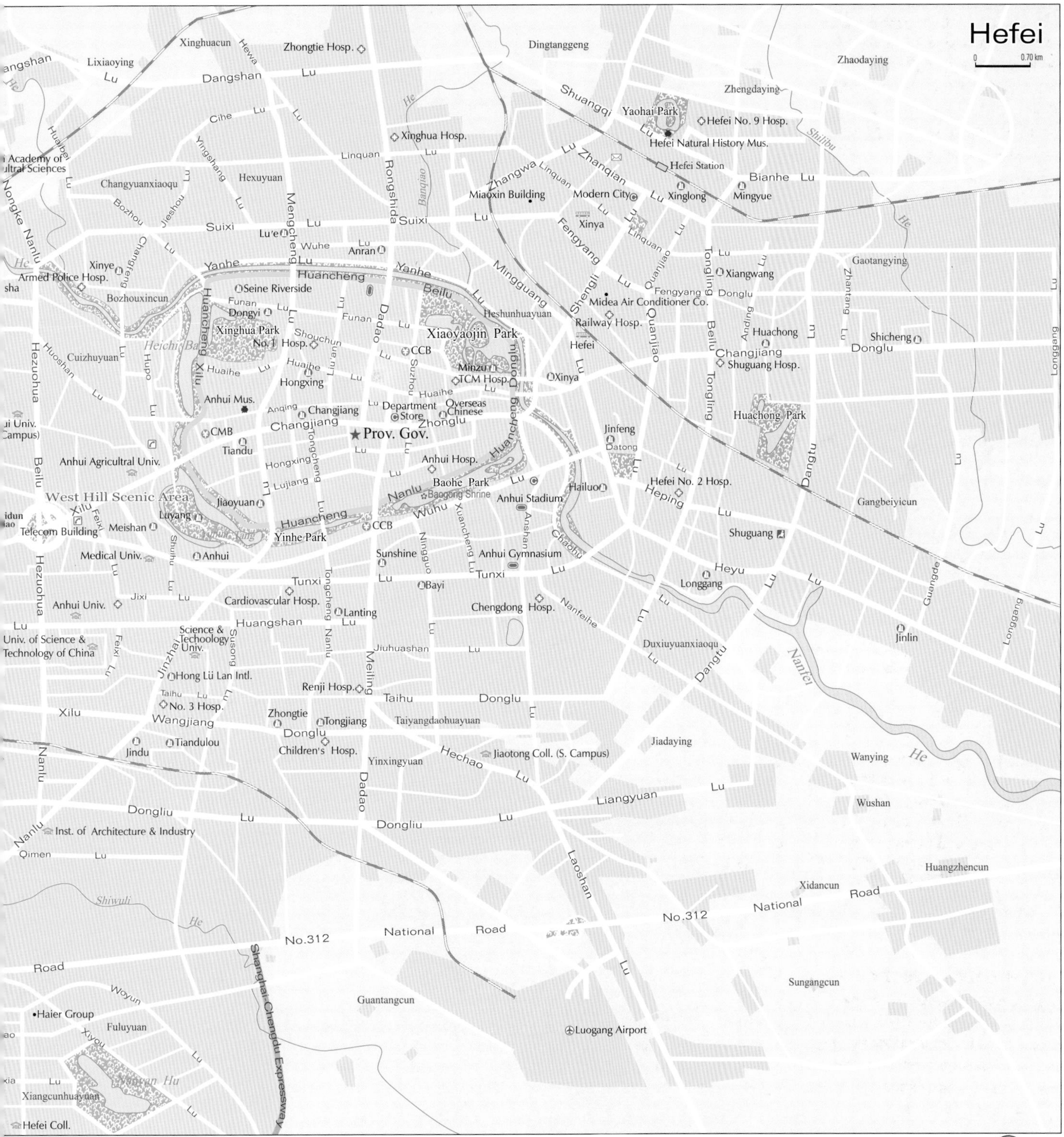

Hefei

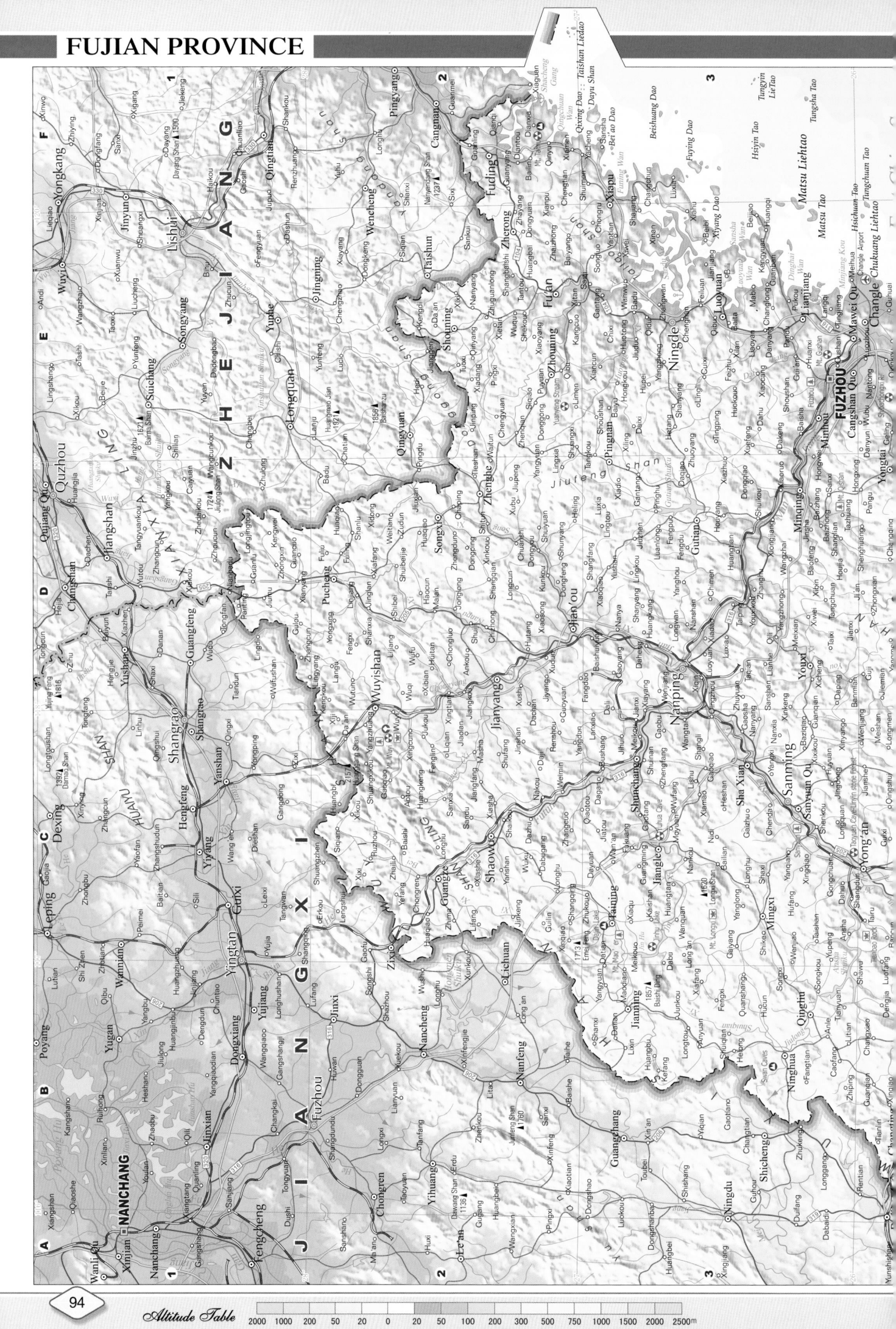

Altitude Table

2000 1000 200 50 20 0 20 50 100 200 300 500 750 1000 1500 2000 2500m

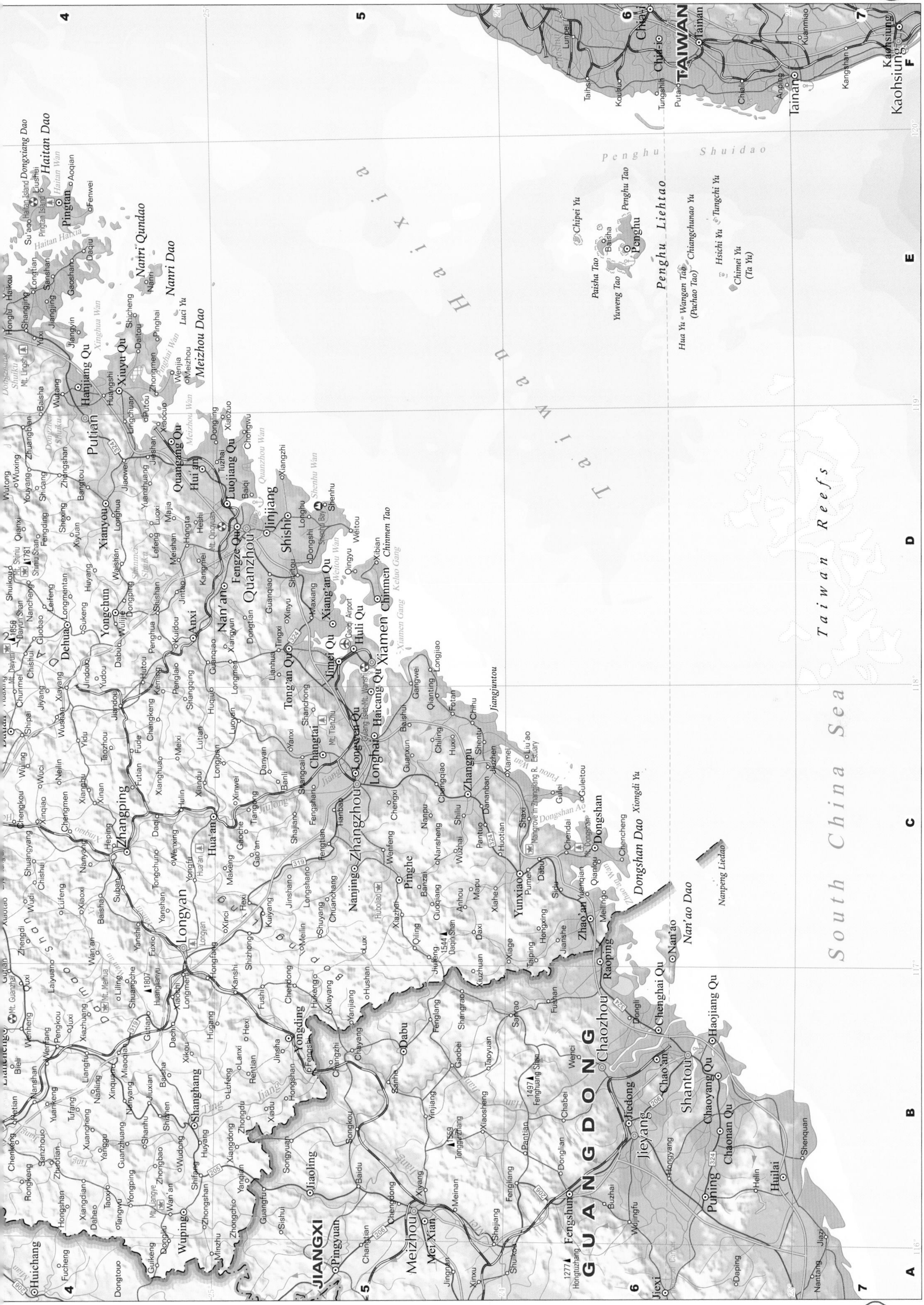

TAIWAN

Tainan

Kaohsiung

Penghu   Shuidao

Penghu Liehtao

Taixi   Reefs

S o u t h   C h i n a   S e a

Haitan Dao

Pingtan

Nanri Qundao

Nanri Dao

Meizhou Dao

Putian

Quanzhou

Jinjiang

Shishi

Xiamen

Nan'an

Anxi

Longyan

Zhangzhou

Longhai

Zhangping

Hua'an

Nanjing

Pinghe

Zhao'an

Dongshan

Nan'ao

Chaozhou

Shantou

Chenghai Qu

Chaoyang Qu

Puning

Jieyang

Jiexi

Meizhou

Mei Xian

G U A N G D O N G

J I A N G X I

Huichang

Scale   1:1 800 000

0   18   36   54   72   90 Km

Fujian Province

With Fuzhou as its capital, Fujian Province, which is abbreviated as "Min", is located on the southeast coast of China, facing Taiwan across the Taiwan Haixia (Str.). It covers an area of over 120,000 square kilometers, and has a population of 33.50 million, including such ethnic groups as Han, She, Hui, Tujia, Miao and Zhuang. Fujian is the renowned hometown for many overseas Chinese.

■ Geographical Features

Topography Mountains and hills take up most part of Fujian's total area. With Wuyi Shan on the west, and Daiyun Shan in the middle, both run from northeast to southwest, its terrain gradually descends from northwest to southeast. Plains like Fuzhou Pingyuan, Putian Pingyuan, Quanzhou Pingyuan and Zhangzhou Pingyuan all lie along coastal area. Major rivers are Min Jiang, Jin Jiang, and Jiulong Jiang, of which Min Jiang is the largest. Long Hu and Xi Hu are two major lakes in Fujian. A sinuous coast line with many gulfs provides Fujian with many favorable seaports like Mawei, Xiamen and Dongshan. Chinmen Tao, Dongshan Dao and Haitan Dao are three major islands among many along the coast.

Climate Subtropical humid monsoon climate rules the area, which blurs the seasonal difference, and brings to Fujian plenty of rains. Annual rainfall in this region is between 1,000~1,900mm. The average annual temperature is between 17~22℃, with an average temperature in January between 6~12℃, while in July between 28~29℃.

■ Natural Resources

Over 110 kinds of minerals have been found in Fujian, among which the reserves of tungsten, iron, molybdenum, columbium, tantalum, rare earth, pyrophyllite, barite, kaolin, granite, fluorite, limestone and coal are particularly important.

Extensive river system provides Fujian with rich water resources, and a water power potential of 10.5 million kilowatt.

As a major forest zone in South China, Fujian's forest cover rate is around 60.52%, the largest in China. Thousands of wild animals, together with over 5,000 species of wild plants and over 750 species of fish live in the area.

Sinuous coast line and sharp fall of sea tide provides Fujian with a potential tide energy capacity of 15 million kilowatt. The region is also rich in terrestrial heat resources, up till now, over 100 hot springs have been found, most of which hold water as hot as 40~60℃.

■ Agriculture

Double or even triple cropping harvest system is applied in Fujian, a province known for its production of rice, wheat, sweet potatoes, sugar cane, tobaccos, and hemps. Longan, orange, lichee, banana, loquat, pineapple, olive, and grapefruits are also grown here. Fujian is the leader in China's Longan output. Prosperous aquaculture industry is developed along coastal area, an area rich in the production of hairtail, yellow-fin tuna, eel, shellfish and laver.

■ Industry

Relying on its rich resources of agriculture, aquaculture and forestry, Fujian's light industries such as sugar-making, tea-making, food production, textile, and paper-making play important roles in China. Metallurgy, machinery, electronics, chemical industry as well as other heavy industries are being developed recently. Canned food, clothes, shoes, plastic commodities, ceramic building materials and sanitation materials are its major export products.

■ Transportation

Railway Yingtan–Xiamen railway runs through the province from north to south, and is joined by an extensive railway system made up of Hengfeng–Nanping, Zhangping–Longchuan and Zhangping–Quanzhou railways, connecting Fujian conveniently with Guangdong and Jiangxi.

Highway Centered round Fuzhou, Xiamen, Quanzhou, Nanping and Yong'an, national highway system connects every city and county in Fujian. Four express highways including Fuzhou–Quanzhou, Quanzhou–Xiamen, Fuzhou–Ningde and Longyan–Zhangzhou have also been put into use.

Airways Two international airports have been built in Fuzhou and Xiamen, providing flight courses to Beijing, Shanghai, Guangzhou, Hong Kong and over 40 other cities in China as well as destinations in Philippines, Malaysia and Singapore.

Waterway Fuzhou port is one of China's ten major container loading ports. Xiamen, Quanzhou and Mawei have all been important seaports historically. Freights from Fujian go directly to Dalian, Shanghai, Hainan, Hong Kong and other domestic seaports as well as neighbouring countries like Japan.

■ Places of Interest

Fujian has beautiful natural scenery. Mt. Wuyi, a typical Danxia physiognomy, lies to the south of Wuyishan City. With clean water running through reddish rocks, the place holds rich propagation species, and is included in the World Heritage List and World Network of Biosphere Reserves by UNESCO. Gulang Islet is a fantastic small island southwest to Xiamen. The scenic Mt. Wanshi is located to the east of Xiamen. Mt. Qingyuan is at the north of Quanzhou. Its three peaks provide three distinctive views. Mt. Taimu stands to the south of Fuqing city, and is surrounded on three sides by the sea. Because of its wonderful natural scenery, many renowned Buddhist temples were built in this province, such as Xuefeng Temple, Wanfu Temple, Guanghua Temple and Nanputuo Temple. Fujian also has many cultural relics such as engravings on Mt. Jiuri, ancient city of Chongwu and Zheng Chenggong's tomb.

■ Local Products

Fujian is the home of Wulong Tea, and produces many world renowned brands of black teas as well as a great variety of fresh fruits such as orange, Longan, lichee, olive, loquat and banana, and the province is also known for producing preserved fruits. Narcissus grown in Zhangzhou is known as China's top ten flowers. Fujian cuisine is one of the eight most famous cuisines in China. Lacquerworks, stone carvings, bead embroidery, puppet making and clay sculpture are traditional local handicrafts.

Mount Wuyi

Fuzhou

0   0.60 km

Fuzhou Natl. Forest Park
Douding Shuiku
Efeng
Banzhong
Xiangfeng
Xiazhang
Xili
Dongyuan
Tingkeng
Xiachiqiao
Xiushan
Xiajing
Dongyuan
Yangting Shuiku
Houban
Xiafang
Xushan
Panli
Quantou
Nainaiping
Sanshan Cemetery
Chixing
Guoqian
Shanbei
Jiaptian Shan
Baitalong
Zong'an
Nanping
Lijia
Guihunanjun Housing Theme Park
Quantou Shan
Licuo
Dafuling
Lin Zexu Tomb
Dongpu
Wuyi Nursery
Golf Club of Dengyun Mtn. Villa
Lianjiangyuan
Ma'ancun
Lijing
Luohan Shan
Henglu
Qinhu
Tingxia
Fuzhou Station
Dengyun Shuiku
Wufengkeng
Changguan
Fujian Sports Center
Jinhui
New Huadu Shopping Center
Baoshan
Helin
Shangpuling
Dafu Shan
Beihuan
Zhonglu
Beizhan
Fuzhou East Station
Shangdun
North Temple
Pingshan Park TCM Inst.
Ping Shan
Nanyang
Fuzhou P.O.
Tianfeng
Huada
Hualin
ABC
Commercial Bank
Dongshan
Shangbaofu
Prov. Gov.
Hot Spring Hotel
Sanba Lu
Xiwei
Banqiao
Dongtou
Tomb of Shen Baozhen
Meifeng
Sheshan
Zuohai Park
CCB
Intl. Conference & Exhibition Center
Jinjishan Park
Dangnan
Houxiang
Chibian
Tomb of Zhang Jing
Lihu Shuiku
Lakeside Hotel
Sun Yatsen Memorial Hall
Wenquan Park
Huamei
Dizang Temple
Huagong
Hengyu
Shanxi
Tomb of Ye Zugui
Xihu Park
Hubin
Minjiang
Foreign Trade Center Hotel
Wenquan
Taixi
Fuzhou Automobile Factory
Jinniushan Park
Wenlinshan Park
Jianxin Hosp.
Bamin
Kaiyuan Temple
Provincial Hosp.
Donghu
Puxiaxincun
Donglu
Xizhan
Houxian
Former Residence of Lin Zexu
ABC
Fuxin
Zhonglu
Fuxin
Longxiang
Fangli
Walmart Super Center
Xihong
Hongshan
Fujian Art Theatre
White Pagoda
Huawei
Fuma
Wuliting
Fujian Cancer Hosp.
Hongshan Bridge
Yangqiao
Fuzhou Univ.
Hongshan Hosp.
Black Pagoda
Xiehe Hosp.
Gutian Telecom. Center
ICBC
ABC
Minjiang
Bao'en Pagoda
Fuyu
Mun. Gov.
Wu Shan
Children Hosp.
Sunshine Holiday
Wangzhuangxincun
Qianyu
Honngguang
Zhenban
Shantoujiao
Jiangbin
Minjiang Univ.
Yidu
Jiaotong
Medical Univ.
Walmart Super Center
Nanzhan
Guohuo
Donglu
Jin'an Hosp.
Lianyang
Jintang
Marong
Minjiang Park
Chating Park
Guohuo
Fujian People's Hosp.
Fuzhou No.1 Hosp.
Fuzhou Mus.
Guangminggang Park
Yafeng Park
Xinzhangzhou
Xinchuan
Dadao
Xiangban
Changting
Zhenwu
Xilu
ICBC
Yangzhongzhou
Bosheng
Yafeng
Eyu Park
Yanzhou
Jinshan
Fujixincun
Hexia
Daliang
CCB
Taijiang Hosp.
Paiwei
Shuguang
Aofeng
Yangli
Central Square
Jiangbin
Jiefang Bridge
Jiangbin
Zhongdadao
Hengjiang Zhou
Youxizhou Bridge
Xidadao
Zhong Zhou
Fuzhou No.2 Hosp.
Jiangbian
Jiukongzha
Diwai
Jiangxin Park
Sanxianzhou Bridge
Longtan
Yantaishan Park
Tian'an Church
Zhongdun
Nanshe
Puxia Zhou
Gangtou
Fujian Normal Univ.
Xiaohu
Fuzhou People's Stadium
BOC
Maidelong
Dacheng
Jinpuxiaoqu
Youxizhou
Licuoshan
Chang'anshan Park
Shangsan
Agricultural Sch.
Green Island H.
Chengnan Hosp.
Puxia
Xindang Zhou
Lutou
Dibianli
Wujiangding
Bailuling
Social Welfare Institution
Dongsheng Park
Lin Zexu Square
Gaishanzhen
Shangyushan
Pushang
Fenggao
Sch. for the Blind
Niutou Shan
Guozhai
Xiuzhai
Jiangbian
Qi'an
Miaofeng Temple
Gaogaishan Park
Fuzhou-Quanzhou Expressway
Linpu
Gaogai Shan
Guangqiao
Lianban
Wanbian
Yangxia
Panyu
Yixun
Tianfu
Paixia
Chengmen Ding
Huang Shan

ZHEJIANG

ANHUI

HUBEI

HUNAN

NANCHANG

Altitude Table

50	20	0	50	100	200	300	500	750	1000	1500	2000	2500 m

Scale 1:1 800 000

0   18   36   54   72   90 km

Jiangxi Province

With Nanchang as its capital, Jiangxi Province, which is abbreviated as "Gan", is located to the south of Chang Jiang (Yangtze River), along Gan Jiang (river). It covers an area of over 160,000 square kilometers, and has a population of 43.02 million, including such ethnic groups as Han, She, Hui, Mongol, Miao, Man and Zhuang.

■ Geographical Features

Topography Mountains and hills take up most part of Jiangxi province. With mountains like Huaiyu Shan, Wuyi Shan, Jiuling Shan, Luoxiao Shan, Jiulian Shan, and Dayu Ling circles around Jiangxi on the east, south and west, Jiangxi's terrain is like a basin opens up in the north, where lie Poyang Hu (L.) and its lake side plain — part of middle and lower Yangtze valley plains. Gan Jiang, Fu He, Xin Jiang and Xiu Shui are major rivers in this province, all of which flow to Poyang Hu, the largest fresh water lake in China.

Climate Subtropical humid monsoon climate rules the area, which brings about adequate sunshine, plenty of rainfall and a mild climate with distinctive seasonal difference. Annual rainfall in this area is between 1,400～1,900mm. The average annual temperature is between 16～20℃, with an average temperature in January between 4～9℃, while in July between 28～30℃.

■ Natural Resources

By now over 140 kinds of minerals were found in Jiangxi, a province most famous for its production of minerals like copper, tungsten, uranium, rare earth and tantalum. The reserves of accompanying sulfur, flux dolomite, halite and serpentine found in the region are among China's top five.

With over 2,400 rivers and many lakes, the province is rich with water resources.

Jiangxi's forest cover rate is around 53.37%, including firs, pine trees, camphor tree, cypress, wingceltis, and bamboos, among which firs and pine trees take up the most part. The province hosts abundant birds and fish with high economic values.

■ Agriculture

Jiangxi is one of China's major production bases of grain and by-products. Rice is the main grain crop planted in Poyanghu Pingyuan (Pln.). Other grain crops include wheat, beans and sweet potatoes. Main cash crops are cotton, rape and other oil bearing crops, hemp, orange, and sugar cane. Jiangxi leads in China in the production of rape seeds and sesame. Animal husbandry in this area is quite popular and well developed, and the province produces well known strains of pigs, chicken and geese. Poyang Hu is one of China's major production areas of fresh water fish.

■ Industry

The production of coal, non-ferrous metal and steel, machinery, electronics, foods, textile, paper, chemicals and medicine are chief industries developed in Jiangxi, a province most famous for the production of machines, textile, food and porcelain.

■ Transportation

Railway Except dozens of branch lines, six main stems including Beijing–Kowloon, Hangzhou–Zhuzhou, Yingtan–Xiamen, Wuhu–Guixi and Wuchang–Jiujiang railways run through Jiangxi. 1/3 of Beijing–Kowloon line runs across this province from north to south.

Highway Centered round Nanchang, Ganzhou, Shangrao, Ji'an and Jiujiang, nearly 100 national and provincial highways run across Jiangxi, reaching every city and county in this region. Express highways like Nanchang–Jiujiang, Nanchang–Ganzhou and Jiujiang–Jingdezhen have all been put into use.

Airway Nanchang Airport offers fight courses to Beijing, Shanghai, Guangzhou, Hong Kong and 20 other major cities in China.

Waterway Gan Jiang, Fu He, Xin Jiang and Xiu Shui as well as Poyang Hu and Chang Jiang are all open to navigation. Nanchang and Jiujiang are important river ports that provide freights to river ports along Chang Jiang like Wuhan, Chongqing, Nanjing, and Shanghai as well as to ports in Japan, Southeast Asia and many other regions around the world.

■ Places of Interest

Jiangxi is most famous for its wonderful natural scenery. Mt. Lushan is located to the south of Jiujiang, it is a renowned summer reserve and is included in the World Heritage List by UNESCO. Mt. Jinggang, a national nature reserve, is located at the middle part of Luoxiao Shan. It is covered with lush forests and hosts rich animal resources. Longhu Mountain is the birth place of Taoism and has many cultural relics. Mt. Sanqing is another Taoist place known to many. Tengwang Pavilion is one of China's three most famous towers. As the earliest base of Chinese revolution, Jiangxi has many revolutionary relics like Nanchang, Ruijin and Anyuan.

■ Local Products

Jiangxi is traditionally known for its production of green tea, black tea, orange, locus roots, lily bulbs, bamboo shoots, black-bone chicken, whitebait, sturgeon and other aquatic products. Local flavours like salted duck, ham, chilli paste and rice noodle are liked by many. Porcelain produced in Jingdezhen is world famous. Inkstone produced in Wuyuan is one of China's four most famous inkstones. Other traditional local handicrafts are: brush pen, porcelain painting, bamboo bed shade, wood carving and camphor suitcase.

Mount Lushan

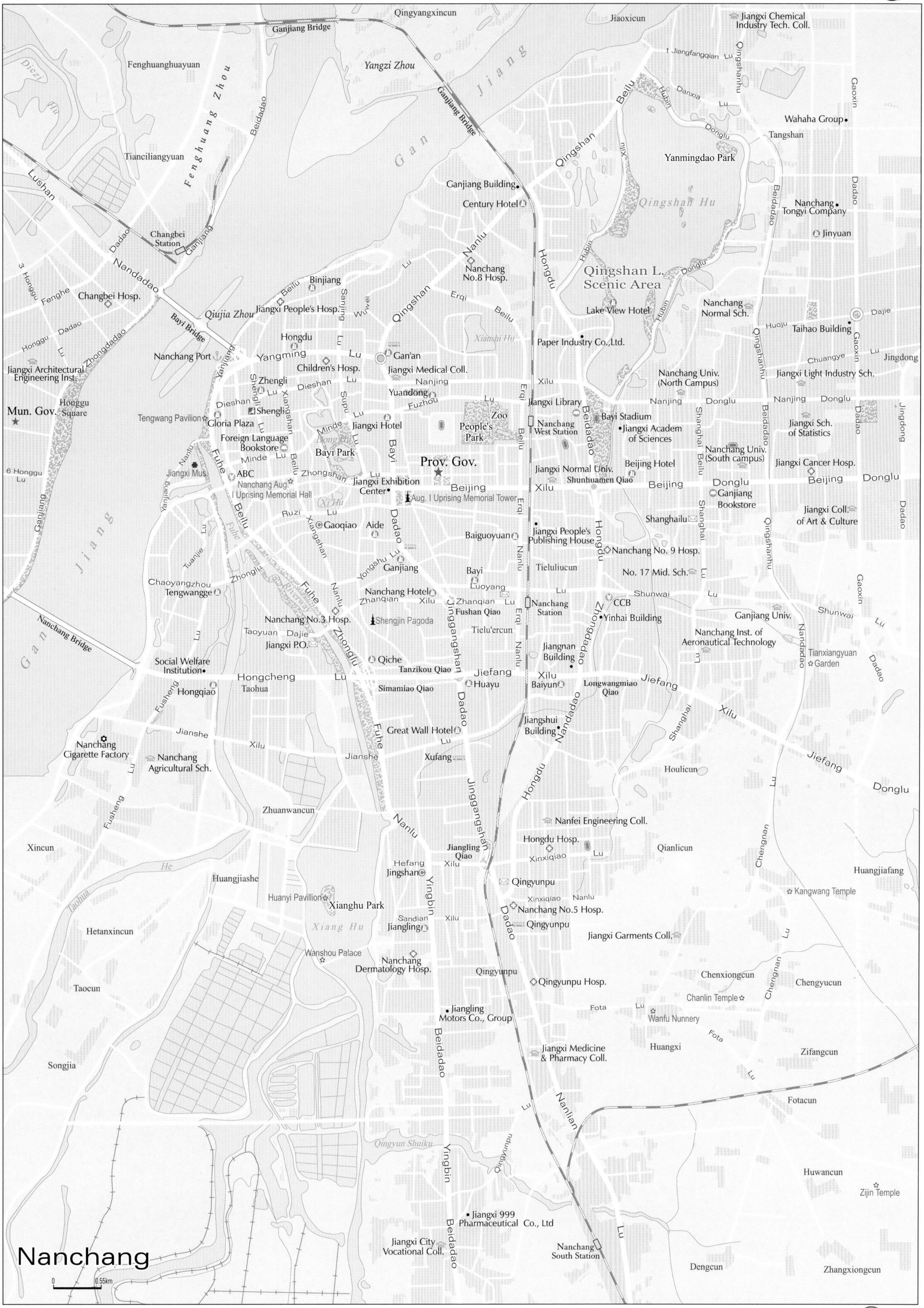

Qingyangxincun
Ganjiang Bridge
Jiaoxicun
Jiangxi Chemical Industry Tech. Coll.

Fenghuanghuayuan
Yangzi Zhou
Jiangfangqian
Qingshanhu
Gaoxin

Fenghuang Zhou
Gan Jiang
Beilu
Hubin
Danxia
Lu

Tianciliangyuan
Lushan
Dieziji
Beidadao
Qingshan
Donglu
Wahaha Group
Tangshan

Changbei Station
Ganjiang
Yanmingdao Park
Nanchang Tongyi Company

Changbei Hosp.
Nandadao
Qingshan Hu
Jinyuan

Hongu
Dadao
Ganjiang Building
Nanlu
Nanchang No.8 Hosp.
Hongdu
Qingshan L. Scenic Area
Nanchang Normal Sch.

Binjiang
Beilu
Century Hotel
Lake View Hotel
Qingshanhu
Dajie

Qiujia Zhou
Jiangxi People's Hosp.
Erqi
Beilu
Paper Industry Co.,Ltd.
Huolu
Taihao Building
Jingdong

Hongdu
Xianshi Hu
Nanchang Univ. (North Campus)
Chuangye
Gaoxin
Jiangxi Light Industry Sch.

Yangming
Gan'an
Jiangxi Medical Coll.
Xilu
Nanjing
Donglu
Nanjing
Donglu

Children's Hosp.
Nanjing
Jiangxi Library
Bayi Stadium
Jiangxi Sch. of Statistics

Nanchang Port
Zhengli
Dieshan
Yuandong
Fuzhou
Zoo
Nanchang West Station
Jiangxi Academ of Sciences
Nanchang Univ. (South campus)
Jiangxi Cancer Hosp.

Tengwang Pavilion
Shengli
Minde
Lu
People's Park
Jiangxi Normal Univ.
Beijing Hotel
Donglu
Donglu

Gloria Plaza
Bayi Park
Zhongshan
Prov. Gov.
Beijing
Shunhuamen Qiao
Beijing
Beijing

Foreign Language Bookstore
Jiangxi Mus.
ABC
Jiangxi Exhibition Center
Aug. I Uprising Memorial Tower
Shanghailu
Ganjiang Bookstore
Jiangxi Coll. of Art & Culture

Nanchang Aug. I Uprising Memorial Hall
Ruzi
Gaoqiao
Aide
Baiguoyuan
Jiangxi People's Publishing House
Nanchang No. 9 Hosp.

Chaoyangzhou
Tengwangge
Yongshu Lu
Ganjiang
Bayi
Luoyang
Tieluliucun
No. 17 Mid. Sch.

Nanchang No.3 Hosp.
Shengjin Pagoda
Nanchang Hotel
Zhanqian
Xilu
Zhangjan
Nanchang Station
CCB
Ganjiang Univ.
Shunwai

Jiangxi P.O.
Taoyuan
Dajie
Fushan Qiao
Tielu'ercun
Yinhai Building
Nanchang Inst. of Aeronautical Technology
Tianxiangyuan Garden

Social Welfare Institution
Qiche
Tanzikou Qiao
Jiefang
Jiangnan Building
Xilu

Hongcheng
Simamiao Qiao
Huayu
Baiyun
Longwangmiao Qiao
Jiefang

Hongqiao
Taohua
Great Wall Hotel
Jiangshui Building
Houlicun
Jiefang

Nanchang Cigarette Factory
Nanchang Agricultural Sch.
Jianshe
Xufang
Donglu

Zhuanwancun
Nanfei Engineering Coll.

Xincun
Jiangling Qiao
Hongdu Hosp.
Qianlicun
Huangjiafang

Huangjiashe
Hefang
Jingshan
Xinxiqiao
Qingyunpu
Kangwang Temple

Xianghu Park
Jiangling
Xinxiqiao
Nanchang No.5 Hosp.
Jiangxi Garments Coll.

Hetanxincun
Xiang Hu
Wanshou Palace
Qingyunpu
Chenxiongcun
Chanlin Temple
Chengyucun

Taocun
Nanchang Dermatology Hosp.
Qingyunpu
Qingyunpu Hosp.
Wanfu Nunnery

Jiangling Motors Co, Group
Jiangxi Medicine & Pharmacy Coll.
Fota
Huangxi
Zifangcun

Songjia
Qingyun Shuiku
Fotacun

Huwancun
Zijin Temple

Nanchang

Jiangxi 999 Pharmaceutical Co., Ltd
Jiangxi City Vocational Coll.
Nanchang South Station
Dengcun
Zhangxiongcun

0   0.55km

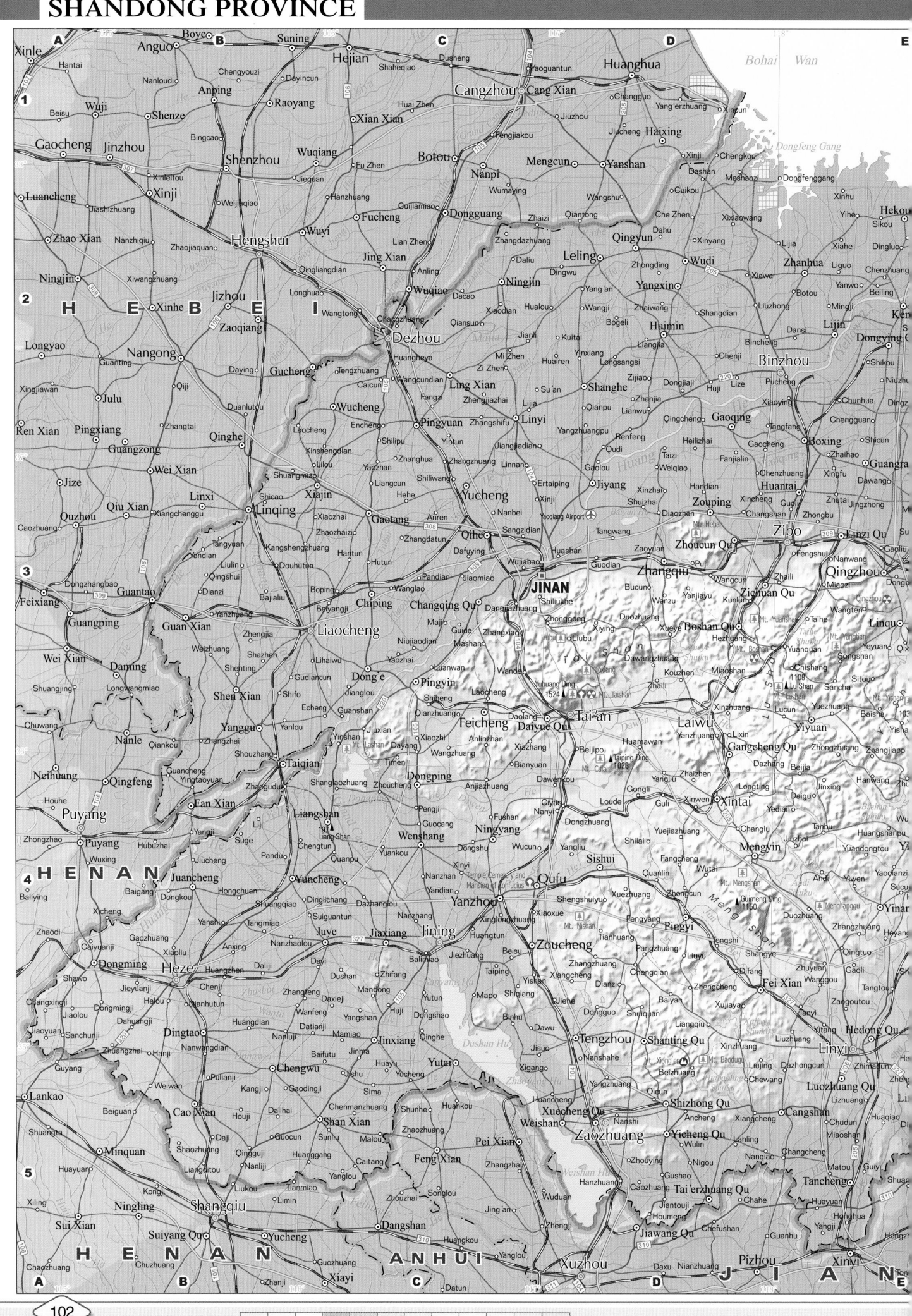

Altitude Table   100 50 20 0 50 100 200 300 500 750 1000 1500 2000 m

F   G   H   I

Bo Hai

Yellow Sea

Beihuangcheng Dao
Nanhuangcheng Dao

Qundao

Daqin Dao
Bohai Haixia
Tuoji Dao

Houji Dao
Miao Dao Dazhushan Dao
Changdao Island Beichangshan Dao
Daheishan Dao Nanchangshan Dao
Changdao
Miaodao Haixia

Sang Dao **Penglai** oXingang
Beigou
Huangheyingo Langao Longshandian Chaoshui
Longkou Xiaomenjie Bajiao Zhifu Dao *Yantai Gang*
Longkou Gang Lutou Xiadingjia Gusidian Daluhang Zhichu Kongtong Dao **Zhifu Qu** Chu Dao
Xinzhuang Huangshanguan Fengyi Guxian **Fushan Qu** Yangmadao **Weihai** Liugong Island Liugong Dao Jiming Dao
Mt. Laoshan Zhaili Fushan **Yantai** Jianggezhuang *Wehai Gang* Haopo Longxudao
Sanshandao Jincheng Linglong Ai Shan 814 Songshan Miaohou Laishan Airport **Muping Qu** Wangtuan Caomiaozi Chengshan
Diaolongzuo Canzhuang Sikou Xicheng **Qixia** Yuandgezhuang Gaoling Taibo Ding Poyu Yaxi
Furong Dao Pinglidian Qishan Yangchu Guanshui Tiekou Taibo Ding 922 Tianfushan **Wendeng** **Rongcheng**
Zhuyou Liangguaji Biguo Shewopo Buxitou Mt. Kunyu Jugezhuang Geju Gaocun
Laizhou Chengguo Chaipeng Qinglong Yukeding Xujiadian Shuidao Kouzio Tengjia
Wenfenglu Guojiadian Xiluo Hetoudian Facheng Mashidian Fengjia Zetou Sengcun Houjia Shangzhuang
Xiaying Tushano Xiaqiu Jiudian Dazé Shan 736 **Laiyang** Longwangzhuang **Rushan** Nanhuang Xiaoguan Bukou Ningjin
Qingxiang Tonghe Dianzio Guliu Zhuwu Rushanzhai Xijia Chishano
Hubu Zhugou Zhangshe Cuizhao **Laixi** Lugezhuang Quanshuitou **Haiyang** Rushankou Baishatan Zeku Renhe Shidao *Moye Dao*
Changyi Gudi Magezhuang **Pingdu** Tuanwang Dakuang Fengcheng Daxinjia Xiaoshikou *Jinghai Wan* Jinghai Mt. Chistan Shidao Wan
Hanting Qu Songzhuang Mincun Tonghe Guxian Radingo Xiao Dayanjiao *Nanhuang Dao* *Yishanzi Dao* *Sanshanzi Dao*
Weifang Shibu Zhongzhuang Guozhuang Xlagezhuang Xuefang Xin an *Sushan Dao*
Changle Beimeng Cuijiaji Llandi Liujiazhuang Taizhi Huashan Wangcun *Dingzi Gang*
Wangliu **Fangzi Qu** Jingshanwa Nancun Beiwangzhu Lingshan Dianji *Tubu Dao*
Masong Zhaoge Zhangling Caijiazhuang Madian Mt. Mashan Wenquan Tianheng *Tianheng Dao*
Honghe **Anqiu** *Yiashan Shuiku* Shuangyang Lencun Aoshanwei Tianheng
Linghe **Gaomi** Hujiazhuang **Jimo** *Laoshan Wan*
Jinzhr Guanzhuang Zhugou **Chengyang Qu** Liuting Airport *Ma'er Dao* *Qianli Yan*
Wenquan **Jiaozhou** Yuangezhuang Liuting Lao Shan 1132 *Daguan Dao* *Changmen Yan*
Wujiaolou Shiqiaozi Tuzhuang Hongdao Mt. Laoshan
Fuguanzhuang Xiangzhou Batchihe Wangwu **Licang Qu** Shazikou
Mengtuan Puji Xinxing Wangtai **Laoshan Qu**
Dongguan Kushan Licha Huangshan **Qingdao**
Zhucheng Zhigou Luwang Mt. Zhushan *Dagong Dao*
Zhaoxian Xumeng Huanghua Taoyuan **Huangdao Qu** Xuejiadao *Chaolian Dao*
Yuli **Wulian** Gaoze Shimei Lingshanwei
Zhaoshan Mt. Wulian Songbai Shihetou **Jiaonan** *Lingshan Wan*
Shibuzi Shichang Wulian Shan 515 Taolm Dacun Zhangjialou
Ju Xian Qiaoshan Haiqing Zangnan Gounanya
Changling Liwuguan Langya *Lingshan Dao*
Chentuan Xinyang Shuqishan Liangcheng *Rizhao Seashore*
Zhonglou Huangdun **Donggang Qu** Heshan
Wentuan Kuishan Gaoking
Laopo Zhulu Jufeng **Rizhao** Taoluo
Pingshang Hushan *Ping Dao* *(Pingshan Dao)*
Junan Zhuanggang Andongwei
Zhubian **Lanshan Qu**
Lizhuang *Haizhou Wan* *Dashan Dao*
Haitou *Cheniu Shan (Danian Shan)*
Ganyu *Dongxi Liandao*
Lianyun Qu Lianyungang *Yellow Sea*
Dunshang Yuntai Shan 625
Haizhou Qu **Lianyungang**
Banpu Xuwei
Fangshan Muxu
Qingyihu Chenjiagang
Guanyun Yangji

Huanghe Kou Xianhe Huanghe Delta Huanghe Estuary Xiazhen
Laohuanghe Kou *Huanghekou*
Laizhou Wan *Changbei Gang* Dajiawa Chahe Yangzi
Houzhen Longchi Qingxiang
Shouguang Daotian Pozi Gudi
Tianma

F   G   H   I

Shandong Province

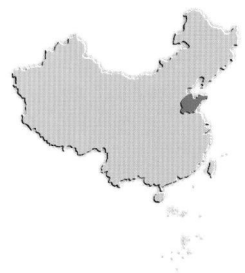

With Jinan as its capital, Shandong Province, which is abbreviated as "Lu", is located on the north of China's coast line, along the lower reaches of Huang He (Yellow River), bordering on Yellow Sea and East China Sea. It covers an area of over 150,000 square kilometers, and has a population of 91.08 million, including such ethnic groups as Han, Hui, Man, Korean and Mongol.

■ Geographical Features

Topography Plains and hills take up most part of Shandong. With Tai Shan (Mt.), Lu Shan, Meng Shan and Qi Shan in the middle, Huabei Pingyuan (Pln.) on the northwest, and Shandong Peninsula on the east, its terrain descends from middle to the outside circle. There are many rivers in the province, including Huang He which runs from west to east, and Jinghang Yunhe (Grand Canel) which runs from north to south. Most rivers in this region are branches of Huang He, Hai He, or Huai He. Major lakes are: Nanyang Hu, Dushan Hu, Shaoyang Hu, and Weishan Hu.

Climate Warm temperate semi-humid monsoon climate rules the area, which brings about distinctive seasonal difference. Annual rainfall in this area is between 550~950mm. The average annual temperature is between 11~14℃, with an average temperature in January between -5~1℃, while in July between 24~28℃.

■ Natural Resources

By now over 100 kinds of minerals were found in Shandong, of which the reserves of gold, gypsum and sulfur are ranked as China's No.1. The total output of gold here takes up over 25% of China's total. Reserves of oil, cobalt, hafnium, diamond, and porcelain clay are ranked as second largest of their kinds in China. Shengli Oilfield is China's second largest, while Yanteng Coal Mine is one of China's major coal mines. Coastal area along the peninsula is one of China's major production bases of sea salt.

Shandong's forest cover rate is around 12.58%. There are more than 400 species of wild animals and over 200 marine lives living in this region, including 40 aquatics of economic value. There are also over 640 species of natural cash plants, over 600 species of trees, over 800 species of medicinal herbs and over 30 Species of aquatic plants growing here.

■ Agriculture

As a major agricultural province, Shandong's grain output ranks the second in China, and its outputs of vegetables, fruits, meat and aquatic products all lead in the country. Main crops here are: wheat, corn, soybean, sweet potato, broomcorn, cotton, tobacco and peanuts. Shandong is a major production base of cotton and the largest vegetable production area in China. Major vegetables are: Chinese cabbage, radish, Chinese onion, garlic, ginger and hot pepper. The province is also famous for its prolific production of tasty fruits like apple, watermelon, pear, peach, cherry and Chinese dates. Animal husbandry in this area mainly concerns raising pigs, cows, and sheep, and the province produce first class strains of pigs, cows, sheep, donkey, chicken and duck. Aquatic products like fish, shrimp, crab, turtle, abalone, and sea cucumber are abundant in this region.

■ Industry

Shandong is most advanced in the production of energy and raw materials. Major industries include: machinery, power generation, oil production, chemicals, metallurgy, building materials, electronics, textiles and food production. Its outputs of alkali, salt, paper, liquor and beer all rank as China's first, while the outputs of coal, oil, fertilizer and cement are very considerable.

■ Transportation

Railway Beijing–Shanghai and Beijing–Kowloon railways run across the province from north to south, while Jinan–Qingdao railway runs from east to west. These trunk lines are joined by over 20 provincial railways.

Highway Centered round Jinan, Weifang, Linyi, Tai'an and Jining, several national highways run across the whole province, connecting every city and county. Express highways like Jinan–Qingdao, Qingdao–Yantai, Jinan–Dezhou and Jinan–Linying have been put into use.

Airway With nearly ten airports in the province, it is conveniently connected with over 30 major cities in China as well as destinations in Japan, R.O. Korea and Singapore.

Waterway: There are nearly 30 ports along its coast, a figure no other province can surpass. Qingdao, Yantai and Rizhao are major deep water sea ports with ocean routes connecting with dozens of countries including Japan, Korea, Singapore and Malaysia.

■ Places of Interest

Shandong has beautiful natural scenery and rich historical and cultural relics. Mt. Taishan borders on Jinan and Tai'an. It is esteemed as the No. 1 of the Five Sacred Mountains in China. Mt. Laoshan, a renowned scenic spot bordering on sea, is located to the northeast of

Qingdao. Jinan is known as "the city of springs". Daming Lake is filled by spring waters and is a major tourist destination in Jinan. Confucius Temple is located in Qufu City. There are over 50 gateways, over 400 rooms and over 2,000 steles in this majestic ancient architectural complex. Old homes and family cemetery of the Confucius' offsprings are also there. Mt. Taishan, Temple, Cemetery and Mansion of Confucius have been included in the World Heritage List by UNESCO. Other tourist attractions are: Penglai Pavilion and Mt. Qianfo.

■ **Local Products**

Peony, rose and China rose are well known flowers of Shandong. Donkey-hide gelatin produced in Dong'e is a traditional rarity of Chinese medicine. Hops, beer and mineral water produced around Qingdao are famous drinks. Abalone, sea cucumber, scallop, prawn, dried shrimp and herring seeds are well known local aquatic products. Local flavours like braised chicken, battercake, broomcorn maltose and starch noodles are liked by many. Clocks, embroidery, porcelain, kite, shell carving, and grass weavings are traditional local handicrafts.

Temple of Confucius in Qufu

Jinan

0 0.88km

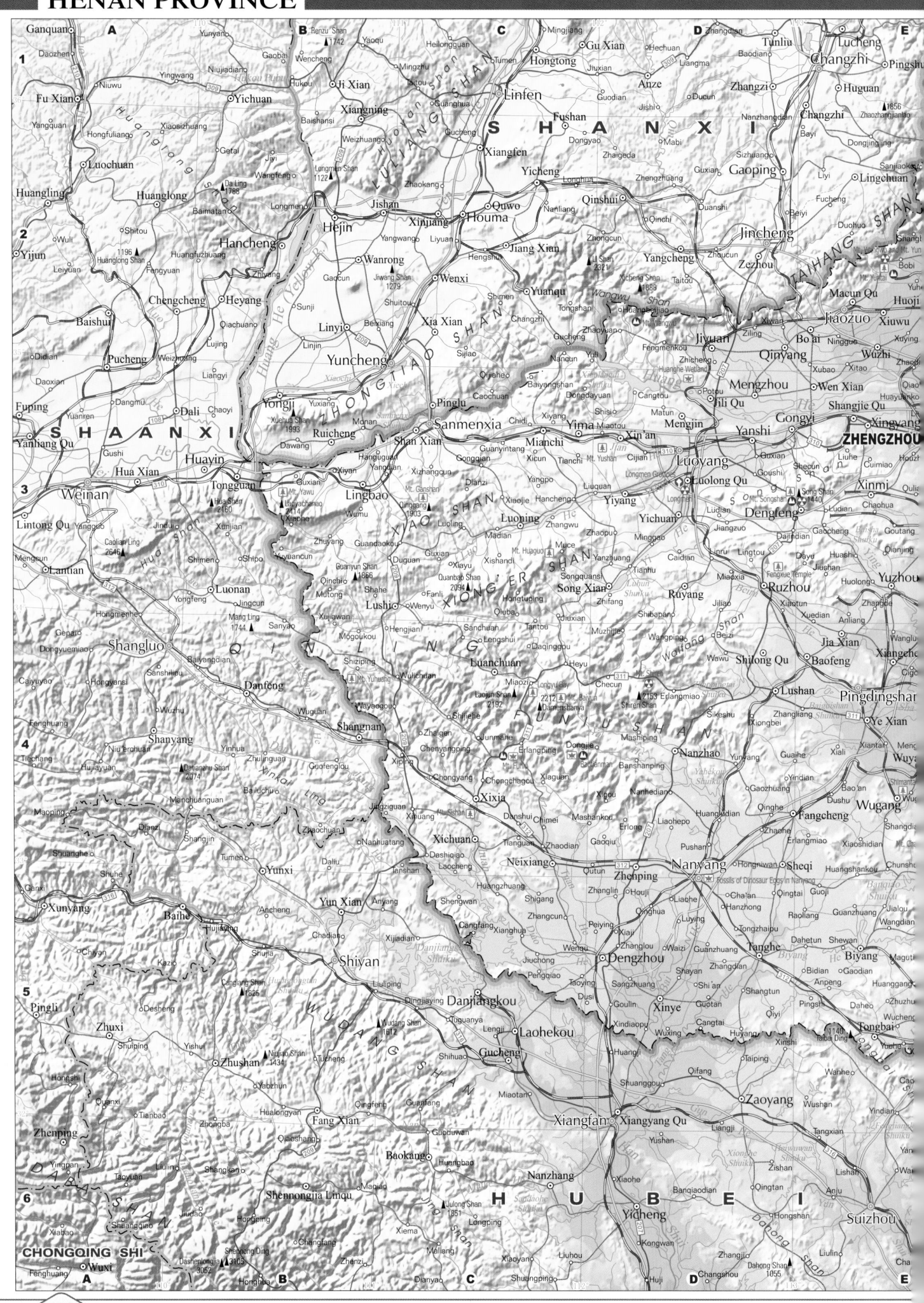

Altitude Table

0   50   100   200   300   500   750   1000   1500   2000   3000 m

Scale 1:2 100 000

0 21 42 63 84 105 km

Henan Province

With Zhengzhou as its capital, Henan Province, which is abbreviated as "Yu", is located along the middle and lower reaches of Huang He (Yellow River), and is traditionally known as the "Central Plain" of China. It covers an area of over 160,000 square kilometers, and has a population of 97.68 million, including such ethnic groups as Han, Hui, Man, Miao and Mongol.

■ Geographical Features

Topography With Funiu Shan (Mt.), Xiao Shan, Xiong'er Shan and Waifang Shan on the west, and Taihang Shan, Tongbai Shan and Dabie Shan on the north and south, Henan's terrain descends from west to east. Huanghuai Pingyuan is part of Huabei Plain, while Nanyang Pendi is the largest basin of the area. Most rivers here are branches of Huang He, Huai He, Wei He and Han Shui, of which Huai He has most branches. Few natural lakes can be found here, but many reservoirs have been built.

Climate As Henan is situated on the transitional zone between warm temperate zone and subtropical zone, humid and semi-humid continental monsoon climate rules the area, which brings about distinctive seasonal difference. Annual rainfall in this area is between 700～1,100mm. The average annual temperature is between 13～15℃, with an average temperature in January between 0～2℃ in the south and between -2～0℃ in the north, while in July between 26～28℃ in the whole region.

■ Natural Resources

By now over 100 kinds of minerals have been found in Henan, among which the reserves of minerals like molybdenum, alkali, pearlite, asbestos, refractory clay, oil, natural gas, gold, silver, antimony and over 40 others are among China's top ten. Minerals like aluminium, copper, lead, zinc, tungsten, fluorite, graphite and gems have all been found in this province. Henan's forest cover rate is around 12.52%, mostly paulownia and pine trees. Tea, tung, sumach, walnut and other fruit trees were also planted here. There are more than 400 species of land vertebrates and over 3 600 species of higher plants living in this area, including over 800 species of medicinal herbs.

■ Agriculture

Henan has been an agricultural province with a long history. As a major production region of grain, oil, cotton and tobacco in China, Henan applies double cropping harvest system in most part of the province. Major crops are: wheat, corn, sweet potato, soybean, millet, broomcorn, cotton, peanut, tobacco, sesame and jute. Xuchang area is most famous for tobacco. Animal husbandry in this area mainly concerns raising pigs and cows, and the province produces first class strains of pigs, cows, sheep, and donkeys.

■ Industry

Henan is a major production region of coal and oil. Thanks to its rich mineral resources and prolific agriculture, Henan's industrial system mainly contains textile, food processing, coal and oil mining, power generation, metallurgy, chemicals, building materials, machinery and electronics. Coal mines in Pingdingshan and Jiaozuo are well known for their enormous output.

■ Transportation

Railway Six main stems including Beijing-Guangzhou, Beijing-Kowloon, Lanzhou-Lianyungang, Jiaozhuo-Liuzhou and Xinxiang-Taiyuan run through Henan, and are joined by many other branch lines.

Highway Centered round Zhengzhou, Kaifeng, Luoyang, Anyang, Nanyang and Xinxiang, several national highways run across the whole province, connecting every city and county. There Express highways including Zhengzhou-Kaifeng, Luoyang-Anyang, Luohe-Xinyang have been put into use.

Airway As an important air terminal in China, Zhengzhou has flight courses to Beijing, Guangzhou, Wuhan, Kunming and 30 other major cities in China.

Waterway Parts of Huang He, Huai He, Ying Shui and Sha He are navigable. Zhoukou and Luohe are important river ports.

■ Places of Interest

There are eight most famous ancient capitals in China, of which four are located in Henan. Anyang was the earliest capital of ancient China, the remains of Shang Dynasty has been found there. Kaifeng used to be called "Bianliang" in ancient times. Since 364 BC, it has been capital for seven dynasties. Longmen Grottoes is located to the south of Luoyang, a city that had been capital for nine dynasties. The Grottoes run continuously for over 1 kilometer long with over 2,100 grottoes holding over 100 thousand statues. It is one of China's four famous art grottoes and is included in the World Heritage List by UNESCO. As one of the Five Sacred Mountains in China, Mt. Songshan is esteemed as Zhong Yue (Middle Mountain). The mountain, with a cluster of 72 peaks, is located to the northwest of Dengfeng City. The legendary martial arts center Shaolin Temple is built on the mountain. Other tourist attractions include: Mt. Jigong, Baima Temple, Baogong Temple and Mt. Jiugong.

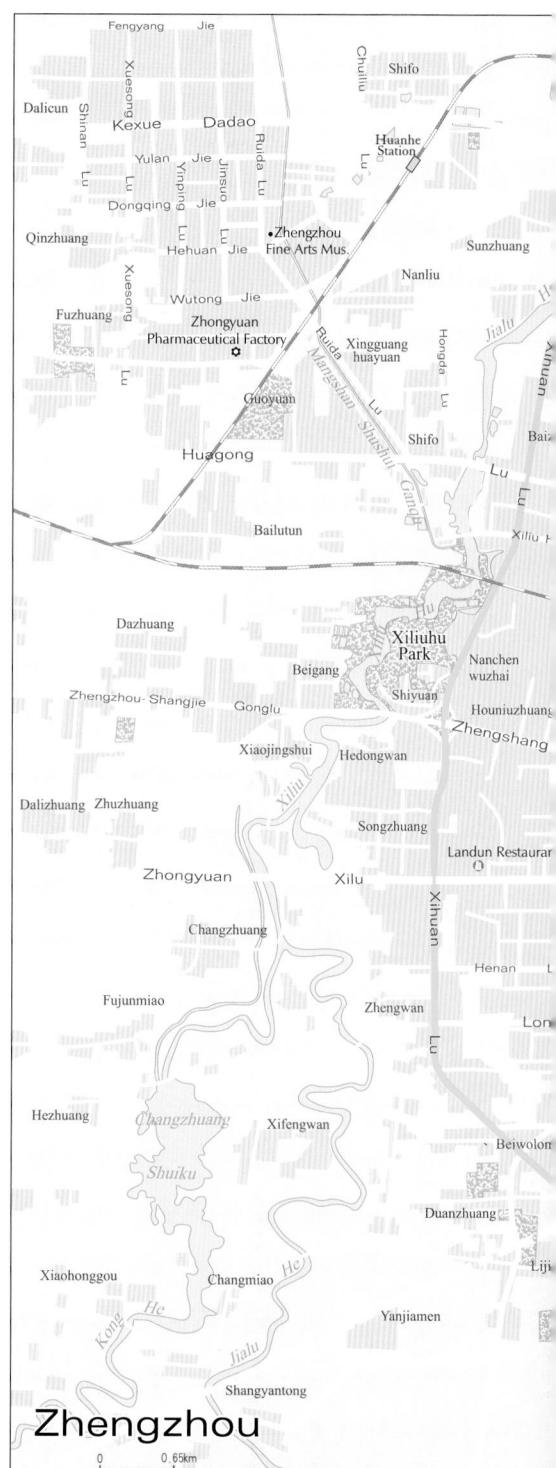

Zhengzhou

■ Local Products

Chinese dates, watermelon, pear, persimmon, paulownia, tobacco and sheep skin are well known local agricultural products of Henan. Green tea produced in Xinyang is ranked as one of China's top ten. The province is also famous for its production of liquor and Chinese medicinal herbs. Local flavours like roast duck, baked chicken, carp and dried bean curd are liked by many. Tang Tricolor, embroidery, jade carving, inkstone, porcelain, palace lantern, and feather painting are traditional local handicrafts.

Longmen Grottoes

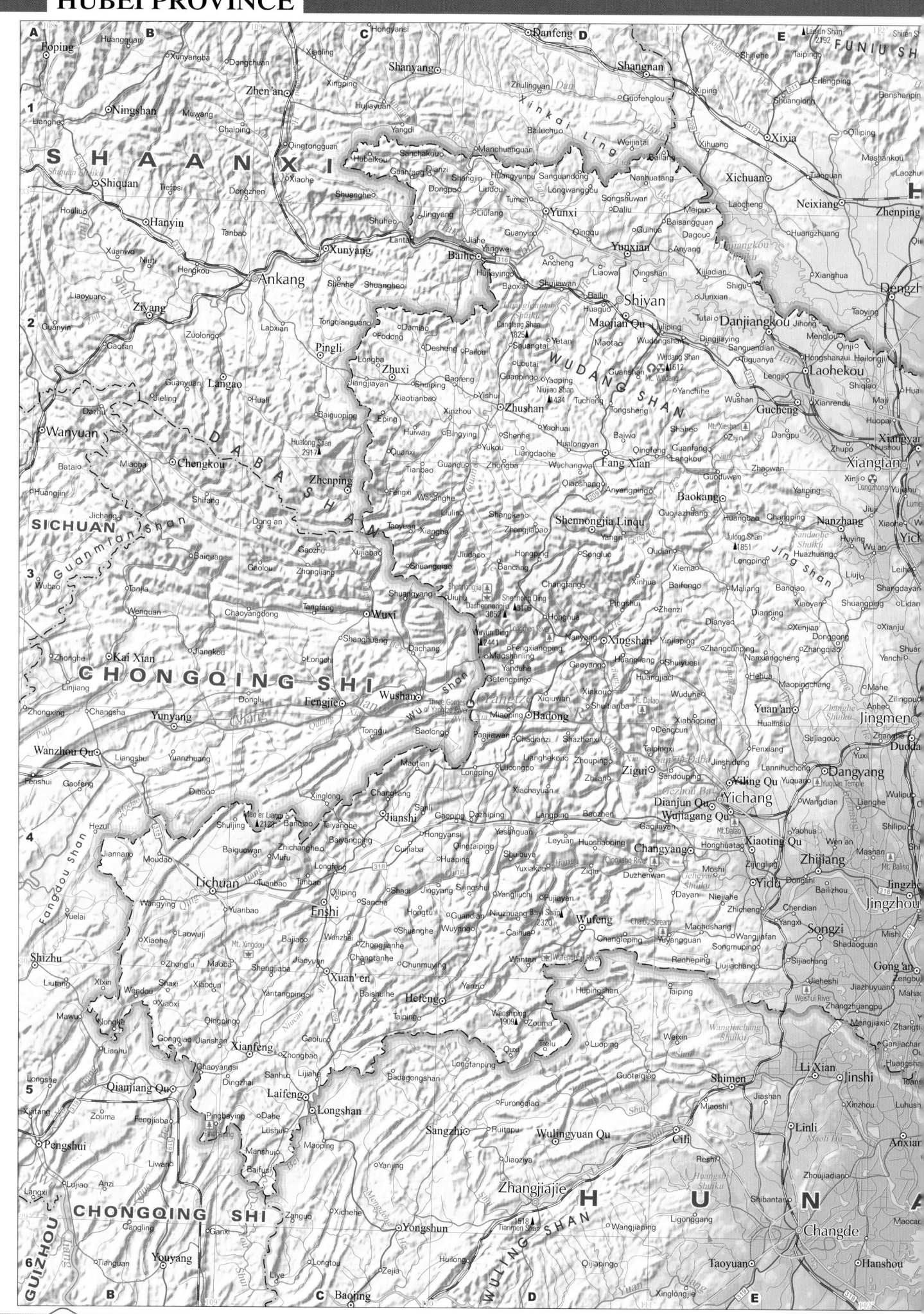

Altitude Table

| 0 | 50 | 100 | 200 | 300 | 500 | 750 | 1000 | 1500 | 2000 | 2500m |

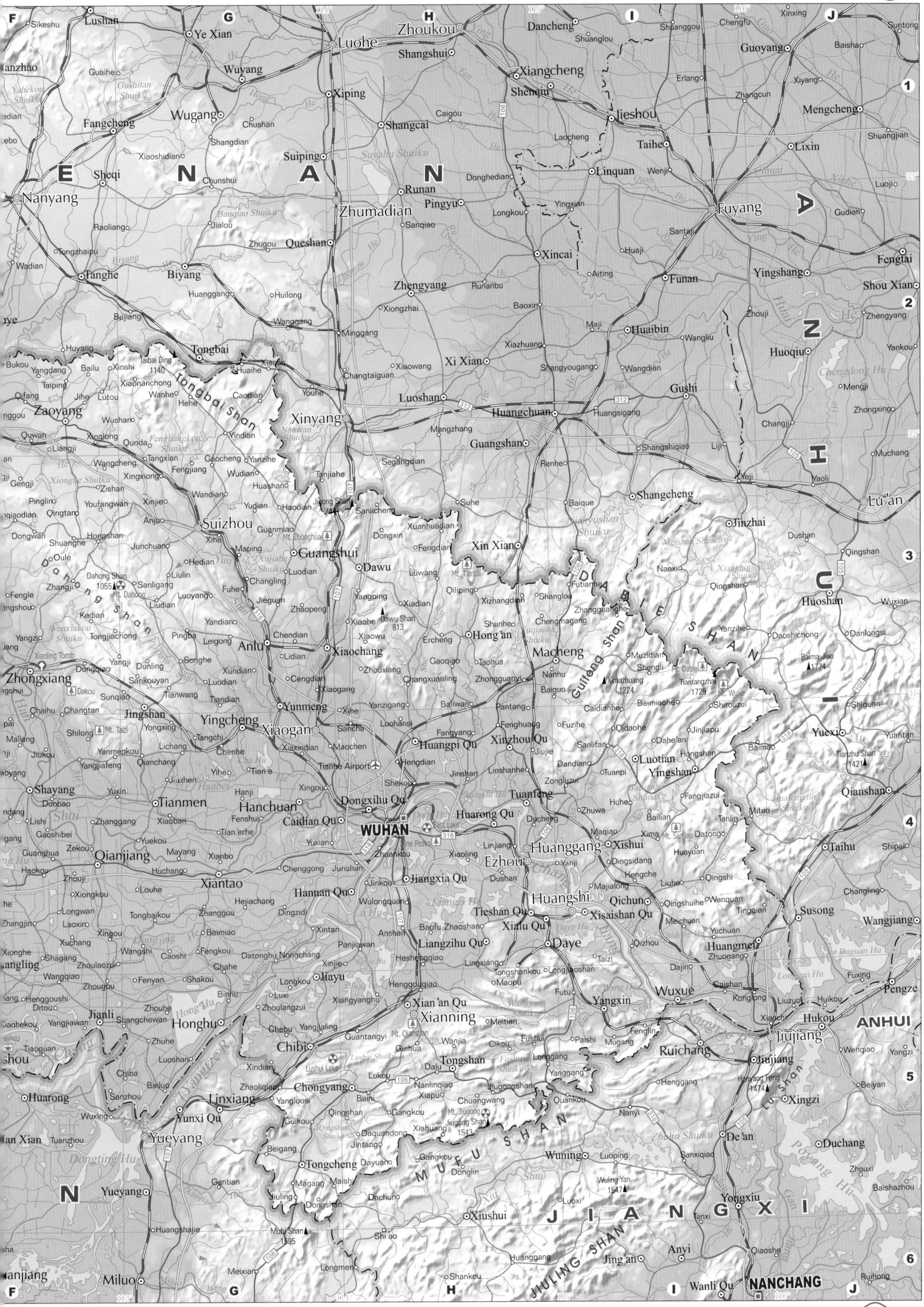

Hubei Province

With Wuhan as its capital, Hubei Province, which is abbreviated as "E", is located on the north bank of Dongting Hu (L.), along Chang Jiang (Yangtze River). It covers an area of over 180,000 square kilometers, and has a population of 60.01 million, including such ethnic groups as Han, Tujia, Miao, Hui, Dong, and Man.

■ Geographical Features

Topography With mountains like Wu Shan, Daba Shan, Wudang Shan, Jing Shan, Dahong Shan, Tongbai Shan and Dabie Shan circles around Hubei on the east, north and west, its terrain generally slopes from the west to the east in the shape of an irregular basin. Jianghan Pingyuan (Pln.) on the southeast is the major agricultural area. Chang Jiang and its largest branch Han Shui are the two major rivers in Hubei. There are many lakes in the province, including: Hong Hu, Liangzi Hu, Dong Hu, Futou Hu, Xiliang Hu, Chang Hu, among which Hong Hu is the largest lake in Hubei.

Climate Subtropical humid monsoon climate rules the area, which brings about adequate sunshine, plenty of rainfall and hot and rainy summers, making Wuhan one of China's three notorious "ovens". Annual rainfall in this area is between 750～1,600mm. The average annual temperature is between 13～18℃, with an average temperature in January between 1～6℃, while in July between 24～30℃.

■ Natural Resources

By now over 130 kinds of minerals have been found in Hubei, among which the reserves of minerals like phosphor, rutile, garnet, and montmorillonite clay are the largest in China. Reserves of iron, manganese, chrome, vanadium, titanium, copper, aluminium, zinc, lead, nickel, tungsten, coal and natural gas have all been found in Hubei.

With over 1,190 rivers and over 300 lakes, Hubei is rich with water resources. Because many rivers run through mountainous areas, the province also holds great hydropower potentials. The famous Sanxia (Three Georges Dam) Project, Gezhouba, Danjiangkou and Geheyan hydropower stations were all built here.

Hubei's forest cover rate is around 25.98%. There are more than 700 species of wild animals, over 3,700 species of plants and over 170 species of fish live in this area, including over 50 species of rare animals under national protection, over 1,800 species of medicinal herbs and over 50 species of fish of economic value.

■ Agriculture

Hubei is an important production base of grain, cotton, oil, pig, poultry and aquatic products, with rice, corn, wheat, potatoes, beans, millet and broomcorn as its major grain crops, and cotton, rape seeds, peanuts, sesame, jute, ramee and tobacco as its major cash crops. Jianghan Plain is the renowned production area of rice, wheat, cotton, ramee and sesame. Tea, tung oil, crude lacquer and herbs are produced mainly in the mountainous area on the west of the province. Pigs, cows and sheep are raised here, and the place is also famous for production of freshwater fish, water fowl, pearl, locus root, and water chestnut. The Sanxia (Three Georges) area of Chang Jiang is the major breeding area of freshwater fish in China.

■ Industry

With Wuhan, Huangshi and Shiyan as its industrial centers, Hubei leads China's industry in the production of steel, automobile, textile, pesticide, chemical fertilizer and hydropower. The province is particularly well known for its production of steel and automobile.

■ Transportation

Railway Centered round Wuhan and Xiangfan, five main stems including Beijing–Guangzhou, Beijing–Kowloon, Jiaozhuo–Liuzou, Hankou–Danjiang and Xiangfan–Chongqing meet in Hubei, and are joined by provincial trunk lines like Wuhan-Jiujiang.

Highway There are many national highways running across Hubei. Centered round Wuhan, Xiangfan and Yichang, highways can reach every city and county in the province. Two express highways of Yichang–Huangshi, Huangshi-Huangmei have all been put into use.

Airway Tianhe Airport is one of China's most important air harbors. Domestic flight courses connect Hubei with Beijing, Shanghai, Guangzhou, Hong Kong and 50 other major cities in China, while international flight courses connect the province with Japan.

Waterway Half of Hubei's cities and counties lie along two major waterways: Chang Jiang and Han Shui. Wuhan is one of China's most important river ports. Other major ports in the province are Jingzhou, Huangshi and Yichang.

■ Places of Interest

Hubei boasts beautiful natural scenery. The world renowned Three Georges begins from east Chongqing and ends at west Hubei along Chang Jiang, including three uniquely majestic and gorgeous river valleys. Mt. Wudang, which is located in Danjiangkou, is a famous sacred place of Taoists. Mt. Jiugong is located in Tongshan County, it is known for its pine trees, bamboos, hot springs and waterfalls.

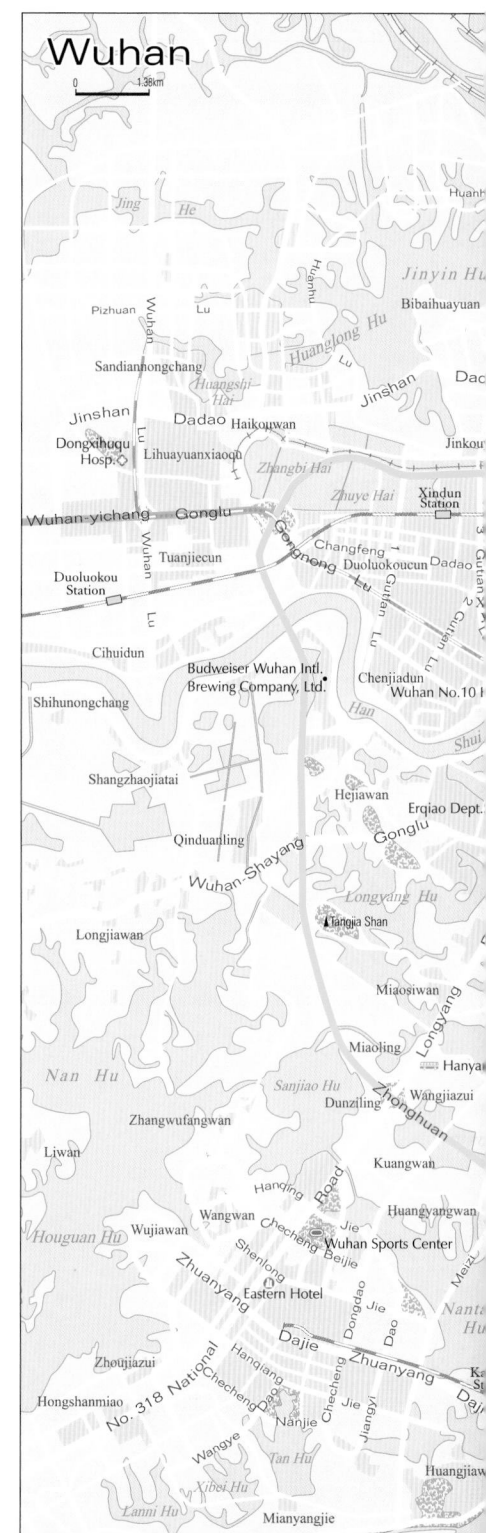

Shennongjia is at the northwest of Hubei. Its intact primitive forest has made it a national natural reserve. It is also known for traces of "wild man", and is now included in World Network of Biosphere Reserves by UNESCO. Xian Ling Tomb, which is located in Zhongxiang city, is the largest emperor's tomb of Ming Dynasty. Other cultural relics include: Quyuan's hometown, Guqin Pavilion, Yellow Crane Tower and Chibi.

■ Local Products

Whitebait and Wuchang fish are world renowned delicacy. Hubei is also famous for the production of orange, loquat, Chinese dates, tea, tung oil, sesame crackers and other local cakes. Shell carving, lacquerwork, bamboo ware, silk and fan are traditional local handicrafts.

Mount Wudang

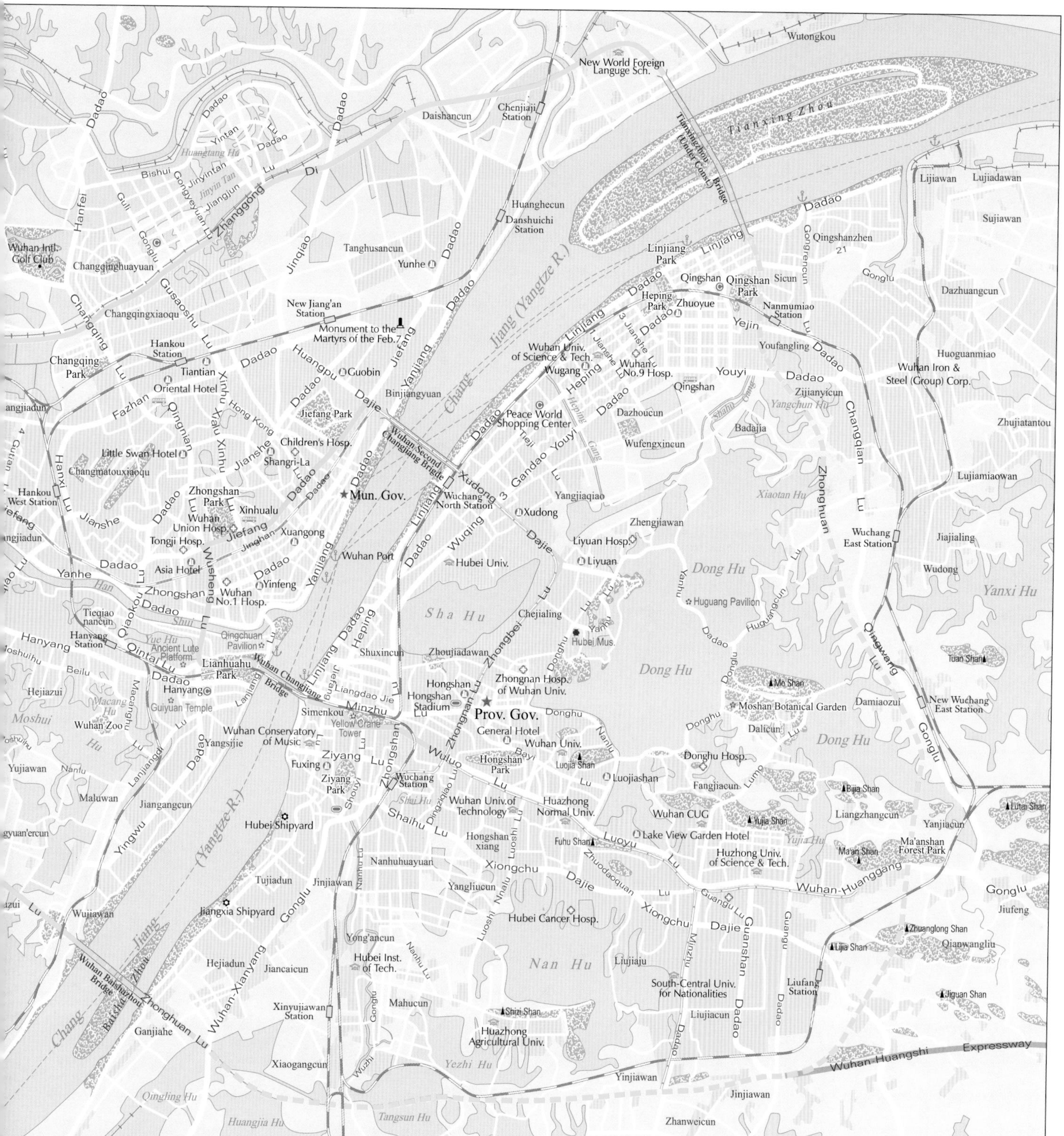

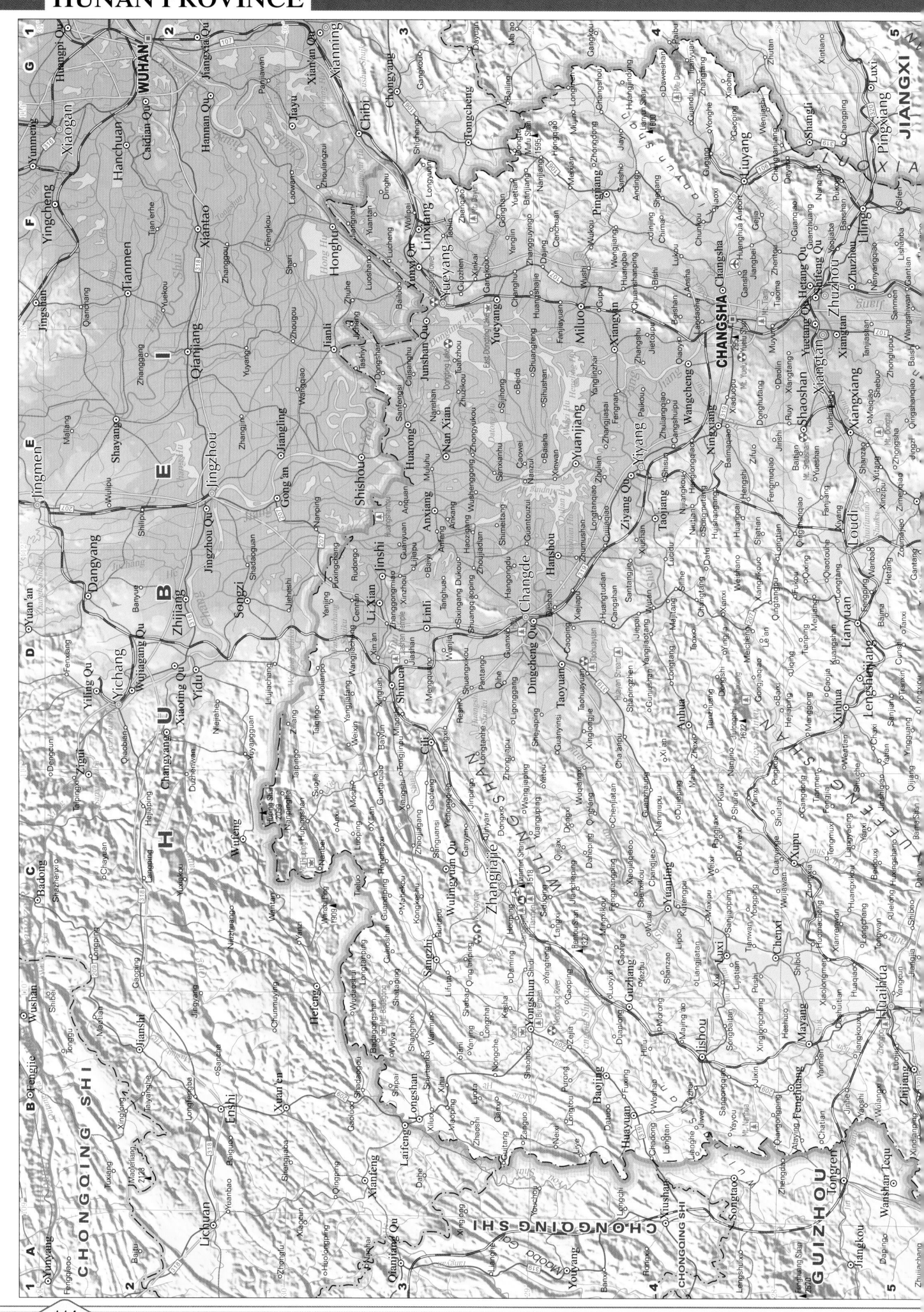

Altitude Table

0 50 100 200 300 500 750 1000 1500 2000 3000 m

GUIZHOU

JIANGXI

GUANGDONG

GUANGXI ZHUANGZU ZIZHIQU

H U N A N

N A N   L I N G

Major places: Hengyang, Shaoyang, Changning, Yongzhou, Lingling Qu, Chenzhou, Suxian Qu, Zixing, Yizhang, Shaoguan, Ruyuan, Yingde, Lechang, Renhua, Shixing, Qujiang, Lianzhou, Yangshan, Qingxin, Qingyuan, Huaiji, Hezhou, Fuchuan, Gongcheng, Pingle, Guilin, Lingui, Xing'an, Lingchuan, Quanzhou, Shuangpai, Dao Xian, Jianghua, Jiangyong, Jianghua, Guanyang, Ziyuan, Longsheng, Sanjiang, Rong'an, Rongshui, Yongfu, Liuzhou, Liujiang, Laibin, Wuxuan, Chengbu, Xinning, Wugang, Dongkou, Hongjiang, Huitong, Jingzhou, Tongdao, Suining, Hengyang, Qidong, Hengnan, Leiyang, Ningyuan, Xintian, Jiahe, Lanshan, Linwu, Yizhang

Hunan Province

With Changsha as its capital, Hunan Province, which is abbreviated as "Xiang", is located on the south bank of Chang Jiang (Yangtze River). It covers an area of over 210,000 square kilometers, and has a population of 65.99 million, including such ethnic groups as Han, Tujia, Miao, Dong, Yao, Bai, Hui and Zhuang.

■ Geographical Features

Topography With mountains on the east, south and west, Hunan's terrain generally slopes from the south to the north in the shape of a horsehoof-like basin. Mountains like Luoxiao Shan, Nan Ling, Wuling Shan and Xuefeng Shan circle around Hunan, with elevation varies from 500m to 1,500m. Dongtinghu Pingyuan on the north is part of middle and lower Yangtze valley plains. Hengyang Pendi (Bsn.) and Zhuzhou Basin are below 50m in altitude. Xiang Jiang, Zi Shui, Yuan Jiang and Li Shui are major rivers in Hunan, among which Xiang Jiang is the largest in the province. Dongting Hu is the second largest fresh water lake in China. It now consists of four major lakes: Dong Dongting Hu, Xi Dongting Hu, Nan Dongting Hu, and Datong Hu.

Climate Middle subtropical humid monsoon climate rules the area, which brings about plenty of rainfall and distinctive seasonal difference. Annual rainfall in this area is between 1,200~1,700mm. The average annual temperature is between 15~18.5℃, with an average temperature in January between 3~8℃, while in July between 27~30℃.

■ Natural Resources

By now over 140 kinds of minerals have been found in Hunan, among which the reserves of minerals like tungsten, bismuth, graphite, manganese, vanadium, stibium, cesium, lithium, arsenic, dolomite, diamond, Glauber's salt and 60 others are among China's top ten. The reserves of tungsten, bismuth, stibium, cesium, lithium, arsenic, non-crystalloid graphite, and barite are of global significance, especially reserves for stibium, which takes up 70% of world's total.

Extensive river system provides the province with plenty of hydropower potentials, mostly around upper reaches of rivers.

As a major wood producing area in southeast China, Hunan's forest cover rate is around 38.9%, mostly firs, pine trees, camphors, and bamboos. There are more than 570 species of wild animals and over 5,000 species of plants living in this area, including over 1,000 species of wild cash plants.

The area is also rich in geothermal resources, up till now, over 160 hot springs have been found.

■ Agriculture

As one of China's major grain production base, grain farming plays an important role in Hunan's agriculture, with rice, wheat and potatoes as its major crops, of which the production of rice is the largest in China. Industrial crops include rape, cotton, ramie and tea. As one of China's exporting base for ramie, tea and oranges, Hunan's production of ramie is the leader in China, and its production of tea is the second largest in China. Animal husbandry in this area also leads in China. Pigs, buffalos, cows, horses, sheep, goose, and ducks are raised here, and the province produce first class strains of pigs, chicken and geese.

■ Industry

Hunan is one of China's nonferrous metal production bases, with Zhuzhou as its metallurgy center, stibium, lead and zinc produced in this province is well known throughout the world. The province has fairly well developed machinery, electronics, chemical, building material, food, textile and paper-making industries, while its production of textile, food, and cigarettes developed very quickly these years.

■ Transportation

Railway Five main stems including Beijing–Guangzhou, Zhuzhou–Guiding, Hengyang–Aikou, Jiaozuo–Liuzhou, and Hangzhou–Zhuzhou railways run through Hunan, and are joined by many other branch lines.

Highway Every city and county in this region is connected by national highway or provincial highway. Three express highways have been built: Changsha–Xiangtan–Chenzhou, Changsha–Yiyang–Changde, Changsha–Xiangtan–Shaoyang–Huaihua.

Airway Changsha has flight courses to Beijing, Shanghai, Guangzhou and 40 other cities in China. Non-stop Flight courses has also been opened to Thailand and R.O. Korea.

Waterway Freights can go from the four major rivers through Chang Jiang to the East China Sea.

■ Places of Interest

Hunan has not only beautiful natural scenery, but also rich cultural relics. Wulingyuan Scenic Area, which consist of Zhangjiajie National Forest Park, and the Suoxiyu and Tianzishan Natural Resources Reserves, presents an unique landscape of incredible Karst physiognomy, beautiful waters, deep gorges, and lush forests, and is included in the World Heritage List by UNESCO. Mt. Hengshan is located in Hengyang, Being one of the five sacred mountains in China, it is esteemed as Nan Yue (South Mountain). The mountain range runs for 150 km, and have a cluster of 72 peaks. It is a nice summer getaway and the only place in south China to watch snow in winter. Mt. Shaoshan is in Xiangtan, Mao Zedong's childhood home there attracts many visitors each year. Yueyang Tower is on the west gate of the ancient city of Yueyang, it is one of the three famous towers in China. Dongting Lake is in the north of the province, there are many cultural relics around the lake area. Mawangdui Tombs of Han Dynasty in Changsha has been a remarkable archaeological discovery. There are many other cultural relics like Emperor Yan's tomb, Yuelu Academy and Wuxi Steles in Hunan.

■ Local Products

Hunan style embroidery is one of China's four most distinguished embroidery styles. The production of fireworks, porcelain, bamboo carving, and fan are traditional local handicrafts. Locus roots and seeds, tea, and orange are special local agricultural products, of which the production of locus roots and seeds are the largest in China. Hunan cuisine is one of the eight most famous cuisines in China. Local flavours like rice noodles, preserved hot pepper and rice cakes are liked by many.

Zhangjiajie

Changsha

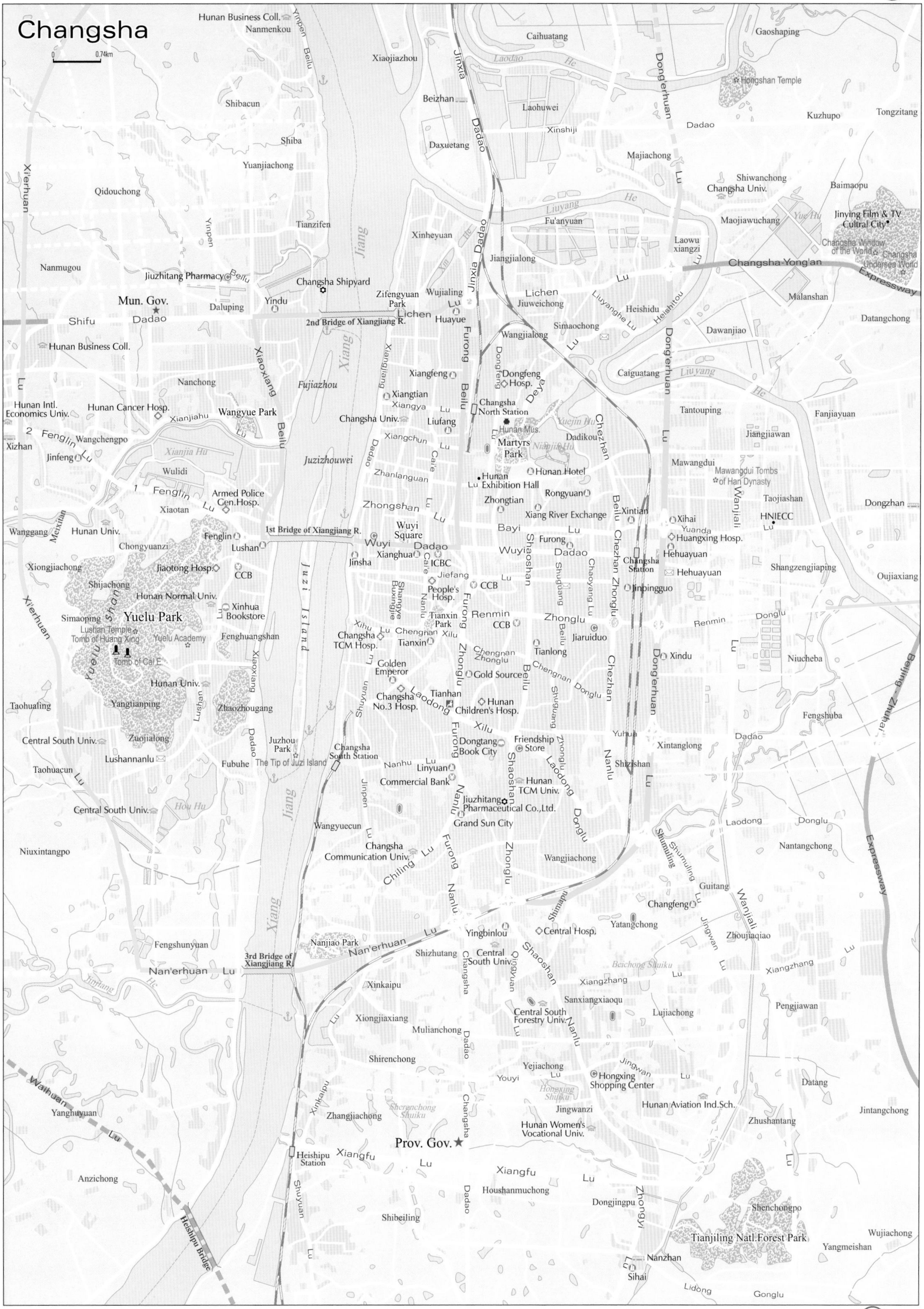

0   0.74km

Hunan Business Coll.
Nanmenkou
Xiaojiazhou
Caihuatang
Gaoshaping
Laodao He
Dong'erhuan
Hongshan Temple
Shibacun
Beizhan
Laohuwei
Kuzhupo
Tongzitang
Shiba
Daxuetang
Xinshiji
Dadao
Yuanjiachong
Majiachong
Shiwanchong
Baimaopu
Tianzifen
Xinheyuan
Fu'anyuan
Lu
Changsha Univ.
Jinying Film & TV
Cultral City
Qidouchong
Yue Hu
Maojiawuchang
Malanshan
Nanmugou
Jiangjialong
Lichen
Laowu xiangzi
Changsha Window of the World
Jiuzhitang Pharmacy
Changsha Shipyard
Zifengyuan Park
Wujialing
Jiuweichong
Heishidu
Changsha-Yong'an Expressway
Changsha Undersea World
Mun. Gov.
Daluping
Yindu
Lichen
Huayue
Furong
Wangjialong
Simaochong
Heishitou
Datangchong
Shifu
Dadao
2nd Bridge of Xiangjiang R.
Liuyanghe Lu
Dongerhuan
Liuyang He
Dawanjiao
Hunan Business Coll.
Xiangfeng
Dongfeng Hosp.
Caiguatang
Tantouping
Nanchong
Xiangtian
Xiangya
Fanjiayuan
Hunan Intl. Economics Univ.
Hunan Cancer Hosp.
Xianjiahu
Changsha Univ.
Liufang
Changsha North Station
Yuejin Hu
Dadikou Lu
Jiangjiawan
Fenglin Lu
Wangchengpo
Xiangchun
Zhanlanguan
Hunan Mus.
Martyrs Park
Nianjiu Hu
Mawangdui
Mawangdui Tombs of Han Dynasty
Xizhan
Jinfeng
Wulidi
Juzizhouwei
Hunan Hotel
Taojiashan
Fenglin
Armed Police Gen.Hosp.
Zhongshan
Hunan Exhibition Hall
Zhongtian
Rongyuan
Xiang River Exchange
Xintian
Xihai
HNIECC
Dongzhan
Xiaotan
Wuyi Square
Bayi
Furong
Yuanda
Huangxing Hosp.
Hehuayuan
Wanggang
Hunan Univ.
Chongyuanzi
Fenglin
Lushan
Wuyi Dadao
Xianghua
Wuyi
Shaoshan
Dadao
Changsha Station
Jinpingguo
Hehuayuan
Shangzengjiaping
Oujiaxiang
Xiongjiachong
Jiaotong Hosp.
CCB
Jinsha
Jiefang
ICBC
Chengnan
CCB
Shugang
Chaoyang Lu
Xindu
Niucheba
Shijiachong
Hunan Normal Univ.
Xinhua Bookstore
People's Hosp.
Shangye Buxingjie
Tianxin Park
Renmin
CCB
Zhonglu
Jiaruiduo
Renmin
Fengshuba
Simaoping
Lushan Temple
Tomb of Huang Xing
Yuelu Academy
Fenghuangshan
Xihu
Changsha TCM Hosp.
Tianxin
Chengnan Zhonglu
Tianlong
Chengnan Donglu
Yuelu Park
Tomb of Cai E
Golden Emperor
Tianhan
Hunan Children's Hosp.
Xilu
Gold Source
Yuhua
Shizishan
Xintanglong
Taohualing
Hunan Univ.
Yangtianping
Changsha No.3 Hosp.
Furong
Donglu
Central South Univ.
Zuojialong
Friendship Store
Dongtang Book City
Hunan TCM Univ.
Laodong
Donglu
Lushannanlu
Fubuhe
The Tip of Juzi Island
Changsha South Station
Nanhu
Linyuan
Commercial Bank
Jiuzhitang Pharmaceutical Co.,Ltd.
Shumuling
Guitang
Nantangchong
Niuxintangpo
Central South Univ.
Hou Hu
Wangyuecun
Grand Sun City
Wangjiachong
Changfeng
Zhoujiaqiao
Fengshunyuan
Changsha Communication Univ.
Chiling
Furong
Zhonglu
Central Hosp.
Yatangchong
Jingwan
Nanjiao Park
Nan'erhuan
Shizhutang
Central South Univ.
Shaoshan
Xiangzhang
Xiangzhang
Pengjiawan
3rd Bridge of Xiangjiang R.
Nan'erhuan Lu
Xinkaipu
Changsha
Qingyuan
Beichong Shuiku
Jinfang
Xiongjiaxiang
Mulianchong
Dadao
Central South Forestry Univ.
Sanxiangxiaoqu
Lujiachong
Shirenchong
Youyi
Yejiachong
Hongxing Shopping Center
Hunan Aviation Ind.Sch.
Datang
Jintangchong
Waihuan Lu
Yanghutyuan
Shenchong Shuiku
Changsha
Jingwanzi
Hongxing Shichang
Anzichong
Zhangjiachong
Prov. Gov.
Hunan Women's Vocational Univ.
Zhushantang
Heishipu Station
Xiangfu
Lu
Xiangfu
Lu
Shenchongpo
Heishipu Bridge
Shibeiling
Houshanmuchong
Dongjingpu
Tianjiling Natl. Forest Park
Wujiachong
Nanzhan
Sihai
Lidong
Gonglu
Yangmeishan
Jinmang He
Xiang Jiang
Juzi Island
Shuyuan

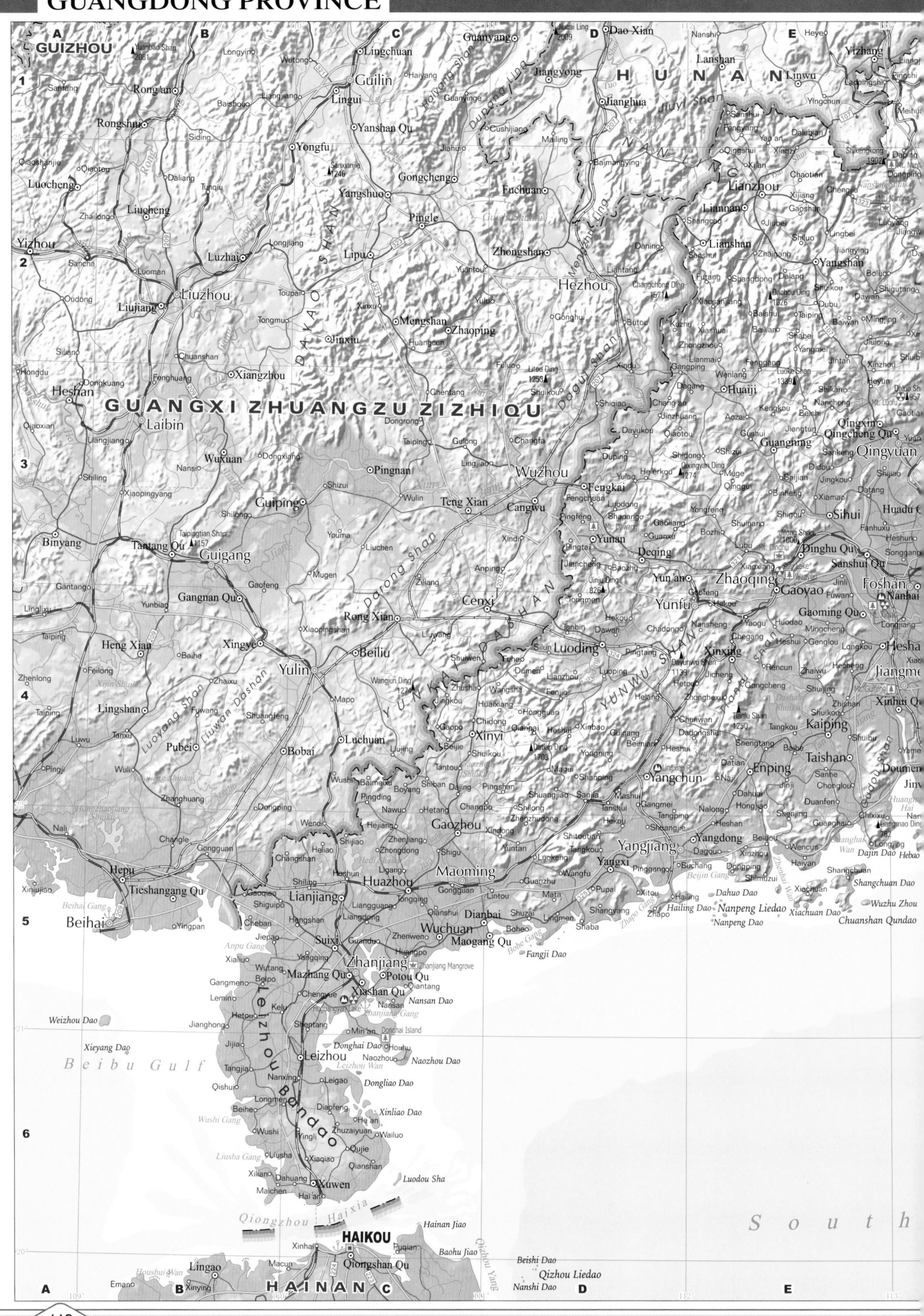

Altitude Table 3000 2000 1000 200 50 20 0 50 100 200 300 500 750 1000 1500 2000 2500 m

Scale 1:2 400 000

| 0 | 24 | 48 | 72 | 96 | 120km |

Guangdong Province

With Guangzhou as its capital, Guangdong Province, which is abbreviated as "Yue", is located on the coast of South China Sea, facing Hong Kong and Macau. It covers an area of over 180,000 square kilometers, and has a population of 77.23 million, including such ethnic groups as Han, Zhuang, Yao, Tujia, Miao, Dong and She. It is the renowned hometown for most overseas Chinese.

■ Geographical Features

Topography 2/3 of Guangdong's total area is covered by mountains and hills, with Nan Ling, Yunwu Shan, Qingyun Shan, Jiulian Shan, Luofu Shan and Lianhua Shan as its major mountains. Guangdong's terrain gradually descends from north to south, intersected by basins like Xingning, Meizhou and Luoding. Zhujian Delta and Chaoshan Pingyuan (Pln.) along the south coast are renowned land of abundance. Mesas are found on Leizhou Bandao (Pen.). Zhu Jiang, Han Jiang, Moyang Jiang, and Jian Jiang are major rivers in this region, of which Zhu Jiang, a combination of Xi Jiang, Bei Jiang and Dong Jiang, is the third largest river in China. A sinuous coast line provides Guangdong with many islands like Chuanshan Qundao, Gaolan Liedao, Wanshan Qundao, Dongsha Qundao, Hengqin Dao, Nansan Dao and Donghai Dao.

Climate With Tropic of Cancer going through the area, subtropical humid monsoon climate rules most part of Guangdong, giving the area prolonged summers and warm winters. Annual rainfall in this region is between 1,400~2,000mm. The average annual temperature in most part of the province is above 19℃, with an average temperature in January between 8~16℃, while in July between 27~29℃.

■ Natural Resources

Over 120 kinds of minerals have been found in Guangdong, mostly non-ferrous metals, among which the reserves of minerals like ferrous sulfide, turf, lead, columbium, germanium, bismuth, thallium, oil shale, Kaolin, and porcelain clay are bounteous. Nanhai oilfield, including Zhujiangkou, Beibu Wan (G.) and other offing basins, holds rich resources of oil and natural gas.

Abundant rainfall gives the area an extensive river system with plenty of water resources.

Guangdong's forest cover rate is around 45.81%. There are more than 800 species of wild animals living in this area, among which over 40 are rare animals under national protection. Over 8,000 species of plants grow here, including over 200 kinds of fruits. Over ten natural protection zones for rare animals and plants have been established in Guangdong.

The province is rich for aquaculture resources.

There are over 800,000 hectares sea water aquatics breeding area and over 400,000 hectares fresh water aquatics breeding area. Among over 800 species of fish living in this region, over 200 have economic values.

Guangdong is also rich with geothermal resources, and over 200 hot springs were found here.

■ Agriculture

Farming plays an important role in Guangdong's agriculture. As the largest rice producing region in China, Guangdong applies double or even triple cropping harvest system, with rice, wheat and potatoes as its main grain crops and peanut, beans, sugar canes, mulberry and hemps as its major economic crops. The province is also China's largest fruit producing region, which is most well known for the production of lichee, banana, orange, pineapple, longan, parambola and papaya. Zhujiang Delta is the most famous production base for mulberry, grain, fruits and sugar, while Leizhou Peninsula mainly produces tropical products like rubber, coffee and coco.

Cows, pigs, and sheep are raised in Guangdong. Prawns, Pearls, grouper, abalone and laver are chief seawater aquaculture products, while carps are raised in fresh water.

Sculpture in Guangzhou

■ Industry

Light industries like the production of family gadgets, commodities, electronics, textile, food and medicine play important roles in Guangdong's industrial system, supplemented by machinery, power industry, building materials, shipbuilding and other industries. Shipbuilding and chemical industry here are fairly well known, and the province leads China's industry in the production of family gadgets, electronics, computer components, plastics and clothes.

■ Transportation

Railway Two main stems, Beijing–Guangzhou and Beijing–Kowloon railways, run through Guangdong, and are joined by Guangzhou–Shenzhen, Sanshui–Maoming, Guangzhou–Meizhou-Shantou, Zhanjiang–Hai'an and other branch lines.

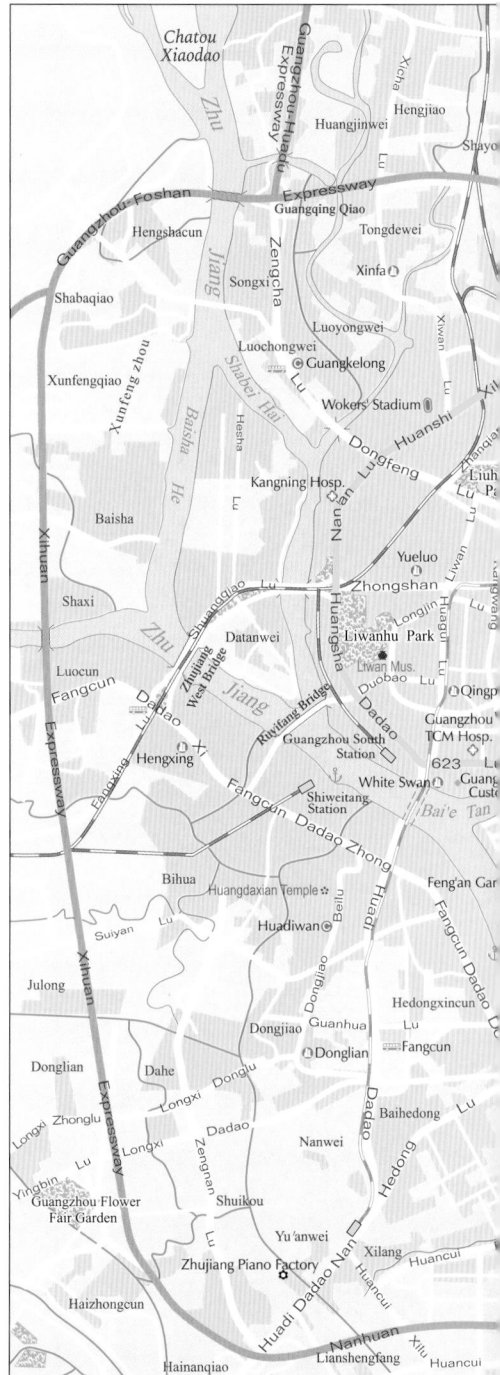

Highway Many national highways run through Guangdong. Express highways like Guangzhou–Zhanjiang, Guangzhou–Shaoguan, Guangzhou–Shenzhen and Shenzhen–Shantou further improve highway transportation here, providing the province with one of China's most developed highway system.

Airway Airports were built in Guangzhou, Shezhen, Zhuhai, Zhanjiang and Shantou, with flight courses connecting the province with over 70 cities in China and over 10 cities abroad.

Waterway Guangdong has a well developed sea transportation system. Ocean routes connect the province with ports all over the world. Deep sea ports like Huangpu, Zhanjiang, Shantou and Shekou can harbor ships over ten thousand tons.

■ Places of Interest

Guangdong boasts not only beautiful natural scenery but also rich cultural relics. Zhaoqing scenery spot consists of a large beautiful lake Xinghu Lake and the fantastic Mt. Dinghu. 7 limestone hills stands around Xinghu Lake in the shape of Big Dipper, thus called Qixing Yan (Seven Star Hills). Mt. Danxia is located on the border of Renhua and Qujiang. Mt. Xiqiao, a dead ocean volcano formed 70 or 80 million years ago, is in Foshan, where many ancient cliff engravings can be found. Ancient gardens in Guangdong have a distinctive local style. Qinghui Garden in Shunde, Yuyin Shanfang in Panyu, Keyuan Garden in Dongguan, Liangyuan Garden in Foshan are the four most famous gardens of the province. Splendid China, the Chinese folk culture villages in Shenzhen, holds miniatures of China's most

famous scenic spots and architectures with distinctive minority styles. Other cultural relics include Xihan Dynasty tomb of King Nanyue, the Opium Destroying Pool, Sun Yat-sen's Memorial Hall and Mt. Yuexiu.

■ Local Products

Banana, orange, and Lichee are most famous Guangdong fruits. Local black tea is also well known. Grouper, crab, oyster, and lobster produced here are well known. Guangdong cuisine is one of the eight most famous cuisines in China. Sausages, moon cakes, rice cake, shrimp dumpling, and steam vermicelli roll and other local flavors are liked by many. Guangdong style embroidery is one of China's four most famous embroidery styles. Porcelain ware, fan, ink stone are traditional local handicrafts.

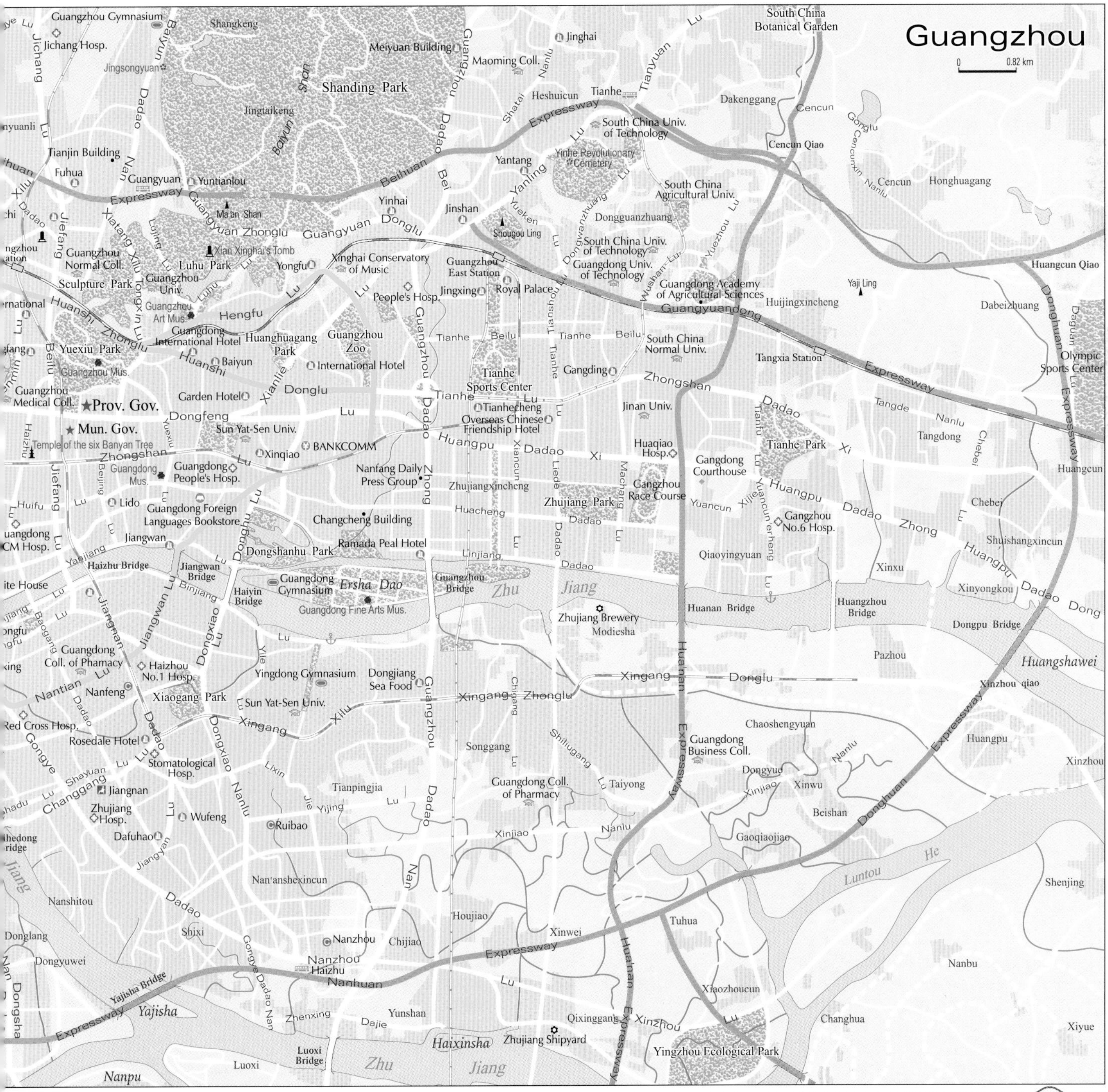

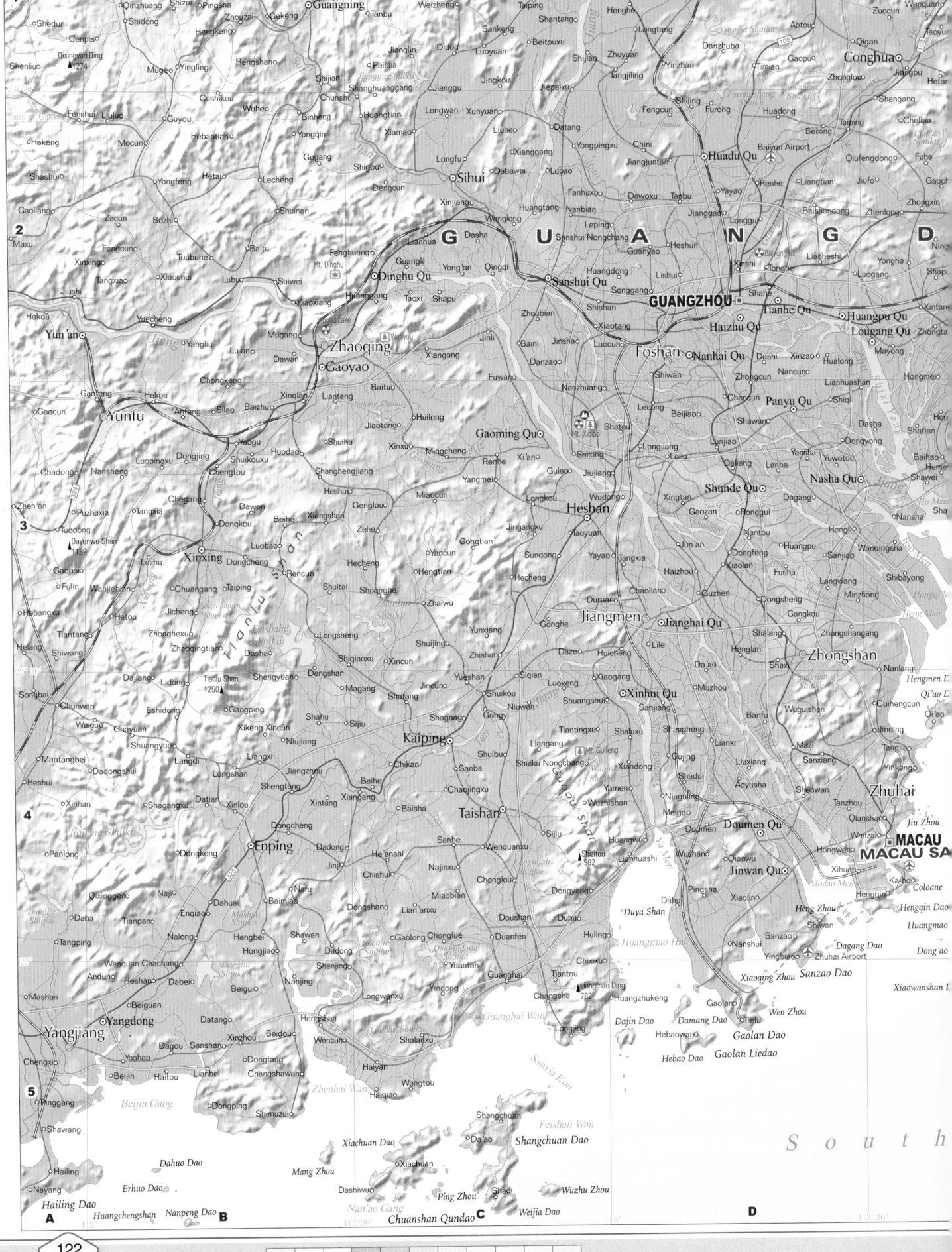

Altitude Table

200 50 20 0 50 100 200 300 500 750 1000 1500m

Zhujiang Delta

The extensive flat land around Zhu Jiang estuary in Guangdong Province is referred to as Zhujiang Delta. This delta plain is composed by a larger alluvial delta made by Bei Jiang and Xi Jiang and a smaller alluvial delta made by Dong Jiang. Zhujiang Delta, in its broad sense, extends to Gaoyao in the west, Qingyuan in the east, Huizhou in the north and reaching the sea in the south, covering an area of 11,000 square kilometers.

The flat Zhujiang Delta is low in altitude, and has extensive river system. Lying at an area south of Tropic of Cancer, the Delta is a traditionally renowned land of abundance for its rich production of rice, fish, silk, sugar, fruits and flowers. It is one of China's most prosperous areas, and is rightly called the "Golden Delta of Guangdong".

As an open up zone in coastal area, Zhujiang Delta is quite well developed in agriculture and is a major production zone of grain, sugar, fresh water aquatics, silk and fruits in Guangdong. The integrated agriculture-aquaculture model developed in this area has successfully created a positive artificial ecosystem well known throughout the world. As this area is close to Hong Kong and Macau, it is easy for local products to be exported.

The Delta area is also a renowned production base of clothes, family gadgets, hard ware, chemicals for daily use, plastic commodities, sugar, food and paper.

There are many important commercial cities in the Delta area. Guangzhou, the capital of Guangdong Province, is the center of economy here which attaches primary importance to the development of finance, trade, science and technology, commerce, service, transportation, energy and telecommunication. The two special economic zones, Zhuhai and Shenzhen, play important roles in introducing new technology and exporting local products. Foshan, Dongguan, Jiangmen and Zhongshan are known as the "Four Small Tigers" of Guangdong for their fast economic development.

As one of China's earliest tourist attractions, Zhujiang Delta has many ports of entry and enjoys perfect travel and hospitality service system. Guangzhou, Zhaoqing and Foshan are listed as historical and cultural city of tourism under national protection. Shenzhen, Zhuhai, Zhongshan, Jiangmen and Huizhou are selected as tourists' best choices. Famous tourist spots in this area include Baiyun Hill, Mt. Xiqiao, and Sun Yat-sen's Memorial Hall, etc.

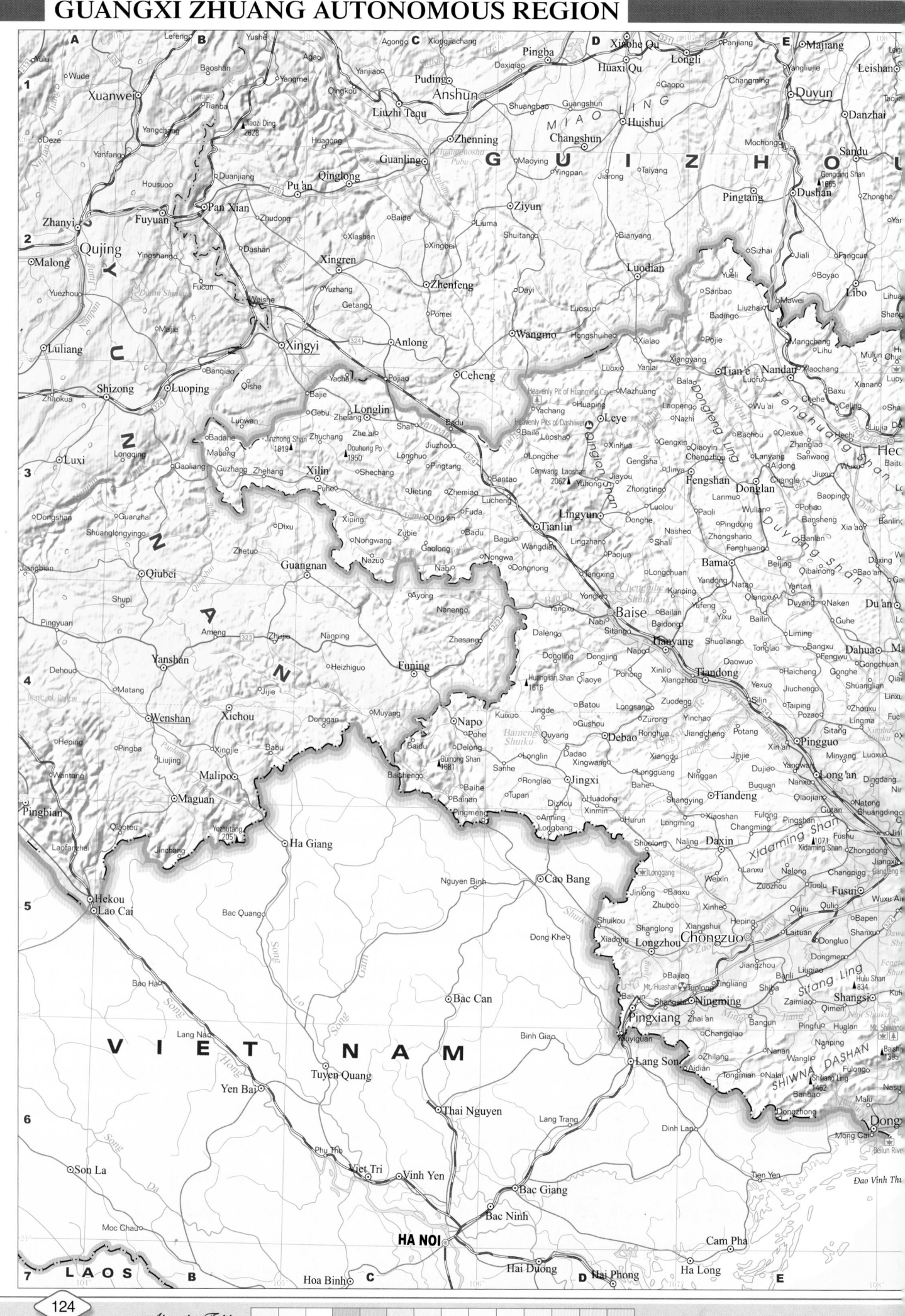

Altitude Table

| 200 | 50 | 20 | 0 | 50 | 100 | 200 | 300 | 500 | 750 | 1000 | 1500 | 2000 | 2500 | 3000m |

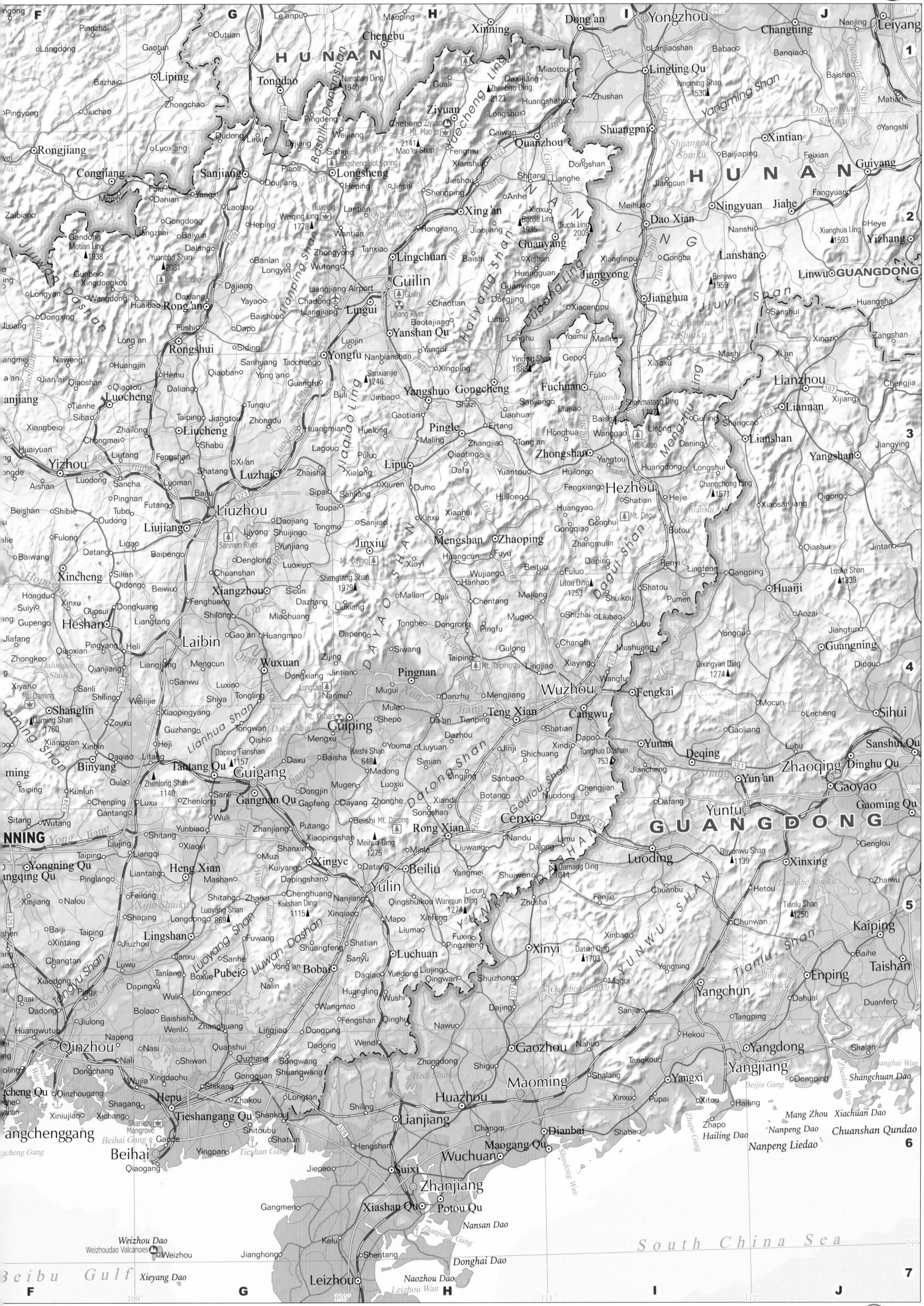

Scale 1:2 400 000 0 24 48 72 96 120 km

Guangxi Zhuang Autonomous Region

With Nanning as its capital, Guangxi Zhuang Autonomous Region, which is abbreviated as "Gui", is located on the south border of China. It covers an area of over 230,000 square kilometers, and has a population of 48.30 million, including such ethnic groups as Han, Zhuang, Yao, Miao, Dong, Mulao, Maonan, Hui, Buyei, and Gin, among them Zhuang people take up 1/3 of the total population.

■ Geographical Features

Topography Mountains and hills take up a large part of Guangxi's total area. With Haiyang Shan, Yuecheng Ling in the northeast; Yunkai Dashan, Liuwan Dashan and Shiwan Dashan in the south; Duyang Shan, Fenghuang Shan, and Jiuwan Dashan in the northwest; and Dayao Shan and Daming Shan in the middle, its terrain gradually descends from the northwest to the southeast. Major rivers are Xi Jiang, Liu Jiang, Yu Jiang, Gui Jiang and Ling Qu. Plains can only be found in river valleys. Guangxi has a sinuous coast line, thus many seaports like Beihai, Fangchenggang, etc. Weizhou Dao and Xieyang Dao are two major islands along the coast.

Climate With Tropic of Cancer go through the autonomous region, subtropical humid monsoon climate rules the area, bringing about abundant rainfall and high temperature together with a clear distinction between dry and wet seasons. Summer here is long and hot, while winter sometimes can be very cold. Annual rainfall in this area is between 1,000~2,000mm. The average annual temperature in most part of the province is between 17~23℃, with an average temperature in January between 6~16℃, while in July between 25~29℃.

■ Natural Resources

Nearly 100 kinds of minerals have been found in the autonomous region, of which over 50 kinds are ranked as top ten in China. With rich reserves for a great variety of high purity non-ferrous metals, Guangxi holds the largest reserves of manganese, tin, arsenic and bentonite in China, and has many major mines.

As a major forest region in south China, Guangxi has an extensive growth of secondary forests and artificial forests. Guangxi's forest cover rate is around 34.37%. Evergreen broadleaf trees are found in natural forests, while artificial forests mainly consist of industrial trees like oil tung, aniseed, and cinnamon as well as pine trees and firs.

There are more than 530 species of birds, over 500 species of sea fish, over 200 species of fresh water fish, over 110 species of wild animals and over 150 species of amphibian living in this area, among them over 140 kinds have been listed as first grade or second grade rare animal under national protection. Nearly 8,000 species of plants have been found here, including over 3,600 species of Chinese medicinal herbs, and over 40 species of rare plants.

■ Agriculture

Guangxi is one of China's major rice producing regions, and the farming of grain crops plays an important role in local agriculture. Major crops here include mainly rice, corn, soybean, potato, sugar cane, peanut, mulberry, and hemp. The northwest part of Guangxi is a grain farming area, while south Guangxi mainly produces sugar canes, banana, pineapple, rubber and sisal. Rich resources of sea fish can be found along Beibu Way(G.), where pearl and oyster are also bred.

■ Industry

Guangxi has built up a complete industrial system including machinery, metallurgy, power, building material, rubber, electronics, medicine, textile, paper making, brewery, and food production. It is a major sugar production base in China, with an annual sugar output higher than that of any other provinces. Guangxi is also a leader in the production of mini cars and heavy-loading trucks.

■ Transportation

Railway Centered round Liuzhou, trunk lines like Nanning–Kunming, Hengyang–Aikou, Guiyang–Liuzhou, Litang–Zhanjiang, Jiaozuo–Liuzhou, and Nanning–Fangchenggang connect Guangxi conveniently with the outside.

Highway Centered round Nanning, numerous national highways and local highways have the whole autonomous region well connected. The completion of the express highway connecting Guilin–Liuzhou–Nanning–Qinzhou–Beihai further improves local highway transportation.

Airway Airports have been built in Nanning, Guilin, Beihai, Liuzhou and Wuzhou, with flight courses connecting Guangxi with most major cities in China as well as neighbouring countries like Vietnam, Thailand and Japan.

Waterway Seaports like Beihai, Fangcheng-gang, and Qinzhou provide freights to ports all over the world. River ports like Wuzhou, Liuzhou and Nanning are also very busy. Wuzhou is directly connected with Hong Kong and Macau.

■ Places of Interest

Gorgeous natural scenery and spectacular Karst physiognomy make Guangxi a great tourist attraction. As a famous national historical and

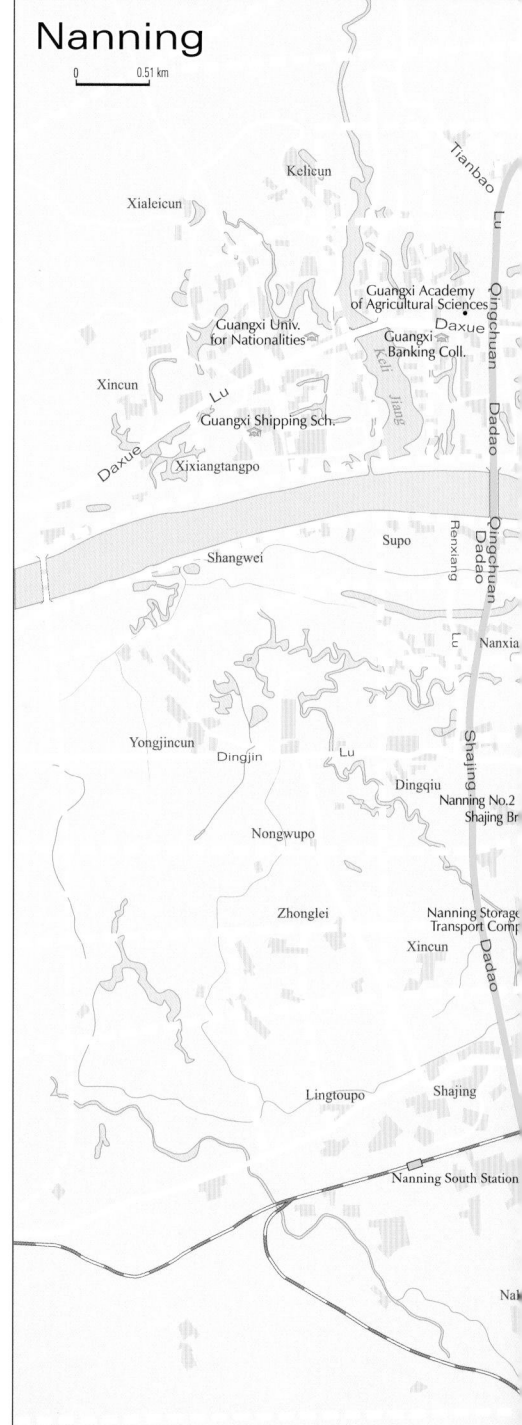

cultural site with incomparable Karst scenery, Guilin is justifiably called the most beautiful city in China. Scenery along Li Jiang between Guilin and Yangshuo is most extraordinary, with the river winds through fantastic mountains and hills like a green silk scarf. West Mountain in Guiping is also well-known for its beautiful scenery. Mt. Huashan, which stands in Ningming County, is most notable for the dazzling frescos of people and different images with a distinctive Zhuang ethnic flavour. Cultural relics like Baise, Longsheng, Zhenwu Pavilion, Liuhou Temple and Confucian Temple are all renowned tourist attractions, while Chengyang Bridge and Mapang Drum-Tower show distinctive characteristic of Dong ethnic architecture style.

■ Local Products

Guangxi is famous for producing Chinese medicinal herbs like pseudo-ginseng, aniseed and momordica grosvenori as well as taros, grapefruit, jackfruit and other fruits. Tea and wine produced here enjoy good fame traditionally. Local flavours like rice noodles and other rice dim sum are liked by many. Pearls produced in Hepu is called "Nan Zhu" (south pearl), which is considered of top grade world wide. Embroidery, shell carving, stone carving, pottery, fan, copper painting are traditional local handicrafts.

Scenery of Lijiang River

Beibu Gulf

A

B

1

2

3

Lingaojiao
Meixia
Wenlian
Diaolou
Gaoshan Ling 190▲
Hongpaio
Bopu Gang
Linchang Jiao
Bingma Jiao
Longmen
Eman
Meiliang
Xinying
Lingao
Bolian
Wuxin
Tougu
Longmen Gang
Lanxun
Meiwen
Baomei
Meitai
Huang
Songlin
Guangcun
Houshui Wan
Sandu
Rongbai
Mutang
Xinfang
Fu'an
Duoweno
Hezh
Ganchongo
Yangpu
Xinying
Zhonghe
Dongcheng
Jialai
Longb
Yangpu Wan
Baimajing
Xinzhou
Changpo
Dongfeng
Nanbao
Dongjia
Dachan Jiao
Songming
Wangwu
Youlun
Dunmu
Luoji
Ma'ar 305
Paipu
Wengui
Shirong
Daxing
Mupai
Chahu
Heshe
Wenqing
Gaoshan Ling 113▲
Dajiang
Fengshi Ling 193
Zhong
Haitou Gang
Hongkan
Fuke
Dacheng
Baodao
Danzhou
Kunlun Nongchang
Meihe
Haitou
Nanluo
Da'an
Shuiwei
Fuqi
Yaxing
Edacun
Changtian
Nada
Tingpai Ling 401▲
Lanyang
Daodia
Haiwei
Xincun
Jilong
Hesheng
Nanfeng
Lanyang Hot Springs
Songteo
Daxian
Bangxi
Nanlingo
Chaying
Shiqiu
Dayao
Fanjia
Jia
Changhua Gang
Changhua
Xianfeng
Sanjia Ling 402▲
Shiyuetian
Taipo
Baomei Ling 844▲
Qifang
Guangya
Fulong
Nanjio
Limush
Jia
Sigengsha Jiao
Changcheng
Baoping
Jinbo
Xinjian
Da'an
Yingxiao
Changhua Jiang
Chahe
Changjiang
Qingsong
Nancha
Baisha
Yuanmen
Xishui
Baisha
Luoreno
Mt. Limu ▲
Limu Ling 1411▲
Sanjia
Shilu Shuiku
Beili Gang
Dontou
Datian
Qicha
Jinbingcun
Futou Ling 1437▲
Zhibao
Nankai
Gao'an
Yingge Ling 1811▲
Qiongzhong
Puqou Wan
Xinjie
225
Xinningpo
H   a   i   n   a   n   D
Hongmao
Basuo Gang
Dongfang
Datian
Donghua
Guangba
Exlan
Wangxia
Mahuo Ling 1546▲
Shiyun
Changzhe
Yulin Jiao
Luodai
Yudao
Yapo
Nanfang
Maoyang
Maodan
Mt. Wuzhi
Shuang Zhou
Nadou
▲682
Guanyin Feng
Luowang
Datian Eld's Deer
Mt. Bawang
Houxian Ling 1654▲
Shuimano
Mt. Wuzhi Wuzhi Shan 1867▲
Shang
Tongtian Gang
Xinlong
Gong aio
Nanmei
Sanping
Maodao
Wanchong
Hongshan
Diaoluos
Bacun
Daguangbu Shuiku
Dapo
Baichao
Nanlongo
Jiangbian
Chong'e
Fanyango
Maodao
Wuzhishan
Nansheng
Shimei
Gan'en Jiao
Gong'ai Nongchang
Chahekou
Shanrong
Ledong
Da'an
Mao'an
Qixianling Hot Springs
Ganchengo
Banqiao
Zhongsha
Tianchi Linchang
Kafaling Linchang
Baoguo
Taoxing Shuiku
Nangango
Jianfeng Ling 1412▲
Mt. Jianfeng
Ronglu
Saoshuo
Zhizhong
Mazui Ling 1317▲
Baoting
Shiling
Lingtou
Jianfeng
Qichang
Leguang Nongchang
Shiluo
Hekouo
Baisha Gang
Shandao
Changmao Shuiku
Baolun Nongchang
Baowen
Maogan
Xiangshui
Jiamao
Liugong
Foluo
Xinjian
Baogao
Baowei Ling 564▲
Da'an Shuiku
Baowen
Jian Ling 1019▲
Baoshio
Sandao
Yingz
Xinmin
Xinggou Shuiku
Qianjia
Zhipao
Zhanano
Xinzhong
Luokui
Yang Jiang
Yinggehai
Huangliu
Guan'an
Yaliang
Sanmudong
Nanlino
Tianza
Yingge Zui
Liguoo
Leluo
Jiusou Nongchang
Sanjiaotu
Licai Nongchang
Gaofeng
Haitangwan
Wanglou Gang
Jiusuo
Fengling
Yacheng
Gaofengdui
Lingshui
Dongluo Wan
Meishan
Baogango
Zhaye
Zhongliao
Niuqi Zh
Bitou Jiao
Fenghuang Airport
Fenghuang
Lizhigou
Linwang
Xigu Dao
Yazhou Wan
Tianya
225
Tielu
Dongluo Dao
Nanshan
Tianya Haijiao
Shigui
Nanshan Jiao
Sanya Tropical Seashore
Hexi
Sanya
Liupan
Ximao Zhou
Sanya Gang
Anyouo
Yalong
Dongmao Zhou
Luhuitou
Liudao
Yulin Gang
Yalong Wan
Luhuitou Jiao
Sanya Coral Reef
Yalong Jiao
Jinmu Jiao

A

B

Altitude Table

| 6000 | 5000 | 4000 | 3000 | 2000 | 1000 | 200 | 50 | 20 | 0 | 50 | 100 | 200 | 300 | 500 | 750 | 1000 | 1500 | 2000 m |

Leizhou Bandao
GUANGDONG
Xuwen
Maichen
Dongjiao
Longtang
Kilian
C
Luodou Sha
D
1

Jiaowei Gang
Hai'an
Paiwei Jiao
po
Hai'an Gang
Santang
Qiongzho
Haixia
Hainan Jiao
Kuangchang
111°

Qiongzh
Xinbu
Dongying
Xinbuhao
Qixing Ling 117
Dongpo
Qiaopo
20°

Xinhai
Haikou Gang
Puqian Wan
Puqian
Longfeng
Baohu Jiao
Huxincun
Beishi Dao
Changliu
Dongbai
Jinshan
Fengpo
Baohu Shan 207
Pingshi
Nanshi Dao
Fengnan
HAIKOU
Lingshan
Yenhai
Luodou
Wengtian
Shuangfan
Qizhou Liedao
Chengmai Wan
Dongshui
Haixiu
Qiongshan Qu
Meilan Airport
Hushan
Daodong Linchang
Qiaotou
Macun
Laocheng
Shishan
Chengxi
Meilan
Sanjiang
Fengwei
Longma
Dafeng
Volcano Zone at Shishan Mts.
Dongzhaigang
Danhuao
Tianwei
Bailian
Haikou Volcanoes
Longqiao
Baoluo
Dazhipo
Gongpo
Qizhou Yang
Nanxing
Mei'an
Yongxing
Shizilu
Yunlong
Hongqi
Xianlai
Ergongdui
Changsa
Baitu
Fushan
Fu'ano
Luojing
Dabao
Yahuai
Donglu Shuiku
Donglu
Gengxin
Meiting
Dongxing
Qingcao
Sanmenpo
Tanniu
Baofang
Songliu
Dala
Yongfa
Dongshan
Ziluan
Xiangou
Tanwen
Xingiao
Beijia
Baoling Shuiku
Houling
Mt. Tonggu
Ruixi
Ding'an
Xinmin
Dapo
Wencheng
Dongge
Longtou
Honghai
Tonggu Zui
Taiping
Longzhou
Pinghe
Jiazi
Nanyang
Touyuan
Taishan
Xinwu
Changwen
Xinzhu
Longhu
Yongfeng
Wenchang
Dongjiao
Jinji Ling 203
Shifu
Dalupo
Fuwen
Leiming
Sanjiu
Penglai
Dianchang
Maihao
Wenru
Xinxing
Pozhai
Huangzhu
Wugailing Po 269
Dayang
Wenlin
Huiwen
Lingweio
Lingshang
Bowen
Nanfu Shuiku
Yuying
Xichang
Datong
Longmen
Honghualing
Yantang
Chongxing
Yandunxu
Fengjia Wan
Tunchang
Longhe
Lulin
Dalu
Nanchang
Fengjia
Tunjiao
Hanlino
Lingkou
Wenfeng
Changpo
3
Huangling
Poxin
Xinshi
Tayang
Gangmenkou
Luzhao
Nanlu
Zhongjian Nongchang
Luoling
Panshui
Tanmen
Fengmu
Wupo
Miaocun
Shibi
Wanquan
Jinmen Gang
Longjiang
Zhongyuan
Bo'ao
111°

Dongtai Nongchang
Wenshi
Chaoyang
Jiuqujiang
Bo'ao Gang
D

Zhongping
Huishan
Yangjiang
Sanletang
Longgun
South China Sea
Luping
Yanyuan
Hongpodui
Mulang Shuiku
Shangen
Lintian
Dafao
Luma
Heping
Bitang
Jiachao
Lelai
Heleo
Gangbei
Napping
Sangengluo
Xiasan
Hou'an
Gangbei Gang
Shifu
Damao
Changfeng
Bai an Dao
Changxing
Niulou
Wanning
Dahua Jiao
Niushang Ling 1288
Xinglong Nongchang
Chunyuan
Xiaudier Shuiku
Gaolong
Lianhua
Dong'ao
Dazhou Dao
Nanqiao
Qiaohai
Zhouzai Dao
Dazhou Island
Benhao
Yangmei
Xinmei
Timeng
Guangpo
Lingshui
Wenluo
Sancar
Li'an
Lingshui Jiao
Xincun
Nanwan
Li'an Gnag

Scale 1:1 000 000
0 10 20 30 40 50km

HAINAN Province inset:
E **NANNING** GUANGXI ZHUANGZU ZIZHIQU
F **GUANGZHOU** **MACAU** MACAU SAR
HONG KONG HONG KONG SAR
G Taiwan Tao Kaohsiung TAIWAN Chihsing Yen
4
HA NOI Beibu Gulf Zhanjiang
Dongsha Qundao
Qion Haixia
HAIKOU
HAINAN Hainan Dao
Sanya
Luzon
5
Xisha Qundao
Bei Jiao
Yongxing Dao
Zhongsha Qundao
Yinji Tan
Balintang Chan.
VIETNAM
Zhongjian Dao
Bofu Ansha
Huangyan Dao
MANILA
LAOS
CAMBODIA
South China Sea
Mindoro I.
6
Liyue Tan
Zhongye Qunjiao
Haima Tan
PHILIPPINES
T. P. Ho Chi Minh
Nansha Qundao
Xianbin Jiao
Palawan
Yinqing Qunjiao
Andu Tan
Cagayan Sulu
Sulu Sea
7
Wan'an Tan
Nanwei Tan
Nan'an Jiao
BANDAR SERI BEGAWAN
BRUNEI
Zengmu Ansha
Laut Sulawesi
MALAYSIA
Kep. Natuna
INDONESIA
Pulau Kalimantan
G
8
HAINAN PROVINCE 1:20 000 000

Hainan Province

With Haikou as its capital, Hainan Province, which is abbreviated as "Qiong", is located on the South China Sea, facing Guangdong across the Qiongzhou Haixia (Str.). Traditionally, Hainan had been under the jurisdiction of Guangdong Province, In 1988, it was established as the newest province in China. It covers an area of over 34,000 square kilometers, and has a population of 7.9 million, including such ethnic groups as Han, Li, Miao, Zhuang, and Hui. It is the main residential area of Li nationality and a renowned hometown for most overseas Chinese.

■ Geographical Features

Topography Hainan Dao is the second largest island in China. Mesas and plans take up 2/3 of the island's total area. With Wuzhi Shan (Mt.) and Limu Ling (Mt.) in the middle, Hainan's terrain descends from middle to the outer circle in the shape of a pear. Major rivers are Nandu Jiang, Changhua Jiang and Wanquan He. Few lakes are found on the island. Reefs and coral islands like Xisha Qundao, Dongsha Qundao and Nansha Qundao lies around Hainan Dao, of which Yongxing Dao is the largest. Zengmu Ansha (Reef) is the southernmost territory of China.

Climate Tropical humid monsoon climate rules Hainan, which brings about frequent typhoons and storms. Though temperature in this province is hot all year round, there are plenty of rainfalls and a clear distinction between rainy season and dry season. Annual rainfall in this area is between 1, 500~2, 000mm. The average annual temperature in most part of the province is between 22~27℃, with an average temperature in January and February between 16~21℃, while in July and August between 25~29℃.

■ Natural Resources

Over 90 kinds of minerals have been found in Hainan, among which the reserves of iron is the largest and of the best quality, while the reserves of minerals like titanium, zirconium, quartz, sapphire, oil, natural gas, and oil shale are bounteous.

Hainan's forest cover rate is around 39.56%, of which natural tropical forests take up 17% of the island's total area. There are more than 1,400 species of trees in the province, of which 460 are national commodity trees. Over 500 species of wild animals and over 4,000 species of plants live on this island, among which over 20 are rare plants under national protection.

Hainan has rich aquatic resources. Over 800 species of fish, shrimps, shellfish and seaweeds are found in Nansha Quandao, Dongsha Qundao and Xisha Qundao. The province also boasts rich sea salt resources. Yinggehai, Dongfang and Yuya are major slat fields.

■ Agriculture

As the largest production base of tropical crop, Hainan raised large quantity of tropical crops with high economic values like rubber, coconut, areca, pepper, coffee, cashew, coco, pineapple, lichee, logan and banana. Rare woods, medicinal herbs and bines are found in tropical rain forests. Double or even triple cropping system is applied in Hainan.

Major crops here are rice, sweat potato, cassava, sugar cane, peanut and tea. Pig, cow, and sheep are raised here, and the province produces some first class strains. The vast South China Sea fishery produces rich aquatic products like fish, shrimps, crabs, pearl and seaweeds.

■ Industry

Hainan is the largest special economic zone in China and the only province that has been given that status. Ever since China's reform and opening up to the outside world, Hainan's industry has developed very quickly in fields like rubber products manufacturing, electronics, family gadgets, mining, metallurgy, chemical fibre, forest industry, sugar making, salt processing, and canned food production, among which sugar making has become one of its pillar industries, while rubber products manufacturing ranges a large variety.

■ Transportation

Railway Sanya-Dongfang-Changjiang railway is now in use, so is the train ferry cross Qiongzhou Haixia.

Highway Highway transportation plays a major role in the transportation system on this island. Three national highways run across the island from north to south, connecting over 300 townships and tourist attractions. Round-island express highway has been put into use.

Airway Meilan and Fenghuang Airports have flights to over 40 major cities in China as well as destinations in Singapore, Thailand and Malaysia.

Waterway Sea transportation is a major way for Hainan to connect with the outside world. There are over 60 natural harbors around the island, and over 20 sea ports have been built, including Haikou, Sanya, Basuo, Yangpu and Qinglan. Nearly 70 international sea routes start from Haikou and Sanya.

■ Places of Interest

With favorable climate and evergreen vegetation, Hainan exhibits unique tropical and subtropical scenery of island. Tropical Seashore of Sanya are well known winter resorts with fine white sands and clean sea water. Wugong Temple, being composed of a series of ancient architecture complex, is 5 kilometers south to Haikou. Tianya Haijiao, which means the end of the world and corner of sea, is located in the southwest seaside of Sanya city. The blue sea and azure sky, the misty waves and dots of sails, together with the coconut trees dancing in the breeze and grotesque stones standing around have here formed a nice poetic picture. Those huge stones engraved with Chinese

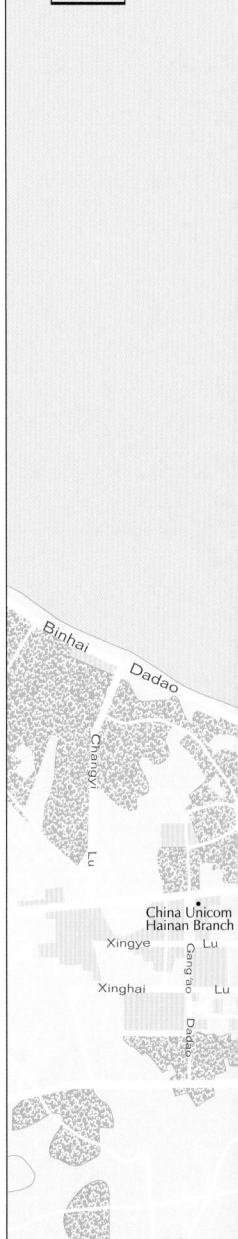

Haikou

Characters of "Tianya", "Haijiao", and "Nantian Yizhu" stand by the South China Sea became a unique scene in Hainan Island. Other tourist attractions include: Hairui's Cemetery, Wenchang Tower and Tropical Arboretum.

■ Local Products

Tropical products like coconut, pineapple, cashew, coffee, rubber, coco and pepper are prolific. Tea and traditional Chinese medicinal herbs produced here enjoys great renown. Coconut shell carving, cow horn carving, shell carving, wood carving, butterfly samples and pearl jewelry are traditional local handicrafts.

Sanya Seashore

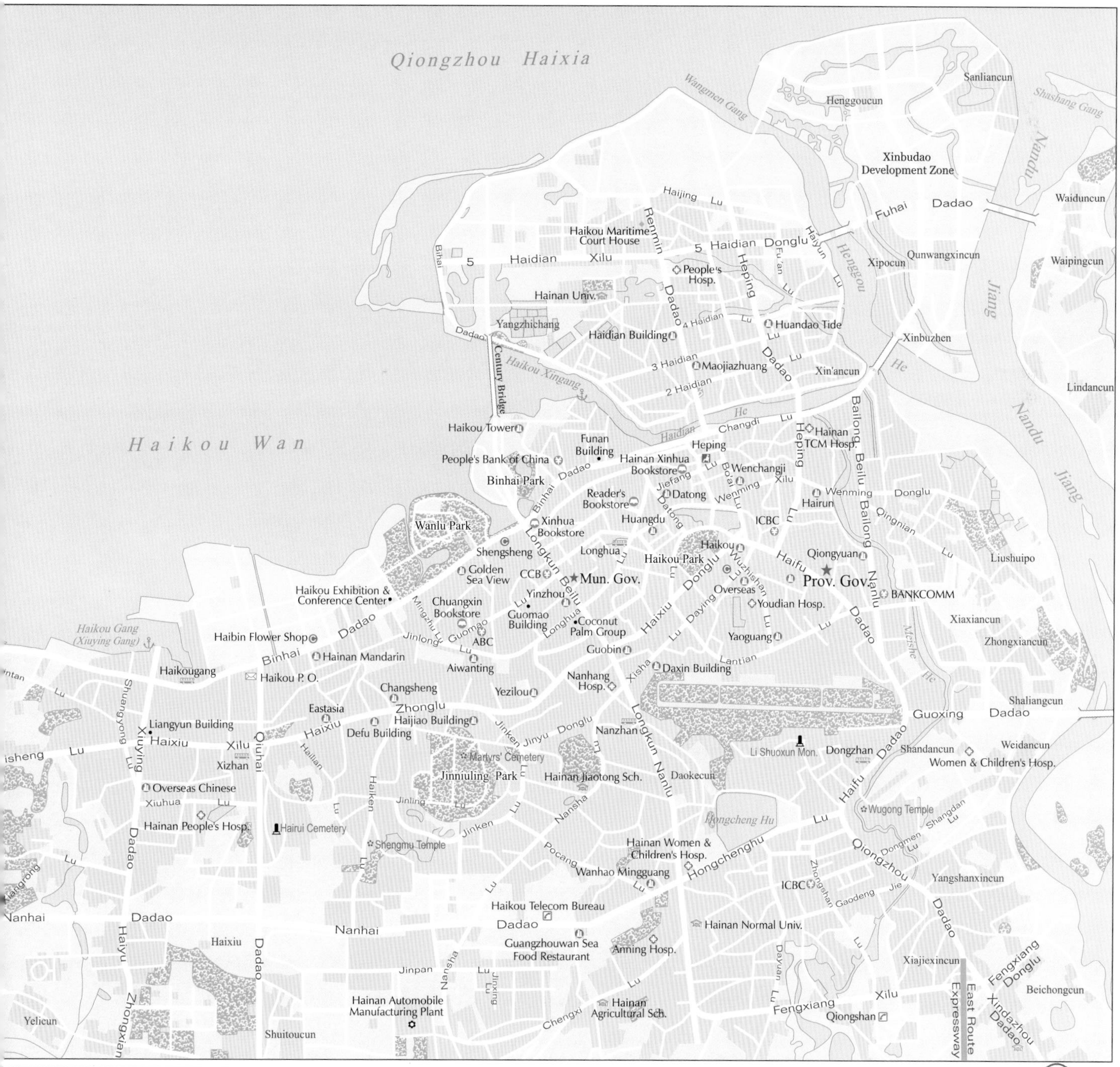

Qiongzhou Haixia

Wangmen Gang

Sanliancun

Shashang Gang

Henggoucun

Xinbudao Development Zone

Nandu Jiang

Waiduncun

Haijing Lu

Fuhai Dadao

Waipingcun

Haikou Maritime Court House

5 Haidian Donglu

Xipocun Qunwangxincun

5 Haidian Xilu

Renmin Dadao

Heping

People's Hosp.

Hainan Univ.

Huandao Tide

Xinbuzhen

Hengou He

Yangzhichang

4 Haidian Lu

Lindancun

Haidian Building

3 Haidian

Maojiazhuang

Xin'ancun

Bailong Beilu Bailong

Nandu Jiang

Century Bridge

Haikou Xingang

2 Haidian

He

Haidian

Changdi

Heping

Hainan TCM Hosp.

Haikou Tower

Funan Building

Heping

Qingnian

Haikou Wan

People's Bank of China

Hainan Xinhua Bookstore

Wenchangji

Binhai Park

Binhai Dadao

Jiefang

Wenming Xilu

Qiongyuan

Reader's Bookstore

Datong

Wenming

Donglu

Liushuipo

Wanlu Park

Xinhua Bookstore

Huangdu

ICBC

Hairun

Shengsheng

Longhua

Haikou

Qiongyuan

Haikou Gang (Xiuying Gang)

Golden Sea View

CCB ★ Mun. Gov.

Haikou Park

Youdian Hosp.

Prov. Gov. ★

BANKCOMM

Haikou Exhibition & Conference Center

Chuangxin Bookstore

Yinzhou

Overseas

Xiaxiancun

Zhongxiancun

Haibin Flower Shop

Binhai Dadao

Guomao Building

Coconut Palm Group

Yaoguang

Haikougang

Hainan Mandarin

ABC

Guobin

Daxin Building

Shaliangcun

Aiwanting

Nanhang Hosp.

Lantian

Guoxing Dadao

Haikou P. O.

Changsheng

Yezilou

Eastasia

Zhonglu

Weidancun

Liangyun Building

Haijiao Building

Nanzhan

Daokecun

Li Shuoxun Mon.

Dongzhan Dadao

Shandancun

Women & Children's Hosp.

Haixiu Xilu

Defu Building

Xizhan

Martyrs' Cemetery

Jinniuling Park

Hainan Jiaotong Sch.

Overseas Chinese

Wugong Temple

Xiuhua

Hainan People's Hosp.

Hairui Cemetery

Hongcheng Hu

Hainan Women & Children's Hosp.

Qiongzhou

Yangshanxincun

Shengmu Temple

Wanhao Mingguang

ICBC

Haikou Telecom Bureau

Dadao

Guangzhouwan Sea Food Restaurant

Anning Hosp.

Hainan Normal Univ.

Xiajiexincun

Nanhai Dadao

Haixiu

Nanhai

Hainan Automobile Manufacturing Plant

Hainan Agricultural Sch.

Fengxiang Xilu

Qiongshan

Beichongcun

Yelicun

Shuitoucun

SICHUAN

GUIZHO

YUNNAN

Qingplan, Piankou, Tumen, Nanbao, Bazi, Jiange, Zhuyuan, Hongyano, Yuanba Qu, Gaoyang, Puji, Leba, Shikuang, Banqiaokou, Nixi

Beichuan, Xuanping, Wudu, Xiaoxibao, Hekou, Wulian, Ximiao, Yunji, Pu'an, Mumao, Lijiang, Zhengzhi, Dongxi, Mumen, Changchi, Wangcang, Xiallang, Xinchang, Yaohong

Jiangyou, Yong'an, Anchang, Qingliang, Longfeng, Zhanqi, Xuzhou, Kaifeng, Dongqingo, Cangxi, Qianfo, Shitan, Enyang, Sima, Yuanshan, Tiefo, Miaoya

Gaochuan, Zitong, Xinqiao, Xujia, Yuanshan, Siyi, Jinxian, Bazhong, Qingjiang, Liangyong, Dingshan, Qiujia, Hujia

An Xian, Xiushui, Shima, Shiban, Renhe, Shengzhong, Langzhong, Sanjiao, Chaba, Ma'an, Xiangtan, Pingchang, Shuangha, Beimiao

Mianzhu, Jinshang, Jinfeng, Huanglu, Luxi, Longshu, Heiping, Shengzhong, Nanbu, Nanmu, Fuxing, Jincheng, Yongle, Hanshui, Pujia, Yiha, Luojiang

Luojiang, Deyang, Xinhua, Santai, Yanting, Fuyi, Fuhu, Jianxing, Panlong, Yilong, Xujia, Xiaoshui, Yongxing, Laolin, Shiti, Guancun, Dazho, Da Xian

Shifang, Sanjie, Zhongjiang, Jianping, Lingxing, Tongshe, Yulong, Jinkong, Fengming, Wangjia, Yingshan, Xiaoqiao, Sanhui, Jingshi, Shiban, Mal

Guanghan, Qingbaijiang Qu, Jinhua, Renhe, Xichong, Longmen, Peng'an, Heshu, Wangjiang, Linbao, Zhaojia, Heshi

Xindu Qu, Jintang, Qingquan, Guanqiao, Shehong, Pengxi, Nanchong, Changle, Luojia, Huaqiao, Qu Xian, Dazhuo, Shiqiaopu, Bishan, Yuanyi

CHENGDU, Luodai, Wufeng, Cangshan, Yufeng, Guihua, Dashi, Longpan, Jialing Qu, Shengguan, Goujiao, Shisuno, Langya, Qingshui, Qiqi, Pingjin

Longquanyi Qu, Jiajia, Sanhe, Yunlong, Liang'an, Lianhua, Baima, Suining, Sanfeng, Liemian, Longkong, Yuechi, Guang'an, Qianfeng, Ganzi, Wenxing, Shaping, Pushun, Yunlong Qu

Jianyang, Yucheng, Shijia, Tongjia, Lezhi, Dongchan, Anju Qu, Guxi, Baolong, Wanshan, Wusheng, Luodu, Gaodeng Shan, Linshui, Xingren, Dianjiang, Gao'an, Ba

Wengong, Longma, Ziyang, Danshan, Dongshan, Yuanda, Anyue, Chongkan, Tongnan, Taihe, Shayu, Longshi, Huangtuo, Qinghua, Hellu, Fenghe, Chengxi, Gaofeng, Gangjia

Renshou, Beidou, Yingjie, Nanjin, Xunlong, Baizi, Tai'an, Gaolou, Dashi, Gaolong, Guandu, Jiulong, Shiyan, Heyou, Sanxi, Rer, Xumir

Fujia, Qiuxi, Zhenzi, Hulongo, Tangba, Shaoyun, Tongxi, Hechuan Qu, Liuyin, Honghuo, Huangyin, Tongjing, Feilong, Shetang, Shu

Gude, Shuanglong, Gaoliang, Zhouli, Wofo, Xiaodu, Taiping, Jiuxian, Yanjing, Qingbing, Xinglong, Bake, Diuzhou, Yunji, Zhenxio, Nantuo, Zhanpu

Wangyang, Lianjie, Zizhong, Shuangcai, Lijia, Zhong'o, Wugui, Pingtan, Tongliang, Mt. Jinyun, Beibei Qu, Shuitu, Mu'er, Shichuan, Changshou Qu, Lidu, Qingxi, Fen

Xinchang, Shuanghe, Shizi, Tieshan, Baoding, Yongxi, Dalu, Qinglong Lake, Yubei Qu, Caijiagang, Jiangbei Airport, Shantuo, Shituo, Fuling Qu

Neijiang, Wujia, Hebaoo, Sanqu, Shima, Wangu, Xiquan, Qingmuguan, Huixing, Xinmao, Linshi, Mt. Wu

Panlong, Guchang, Longshi, Yulong, Bishan, Jiangbei Qu, Mudong, Shuanghekou, Mawu, puzi, Shuanghe

Rong Xian, Weiyuan, Lingjia, Rongchang, Honglu, Shuangqiao Qu, CHONGQING, Nan'an Qu, Wubu, Mingjia, Tianci, Jubao, Baisha, Shixi, Pingqiao, Baiyun, Wulo

Changshan, Dujia, Xinqiao, Zigong, Gongjing Qu, Shuanghe, Anfu, Shuanghe, Mafang, Laifeng, Shiban, Dadukou Qu, Jiulongpo Qu, Yajiang, Changba, Guang

Nixi, Yongxing, Fushan, Daguan, Yantan Qu, Longchang, Baofeng, Linjiang, Wutan, Degan, Tongguanyi, Banan Qu, Tianxingsi, Shiqiang, Shuijiang, Longddr

Guanyin, Kongtan, Dengguan, Fushun, Daisi, Xuantan, Ji'an, Hegemou, Youxi, Yipin, Shengdengshan, Xianfeng, Jielong, Daguan, Nanchuan Qu, Yuquan

Lichang, Zhaohua, Huaide, Shidong, Zhaoya, Zhuyang, Lishi, Liangcha, Jiasu, Xihu, Guangxing, Shentong, Longsheng, Wenfeng, Sanguan, Yangxi, Loul

Xiangbi, Nanxi, Luzhou, Foyino, Wanglong, Tanghe, Piluo, Jiaping, Qijiang, Nantong, Nanping, Jinfo Shan, Mazui, Daozhen

Pingshan, Yibin, Jiang'an, Naxi Qu, Baijie, Hejiang, Hutouo, Fubao, Bailu, Caijia, Zhuangtang, Fuhuan, Gaishi, Jinshan, Toudu, Zheng'an

Shuifu, Shahe, Changning, Shangma, Huguo, Guandu, Zhongshan, Bailin, Mt. Simian, Dongxi, Dingshan, Xinzhou, Mugua, Anchang

Shuanglong, Gao Xian, Chishui, Hushi, Simianshan, Fujia, Zhaiba, Shihao, Songkan, Xiaoya, Miaotang

Yanjin, Gong Xian, Gongquan, Maling, Xingwen, Shuiwei, Tucheng, Xishui, Sanchahe, Wenshui, Xianyuan, Xinzhan, Lejian, Jiuci

Junlian, Luochang, Didong, Shilin, Xuyong, Deyue, Yongle, Xijiu, Sangmu, Erli, Sanhe, Chumi, Kuankuo, Wangcao, Yong'an

Luobiao, Lianghe, Yibin, Jiusicheng, Hongqiao, Xiyong, Tongzi, Qinggangtang, Liudu, Tuping

Altitude Table 0 100 300 500 750 1000 1500 2000 2500 3000 3500m

Scale 1:1 800 000   0   18   36   54   72   90km

Chongqing Municipality

Chongqing is abbreviated as "Yu". As a linking zone between east China and west China, it is located on the northeast corner of southwest China, along the upper reaches of Chang Jiang (Yangtze River). It covers an area of over 82,300 square kilometers, and has a population of 31.3 million, including such ethnic groups as Han, Tujia, Miao, Hui, Mongol and Yi.

■ Geographical Features

Topography Mountains and hills take up most part of Chongqing. With mountains like Daba Shan, Wu Shan, and Dalou Shan circle round Chongqing on the east, south and west, Chongqing's terrain slopes from south and north to the Chang Jiang river valley, intersected only by basins like Liangping and Xiushan. The main stream of Chang Jiang runs across Chongqing from southwest to northeast. Other major rivers include Jialing Jiang, Wu Jiang, Qi Jiang, Qu Jiang and Daning He, which cut out many deep valleys in the mountains.

Climate Subtropical humid monsoon climate rules the area, which blurs the seasonal difference, and brings to Chongqing little snow but plenty of clouds and mists. Annual rainfall in this region is between 1,000~1,400mm. The average annual temperature is between 13~18℃, with an average temperature in January between 1~8℃, while in July between 21~29℃. Chongqing is one of China's three "ovens".

■ Natural Resources

Chongqing boasts rich reserves of natural resources. Over 70 kinds of minerals have been found here, among which the reserves of minerals like coal, natural gas, manganese, mercury, aluminium, strontium, barium, halite, barite, limestone, fluorite, and silicon are bounteous, especially that of first grade strontium, which is the largest in China. Mercury found in Xiushan and Youyang are of enomous quantity.

Forest cover rate in this region is around 21%, as most of the mountainous area in Chongqing is covered by forests. There are more than 4,000 species of plants, including over 2,000 species of Chinese medicinal herbs, mostly Chinese goldthread, dangsen, honeysuckle, and caladium. Over 600 species of animals live here, among which over 100 are rare animals under national protection.

■ Agriculture

Chongqing is one of China's major production bases of grain and pork. Main grain crops are: rice, wheat, corn and sweet potato; main economic crops are: rape, peanuts, tung tree, mulberry, hemp, and tobacco; fruits like orange, grapefruit, peach and plum are also grown here. Pig, cow, sheep, and rabbit are raised here, and this region produces first class strains of pig, and rabbit.

■ Industry

Chongqing has been one of China's traditional industrial centers, and is now the largest economic center in southwest China. Main industries here include: machinery, chemical, metallurgy, textile, building material, food processing, automobile, motorcycle, pharmacy, electronics, power engineering, war industry and hi-tech industries like information engineering, biotechnology, and environmental protection. Chongqing has the largest aluminium processing factory in Asia. Motorcycles produced here takes up 1/3 of China's total output, and 1/2 of its motorcycles are exported, making Chongqing one of China's top ten electromechanical products exporting bases.

■ Transportation

Railway Three main stems including Chengdu-Chongqing, Xiangfan-Chongqing, and Chongqing-Guiyang railways run through Chongqing, and are joined by branch lines of Baoji-Chengdu, Chengdu-Kunming, and Beijing-Guangzhou railways, connecting Chongqing conveniently with the rest part of China.

Highway A convenient network made up by national highways and provincial highways has been completed. Express highways like Chengdu-Chongqing, Chongqing-Fuling, Chongqing-Guiyang have been put into use.

Airway Over 50 domestic and international flight courses are available at Jiangbei Airport.

Waterway Dozens of ports and docks have been built along Chang Jiang. Freights weighting thousands of tons can go directly to seaports like Wuhan and Shanghai, and therefore to the rest of the world.

■ Places of Interest

Chongqing has beautiful natural scenery and rich cultural relics. Three Gorges of Chang Jiang is not just a natural wonder of spectacular

scenery, but an area surrounded by rich cultural relics and fantastic legends. Xiaosanxia (minor three gorges) lies in Wushan County, which are three beautiful valleys along Daning River. Mt. Jinyun is a Buddhist place with over 1,500 years of history. Mt. Simian in Jiangjin is not only covered with primitive forests, but also decorated by lakes and waterfalls. Mt. Jinfo, a national nature reserve and national forest park, is located in Nanchuan. Dazu Rock Carvings can be found in Dazu County. These treasures of China's early rock carving art were finished in late Tang Dynasty and are now included in the World Heritage List by UNESCO. Other cultural relics can be found in Fuling, Fengdu, Zhongxian, Wanzhou and Yunyang.

■ Local Products

The famous Chongqing hotpot boasts a long history. Other local flavors like pickles, beef jerk, lobster sauce and rice candy are all well known in China. Grapefruits, peach and orange produced here are of high quality. Embroidery, silk, and bamboo products are traditional local handicrafts.

Three Gorges of Yangtze River

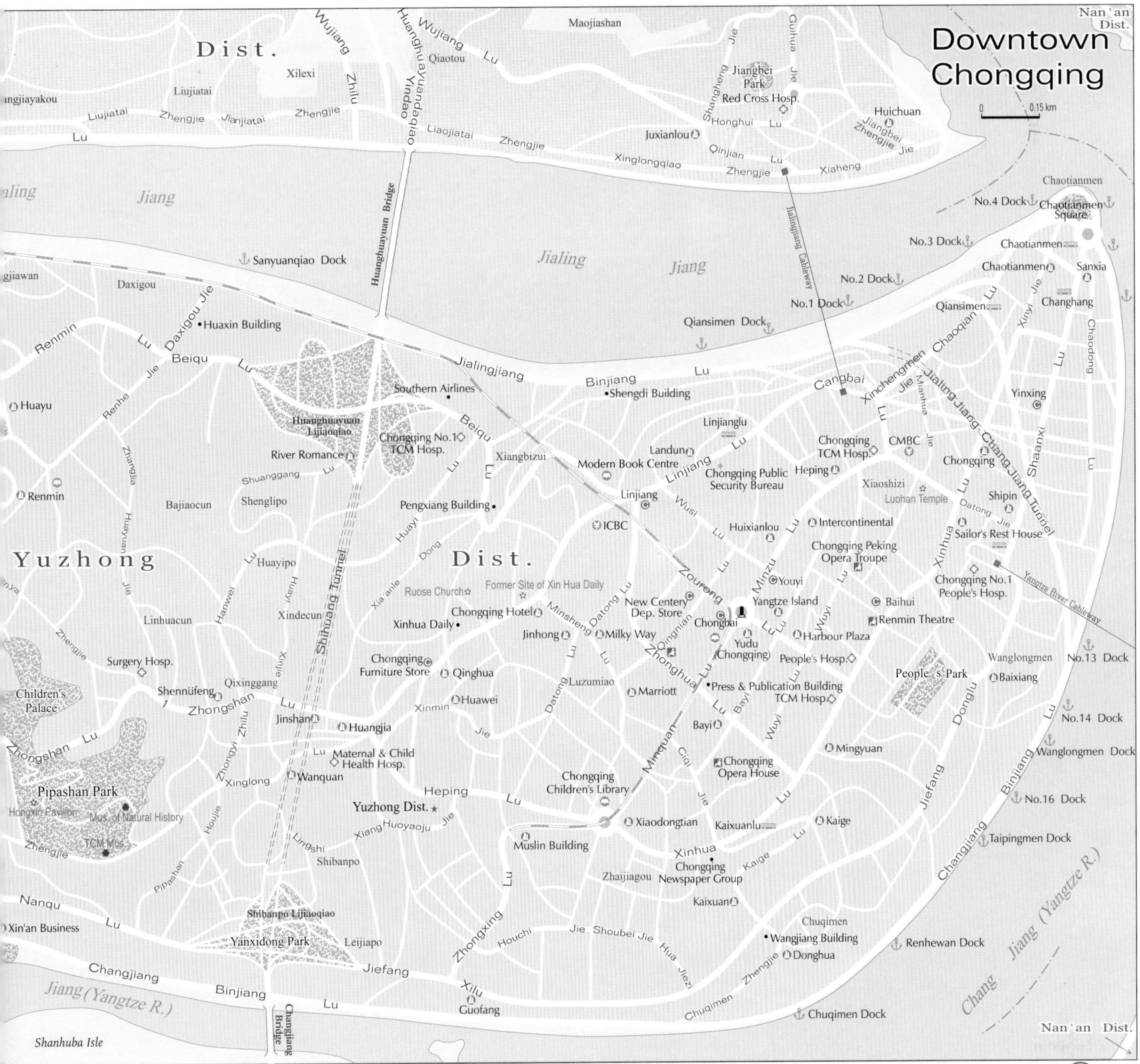

Downtown Chongqing

[Map of Downtown Chongqing showing Yuzhong District, Jiangbei District, Nan'an District, the Jialing Jiang and Chang Jiang (Yangtze R.), and numerous streets, landmarks, and docks.]

Chongqing

0   0.53 km

Yubei Dist.

Jiangbei Dist.

Shapingba Dist.

Jiulongpo Dist.

Dadukou Dist.

Banan

Geleshan Forest Park

Huangpoding
Buyunqiao
Baigong Hall
Hailuoshi
Zhazi Cave
Southwest Univ. of Political Science & Law
Martyrs' Cemetery
Longjingwan
Huashengbao
Geleshan
Lishuwan Station
Linyuan
611 Baipo Ding
Zhongqushan Tunnel
Coll. of Communication
Shandong
Caofangwan
Chongqing East Station
Pengjiagang
Huayan Temple
Gonghecun
Hongbin
Huayan Hosp.

Shuangbei
Jialing Group
Guihuayuan
Dengzhanwan
Banbianjie
Shimahe
Jiajie Tongjiaqiao Zhengjie
Baolun Temple
Citong Gonglu
Fenghuangshan Park
Jiaolong Lu
Laodong Lu
Pingqiao
Chongqing Univ.
Yinhe Theatre
Shayang Lu
Yubei Lu
Hongxiang
Dianli Hosp.
Shazhong
Huashan
Zaozibao Chongqing Univ.
Chongqing Grand Hotel
Yinshan
People's Hosp.
Liyuan
Jintaiyang
Tiancheng
Xiaojiang
Xinjie
Shapingba
Shaping Park
Fuyuansi
Ronghu
Jinlongyufeng Restaurant
Shilianpan
Blue Sky
Shixiao
Tianxingqiao Zhengjie
Southwest Pharmaceutical Co.,Ltd.
Lizilin
Moon Light
Xi'nan Hosp.
Third Military Medical Univ.
Damianpo
Gaojuepu
Longma
Fengtian
Fengmingshan
Xinqiao Hosp.
Shixin
Lanhuacun
Jiulongpo
Gree Electric Appliance Inc.
Sunhe
Shizushan
Ertang
Dadao
Xiangbiju
Huju
Hi-Tech Park
Dadao
Chentuo
Xinlongyicun
Mongshi Shuiku
Tiandengbao
Shuangshan
Dazhong
Wangjiayan
Baqiao
Jiutian
Baqiao Jie
Masangxi Bridge
Darenbao
Longjingwan

Chongqing-Chengdu Changshou Expressway
Zhengjie Tongjiaqiao Zhengjie
Yanggong
Qiao
Buxing Jie
Hanyu
Longquan Lu
Gaotanyan Zhengjie
Dadao
Tianma Lu
Xiajiawan
Dachuan
Yulingdong
Peace
Anhua
Bailin
Yingbin
Chengdu-Chongqing
Chongqing North Station
Xiaolongkan
Zhengjie
Shangtuwan Lu
Xiatuwan
Pingdingshan Park
Shikuo
Gaomiaocun
Shiyang
Yugao Park

Binjiang
Gaojiahuayuan Bridge
Shapingba Jiang
Huagongcun
Former Residence of Xu Beihong
Shimen Park
Shimen
Chongda Hosp.
Chongda
Cancer Hosp.
Shimen Bridge
Dist.
Guihuacun
Shangtuwan Lu
Luojiawan
Jinyinwan
Shiqiaozhen
Chongqing Jiaotong Univ.
Wujiu
Yuzhou Lu
Yuzhou
Yiping
Keyuan Lu
South Garden
Olympic Stadium
Xiechen Lu
Chenjiaping
Shipingqiao
Taohua
Xijiao Hosp.
Xiangbiju

Chongqing Hechuan Expressway
Songshi
Dadao
Huayucun
Hongshi Lu
Jiangling
Lanjian
Hong'ensi Park
Dashikuai Hosp.
Yijiacun
Dashibayicun
Dashiba Lu
Zhengjie
Yiran
Tianfu Cola Group
Yuanjie
Yangjiaping
Yangxin
Huafu
Jianshe
Zhigang

Hongyan Shuiku
Beibuxinqu
Panjiang
Yancheng
Tiexin
Shubei
Huahui Park
Guanyinmiao
Lanjian
Jiangbei Dist.
Yijiacun
Longyin Lu Hongyan Lu
Hongyan Revolutionary Mus.
Chongqing Normal Univ.
Taiyangwan
Hutouyan
Hualongqiao
Shiyou Lu
Baiyun
Hualongqiao Zhengjie
Jiukengzi
Taping Hosp.
Great Wall
Chongqing Medical Univ.
Caiyuan
Dashi
Yuzhou
Dahe
Keyuan Lu
Chongqing Telecom Comp.
Yuanlin
Honglou
Jiangzhou
Yuanjiagang
Xialiuwan Zhengjie
Egongyan
Chongqing Construction Hosp.
Laodongcun
Jianshe
Yangjiaping Zhengjie
Heshangshan
Yuxi Hosp.
Xiche
Wangjiagou
Yangjiu
Zoo
Changjiang erqiao

Chuangshiji
Honglin
Longhua Lu
Xinpai
Jinlong
ICBC
Dadao
Longxi
Hefu
Huahuang
Donghe G
Waimao
Jianxin
Sichou
Chunhuiyuan
Jialing Park
Jiangbei Dist.
Wanshouqiao
Jianxin Xilu
Fuka
Lijiaping
Chongqing Technology Don & Business Univ.
Jialing Jiang
Intl. Exhibition & Conference Centre
Fotuguan Park
White Rose
Changjiang Lu
Honglou
Danyang Lu
Egongyan Bri
Yangjiaping Zhengjie

Chang Jiang
Yejin Hosp.
Yugangcun
Huangnigou
Yuejin
TCM Hosp.
Yueguanghuayuan
Dadukou Dist.
Dadukou Park
Caiyuan
Ganjie
Ganghua Zhilu
Baqiao Jie
Baihuacun
Chongqing Iron & Steel (Group)Co., Ltd.
Xiliutuo
Jiangjiawan
Linjiangcun
Daguangm
Yinqiao
Jiulongcun
Wangjiatian
Mawangp
Huaxi
Lijiatuo Changjiang Bridge

No. 319 National Road
Shaxiao Jieshi

136

QINGHAI · **GANSU** · **QINGHAI** · **QINGHAI**

BAYAN · **HAR SHAN** · **A NYEMAQEN SHAN**

XIZANG (TIBET) · **ZIZHIQU**

HENGDUAN SHAN · **SHALULA SHAN** · **DAXUE SHAN** · **ZHEDUO SHAN** · **KONGGAR SHAN**

INDIA · **MYANMAR** · **YUNNAN**

Geqen · Qingshuhe · Bênmana · Yigxung · Kyinzhio · Tanglag · Gadè · Nguraxoima · Gahai · Lhamosi · GQINGHAI · Magu

Dámjong · Acho · Xogba · Parongsi · Dagtogo · Darlag · Kanglung · Xia Zanggor · Basar · Murge · Waiwaincang · Qamme · Zoigê Wetlands · Lingwa · Maima

Longbao · Chindu · Chomsakongma · Sangruma · Tarlagjimdo · A · Boiba · Marzhingo · Sogruma · Jigzhi · Qoijema · Tenggor

QINGHAI · Gêmang · Q I N G H A I · 5369 Nyainbo Yuzê Feng · Waqên

Yushu · Qatog · Udoima · Ju'nyung · Waxu · Nyidoi · Dajdoi · Dakar · Gyimkar · Chubgên · Baima · Aba · Mêgor · Hongyuan

Shanglaxiu · Zenda · Sêrxü · Chomsagabma · Aqu · Choxigabma · Kêgor · Nyainlungo · Shang Dokog · Namda · Kogbo · Rongwam · Anqgu

Gyobreg · Calungtang · Pênda · Logung · Lamdoo · Sanchahe · Wointog · Nyangug · Zhong Zakog · Nyikog · Xorg · Sêrtar · Zamtang · Shang Zamtang · Zongbur · Sarzê · Rangkou · Shuangsi

Nangqen · Ji'nyinsib · Xiao Surmango · Gosu · Mani · Yilhung · Ranchang · Zamtang · Sizhai

Doingêrxu · Mianda · Wojbodoi · Dêge · 6168 Que'er Shan · Zinkog · Sênkar · Garzê · Wengda · Sili · Barkam

Riwoqê · Derdoino · Cêrwai · Gantog · Horbo · Nyamgyi · Dagaing · Zangmai · Akorio · Jinchuan · Lianghe

Qamdo · Jomda · Toba · Qu'nyido · Baiyu · Zomdo · Luhuo · Yi'ngoi · Xuxur · Anning · Malêo · Siguniang

Morri · Gyangbê · Bdloo · Barong · Acab · Ximlong · Kangsaro · Dawu · Shachong · Sênggezong · Danba · Xiaojin · Dawê · Hanmiu

Gonjo · Lha gyai · Chagan Sumdo · Youyi · Jaggongo · Donggu · Ran'an · Kongyuo · Qiaoqi · Baoxing

Baxoi · Meiyu · Qamdun · Gajê · Peca · Heping · Garwao · Pâmai · Haizi Shan 5820 · Zhonggu · Lingguan · Lushi

Nagjog · Tanggar · Gyizhong · Qangsumo · Samar · Qowo · Hongleng · Mt.Konggar · Kangding · Tianquan

Gyari · Sayol · Co'nga · Zangxoi · Sangdo · Litang · Yajiang · Wachai · Luding · Yingjing

Jidaro · Yugug · Rawu · Markam · Zogang · Batang · Chuwanang · 6204 Ga'nyên · Zhamla · Gyawa · Marlamco · Ranran Niuchang · Sade · Lugba · Xinmin · Hanyuan · Shimian

Bidaqiao · Goqên · Kyengmai · Qizhong · Yanngang · Zongza · Dingpur · Zhongdam · Sumdo · Nabo · Dêwo · Posarong · Tanggo · Caoyuanzi · Hongbao · Tianba

Xiangcheng · Daocheng · Jiulong · Sanyanlong · Tuowu · Ganluo

Zayu · Xia Zayu · Foshan · Derong · Bunde · Ringgo · Baisi · Tangyang · Naiqu · Sarye · 4791 Huatou Jian · Yuexi · Mianning

Walungo · 6740 Mdoing Xueshan · Dêqen · Gexoi · Siwa · Dongsib · Kalao · Jinping Shan 4193 · Zi'ero · Xide · Niuniuba

Bingzhongluo · Yanmen · Bamzerago · Gaica · Gaqag · Goyagtang · Wujiao · Kejer · Ruanxingou · Zhoujiaping · Luoha · Zhagjue

Nai Ga · Gongshan · Myixar · Xamgyi'nyilha · Muli · Baima · Xichang

Shingbwiyang · Putao · Tapu · Maji · Luguhu · Jmhe · Baiwu · Jatie · Butuo · Tuojue

Makaw · Lazo · Welatam · Judieng · Sanba · Culyu · Boda · Meiyu · Yanyuan · Nanbe · Dechang · Puge · Luoj

4579 Bilou Xueshan · Weixi · Fugong · 5396 Haba Xueshan · Yulong Xueshan 5596 · Taomaping · Ninglang · Hongbao · Puwei · Ningnan

4247 · Jianchuan · Yulong · Lijiang · Yongsheng · Huaping · Xiqu · Yanbian · Huili · Huidong

Xuebang Shan · Lanping · Heqing · Chenghai · Wenguan · Miyi · Huangbaio · Qiao

Chenggan · Eryuan · Songgui · Wanbi · Yongxing · Yongren · Panzhihua · Renhe Qu · Dong Qu · Lunan Shan 3078 · Jiangzhou · Luozuo · Yangjiaba · Tong'an · Luhe

Dabaicao Ling 3657 · Lihong · Yuza · Pulong · Dongchuan · Yongren

Altitude Table

0 100 300 500 750 1000 1500 2000 2500 3000 4000 5000 6000 7000m

Scale 1:3 500 000

Sichuan Province

With Chengdu as its capital, Sichuan Province, which is abbreviated as "Chuan" or "Shu", is located on the southwest of China, along the upper reaches of Chang Jiang (Yangtze River). It covers an area of over 480,000 square kilometers, and has a population of 85.29 million, including such ethnic groups as Han, Yi, Tibetan, Qiang, Miao, Hui, and Mongol.

■ Geographical Features

Topography With mountains like Min Shan, Qionglai Shan, Daxue Shan, Shaluli Shan, and Xiaoxiang Ling in the west and Sichuan basin in the east, Sichuan's terrain gradually descends from west to east. The altitude of mountainous area in this region is around 1,000~3,000m, while that of the basin is around 250~750m. Except Songpan Caodi(Grassland), a pasture in the north that belongs to Huang He (Yellow River) drainage area, the rest of the province are all in Chang Jiang drainage area. Rivers like Yalong Jiang, Min Jiang, Dadu He, Tuo Jiang, Jialing Jiang, Fu Jiang and Qu Jiang are all branches of Chang Jiang. There are over 1,000 lakes in Sichuan, including Qiong Hai and Lugu Hu.

Climate Sichuan covers both Eastern Monsoon Area and Qingzang Plateau, and therefore has diversified climate. Subtropical moist monsoon climate rules the eastern basin area, bringing about mild temperature and an annual rainfall of 800~1,200mm, together with an average annual temperature of 16~18℃. Temperate subtropical highland climate rules the west part of Sichuan, bringing colder temperature and strong sunshine to this area. A vertical change of climate occurs in mountainous areas, climate change from warm temperate to temperate, cold temperate and even to sub-frigid zone as altitude goes up. Average annual temperature in this area is between 6~12℃.

■ Natural Resources

Over 120 kinds of minerals have been found in Sichuan, a province holding the largest reserves of vanadium, titanium, ferrous sulfide, optic fluorite, gritstone, clay, and gangue quartz in China. The reserves of Glauber's salt, halite, asbestos, white isinglass, cadmium, iodine, beryllium, lithium, strontium and mercury found in Sichuan are all listed as China's top three.

Sichuan has rich water resources. Over 340 rivers have drainage area larger than 500 square kilometers. As most of its major rivers run through mountainous area, the province holds 1/5 of China's hydropower potentials.

Sichuan's forest cover rate is around 24%, making up for most part of southwest China's forest area. There are more than 10,000 species of plants grown here, including over 3,500 species of Chinese medicinal herbs, and over 1,100 species of vertebrate, among which over 50 are rare animals under national protection.

■ Agriculture

Throughout history, Sichuan has been an affluent area with well developed agriculture. It is one of China's major production bases of grain, oil and pig. Main grain crops are: rice, wheat, buckwheat, barley, broomcorn and potatoes, among which rice planting take up the largest part. Main economic crops are: rape, cotton, peanut, sesame, and sugarcane, the production of which all lead in China. Mountainous area in west Sichuan is the major pasturing and forest area. Pig, cow, sheep and horse are raised here, while the outputs of tung oil, raw lacquer, and insect wax in this area are the largest of China.

■ Industry

Sichuan has the most advanced and complete industrial system in west China. Major industries are: electronics, machinery, metallurgy, chemicals, energy, building material, forestry, textile, sugar-making, and food production. Sichuan plays an important role in China's metallurgy, chemicals, machinery, space navigation, and electronics industries, and the province is most well known for its production of steel and chemicals, as well as for space craft launching, and hydropower station.

■ Transportation

Railway Seven main stems including Baoji-Chengdu, Chengdu-Chongqing, Chengdu-Kunming, Chengdu-Dazhou, and Dazhou-Wanzhou railways run through Sichuan, and the newly built Baoji-Chengdu double-track railway can connect with China' major trunk line Lanzhou-Lianyungang railway.

Highway Centered round Chengdu and Nanchong, Sichuan's highway system extend in all directions, reaching every city and county within the province. Major highways are: Sichuan-Tibet, Sichuan-Qinghai, Sichuan-

Gansu, Sichuan-Shaanxi, and Sichuan-Chongqing. Express highways like Chengdu-Chongqing, Chengdu-Guang'an, Chengdu-Ya'an and Neijiang-Yibing have been put into use.

Airway Shuangliu Airport in Chengdu is one of China's four major air terminals. Over 140 flight courses connect Sichuan with many domestic and international cities.

Waterway Chang Jiang and its major branches in Sichuan provide the province with an extensive water navigation system. Major river ports are Yibin, Luzhou, Leshan, Hejiang and

Calcareous tufa streams of Huanglong

Nanchong.

■ Places of Interest

Tourism in Sichuan is quite well developed. Jiuzhaigou, Huanglong, Mt. Emei-Leshan Giant Buddha, Mt. Qingcheng–Dujiangyan are all included in the World Heritage List by UNESCO. The fantastic Jiuzaigou lies along Minjiang River. Emei Mountain is one of China's Four Sacred Buddhist Mountains. Huanglong is a 7,000m long, 300m wide calcified valley with spectacular scenery. Leshan Giant Buddha is 71 meters tall. It is the largest stone Buddha statue in the world.

Wolong Nature Reserve lies in Wenchuan County. It is the ideal home for pandas. Dujiangyan lies in Dujiangyan City. It is one of China's four major ancient irrigation works. Other culture relics in Sichuan include: Qingcheng Mountain, Gongga Mountain, Xiling Xueshan, Du Fu's Thatched Cottage, Libai's hometown and Temple of the Marquis of Wu.

■ Local Products

Sichuan is most well known for its production of bristle, tung oil, insect wax and raw lacquer. Liquor produced here enjoys high reputation. The province is also famous for its production of orange, longan, pear and apple. Spicy Sichuan cuisine is one of the eight most famous cuisines in China. Rice dumpling, wonton, spicy horsebean, preserved egg, salted duck and other local flavors are liked by many. Embroidery, silk, paper-cutting, lacquer ware, bamboo ware, fan and bamboo painting are traditional local handicrafts.

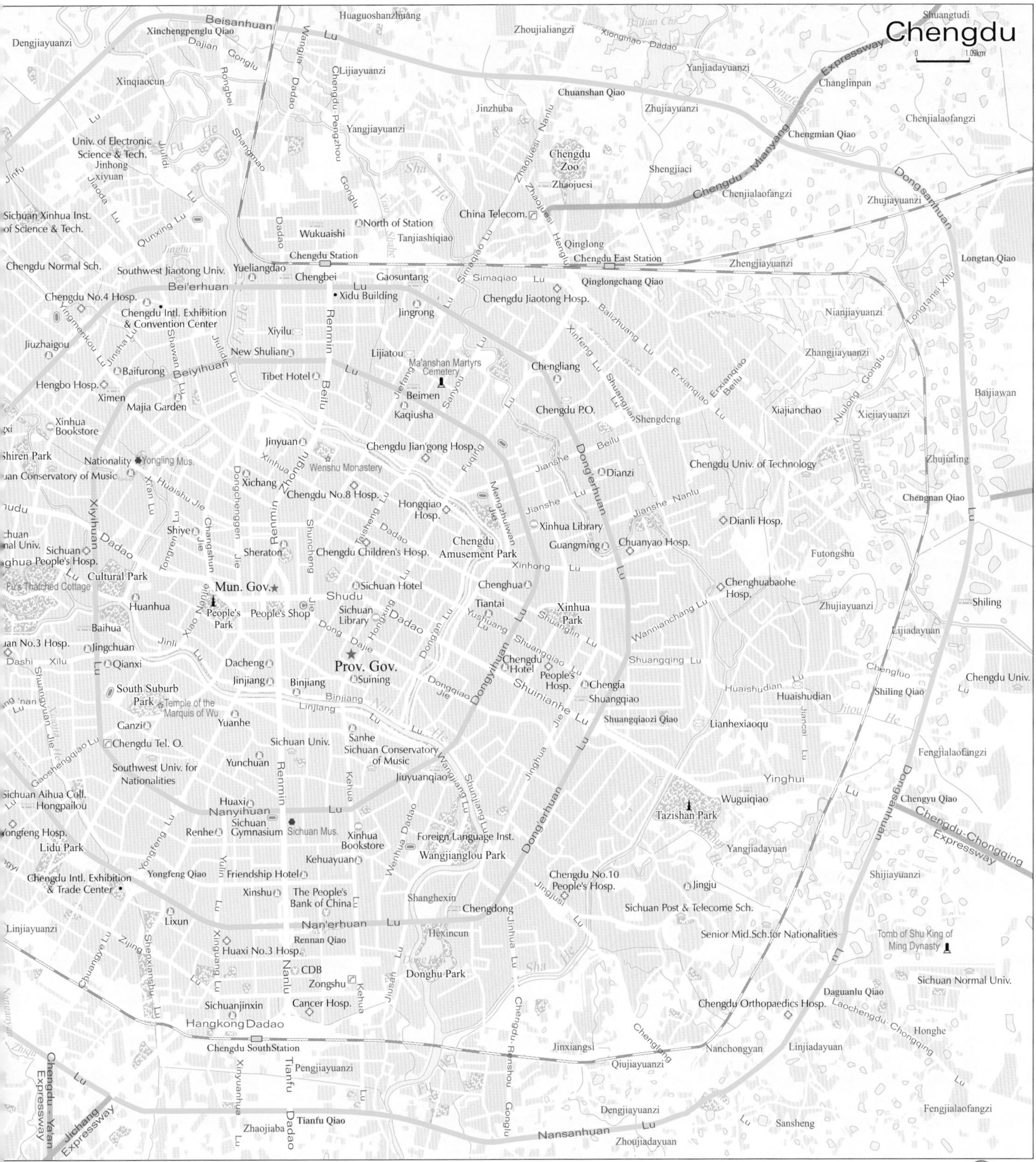

Chengdu

1.09km

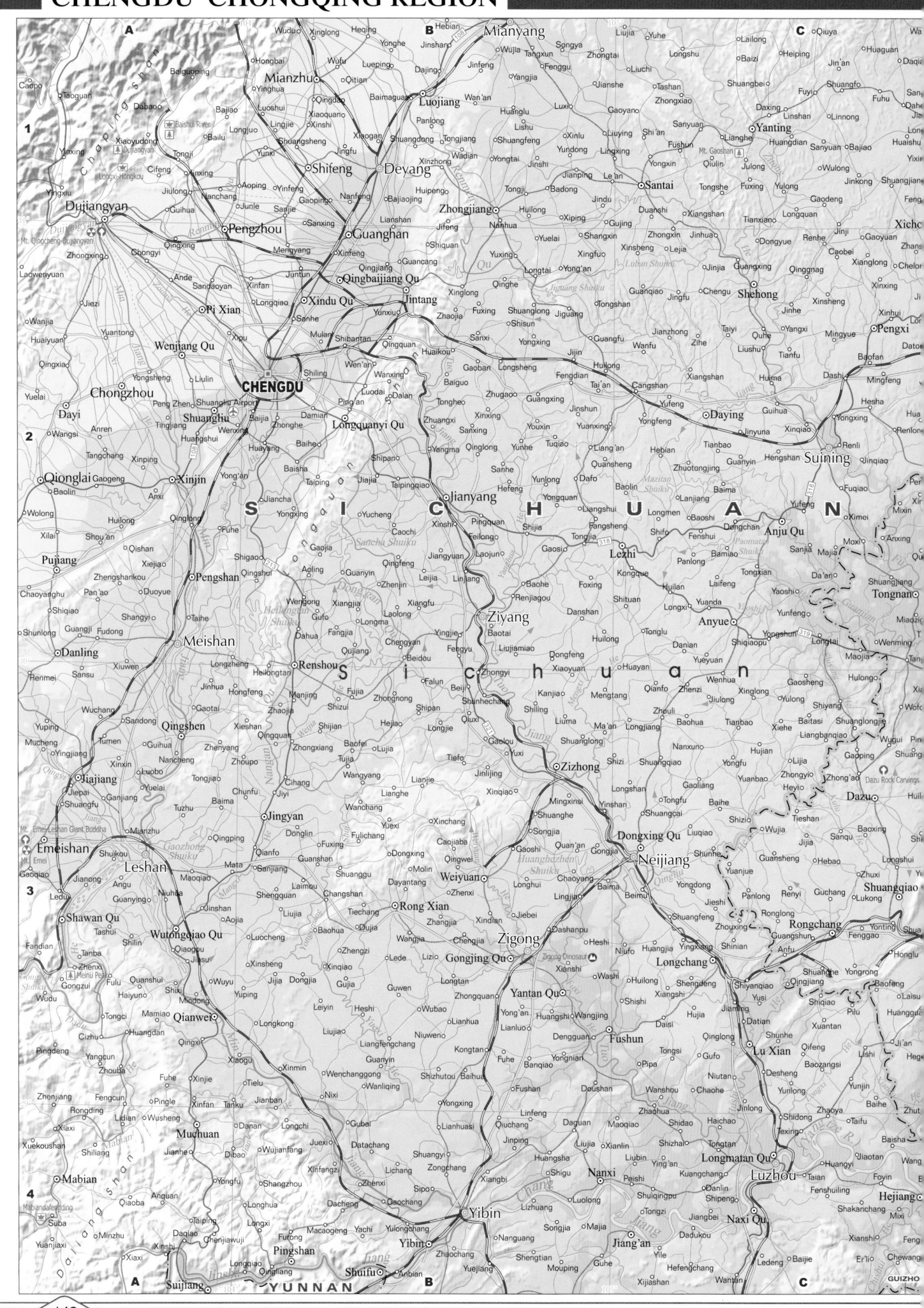

Altitude Table

0 100 300 500 750 1000 1500 2000 2500 3000 3500 m

Chengdu-Chongqing Region

Chengyu Area refers to the area around Chengdu and Chongqing. This is the most developed and most densely populated economic area of southwest China.

Chengyu Area is located at the bottom of Sichuan Pendi (Bsn.), and is divided in the middle by Longquan Shan. The east part is a hilly area, while the west part is the prolific Chengdu Pingyuan (Pln.), which covers over 6,000 square kilometers. Dujiangyan irrigation work was built here during the Warring States Period. Major rivers here are Chang Jiang (Yangtze R.) and its branch Jialing Jiang.

Subtropical humid monsoon climate rules the area, which brings an annual rainfall of above 1,000mm. The average temperature in January between 2~6℃, while in July above 24℃.

This area has been traditionally a farming area and a major production base of grain, cotton, meat, pod and orange. The irrigation area of Dujiangyan has now quadrupled. Rice, wheat, rape, peanut, cotton, hemp, sugar cane, tea and orange are mainly planted in the hilly terrace of Chuanzhong Qiuling (Hills). Areas along Tuo Jiang (R.) mainly produce sugar cane and mulberry. Tea, bamboo and orange produced in this region are largely sold to other provinces.

Chengyu Area is an important industrial base of southwest China. Abundant reserves of coal, iron, aluminium, Glauber's salt and limestone have been found here. Chongqing is both the economic center in the area along upper reaches of Chang Jiang and the largest commercial city of southwest China. Machinery, chemical industry, metallurgy, food production, textile, electronics, space technology, sugar making, salt production and silk production in this region are all well known. Chongqing and Chengdu are also the industrial bases of heavy loading trucks, large automatic instruments and electronics.

Chengyu Area is also the hinge of transportation in southwest China. Chengdu is the largest transportation hub of southwest China, railway system here are connected with every other part of China, while highway system here extends to all directions. Shuangliu Airport is one of China's four major air terminals which provide over 50 domestic flight courses and several international flight courses. Chongqing is the linking zone between the well developed east China and west China that has abundant resources. Not only do many main stems of railway and highway meet here, also it is the largest river port in this area and the only port in southwest China that have freights go directly to the sea. Jiangbei Airport provides flights to Beijing, Shanghai, Guangzhou and other major cities in China.

There are many scenic spots and cultural relics in Chengyu Area, among which Dazu Rock Carvings, Mt. Emei-Leshan Giant Buddha and Mt. Qingcheng -Dujiangyan are all listed in the World Heritage by UNESCO. Other than these, many national nature reserves together with homes and temples for China's most famous poets, Taoist sacred places as well as Buddhist sacred places can all be found in this area.

Scale 1:1 100 000
0 11 22 33 44 55km

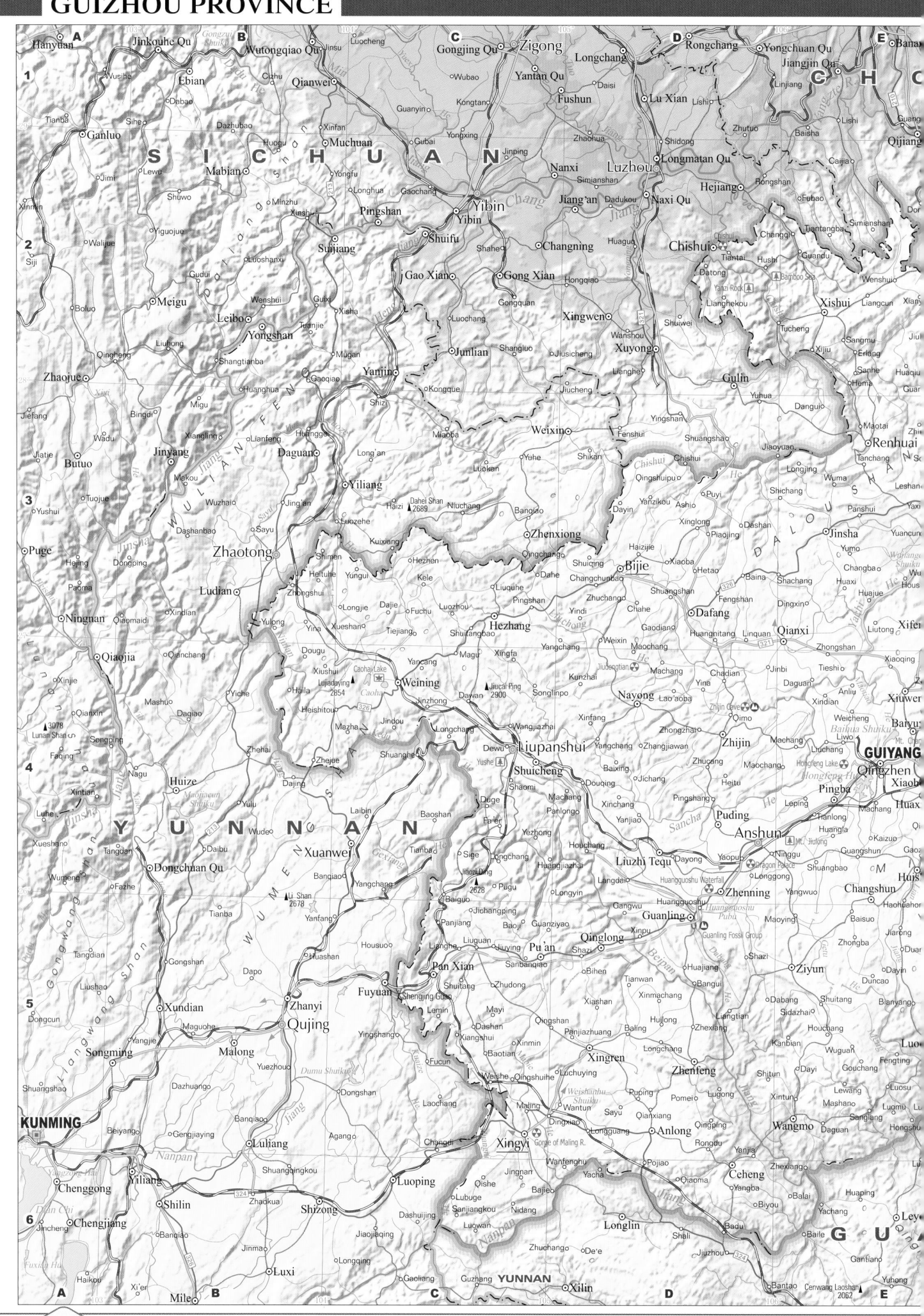

Altitude Table

0   100   300   500   750   1000   1500   2000   3000   4000   5000m

HUBEI

HUNAN

GUANGXI ZHUANG ZIZHIQU

Guizhou Province

With Guiyang as its capital, Guizhou Province, which is abbreviated as "Gui", is located on the east of Yungui Gaoyuan (Plt.), southwest of China. It covers an area of over 170,000 square kilometers, and has a population of 37.87 million, including such ethnic groups as Han, Miao, Buyei, Dong, Tujia, Yi, Li, Gelao, Sui, Bai, Hui, and Zhuang. Minority ethnic groups take up a large part of its population.

■ Geographical Features

Topography The average altitude of Guizhou is about 1,100m above sea level. With rugged Dalou Shan (Mt.) and Wumeng Shan to the west and Miao Ling (Mt.) in the middle, its terrain gradually descends from west to east, intersected only by basins like Guiyang, Anshun, Duyun and Kaili. 90% of its total area are covered by mountains and hills, of which 70% are karst topography, providing the area with one of the world most typical karst physiognomy. Major rivers in this province are Wu Jiang, Chishui He, Qingshui Jiang, Hongdu He, Nanpan Jiang, Beipan Jiang and Duliu Jiang, among which Wu Jiang is the largest. Of those few lakes in this province, Cao Hai is the largest.

Climate Subtropical highland humid monsoon climate rules the area, which blurs the seasonal difference, and brings to Guizhou plenty of rainfall. Annual rainfall in this region is between 1,100～1,400mm. The average annual temperature is between 10～20℃, with an average temperature in January between 3～6℃, while in July between 22～26℃.

■ Natural Resources

Rich reserves of a large variety of minerals have been found in Guizhou. By now over 110 kinds of minerals have been found, among which the reserves of minerals like coal, phosphor, mercury, antimony, manganese, bauxite, ferrous sulfide, barite, dolomite, gritstone, limestone, concrete and other building materials are bounteous, especially those of phosphor and barite, which are the largest in China. Places like Tongren, Kaiyang and Xiuwen are famous for their abundant reserves of mercury, phosphor and bauxite respectively.

Guizhou's forest cover rate is around 20.81%. Tung oil, raw lacquer, bamboo, wood for construction use and other forest products from this area are well-known.

There are more than 1,000 species of wild animals and over 3,800 species of plants living in this area, including over 600 species of cash plants and around 2,600 species of Chinese medicinal herbs, some of which are world famous.

■ Agriculture

Double cropping harvest system is applied in Guizhou, with rice, corn, wheat and potatoes as major grain crops, and tobaccos, rapes, ramees and beets as major industrial crops. Rice and rape are common crops found in basins and southeast area, while corn was planted in the northwest. Tobacco and tussah produced in this province is well-known throughout China. Cows, pigs, and sheep are also raised in this area, with bristle as a major export product.

■ Industry

Guizhou is the production base of energy, machinery, raw materials and defence industry (aviation, space technology and electronics) in Southwest China. Liupanshui is a chief coal producing area, while machinery industry is mainly developed around Guiyang, Zunyi, Anshun, and Duyun. Metallurgy, chemical fertilizer production and power stations are also developed here, with Wujiangdu Hydropower Station as the most famous one. The production of alcohol, tobacco, beverage, textiles and leather are important light industries in this region. Guizhou is the leader in the production of raw coal, aluminium ingot, cigarette and alcohol in China.

■ Transportation

Railway Five main stems including Guiyang–Liuzhou, Chongqing–Guiyang, Zhuzhou–Guiding, Guiyang–Kunming, and Nanning–Kunming railways run through Guizhou, and are joined by many other branch lines and leased lines.

Highway Centered round Guiyang, Zunyi and Anshun, and framed by national highways, Guizhou's highway system extends in all directions. Express highways connecting Guiyang with Huangguoshu, Zunyi and Duyun have all been put into use.

Airway Nonstop flight courses connect Guiyang with Beijing, Shanghai, Guangzhou and over 30 other cities in China.

■ Places of Interest

Guizhou is famous for its gorgeous karst caves and other spectacular natural sceneries as well as its rich cultural and revolutionary relics. Huangguoshu Waterfall, the biggest waterfall in China, is located between Zhenning and Guanling. Located to the southwest of Anshun is Dragon Palace, an extensive karst cave system with subterranean lakes; while another grandeur karst cave system— Zhijin Cave, which exhibit almost all forms of karst caves ever found in the world lies to the north of Anshun. Hongfeng Lake is the largest artificial lake in Guiyang. Wuyang River lies on the east of Guizhou. It is famous for gorgeous valleys along its shore. Mt. Fanjing National Nature Reserve holds a well preserved subtropical ecosystem, and is included in UNESCO's World Network of Biosphere Reserves. Other tourist attractions include some other national nature reserves and revolutionary sites, including the site for Zunyi Meeting.

■ Local Products

Moutai, the so called "national liquor" of China, is undoubtedly the most prominent local product. Except that, Dong Jiu, Duzhong, and Xishui are all well-known liquor brands. Guizhou is also famous for its tea. Local flavors such as ham, noodle, pickle vermicelli and other minority flavours are liked by many. Minority handicrafts like embroidery, lace, painting, musical instrument, lacquerwork, and inkstone all have their unique characteristics.

Huangguoshu Waterfall

Guiyang

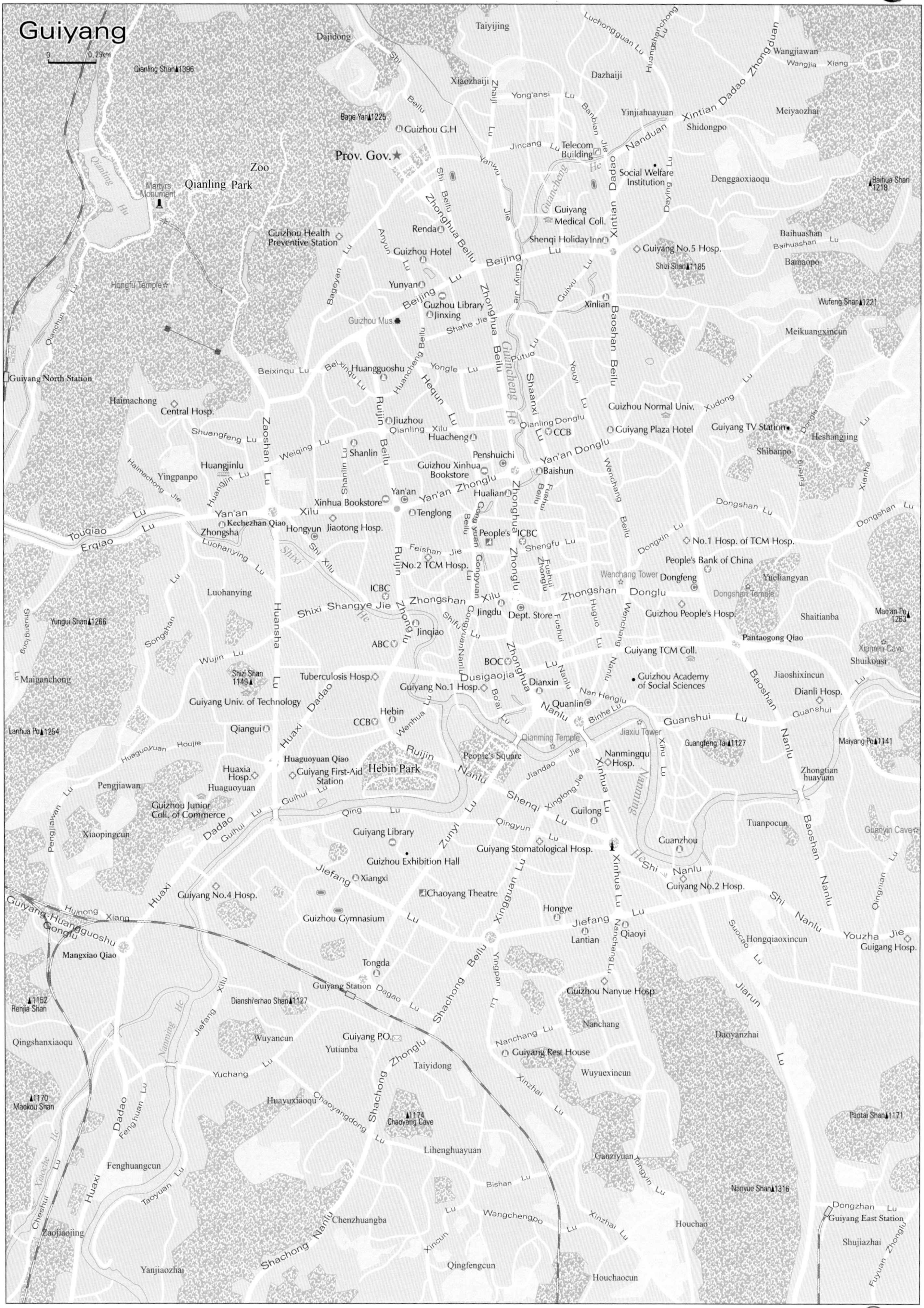

0   0.29km

Qianling Shan▲1396
Dajidong
Taiyijing
Luchongguan Lu
Huangnanzhong
Wangjiawan
Wangjia Xiang
Xiaozhaiji N
Dazhaiji
Zhongduan
Xintian Dadao
Meiyaozhai
Bage Yan▲1225
Yong'ansi Lu
Yinjiahuayuan
Shidongpo
Guizhou G.H
Jincang Lu
Telecom Building
Nanduan
Denggaoxiaoqu
Prov. Gov. ★
Baihua Shan▲1218
Zoo
Martyrs Monument
Qianling Park
Social Welfare Institution
Guiyang Medical Coll.
Guizhou Health Preventive Station
Renda
Guizhou Hotel
Shenqi Holiday Inn
Guiyang No.5 Hosp.
Baihuashan Lu
Baihuashan Lu
Hongfu Temple ☆
Yunyan
Beijing Lu
Shizi Shan▲1185
Bamaopo
Wufeng Shan▲1221
Guzhou Library
Jinxing
Xinlian
Meikuangxincun
Guizhou Mus.
Shahe Jie
Guiyang North Station
Huangguoshu Lu
Yongle
Youyi Lu
Guizhou Normal Univ.
Xudong
Haimachong
Central Hosp.
Beixinqu Lu
Jiuzhou
Qianling Xilu
Huacheng
Shaanxi
Qianling Donglu
CCB
Guiyang Plaza Hotel
Guiyang TV Station
Heshangjing
Shuangfeng Lu
Zaoshan
Shanlin
Penshuichi
Yan'an Donglu
Shibanpo
Huangjinlu
Huangjin Lu
Guizhou Xinhua Bookstore
Baishun
Dongshan Lu
Yingpanpo
Xilu
Yan'an
Xinhua Bookstore
Hualian
No.1 Hosp. of TCM Hosp.
Yan'an Zhonglu
Haimachong Jie
Tenglong
People's
ICBC
Shengfu Lu
Yan'an Zhongsha
Kechezhan Qiao
Hongyun Jiaotong Hosp.
Shi Xilu
Feishan Jie
No.2 TCM Hosp.
Wenchang Tower
Dongfeng
Yuchiangyan
Touqiao
Erqiao
Luohanying Lu
Ruijin
Zhongshan
Dongshan Temple
Maganpo▲1263
Shaitianba
Luohanying
Shixi Shangye Jie
Jingdu
Dept. Store
Guizhou People's Hosp.
Xigntien Cave
Shuikoushi
Yungui Shan▲1266
Songshan
ABC
Jinqiao
Jingdu
Guiyang TCM Coll.
Pantaogong Qiao
Jiaoshixincun
Dianli Hosp.
Maiganchong
Wujin Lu
Tuberculosis Hosp.
BOC
Dusigaojia
Dianxin
Guizhou Academy of Social Sciences
Guanshui Lu
Guanshui
Lanhua Po▲1254
Shizi Shan 1149▲
Guiyang Univ. of Technology
Hebin
CCB
Wenhua
Guiyang No.1 Hosp.
Nan Henglu
Nanlu
Quanlin
Binhe Lu
Jiaxiu Tower
Guangfeng Tai▲1127
Maiyang Po▲1141
Qiangui
Huaxi
Ruijin
Qianming Temple
Nanmingqu Hosp.
Zhongtian huayuan
Huaguoyuan Qiao
Huaxia Hosp.
Guiyang First-Aid Station
Hebin Park
People's Square
Nanlu
Guilong
Guanzhou
Tuanpocun
Guanyin Cave
Pengjiawan
Huaguoyuan
Guihui
Qing Lu
Shenqi
Xingde Jie
Jiandao
Xinhua Lu
Guizhou Junior Coll. of Commerce
Xiaopingcun
Dadao
Guihui
Guiyang Library
Guangzhou
Zunyi
Qingyun Lu
Guilong
Guiyang Stomatological Hosp.
Guiyang No.2 Hosp.
Shi Nanlu
Qingnian
Guizhou Exhibition Hall
Xiangxi
Jiefang Lu
Chaoyang Theatre
Hongye
Jiefang Lu
Lantian
Qiaoyi
Hongqiaoxincun
Youzha Jie
Guigang Hosp.
Guiyang-Huangguoshu Gonglu
Guiyang No.4 Hosp.
Huinong Xiang
Guizhou Gymnasium
Mangxiao Qiao
Tongda
Guizhou Nanyue Hosp.
▲1152 Renjia Shan
Dianshi'erhao Shan▲1127
Guiyang Station
Dagao Lu
Shachong Beilu
Yingpan
Nanchang Lu
Nanchang
Daoyanzhai
Qingshanxiaoqu
Jiefang Xilu
Wuyancun
Guiyang P.O.
Yutianba
Guiyang Rest House
Wuyuexincun
▲1170 Maokou Shan
Yuchang
Taiyidong
Xinzhai Lu
Huayuxiaoqu
Shachong Zhonglu
Paotai Shan▲1171
▲1174 Chaoyang Cave
Chaoyangdong
Lihenghuayuan
Fenghuangcun
Bishan
Nanyue Shan▲1316
Dongzhan Lu
Guiyang East Station
Zaojiaojing
Chenzhuangba
Wangchengpo
Houchao
Jiarun Lu
Fuyuan Zhonglu
Shujiazhai
Yanjiaozhai
Qingfengcun
Houchaocun

Altitude Table
50 20 0 100 300 500 750 1000 1500 2000 2500 3000 4000 5000 6000 7000 m

VIET NAM

LAOS

GUANGXI ZHUANGZU ZIZHIQU

GUIZHOU

Yungui Gaoyuan

CHONGQING SHI

KUNMING
GUIYANG
NANNING
HA NOI

Beibu Gulf

Scale 1:3 500 000

| 0 | 35 | 70 | 105 | 140 | 175 km |

Yunnan Province

With Kunming as its capital, Yunnan Province, which is abbreviated as "Dian" or "Yun", is located on the southwest of Yungui Gaoyuan (Plt.), Southwest of China. It covers an area of over 380,000 square kilometers, and has a population of 41.76 million, including such a great variety of ethnic groups as Han, Yi, Bai, Hani, Zhuang, Dai, Miao, Hui, Lisu, Lahu, Va, Naxi, Yao, Jingpo, Tibetan, Blang, Buyei, Achang, Pumi, Mongol, Nu and Jino. Yunnan is a typical multi-ethnic group province.

■ Geographical Features

Topography Mountains and hills take up 90% of Yunnan's total area. With Gaoligong Shan, Nu Shan and Yun Ling and many other mountains in the west and Wulian Feng, Wumeng Shan in the northeast, its terrain gradually descends from the northwest to the southeast. Rivers like Jinsha Jiang, Lancang Jiang, Yuan Jiang, and Nu Jiang all run to the Pacific Ocean or Indian Ocean. Lakes are everywhere to be found in Yunnan, with Dian Chi as the largest of the province and Er Hai as the largest in west Yunnan.

Climate Subtropical and tropical highland humid monsoon climate rules the area, which blurs the seasonal difference. Annual rainfall in this region is between 1,000mm～1,500mm. The average annual temperature in most part of the province is between 13～20℃, with an average temperature in January between 8～12℃, while in July between 18～24℃, though mountainous area is much colder.

■ Natural Resources

Over 150 kinds of minerals have been found in Yunnan, a province most famous for its rich reserves of non-ferrous metals. Yunnan holds the largest reserves of lead, zinc, and tin in China. The reserves of halite, kalium salt, Glauber's salt, ferrous sulfide, asbestos, mica, graphite, diatomite, gritstone, and basalt here are all ranked as China's top ten. Marbles found in Dali is particularly celebrated for its fine quality and unique patterns.

Rich hydropower is found in northwest Yunnan along rivers of Jinsha Jiang, Lancang Jiang, and Nu Jiang.

Yunnan's forest cover rate is around 33.64%, mostly pine trees, spruce, and firs. There are more than 2,860 species of wild animals, over 10,000 species of insects and over 18,000 species of plants living in this area, including over 2,000 species of Chinese medicinal herbs, over 360 species of spiceberries and over 2,000 species of ornamentals, making this province the most diversified biosphere in China.

■ Agriculture

Yunnan encourages an all-round development in farming, forestry, animal husbandry, sideline occupations and fishery. Grain crops like rice, corn, wheat, beans and potato are grown in southeast hills and basins, together with tobacco, sugar cane, tea, cotton and hemp. Yunnan is China's No. 1 tobacco producing province. Industrial crops like rubber, coffee, oil palm, cinchona, pepper, sisal, and citronella are planted in valleys and basins in the south together with banana, pear, nuts and other fruits. Animal husbandry plays an important role in northwest Yunnan, with cow, buffalo, yak and horse as the main livestock. Lijiang horse is a well-known strain.

■ Industry

The province is known as "land of non-ferrous metals", and is very famous in China for the production of copper, tin and lead. Heavy industries like machinery, metallurgy, steel, coal and power industry are developed in Yunnan, whose manufacturing of cigarettes, tea and sugar are well-known throughout China.

■ Transportation

Railway Five main stems including Chengdu-Kunming, Nanning-Kunming, Guiyang-Kunming, and Neijiang-Kunming railways connect Yunnan with domestic cities and neighbouring countries, and are joined by many provincial branch lines.

Highway Centered round Kunming and Dali, Yunnan's highway system extends in all directions. Express highways connecting Kunming with other major cities have been put into use.

Airway Flight courses not only connect Kunming with some major cities in Yunnan, but also link it with Beijing, Shanghai, Guangzhou, and over 60 other cities in China, as well as destinations in Thailand, Myanmar, Singapore, and Laos.

Waterway Freights can sail from Shuifu port to Shanghai port directly. Other major ports are Simao and Jinghong.

■ Places of Interest

As Yunnan holds the largest number of minority ethnic groups in China, the fascination of multiple cultures adds attraction to its legendary scenery. The tremendous Dianchi Lake lies to the southwest of Kunming, circled by four wonderful hills on four sides. The spectacular karst physiognomy, namely Stone Forest, is located in Shilin Yi Autonomous County, and its charm is enhanced by numerous beautiful legends. Xishuangbanna National Nature Reserve exhibits the enchanting beauty of tropical rainforest together with a rich array of wild animals and plants. The place is also enchanted by traditional ethnic culture. Old Town of Lijiang and Three Parallel Rivers

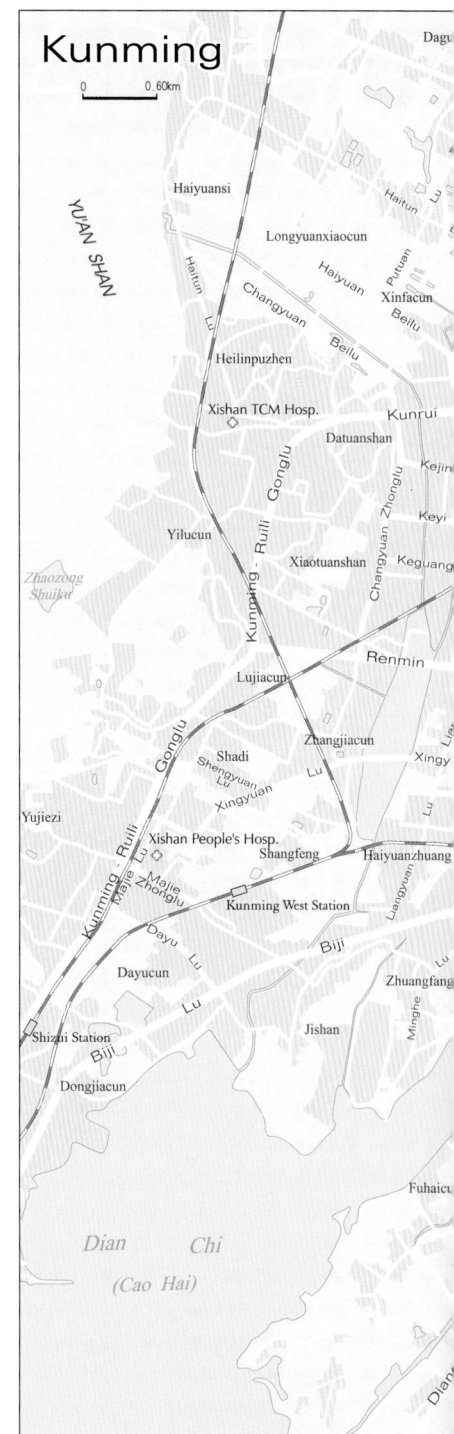

have been included in the World Heritage List by UNESCO. Tourist attractions like Tengchong, Ruili, Dali and Jianshui all enjoy world renown.

■ Local Products

Yunnan is most famous for producing quality cigarettes, teas, herbal medicines and flowers. Stone carving, bronze ware, carpet and silk are traditional local handicrafts. Tasty local flavor like ham, preserved beancurd, cakes and rice noodle are worth trying.

Heilong (Black Dragon) Pool of Lijiang

A B C D E

1

Piyalma Moyu
Hotan
Duwa Zawa
Lop Qira Damiku
Hotan Xanbabazaro Oytograk
Yutian Minfeng Rokiya
Andirlangar
Yawatongguzlangar Koramlik Togkuzdaban *Shan*
Aqqan
Oyyaylak

XINJIANG UYGUR ZIZHIQ

K U N L U N *Shan*
Qakar
Yeyik
Sicha Xuefeng 6748
Nur Aqqan
Muz Tag 6973
Kaxtexi Buya
Muz Tag 6638 *Kaxtexi shan*
K U N L U N *SHAN*

2
Kara-itagh
Qangri Muztag 6920
Usfun Tag
Tuanjie Feng 6644 Chalukou
Hechakou
Keriya Shankou
Rola
Rola Kangri 60
KARAKORUM SHAN
Hongshantou
Jasammari
6356 Tozê Kangri
Dongbol
Qangringngoinza
Kongka Shankou
Chaggar 6613
Deyu Co
Qoltên Co
Gyanang Co
Xueyuan Hu
Longwei Co
Linggo Co

Nêsu
Karnag *Qingzang*
6460 Zangsêr Kangri
Nagdê Kangri 6004
Bangkor
Bangong Lake
Lhariihaxing Domar
3
KASHMIR (Area actually controlled by India)
Rutog
Risum
Gogarngü
Mayêr Kangri 6266
Garco Shuan Zaqungnggom 6304
Lugu
Chagbo
Dêlê Rabang
6418 Tachagpu Shan
Xiangian Samen
Kongmo
Chamdong
Rongma
Sêrgyog 5540
Zhaxigang Gar Bibgya Garla Caka Oma Ombudangsang Qungcang Xugba
Gola Zesum 6112 Zoco Qangba Nyêr Co Gêrzê Qiangtang Ngoqu Chamma
Qusum Günsa Xungba Ramangzalê Xiede
Sumdeling Naggorgor Marlao Naggor Marmê Oidê Dongco Zhongcang 5289 Muggargoibo Urdoi Cozhelhoma Gab'aluma
Diyag Lugba Qarigzê Sogdoi Yagra Tiurio Kurqên Namoqê Xagzi Bugkamba Asog Nyima Sinya Yuzhrom
Tarejong Zanda Gyanabung Moincêr Lodo Ringtor Lungkugo Asog Ombu Goilung Dê'ngu Mayoin
Bulingo Daba 6656 Kangrinboqê Feng Ripor Rigar Tarunha Cêri Gyungcang L'adoi Chowa Xagoo Xai
Dongbo Kyunglung Baga Hor Kaigoin Lunggar Dagxung Coqên Domar Kanglung
4
Mapam Yumco Kunggyü Nyogzê Pungzhango Gêma Gyangrang Qulho Nyigo D'argo Ngangzê Shan Kyag Xiang Jaggang
Chamoli Nairona'nyi 7694 Parbugleo Gala Moqêndo Lungdingiê Goin'gyibug Oomai Qanoiapoia
Burang Horba Bobdoi Garqung Chaqung Caze Darog Mubagêqên Qêqung
Almora Paryang 7095 Loinbo Kangri Amjogxung Dagmoxar Qingtiio Nya
Naggu Zhuzhu Saincang Xungba Lugba Xeitapu Kangri 6310 Yagmo
H I M A L A Y A Zhongba Qêra Darog Nartang Dan
Paingi Yagra Ru'gyog Targyailing Qu'gO S H A N
5
Rampur Mahendranagar Xarba La Lhagang Saga Darqung Kyêrdo Sangsang Xaitongn
Jumla Changgo Kungtang Abqên Zhêba Xaru Qu'go Ngamring Zhaxigang Xiga
Tibrikot Gyirong Mainpu Suroo Xiqên Rasa Geding
Bareilly Chāmeo Gongpu Borong Nailung Domblangma Peak Tingri Gyaco Chāmeo Mabja Sai Xia Lalho
Budaun Shāhjahānpur Sallyana Pokhara Ganggar Xixabangma Feng 8027 Yarlêb Zhaxizomo Cōgo Zhig Kon Changlung
Nepālganj Nyalam Oowowuyan Feng Dingye Saro Oudêng Gamba
Nanpara Gyirong 8201 Domblangma Feng 8844.43 Makalu Shan 8463 Riwo Kyungo Qudêng
Sitāpur Butwal KATHMANDU
6
I N D I A Hetaudā Sindhulimādī Yado
Etāwah Gonda Nautanwa Gangtok
Lucknow Kālī Janakpur Dhankuta Kalimp
Kānpur Faizābād Gorakhpur Motihari Siligur
Rāe Bareli Azamgarh Muzaffarpur Darbhanga Kishanganj
BANGLA

A B C D E

Altitude Table

0 100 300 500 750 1000 1500 2000 2500 3000 4000 5000 6000 7000 m

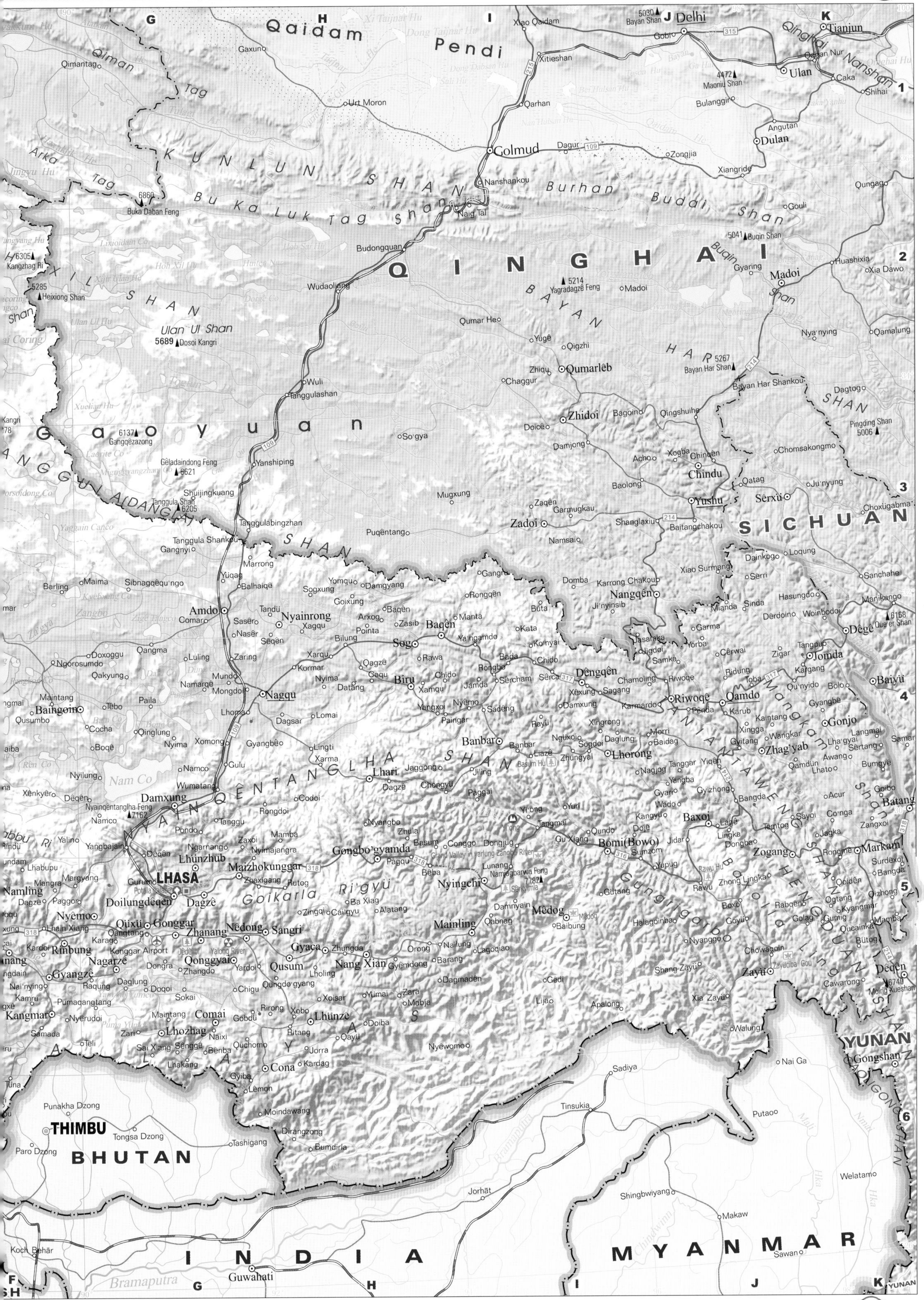

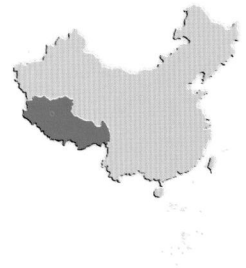

Xizang (Tibet) Autonomous Region

With Lhasa as its capital, Xizang (Tibet) Autonomous Region, which is abbreviated as "Zang", is located on the southwest part of Qingzang Gaoyuan (Plt.), along the southwest border of China. It covers an area of over 1.2 million square kilometers, and has a population of 2.59 million, including such ethnic groups as Tibetan, Han, Hui, Monba, Lhoba and Naxi, among which Tibetan take up 95% of the total population.

■ Geographical Features

Topography The average altitude of Xizang ranges from above 5,000 meters in the west to around 4,000 meters in the east, and is named "the roof of the world". On the south border are Himalayas and Gangdise Shan (Mt.), among which the Qomolangma Feng (Peak) on the Sino-Nepal border is 8844.43m in altitude, the highest peak in the world. Kunlun Shan, Hoh Xil Shan and Tanggula (Dangla) Shan are on the north border, while Hengduan Shan is on the southeast border. Highland lakes like Nam Co (L.), Siling Co and Zhari Nam Co are surrounded by these mountains, of which Nam Co is the second largest salt lake in China. Major rivers in this region are: Yarlung Zangbo Jiang, Nu Jiang, Lancang Jiang and Jinsha Jiang.

Climate Arid highland climate here are characterized by sharp vertical change in temperature. Such climates as tropical, subtropical, temperate highland, sub-frigid highland, frigid highland are found from southeast to northwest as altitude goes up. In general, long hours of sunshine here are balanced by low temperature, sparse rainfall, low oxygen and low air pressure, causing sharp change in daily temperature. Annual rainfall in this region is between 50∼500mm. The average annual temperature in January here is between-4∼-10℃, while in July around 15℃. On the north highland, there is a half-year frozen period.

■ Natural Resources

The reserves of borax, copper, lithium, arsenic, magnesite, barite, white isinglass, and turf are ranked as China's top five. Other major minerals are: salt, natural alkali, Glauber's salt, manganese, chrome, sulfur, diatomite, Iceland spar and corundum.

As one of the major primitive forest zones in China, Xizang's forest covers a total area of 4.09 million hectares, mostly pine trees, firs, and cypress. Exuberate grass make this region one of China's major pastures. There are 3,000 species of animals and over 5,000 species of higher plants live in this region, of which over 1,000 are natural medicinal herbs and over 400 are medicinal herbs in common use.

As the annual sunshine time here is between 3,100∼3,400 hours, Xizang has rich heat energy resources. Geothermal reserves here are the largest of its kind in China. Over 600 geothermal sites have been found, among which the renowned Yangbajing Geothermal Power Station generates a heat energy capacity equal to that generated with 4.7 million tons of standard coal.

■ Agriculture

Animal husbandry plays an important role in Xizang's economy. As one of China's major pastures, Xizang raises diversified stocks such as yak, pien niu, sheep, goat, pig, horse, donkey and mule. Yak hair and cashmere produced in this region are popular in the world market. Major crops farmed here are: highland barley, pea, wheat, buckwheat, rape, beet, benne, tea and some subtropical fruits. The southeast part of Xizang is a major natural forest area producing medicinal herbs like caladium and snow lotus.

■ Industry

Supported by its rich reserves of solar energy, geothermal energy and minerals, Xizang's industries mainly consist of power generating, mining, pharmacy, wool weaving, paper making and diary food production. Factories have been built for auto repairing and the production of carpet, building materials, chemicals, farm tools, and foods. Borax produced here plays an important role in China.

■ Transportation

Highway and airway are main traffics here. Xining-Lhasa railway has now reached Lhasa.

Highway Centered round Lhasa, Xigazê, Qamdo, and Nagqu, highways like Qinghai-Xizang, Sichuan-Xizang, Yunnan-Xizang, and Xinjiang-Xizang formed a diamond shaped highway network in this region.

Airway Lhasa has flights to Chengdu, Beijing, Shanghai and most other major cities in China as well as to Kathmandu in Nepal.

■ Places of Interest

Xizang holds great attraction for scholars, tourists and explorers from China and abroad for its majestic and grand scenery, and mysterious religious culture. Potala Palace, the greatest monumental structure in the whole region, is located on the Red Hill of Lhasa. This grand structure exhibits both Han and Tibetan architectural styles and functions as a palace, a temple and the destination of religious pilgrims. Jokhang Temple in the center of Lhasa is the spiritual center of Xizang. The statue of Jowo Sakyamuni worshiped in this temple was brought by Princess Wencheng from Chang'an in Tang Dynasty. Barkhor Street around this temple is considered as the "Sacred Road" by the Tibetans. Norbulingka in Tibetan means "precious park". Located on the west suburb of Lhasa, it had been the summer palace of past Dalai Lamas. All these sites have been included in the World Heritage List by

UNESCO. Tashilumpo Monastery to the west of Xigazê is the largest temple there and one of the six largest monasteries for the Ge-lug-pa Sect of Lamaism in China. The spectacular "U" shaped Yarlung Zangbo Valley is on the southeast part of Yarlung Zangbo Jiang. Qomolangma Feng, the highest peak in the world, is located on the Sino-Nepal border. It has always been the dream of every mountain climber to conquer this snow covered peak.

■ **Local Products**

Rare medicinal materials like angelica, glossy ganoderma, aweto, caladium, saffron, ginseng, and some animal parts for medical use are traditional local products. Ghee tea, Kase, highland barley cake, and highland barley liquor are unique Tibetan flavours. Carpets, boots, clothes, aprons in Tibetan style are popular local handicrafts. Potteries, gold, silver and copper wares, and wooden bowls are traditional local handicrafts.

Potala Palace

NEI MONGOL (INNER MONGOLIA) ZIZHIQU

NINGXIA HUIZU ZIZHIQU

SHAN XI

YAN'AN

HUANG

Mu Us Shadi

Ordos

YINCHUAN

Yan'an

Yulin

Suide

Tengger Shamo

Helan Shan

Hengshan

Altitude Table

0   100   300   500   750   1000   1500   2000   2500   3000 Km

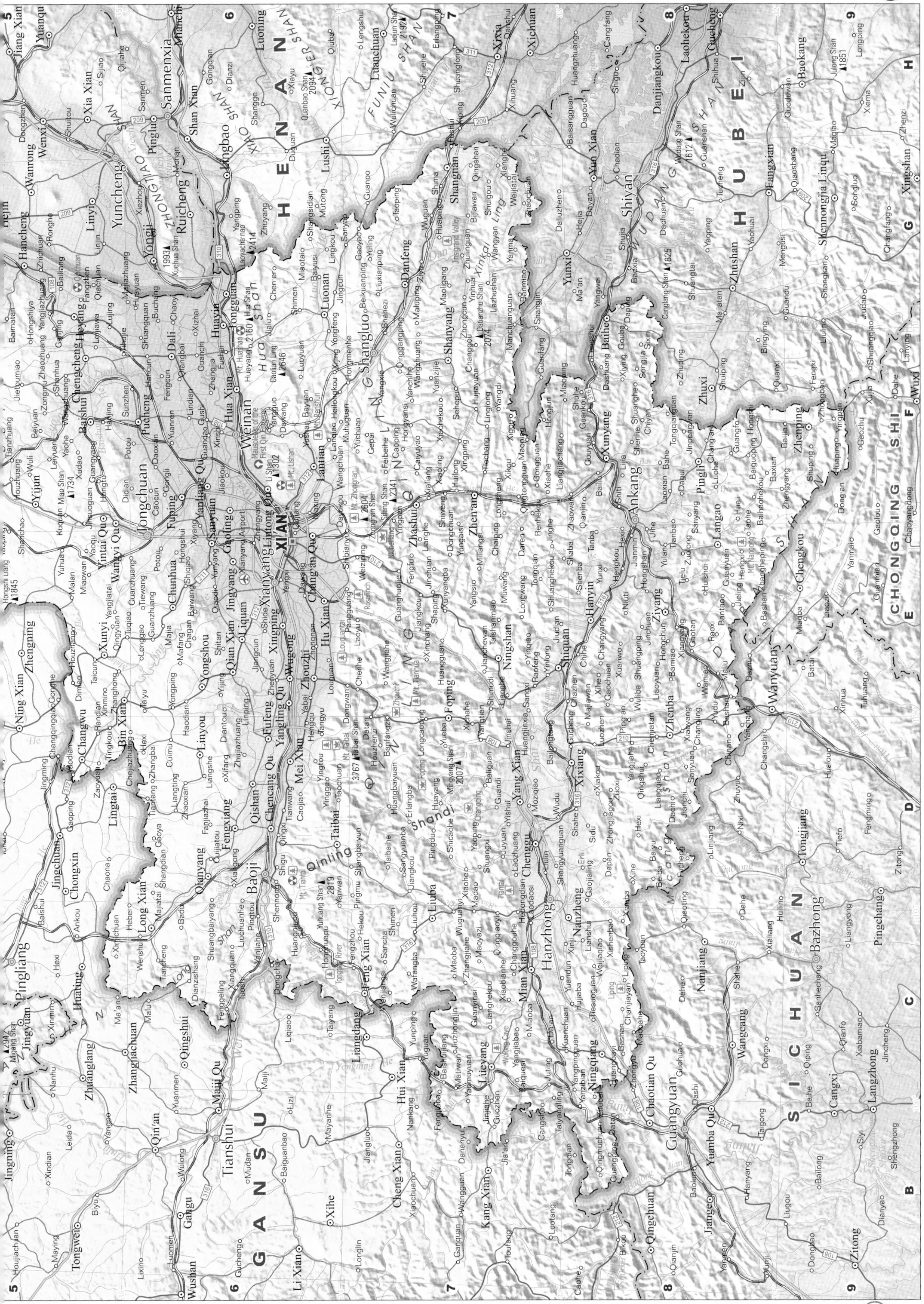

Shaanxi Province

With Xi'an as its capital, Shaanxi Province, which is abbreviated as "Shaan" or "Qin", is located along the middle reaches of Huang He (Yellow River), with Huangtu Gaoyuan (Plt.) on the north. It covers an area of over 190, 000 square kilometers, and has a population of 36.42 million, including such ethnic groups as Han, Hui, Man, Mongol, and Tibetan.

■ Geographical Features

Topography With Huangtu Gaoyuan on the north and Qin Ling (Mts.), Daba Shan (Mt.) on the south, Shaanxi's terrain descends from both sides to the middle where the fertile alluvial plain of Guanzhong Pingyuan lies. Hills, highlands and valleys are everywhere in the north, while basins can be found in the south mountainous area. Qin Ling is the dividing line between north and south in climate and the watershed between Chang Jiang (Yangtze River) and Huang He (Yellow River). Rivers north of Qin Ling are branches of Huang He, including Wei He (the largest branch of Huang He), Jing He, Luo He and Wuding He; while rivers south of Qin Ling are branches of Chang Jiang, including Han Shui (the largest branch of Chang Jiang), Dan Jiang and Jialing Jiang.

Climate Located on the transition zone between the humid southeast and the arid northwest, Shaanxi's climate changes from temperate semi-arid monsoon climate in the north to warm temperate semi-arid and semi-humid monsoon climate in the middle till subtropical humid monsoon climate in the south. North part of the province has distinctive seasonal difference with dry winters and rainy summers, while the south part has plenty of rainfall. Annual rainfall in this area is between 500~1000mm. The average annual temperature is between 9~16℃, with an average temperature in January between -11~3.5℃ in the north, while in July between 21~28℃.

■ Natural Resources

By now over 130 kinds of minerals were found in Shaanxi, among which the reserves of minerals like coal, iron, manganese, copper, mercury, molybdenum, strontium, rhenium, natural gas, limestone, cement stone and dozens of others are among China's top three. As an important energy base in China, Shaanxi has supreme-sized power coal fields and natural gas fields up to international standard.

With 1,450 reservoirs and nearly 30 hydropower stations, Shaanxi's water resources are comparatively rich.

Shaanxi's forest cover rate is around 28.74%, mostly firs, pine trees, cypress, birch, poplars and paulownia. There are more than 750 species of wild animals and over 3,300 species of plants living in this area, including nearly 30 species of rare animals.

■ Agriculture

Shaanxi is a traditional agricultural region. Most of its farm lands are dry land. Crops harvest once a year in north Shaanxi, where millet, glutinous millet, corn, potato, benne, tobacco and beet are planted. Triple harvests in two years are practiced in Guanzhong Pingyuan, a well known production area of wheat and cotton. South part of Shaanxi carries out double harvest system. Rice, orange, palm and corn are grown here, and the area ranks first in raw lacquer output in China. Sheep, goat, cow, donkey, pig and horse are raised in the province. It not only raises more milk goats than any other provinces in China, but also produces first class strains of cow and donkey.

■ Industry

As a well developed province in west China, Shaanxi's industries mainly consist of machinery, textile, energy, electronics, space technology, chemicals, pharmacy and food production, of which machinery and textile are of primary importance. Shenfu, Tongchuan and Hancheng are well known coal fields. As a major production base of machinery and electronics, Shaanxi produces some very competitive industrial products, including: aeroplanes, high voltage electricity transmission and transformation equipments, engineering machinery, new materials, family gadgets, computer, communication instruments, medicines and chemicals.

■ Transportation

Railway The main stem Lanzhou-Lianyungang railway runs through Shaanxi from west to east, and is joined by Baoji-Chengdu, Yangpingguan-Ankang, Xiangfan-Chongqing, Houma-Xi'an and Xi'an-Yan'an railways from north or south. Short distance conveyance railways include: Xi'an-Ankang, Meijiaping-Qianhezhen and Xi'an-Huxian.

Highway Centered round Xi'an, nearly 10 national highways and over 50 provincial highways, together with express highways like Xi'an-Baoji and Xi'an-Tongchuan, connect every city and county in the area.

Airway Xianyang International Airport is an important hub of air transportation in West China. Flight courses here can reach Beijing, Shanghai, Guangzhou and over 50 other major cities in China as well as international destinations in Japan and R.O. Korea.

■ Places of Interest

With its long history, Shaanxi holds numerous historical and cultural relics. Mt. Huashan is located to the southwest of Huayin County. As one of the Five Sacred Mountains in China, Mt. Huashan, a legendary place known for its spectacular steepness, is esteemed as Xi Yue (West Mountain). Mt. Lishan and Huaqing Hot Spring are to the east of Xi'an. Huaqing Hot Spring has been an imperial resort for several dynasties, while Mt. Lishan is where "Xi'an Incident" took place. Mausoleum of the First Qin Emperor, which is included in the World

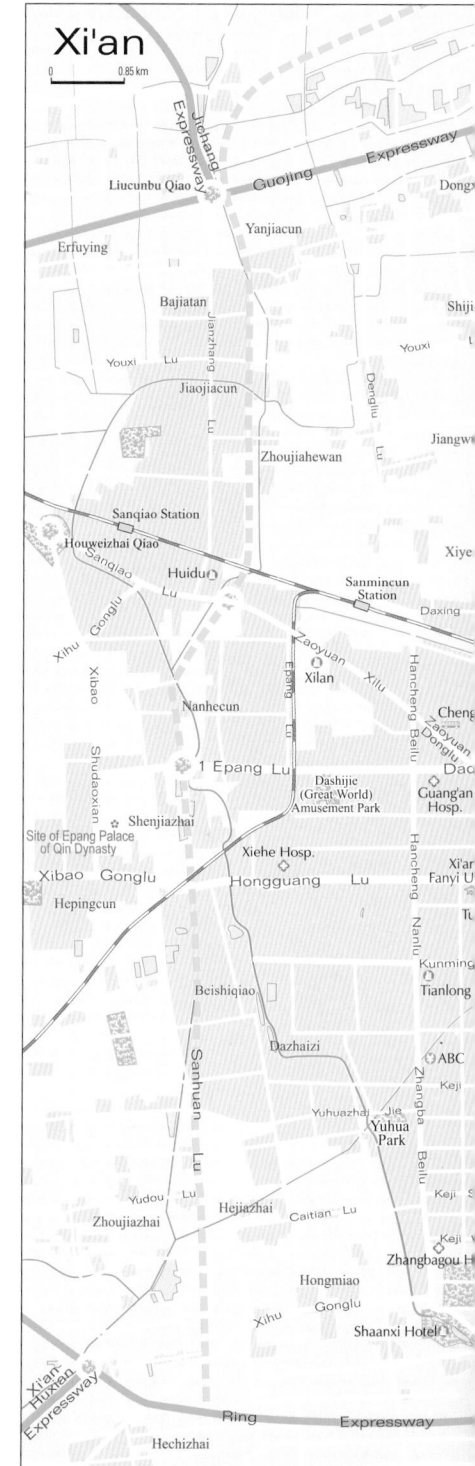

Heritage List by UNESCO, is close to these two sites. The grand terracotta army in neat formation excavated here was built around 300 B.C. Forest of Stone Steles is now part of Shaanxi Museum. It is a treasury of Chinese calligraphy. Banpo Museum on the east suburb of Xi'an kept the remains of primitive matriarchal villages built 6,000 years ago. Dayan Pagoda and Xiaoyan Pagoda are on south Xi'an. They are excellent models of brick pagoda constructed in Tang Dynasty. Other tourist attractions include: remains of imperial palaces and tombs from Qin, Han and Tang dynasties as well as some relics of Chinese revolution.

■ Local Products

Jade carving, clay sculpture, fake Tang tri-color, embroidery, pyrographed chopsticks, green porcelain bowl, and shadow play figure are traditional local handicrafts. Pomegranate, persimmon, walnut, chestnut, and kiwi fruit are renowned local fruits. Local flavors like rice wine, dried hot pepper, braised mutton with pancake are liked by many. Liquor brewed in Fengxiang County enjoys high renown traditionally.

Pits of Terracotta Warriors and Horses

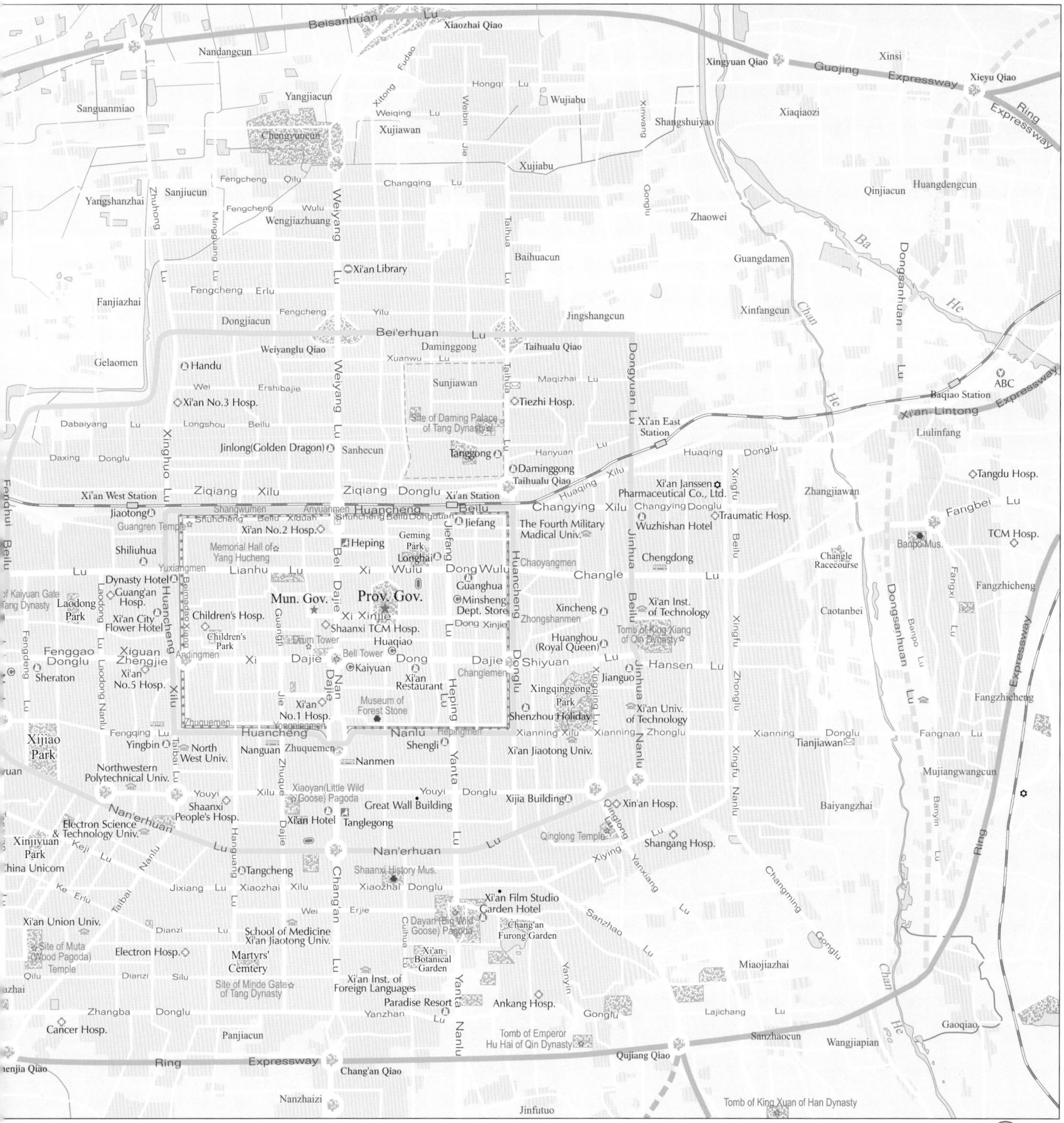

A B C D E

XINJIANG UYGUR ZIZHIQU

MONGOLIA

Wupu
Hami ○ Taojiagong
○ Daquanwan ○ Qincheng
○ Naphu
○ Luotuoquanzi
○ Yandun
○ Koshui

Sanzuohulishan ○
Argaltin Sair ○ Hulqut ○

Ejin Qi ○
○ Jargalang
Saihan Toroi ○
○ Bayan Bogd
Hol Barun Sum ○

○ Wytongdaquan
○ Mingshui

Yamansuo ○

Xingxingxia ○

Jinwozi ○
Malianjing Daoban ○

Dongfengquan ○
○ Hongshishan

Shibanjing ○
Mazongshan ○
Luanshanzi ○
Mazong Shan 2583 ▲

Lujing ○

Bor Ul Shan

○ Jongstin But

Tiancango ○
Dingxin ○
○ Dazhuangzi

Badai

Bai Shan ▲ 2017

BEI SHAN

Shibandun ○
Yin'aoxia ○

Beishan Meikuang ○ Liangjianfang ○

Mazongshan ○

Xihu ○
Guazhou ○ Nancha ○
Bulongji ○ Qiaowan
○ Huangzhawan

Huahai ○
Xiaojinwan ○

Xiba ○
Heli ○
○ Qagan Tolgoi

512

Yumen ○
Qiaozi ○
Tashi ○
Changmadaba ○
Chijin ○
Qingyuan ○
Jiayuguan ○ Huaimao ○
Jiuquan ○
Huangnibao Yanchi ○ Luocheng ○
Jinta ○

Dunhuang ○
Mogao ○ Mogao Caves
Dunhuang Xihu L. ○
Mingsha Shan
Nanhu ○ 1758 ▲ Heishi Feng
Shazaoyuan ○

Dongbatu ○
Yingzui Shan

Changma ○
Yaomo Shan

Laojunmiao ○
4587 ▲ Yu'ermeng

Jingtie Shan 5206 ▲
Xidong ○
Shangba ○
Xiaheqing ○
Qilian Shan 5647 ▲

Gaotai ○ Pingchuan ○
Minghai ○ Heiquan ○
Banqiao ○ Longs

Linze ○ Dongda Shan 3816
Wujiang ○

Zhangy

Changmadaba ○
Shan

Yingzui Shan 3426

Yema Shan

Daxue Shan 5483

Shibaocheng ○
Dagongcha ○

QILIAN

Sanchakou ○
Oiqingo ○

Jinfosi ○
Hongyazi ○
Qilian ○
Tunsheng ○
Luotuo ○

Hei Shan 3204 ▲

Baiyin ○
Huazhai ○

Sunano ○
Heping ○
Xishui ○

Dadun

Wutonggou ○
Minzhu ○
Aksay ○
Subei ○

Hongliuxia ○

Yanchiwan ○

TULAI

Tuolai Nanshan 5148 ▲

Sur ○

NANSHAN

Tulai Muchang ○
Bianmagou ○

Xiaosalong ○
Balguanmen Hongshiwo ○
Yangge ○

Yeniugou ○

QILIA

Qilian ○

Heping ○
Altun Shan 5798 ▲ Shan

DANGHE

Dushanzi ○

NANSHAN

SHULE NANSHAN

TULAI

DATONG SHAN

Muri ○
Alizha ○

Tannanba

Sandaoban ○

Yema
Nanshan

Tuanjie ○
Jianshe ○

Huiten Golo ○

5808 ▲
Kangze gya

Longmen ○

Sidaoban ○
Dingzikou ○

Huahaizi ○
Hongyazi ○

Haizeletuobie ○

Zhugkyung ○

Shuiyazidun ○

Serteng Shan

Taijun

Daba

Shan

Yiligou ○

Qaidam

Chalengkou ○

Luliang Shan 4110 ▲
Yuke Qaidam
Da Qaidam ○

Shan

Jun Ul

Bayan Shan 5030 ▲
Shan

Karmar ○
Tianjun ○ Jianghe ○
Gangc

315

QINGHAI

Yiliping ○

pendi

Xiao Qaidamo ○
Xitie Shan 4037 ▲
Xitieshan

Delhi ○
Hoit Taria ○
Suj ○

Tianpeng ○
Nur ○
Opga ○
Ulan ○

Jirmeng ○
Haixin Shan 3266 ▲

NANS

Jiang

Gando ○

Taijun He

Tart ○

4472 ▲
Maomu Shan

Qagan ○
Caka ○
Xiangpi Shan 4451 ▲

Heimahe ○

Tie

Urt Moron ○

Da Juh ○

Xarag ○

109

Parxixingka Nongchang ○
Qoijie ○

Golmud ○
Darhan ○

Dagur ○

Nomhon ○

Dulan ○
Reshui ○

Daheba ○

Golmud ○

109

Jun ○

Xinghai ○

Nanshankou ○

QINGHAI

Xiangride ○ Xang ○

Ngola Shan

Nali Tal ○

BURHAN BUDAI SHAN

Gouli ○

KUNLUN

Kunlun Shankou ○
Budongquan ○

Har Axrag ○

Buqing Shan 5041 ▲
Buqing Shan

Zuimatan ○
Jirmainna ○

Wenquan ○

SHAN

Yagradagze Feng 5214 ▲

Huashixia ○

Xia Dawo ○

A N E

Hol Sir Hu ○

Gyaring ○

Madoi ○

6282 ▲
maden Kangri

Wudaoliang ○

Madoi ○

Heiho ○

Qumur ○

Fenghuo Shankou ○

BAYAN HAR SHAN

Nya'nying ○ Changmahe ○

Yigxung ○

Qumarhe ○

Yuge ○

Bayan Har Shan 5267 ▲
Bayan Har Shankou ○

Chalaxung ○

G

Tangxung

Wuli ○

Chaggur ○
Oelungbo ○

Milagabmo ○

BAYAN

Dagtogo ○

Tanggulashanp

Qumarleb ○

Bagoin ○
Qingshuihe ○

Sangruma ○

HAR

Darl

SICHUAN

Pingding Shan 5006 ▲

Zhidoi ○

A B C D

Altitude Table

0 100 300 500 750 1000 1500 2000 2500 3000 4000 5000 6000 m

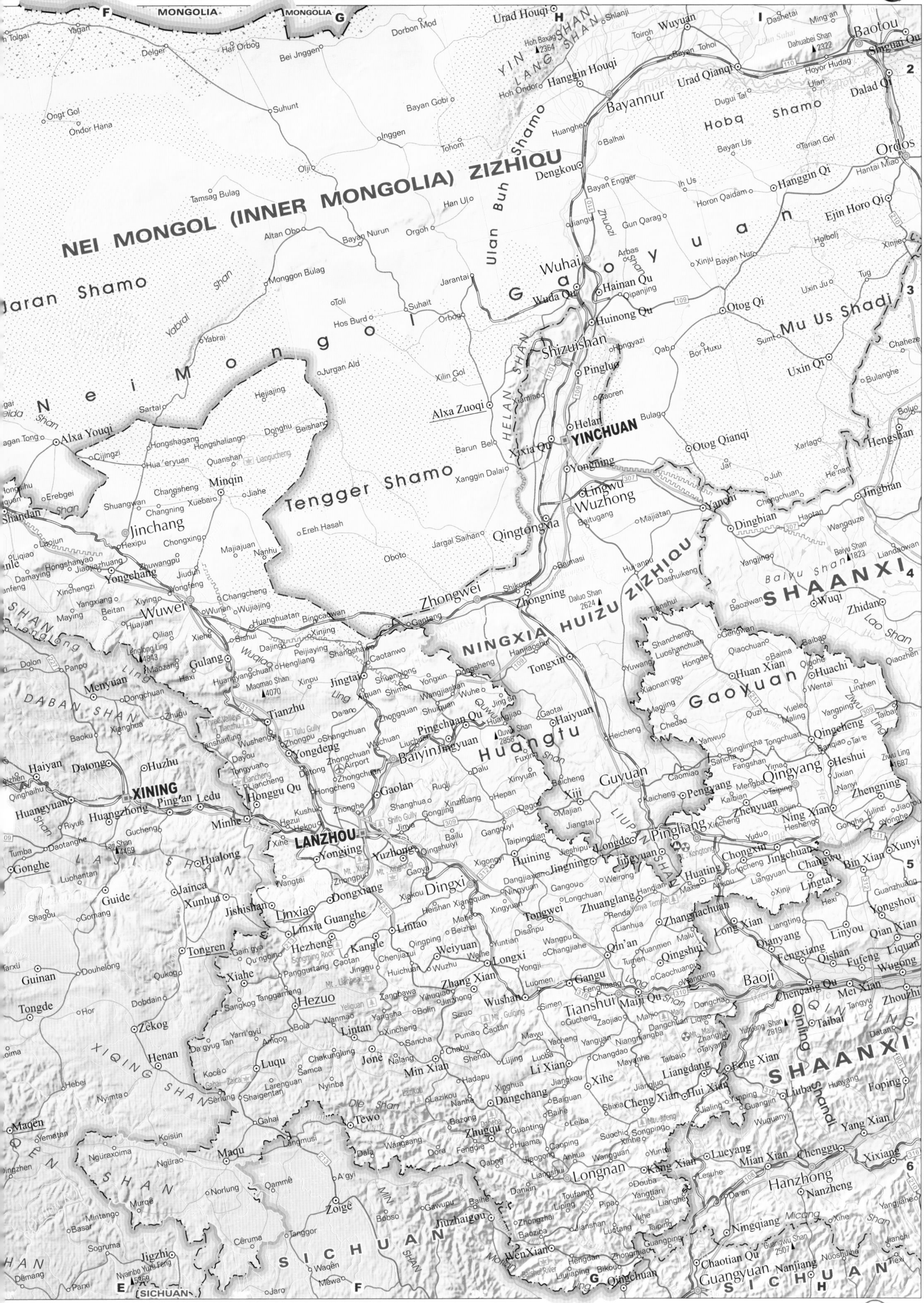

NEI MONGOL (INNER MONGOLIA) ZIZHIQU

Scale 1:4 000 000

0   40   80   120   160   200 km

Gansu Province

With Lanzhou as its capital, Gansu Province, which is abbreviated as "Gan" or "Long", is located in northwest China, along the upper reaches of Huang He (Yellow River). It covers an area of over 390,000 square kilometers, and has a population of 25.81 million, including such ethnic groups as Han, Hui, Dongxiang, Tibetan, Tu, Man, Mongol, Bonan, Yugur, Salar, and Kazak.

■ Geographical Features

Topography Mountains and highlands take up most part of Gansu, and give it an average altitude of above 1,000 meters. Most of the middle and east part of it is of special loess topography. Gobi desert can be found west to Zhangye. West to Wuqiao Ling (Mts.), and between Qilian Shan (Mt.) and Beida Shan is the well known Hexi (or Gansu) Corridor where green land and Gobi Desert intermittently spread. It was the route of ancient "Silk Road". The south mountainous area is the continuation of Qin Ling. Dang He, Shule He, Hei He and Shiyang He are major rivers in the inner flowing area, while Xihan Shui, Bailong Jiang (both branches of Chang Jiang), Huang He and its branches like Tao He, Huang Shui and Jing He are major rivers in outer flowing area. Oases are found along the middle reaches of inner flow rivers.

Climate Typical temperate continental climate rules the area, bringing about frequent storms and sharp change in temperature in summer, while winter here is dry and cold. Annual rainfall in this region is between 30～800mm. The average annual temperature here is between -1～14℃, with an average temperature in January between -14～3℃, while in July between 11～27℃.

■ Natural Resources

By now over 170 kinds of minerals have been found in Gansu, among which the reserves of minerals like nickel, cobalt, platinium, construction clay, and serpentine are ranked as China's No. 1. The province also has rich resources of coal, oil shale, turf and oil.

Gansu's forest acreage is around 4.83%, much lower than the average forest cover rate in China, though the proportion of shelter forest is higher than the national average. Trees here are mostly firs, pine trees, paulownia, poplar, narrow-leaved oleaster, purple willow and economic trees like walnut, orange, Chinese dates, sumach and tung trees. There are more than 650 species of wild animals and over 1,200 species of wildings living in this area, of which 950 are medicinal herbs. As the annual sunshine time here is between 2,900～3,300 hours, Gansu has rich solar energy resources, and solar cooker is more popular here than in most other places in China.

■ Agriculture

Grain farming is the major agriculture developed in Gansu, with wheat, corn, millet, broomcorn, highland barley and potato as its major crops. Oil plant, beet, cotton, medicinal herbs, hemp, tobacco, vegetables and fruits are also grown in this region. Oases along Hexi Corridor are the major production base of commodity grain. Cotton is grown in Anxi; highland barley and potato are planted in southwest part; while broomcorn and millet are grown in the east. Fruits are mainly grown in areas around Lanzhou. Gannan Gaoyun (Plt.) is a major pasturing area raising yak, cow, pig, horse, sheep and camels, of which horse and sheep here are of quality strains. Sheep skin, leather and casing for sausages are important local products.

■ Industry

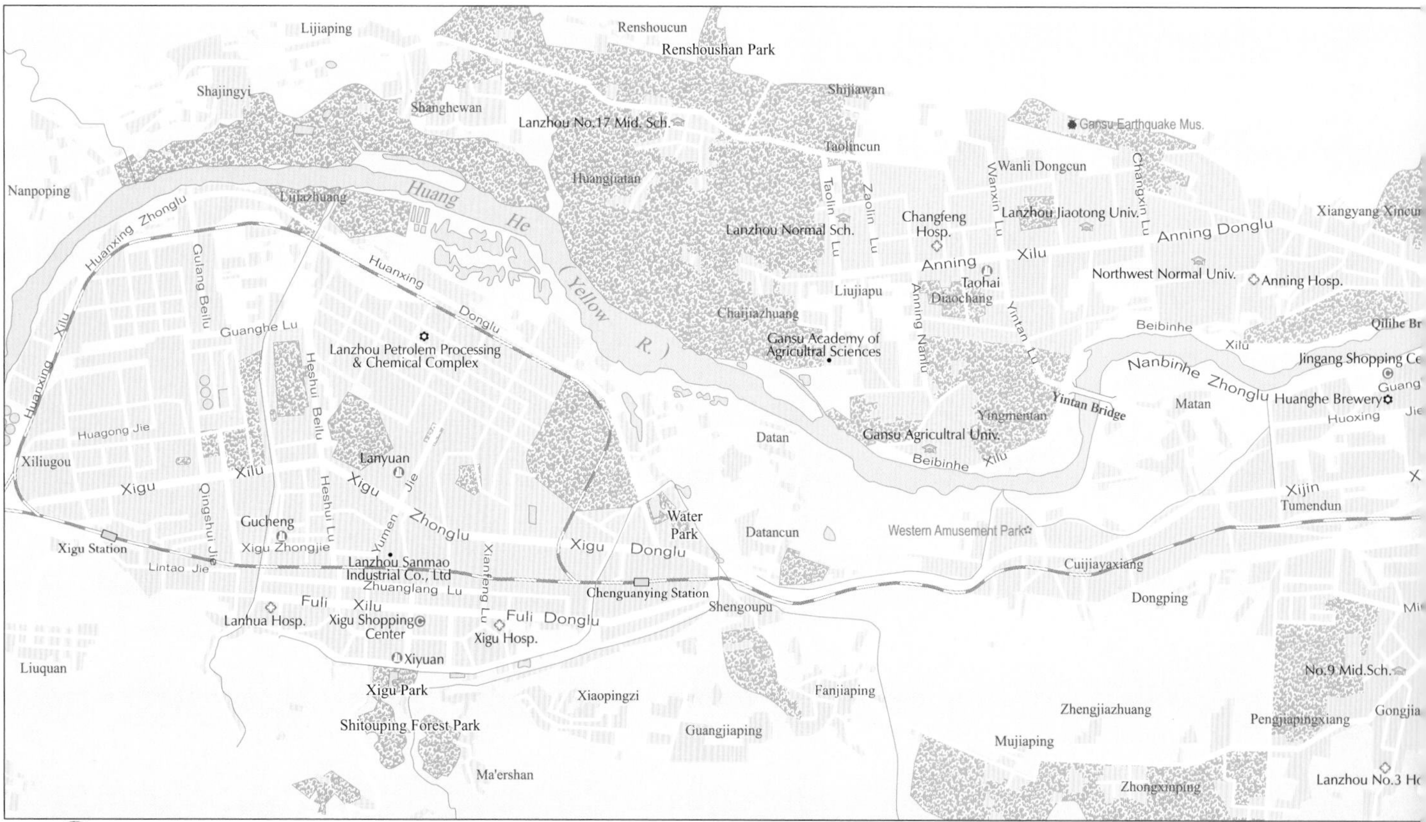

Nonferrous metal metallurgy, oil exploitation and refinement, production of petrochemicals and relative machineries, wool weaving, pharmacy, power engineering, and nuclear industry are supporting industries of Gansu. The output of nickel, aluminium and copper here play important roles in China's economy. Oil refining and petrochemical industry developed in areas around Lanzhou is quite prosperous. Jiayuguan is the largest production base of steel in northwest China. Liujiaxia and Yanguoxia hydropower stations as well as Jiuquan Space Launching Center are well

known.

■ Transportation

Railway main stems like Lanzhou-Lianyungang, Baotou-Lanzhou, Lanzhou-Xining and Lanzhou-Ürümqi railways center round Lanzhou.

Highway Centered round Lanzhou, national highways as well as provincial highways connect every city and county in the province. Express highways connecting Lanzhou with Baiyin, Hami and Baoji are in use.

Airway Lanzhou Airport provides flight courses to inner-province destinations like Jiayuguan, Dunhuang, Tianshui as well as Beijing, Shanghai, Guangzhou and 30 other major cities in China.

■ Places of Interest

Gansu province was the place where the main traffic line in ancient time between China and western countries-the famous Silk Road- passed through. With rich cultural resources, the province has many places of interest and historical monuments.

Mogao Caves southeast to Dunhuang is a world renowned art treasury listed in the World Heritage by UNESCO. The completion of this project lasted for more than 1,000 years. The total number of grottoes here is 492, in which there are over 3,000 sculptures and 45,000 square meters of murals exhibiting scriptures, the biography and stories of the Buddha, and other Buddhist historical records. Mt. Maiji is located 50 kilometers from Tianshui. Grottoes here are one of China's four most famous grottoes. There are 194 grottoes, more than 7, 200 statues found, of which more than 1,000 are taller than 1m. Labuleng Monastery built in early Qing Dynasty is located in Xiahe County. It is one of the six great monasteries of Tibetan Buddhism in China. Jiayuguan Pass is the western terminus of the famous Great Wall. Cleft between Qilian Shan and Mazong Shan, the whole structure is magnificently designed. As this was an important strategic point on the Silk Road, the pass was built with high towers providing distant views in all directions. Other tourist attractions are: Confucian Temple, and Haizang Temple in Wuwei, Dafo Temple in Zhangye, Nanguo Temple and Fuxi Temple in Tianshui, as well as many others.

■ Local Products

Moonlight cups produced in Jiuquan have been legendary wine cups in China. Inkstone, water pipe, lacquer carving, pebble carving, and gourd carving are traditional local handicrafts. Angelica produced in Minxian County is of first class. Melon, pear, Chinese date, apple, melon seeds and Jew's-ear are well known local agricultural products. Local flavours like noodles, beef pancake, and preserved ham are liked by many.

Jiayuguan Pass

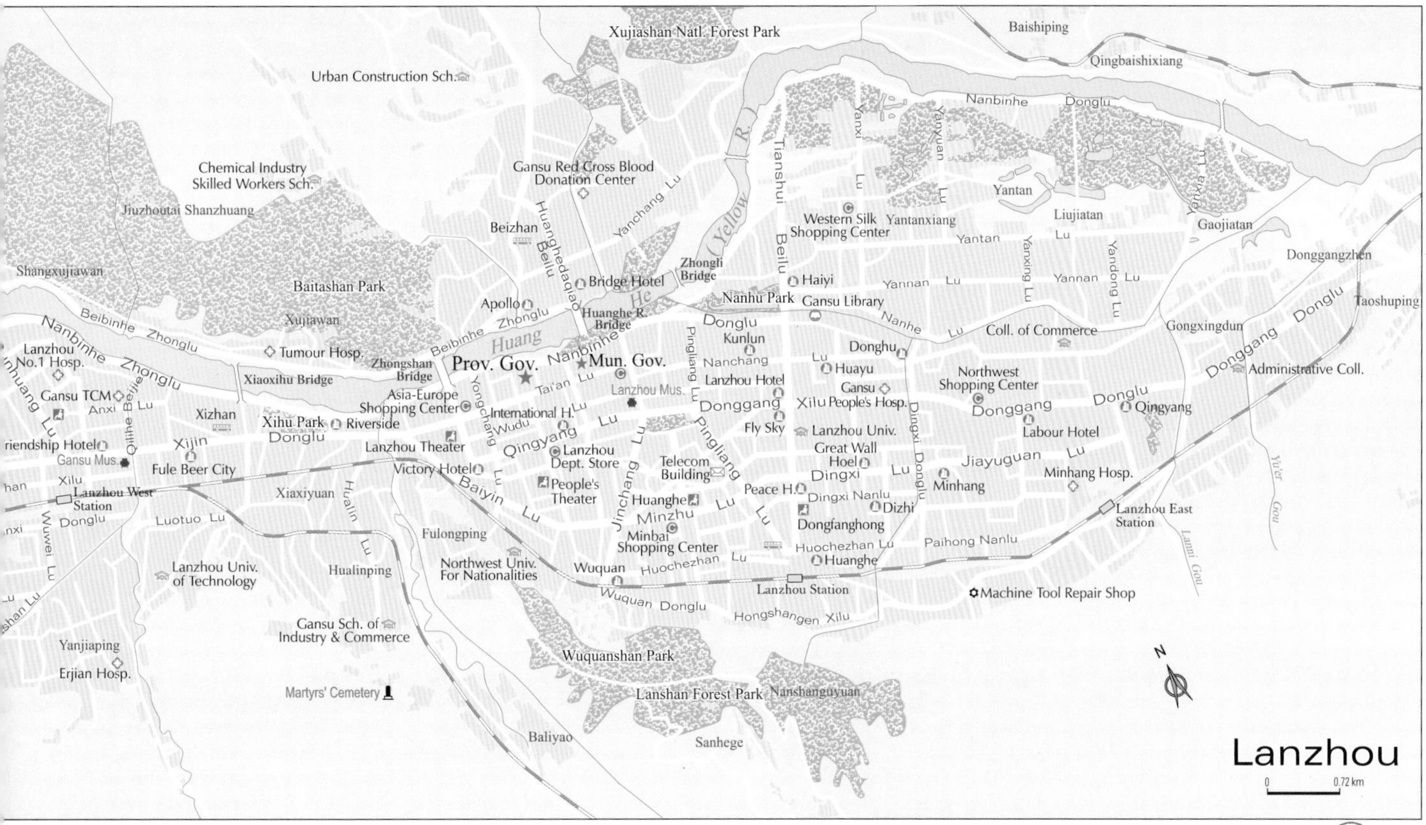

Lanzhou

Kumtag Shamo

A   B   C   D   E   F   G   H

1   36 Tuanchang   Dongluk   Aksay   Subei   Yema

▲4244   Baxborgan   Heping   Altun Shan 5798▲   Dunge 1 Daoban   Dushanzi   Yem

Luotuo Feng   Xiyajialəkə Shan 4622   Xorkol   Qingxinjie Shan 4054   Hondi Yanchang   4 Daoban   Yanchiw

2   Karaqalə   Suuxqi   Obo liang   Jiameihuo   Dingzikou   Huahaizi   Dushanzi

Bax Bulak   Yetimbulak   Mangnai   Niubiziliang   Lenghu   Chalukou   Mahai   Ige

Hongliuquan   Shuiyazidun   Nanbaxian   Lüliang Shan 4110   Da Qaidam

XINJIANG UYGUR ZIZHIQU   Gas   Youshashan   Changweiliang   Chalengkou

Aralo   Youquanzi   Dafengshan   Obo liang erhao   Pomenheqiao

Huanggualiang   Yiligou   Shenglikou

3   Qimantag   Lao Mangnai   Shuizhan   Yiliping   Xiao Qaidam   Yangchangzigou

Ziliujing   Xi Taijnar Hu   Xitieshan 4037   Dame

Gaxun   Sebei   Xitieshan   Tazian

Qaidam Pend

4   5866▲ Qimanleikè Tag   Behleg   Denggin Nomor   Bulangtai   Urt Moron   Karakazan   Qarhan   Reshui

ARKA TAG   Hureng Tohoi   Da Juh   Xiaoqiao   Dagur

KUNLUN TAG   6860   Urt Moron   Toroi   Golmud   Gayag

Buka Daban Feng   Hoit Tohig   Nanshankou   Naij Gu

5   Kangzhag Ri 6305▲   KUNLUN SHAN   Xiaoshazigou   Naij Tal   Kaihuan

HOH XIL SHAN   BUKA LUK TAG   Kunlun Shankou   Norzagabma

5285 Heixiong Shan   Hoh Xil   Hoh Sai Hu   Haiding Hu   Budongquan   BAYAN

Qingzang   Wudaoliang   Bi'aqie   Cochiyarlung   Yagradagzê Feng 5214▲

6   Dosoi Kangri 5689▲   Yugêzibo   Bêru'ogma   Qumarhe   Lungmar   Karx

Gaoyuan   Erdaogou Bingzhan   Fenghuo Shankou   Longqiongjibao   Zhigoikongma   Yugê   Qigzhi

Purog Kangri 6278▲   Carumarcha   Dangzhadara   Gogarlungring   Chaggur   Zhiqu   Sêrwolungwa

Wuli   Qêlungringkong   Machangchak   Qumarlêb

7   6137▲ Ganggênzazong   Gepaitang   Tanggulashan   Zhiqutong   Mugquka   Qurūgagka   Caipuzhangtong   Zhidoi   Dakog   Qang

Nyaxi   So'gya   Risangtar

Garqu Yan   Nyêxukongma   Doicê   Niandahai

Gêladaindong Feng 6621▲   Yanshiping   Biqu   Baquka   Damjong   Lixin

Shuijingkuang   Shanalongren   Ngamnaxung   Lungmugnang   Lungmug

Tanggula Shan 6205   Wenquan   Luringma   Mugxung   Ramda   Daoongyong   Longbao

8   Tanggula Bingzhan   Cha'angmadengma   Qu'angayong   Chadam   Zaqên   Daconngyong   Yaigê

Gangnyi   Tanggula Shankou   Puggêntang   Zarikando   Garmugkau   Zadoi   Lungmarda   Lungyê

Barling   Kyêbxiang Co   Suolagongma   Jiri'gya'nyag   Aôoi   Sêqu   Namsai

Domar   Baleqie   Damyang   Gyedoi   Domba

XIZANG (TIBET) ZIZHIQU   Comar   Amdo   Zhoxog   Garlung

Nyainrong   Zasib   Manta   Buta   Gaxiung

Ngorosumdo   Doxoggu   Qangma   Bilung   Jinyinshi   Lugoosh

9   Maintang   Zaring   Kormar   Qagzê   Sog   Baqên   Yangamdo   Gyalqên   Rongbo   Chido   Abao   Jiqiu

Baingoin   Namargê   Naqu   Biru   Dêngqên

Paila   Zhoma   Lomai

B   C   D   E   F   G   H

Altitude Table
750 1000 1500 2000 2500 3000 4000 5000 6000 7000 m

Qinghai Province

With Xining as its capital, Qinghai Province, which is abbreviated as "Qing", is located in Northwest China, on the northeast part of Qingzang Gaoyuan (Plt.). It covers an area of over 720,000 square kilometers, and has a population of 4.92 million, including such ethnic groups as Han, Tibetan, Hui, Tu, Salar, Mongol, and Man.

■ Geographical Features

Topography Large area of steep mountains and highlands in Qinghai are intersected by basins and valleys in between, giving it an average altitude of above 3,000m. Qinghai's terrain is framed by Qilian Shan (Mt.) in the north, Kunlun Shan in the middle and Tanggula (Dangla) Shan in the south. Basins like Qaidam Pendi, Qinghaihu Pendi, Gonghe Pendi and Hoh Xil Pendi distribute among these mountain ranges. China's three major rivers including Chang Jiang (Yangtze River), Huang He (Yellow River) and Lancang Jiang all start here. Other major rivers in this region are Huang Shui, Datong He, Za Qu, Tongtian He, and Shule He. Numerous lakes can be found here, including Qinghai Hu, Gyaring Hu, Ngoring Hu, Dabsan Hu, and Hoh Xil Hu, among which Qinghai Hu is the largest inland salt lake in China, while Gyaring Hu and Ngoring Hu are a pair of largest fresh water lakes in the province.

Climate Typical continental highland climate here are characterized by sharp change in daily temperature. Summer here is short and dry, while winter is long and cold. Annual rainfall in this area is between 50~400mm. The average annual temperature here is between -5~8℃, with an average temperature in January between -18~-7℃, while in July between 5~21℃.

■ Natural Resources

By now over 120 kinds of minerals have been found in Qinghai, among which the reserves of minerals like potassium, sodium chloride, kalium, magnesium, asbestos, Glauber's salt, quartzite, and limestone are ranked as China's No. 1. The province also has rich resources of nonferrous metals and rare metals like copper, lead, zinc, and gold dust. Large reserves of oil and natural gas have been found in Qaidam Pendi.

Numerous rivers with sharp falls provide the province with abundant hydropower resources. The 270 meters flow of Huang He between Longyang Xia and Sigou Xia can afford several large hydropower stations in rundles. Up till now nearly 180 hydropower stations have been built in this province.

Qinghai's forest cover rate is around 0.43%, mostly firs, poplar, dryland elm, buckthorn and Chinese prickly ash. There are more than 270 species of land vertebrates and nearly 2,000 species of wildings living in this area, of which about 700 are medicinal herbs, including over 50 species of rare medicinal herbs like snow lotus, aweto, liquorice, caladium, angelica and medlar.

There are rich resources of solar energy and wind energy as well as diversified high quality easy-to-exploit salt lakes in this area.

■ Agriculture

As one of China's four major pastures, Qinghai raises diversified stocks such as sheep, goat, yak, pien niu, cow, horse, donkey and camel, of which yaks and Tibetan sheep are of the majority. Horses raised in Hequ, Yushu and Haomen, together with pigs raised in Huzhu and camels raised in Qaidam are of quality strains. As one of China's major production areas of wool, Qinghai produces famous livestock products like wool, lamb skin, camel hair, cashmere, cowhide, beef and mutton. Qaidam Pendi, Hainan Zangzu Zizhizhou (Aut. Pref.), and valleys in the northeast are major farmlands in this province. Major crops are: wheat, highland barley, millet, potato, oat, buckwheat, raw oat, horsebean, pea, rape, beet and benne. Fisheries are found in Qinghai Hu, Gyaring Hu, and Ngoring Hu.

■ Industry

Supported by its rich reserves of energy and salt resources, Qinghai's industries mainly consist of metallurgy, oil exploitation and refinement, power engineering, building materials production, textile, leather processing, paper making and salt industry. Longyangxia Hydropower Station and Golmud Oil Refinery are well known in China.

■ Transportation

Railway Lanzhou-Qinghai railway is the artery line connecting Qinghai with the outside world. Qinghai-Xizang railway has now reached Lhasa.

Highway Centered round Xining, several national highways and provincial highways connect every part of the province efficiently.

Airway Xining has flights to Beijing, Shanghai, Guangzhou and dozens of other major cities in China.

■ Places of Interest

Qinghai Province is attractive not only for its unique highland scenery but also for its colorful local customs. Located 150 kilometers from Xining, Qinghai Lake covers an area of 4,500 square kilometers. The beauty here lies

Qinghai Lake

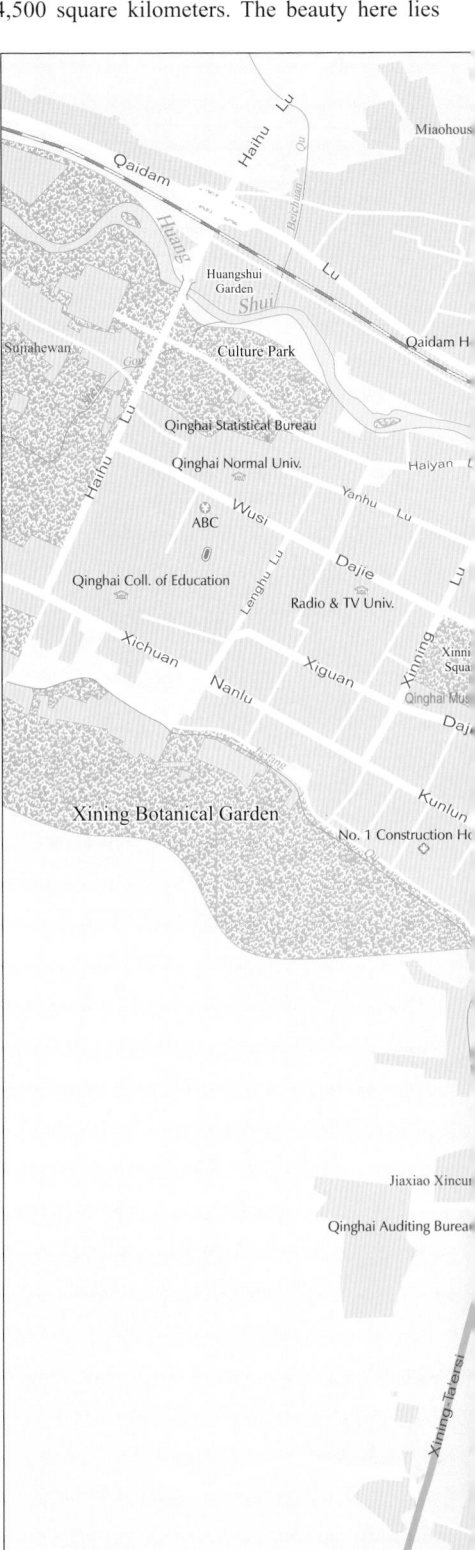

Xining

in its salty vastness and the remote peace that it instills. Highlights of the lake include the Bird Island and a peninsula in the westernmost part of the lake. Bird Island is located in the northwestern corner of Qinghai Lake. It is a natural habitat of more than 100,000 migrant birds from southern China and the Indian Ocean. Mengda National Nature Reserve is located in Xunhua Salar Zizhixian, with a pond of 20 hectares, and is surrounded by ancient trees of 540 species. Located in Huangzhong County, Kumbum Monastery is under national protection because it is the birthplace of

Tsongkhapa, founder of the Ge-lug-pa (or Yellow) Sect and one of the six largest monasteries for the Ge-lug-pa Sect of Lamaism in China. Situated on Dongguan Boulevard in downtown Xining, Dongguan Mosque is one of the four largest mosques in northwest China. It was built in the style of palace in ancient China, accompanied by two-story buildings on both sides. Other tourist attractions are: the Salt Bridge, A'nyemaqen Mountain, sources of Chang Jiang and Huang He, Temple of Princess Wencheng and Daotang River.

■ Local Products

Wool, cashmere, lamb skin, thick caddice, carpet, yak hide and marmot skin are famous local products. Squamaless carp in Qinghai Hu is well known for its tender and fresh taste. Liquor made from highland barley is a special local treat. Local flavours like boiled mutton, horse entrails, beef jerky and mature vinegar are known to many. Painted swan egg, golden bell and porcelain urns modeled on Kumbum Monastery style, silver ware and Tibetan knives are traditional local handicrafts.

NEI MONGOL (INNER MONGOLIA) ZIZHIQU

Nei Mongol Gaoyuan

Mu Us Shadi

Ulan Buh Shamo

Tengger Shamo

NEI MONGOL (INNER MONGOLIA) ZIZHIQU

HELAN SHAN

Shizuishan

Yellow R.

YINCHUAN

Huinong Qu

Pingluo

Helan

Xixia Qu

Jinfeng Qu

Yongning

Lingwu

Wuzhong

Qingtongxia

Zhongning

Zhongwei

Shapotou Qu

Niushou Shan

Hainan Qu

Alxa Zuoqi

Otog Qianqi

Yanchi

Dingbiano

King's Mausoleum of western Xia Dynasty

Mt.Helan

3556 Helan Shan

G A N S U

Altitude Table

0 100 300 500 750 1000 1500 2000 2500 3000 4000 m

SHAANXI

GANSU

Huangtu Gaoyuan

Huangtu Gaoyuan

Haiyuan Gaoyuan

LIUPAN SHAN

Quwu Shan

Qingyang

Pingliang

Zhenyuan

Huan Xian

Guyuan

Tongxin

Pengyang

Longde

Jingyuan

Jingning

Huining

Dingxi

Jingchuan

Chongxin

Huating

Zhuanglong

Xiji

Pingchuan Qu

Baiyin

Scale 1:1 200 000

0 12 24 36 48 60 Km

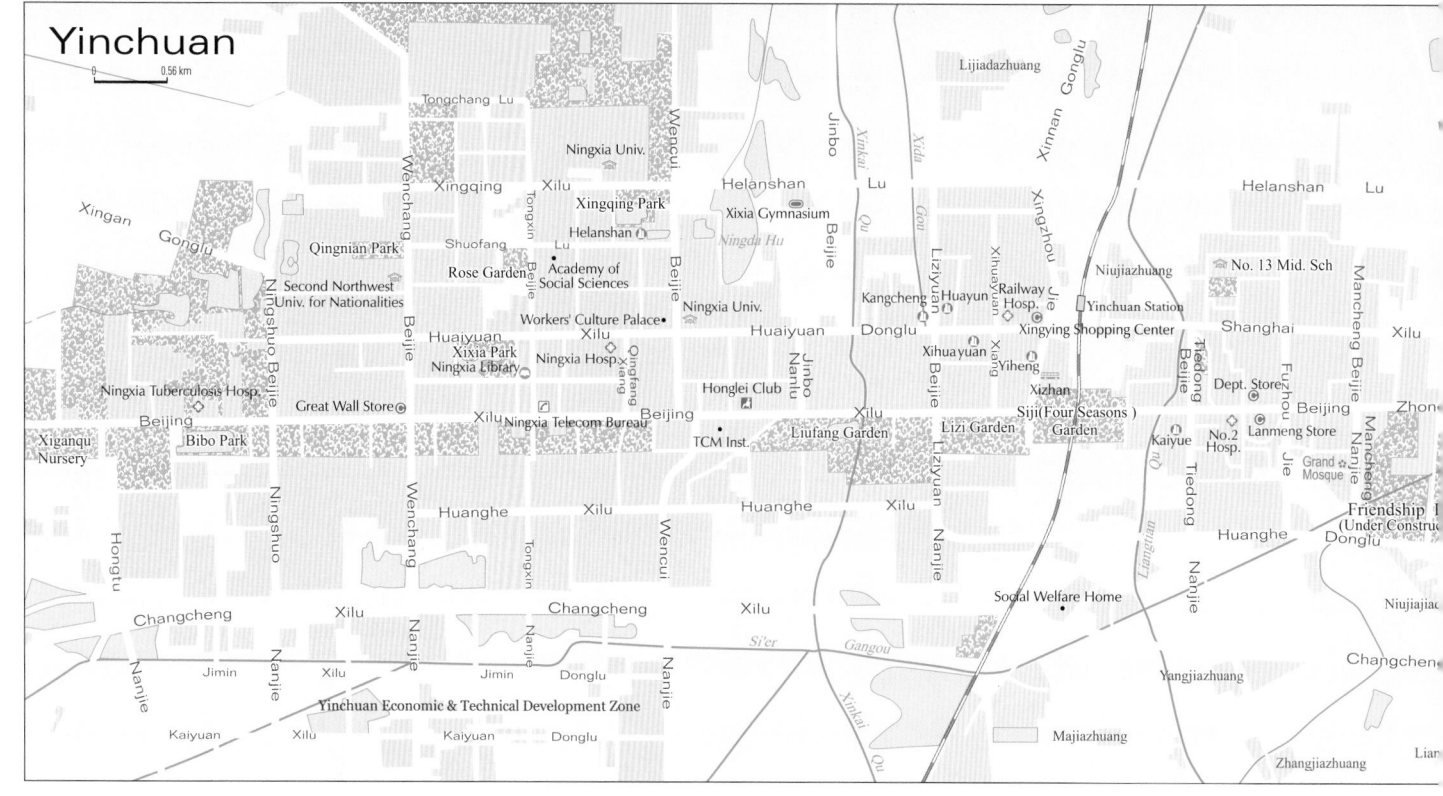

Ningxia Hui Autonomous Region

With Yinchuan as its capital, Ningxia Hui Autonomous Region, which is abbreviated as "Ning", is located in Northwest China, along the upper and middle reaches of Huang He (Yellow River). It covers an area of over 66,000 square kilometers, and has a population of 5.8 million, mostly Hui and Han, of which Hui people take up 1/3 of the total population. Other ethnic groups living in this area include Man, Mongol, Dongxiang, Tujia, and Zhuang.

■ Geographical Features

Topography   The average altitude of Ningxia is above 1,000m, as plateau and mountainous area take up 3/4 of its total area. With Huangtu Gaoyuan (Plt.) and Liupan Shan (Mt.) to the south and Ningxia Pingyuan (Pln.) to the mid-north, Ningxia's terrain descends from south to north, broken only by two mountains of Helan Shan and Niushou Shan on the northwest. Huang He (Yellow R.) runs through the mid-north part of the autonomous region, and is divided into several branches including Qingshui He, Kushui He and Hulu He.

Climate   Temperate semi-humid and semi-arid continental climate rules the autonomous region, bringing about very few rainfall and strong frequent winds together with sands. Summer here is short and cool, while winter is long and cold. Annual rainfall in this region is between 200~600mm, and varies greatly in different years. Sharp difference occurs in annual and daily temperature. The average annual temperature here is between 5~10℃,

with an average temperature in January between -10~ -7℃ , while in July between 17~24℃.

■ Natural Resources

Over 50 kinds of minerals have been found in the autonomous region, most of which are energy or nonmetal resources. Large reserves of easy-to-exploit diversified quality coals are found here, among which Taixi coal, the so-called " king of coals" is most famous. Ningxia also has rich resources of oil and natural gas. Reserves of gypsum, China clay, barite, quartz and limestone are also found here.

Ningxia's forest cover rate is around 2.20%.

Nearly 400 kilometers of Huang He run through Ningxia, bringing rich hydropower resources and an irrigation capacity of four billion cubic meters to this region. However, the per capita water resource possession is still lower than that of China's average quantity.

■ Agriculture

By drawing water from Huang He into agricultural irrigation, Ningxia became one of China's production bases of commodity grain. Rice, wheat, corn, broomcorn and glutinous millet are planted together with benne, beet, rape, medlar and various fruits. Sheep is the chief stock for animal husbandry in this region, which is a major production base of sheep skin in China. First grade sheep skins produced here play important roles on international market. Cow, horse, mule, donkey and camel are also raised here, making the province one of China's major production bases of dairy cow and meat cow. Aquatic breeding is developed along Huang He.

■ Industry

Supported by its rich resources of coal, electricity and hydropower, Ningxia has built up a relatively complete industrial system composed by petro-chemical industry, metallurgy, machinery, pharmacy, building materials production and agricultural by-products processing. The production of wine, potato starch, Muslim meat and dairy products, aquatics and processed fruits and vegetables are fairly well developed. Bio-pharmacy based on processing of medicinal herbs like medlar, liquorice and Chinese ephedra are making a start.

■ Transportation

Railway   Two main trunk lines of Baotou-Lanzhou and Baoji-Zhongwei railways run through the autonomous region and are

Xi Hu
Xihu Amusement Park
Jinjiazhaizi
Zhaojiashatan
Lu
Beiwangzhuang
Baliqiaosandui
Daziqukou
Helanshan
Manchun
No.109 National Road
Beita Hu
Helanshan — Lu
Xinshuiqiaojiudui
Beitacun
Beibaozhuang
Haibao Tower
Manchunshidui
Yinxin Gangou
Qu
Tanglai
Shanghai
Fengjiazhaizi
Xilu
Shanghai
Haibao Park
Lisheng Xiang
Shanghai
Yinjiazhuang
Donglu
Fengcheng Hosp.
Gonglu
Yinxin
Beijing
Zhonglu
Sun God Hotel
Shanghai
Gongda
Manchun Mid. Sch.
Ningxia Meteorological Bureau
Ning'an Dajie
Minsheng Chengshihuayuan
Huanghe
Amusement Park
Donglu
Fukang
Yinzuo
Chengyuan
Beijie
Beijing
International Hotel
Gonglu
demy of Agriculture & Forestry Sciences
Xiyuan Xiaoqu
Zhongshan Park
Yinchuan Gymnasium
Honghuasandui
Islamic Scripture Coll.
Qinghe
Hubin
Aut. Reg. Gov. ★
Ningxia Stadium
Hubin Jie
No.3 Hosp.
Manchunyidui
Ningxia Univ.
Huanghe Donglu
TCM Hosp.
Yiyuan
Wenhua Jie
Zhongshan
Lijing
Lijinghu Park
Great Wall Hotel
Jiefang
Xijie
Dept. Store
Jiefang
Dongjie
You'aibadui
Changcheng Huayuan
Nanjie
Xinhua
Yinchuan Hotel
★ Mun. Gov.
Zhengyuan
Jian Hu
Nanxun
Xinhua Dept. Store
Changcheng
Xinhua Mus.
Xijie
Xilu
Exhibition Hall
Dongjie
Jinling
Yinchuan-Tonggui Gonglu
Zhonglu
Changxing Xiaoqu
Yinshui
Nanxun Donglu
Xinhua Nanjie
Guodi Hu
Zhengyuan
Dianli
Nanxun
Dongjie
Huayan Hu
Changcheng
Nanguan Mosque
Donglu
Wuxing(Five-star)
Huayanhuzhuang
Baixing Shopping Centre
Aviation Building
Yingbin Square
Kongjiazhuang
Bao Hu
Qu
Qinghe
You'ai Xiang
Yinchuan-Gujiaozi Gonglu
Baoqing
Xilu
Nanjie
Daxin
Baoqing
Xilu
Huanhu Xilu
Liangjiazhuang
Guanghuamencun
Shengli Nanjie
Lijing Nanjie
Huanhu Donglu
Ningxia Medical Coll.
Taqiao Jiudui
Qishi'er Lianhu
Hosp. of Ningxia Medical Coll.
No.5 Hosp.
Kongque Hu

---

connected with national main stems like Lanzhou–Ürümqi, Lanzhou–Xining, Lanzhou–Lianyungang and Beijing–Baotou railways. Short distance branch lines like Pingluo–Luqigou railways are also in use.

Highway Centered round Yinchuan, every county and town in this region connected by national highways and regional highways. Shizuishan–Zhongning express highway has been put into use.

Airway Yinchuan has flight courses to Beijing, Shanghai, Guangzhou and other major cities in China.

■ **Places of Interest**
With a rich heritage combining the cultures of Western Xia Dynasty, the migrants, the boundary areas, and Islam, Ningxia has rich tourism resources. The King's Mausoleums of Western Xia Dynasty, often called the Pyramids of China, are located to the west of Yinchuan, facing Helan Mountain, where ten

thousands of cliff carvings by ancient nomads are found. Located on the hillside east to Qingtongxia City, the Pagoda 108 consists of 108 pagodas. It is the only ancient pagoda complex found in China. Chengtiansi Pagoda on the southwest of Yinchuan was built in 1050. It is the only pagoda of Western Xia Dynasty that has construction date recorded. Mt. Xumi Grottoes lying at the eastern foot of Mt. Xumi, 55 kilometers northwest of Guyuan County, is a gateway on the ancient Silk Road and is one of the earliest grottoes found in China. The Sand Lake north of Yinchuan is a lake dotted with sands. It combines the lush southern-type view with the northern-frontier scene beyond the Great Wall. Other tourist attractions include: Nanguan Mosque, Gaomiao Temple, Western China Film City, and remains of Great Wall.

■ **Local Products**
Sheep skin, medlar and blue inkstone are three most famous local products. Tribute Chinese dates, red melon seeds, tremella, locus roots,

carp, rabbit meat and donkey-hide gelatin are well known local agricultural products. Local flavors like Muslim pastry and specially prepared beef and mutton are liked by many. Jacquard blanket, archaize carpet, Islam porcelain, and stone carving are traditional local handicrafts.

King's Mausoleum of Western Xia Dynasty

A   B   C   D   E   F   G   H   I

Yefezkazgen

Atasu   Zharyk

Karazhal   Agadyr'

K A Z A K H S T A N

Kazakhskiy melkosopochnik

Mointy   Aktogay   Ayaguz   Zharma   Kokpekty   Kurchum

Balkhash   Urdzhar   Oz. Zaysan

TARBAGATAI SHAN

Saryshagan   Sasykkol

165 Tuanc   Sban   Tacheng(Qoq

Kamkaly   Ulanbel   Saryyesik-Atyrau   Sarkand   Andreyevka   Terekti   Emin   Dorbiljin   Hujir

Zhanatas   Taldykorgan   Lepsy   Ucharal   Küp   Yumin

Karatau   Bakanas   Tekeli   Mao'ergou   Toli

Moyynkum   Saryozek   Jiyek   Tiechar

Moyynkum   ALATAW   SHAN   Bole(Bortala)   Sh

Taraz   Kazan   Qagan Tungge   Alataw Shankou

Lugovoye   Chilik   Zharkent   Wenquan(Arixang)   Wutai   Jinghe(Jing)   Todog   Sikes

BISHKEK   Almaty   Daxigou   Songshutou   BOROHORO   SHAN   Baiyang

Kara-Balta   Tokmak   Horgos Kou'an   Dalt

Shymkent   Talas   Balykchy   Huocheng   Yining(Gulja)   Nilka   Ulastal   ERENHABI

Chirchik   Ysyk-köl   Karakol   Qapqal   Yining(Gulja)   Turgen   Narat

TOSHKENT   Toktogul   Kah Xiang   Baytokay   Gongliu   NARAT SHAN   Bayan Golo   Bay

Namangan   West Tianshan Mountain   Zhaosu(Mongolkire)   Tekes(Kunes)   Honggorso

Almalyk   UZBEKISTAN   Qagan Usu   (Tokkuztara)   (Torkuztar)   Kokterak   Bayan

KYRGYZSTAN   Naryn   Qagan Usu   4220   Dalarqa   Keyi

TAJIKISTAN   Jalal-Abad   TIAN   6995   Hantang Feng   Baicheng(Bay)   Kizil   Agi   Yeng

Khudzhand   Kokand   Margilan   Osh   Naryn   744   Tomur Feng   Laoputai   Daqiao   Qargio   Kuqa(Toksu)   Qiman   Lu   Lunnar

Khaydarken   Turugart Kou'an   NANMAL   Tumxiawat   Wensu   Xinhe(Toksu)   Tarim

Sary-Tash   Talkiydi Shankou   Karagulak   Aqegi   Jam   Xayar

SHAN   Kufansarak   Wushi   Aksu   Aral   Tarim

Uluggat   Toyun   Terak   KARATEKTI   SHAN   Awat   14 Tuanchang   Hada

Arkaxtam   Kansu   Kazajol   Piqan   Kalpin   Goruqol   **T a r i m**

Wuqia(Ulugat)   Artux   Xekarkol   Sanchakou   Aqal

Kashi(Kaxgar)   Kizilsu   Odaklik   Bachu(Maralwexi)   Tumxuk   Taklimaka

Bostanterag   Shufu   Shule   Jiashi(Payzawat)   qongkuroak   Aksakmaral

TAJIKISTAN   Muji   Akto   Yopurga   Bayawat   Tumantal   **T a k l i m a k a**

Qiruk   Bulungkol   Sogat   Elixku   Gazkol   Minfengchakou

Uzbel Shankou   Yengisar   Markit   Tazhong

Murgab   7649   Kongur Shan   Kizilto   Kizil   Shache(Yarkant)   1413 Gudong Shan   Mazar tag

Muztagata Shan   7509   Qarak   Karasu   Daryaboyi

Tagarma   Qarlung   Zepu(Poskam)   Maxut   Kizillik

Khorugh   Koguxluk   Koxrap   Qipan   Yecheng(Kargilik)   Kizilik   Andir Nongchang

AFGHANISTAN   Taxkorgan   Semuqi   Uxxarbax   Pishan(Guma)   Karasay   Qongmazar   Andirlangar

Daftar   Kokyar   Muji   Piyalma   Moyu(Karakax)   Paxxiyim

Mintekse Daban   Issikbulak   Xihxu   Koxtag   Kiliyang   Hotan   Qira   Yengibag   Minfeng(Niya)   Oyya

Kunjirap Dabam   Kangkur   Duwa   Hotan   Lop   Yutian(Keriya)   Yeyik   Sicha Ko

Chitral   Hunza   Kunjirap Kou'an   Jichtong Tag 3870   Satemalanggar   Aqqan   Koyak

Kalam   Mazar   KARAKORUM   Buya   Qakar   Bosian   Kaxtexi shan   Nur

Gilgit   (Area actually controlled by Pakistan)   Yatru Gou   Haxak   KARATAG SHAN   Dahongliutan   6048   Jiandao Feng   Qong Muztag 6920   Wolong Gang 5868

6667   8611   Broad Feng   Qogri Feng   6838   Muz Shan

Mardan   8051   Qosherrum Shan   Chaluchukou

Peshawar   8080   Karakorum Shankou   Shenxianwan   6644   Tuanjie Feng   Tielongtan   Keriya Shankou

PAKISTAN   Cease-fire line between India and Pakistan   Hechakou   Bogeda Co

Cease-fire line between India and Pakistan   Hongshantou   Barah Co

Srinagar (Area actually controlled by India)   **X I Z A N G (T**

ISLAMABAD   Kongka Shankou   Sumxi

Rawalpindi

C   D   E   F   G   H   I

Altitude Table   200 100 0 100 300 500 750 1000 1500 2000 2500 3000 4000 5000 6000 7000 m

RUSSIA

MONGOLIA

HANGAY NURUU

Ölgiy Hovd Hyargas Nuur Songino
Uliastay
Dzavhan Gol Tsagaanhayrhan Tsetserleg
Har Nuur Doigoh Nuur Bayanbulag
Hovd Har Us Nuur Bayanhongor
Altay Shan Arxant Daban
Altay Tseel Chandmani Bogd
Bayan Qbo Bulgan Bayan-Öndör
Fuhai (Burultokay) Karatingke
Qinghe Qinggil Agax Obo
Haramgalo Sartakay
Urho Qu Bulgan

Junggar Pendi
Baijiantan Qu
Gurbantünggüt Shamo
Dishui Quan
Hoboksar
Shawan Manas Wujiaqu Fukang Qitai Mori Barkol Yiwu (Araturuk)
Shihezi Huitubi Changji Miquan Jimsar Xialaoba Dahe Barkol Xiamaya
ÜRÜMQI Urumqi Xishan Tianshan Argalin Sair
Dabancheng Qu Qiqiaojing Yiwanquan Hami (Kumul) Hongshishan
TIAN SHAN BOGDA HAN Shanshanzhan Erpu Wupu Qincheng NEI MONGOL (INNER MONGOLIA) ZIZHIQU
Turpan Qltim Daquanwan Wutongdaquan
Toksun Shanshan (Piqan) Xarhu Nanhu Yandun Kushui
Turpan Pendi Kumtag Desert Shuangjingzi Mazongshan Shibanjing
Hejing Qol Tag Yamansu Xingxingxia NEI MONGOL (INNER MONGOLIA) ZIZHIQU
Hoxud Bohu (Bagrax) BEI SHAN
Korla Bosten (Bagrax) Hu Liuyuan Qiaowan Huahai
K U R U K T A G Guazhou Yumen Jiayuguan Jinta
Yuli (Lopnur) Dongdashankou Heishan Ling Bai Shan Shule He Yumen Jiuquan
Tuanjiecun Ak Tag Xihu Dunhuang Changma Laojunmiao Qingshui
Daxihaizi Shuiku Lop Nur Yingzui Shan QILIAN SHAN
Kumtag Shamo Aksay Subei yema shan SHULE NANSHAN
Tokum Lop Nur Wild Camel DANGHE NANSHAN Yagkeng
Donglук Danghe He Yanchiwan Har Hu
Ruoqiang (Qarkilik) Simola Anba Shan Huahaizi Teijin babao shan
ASYIN TAG Xorkol Qingxinjie Shan Dingzikou Suleng Shan Teijin Joe
Luotuo Feng Yiyajielake Shan Da Qaidam Delingha
Mt. Altun Suuxan ALTUN SHAN Yetimbulak Huanggualiang Jun Ul Shan Ulan
Kaxsay Xorkol Gas Gas Hure Hu Xi Taijnar Hu Xitieshan Ulan
Qiemo (Qarqan) Lao Mangnai Dong Taijnar Hu Dabsan Hu Bei Hulsan Hu Toson Hu Qaidam He
Munabulak Taixin He Qarhan Nan Hulsan Hu Angutan
QIMAN TAG Oimanteg Urt Moron Dulan
Zuyan Shan Hureng Tohoi Toroi Golmud Nomhon
Muztag Feng BUKALUK TAG Nanshankou
Pingzhang Ling Jingya Hu BURHAN BUDAI SHAN
Hei Shan KUNLUN SHAN Buka Daban Feng QINGHAI
Lixioidain Co Kunlun Shankou Huiten Nur Qumar He Gyaring
Budongquan Madoi
HOH XIL SHAN Hoh Xil Hu Ngoring Hu
Dogaicoring Qangco Xijir Ulan Hu Dorge Co Qumar Qu Yojilangleb
Rola Co Beilu Yogilangleb
Dongbolhai Shan Ulan Ul Hu Tongtian Qu-garma Chaggur Qumarleb
Margai Caka Ulan-ul shan Naij Co Serwolungwa Chalapem
ZIZHIQU Qumar Qu Tanggula Yan Qumaqu SICHUAN
Purog Kangri Zhidoi Chindu
Lixin

Xinjiang Uygur Autonomous Region

With Ürümqi as its capital, Xinjiang Uygur Autonomous Region, which is abbreviated as "Xin", is located along the northwest border of China. It covers an area of over 1.6 million square kilometers, and has a population of 18.89 million, including such ethnic groups as Uygur, Han, Kazak, Hui, Kirgiz, Mongol, Dongxiang, Tajik, Xibe, Man, Tujia, Uzbek and Russ, among which Uygur take up 45% of the total population.

■ Geographical Features

Topography Xinjiang's topography features three broadly parallel mountain ranges with two basins lying between them. Running in the middle, the Tian Shan (Mountains) divide Xinjiang into north and south. North across the Junggar Pendi (Basin) is Altay Shan. Across the Tarim Pendi to the south are Kunlun Shan, Karakorum Shan and Altun Shan. Taklimakan Shamo (Desert) in the south is China's largest and the world's second largest desert of shifting sands, while Gurbantunggut Shamo (Desert) in the north is the second largest desert in China. There are also Turpan Pendi and Ili Valley. Major rivers are Tarim He, Ili He, Ertix He, and Manas He, of which Tarim He is the longest inland river in China, while Ertix He is the only river in China that belongs to Arctic Ocean water system. Tian Chi, Bosten (Bagrax) Hu and Aydingkol Hu are major lakes in the area, of which Aydingkol Hu at 155 meters below sea level is the lowest lake and the lowest lying place in China.

Climate Typical arid continental climate rules the area, bringing about strong sunshine, minimum rainfall and a sharp change in daily temperature. There is also a sharp difference in temperature between the south and the north. Annual rainfall in the whole area is between 50～150mm. The average annual temperature in the south is between 7～14℃ , with an average temperature in January around -10℃ , while in July 25℃ . In the north, the average annual temperature is between -4～9℃ , with an average temperature in January around -20℃, while in July 20℃ .

■ Natural Resources

Rich reserves of oil, natural gas, coal, gold, chrome, copper, nickel, rare metal, asbestos, Glauber's salt, limestone, natrium saltpeter, crystal, Iceland spar, agate and jade have been found in Xinjiang. There are also plenty of easy-to-exploit quality lake salt resources in this region.

With rainfall and melting glacier as the major source of water, this region is poor in water resources.

Xinjiang's forest cover rate is around 1.08%, mostly firs, poplar, and pine trees. There are more than 580 species of wild animals and over 3000 species of wildings living in this area, of which over 300 are of medical use or economic value.

As the second largest pasturing area in China, the region has extensive grassland.

As the annual sunshine time here is between 2，600～3，400 hours, Xin jiang has rich heat energy and wind energy resources.

■ Agriculture

Xinjiang depends on oasis irrigation agriculture, with wheat as its major grain crop. Other crops are: corn, broomcorn, rape, benne, sesame and beet. Manas He drainage area, Turpan Pendi and south Xinjiang are major production base of plush cotton in China. Mulberries are planted in the south, where fruits abound. Animal husbandry in Xinjiang is quite well developed. Stocks such as sheep, cow, and horse are raised here, and the region produces first class strains of these stocks.

■ Industry

Xinjiang industries mainly include coal mining, oil exploitation and refinement, sugar making, textile, and food production. Light industrial products like liquor, canned food, beverage, dairy products, daily chemicals, essence and spices, precious stone processing in this region is also famous. Sugar, and articles with ethnic characteristics are known for their distinctive quality. Functional foods and beverage made by Uygur medicinal herbs are gaining popularity.

■ Transportation

Railway Main artery line Lanzhou−Ülümqi railway is connected with Baotou−Lanzhou and Lanzhou−Lianyungang railways. Nanjiang railway which connects Ürümqi to Kashi (Kaxgar) via Korla, and Beijiang railway which connects Ürümqi to Alataw Shankou are two major regional railways.

Highway Centered round Ürümqi, several national highways and provincial highways connect every city and county of the region. Express highway connecting Ürümqi with Hami (Kumul) and Korgas has been put into use.

Airway Ürümqi International Airport is one of China's major gateway airports. Domestic flights here can reach Beijing, Shanghai and over 40 other major cities in China, while international airlines connect the region with destinations in Middle and Far East. There are also airports in Kashi (Kaxgar), Yining (Gulja), Altay, Korla, Hotan and Tacheng (Qiqek).

■ Places of Interest

With ancient memories of the Silk Road, Xinjiang is where east meets west, where Asia connects with Europe. It is a place rich in cultural and ethnic diversity. Tian Chi (Heavenly Lake), a highland moraine lake formed more than two million years ago in the Quaternary glacial epoch, is situated in the Tianshan Mountain range, 115 Kilometers northeast of Ürümqi. The lake is deep, calm and limpid. When the peaks and the clouds are mirrored in the glittering water, it is so extremely beautiful that one feels like they are in paradise. Kanas Lake, a deep water lake, is located in Burqin County. It is a national nature reserve. Flaming Mountains of Turpan is so called for the deeply fissured red sandstone slopes which twist heavenward like flickering flames, as if the desert from which they spring was itself ablaze. The famous "Ghost Town" is northeast to Karamay. In the remote past, this area was once a vast fresh water lake and became land during the orogenic movement. The deposit at bottom of the lake through a long, long time of weathering and erosion became a fortress-like town known as the "Ghost Town". Other major tourist attractions are: Kirzil's Thousand Buddha Cave, the ancient cities at Jiaohe and Gaochang, the ruins at Loulan, Tomb of Xiangfei and the Idgar Mosque.

■ Local Products

Hami melon, grape, apple, pear, and apricot are famous local fruits, while Chinese ephedra, bluish dogbane, lavender, liquorice, caladium, and snow lotus are well known local medicinal herbs. Local flavours like roast lamb, roasted mutton cubes, specially cooked rice and crusty pandcake are liked by many. Carpet, embroidered hat, ethnic musical instruments, knife and jade are traditional local products.

Tian Chi (Heavenly Lake) of Mount Tianshan

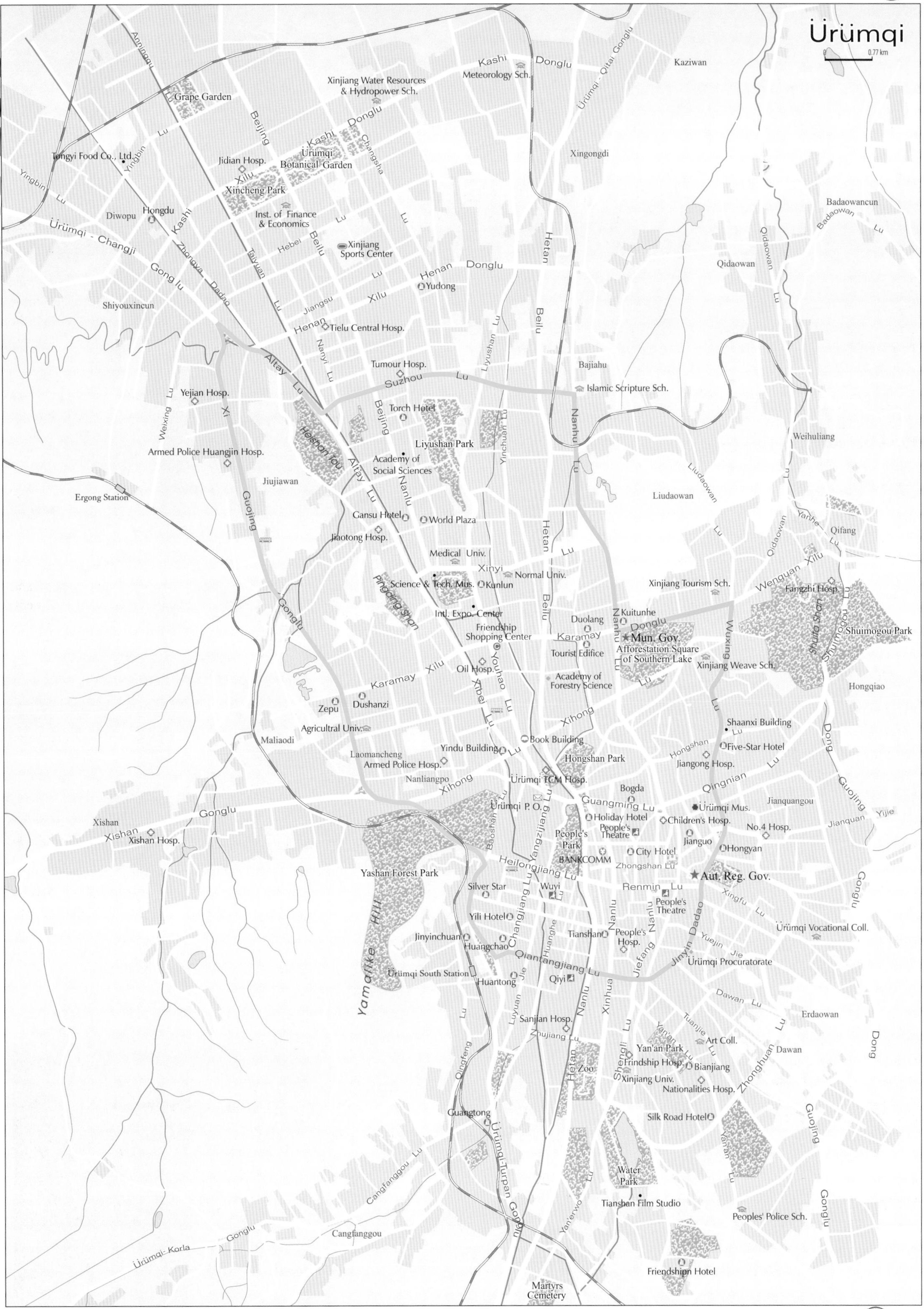

Ürümqi

0.77 km

Kashi Donglu
Meteorology Sch.
Kaziwan

Xinjiang Water Resources & Hydropower Sch.

Grape Garden

Tongyi Food Co., Ltd.

Jidian Hosp.

Ürümqi Botanical Garden

Xincheng Park

Xinjiang Sports Center

Diwopu

Hongdu

Ürümqi - Changji Gong lu

Shiyouxincun

Inst. of Finance & Economics

Xingongdi

Badaowancun

Badaowan Lu

Qidaowan

Yudong

Henan Donglu

Tielu Central Hosp.

Tumour Hosp.

Suzhou Lu

Bajiahu

Islamic Scripture Sch.

Weihuliang

Yejian Hosp.

Torch Hotel

Liyushan Park

Armed Police Huangjin Hosp.

Academy of Social Sciences

Jiujiawan

Liudaowan

Qifang

Ergong Station

Gansu Hotel

World Plaza

Jiaotong Hosp.

Medical Univ.

Xinyi

Normal Univ.

Science & Tech. Mus. Kunlun

Intl. Expo. Center

Friendship Shopping Center

Oil Hosp.

Karamay Xilu

Zepu Dushanzi

Agricultral Univ.

Maliaodi

Xinjiang Tourism Sch.

Fangzhi Hosp.

Shuimogou Park

Hongqiao

Duolang

Karamay

Tourist Edifice

Academy of Forestry Science

Z Kuitunhe

Mun. Gov.

Afforestation Square of Southern Lake

Xinjiang Weave Sch.

Shaanxi Building

Five-Star Hotel

Jiangong Hosp.

Book Building

Yindu Building

Laomancheng Armed Police Hosp.

Nanliangpo

Ürümqi TCM Hosp.

Hongshan Park

Hongshan

Bogda

Guangming Lu

Ürümqi Mus.

Jianquangou

Qingnian

No.4 Hosp.

Jianquan Yijie

Xishan

Xishan Hosp.

Ürümqi P.O.

Holiday Hotel

People's Theatre

Children's Hosp.

City Hotel

Zhongshan Lu

Jianguo

Hongyan

Yashan Forest Park

Silver Star

Wuyi

Aut. Reg. Gov.

BANKCOMM

People's Park

Renmin

People's Theatre

Ürümqi Vocational Coll.

Yili Hotel

Jinyinchuan

Huangchao

Tianshan

People's Hosp.

Jinyin Dadao

Yuejin Jie

Ürümqi Procuratorate

Ürümqi South Station

Huantong

Qiyi

Dawan Lu

Erdaowan

Sanjian Hosp.

Yan'an Park

Art Coll.

Dawan

Friendship Hosp.

Bianjiang

Xinjiang Univ.

Nationalities Hosp.

Guangtong

Silk Road Hotel

Water Park

Tianshan Film Studio

Peoples' Police Sch.

Cangfanggou

Ürümqi - Korla

Cangfanggou

Martyrs' Cemetery

Friendship Hotel

Yamalike Hill

A B C

G U A N G D O N

1

Yazai Shan
Xiaochan Dao
Xili
Meilin Shuiku
Meilin
Guangzhou-shenzhen
Bao'an Qu
Luohu Qu
Shenzhen
Nanshan Qu
Futian Qu
San Uk Lir
Qianhai Wan
Dachan Dao
Luo Hu
Hung Lung H
Ma Tso Lung
Ma Zhou
Shenzhen Wan
Lok Ma Chau
Sheung Shui
Chau Tau
Kwa Tung Shek Wu Hui
Shekou Wan
Mai Po
San Tin
Yeuk
Kam Tsin
Fanling
Wo Hop She

Shekou Wan
Sha Kiu Tsuen
Tsim Bei Tsui
Mai Po
Shek Wu Wai Hang Tau Tai Po
Kai Leng
Wo Shang Wai
Lau Fau Shan
Fairview Park
Tsin Keng San Wat
Ying Pun
Hang Hau Tsuen
Nam Sang Wai
San Wai Tsuen
Ngau Tam Mei
Pak Tai To Yan
480
Tin Shui Wai
Mo Fan Heung
Kai Kung Leng
Ta Shek Wu
Wai Tau Tsuen
Fung Kong Tsuen
572
Wang Chau
A Kung Tin
Chung Uk Tsuen
Sheung Pak Nai
Ngau Hom Sha
Kam Tin
Ha Che
Ha Tsuen
Wong Uk Tsuen
Lam Tsuen Valley
Wang Toi Shan
Chai Kek
Yuen Long
Kam Hing Wai
2
Ha Pak Nai
Tong Yan Tin Lin Tsuen
Shap Pat Heung
Kam Tsin Wai
Pat Heung
Wong Chuk Yuen
Tai Om Shan
Hung Shui Kiu
San Tsuen
Tai Kwai Tsuen
Nam Hang Tsuen
Shek Kong
NEW TERRITORIE
Nim Wan
Tuen Tsz Wai
Lam Tei
Pak She Tsuen
Ma On Kong
Kap Lung
Lan Kok Tsui
Kei Lun Wai
Fu Tei Chung Tsuen
Tai Tong Tsuen
Tin Fu Tsai
Tai Mo Shan
957
Leung King Estate
Yeung Ka Tsuen
Tsuen Kam Au
Tai Lang Shui
Yeung Siu Hang
San Hui Village
Sheung Fa Shan
Chuen Lung
Wo Yi Hop
Castle Peak 583
Tuen Mun
Tai Lam Chung Reservoir
Nam Long
Tsing Fai Tong
Tso Kung Tam
Tap Shek Kok Lung Kwu Tan
San Shek Wan
So Kwun Wat
Sham Tseng
Chai Wan Kok
Sheung Kwa
San Tsuen
Siu Lam
Tai Lam Chung
Ting Kau
Chung
Lingding Yang
Mong Hau Shek
Pearl Island
Tsing Lung Tau
Nga Ying Chau
Tsuen Wan
Lungkwu Chau
Tai Lam Kok
Pak Wan
Kwai Chu
Urmston Road
Ma Wan Channel
Ma Wan
Kam Chuk Kok
Pak Chau
San Po Tsun
Tsing Yi
So
Sha Chau
The Brothers Siu Mo To
Cheung Sok
Tso Wan
Tang Lung Chau
Lun Chi Kok
Tai Mo To
Ngong Shuen Au
3
Sham Shui Kok
Yam O
Pa Tau Kwu
Ngong Shuen Chau
Chek Lap Kok
Yi Pak Au
Hong Kong Disneyland
Hong Kong International Airport
North Lantau Highway
Tai Pak Wan
Discovery Bay
Sai Ying
Sha Lo Wan
Ngau Kwu
Nim Shue Wan Village
Siu Kau Yi Chau
Central Dis
Sham Shek Tsuen
Tung Chung
Hung Fa Ngan
Tai Lei
Peng Chau
Kau Yi Chau
Green Island
Kennedy Town
Nim Yuen
Lung Mei Tsuen
Wang Tong
Tai Shui Hang
Pok Fu Lam
Sai Tso Wan
LANTAU ISLAND
Mui Wo
Man Kok
Tei Tong Tsai
Tai Tung Shan 869
Nam Shan
Silver Mine Bay
Chau Kung To
Wah Fu Aberd
Ngong Ping
Fung Wong Shan
Shui Tseng Wan
Hei Ling Chau
Tai O
Hang Mei
Luk Wu
Tiantan Grand Buddha 934
Pui O Wang Tong
Chi Ma Wan
Pak Kok
Magazine Island
Keung Shan
Ham Tin
Ap Lei C
Yi O
Pui O Wan
Shek Kok Tsui Pak Kok San Tsuen
Luk Chau
Man Cheung Po
Tai Hom Sham 466
Shek Pik
Tong Fuk
Cheung Sha
Cheung Sha Wan
Yung Shue Wan
Tai Wan San Tsuen
Shek Pik Reservoir
Chi Ma Wan Peninsula
Shui Hau
Mong Tung Wan
Sea Ranch
Tai Long
Luk Chau Village
Kai Yet Kok
Tsin Yue Wan
Tung Wan Mei
Cha Kwo Chau
Adamasta Channel
Ha Mei Wan
Loso Shing Sok Kwu
4
Tai Long Wan
Lo Kei Wan
Shek Kwu Chau
Cheung Chau Wan
Tung Wan
West Lamma Channel
Fan Lau
Nam Tam
Fan Lau Kok
Siu A Chau
Cheung Chau
Lamma Island
Dayu Haixia
Yuen Chau Cheung Muk Tau
Niutou Dao
Tai A Chau
Soko Islands
Yuen Kong Chau
Tai Kok
Zhongxin Zhou
Tau Lo Chau
Gui Shan
5
Guishan Dao
Zhenxiang Dao Zhizhou Cun Dazhi Zhou
A Xiaozhi Zhou B Wailingding Dao C

K
o
u

Z
h
u
j
i
a
n
g

Neilingding Dao
Dongjiao Zui
Lingding Yang

Shenzhen Wan (Deep Bay)

Altitude Table
50 20 0 20 50 100 200 300 500 750 1000m

Scale 1:200 000

0 2 4 6 8 10 km

Hong Kong Special Administrative Region

Hong Kong Special Administrative Region is abbreviated as "Gang". Located to the east of Zhu Jiang (R.) Estuary, it is made up of Hong Kong Island, Kowloon, New Territories and other separate islands, covering an area of over 1,103 square kilometers. The SAR government is stationed on Hong Kong Island. There are over 6.8 million people living in Hong Kong, 90% of which are Chinese, others are English, Americans, Filipinos and Indians.

Hong Kong is traditionally an indivisible part of China. It was a small port in ancient times which got its name in Ming Dynasty for transferring fragrant woods produced in Dongguan County, Guangdong Province. In mid and late 19th century, Hong Kong area was ceded and leased to Great Britain. On 19, Dec. 1984, China and Great Britain signed the joint declaration on Hong Kong issues. On 1, July, 1997, Hong Kong reverted to Chinese sovereignty, and became a highly autonomous region of the People's Republic of China – Hong Kong Special Administrative Region.

Night Scenery of Hong Kong

■ **Geographical Features**

Topography As the extending part of Lingnan Qiuling (Hills), Hong Kong is featured with hills, islands and bays. Lantau Island is the largest island in Hong Kong, the second being Hong Kong Island, on the north of which is the renowned port Victoria. Kowloon peninsula is across Mawan Strait to the north. Some short rivers can be found there. There is also a fresh water lake on the north and a reservoir on the east.

Climate Subtropical marine monsoon climate rules the area, bringing about frequent typhoons and storms and an annual rainfall of above 2,200mm. The average annual temperature in this region is around 23℃, with an average temperature in January and February around 15℃, while in July and August around 28℃.

Northern Hong Kong Island

■ Economy

As the transportation hub of Southeast Asia, Europe, America and Oceania, Hong Kong is well developed in processing, trade and finance, and is well known as the "Oriental Pearl" and the "Paradise for Shoppers and Tourists".

Hong Kong has transited from a carrying trade port to a processing base of export goods. Trade and logistics, financial services, tourism and professional and other producer services are now four economic backbones of Hong Kong, while electronics, clothing, textile yarn and fabrics, toys and games, footwear, watches and clocks are its major export goods.

Agriculture in Hong Kong mainly consists of by-products production, fishery and horticulture.

As the center of world trade, finance and shipping, Hong Kong is quite well developed in service industries like air-ferry, ocean-shipping, tourism, as well as finance and banking.

With its strategic location, Hong Kong is both a free trade port and the second largest air terminal in Asia. Ever since the 1980s, Hong Kong has become the second largest and busiest container terminal in the world, with around 20 ocean routes to over 100 countries and regions. Victoria is the third largest natural port in the world. Hong Kong International Airport is the busiest and the most advanced airport in the world, harboring flights of every major airline companies in the world. Beijing-Kowloon and Guangzhou-Kowloon railways connect Hong Kong with mainland China.

■ Tourism

Victoria Peak is located on the west of Hong Kong Island, whose peak provides the best bird view of Hong Kong. Ocean Park, situated on the southern side of Hong Kong Island, is one of the world's acclaimed educational theme parks covering more than 870, 000 square meters of land. Ching Chung Koon, located at Tuen Mun New Town, embodies all the charm and visual delights of traditional temples in Mainland China. Tiantan Buddha, the largest copper statue of Buddha in the world, is located on Lantau Island. Other tourist attractions are: Hong Kong Disneyland, Lantau Peak, Repulse Bay, Stanley Market, Temple Street, Avenue of Stars, Hong Kong Gold Coast and Ngong Ping 360.

As a gourmand's paradise, Hong Kong provides tourists with the best and the most diversified cuisines in the world.

Ocean Park

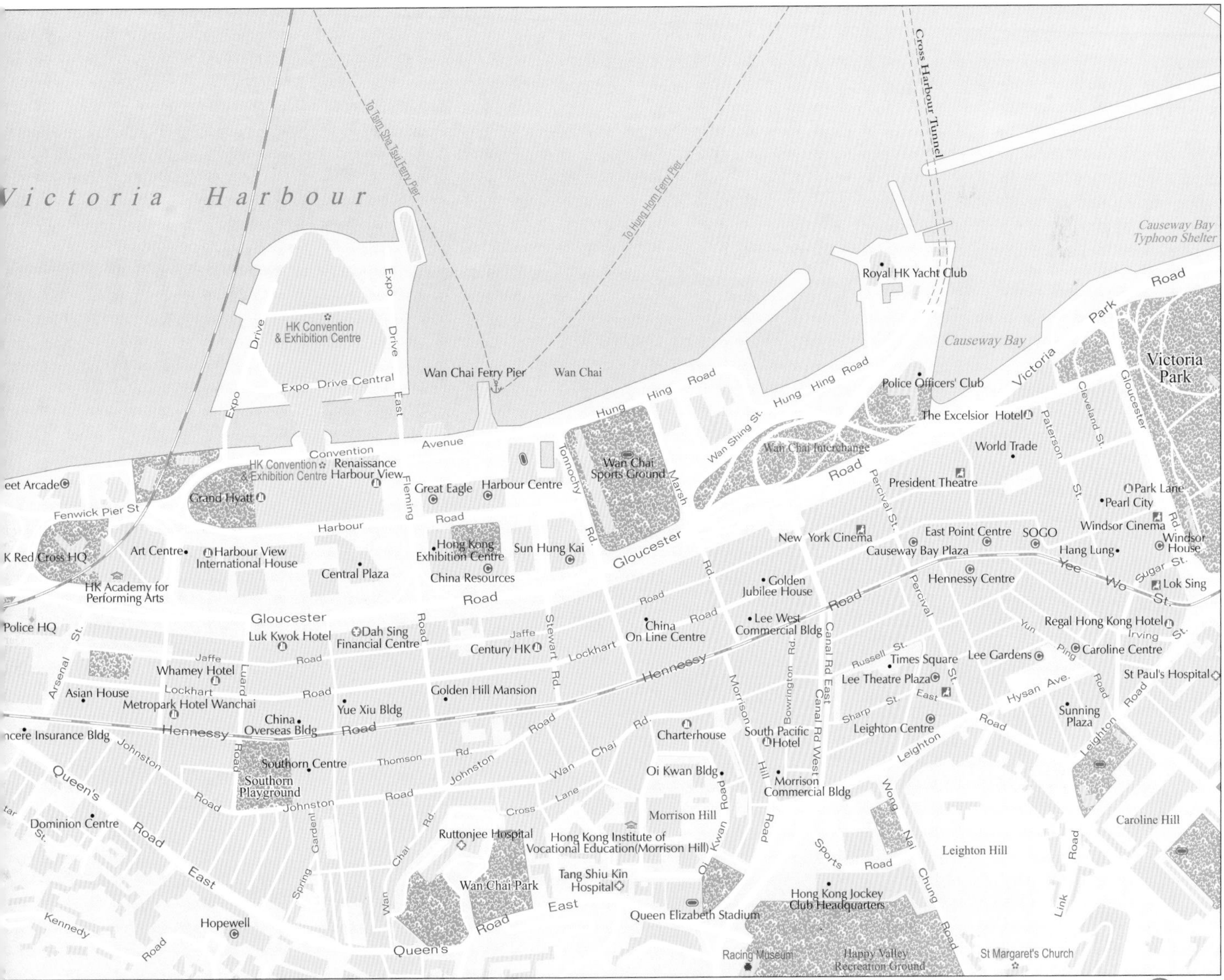

Terminal 2
Terminal 3
Terminal 4
Terminal 6
Terminal 7
Terminal 8
Container Terminal
Ngong Shuen Chau

Chung Shan Terrace
Kwai Chung Hosp.
Princess Margaret Hosp.
Ching Lai Court
Lai Chi Kok Hosp.
Mei Foo Sun Chuen
Lai Chi Kok Park

Castle Peak Rd.
Kwai Chung Rd.
Mei Lai Rd.
Kwai Tsing Container Port Rd. South
Container Port Rd.
Hing Wah
Kwai Chung Road
Castle Cheung Road
Ching Cheung Road

Tai Po Road
Caritas Hosp.
So Uk Estate
Kwong Lee Rd.
Lai Sun
Un Chau St.
Shek Kip Mei
Trade Square
Precious Blood Hosp.
Lai Kok Estate
Sham Shui Po
Nam Cheong Station
Nam Cheong Estate
Tung Chau Street Park
Nam Cheong Park
Tai Kok Tsui
Olympian City
HSBC Centre
Olympic Station
Cherry Street Park
Charming Garden

Tai Wo Ping
Chak On Estate
Cornwall Street
Beacon Hill
Hong Kong Baptist Un.
Junction Road
Shek Kip Mei Park
Festival Walk
Kowloon Tong Station
City Univ. of Hong Kong
HK Institute of Vocational Education (Lee Wai Lee)
Nam Shan Estate
Tai Hang Tung Estate
Police Sports & Recreation Club
Fa Hui Park
Newton Hotel-Kowloon
Boundary Street
Kowloon Tong Sch.
Concourse
Prince Edward Road West
Grand Century Place
Kowloon Hosp.
Pioneer Centre
Eye Hosp.
Mong Kok Station
Perth Street
Sports Ground
Mong Kok Rd.
Mong Kok
Argyle St.
Kwong Wah Hosp.
The Open Univ. of Hong Kong
Ho Man Tin
YMCA
Oi Man Estate
King's Park
Bianchi Lodge
Queen Elizabeth Hosp.
Yau Ma Tei
Dorsett Seaview Hotel
Diocesan Girls' Sch.
Gun Club Hill Barracks
The Hong Kong Polytechnic Univ.
Kowloon Station
Hung Hom Station
HK Mus. of History
Hung Hom
Hong Kong Coliseum
China HK City
Royal Pacific Hotel
Kowloon Park
Knutsford Hotel
HK Science Mus.
Prince Hotel
Royal Garden
Tsim Sha Tsui Centre
Gateway Hotel
Shangri-La
Harbour City
Holiday Inn
Peninsula
TST East Station
Hong Kong Hotel
New World Renaissance
Space Mus.
New World Centre
HK Cultural Centre
HK Museum of Art.
Tsim Sha Tsui
Kowloon Public Pier

New Yau Ma Tei Typhoon Shelter

West Kowloon Highway

Western Harbour Tunnel

Sai Ying Pun
Sun Yat-Sen Memorial Park
HK Macau Ferry Terminal
Sheung Wan
Shun Tak Centre
Four Seasons Hotel
ifc Mall
Hong Kong Station
Central District
Sai Wan
Connaught Road West
Des Voeux Road West
Queen's Road West
Belcher Bay Park
The Belcher's
Belcher's
Kwun Lung Lau
The Univ. of Hong Kong
Realty Gardens
Mount Davis
Lung Fu Shan
Hong Kong Central Hosp.
HSBC
HK Zoological & Botanical Gardens
Central Government Offices
Canossa Hosp.
Hong Kong Park
Victoria Peak ▲552
Victoria Peak Garden
The Peak
Peak Tramway
Queen Mary Hosp.
Pok Fu Lam Country Park
Pok Fu Lam
Strawberry Hill
▲Mount Gough
Aberdeen Country Park

Des Voeux Road Central
Queen's Road Central
General Post Office
City Hall
Central
HK Red Cross HQ
Admiralty Centre
Metropark Hotel Wanchai
Pacific Place
Magazine Gap Road
Stubbs Road

Victoria Harbour
Wan Chai
HK Convention & Exhibition Centre
Grand Hyatt
Central Plaza
Gloucester Road
Luk Kwok Hotel
Hennessy Road
Ruttonjee Hosp.
Wan Chai Park
Old Wan Chai Post Office
Queen's Road East
The Excelsior
Causeway
Time Square
Charterhouse
Tang Shiu Kin Hosp.
St. Margaret's
Happy Valley Recreation Ground
HK Sanatorium & Hosp.

Cross Harbour Tunnel

HONG KONG

Hong Kong
Island • Kowloon

0.34 Km

Our Lady of
Maryknoll Hosp.
Fung Tak
Estate
Yuen
Chuk Yuen
South Estate
Ma Court
Road
Yuen Tak
Fung
Road
Lung Poon
Court
Fu Shan Estate
Tak Shing Tunnel
King Shan Court
Tsz Wan Village Road
Ma Tau Hom Rd.
Fung
Tak
Ma On Shan Country Park
Mei St.
Wong Tai Sin
Cheung
Lung
▲Fei Ngo Shan
Wong Tai Sin Temple
Palza Hollywood
Hammer Hill Road
Sports Ground
Morse Park
San Po Kong
Fei Wan Rd.
Hong Kong
Buddhist Hosp.
Tung Tau
Estate
Road
San Po Kong Bldg.
Rhythm Garden
Choi Hung Estate
ok
Park
Hung
Mei Tung
Estate
Choi Wan Estate
Water
Bay
Clear
New
Water
Bay
Road
Kowloon Wall
City Park
Choi Wan
Ping Shek Estate
Clear
Lee
Shun Lee
Estate
On
Kowloon
City
Road
L   O   O   N
Regal Oriental Hotel
Tung Tau
Estate
Richland
Garden
Kwun
Kai Yip Estate
Tong
Shun Lee
Road
Tseung Kwan O
Tsin
Wai
Road
Far East Flying &
Technical Sch.
Road
L   O   O   N
Kwun
Kai Cheung
Kwong
Kowloon Bay
Sports Ground
Amoy Plaza
Jordan Valley
Shun Tin Estate
Tsui Lam Estate
Tong
Lam
Hing
St.
Wang
International Trade &
Exhibition Centre
Telford
Gardens
Amoy Gardens
Sau
n-Kwong Road
creation Ground
Kowloon Bay
Telford Plaza
Ngau
Chun
United Christian
Hosp.
Mau
Ma Tau Kok
Sheung Yuet Rd.
Road
Sau Mau
Ping Estate
Ping
Newport Centre
Kai Fuk Rd.
Lok Wah
North Estate
Ning
Hiu
Po
Lam
Road
Ma Tau Kok
Road
Pacific Trade Centre
Ngau Tau Kok
Wo Lok
Estate
Road
Kwong
Kowloon City
Ferry Pier
Garden Estate
Hong Ning Road
Recreation Ground
Tsui Ping
Estate
HK Inst. of Vocational
Education(Kwun Tong)
Hoi Sham Park
To Kwa Wan
Typhoon Shelter
Hoi Bun
Road Park
Yue Man Centre
Kwun
Tong
Hing Tin Estate
Wing Fai
Kwun Tong
Yuet Wah St.
Tseung
Tak
Lam Tin
Kwun Tong Tai Wan
Kowloon Bay
Millennium City
APM
Road
Kwun Tong
Recreation Ground
Kwan
Tak Tin St.
Lam Tin Park
Ng Kwai Shan▲304
unghom
square
Hung Hom Estate
Hutchison Park
Kowloon Bay
King
Kwun Tong
Industrial Centre
O
Tak Tin
Estate
United
uilding
Zung Fu
Tai Wan Shan Park
Laguna
Park
Fat
Lin
Ping Tin
Estate
Kin Ming Estate
Whampoa
Oriental Golf City
Sin
Lei
Harbour Plaza
Sai Tso Wan
Yue
rbour Plaza
Metropolis
Cha Kwo Ling
Road
Mun
Hung Hom Ferry Pier
Yau Tong
Estate
Ko Yee Estate
Cha
Kwo
Ling
Kwun Tong Tsai Wan
Ko Fai Rd.
North Point Ferry Pier
Tung Yuen St.
Pau Toi Shan
▲222
North Point
Corridor
Shung Shun
Eastern
Island
Tsau Wan
Sam Ka Tsuen
Provident Centre
Road
Eastern Harbour Tunnel
The South
China Hotel
Java
Harbour Plaza
City Garden
Bedford
Gardens
Eastern Harbour Centre
North Point Centre
Newton
Pak Fuk Road
King's
Quarry
Bay Park
Island
Sea View Estate
Temple
Road
Pacific Palisades
Devon Hse
Taikoo Shing
Cityplaza
Lei King Wan
Lei Yue Mun
Causeway Bay
yphoon Shelter
HK Shue Yan College
Choi Sai Woo Park
Eastern Centre
King's Road
Eastern Magistracy
Viking Villas
Braemar Hill Mansions
Kornhill Plaza
Shaukeiwan Typhoon Shelter
Victoria
Park
Road
Hing Fat
Tin
Hau
Sai Wan Ho
Eastern
Shau
Kei
Tung Yuk Court
Kung
Corridor
Ngam
A Kung
Ngam
HK Mus. of Coastal Defence
Pak Sha Wan
Central Library
Yue Street
Ho
Wan
Kornhill
Tung
Hei Court
Lin Fa Kung
Tai Hang
Lai Tak Tsuen
Yiu Tung
Estate
Shau Kei Wan
Ming Wah Dai Ha
Island
St Paul's Hosp.
Lei Yue Mun Park
& Holiday Village
Caroline Hill
Tung Wah
Eastern Hosp.
Hang
Sir Cecil's Ride
Chai
Elm Tree Towers
HK Inst. of Vocational
Education(Chai Wan)
Hong Kong
Stadium
I   S   L   A   N   D
Tai Tam Country Park
Chai Wan Au
Jardine's Lookout
Wan
Pamela Youde
Nethersole Eastern Hosp.
appy Valley
Mount Butler▲
Jardine's Lookout
Mount Parker▲
Chai Wan
Eastern
Corridor

Altitude Table

20 0 20 50 100 200 300 m

Zhujiang Kou

E

D

C

B

A

4 5 6 7

Macau International Airport

Macau International Airport

Airport

Baía de Ka Hó

Porto de Ká Hó

Fábrica de Cimentos

132 Monte Ka Hó

Povoação de Ká Hó

Parque de Merendas do Altinho de Ká Hó

Hotel China

Ds Meteorológicos e Geofísicos

160 Taipa Grande

Casa Museu da Taipa

Praia de Nossa Senhora da Esperança

Jardim Cidade das Flores

P
A
I
P
A
T

Tapa Pequena
112

Hyatt Regency Macau

Grandview Hotel

Jockey Clube de Macau

Estádio de Macau

Ponte Flôr de Lótus

Dique Ouste

Haibin

Ciganda

Ciganda

Ciganda

Huandan

Huandan

Central Térmica de Ká Hó

Heliporto

Reservatório de Seac Pai Van

Barragem de Ká Hó

Barragem de Hác Sá

Parque de Merendas da Barragem de Hác Sá

Praia de Hác Sá

Povoação de Hác Sá

Parque de Hác Sá

Baía de Hác Sá

Kartódromo de Coloane

Seac Pai Van Park

Seac Pai Van

Estátua da Deusa A-Má

Parque de Merendas do Alto de Coloane

C O L O A N E

172 Coloane Alto

Parque de Merendas do Trilho de Coloane

Pousada de Coloane

Choc Van

Baía de Cheoc Van

Parque Industrial de Concórdia

Coloane

Morro de Antihalja
122

Tai Van

Lai Chi Van

Povoação de Lai Chi Van

Baoqing Lu

Huoshao Shan
101

Cushahuan

Cushaqiag
158 Houshan

Dajiao Ding
106

Shishan

G U A N G D O N G

Yanghuan

Fengchuiluodai
195

Miaoren Wuji
218

Scale 1:31 000

0   0.31   0.62   0.93   1.24   1.55 km

Macau Special Administrative Region

Macau Special Administrative Region is abbreviated as"Ao". Located to the west of Zhu Jiang (R.) Estuary, it is composed of Macau Peninsula and the islands of Taipa and Coloane, covering a land area of over 27.3 square kilometers. The SAR government is stationed on Macau Peninsula. There are 445 thousand people live in Macau, 97% of which are Chinese, others are mostly Portuguese.

Ruins of St. Paul's Catholic Church

Macau is traditionally an indivisible part of China. It was a small fishing village belonging to Xiangshan County (Zhongshan City), Guangdong Province in ancient times. In 1553, it was taken by Portuguese, and was later claimed a "colonial free port" till 1887, when it was put absolutely under Portuguese control. On 13, April, 1987, China and Portugal signed the joint declaration on Macau issues. On 20, Dec. 1999, Macau reverted to Chinese sovereignty, and became a highly autonomous region of the People's Republic of China – Macau Special Administrative Region.

■ Geographical Features

Topography Macau used to be a small island in the sea, and was later connected with the continent by land reclamation as well as sands brought by Zhu Jiang. Most part of the peninsula is composed of flat land and low hills. Macau's highest point is at Coloane Alto (172 meters above sea level). There are many natural deep gulfs around Macau.

Climate Subtropical marine monsoon climate rules the area, bringing frequent typhoons and annual rainfall of above 2,000 mm. The average annual temperature here is around 22℃, with an average temperature in January around 14.5℃, while in July around 29℃.

■ Economy

Macau is well known for its gambling industry and is called the "Far East Monte Carlo". Tourism is another source of gaining foreign currency and pillar of Macau's economy. As Macau has barely any natural resources, it had been a consumption city for a long time, only producing firecrackers, matches, incense, and other minor traclitional handicrafts. However, its economy have been taking on a new face ever since 1960's. Today Macau's economy system mainly consists of four types: gambling, export-oriented processing, finance and real estate.

Transportation plays an important role for this small peninsula. As an international free port, Macau can harbor freights weighing over 3000 tons and connects the east with the west in trading. Macau International Airport has flights to many major cities all over the world. The newly built Lianhua Bridge brings Macau closer to mainland China.

■ Places of Interest

In the past 400 years, Macau has been one of the busiest centers of exchange between the east and the west. Historic center of Macau is listed in the World Heritage by UNESCO. The Ruins of St. Paul's Catholic Church, the first of its kind built in the Far East, is located on a small hill. Other tourist attractions include: The Leal Senado Building, Na Tcha Temple, Casa Garden and A Ma Temple.

Ponte da Amizade (Friendship Bridge)

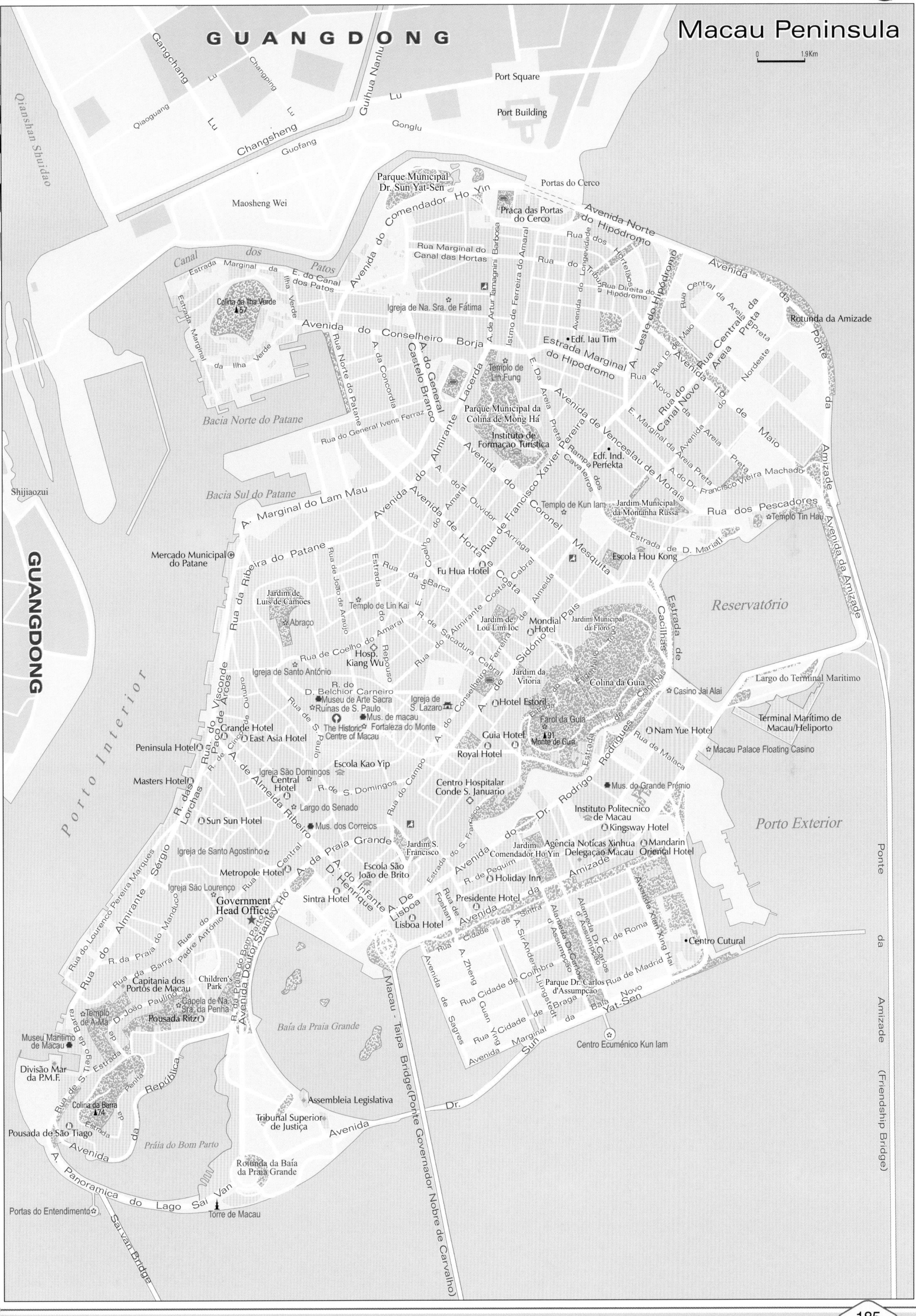

Macau Peninsula

0   1.9Km

GUANGDONG

GUANGDONG

Qianshan Shuidao

Gangchang
Changping
Lu
Guilha Nanlu
Lu
Port Square
Port Building
Qiaoguang
Lu
Changsheng
Gonglu
Guofang
Maosheng Wei

Parque Municipal
Dr. Sun Yat-Sen
Portas do Cerco
Praça das Portas
do Cerco
Avenida Norte
do Hipódromo
Ho Yin

Canal   dos   Patos
Estrada Marginal da
E. do Canal
dos Patos
Rua Marginal do
Canal das Hortas
Rua
Rua Direita do Hipódromo
Avenida Central da Areia Preta
Rotunda da Amizade
Colina da Ilha Verde
▲57
Igreja de Na. Sra. de Fátima
Avenida do Conselheiro Borja
Edf. Iau Tim
Estrada Marginal
do Hipódromo
Bacia Norte do Patane
Rua Norte do Patane
Templo de
Lin Fung
Parque Municipal da
Colina de Mong Há
Instituto de
Formação Turística
Edf. Ind.
Perfekta
Bacia Sul do Patane
A. Marginal do Lam Mau
Avenida de Venceslau de Morais
Shijiaozui
Rua dos Pescadores
Templo de Kun Iam
Jardim Municipal
da Montanha Russa
Templo Tin Hau
Mercado Municipal
do Patane
Escola Hou Kong
Rua da Ribeira do Patane
Fu Hua Hotel
Reservatório
Jardim de
Luis de Camões
Templo de Lin Kai
Abraço
Jardim de
Lou Lim Ioc
Mondial
Hotel
Jardim Municipal
da Flora
Hosp.
Kiang Wu
Jardim da
Vitória
Colina da Guia
Largo do Terminal Marítimo
Igreja de Santo António
Museu de Arte Sacra
Ruínas de S. Paulo
Igreja de
S. Lazaro
Hotel Estoril
Farol da Guia
Terminal Marítimo de
Macau/Heliporto
Grande Hotel
East Asia Hotel
Mus. de macau
The Historic
Centre of Macau
Fortaleza do Monte
Guia Hotel
Monte de Guia
Nam Yue Hotel
Macau Palace Floating Casino
Peninsula Hotel
Royal Hotel
Casino Jai Alai
Masters Hotel
Igreja São Domingos
Central
Hotel
Largo do Senado
Centro Hospitalar
Conde S. Januario
Mus. do Grande Prémio
Porto Exterior
Sun Sun Hotel
Mus. dos Correios
Instituto Politecnico
de Macau
Kingsway Hotel
Porto Interior
Igreja de Santo Agostinho
Jardim S.
Francisco
Jardim
Comendador Ho Yin
Agência Notícias Xinhua
Delegação Macau
Mandarin
Oriental Hotel
Metropole Hotel
Escola São
João de Brito
Holiday Inn
Igreja São Lourenço
Sintra Hotel
Presidente Hotel
Government
Head Office
Lisboa Hotel
Centro Cutural
Capitania dos
Portos de Macau
Children's
Park
Capela de Na.
Sra. da Penha
Pousada Ritz
Parque Dr. Carlos
d'Assumpção
Museu Marítimo
de Macau
Templo
de A-Ma
Baía da Praia Grande
Centro Ecuménico Kun Iam
Divisão Mar
da P.M.F.
Colina da Barra
▲74
Assembleia Legislativa
Pousada de São Tiago
Tribunal Superior
de Justiça
Ponte   da   Amizade   (Friendship Bridge)
Portas do Entendimento
Sai Van Bridge
Rotunda da Baía
da Praia Grande
Torre de Macau
Práia do Bom Parto
A. Panoramica do Lago Sai Van

A   B   C   D

Jianshe   Guji   Changle   Hsichuan Tao   Chukuang Liehtao   Tungchuan Tao

Longmen   Qingkou   Jiangtian

Taoyuan   Taihua   Changqing   Yongtai

Shangjing   Songkou   Dayang   Jingyang   Fuqing   Dalian Dao

Datian   Daiyun Shan   Shuikou   Youyang   Zhuangbian   Su'ao   Dongxiang Dao

Shipai   1856   Chishui   Wutong   Yuxi   Haitan Dao   Haitan Wan

1

Yigu   Xiayang   Dehua   Leifeng   Fengshan   Longtian   Gaoshan   Pingtan   Niushan Dao

Xianghu   Dongzhen Shuiku   Putian   Daqiu   Cao Yu

F U J I A N   Duwei   Hanjiang Qu   Tang Yu

Penghu   Xianyou   Huangshi   Fenwei

Gande   Yongchun   Jiaowei   Xiuyu Qu   Shicheng

Fude   Huoju   Luoxi   Putou   Pinghai

Xianghua   Jingu   Shishan   Tulingo   Wenjia   Lusi Yu   Nanri Dao

Xiandu   Meishan   Quangang Qu   Pinghai Wan

Anxi   Guangqiao   Hui'an   Meizhou Dao   Wuchiu Yu

Luoyan   Nan'an   Luojiang Qu   Xinfeng

Fengze Qu   Chongwu   Hsin

Yanxi   Quanzhou   Quanzhou Gang   Hsiangshan

Fengshan   Guangqiao   Jinjiang   Chunan   Paoshan

Changtai   Guankou   Shuitou   Shishi   Toufen

Zhangzhou   Jimei Qu   Maxiang   Sanwan   Hsihu

Haicang Qu   Tong'an Qu   Dadeng Dao   Shenhu Wan   Houlung   Miaoli

2

Longhai   Huli Qu   Weitou Wan   Shenhu   Tunghsiao   Tunglo   Chunghsin

Xiamen   Hsiaochinmen Tao   Chinmen Tao   Yuanli   Tahu   Pafen

Gangwei   Chinmen   Haokedun   Tachia   San-i   Cholan

Xiamen Gang   Liaoluo   Taan   Waipu

Changqiao   Liaoluo Wan   Taichung kang   Chingshui

Fotan   Dongding Dao   Wuchi   Tantzu   Taichung   Kuk

Zhangpu   Nanding Dao   Taichung   Taiping   Heping

Jiuzhen   Shentu   Jiangjun Tou   Hsienhsi   Lukang   Changhua   Wufeng

Liu'ao   Fuhsing   Fengyuan   Koohsing

Guleli   Futou Wan   Hsihu   Yuanli   Tsaotun   Nantou   Puli

Hong Yu   Fangyuan   Peitou   Tienchung   Mingchien   Yuchih

Tacheng   Chitang   Hsilo   Ershui   Shuili

Fengjungo   Lunpei   Huwei   Chu Shan   Hsin-i

Chipei Yu   Taihsi   Ssuhu   Yuanchang   Yunlin   Hsitouo

Paisha Tao   Niao Yu   Hsialun   Peikang   Touhan   Kukeng

Yuweng Tao   Paisha   Hsiyu   Meishan   Chuch'i   Hsiukulua

3

Wai'an   Huhsi   Penghu Tao   Kouhu   Chiali   Fanlu   Yu Shan   38

Penghu   Waishantingchou   Potzu   Chia-i   Alishan   Wufeng   3952

Penghu Liehtao   Tungshiho   Houpi   Chia-i   Kuantzuling   Tapu

Hua Yu   Wang'an   Yenshui   Sanmin   Taoyuan

Wangan Tao   Chiangchunao Yu   Peimeio   Putaio   Tainan   Fuhsing   Tienchih

(Pachao Tao)   Hsuehchia   Tapu   Nanhsi   Peinan Chushan

Mao Yu   Mashakou   Matou   Tsengwen Shuiku   4293

Chimei   Tungchi Yu   Chiali   Shanhua   Yuching   Chianhsien   Sentao

Chimei Yu   Hsichi Yu   Chiku   Shanhu Tan   Tanei

(Ta Yu)   Anping   Tsochen   Taolino

Anping Kang   Hsinhua   Shanlin   Liukuei

Taiwan Reefs   Tainan   Kuanmiao   Neimen   Chishan   Meinung   Chiuliao

Hunei   Alien   Chunhua   Kaoshuo   Likang   Wutai

Luchu   Wushantien Shuiku   Likang

Yungan   Nantzu   Chiuju   Chiuju   Santi

Nantzuo   Kaohsiung   Neipu   Taiwu   Chihpe

4

Kaohsiung   Pingtung   Peitawu Shan   3090

Kaohsiung Kang   Kaohsiung   Hsinyuan   Lai-i

Chichin   Kaohsiung Airport   Taiwu   Chin

Hsiaokang   Tachu

Linyuan   Tungkang   Hsinpi   Kutzulun

Linpien   Chiatung   Chunjih   Chialo   Tawu

Liuchiu Yu   Liuchiu   Fangshan

Fangshan   Shihtzu   Hsuhai

Fengkang   Mutan   Kangtzu

Checheng   Manchou

5   Hengchun   *S o u t h   C h i n a   S e a*   Maopitou   Nan Wan   Oluanpi

A   B   C   D   Chihsing Yen

Taiwan Haixia

Pinghai Wan   *Xinghua Wan*   *Nanri Qundao*

Penghu shuitao   *Alishan*   *T a i w a n*   *S H A N   C H*

Altitude Table

7000 6000 5000 4000 3000 2000 1000 500 200 100 50 20 0 50 100 200 300 500 750 1000 1500 2000 2500 3000 m

East China Sea

Chihwei Yu

Huangwei Yu

Tiaoyu Tao   Peihsiao Tao
Nanhsiao Tao

Pengchia Yu

Mienhua Yu

Huaping Yu

Fukuei Chiao   Shihmen
Sanchibo   Chinshan
Tanshui   Yangmingshan
nshui Kang   Wanli
iwei   Hsiafu Pali   Peitou   Chilung Kang
Airport   Sanchung   Nanking   Chilung
yuan   Taipei   Chinkuashih
TAIPEI   Shuanghsi   Santiao Chiao
Yingko   Pinghsi   Maoao
Tahsi   Hsintien   Shihting   Huoshaoliao
mei   Hsiungkung   Touchen   Kenghsin
gtan   Wulai   Kueishan Tao
Fuhsing   Chiaohsi
Niaotsui   Shuanglienpi   I-lan   Chuangwei
hher   Taman Shan   Yuanshan   Wuchieh
iienshih   2130   Tatung   Tungshan
Kunghsi   Mingchih   Suao   Suao Kang
Chlutse   Nana   Wushih Pi
h Shan   Ssuchi   Meitan
84   Nanhu Tashan   Tachoshulo
3740   Hojen
Huanshan
Lishan   Tienhsiang
Tayuling   Chilai Chushan   Hsiuluan   Hsincheng
3559   Lushan   Hsincheng
feng   Hualien   Hualien Kang
Chiaon   Wenlan
Shoufeng   Lingting
Hsikou   Shuilien
asashe   Fenglin   Chialulan
Wanjung   Kuangfu
Huyuan   Fengpin
Juisui   Shihti
Chohsi   Tafeng
Yuli
Autung   Changpin
ingshui   Chuhu
Fuli   Tuwei
shang   Hsinkang Shan
1682   Chengkung
uanshan
hmei
Tungho
eh   Tulan
aitung
Taitung Kang
Lutao   Lu Tao
(Huoshao Tao)

Yonakuni-jima

J A P A N

Ryūkyū - guntō

Sakishima-shotō

Iriomote-jima   Ishigaki   Ishigaki-jima

Yaeyama - rettō

P A C I F I C   O C E A N

Tropic of Cancer

Lan Yu
Lanyu
Hsiaolan Yu

Taiwan Province

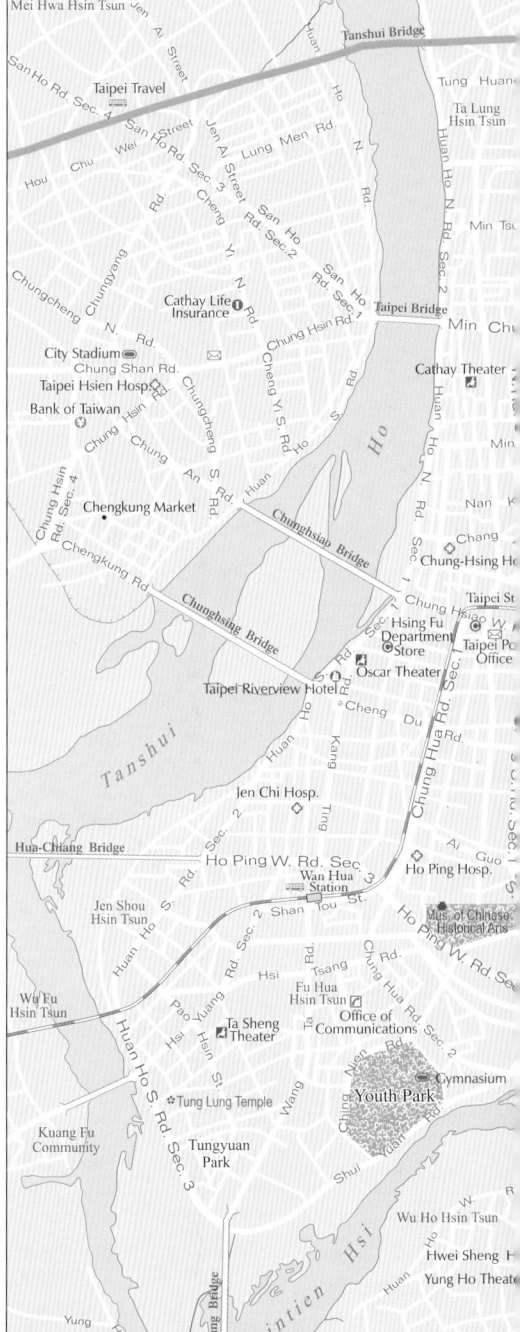

With Taipei as its capital, Taiwan Province, which is abbreviated as "Tai", is located on the southeast offshore area of China. It is traditionally an indivisible part of China. In 1895, Taiwan was seized by Japanese, but was returned to China in 1945 when Anti-Japanese War ended. The province is made up by over 80 islands including Taiwan Tao, Penghu Liehtao, Lan Yu, Tiaoyu Tao, and Chihwei Yu, covering an area of over 36,000 square kilometers, of which Taiwan Tao takes up 35,800 square kilometers. It has a population of 22.28 million (including population on Matsu Tao and Chinmen Tao), including ethnic groups of Han and Gaoshan.

■ Geographical Features

Topography Taiwan Tao is the largest island of China. 2/3 of the island is covered with mountains and hills, flat land can only be found along the west coast. Mountains like Hai'an Shan, Chungyang Shan, Yu Shan, Ali Shan and Hsueh Shan run parallel from northeast to southwest, forming a terrain sloping downward from the middle to both sides, intersected by numerous basins and narrow plains, such as Tainan Plain, Pingtung Plain, I-lan Plain, Yanhai Plain, Taipei Basin and Taichung Basin. There are many volcanoes on the island, including Datun Volcanoes, Chilung (Keelung) Volcanoes and Penghu Volcanoes. Major rivers are Choshui Hsi, Kaoping Hsi and Tsengwen Hsi. Few lakes are found in Taiwan, of which Jihueh Tan is the largest natural lake, while Shanhu Tan and Tsengwen Shuiku are artificial lakes. Islands like Penghu Liehtao, Lan Yu, Tiaoyu Tao, and Chihwei Yu lines around Taiwan Tao.

Climate Subtropical humid monsoon climate rules the area. Annual rainfall in this region is above 2,000mm. The average annual temperature is between $20\sim25°C$, with an average temperature in January between $13\sim20°C$, while in July between $24\sim29°C$.

■ Natural Resources

Coal, oil, natural gas, sulfur, salt, gold and copper are main minerals exploited in Taiwan, of which coal is the most important. Coal fields are usually found in the north, while Tatun Shan area stores China's largest sulfur resources.

Because of the mountainous topography, most rivers are short and with great falls, providing Taiwan with rich hydropower resources.

As a major forestry area in southeast China, Taiwan's forest cover rate is around 55%, mostly firs, pine trees, and Nanmu trees. Camphors, tung trees, rubber trees and other economic trees were planted there together with herbal plants like lemon gum, nutmeg and cinchona.

Situated on the Circum-Pacific Volcanic Belt, Taiwan has many volcanoes and hot springs, providing rich resources of geothermal energy. It also has rich marine product resources and sea salt resources because the island dwells on an area where warm current meets cold current.

■ Agriculture

Taiwan is one of China's major production areas of rice and sugar. Main crops here are: rice, wheat, sweat potatoes, sugar cane, peanut, hemp, and tea. The province is also well known for its production of tropical fruits like banana, pineapple, orange, grapefruits, longan and lichee. Kaohsiung, Chilung (Keelung), Suao, Hualien, Hsinkang and Penghu are renowned fisheries for sea fish, shellfish, shrimps and coral.

■ Industry

Textile and food processing are traditional industries in Taiwan. Light industries in the province have always been well developed. By late 1970s, local government begins to put emphasis on the development of heavy industries, mainly manufacturing industries like electro-machinery and chemical production. Most automobiles, aeroplanes, ships, petro-chemicals, steel, electro-implements, computers, electronics, textiles and clothes,

Taipei Imperial Palace

sports goods, shoes, toys, foods, and handicrafts produced here are sold abroad.

■ Transportation

Railway Around-island railway network has been completed. Electric railway from Chilung (Keelung) to Kaohsiung is joined by Taitung railway, Beihui railway and Nanhui railway.

Highway A convenient highway system made up by express highways, around-island highway, cross-province highway and coastal highways have been completed.

Waterway Sea transportation centers round Chilung (Keelung), Kaohsiung and Hualien. Other major ports include: Taitung, Suao, and Makung in Penghu.

Airway Dozens of international airports were built in Taoyuan, Kaohsiung and other places, providing flight courses to America, Japan, and Southeast Asia.

■ Places of Interest

Located on the Circum-Pacific Volcanic Belt, Taiwan is endowed with an unique scenery characterized by karst physiognomy and abrasion landform. Jihueh Tan, the largest and the only natural mountain lake in Taiwan is situated in Nantou County. It is a renowned summer resort. Mt. Ali, a natural forest park famous for its spectacular trees, clouds and sun rise, is located northeast to Chia-i County. Mt. Yangming is to the north of Taipei. It is China's only tourist spot exhibiting all kinds of volcanic features, and is most well known for its natural valleys, hot springs and waterfalls. Lin's Garden in Taipei is the largest architectural complex remains of Qing Dynasty, and is an exemplary exhibition of Chinese classic garden. Other tourist attractions include: Mt. Yushan, Meeting Bagua, Gugong Museum, and Mazu Temple.

■ Local Products

Corals produced in Penghu are very popular throughout the world. Nantou is the world largest supply center of butterfly samples. Camphors and spices produced in Taiwan are well known throughout the world. Local handicrafts include: stone carvings, jade ware, artistic porcelain, kite, shell carving, and knives. Many local teas are of first class quality.

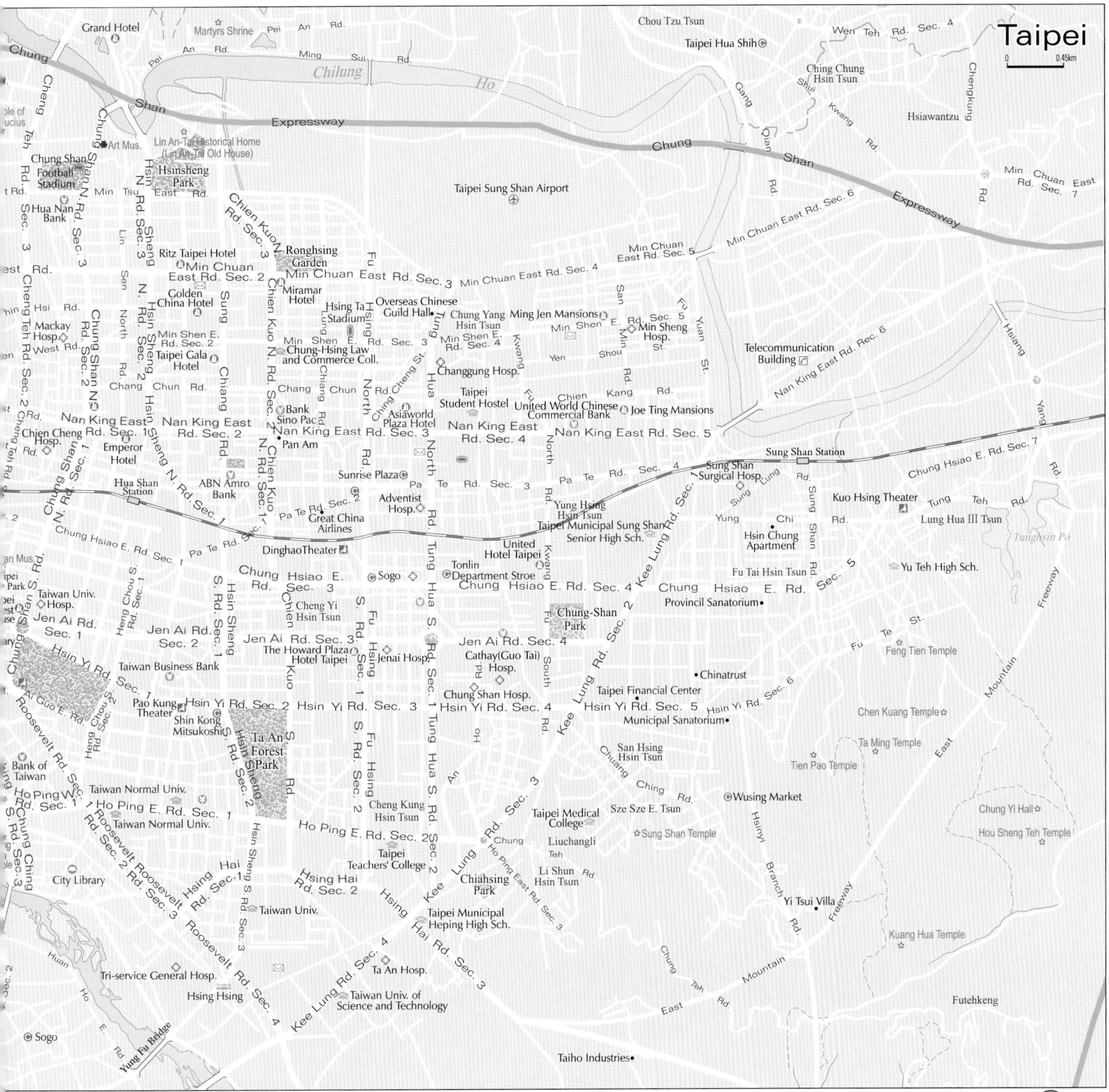

Taipei

Introduction To The Index

The index includes about 24,000 place names shown on the 34 maps of provinces, autonomous regions, municipalities and special administrative regions in China. For the romanization of place names in this Atlas, the *Pinyin* system has been adopted.

Each entry includes the name, the abbreviation of administrative division, a page number and a grid reference:

| Yanqing [BJ] | 36 | B3 |
| Hangzhou [ZJ] | 84 | E2 |

Names are referenced by alphanumeric grid, which indicates the location of symbol center for point elements such as city and peak, and the location of the first alphabet for linear or area elements such as sea, river, and mountains. For each place in the Atlas, only one entry has been included in the index.

Names in the index are arranged in alphabetical order.

Abbreviations

AH--------Anhui	HI--------Hainan	SC--------Sichuan
BJ--------Beijing	HL--------Heilongjiang	SD--------Shandong
CQ--------Chongqing	HN--------Hunan	SH--------Shanghai
FJ--------Fujian	JL--------Jilin	SN--------Shaanxi
GD--------Guangdong	JS--------Jiangsu	SX--------Shanxi
GS-------- Gansu	JX--------Jiangxi	TJ--------Tianjin
GX--------Guangxi	LN--------Liaoning	TW--------Taiwan
GZ--------Guizhou	MC--------Macau	XJ--------Xinjiang
HB--------Hubei	NM--------Nei Mongol	XZ--------Xizang
HEB--------Hebei	NX--------Ningxia	YN--------Yunnan
HEN--------Henan	QH--------Qinghai	ZJ--------Zhejiang
HK--------Hong Kong		

Glossary in *Pinyin* and *English*

Ansha/Shoal,Reef	Jiao/Reef	Shandi/ Mountain land
Arxan/Hot spring	Jie/Street (St.),Avenue (A.)	Shang/Upper
Bandao/Peninsula (Pen.)	Jing/Well	Shankou/Pass
Bei/North	Kou/Mouth	Shanmai/Mountains (Mts.)
Bulag/Spring	Liedao/Islands (Is.)	Shi/City
Chuan/River (R.)	Ling/Mountains (Mts.),Ridge	Shui/River (R.)
Co/Lake (L.)	Linqu/Forest region	Shuidao/Channel (Chan.)
Chi/Lake (L.)	Lu/Road (Rd.)	Shuiku/Reservoir (Res.)
Da/Greater,Grand	Moron/River	Tag/Mountain
Daban/Ridge,Pass	Muchang/Pasture	Tan/ Beach
Dalai/Sea,Lake	Nan/South	Tan/Pool
Dao/Island (I.)	Nei/Inner	Ul/Mountain
Dian/Shallow lake	Nongchang/Farm	Wai/Outer
Ding/Peak,Top	Nur/Lake (L.)	Wan/Gulf (G.),Bay
Dong/East	Pao/Lake (L.)	Xi/West
Feng/Peak,Mount	Pendi/Basin (Bsn.)	Xi/Stream,Brook
Fenhongqu/Flood diversion area	Pingyuan/Plain (Pln.)	Xia/Gorge,Valley
Gang/Harbour,Port	Po/Lake (L.)	Xia/Lower
Gaoyuan/Plateau (Plt.)	Pubu/Waterfall	Xian/County (Co.)
Gobi/Gobi,Semidesert	Qi/Banner (B.)	Xueshan/Snowberg
Gol/River (R.)	Qian/Front	Yan/Rock,Crag
Gonglu/Highway	Qiao/Bridge	Yanhu/Salt lake
Gou/River (R.),Ditch	Qiuling/Hills	You/Right
Guan/Pass	Qu/River (R.)	Yu/Island (I.)
Hai/Sea	Qu/Irrigation canal	Yunhe/Canal
Haixia/Strait (Str.),Channel (Chan.)	Quan/Spring	Zangbo\River
He/River (R.)	Qundao/Islands (Is.)	Zhaoze/Swamp,Marsh
Hou/ Back	Qunjiao/Reefs	Zhong/Central,Middle
Hu/Lake (L.)	Shadi/Sandy land,Desert	Zuo/Left
Hudag/Well	Shamo/Desert (Des.)	
Jiang/River (R.)	Shan/Mountain (Mt.),Mountains (Mts.)	

1

129 Tuanchang[XJ]	172	J3
14 Tuanchang[XJ]	172	H5
150 Tuanchang[XJ]	172	K3
165 Tuanchang[XJ]	172	J2
32 Tuanchang[XJ]	172	K5
36 Tuanchang[XJ]	172	L6

A

A Chau[HK]	176	D2
A Kung Tin[HK]	176	C2
Aba[SC]	138	G3
Abag Qi[NM]	58	K5
Abao[QH]	164	H9
Aberdeen Reservoirs[HK]	176	D4
Aberdeen[HK]	176	D4
Abqên[XZ]	152	D5
Acab[SC]	138	E4
Acheng Qu[HL]	70	D6
Acho[QH]	164	I7
Acur[XZ]	152	K4
Adamasta Channel[HK]	176	C4
Adoi[QH]	164	G8
Agang[YN]	148	J5
Agax Obo[XJ]	172	M2
Agi[XJ]	172	I5
A'gyirong[SC]	138	I2
Ahati Shan[QH]	164	C2
A'hati Shan[XJ]	172	M6
Ahu[JS]	80	D2
Ai Shan[SD]	102	G2
Aibag He[NM]	58	I7
Aicheng[JX]	98	C2
Aidian[GX]	124	E6
Aidong[GX]	124	E3
Aiguo[SH]	74	B2
Aihuan[ZJ]	84	F4
Aihui[HL]	70	D4
Aikou[CQ]	132	E5
Aikou[JX]	98	C2
Ailao Shan[YN]	148	G6
Ailao Shan[YN]	148	G6
Ainishan[YN]	148	G6
Aishan[GX]	124	F3
Aiting[AH]	90	B4
Aiwan Wan[ZJ]	84	F4
Aiyang[LN]	62	H4
Aizhai[HN]	114	B4
Aji[LN]	62	G2
Ak Tag[XJ]	172	N5
Ake[YN]	148	K6
Akori[SC]	138	G4
Akqi[XJ]	172	G5
Aksakmaral[XJ]	172	G6
Aksay[GS]	160	B3
Aksayqin Hu[XJ]	172	G8
Aksu[XJ]	172	H5
Akto[XJ]	172	E6
Aktübek Kou'an[XJ]	172	J1
Akungtien Shuiku[TW]	186	D4
Alag Hu[QH]	164	J5
Alakak[XJ]	172	K2
Alatang[XZ]	152	H5
Alataw Shan[XJ]	172	G3
Alataw Shankou[XJ]	172	I3
Alaying[HN]	114	B5
Aldar[NM]	58	N4
Ali Shan[TW]	186	D3
Alien[TW]	186	D4
Alishan[TW]	186	D3
Alizha[QH]	164	L3
Altan Had[NM]	58	M4
Altan Hil[NM]	58	K5
Altan Obo[NM]	58	F7
Altan Qog[NM]	58	D8
Altay Shan[XJ]	172	K1
Altay Shan[XJ]	172	L2
Altay[XJ]	172	L2
Altun Shan[GS]	160	A3
Altun Shan[QH]	164	D2
Altun Shan[XJ]	172	L6
Alxa Youqi[NM]	58	D8
Alxa Zuoqi[NM]	58	F8
Amdo[XZ]	152	G3
Ameng[YN]	148	J7
Amjogxung[XZ]	152	E5
Amo Jiang[YN]	148	G7
Amqog[GS]	160	F5
Amu Co[XZ]	152	F3
An He[JS]	80	D3
An Xian[SC]	138	J4
Anbian[SN]	156	E3
Anchang[GZ]	144	F2
Ancheng[HB]	110	D2
Ancheng[SD]	102	D5
Anda[HL]	70	C5
Andi Shuiku[SD]	102	E4
Andi[SD]	102	E4
Andi[ZJ]	84	D4
Anding[HN]	114	F4
Anding[JL]	66	C2
Anding[SN]	156	F3
Andir Nongchang[XJ]	172	I7
Andirlangar[XJ]	172	I7
Andongwei[SD]	102	F4
Andu Tan[HI]	128	F7
Andun[GD]	118	H3
Anfen[SX]	54	C6
Anfeng[HEN]	106	F1
Anfeng[HN]	114	E3
Anfeng[JS]	80	D2
Anfeng[JS]	80	F4
Anfengshan Shuiku[JS]	80	D2
Anfengtang Shuiku[AH]	90	C4
Anfengtang[AH]	90	C4
Anfu[CQ]	132	B4
Anfu[JX]	98	B4
Anfu[JX]	98	C5
Ang'angxi Qu[HL]	70	B5
Angou[SN]	156	G4
Anguli Nur[HEB]	48	B2
Anguo[HEB]	48	C5
Angutan[QH]	164	K4
Anhe[GX]	124	H2
Anhe[HB]	110	F3
Anhe[SN]	156	G4
Anhou[FJ]	94	C5
Anhua[GS]	160	G6
Anhua[HN]	114	D4
Anji[ZJ]	84	D2
Anjiang[HEB]	48	E3
Anjiang[HN]	114	C5
Anjiazhuang[SD]	102	C4
Anjiazhuang[SX]	54	B4
Anjiazhuang[TJ]	42	B2
Anju Qu[SC]	138	K5
Anju[HB]	110	G3
Anju[SX]	54	C6
Ankang[HN]	114	E3
Ankang[SN]	156	F8
Ankang[YN]	148	E7
Ankou[FJ]	94	D2
Ankou[GS]	160	H5
Ankou[JL]	66	F5
Ankou[ZJ]	84	D4
Anle[FJ]	94	B3
Anle[YN]	148	G5
Anlelin[JX]	98	B2
Anlezhuang[TJ]	42	B2
Anliang[HEN]	106	E3
Anling[HEB]	48	D6
Anling[HEN]	106	F4
Anling[ZJ]	84	E4
Anlinzhan[SD]	102	C3
Anliu[AH]	90	B3
Anliu[GZ]	144	E4
Anlong[GZ]	144	D5
Anlu[HB]	110	G3
Anmin[LN]	62	H2
Anmin[LN]	62	H5
Anmin[ZJ]	84	D4
Annanba Shan[GS]	160	A3
Annanba Shan[QH]	164	E1
Anning He[SC]	138	H9
Anning[GX]	124	D5
Anning[SC]	138	H4
Anning[YN]	148	H6
Anpeng[HEN]	106	E5
Anping Kang[TW]	186	D3
Anping[HEB]	48	C5
Anping[HEN]	106	G4
Anping[TW]	186	D3
Anpu Gang[GD]	118	B5
Anqing[AH]	90	D6
Anqiu[SD]	102	F3
Anqog[SC]	138	H3
Anquan[HN]	114	E3
Anren[HN]	114	F6
Anren[SD]	102	C3
Ansai[SN]	156	F4
Ansha Shuiku[FJ]	94	B3
Ansha[FJ]	94	C3
Ansha[HN]	114	F4
Anshan[HB]	110	H4
Anshan[HEB]	48	F4
Anshan[HN]	114	C6
Anshan[LN]	62	F3
Anshu[JL]	66	F5
Anshun[GZ]	144	D4
Anting[SH]	74	C2
Antu[JL]	66	I4
Anwo[SX]	54	C6
Anxi[FJ]	94	D4
Anxi[HN]	114	C3
Anxiang[HN]	114	E3
Anxin[HEB]	48	C5
Anxing[SD]	102	B4
Anyang He[HEB]	48	B7
Anyang He[HEN]	106	F1
Anyang[HB]	110	E2
Anyang[HEN]	106	F1
Anyang[HEN]	106	F1
Anyangping[HB]	110	D3
Anye[SX]	54	B4
Anyêmaqên Shan[GS]	160	D5
A'nyêmaqên Shan[QH]	164	L5
Anyi[JX]	98	C3
Anyou[HI]	128	B3
Anyu[SX]	54	C6
Anyuan[FJ]	94	B3
Anyuan[JX]	98	C6
Anyue[SC]	138	K5
Anze[SX]	54	D5
Anzhou[HEB]	48	C5
Anzhuang[SD]	102	E4
Anzhuangzi[TJ]	42	B4
Anzi[CQ]	132	E4
Anziling[HEB]	48	E3
Ao Jiang[ZJ]	84	E5
Aobaowan[NX]	168	D3
Aocheng[JX]	98	B5
Aohan Qi[NM]	58	M6
Aojiang[ZJ]	84	E5
Aoluguya[NM]	58	O1
Aonan[JX]	98	B5
A'ong Co[XZ]	152	B3
Aoqian[FJ]	94	E4
Aoshang[HN]	114	B6
Aoshanwei[SD]	102	G3
Aoshi[SX]	54	E2
Aotou[FJ]	94	C2
Aotou[GD]	118	F3
Aotou[GD]	118	G4
Aoxi[GZ]	144	F3
Aozai[GD]	118	E3
Ap Chau[HK]	176	E1
Ap Lei Chau[HK]	176	D4
Ap Lei Pai[HK]	176	D4
Apalong[XZ]	152	I5
Aqal[XJ]	172	G5
Aqatag[XJ]	172	G5
Aqqan[XJ]	172	H7
Aqqan[XJ]	172	J7
Aqqikkol Hu[XJ]	172	L7
Aqug[SC]	138	D3
Ar Gol[QH]	164	J3

Ar Gu[XJ]	172	K4	Badu[ZJ]	84	C5	Baijia[JX]	98	B5
Ar Hondlon[NM]	58	M5	Bag Tai[NM]	58	O6	Baijia[SH]	74	C2
Ar Horqin Qi[NM]	58	N6	Baga[XZ]	152	B4	Baijia[SH]	74	C3
Aral[QH]	164	C2	Baga[YN]	148	J7	Baijia[SN]	156	F9
Aral[XJ]	172	H5	Bagerik[XJ]	172	J6	Baijian[TJ]	42	B2
Araltobe[XJ]	172	M2	Bagoin[QH]	164	I7	Baijiankeng[NX]	168	C3
Arda[XJ]	172	K2	Bagong Shan[AH]	90	C4	Baijiantan Qu[XJ]	172	J3
Argalin Sair[NM]	58	C6	Bagong[SX]	54	D6	Baijiaping[HN]	114	D7
Arka Tag[XJ]	172	L7	Bagongqiao[HEN]	106	G2	Baijiatan[NX]	168	C3
Arkaxtam[XJ]	172	D6	Bagongshan Qu[AH]	90	C4	Baijiawan[NX]	168	C3
Arou[QH]	164	M3	Bagou[QH]	164	M5	Baijiaya[SX]	54	B5
Artux[XJ]	172	F6	Bagu[SC]	138	I7	Baijiazhuang[SX]	54	E2
Aru Co[XZ]	152	C3	Bagui[GX]	124	D3	Baijijishangtian[NX]	168	C1
Arun He[NM]	58	O3	Bahe[GX]	124	D4	Baijin[GZ]	144	E4
Arun Qi[NM]	58	O3	Bahe[SN]	156	F8	Baijin[JL]	66	J5
Arxan[LN]	62	F2	Bahechuan[LN]	62	H3	Baijing[SX]	54	E4
Arxan[NM]	58	M4	Bahui[LN]	62	G4	Baijixun[YN]	148	E3
Arxant Daban[XJ]	172	M2	Bai He[HB]	110	D3	Baikalu Shan[HL]	70	B2
Arxog[XZ]	152	H3	Bai He[HEN]	106	D5	Bail Nur[NM]	58	W10
Asar Hao[NM]	58	I8	Bai Shan[GS]	160	A2	Bailan[GX]	124	D4
Asar Hao[NM]	58	W12	Bai Shan[XJ]	172	N5	Bailang[HB]	110	D1
Ashi[GZ]	144	D3	Bai Shui[GD]	118	E2	Baile[GX]	124	D3
Asog[XZ]	152	D4	Bai Shui[HN]	114	E6	Baili Dao[GD]	118	F5
Asog[XZ]	152	D4	Baia da Praia Grande[MC]	182	A2	Baili[AH]	90	B6
Astin Tag[XJ]	172	L6	Baia de Cheoc Van[MC]	182	C7	Bailian[FJ]	94	C3
Atatkan He[XJ]	172	M7	Baia de Hác Sá[MC]	182	C7	Bailian[GD]	118	E2
Autung[TW]	186	E3	Baia de Ká Hó[MC]	182	D5	Bailian[HB]	110	I4
Awang[XZ]	152	K4	Baï an Dao[HI]	128	C3	Bailian[HI]	128	C2
Awat[XJ]	172	H5	Baibao[SN]	156	E4	Bailiang[SN]	156	G5
Awiytan[XJ]	172	L2	Baibei[SX]	54	D4	Bailianhe Shuiku[HB]	110	I4
Ayakkum Hu[XJ]	172	L7	Baibung[XZ]	152	I5	Bailin[CQ]	132	C5
Ayanhe[HL]	70	E4	Baicai[XZ]	152	F5	Bailin[FJ]	94	F2
Aydingkol Hu[XJ]	172	L4	Baicang[HN]	114	D6	Bailin[GX]	124	E4
Ayila Ri'gyuü[XZ]	152	A3	Baicao Ling[YN]	148	G5	Bailin[HB]	110	D2
Ayong[YN]	148	K7	Baicao[HEB]	48	D2	Bailin[HN]	114	F6
Ayuan[NM]	58	O2	Baicaogou[NX]	168	B3	Bailitou[SX]	54	D2
			Baicaokou[SX]	54	D2	Bailiu[SN]	156	F8
			Baicha[HI]	128	A3	Bailizhou[HB]	110	E4
B			Baichangmen[LN]	62	E3	Bailong Gang[SH]	74	D2
			Baicheng（Bay）[XJ]	172	H5	Bailong Jiang[GS]	160	F5
			Baicheng[JL]	66	C2	Bailong[AH]	90	D4
Ba He[SC]	138	M4	Baichengzi[NM]	58	N6	Bailong[GZ]	144	F5
Ba He[SN]	156	F8	Baichi[HEN]	106	F4	Bailong[SC]	138	K4
Ba Shui[HB]	110	I4	Baichihe[SD]	102	F3	Bailongtang[SN]	156	D7
Ba Xiag[XZ]	152	H5	Baicun[GZ]	144	F2	Bailu He[HEN]	106	G5
Babaihu[TJ]	42	C1	Baidag[XZ]	152	J4	Bailu[CQ]	132	F2
Babbu Ri[XZ]	152	F4	Baidaokou[HEN]	106	F2	Bailu[GS]	160	G5
Babian Jiang[YN]	148	G7	Baidi[CQ]	132	F2	Bailu[GX]	124	G3
Babian[YN]	148	G7	Baidian[AH]	90	F6	Bailu[HB]	110	F2
Babu[YN]	148	J7	Baidian[HEN]	106	G5	Bailu[JX]	98	B5
Bacha[HL]	70	G4	Baidishi[HN]	114	D6	Bailu[YN]	148	H5
Bachagou[LN]	62	E5	Baidong[GX]	124	D4	Bailuo[HB]	110	G5
Bachi[GD]	118	H2	Baidu[GD]	118	I2	Baima Hu[JS]	80	E3
Bachigang[HEB]	48	F4	Baidu[GX]	124	C4	Baima Jian[AH]	90	C5
Bachou[GX]	124	E3	Bai'e[JX]	98	C6	Baima Shan[GZ]	144	E2
Bachu(Maralwexi)[XJ]	172	G6	Baifang[HN]	114	E6	Baima Shan[HN]	114	C5
Bacia Norte do Patane[MC]	182	A1	Baifeng[HB]	110	E3	Baima Shan[ZJ]	84	D4
Bacia Sul do Patane[MC]	182	A1	Baifeng[ZJ]	84	F3	Baima[CQ]	132	D4
Bacun[HI]	128	B3	Baifusi[HB]	110	C5	Baima[GS]	160	H4
Bada[XZ]	152	I4	Baifutu[SD]	102	C5	Baima[HEB]	48	E4
Bada[YN]	148	J6	Baigezhuang[HEB]	48	F4	Baima[HN]	114	D5
Bada[ZJ]	84	E3	Baiguan[GS]	160	G6	Baima[JS]	80	E5
Badagongshan[HN]	114	B3	Baiguishan Shuiku[HEN]	106	E4	Baima[QH]	164	M8
Badahe[GX]	124	B3	Baiguo[CQ]	132	D4	Baima[SC]	138	G8
Badai Oroi[NM]	58	M5	Baiguo[GZ]	144	C4	Baima[SC]	138	J3
Badain Jaran Shamo[NM]	58	D7	Baiguo[HB]	110	I3	Baima[ZJ]	84	C3
Badaogou[JL]	66	H6	Baiguoping[SN]	156	F8	Baimajing[HI]	128	B2
Badaogou[JL]	66	J4	Baiguowan[HB]	110	C4	Baimangying[HN]	114	D8
Badaogu[TJ]	42	B3	Baihaohekou[SN]	156	F8	Baimaoping[HN]	114	C6
Badaohao[LN]	62	F3	Baihe[GD]	118	E4	Baimaqiao[HN]	114	E4
Badaohe[HEB]	48	F3	Baihe[GS]	160	G6	Baimaqiao[JX]	98	D3
Badaohezi[JL]	66	G4	Baihe[GX]	124	C4	Baimashi[SX]	54	E2
Badaojuan[NX]	168	B3	Baihe[SC]	138	J2	Baimasi[NX]	168	B3
Badaoka[NM]	58	N1	Baihe[SN]	156	G8	Baimatan[SN]	156	G5
Badaoshao[YN]	148	J6	Baihe[YN]	148	I8	Baimeixu[GD]	118	C4
Badaying[HEB]	48	E2	Baihua Shuiku[GZ]	144	E4	Baimi[SH]	74	C2
Badi[YN]	148	E3	Baihua[GD]	118	G4	Baimian[NX]	168	C5
Bading[GX]	124	E2	Baihuagou[HEB]	48	C2	Baimiao[HB]	110	G4
Badong[HB]	110	D3	Baihugou[HEB]	48	E2	Baimiao[HEN]	106	G3
Badou[AH]	90	D4	Baiji Shan[AH]	90	E7	Baimiaohe[HB]	110	I3
Badu[FJ]	94	E3	Baiji Shan[ZJ]	84	C3	Baimiaotan[HEB]	48	B2
Badu[GX]	124	C3	Baiji[GX]	124	F5	Baimiaozi[NM]	58	X11
Badu[GZ]	144	D6	Baiji[HEN]	106	G4	Baimu[JX]	98	B3
Badu[SN]	156	C6	Baijia[CQ]	132	D3	Baina[GZ]	144	D3

Bainan He[GX]	124	C4	Baishuihe[HB]	110	C5	Baizhu[JX]	98	D4
Bainan[GX]	124	C4	Baishuijiang[SN]	156	C7	Baizhu[ZJ]	84	E4
Bainang[XZ]	152	F5	Baishuijie[JX]	98	C2	Baizhuangzi[TJ]	42	C3
Baingoin[XZ]	152	G4	Baishuitou[TJ]	42	C4	Baizi[CQ]	132	B3
Baini[HB]	110	H5	Baishuiyang[ZJ]	84	E4	Baizuizi[NX]	168	C4
Baipeng[GX]	124	G3	Baishuiyuan[FJ]	94	D3	Baji[HEN]	106	G4
Baipenzhu Shuiku[GD]	118	H3	Baishun[GD]	118	G1	Bajia[HEB]	48	F3
Baiqi[FJ]	94	D5	Baisi[HEN]	106	F4	Bajialiu[SD]	102	B3
Baiqi[HEB]	48	C2	Baisi[SC]	138	F7	Bajianfang[TJ]	42	B2
Baiqi[JL]	66	G3	Baisuo[GZ]	144	E5	Bajiao[GX]	124	D5
Baiqi[LN]	62	G4	Baita He[JX]	98	E3	Bajiao[GZ]	144	F2
Baiqizhai[LN]	62	H2	Baita[FJ]	94	E3	Bajiao[HB]	110	C4
Baiquan[HL]	70	D5	Baita[LN]	62	D4	Bajiao[SC]	138	H4
Baiquanmen[GS]	160	D3	Baita[SD]	102	E3	Bajiao[SC]	138	K4
Baique[HEN]	106	G6	Baitafan[AH]	90	C5	Bajiao[SD]	102	H2
Baiquesi[SN]	156	C7	Baitan[HEN]	106	F3	Bajiao[SX]	54	C2
Bair Ul[NM]	58	K6	Baitang[QH]	164	J8	Bajiao[YN]	148	F6
Bairab Co[XZ]	152	C2	Baitang[SX]	54	D2	Bajiazi[LN]	62	D4
Bairin Youqi[NM]	58	M6	Baitangchakou[QH]	164	J8	Bajiazi[LN]	62	E2
Bairin Zuoqi[NM]	58	M6	Baitao[CQ]	132	D4	Bajie[GZ]	144	D6
Bairo Zangbo[XZ]	152	F4	Baitaozi[NX]	168	B4	Bajileu[JL]	66	E3
Baisangguan[HB]	110	D2	Baitashui[NX]	168	C3	Bake[CQ]	132	D4
Baise[GX]	124	D4	Baitazi[LN]	62	C4	Bakeshu[LN]	62	H2
Baisha Gang[HI]	128	A3	Baitazi[TJ]	42	B2	Bakog[QH]	164	I7
Baisha Shuiku[HEN]	106	E3	Baitian[HN]	114	E5	Bala[GX]	124	E3
Baisha[AH]	90	C3	Baitu[CQ]	132	E3	Balai[GZ]	144	E6
Baisha[CQ]	132	C4	Baitu[GX]	124	F3	Balgan[NM]	58	T11
Baisha[CQ]	132	C4	Baitu[HI]	128	C2	Balgas[SN]	156	F2
Baisha[FJ]	94	B4	Baitu[JS]	80	E5	Balguntay[XJ]	172	K4
Baisha[FJ]	94	C4	Baituguang[NX]	168	C3	Balhai[NM]	58	G7
Baisha[FJ]	94	E3	Baituyao[HEB]	48	C2	Balhaiqê[XZ]	152	G3
Baisha[FJ]	94	E4	Baiwan[GD]	118	E2	Bali[LN]	62	F4
Baisha[GD]	118	F2	Baiwang[GX]	124	F3	Balidian[ZJ]	84	E2
Baisha[GX]	124	G4	Baiwang[SN]	156	E6	Balidianzi[LN]	62	H3
Baisha[GX]	124	I3	Baiwen[SX]	54	C3	Baliguan[SN]	156	D7
Baisha[GZ]	144	G3	Baiwo[HB]	110	D2	Balimiao[SD]	102	C4
Baisha[HI]	128	B2	Baiwu[SC]	138	G8	Baling[GZ]	144	D5
Baisha[HI]	128	B2	Baixi[HN]	114	D4	Balipu[TJ]	42	B1
Baisha[HN]	114	E4	Baixiang[HEB]	48	B6	Baliqiao[TJ]	42	A3
Baisha[JX]	98	C5	Baixing[GZ]	144	D4	Balishao[JL]	66	G5
Baisha[SD]	102	E3	Baiya[NX]	168	B4	Baliu[YN]	148	G7
Baishan[AH]	90	C3	Baiyan[SD]	102	D4	Baliwan[HB]	110	H3
Baishan[AH]	90	D5	Baiyang Dian[HEB]	48	C5	Balizhuang[TJ]	42	C3
Baishan[HL]	70	E5	Baiyang He[XJ]	172	J2	Bam Co[XZ]	152	G4
Baishan[JL]	66	E4	Baiyang[FJ]	94	E2	Bama[GX]	124	E3
Baishan[JL]	66	G6	Baiyanggou[XJ]	172	J3	Bamao[ZJ]	84	E3
Baishan[JL]	66	H5	Baiyangping[HB]	110	C4	Bamencheng[TJ]	42	C2
Baishan[JL]	66	I5	Baiyangshan[HEN]	106	C3	Bameng Shuiku[GX]	124	D4
Baishan[LN]	62	C3	Baiyangshihu[BJ]	36	B3	Bamian Shan[HN]	114	F6
Baishansi[SX]	54	B6	Baiyangyu[SX]	54	E4	Bamian Shan[HN]	114	F7
Baishanzu[ZJ]	84	D5	Baiyazi[NX]	168	B4	Bamian[JL]	66	H2
Baishatan[SD]	102	H3	Baiyi Shan[HB]	110	D4	Bamiancheng[LN]	62	H1
Baishaxu[HN]	114	E7	Baiyi[HN]	114	D3	Bamiao[SN]	156	E8
Baishazhou[JX]	98	D2	Baiyi[SC]	138	M4	Bamudi[BJ]	36	C2
Baishe[JX]	98	D4	Baiyin He[JL]	66	G3	Bamzerag[YN]	148	E2
Baisheng[GX]	124	C4	Baiyin[GS]	160	D3	Banan Qu[CQ]	132	C4
Baishi Ding[FJ]	94	B3	Baiyin[GS]	160	G4	Banba[GX]	124	E6
Baishi Shan[GX]	124	H4	Baiyinna[HL]	70	C2	Banbar[XZ]	152	I4
Baishi Shan[HEB]	48	B4	Baiyu Shan[SN]	156	E3	Banbar[XZ]	152	I4
Baishi[CQ]	132	D3	Baiyu Shan[SN]	156	E3	Banbian Hu[HN]	114	E4
Baishi[CQ]	132	E4	Baiyu[FJ]	94	E3	Banbishan[HEB]	48	E3
Baishi[FJ]	94	C2	Baiyu[HN]	114	C6	Bancang[HB]	110	D3
Baishi[GX]	124	H2	Baiyu[LN]	62	H2	Bancheng[JS]	80	D3
Baishi[GZ]	144	H4	Baiyu[QH]	164	M7	Banchengzi[BJ]	36	E2
Baishi[HN]	114	E5	Baiyü[SC]	138	D4	Bancun[FJ]	94	C4
Baishi[SX]	54	C6	Baiyu[SN]	156	D8	Banfangzi[SN]	156	D7
Baishi[YN]	148	E4	Baiyun Hu[SD]	102	D3	Bang Hu[JX]	98	C2
Baishidu[HN]	114	F7	Baiyun Qu[GZ]	144	E4	Bangang[AH]	90	C4
Baishilizi[HL]	70	D3	Baiyun Yan[GZ]	144	E3	Bangda[XZ]	152	J4
Baishishan[JL]	66	H4	Baiyun Zhang[GD]	118	G4	Bangda[XZ]	152	K5
Baishishui[GX]	124	G5	Baiyun[CQ]	132	D4	Bangdag Co[XZ]	152	B2
Baishitou[XJ]	172	N4	Baiyun[CQ]	132	F2	Bangdong[GZ]	144	H4
Baishiya[GX]	124	F6	Baiyun[GX]	124	D5	Banggu[YN]	148	J7
Baishiyan[YN]	148	I5	Baiyun[GX]	124	G2	Bangkor[XZ]	152	A3
Baishou[GX]	124	G2	Baiyun[HL]	70	D4	Bangma Shan[YN]	148	E7
Baishu[HEB]	48	B4	Baiyun[HN]	114	D3	Bangongo Co[XZ]	152	A3
Baishu[HN]	114	F5	Baiyun[SX]	54	E4	Bangshipu[LN]	62	F4
Baishui He[SN]	156	F5	Baiyunshan Shuiku[JX]	98	C5	Bangtou[FJ]	94	D4
Baishui Jiang[GS]	160	G6	Baiyusi[SN]	156	G6	Bangui[GZ]	144	D5
Baishui[FJ]	94	C5	Baizhang[FJ]	94	D3	Bangun[GX]	124	E5
Baishui[GD]	118	E2	Baizhang[ZJ]	84	D5	Bangxi[HI]	128	B2
Baishui[HN]	114	D6	Baizhi[CQ]	132	E2	Bangxu[GX]	124	E4
Baishui[JX]	98	B3	Baizhong[FJ]	94	D3	Banhu[JS]	80	E3
Baishui[SN]	156	F5	Baizhu[JX]	98	A4	Banjiang[HN]	114	F3

Banjieta[HEB]	48	E2
Banjing[JS]	80	F4
Banlan[GX]	124	E3
Banlan[GX]	124	G2
Banlao[YN]	148	D7
Banli[FJ]	94	C5
Banli[GX]	124	E5
Banling[GX]	124	F3
Banlun[YN]	148	K7
Banmian[FJ]	94	D3
Banmiao[SN]	156	G7
Banmiaozi[JL]	66	G5
Banmu[HEN]	106	F3
Banpo[YN]	148	F7
Banpodian[HEN]	106	F2
Banpu[JS]	80	E2
Banpudian[AH]	90	C3
Banqiao Shuiku[HEN]	106	E5
Banqiao[AH]	90	D4
Banqiao[GS]	160	E3
Banqiao[GS]	160	H5
Banqiao[HB]	110	C4
Banqiao[HB]	110	E3
Banqiao[HEN]	106	F3
Banqiao[HI]	128	A3
Banqiao[HN]	114	E6
Banqiao[JS]	80	D5
Banqiao[JS]	80	E2
Banqiao[YN]	148	F4
Banqiao[YN]	148	I5
Banqiao[YN]	148	J3
Banqiao[ZJ]	84	D4
Banqiaodian[HB]	110	F3
Banqiaoji[AH]	90	C3
Banqiaokou[SC]	138	M3
Banquan[SD]	102	E4
Banshan[HN]	114	F5
Banshanping[HEN]	106	D4
Bansheng[GX]	124	E3
Banshi[JL]	66	K5
Banshi[JX]	98	C6
Banta[AH]	90	E4
Bantao[GX]	124	C3
Bantao[SN]	156	E8
Banxi[CQ]	132	E5
Banxi[GZ]	144	G2
Banyan Hua[NM]	58	V11
Banzai[FJ]	94	C5
Banzhu[ZJ]	84	F3
Banzhuyuan[AH]	90	B5
Bao He[SN]	156	C7
Bao'ai He[GX]	124	D4
Bao'an Qu[GD]	118	F4
Bao'an[CQ]	132	F5
Bao'an[GX]	124	E3
Bao'an[HEN]	106	E4
Bao'an[HN]	114	E7
Baoan[QH]	164	O5
Baochang[JS]	80	G4
Baodao[HI]	128	B2
Baode[SX]	54	C2
Baodi Qu[TJ]	42	B2
Baodian[JL]	66	E3
Baoding[CQ]	132	B4
Baoding[HEB]	48	C5
Baodong[HL]	70	G6
Baodun[JS]	80	F3
Baofang Shuiku[HI]	128	C2
Baofang[HI]	128	C2
Baofeng[CQ]	132	B4
Baofeng[FJ]	94	D3
Baofeng[HB]	110	D2
Baofeng[HEN]	106	E4
Baofeng[JX]	98	C2
Baofeng[NX]	168	C1
Baofeng[YN]	148	E5
Baofeng[YN]	148	H6
Baofu[HB]	110	H4
Baogang[HI]	128	B3
Baogao[HI]	128	A3
Baogunao[YN]	148	I4
Baoguo[HI]	128	B3
Baohu Jiao[HI]	128	C1
Baohu Shan[HI]	128	C2
Baohua[YN]	148	F6
Baoji[AH]	90	D3
Baoji[GZ]	144	C5
Baoji[JS]	80	D3
Baoji[SN]	156	D6
Baojia[CQ]	132	E4
Baojiatun[LN]	62	F2
Baojie Ling[GX]	124	H2
Baojing[HN]	114	B4
Baokang[HB]	110	E3
Baokeng[GD]	118	I2
Baokou[GD]	118	H3
Baoli[LN]	62	G2
Baoling Gang[HI]	128	D2
Baolong[CQ]	132	B3
Baolun Nongchang[HI]	128	B3
Baoluo[HI]	128	C2
Baomei Ling[HI]	128	B2
Baomei[HI]	128	B2
Baomin[JL]	66	D1
Baoping[GX]	124	E3
Baoping[HI]	128	A2
Baoqiao[SH]	74	C2
Baoqing[HL]	70	G5
Baoquan[HL]	70	D4
Baoquanshan[JL]	66	H6
Baoshan Qu[HL]	70	F5
Baoshan Qu[SH]	74	C2
Baoshan[BJ]	36	D2
Baoshan[HL]	70	B4
Baoshan[HL]	70	D5
Baoshan[HL]	70	E4
Baoshan[JL]	66	G5
Baoshan[JX]	98	C5
Baoshan[LN]	62	G4
Baoshan[NM]	58	P3
Baoshan[SH]	74	C2
Baoshan[YN]	148	E3
Baoshan[YN]	148	E5
Baoshan[YN]	148	J4
Baoshi[HI]	128	B3
Baoshi[NM]	58	N5
Baoshou[JL]	66	G3
Baota[SN]	98	C2
Baota[NX]	168	C2
Baotajiang[GX]	124	H2
Baotian[GZ]	144	C5
Baotian[ZJ]	84	E5
Baoting[HI]	128	B3
Baotou[NM]	58	H7
Baotou[NM]	58	V11
Baotun[HEN]	106	F3
Baowei Ling[HI]	128	A3
Baowei[SH]	74	C2
Baowen[HI]	128	B3
Baoxi[ZJ]	84	C4
Baoxia[HB]	110	D2
Baoxin[HEN]	106	F5
Baoxing[HL]	70	F4
Baoxing[SC]	138	H5
Baoxiu[YN]	148	H7
Baoxu[GX]	124	D5
Baoying[JS]	80	E3
Baoying[TJ]	42	A3
Baoyuanzhan[HEB]	48	E1
Baozhen[HB]	110	D4
Baozhen[SH]	74	C1
Baozhimawo[TJ]	42	C2
Baozhu[GD]	118	D3
Baozi[HN]	114	B6
Baoziba[GS]	160	G6
Baoziwan[SN]	156	D3
Bapen[GX]	124	E5
Baqên[XZ]	152	H3
Baqên[XZ]	152	I4
Baqiao[JS]	80	E4
Baqiu[JX]	98	C4
Baquan[SX]	54	D5
Baquka[QH]	164	F7
Barang[XZ]	152	H5
Barkam[SC]	138	H4
Barkol Hu[XJ]	172	N4
Barkol[XJ]	172	N4
Barling[XZ]	152	F3
Barong[SC]	138	E4
Barragem de Hác Sá[MC]	182	C6
Barragem de Ká—Hó[MC]	182	C6
Barun Har Modon[XJ]	172	K4
Barun[NM]	58	T11
Barun[QH]	164	J4
Barun[QH]	164	J5
Basalt Island[HK]	176	F3
Basar[QH]	164	M7
Bashan Shuiku[SD]	102	E4
Bashan[CQ]	132	D3
Bashan[CQ]	132	E1
Bashan[SN]	156	C8
Bashan[SN]	156	E8
Bashiba[JL]	66	D3
Bashili Dananshan[GX]	124	G2
Bashili Dananshan[HN]	114	C6
Basum[XZ]	152	H4
Basuo Gang[HI]	128	A2
Bata[SX]	54	E3
Batai[SC]	138	N4
Batan[JS]	80	F2
Batang[SC]	138	E5
Batangwan[NX]	168	B3
Batou[GX]	124	D4
Batuan[HN]	114	F5
Batuying[LN]	62	D3
Bawan[GD]	118	H3
Bawang[SC]	138	G5
Bawu[JL]	66	E4
Baxian[SN]	156	F8
Baxianzhuozi[TJ]	42	C1
Baxin[YN]	148	H7
Baxin[YN]	148	J7
Baxoi[XZ]	152	J4
Baxolla Ling[XZ]	152	J5
Baxu[GX]	124	E3
Bayan Bogd[NM]	58	D7
Bayan Bulag[NM]	58	U11
Bayan Col[QH]	164	J3
Bayan Engger[NM]	58	G7
Bayan Engger[NM]	58	T11
Bayan Gol[XJ]	172	I4
Bayan Har Shan[QH]	164	J6
Bayan Har Shan[QH]	164	K7
Bayan Har Shan[SC]	138	C2
Bayan Har Shankou[QH]	164	J6
Bayan Huxu[NM]	58	L5
Bayan Kuangqu[NM]	58	H7
Bayan Moron[NM]	58	S12
Bayan Nur[NM]	58	H8
Bayan Nur[NM]	58	K6
Bayan Nur[NM]	58	O5
Bayan Nurun[NM]	58	F7
Bayan Obo[NM]	58	I7
Bayan Obo[NM]	58	U11
Bayan Obo[XJ]	172	K2
Bayan Qogt[NM]	58	J6
Bayan Shan[QH]	164	J3
Bayan Ul[NM]	58	J5
Bayan Ul[XJ]	172	J4
Bayan Us[NM]	58	H7
Bayan Us[NM]	58	U11
Bayan[HL]	70	D5
Bayan[NM]	58	H6
Bayan[NM]	58	X11
Bayan[QH]	164	N4
Bayanhar Shan[QH]	164	H5
Bayannur[NM]	58	G7
Bayannur[NM]	58	T11
Bayawat[XJ]	172	F6
Bayi[NM]	58	T11
Bayi[SX]	54	E6
Baying[JX]	98	C6
Bayna Dulan[NM]	58	J5
Baytic Shan Muchang[XJ]	172	M3
Baytik Shan[XJ]	172	M3
Baytokay[XJ]	172	H4
Bayuan[SN]	156	F6
Bayuquan Qu[LN]	62	F4
Bazhai[GZ]	144	G4
Bazhai[YN]	148	J7
Bazhong[SC]	138	L4
Bazhou[HEB]	48	D4

Bazhou[SX]	54	E4
Bazhuangzhan[NX]	168	C3
Bazhuangzi[TJ]	42	C2
Bazi[GD]	118	G2
Baziqiao[FJ]	94	C3
Bazong[GS]	160	G6
Beacon Hill[HK]	176	D3
Bêba[XZ]	152	H5
Bêca[QH]	164	I8
Behleg[QH]	164	D4
Bei He[HB]	110	C5
Bei Hulsan Hu[QH]	164	H4
Bei Inggen[NM]	58	F7
Bei Jiang[GD]	118	F2
Bei Jiao[HI]	128	F5
Bei Shan[GS]	160	B2
Bei Xi[FJ]	94	C2
Bei'an[HL]	70	D4
Bei'an[BJ]	36	C3
Bei'ao Dao[FJ]	94	F3
Beiba[SN]	156	D8
Beibai[BJ]	36	C4
Beibei Qu[CQ]	132	C4
Beibi[FJ]	94	E3
Beibu Gulf[GD]	118	A6
Beibu Gulf[GX]	124	F7
Beibu Gulf[HI]	128	A1
Beibuzi[NX]	168	B5
Beicai[SH]	74	D2
Beicang[TJ]	42	B3
Beichangshan Dao[SD]	102	G2
Beichangtan[NX]	168	A3
Beichen Qu[TJ]	42	B3
Beicheng[SX]	54	D5
Beichengzi He[JS]	80	E4
Beichuan[SC]	138	J4
Beichuan He[QH]	164	N3
Beichuan He[SX]	54	C4
Beicigou[BJ]	36	C2
Beicun[TJ]	42	C3
Beida He[GS]	160	C3
Beida Shan[NM]	58	D8
Beida[HI]	128	C3
Beida[HN]	114	E3
Beidagang Shuiku[TJ]	42	B4
Beidahu[JL]	66	G4
Beidaihe Qu[HEB]	48	G4
Beidian[HEB]	48	C5
Beidianzi[BJ]	36	E2
Beidianzi[LN]	62	I3
Beidingji[JS]	80	D2
Beidou[GD]	118	E5
Beidou[YN]	148	E5
Beidouxi[HN]	114	C5
Beiershijiazi[LN]	62	C2
Beifang[BJ]	36	D3
Beifei He[AH]	90	C3
Beigang[HB]	110	G5
Beigang[JL]	66	H5
Beigang[JX]	98	C4
Beigang[SH]	74	D1
Beige[YN]	148	I7
Beigou[SD]	102	G2
Beiguan Dao[ZJ]	84	E5
Beiguan[HEN]	106	G3
Beihai Gang[GX]	124	G6
Beihai[GX]	124	G6
Beihai[LN]	62	E6
Beihan[SX]	54	C5
Beihe[GD]	118	B6
Beihuaidian[TJ]	42	C3
Beihuangcheng Dao[SD]	102	G1
Beihujiajuan[NX]	168	C2
Beiji Shan[ZJ]	84	F5
Beijia[HI]	128	C2
Beijia[SD]	102	E3
Beijiang[HL]	70	D3
Beijiang[JS]	80	E3
Beijiao[FJ]	94	E3
Beijie[GD]	118	C4
Beijie[ZJ]	84	D4
Beijin Gang[GD]	118	E5
Beijing[BJ]	36	C4
Beijing[GX]	124	E3
Beijinzhuang[TJ]	42	B3
Beijipo[SD]	102	D3
Beijishan Liedao[ZJ]	84	F5
Beijuma He[HEB]	48	C4
Beikeng[JX]	98	C4
Beikuanping[SN]	156	G7
Beilang[SH]	74	C2
Beili Gang[HI]	128	A2
Beili[GD]	118	I2
Beilian[HL]	70	C4
Beiling[SD]	102	E2
Beiliu Jiang[GX]	124	H5
Beiliu[GX]	124	H5
Beilong Shan[ZJ]	84	E5
Beilonggang[JS]	80	E3
Beilu He[QH]	164	F6
Beilun He[GX]	124	E6
Beilun Qu[ZJ]	84	F3
Beimajuanzi[HEB]	48	E3
Beimazhuang[BJ]	36	D4
Beimeng[SD]	102	F3
Beimian[GD]	118	D4
Beimiao[HEN]	106	G5
Beipan Jiang[GZ]	144	D5
Beipiao[LN]	62	D3
Beiping[SX]	54	D5
Beipo[GD]	118	B5
Beiqiao[SH]	74	C2
Beiru He[HEN]	106	D3
Beisanjia[LN]	62	H2
Beishan Meikuang[GS]	160	D2
Beishan[GS]	160	G3
Beishan[GX]	124	F3
Beishan[HN]	114	D5
Beishan[HN]	114	F4
Beishangmatou[TJ]	42	B4
Beishe[SX]	54	E5
Beishi Dao[HI]	128	D2
Beishi[GD]	118	E3
Beishi[GX]	124	H5
Beishicao[BJ]	36	D3
Beishihe[HL]	70	D4
Beishuang Dao[FJ]	94	F3
Beishuiquan[HEB]	48	B3
Beisijia[LN]	62	D2
Beisijiazi[LN]	62	D3
Beisijiazi[LN]	62	G2
Beisiping[LN]	62	I3
Beisu[SD]	102	C4
Beita[LN]	62	D2
Beitai Ding[SX]	54	E2
Beitaishang Shuiku[BJ]	36	D3
Beitaizi[BJ]	36	D2
Beitan[GS]	160	E4
Beitan[TJ]	42	B2
Beitang Shuiku[TJ]	42	C3
Beitang[TJ]	42	C3
Beitanzhuang[HEB]	48	B5
Beitaoyuan[TJ]	42	B1
Beitian Chi[SX]	54	E5
Beitian[SX]	54	D4
Beitou[GD]	118	G2
Beitouying[HEB]	48	E2
Beituan[FJ]	94	B4
Beitun[XJ]	172	K2
Beituo[GX]	124	I3
Beiwangzhu[SD]	102	G3
Beiwei Tan[GD]	118	H5
Beiwei[HEB]	48	D5
Beiwu[BJ]	36	D3
Beiwu[GX]	124	G4
Beiwudang[SX]	54	C4
Beixiang[GD]	118	F1
Beixiang[SX]	54	B6
Beixiaolou[TJ]	42	A3
Beixiaozhuang[HEB]	48	B6
Beixiazhuang[SX]	54	E3
Beixin[SX]	54	B6
Beixindian[BJ]	36	D2
Beixing[HL]	70	F6
Beixingqiao[JS]	80	G4
Beiya[YN]	148	F4
Beiyang[YN]	148	I5
Beiyangji[SD]	102	C3
Beiyao[TJ]	42	B3
Beiyijing[SX]	54	D3
Beiyinhe[HL]	70	D6
Beiyu[BJ]	36	B4
Beiyuan[JX]	98	B4
Beiyuan[SN]	156	F5
Beiyubu[TJ]	42	B3
Beiyukou[SX]	54	E3
Beizangcun[BJ]	36	C4
Beizhai[BJ]	36	D3
Beizhai[GS]	160	G5
Beizhai[SX]	54	E4
Beizhakou[TJ]	42	B4
Beizhang[ZJ]	84	F3
Beizhen[LN]	62	E3
Beizheng[JL]	66	D3
Beizhihe[BJ]	36	B4
Beizhouzhuang[SX]	54	D2
Beizhuang[BJ]	36	E2
Beizhuang[SD]	102	D5
Beizi[HEN]	106	D4
Bênba[XZ]	152	G5
Bengbeng He[LN]	62	C2
Bengbu[AH]	90	D4
Benhao[HI]	128	B3
Benjiwo[HN]	114	D7
Benmana[QH]	164	K6
Benxi[LN]	62	G3
Benxi[LN]	62	H3
Bênxung[XZ]	152	F5
Benzhuang[GZ]	144	F3
Bêruogma[QH]	164	F6
Bi Qu[QH]	164	D7
Biancang[JS]	80	F3
Biandan Gang[JS]	80	F2
Biandangou[NX]	168	C3
Bianjiang[YN]	148	F7
Bianmagou[QH]	164	L2
Bianmen[LN]	62	H4
Biantan[QH]	164	N4
Bianyang[GZ]	144	E5
Bianyao[SX]	54	E2
Bianyuan[SD]	102	C3
Bianzhangzi[LN]	62	D3
Bianzhao[JL]	66	D3
Biaocun[YN]	148	E4
Biaokou[TJ]	42	C3
Biaoli[AH]	90	B3
Bi'aqie[QH]	164	F5
Bibgya[XZ]	152	B3
Bidi[SX]	54	D6
Bidian[HEN]	106	E5
Bielahong[HL]	70	H5
Bieli[FJ]	94	B4
Bieqiao[JS]	80	E5
Big Wave Bay[HK]	176	E4
Biguo[SD]	102	G2
Bihen[GZ]	144	D5
Bijia Shan[ZJ]	84	G3
Bijiawan[SN]	156	G7
Bijie[GZ]	144	D3
Bikou[GS]	160	G6
Bili[FJ]	94	E3
Biliu He[LN]	62	F5
Bilung[XZ]	152	H4
Biluo Xueshan[YN]	148	E4
Bin Jiang[GD]	118	E3
Bin Xian[HL]	70	D6
Bin Xian[SN]	156	E5
Bincheng[SD]	102	D2
Binchuan[YN]	148	F5
Bingcaowan[GS]	160	F4
Bingfang[JS]	80	G4
Binglie[YN]	148	J7
Binglincha[GS]	160	H4
Bingma Jiao[HI]	128	B2
Bingying[HB]	110	C2
Bingzhongluo[YN]	148	D2
Binhai[HEB]	48	F4
Binhai[JS]	80	E2
Binhe[JS]	80	F2
Binheng[GD]	118	E3
Binhu[HB]	110	G5
Binhu[SD]	102	C4

Binhuai[JS] 80 F2
Binlang Jiang[YN] 148 D6
Binnan[HL] 70 D3
Bintian Shuiku[JX] 98 D2
Binyang[GX] 124 F4
Binzhou[SD] 102 E2
Biqeq[NM] 58 X11
Biqu[QH] 164 E7
Biru[XZ] 152 H4
Bishan[CQ] 132 C4
Bishan[CQ] 132 D3
Bishan[JX] 98 D2
Bishi[HN] 114 F4
Bishui[HL] 70 B2
Bitang[HI] 128 C3
Bitou Jiao[HI] 128 A3
Bixi[JX] 98 B5
Biyang He[HEN] 106 D5
Biyang[HEN] 106 E5
Biyong[HN] 114 B5
Biyou[GZ] 144 D6
Bizhai[YN] 148 E6
Bizhou[HL] 70 C3
Bizhou[JX] 98 B5
Bo Hai[SD] 102 F1
Boai He[YN] 148 L7
Bo'ai[HEN] 106 E2
Boai[YN] 148 L7
Bo'ao Gang[HI] 128 C2
Bo'ao[HI] 128 C2
Bobai[GX] 124 G5
Bobdoi[XZ] 152 D4
Bobi[HEN] 106 E2
Bobso[SC] 138 I2
Boda[SC] 138 G8
Bodu[JL] 66 E2
Bofu Ansha[HI] 128 F5
Bogcang Zangbo[XZ] 152 E4
Bogd Ul[NM] 58 K5
Bogd Ul[NM] 58 L3
Bogda Shan[XJ] 172 L4
Bogeli[SD] 102 D2
Bohai Haixia[LN] 62 E6
Bohai Haixia[SD] 102 G1
Bohai Wan[SD] 102 D1
Bohai Wan[TJ] 42 C4
Bohai[BJ] 36 D3
Bohai[CQ] 132 E5
Bohai[HL] 70 E6
Bohai[TJ] 42 C4
Bohe Gang[GD] 118 D5
Bohe[GD] 118 D5
Bohe[HL] 70 C6
Bohu(Bagrax)[XJ] 172 K5
Boiba[QH] 164 L7
Bola[GS] 160 F5
Bolao[GX] 124 G5
Bole(Bortala)[XJ] 172 I3
Boli[HL] 70 F6
Boli[JS] 80 E3
Bolian[HI] 128 B2
Bolichengzi[JL] 66 E4
Bolin[GS] 160 F5
Bolishan[JL] 66 D4
Bolo[XZ] 152 K4
Boluo[GD] 118 F2
Boluo[GD] 118 G3
Boluo[SN] 156 F2
Boluonuo[HEB] 48 E2
Bomi(Bowo)[XZ] 152 I5
Bong Co[XZ] 152 G4
Bonihe[JL] 66 F4
Boping Ling[FJ] 94 B5
Boping[SD] 102 C3
Bopu Gang[HI] 128 B2
Boqê[XZ] 152 G4
Bor Ondor[JL] 66 C3
Bor Tohoi[NM] 58 W11
Borohoro Shan[XJ] 172 I3
Borong[XZ] 152 D5
Bortala He[XJ] 172 H3
Boshan Qu[SD] 102 D3
Boshan Shuiku[HEN] 106 E5
Boshang[YN] 148 F7

Boshe[ZJ] 84 D3
Bosian[XJ] 172 H7
Bostanterag[XJ] 172 E6
Bosten(Bagrax) Hu[XJ] 172 K5
Bostenhu[XJ] 172 K5
Botang[GX] 124 H4
Botou[HEB] 48 D5
Botou[SD] 102 E2
Bowang[AH] 90 E5
Bowen[HI] 128 C2
Boxing[SD] 102 E2
Boxo[XZ] 152 J5
Boxue[GX] 124 G5
Boyang[GD] 118 C4
Boye[HEB] 48 C5
Boyi[JS] 80 E5
Boyi[SX] 54 D4
Bozdong[XJ] 172 H5
Bozhi[GD] 118 E3
Bozhou[AH] 90 B3
Bozhu Shan[YN] 148 I7
Broad Feng[XJ] 172 F8
Bu Qu[XZ] 152 F5
Buchang[GD] 118 D5
Buchang[SN] 156 G6
Bucun[SD] 102 D3
Budayuan[LN] 62 I4
Budongquan[QH] 164 F5
Bugkamba[XZ] 152 D4
Bugong[SX] 54 C7
Bugt[NM] 58 N3
Bugugou[HEB] 48 E2
Buh He[QH] 164 K3
Buhai[JL] 66 F3
Buhe[HB] 110 F4
Buir Nur[NM] 58 L4
Buir[NM] 58 L3
Bujia[JX] 98 B2
Buka Daban Feng[QH] 164 C4
Buka Luk Tag[QH] 164 D5
Bukou[HB] 110 F2
Bukou[SD] 102 I2
Bulag[NM] 58 L5
Bulang Nur[NM] 58 T11
Bulanggir[QH] 164 J4
Bulanghe[SN] 156 F2
Bulangshan[YN] 148 F9
Bulangtai[QH] 164 E4
Bulaotun[BJ] 36 D2
Buli[GX] 124 H3
Bulin Xil[NM] 58 V12
Buling[XZ] 152 A4
Buliu He[GX] 124 D3
Bulongji[GS] 160 C2
Bulu[ZJ] 84 E4
Bulungkol[XJ] 172 E6
Bumdirla[XZ] 152 H6
Bumgyê[XZ] 152 K4
Bündo[SC] 138 E7
Buqian[GD] 118 G3
Buqing Shan[QH] 164 J5
Buqing Shan[QH] 164 J5
Buquan[GX] 124 E4
Burang[XZ] 152 B4
Burgastai Gou[NM] 58 V11
Burhan Budai Shan[QH] 164 H5
Burhan[NM] 58 M7
Burjang Haizi[NM] 58 H8
Burog Co[XZ] 152 D2
Burqin He[XJ] 172 K1
Burqin[XJ] 172 K2
Burqunji[XJ] 172 N3
Bushang[FJ] 94 C3
Buta[XZ] 152 I3
Butmej[NM] 58 J6
Bütog[XZ] 152 K5
Butou[GX] 124 I3
Butuo[SC] 138 H8
Buxitou[SD] 102 H2
Buya[XJ] 172 H7
Buyant[NM] 58 G7
Buyuan Jiang[YN] 148 G8
Buyun Shan[LN] 62 F4
Buzhai[GD] 118 I3

Buzidian[HEB] 48 E3
Buziwan[SX] 54 E1

C

Caca He[QH] 164 K4
Cacaxingka Nongchang[QH] 164 K4
Cai Xi[ZJ] 84 C4
Caibu[HEB] 48 C7
Caicun[AH] 90 E6
Caicun[SD] 102 C2
Caidian Qu[HB] 110 G4
Caidian[HEN] 106 D3
Caidianhe[HB] 110 I4
Caifang[JX] 98 C6
Caigongzhuang[TJ] 42 B4
Caigou[HEN] 106 F4
Caigyu[XZ] 152 H5
Caihua[HB] 110 D4
Caihuaping[HN] 114 F6
Caijia[CQ] 132 C5
Caijia[JL] 66 E4
Caijiabu[TJ] 42 C3
Caijiagou[JL] 66 G2
Caijiahui[SX] 54 B3
Caijiakou[BJ] 36 B4
Caijiaqiao[AH] 90 E6
Caijiawa[BJ] 36 D3
Caijiaya[SX] 54 C3
Caijiazhuang[SD] 102 F3
Cailikou[HN] 114 D7
Cailing[JX] 98 D2
Cailu[SH] 74 D2
Caimiao[HB] 110 F4
Caipuzhangtong[QH] 164 G6
Caiqiao[HN] 114 D6
Caisanghu[HN] 114 E3
Caishan[HB] 110 I5
Caitang[SD] 102 C5
Caiwan[GX] 124 H2
Caiyu[BJ] 36 D4
Caiyuan[HEB] 48 F3
Caiyuan[JL] 66 F6
Caiyuanji[SD] 102 B4
Caiyuanzi[JL] 66 F3
Caiyuyao[SN] 156 F7
Caizhuang[HEN] 106 F3
Caizhuangzi[TJ] 42 B4
Caizi Hu[AH] 90 D6
Caizi[JL] 66 D3
Caka Yanhu[QH] 164 L4
Caka[QH] 164 L4
Caka[XZ] 152 C3
Calungtang[QH] 164 I8
Cam Co[XZ] 152 C3
Canal dos Potos[MC] 182 A1
Cang Xian[HEB] 48 D5
Cangfang[HEN] 106 C5
Cangji[JS] 80 D3
Cangjiaxia[QH] 164 O4
Cangkutan[NX] 168 C1
Canglang Qu[TJ] 42 B4
Canglang Shan[HB] 110 D2
Canglin[JL] 66 K4
Cangling[CQ] 132 E5
Cangling[YN] 148 G5
Cangnan[ZJ] 84 E5
Cangqiao[SH] 74 C2
Cangshan Qu[FJ] 94 E3
Cangshan[HL] 70 B3
Cangshan[HN] 114 D4
Cangshan[SC] 138 K5
Cangshan[SD] 102 E5
Cangshang[BJ] 36 D3
Cangshe[SN] 156 B7
Cangshuipu[HN] 114 E4
Cangtai[HEN] 106 D5
Cangtou[AH] 90 D5
Cangtou[HEN] 106 D3
Cangwu[GX] 124 I4
Cangxi[SC] 138 K4

Name	Page	Grid
Cangyan[ZJ]	84	E3
Cangyanshan[HEB]	48	B6
Cangyuan[YN]	148	E7
Cangzhen[AH]	90	D4
Cangzhou[HEB]	48	D5
Canzhuang[SD]	102	G2
Cao Xian[SD]	102	B5
Cao'an[AH]	90	D4
Caoba[SC]	138	M4
Caoba[YN]	148	I7
Caobo[HN]	114	F5
Caobu[JS]	80	G4
Caochang[LN]	62	C4
Caochi[SC]	138	J5
Caochuan[SX]	54	C7
Caochuanpu[GS]	160	H5
Caocun[AH]	90	D2
Caocun[SN]	156	F6
Caocun[SX]	54	D5
Caodaokou[TJ]	42	C2
Caodian[HB]	110	G2
Caodian[JS]	80	E3
Caodian[TJ]	42	B2
Caodu He[GX]	124	E2
Caodu He[GZ]	144	F4
Cao'e Jiang[ZJ]	84	E3
Caofang[FJ]	94	B3
Caofeidian[HEB]	48	F5
Caogou[AH]	90	D3
Caogoubu[HEB]	48	B4
Caohai[GZ]	144	C4
Caohang[SH]	74	C2
Caohecheng[LN]	62	H4
Caohekou[LN]	62	G4
Caohezhang[LN]	62	H3
Caohu[XJ]	172	J5
Caoji[AH]	90	B4
Caoji[HEN]	106	H3
Caojia[HN]	114	D5
Caojia[SN]	156	D6
Caojiakou[TJ]	42	C2
Caojialu[BJ]	36	E2
Caojiawu[HEB]	48	D4
Caojiayuan[SX]	54	B4
Caojiazhai[SH]	74	D3
Caojiazhuang[SX]	54	C6
Caojing[SH]	74	C2
Caojing[SH]	74	C3
Caojing[SX]	54	B5
Caolian Ling[SN]	156	F6
Caolin[JX]	98	B5
Caolu[SH]	74	D2
Caomiao[AH]	90	C5
Caomiao[AH]	90	D4
Caomiao[JS]	80	D3
Caomiao[JS]	80	F3
Caomiao[NX]	168	C4
Caomiaozi[SD]	102	I2
Caonian[HEB]	48	F3
Caopie[JS]	80	F4
Caoping[GS]	160	G6
Caoping[HN]	114	D4
Caoping[SN]	156	F7
Caoqiao[JS]	80	D2
Caoshi[AH]	90	C3
Caoshi[HB]	110	G4
Caoshi[LN]	62	I2
Caotan[GS]	160	F5
Caotan[GS]	160	G5
Caotang[CQ]	132	F2
Caotang[GZ]	144	F3
Caotanwo[GS]	160	G4
Caowa[NX]	168	B4
Caowang[SH]	74	C2
Caowei[HN]	114	E3
Caoyan[JS]	80	F4
Caoyuan[HEB]	48	D2
Caoyuan[TJ]	42	B3
Caoyuanzi[SC]	138	G6
Caozhuang[AH]	90	C2
Caozhuang[LN]	62	D4
Caozhuang[SD]	102	D5
Caozhuangtou[SX]	54	D4
Caozili[TJ]	42	B3
Capug[QH]	164	N4
Caqu[XZ]	152	H4
Carumarcha[QH]	164	E6
Castle Peak[HK]	176	B2
Causeway Bay[HK]	176	D3
Cawarong[XZ]	152	K5
Cazê[XZ]	152	E4
Ceheng[GZ]	144	D6
Celing[GX]	124	E3
Cenchuan[HN]	114	F4
Cengang[ZJ]	84	F2
Cengdian[HB]	110	G3
Cengong[GZ]	144	G3
Cenhe[HB]	110	F4
Cennan[HN]	114	D3
Censong[GZ]	144	G4
Centianhe Shuiku[HN]	114	D7
Cenwang Laoshan[GX]	124	D3
Cenxi[GX]	124	H5
Cêri[XZ]	152	D4
Cêruma[GS]	160	F6
Cêrwai[XZ]	152	J4
Cetian Shuiku[SX]	54	E2
Ceyu[HEB]	48	B6
Cezi Dao[ZJ]	84	F2
Cha Hu[HB]	110	G4
Cha Kwo Chau[HK]	176	B4
Cha'an[AH]	90	C4
Cha'an[HEN]	106	D5
Cha'angmadengma[QH]	164	E8
Cha'anpu[HN]	114	D4
Chabaqi[NM]	58	O3
Chabei[GD]	118	I3
Chabu[GS]	160	G5
Chabyêr Caka[XZ]	152	D4
Chadam[QH]	164	G8
Chadao[HEB]	48	C3
Chadian[AH]	144	D4
Chadian[TJ]	42	C3
Chadianzi[HB]	110	D4
Chadong[GD]	118	D4
Chadong[GX]	124	G2
Chadong[HN]	114	B4
Cha'ensi[HN]	114	E5
Chagan[JL]	66	D2
Chagan[SN]	156	E6
Chagbo[XZ]	152	D3
Chagcaka[QH]	164	I9
Chaggar[XZ]	152	A2
Chaggur[QH]	164	G6
Chagmar[QH]	164	L3
Chagna[XZ]	152	D5
Chagou[HEB]	48	F2
Chagou[LN]	62	F4
Chagxê Zangbo[XZ]	152	D5
Chahayang[HL]	70	C4
Chahe[AH]	90	E4
Chahe[GZ]	144	D3
Chahe[HB]	110	G4
Chahe[HI]	128	A2
Chahe[JS]	80	E3
Chahe[JS]	80	F4
Chahe[SD]	102	E2
Chahe[YN]	148	H6
Chahekou[HI]	128	A3
Chahu[HI]	128	B2
Chahua[AH]	90	B3
Chai He[LN]	62	H2
Chai Kek[HK]	176	D2
Chai Wan Kok[HK]	176	C2
Chai Wan[HK]	176	D3
Chaichangtun[BJ]	36	D4
Chaigang[JL]	66	F3
Chaihe Shuiku[LN]	62	H2
Chaihe[NM]	58	N4
Chaiheyuan[NM]	58	N4
Chaihu[HB]	110	F4
Chaijiabang[SH]	74	C3
Chainjoin Co[XZ]	152	E2
Chaipeng[SD]	102	G2
Chaiping[SN]	156	E7
Chaiwan[JS]	80	F4
Chajian[AH]	90	E4
Chakou[AH]	90	E7
Chakou[HEB]	48	B5
Chakou[SN]	156	F4
Chakou[SX]	54	C4
Chakunglung[GS]	160	F5
Chalapem[QH]	164	J6
Chalengkou[QH]	164	F3
Chalin He[HL]	70	E5
Chalin[HN]	114	D6
Chaling[HN]	114	F6
Chalu He[JL]	66	G4
Chaluhe[JL]	66	F4
Chalukou[JL]	66	G3
Chalukou[QH]	164	G2
Chalukou[XJ]	172	G8
Chamco[XZ]	152	E5
Chamdong[XZ]	152	D3
Chamma[XZ]	152	E3
Chamoling[XZ]	152	J4
Chamu Co[QH]	164	D6
Chanfang[HEB]	48	A6
Chang Hu[HB]	110	F4
Chang Jiang(Yangtze R.)[AH]	90	D5
Chang Jiang(Yangtze R.)[CQ]	132	D4
Chang Jiang(Yangtze R.)[HB]	110	H4
Chang Jiang(Yangtze R.)[JS]	80	E4
Chang Jiang(Yangtze R.)[JX]	98	E2
Chang'an Qu[SN]	156	E6
Chang'an[AH]	90	E6
Chang'an[GD]	118	D3
Chang'an[HI]	128	C2
Chang'an[HL]	70	G5
Chang'an[JL]	66	H3
Chang'an[LN]	62	H4
Chang'an[SN]	156	F8
Changba[CQ]	132	D4
Changba[GZ]	144	E3
Changba[GZ]	144	F3
Changba[SC]	138	M4
Changbai Dao[ZJ]	84	G2
Changbai Shan[HL]	70	E7
Changbai Shan[JL]	66	I5
Changbai[JL]	66	I6
Changbaishan Baohuzhan[JL]	66	I5
Changbaishan Tianchi[JL]	66	I6
Changbang[SH]	74	C2
Changbao[GZ]	144	G2
Changbei Gang[SD]	102	E2
Changcao[BJ]	36	B4
Changce[HN]	114	F7
Changcheng[GS]	160	F4
Changcheng[HI]	128	A2
Changcheng[SD]	102	E5
Changcheng[SX]	54	E1
Changchi[SX]	54	E3
Changchong Ding[GX]	124	I4
Changchun[FJ]	94	F3
Changchun[HL]	70	C5
ChangChun[JL]	66	F4
Changchunbao[GZ]	144	D3
Changchunling[JL]	66	F2
Changdang Hu[JS]	80	E5
Changdao[GS]	160	G5
Changdao[SD]	102	G2
Changde[HL]	70	C5
Changde[HN]	114	D3
Changdi[YN]	148	J5
Changdian[LN]	62	H4
Changfa[GX]	124	I4
Changfa[HL]	70	C4
Changfeng[HB]	110	D3
Changfeng[AH]	90	D4
Changfeng[AH]	90	D6
Changfeng[HI]	128	C3
Changgang Shuiku[JX]	98	C5
Changgang[AH]	90	D5
Change[HEN]	106	E4
Changgo[XZ]	152	D5
Changgong[SH]	74	D1
Changgou[SN]	156	F7
Changgouhe[SN]	156	C7
Changguanmiao[SN]	156	D4
Changguo[HEB]	48	E5
Changhai[LN]	62	F5
Changhe[ZJ]	84	F2

Changheying[LN]	62	E3
Changhong[ZJ]	84	C3
Changhu[HN]	114	F3
Changhua Gang[HI]	128	A2
Changhua Jiang[HI]	128	A2
Changhua Jiang[HI]	128	B3
Changhua[HI]	128	A2
Changhua[TW]	186	D2
Changhua[ZJ]	84	D2
Changji[AH]	90	C4
Changji[XJ]	172	K3
Changjiadagou[NX]	168	C5
Changjiahe[GS]	160	G5
Changjiang Kou[SH]	74	D1
Changjiang Qu[JX]	98	E2
Changjiang[GD]	118	F1
Changjiang[HI]	128	B2
Changjiang[JS]	80	F4
Changjie[HN]	114	C4
Changjie[YN]	148	E5
Changjie[ZJ]	84	F3
Changkeng[FJ]	94	C4
Changkeng[ZJ]	84	G3
Changle[FJ]	94	E4
Changle[GX]	124	E3
Changle[NX]	168	B3
Changle[SD]	102	E3
Changle[SX]	54	C7
Changle[ZJ]	84	D2
Changleping[HB]	110	D4
Changli[HEB]	48	G4
Changliang[HB]	110	C4
Changliang[HEB]	48	C2
Changling[BJ]	36	C3
Changling[CQ]	132	E3
Changling[HB]	110	G3
Changling[HL]	70	D5
Changling[JL]	66	D3
Changling[SD]	102	E4
Changling[SN]	156	D8
Changling[SX]	54	E4
Changliu[HI]	128	C1
Changlong[FJ]	94	E3
Changlong[JL]	66	E3
Changlu[SD]	102	D4
Changlung[XZ]	152	F5
Changluo[JX]	98	C6
Changma He[GS]	160	C3
Changma[GS]	160	C3
Changmadaba[GS]	160	C2
Changmahe[QH]	164	L6
Changmao Shuiku[HI]	128	B3
Changmar[QH]	164	N5
Changmei[GX]	124	F3
Changmen Yan[SD]	102	G3
Changming[GX]	124	E5
Changming[GZ]	144	F4
Changning[GS]	160	F3
Changning[HEB]	48	F4
Changning[HN]	114	E6
Changninghe[SC]	138	J7
Changning[SX]	54	D4
Changning[YN]	148	E6
Changpin[TW]	186	E3
Changping Qu[BJ]	36	C3
Changping[GX]	124	E5
Changping[HB]	110	E3
Changping[JX]	98	A4
Changping[JX]	98	B5
Changpo[GD]	118	D4
Changpo[HI]	128	B2
Changpo[HI]	128	C2
Changpu[AH]	90	C6
Changpu[JX]	98	C7
Changqi[GZ]	144	E2
Changqiao[FJ]	94	C5
Changqiao[GX]	124	E6
Changqing Qu[SD]	102	C3
Changqing[FJ]	94	D4
Changqing[GZ]	144	F4
Changqing[NM]	58	T11
Changqing[SX]	54	B7
Changqu[NX]	168	B2
Changrong[JS]	80	F4
Changsa[HI]	128	C2
Changsengling[JL]	66	I5
Changsha[CQ]	132	E3
Changsha[GD]	118	I2
Changsha[HN]	114	F4
Changsha[HN]	114	F4
Changsha[JS]	80	G4
Changsha[JX]	98	C6
Changshan Qundao[LN]	62	F5
Changshan[AH]	90	D4
Changshan[GD]	118	C5
Changshan[HL]	70	B2
Changshan[HL]	70	B5
Changshan[JL]	66	E2
Changshan[JL]	66	G4
Changshan[SD]	102	D3
Changshan[ZJ]	84	C4
Changshantou[NX]	168	B3
Changshanyan[JX]	98	D3
Changshanyu[HEB]	48	E3
Changshaoying[BJ]	36	D2
Changsheng[GS]	160	F3
Changsheng[HL]	70	E4
Changsheng[NM]	58	U10
Changsheng[NX]	168	C2
Changshou Hu[CQ]	132	D4
Changshou Qu[CQ]	132	D4
Changshou[HB]	110	F3
Changshou[HN]	114	F4
Changshu[JS]	80	F5
Changshuihe[HL]	70	D4
Changshun[GZ]	144	E4
Changtai[FJ]	94	C5
Changtan Shuiku[ZJ]	84	F4
Changtan[CQ]	132	E3
Changtan[CQ]	132	E4
Changtan[GX]	124	F5
Changtan[HB]	110	F3
Changtang[GD]	118	H2
Changtang[HN]	114	D4
Changtang[JX]	98	B4
Changtanhe[HB]	110	C4
Changtian[GD]	118	H2
Changtian[HI]	128	B2
Changtian[HI]	128	B3
Changtian[JX]	98	D5
Changting[FJ]	94	B4
Changting[HL]	70	E6
Changtu[LN]	62	H2
Changtu[ZJ]	84	G2
Changtun[HEB]	48	C6
Changtun[TJ]	42	B3
Changweiliang[QH]	164	E2
Changwen[HI]	128	C2
Changwu[SN]	156	D5
Changxiao[FJ]	94	B4
Changxin[NX]	168	C2
Changxin[YN]	148	E4
Changxindian[BJ]	36	C4
Changxing Dao[LN]	62	E5
Changxing Dao[SH]	74	D2
Changxing[HI]	128	C3
Changxing[JL]	66	I4
Changxing[SH]	74	C1
Changxing[SH]	74	D2
Changxing[ZJ]	84	D1
Changxingdao[LN]	62	E5
Changxingji[SD]	102	A4
Changxuanling[HB]	110	H3
Changyang[BJ]	36	C4
Changyang[HB]	110	E4
Changyang[SN]	156	E8
Changyangpu[HN]	114	D5
Changyi[JX]	98	D2
Changyi[SD]	102	F3
Changying[HL]	70	B2
Changyuan[HEN]	106	F2
Changzhao Shuiku[ZJ]	84	F3
Changzhen[SX]	54	C2
Changzheng[HI]	128	B3
Changzheng[SH]	74	C1
Changzhi[GD]	118	I2
Changzhi[SX]	54	C6
Changzhi[SX]	54	E5
Changzhi[SX]	54	E5
Changzhou[GX]	124	E3
Changzhou[JS]	80	E5
Changzhoucun[TJ]	42	C1
Changzhuang[HEN]	106	F4
Changzhuang[SD]	102	C2
Changzhuyuan[HEN]	106	G6
Changzipu[HN]	114	D7
Chanjiayan[SN]	156	C8
Chantang[AH]	90	D3
Chao He[BJ]	36	E2
Chao He[HEB]	48	D3
Chao Hu[AH]	90	D5
Chao'an[GD]	118	I3
Chaobai He[BJ]	36	D3
Chaobai He[HEB]	48	D3
Chaobai Xinhe[TJ]	42	B3
Chaobin[SH]	74	D2
Chaoguan[BJ]	36	E2
Chaohu Nongchang[NX]	168	C2
Chaohu[AH]	90	D5
Chaohua[HEN]	106	E3
Chaolian Dao[SD]	102	G4
Chaonan Qu[GD]	118	I3
Chaonitan[SH]	74	C3
Chaor He[NM]	58	N4
Chaoshui[SD]	102	G2
Chaotian Qu[SC]	138	K3
Chaotian[GD]	118	E2
Chaotian[GX]	124	H2
Chaoyang Nongchang[SH]	74	D2
Chaoyang Qu[BJ]	36	C4
Chaoyang Qu[GD]	118	I3
Chaoyang[AH]	90	D3
Chaoyang[GZ]	144	F5
Chaoyang[HI]	128	C2
Chaoyang[HL]	70	D4
Chaoyang[HL]	70	G5
Chaoyang[JL]	66	G3
Chaoyang[JL]	66	G3
Chaoyang[JL]	66	H3
Chaoyang[LN]	62	D3
Chaoyang[LN]	62	G4
Chaoyang[NM]	58	V11
Chaoyangchuan[JL]	66	J5
Chaoyangdong[CQ]	132	F2
Chaoyangshan[JL]	66	F4
Chaoyangsi[HB]	110	B5
Chaoyi[HN]	114	B6
Chaoyi[SN]	156	G6
Chaoyuan[NM]	58	N3
Chaozha[SH]	74	D2
Chaozhou[GD]	118	I3
Chaozongqiao[TJ]	42	B4
Chapeng[HEB]	48	G4
Chaping Shan[SC]	138	I4
Chaping[FJ]	94	D2
Chaqiao[AH]	90	D6
Chaqigou[NX]	168	C2
Chaqung[XZ]	152	E4
Charen Co[QH]	164	E6
Chasadi[YN]	148	D3
Chashang[SN]	156	G3
Chashang[SX]	54	D3
Chashui[AH]	90	C6
Chatai[JL]	66	D2
Chatan[JX]	98	B6
Chatian[HN]	114	B5
Chatian[ZJ]	84	C5
Chau Kung To[HK]	176	C4
Chau Mei Kok[HK]	176	F1
Chau Tau[HK]	176	C1
Chau Tau[HK]	176	F1
Chawan[AH]	90	E5
Chaxi[HN]	114	D5
Chaying[HI]	128	B2
Chayuan[JX]	98	C5
Chayuan[ZJ]	84	F3
Chazhen[SN]	156	E7
Che Zhen[SD]	102	D2
Cheban[GD]	118	B5
Chebu[HB]	110	G5
Checheng[TW]	186	D4
Checun[HEN]	106	D4

Chedao[GS] 160 H4
Chefushan[JS] 80 C2
Chegang[GD] 118 E4
Chegu[YN] 148 H7
Chehe[GX] 124 E3
Chejiang[HN] 114 E6
Chejiazhuang[SN] 156 D6
Chek Chau[HK] 176 F1
Chek Keng Hau[HK] 176 E2
Chek Keng[HK] 176 E2
Chek Kok Tau[HK] 176 E1
Chek Lap Kok[HK] 176 B3
Chek Mun[HK] 176 E2
Chelu[HL] 70 E4
Cheluwan[NX] 168 B4
Chêm Co[XZ] 152 A2
Chemen[JS] 80 D3
Chen Barag Qi[NM] 58 M3
Chen Shui[HN] 114 B5
Chen Xi[HN] 114 C5
Chenbao[JS] 80 E4
Chenbu[AH] 90 D5
Chencang Qu[SN] 156 D6
Chencheng[FJ] 94 C6
Chencun[ZJ] 84 D4
Chenda[FJ] 94 C3
Chendai[FJ] 94 C6
Chendian[HB] 110 E4
Chendian[HB] 110 G3
Chendong[FJ] 94 B5
Chen'er[SN] 156 G6
Cheng Hu[JS] 80 F5
Cheng Xian[GS] 160 G6
Cheng'an[HEB] 48 B7
Chengbei[CQ] 132 D3
Chengbei[SC] 138 K3
Chengbei[SD] 102 H3
Chengbei[SH] 74 C1
Chengbei[ZJ] 84 D4
Chengbei[ZJ] 84 E4
Chengbihe Shuiku[GX] 124 D4
Chengbu[HN] 114 C6
Chengcheng[SN] 156 F5
Chengchuan[NM] 58 H9
Chengde[HEB] 48 E3
Chengde[HEB] 48 F3
Chengdong Hu[AH] 90 C4
Chengdong[AH] 90 C3
Chengdongshi[JS] 80 E4
Chengdu[SC] 138 J5
Chengfa[JL] 66 G3
Chengfu[AH] 90 B3
Chenggezhuang[BJ] 36 D3
Chenggezhuang[BJ] 36 E3
Chenggong[HB] 110 G4
Chenggong[YN] 148 H6
Chenggu[SN] 156 D7
Chengguan[BJ] 36 B4
Chengguan[SD] 102 E2
Chengguan[TJ] 42 A2
Chengguan[TJ] 42 B2
Chengguo[SD] 102 F2
Chenghai Qu[GD] 118 I3
Chenghai[YN] 148 F4
Chenghai[YN] 148 F4
Chenghuang[GX] 124 G5
Chenghuang[SX] 54 C5
Chengjia[GD] 118 E2
Chengjian[GX] 124 I4
Chengjiang[GD] 118 G2
Chengjiang[JX] 98 C6
Chengjiang[YN] 148 H6
Chengkou[CQ] 132 E2
Chengkou[FJ] 94 C4
Chengkou[GD] 118 F1
Chengkou[SD] 102 D1
Chengkung[TW] 186 E3
Chenglin[TJ] 42 B3
Chenglong[JX] 98 B7
Chenglou[HEN] 106 G3
Chengmagang[HB] 110 H3
Chengmai Wan[HI] 128 B2
Chengmai[HI] 128 C2
Chengmen[FJ] 94 C4

Chengmenwan[NX] 168 B4
Chengnan[AH] 90 C5
Chengnan[FJ] 94 E3
Chengnan[NM] 58 U11
Chengnan[SH] 74 C2
Chengnan[SX] 54 B5
Chengping[LN] 62 H2
Chengqian[SD] 102 D4
Chengqiao[SH] 74 C2
Chengshan[LN] 62 F5
Chengshan[SD] 102 I2
Chengshang[JX] 98 C4
Chengshanjiao[SD] 102 I2
Chengtan Jiang[ZJ] 84 E3
Chengtanjiang[HN] 114 F5
Chengtian[FJ] 94 F2
Chengtun[SD] 102 B4
Chenguang[HL] 70 E6
Chenguang[JX] 98 C7
Chenguantun[TJ] 42 A4
Chenguantun[TJ] 42 B3
Chengwu[SD] 102 B5
Chengxi Hu[AH] 90 C4
Chengxi Hu[AH] 90 C4
Chengxi[CQ] 132 D3
Chengxi[FJ] 94 C5
Chengxi[HI] 128 C2
Chengxiang[JS] 80 D3
Chengyang Qu[SD] 102 G3
Chengyang[NX] 168 C5
Chengyuan[FJ] 94 E2
Chengyue[GD] 118 C5
Chengzhao[ZJ] 84 D5
Chengzhuang[SX] 54 C3
Chengzi Hu[JS] 80 D3
Chengzi[BJ] 36 E2
Chengzi[HEB] 48 E2
Chengzi[YN] 148 C6
Chengzihe Qu[HL] 70 F6
Chengzijie[JL] 66 G3
Chengzitan[LN] 62 F5
Chenhe[HB] 110 G4
Chenhe[SN] 156 E7
Cheniu Shan(Danian Shan)[SD] 102 F5
Cheniu Shan[JS] 80 E2
Chenji[AH] 90 C3
Chenji[HEN] 106 G5
Chenji[JS] 80 D3
Chenji[SD] 102 B4
Chenji[SD] 102 D2
Chenjia[SH] 74 D1
Chenjiadaliang[NX] 168 C3
Chenjiadian[HL] 70 D5
Chenjiagang[JS] 80 E2
Chenjiagou[NX] 168 C3
Chenjiahang[SH] 74 C2
Chenjiang[GD] 118 G3
Chenjiaqiao[SH] 74 C2
Chenjiatan[HN] 114 C4
Chenjiatan[SN] 156 D8
Chenjiatuo[BJ] 36 D3
Chenjiawa[HEB] 48 B3
Chenjiawanzi[NX] 168 C2
Chenjiayao[SX] 54 D1
Chenjiaying[SX] 54 C2
Chenjiayu[BJ] 36 D2
Chenjiazhuang[SX] 54 E3
Chenjiazui[GS] 160 F5
Chenjin[NX] 168 C5
Chenkeng[FJ] 94 B4
Chenliu[HEN] 106 F3
Chenmanzhuang[SD] 102 C5
Chenming[HL] 70 E5
Chenping[GX] 124 F4
Chenqiao[HEN] 106 F3
Chenqing[HL] 70 D4
Chenshi[HEB] 48 C5
Chenshui[NX] 168 A3
Chentaizi[TJ] 42 B4
Chentang[GX] 124 H4
Chentao[JS] 80 E2
Chentuan[SD] 102 F4
Chenwei[JS] 80 D3
Chenxi[HN] 114 C4

Chenyangping[HEN] 106 C4
Chenyu[ZJ] 84 F4
Chenzhazi[HEB] 48 E3
Chenzhou[HN] 114 F7
Chenzhuang[HEB] 48 B5
Chenzhuang[HEB] 48 D5
Chenzhuang[SD] 102 D2
Chenzhuang[SD] 102 E2
Chenzhuang[TJ] 42 A2
Chenzui[TJ] 42 B3
Cheoc Van[MC] 182 C7
Chetian[CQ] 132 F4
Chetian[GX] 124 H1
Chetou[HN] 114 E7
Chetou[JX] 98 C6
Cheung Chau Wan[HK] 176 C4
Cheung Chau[HK] 176 C4
Cheung Lek Mei[HK] 176 D2
Cheung Muk Tau[HK] 176 B4
Cheung Muk Tau[HK] 176 E2
Cheung Sha Wan[HK] 176 B4
Cheung Sha Wan[HK] 176 D3
Cheung Sha[HK] 176 B4
Cheung Sheung[HK] 176 E2
Cheung Sok[HK] 176 C3
Chewang[HEB] 48 B7
Chewang[SD] 102 D5
Chexi[JX] 98 C5
Chi He[AH] 90 D4
Chi Hu[JX] 98 C2
Chi Ma Wan Peninsula[HK] 176 B4
Chi Ma Wan[HK] 176 B4
Chiahsien[TW] 186 D3
Chia-i[TW] 186 D3
Chiali[TW] 186 D3
Chialu[TW] 186 D4
Chialulan[TW] 186 E3
Chian[TW] 186 E3
Chi'an[ZJ] 84 E3
Chiangchunao Yu[TW] 186 C3
Chiaohsi[TW] 186 E2
Chiatung[TW] 186 D4
Chiba[HB] 110 G5
Chibi[HB] 110 G5
Chibuzhang Co[QH] 164 C7
Chicheng[HEB] 48 C3
Chichin[TW] 186 D4
Chidi[HEN] 106 C3
Chido[XZ] 152 I4
Chido[XZ] 152 I4
Chidong Hu[HB] 110 I4
Chidong[GD] 118 C4
Chienshih[TW] 186 E2
Chifeng[GD] 118 I3
Chifeng[NM] 58 M6
Chigu Co[XZ] 152 G5
Chigu[JX] 98 B4
Chigu[XZ] 152 G5
Chihe[AH] 90 D4
Chihe[SN] 156 E8
Chihpen[TW] 186 E4
Chihshang[TW] 186 E3
Chihsing Yen[TW] 186 D5
Chihu[FJ] 94 C5
Chihwei Yu[TW] 186 H1
Chijiang[JX] 98 B6
Chijin[GS] 160 C2
Chijiu[YN] 148 H5
Chiku[TW] 186 D3
Chilai Chushan[TW] 186 E2
Chiling[AH] 90 D6
Chiling[FJ] 94 C5
Chilu[BJ] 36 D4
Chilung Kang[TW] 186 E1
Chilung[TW] 186 E1
Chima[HN] 114 F4
Chimei Yu(Ta Yu)[TW] 186 C3
Chimei[HEN] 106 C4
Chimei[TW] 186 C3
Chimen[FJ] 94 D3
Chinan[SN] 156 D8
Chindu[QH] 164 J7
Chinfeng[TW] 186 D4
Chingshui[TW] 186 D2

Chingshui[TW]	186	E3
Chiniwa[SX]	54	D3
Chinkuashih[TW]	186	E1
Chinlun[TW]	186	D4
Chinmen Tao[FJ]	94	D5
Chinmen[FJ]	94	D5
Chinqên[QH]	164	J7
Chinshan[TW]	186	E1
Chipei Yu[TW]	186	C3
Chiping[SD]	102	C3
Chisha[AH]	90	E6
Chishan Hsi[TW]	186	D3
Chishan[SD]	102	I3
Chishan[TW]	186	D4
Chishang[SD]	102	E3
Chishi[ZJ]	84	D4
Chishiqiao[SX]	54	D5
Chishou[ZJ]	84	D4
Chishui He[GZ]	144	D2
Chishui He[GZ]	144	D3
Chishui[FJ]	94	C4
Chishui[FJ]	94	D4
Chishui[GZ]	144	D2
Chishui[JX]	98	D5
Chishui[SC]	138	K8
Chishuxia[GD]	118	G3
Chisong[JL]	66	H5
Chitang[SH]	74	C2
Chitou Dao[ZJ]	84	E5
Chitu[TJ]	42	B3
Chiuju[TW]	186	D4
Chiuliao[TW]	186	D4
Chiutse[TW]	186	E2
Chiwang[QH]	164	J7
Chixi[FJ]	94	D4
Chixi[FJ]	94	E3
Chixi[ZJ]	84	E5
Chixixu[GD]	118	E5
Chiyan[SN]	156	F8
Chizhong[FJ]	94	D2
Chizhou[AH]	90	D6
Chohsi[TW]	186	E3
Cholan[TW]	186	D2
Chomsagabma[SC]	138	D3
Chomsakongma[SC]	138	D2
Chong'an Jiang[GZ]	144	F4
Chong'an[GZ]	144	F4
Chong'an[NX]	168	C5
Chongchagou[HEN]	106	C4
Chongde[YN]	148	H5
Chong'e[HI]	128	B3
Chongfu[ZJ]	84	E2
Chonggang[NX]	168	C2
Chonggang[YN]	148	E7
Chonghe[HL]	70	D6
Chongkan[CQ]	132	B3
Chongli[HEB]	48	C3
Chongli[HEN]	106	F4
Chongling Shui[HN]	114	E6
Chonglou[GD]	118	E4
Chongluo[FJ]	94	D2
Chongmai[GX]	124	F3
Chongming Dao[SH]	74	C1
Chongming[SH]	74	C1
Chongqing Shuiku[BJ]	36	C4
Chongqing[CQ]	132	C4
Chongren[FJ]	94	C2
Chongren[JX]	98	D4
Chongren[ZJ]	84	E3
Chongru[FJ]	94	E3
Chongshan[JL]	66	I5
Chongshou[ZJ]	84	F2
Chongtou[ZJ]	84	D4
Chongwu[FJ]	94	D5
Chongxian[JX]	98	B6
Chongxin[GS]	160	H5
Chongxin[JL]	66	E2
Chongxing[GS]	160	F3
Chongxing[HI]	128	C2
Chongxing[NX]	168	C2
Chongyang Xi[FJ]	94	D2
Chongyang[HB]	110	H5
Chongyang[HEN]	106	C4
Chongyi[GZ]	144	G4

Chongyi[JX]	98	B6
Chongyü[XZ]	152	I4
Chongzhou[SC]	138	I5
Chongzuo[GX]	124	E5
Choshui Hsi[TW]	186	D3
Chounikeng[BJ]	36	C3
Choushui[JL]	66	H5
Chowa[XZ]	152	E4
Chowagoin[XZ]	152	J5
Choxugabma[SC]	138	E3
Chu Dao[SD]	102	I2
Chu He[JS]	80	D4
Chu Mun Tin[HK]	176	E1
Chu Shan[TW]	186	D3
Chuaigutuan[HEB]	48	B3
Chuan He[YN]	148	F6
Chuan Xi[HEN]	106	C4
Chuanchang[FJ]	94	C5
Chuandong Gang[JS]	80	F3
Chuanfang[YN]	148	G4
Chuanfangyu[TJ]	42	C1
Chuangcheng[JS]	80	D3
Chuangu[TJ]	42	C3
Chuangwang[HB]	110	H5
Chuangwei[TW]	186	E2
Chuangyecun[TJ]	42	C3
Chuanjie[YN]	148	H6
Chuanjing[NM]	58	H7
Chuankou[NX]	168	C5
Chuankou[SX]	54	C5
Chuankou[SX]	54	E4
Chuanli[HEB]	48	B4
Chuannan[ZJ]	84	F4
Chuansha[SH]	74	D2
Chuanshan Qundao[GD]	118	E5
Chuanshan[GX]	124	F2
Chuanshan[GX]	124	G3
Chuanshanping[HN]	114	F4
Chuanshi[FJ]	94	D4
Chuanxing[HN]	114	F6
Chuanyan[HN]	114	D6
Chuanyang He[SH]	74	D2
Chuanyao Gang[JS]	80	G4
Chuanzhusi[SC]	138	I3
Chubqên[QH]	164	M8
Chuchi[TW]	186	D3
Chudian[AH]	90	C3
Chudun[SD]	102	E5
Chuen Lung[HK]	176	C2
Chuhou[SX]	54	B6
Chuhu[TW]	186	E3
Chuji[AH]	90	C3
Chuk Kok[HK]	176	E3
Chukuang Liehtao[FJ]	94	E4
Chulan[AH]	90	D2
Chumda[QH]	164	J7
Chumen[ZJ]	84	F4
Chumi[GZ]	144	E2
Chumiao[HEN]	106	G3
Chunan[TW]	186	D2
Chun'an[ZJ]	84	D3
Chung Hom Kok[HK]	176	D4
Chung Hom Wan[HK]	176	D4
Chung Mei[HK]	176	E1
Chung Pui[HK]	176	D1
Chung Uk Tsuen[HK]	176	D2
Chunghsing[TW]	186	D2
Chungyang Shan[TW]	186	D3
Chunhu[ZJ]	84	F3
Chunhua[JL]	66	L4
Chunhua[JS]	80	D5
Chunhua[SD]	102	E2
Chunhua[SN]	156	E6
Chunjih[TW]	186	D4
Chunkou[HN]	114	F4
Chunmei[FJ]	94	C4
Chunmuying[HB]	110	C4
Chunshucha[NX]	168	C4
Chunshui[HEN]	106	E4
Chuntao[JX]	98	D3
Chunwan[GD]	118	D4
Chunyang[JL]	66	J4
Chunyuan[HI]	128	C3
Chushan[HEN]	106	E4

Chutang[TW]	186	D3
Chutouling[TJ]	42	C1
Chuwanang[SC]	138	E6
Chuwang[HEN]	106	F1
Chuwei[TW]	186	E1
Chuxiong[YN]	148	G5
Chuyang[CQ]	132	G2
Chuzhangdi[HEB]	48	B2
Chuzhib[XZ]	152	F5
Chuzhou Qu[JS]	80	E3
Chuzhou[AH]	90	E4
Ci He[HEB]	48	B5
Ci He[HEN]	106	G4
Ci Xian[HEB]	48	B7
Cibeiyu[BJ]	36	C3
Cicheng[ZJ]	84	F3
Cicun[SX]	54	D5
Cigou[HEN]	106	E4
Cihuai Xinhe[AH]	90	C3
Cijian[HEN]	106	D3
Cijiawu[BJ]	36	B4
Cijingzi[GS]	160	E3
Cikou[HB]	110	H5
Cili[HN]	114	D3
Ciping[JX]	98	B5
Cishan[HEB]	48	B7
Cixi[ZJ]	84	F2
Ciyao[SD]	102	D4
Ciyaopu[NX]	168	C2
Ciyushan[HEB]	48	G3
Ciyutuo[LN]	62	F3
Cizhouzhai[HEN]	106	F2
Cizhu[CQ]	132	C4
Cizhu[CQ]	132	E3
Cizijing[JL]	66	E3
Clear Water Bay[HK]	176	E3
Co Nag[XZ]	152	G3
Co Ngoin[XZ]	152	F4
Co Nyi[XZ]	152	E2
Cocha[XZ]	152	G4
Cochiyarlung[QH]	164	H5
Codoi[XZ]	152	H4
Cogo[XZ]	152	E5
Colina da Barra[MC]	182	A3
Colina da Ilha Verde[MC]	182	A1
Colina da Penha[MC]	182	A2
Colina de Mong Há[MC]	182	B1
Coloane Alto[MC]	182	C6
Coloane[MC]	182	B6
Coloane[MC]	182	B7
Comai[XZ]	152	E4
Comai[XZ]	152	G5
Comar[XZ]	152	G3
Como Chamling[XZ]	152	F5
Cona[XZ]	152	G5
Co'nga[XZ]	152	K5
Conggo[XZ]	152	H4
Conghua[GD]	118	F3
Congjiang[GZ]	144	G5
Congluoyu[SX]	54	B4
Congziyu[SX]	54	D5
Coqên[XZ]	152	D4
Cozhêlhoma[XZ]	152	E4
Cozhêqangma[XZ]	152	E3
Cuicun[BJ]	36	C3
Cuigang[HL]	70	C2
Cuigezhuang[BJ]	36	C3
Cuihuangkou[TJ]	42	B2
Cuijiaba[HB]	110	C4
Cuijiaji[SD]	102	F3
Cuijiamiao[HEB]	48	D6
Cuijiaqiao[HN]	114	E4
Cuijiatou[SN]	156	D6
Cuijiawan[SN]	156	G3
Cuikou[SD]	102	D2
Cuili[GZ]	144	G5
Cuiluan Qu[HL]	70	E5
Cuimiao[HEN]	106	E3
Cuimu[SN]	156	D6
Cuixi[FJ]	94	E3
Cuixinzhuang[TJ]	42	B2
Cuiyan[LN]	62	D3
Cuiyun[YN]	148	F8
Cuizhao[SD]	102	G3

Cuizhenpu[LN]	62	G2
Cunqian[JX]	98	C3
Cunqiao[SH]	74	D2
Cunrui[HEB]	48	C3
Cunshi[HN]	114	D5
Cuocheng[HEN]	106	H4
Cushijiang[HN]	114	D7

D

Da Baicao Ling[YN]	148	G4
Da Haltang He[GS]	160	B3
Da Hinggan Ling[NM]	58	M5
Da Juh[QH]	164	G4
Da Ling[SN]	156	G5
Da Qaidam Hu[QH]	164	H3
Da Qaidam[QH]	164	H3
Da Sui[NM]	58	X10
Da Xian[SC]	138	M4
Da'an Shuiku[HI]	128	B3
Da'an[FJ]	94	C2
Da'an[FJ]	94	E2
Da'an[GS]	160	F4
Da'an[GX]	124	F3
Da'an[GX]	124	H4
Da'an[HI]	128	A2
Da'an[HI]	128	B2
Da'an[HI]	128	B3
Da'an[JL]	66	E2
Da'an[JL]	66	J4
Da'an[SC]	138	K5
Da'an[SN]	156	C7
Da'an[TJ]	42	B4
Da'anshan[BJ]	36	B4
Da'anzhang[NX]	168	B4
Daba Shan[HB]	110	B2
Daba Shan[SN]	156	E8
Daba[JL]	66	D2
Daba[SC]	138	K7
Daba[XZ]	152	A4
Dabai Shan[ZJ]	84	F2
Dabaidi[JX]	98	D5
Dabaiyizi[NX]	168	C3
Dabaizhuang[TJ]	42	B3
Dabalang[HL]	70	F5
Daban Shan[QH]	164	N3
Daban Shankou[QH]	164	N3
Daban[LN]	62	D3
Dabancheng Qu[XJ]	172	L4
Dabang He[GZ]	144	D5
Dabang[GZ]	144	D5
Dabao[HI]	128	C2
Dabao[SC]	138	I4
Dabaodang[SN]	156	G2
Dabaozi[HN]	114	B6
Dabazi[HEB]	48	E2
Dabei Liedao[ZJ]	84	E5
Dabeicha[JL]	66	G6
Dabeicha[LN]	62	I2
Dabeicheng[JL]	66	K4
Dabeihe[BJ]	36	B4
Dabie Shan[AH]	90	B5
Dabie Shan[HB]	110	I3
Dabie Shan[HEN]	106	F6
Dabijiashan[LN]	62	E4
Dabizhuang[TJ]	42	B3
Dabs Nur[JL]	66	D3
Dabu[FJ]	94	C3
Dabu[FJ]	94	C6
Dabu[FJ]	94	D4
Dabu[GD]	118	F2
Dabu[GD]	118	I2
Dabu[HEB]	48	C3
Dabu[JX]	98	C6
Dabugang[FJ]	94	C2
Dabujiang[HN]	114	F6
Dabutou[SX]	54	D5
Dacaigezhuang[TJ]	42	B1
Dacang[YN]	148	F5
Dacao[SD]	102	C2
Dacaodianzi[HL]	70	B2
Dachan Jiao[HI]	128	B2

Dachan[FJ]	94	D2
Dachang[HEB]	48	D4
Dachang[JS]	80	D4
Dachang[SH]	74	C2
Dachanghan[SN]	156	G1
Dachangshan Dao[LN]	62	F5
Dachangtu Shan[ZJ]	84	G2
Dachaoshandong[YN]	148	F6
Dachatun[JL]	66	G4
Dachen[ZJ]	84	E4
Dacheng[HI]	128	B2
Dacheng[JX]	98	C3
Dachi[FJ]	94	B4
Dachi[SN]	156	D8
Dachishan[HEN]	106	E2
Dachou Ding[GD]	118	E2
Dachuan[JL]	66	F6
Dachuan[JL]	66	F6
Dachuan[SC]	138	I5
Dachuantou[LN]	62	H4
Dachun[JX]	98	B2
Dacongyong[QH]	164	H7
Dacun[SD]	102	F4
Dacun[TJ]	42	B4
Dacundian[HN]	114	D6
Dadao[GX]	124	D4
Dade[LN]	62	F2
Dadi[GZ]	144	G4
Dadian[AH]	90	D3
Dadian[SD]	102	E4
Dadianzi[BJ]	36	D2
Dadianzi[LN]	62	H2
Dadiji[YN]	148	G6
Dadingzi[HL]	70	D6
Dadong[BJ]	36	C4
Dadong[GD]	118	I2
Dadong[GX]	124	F5
Dadong[GX]	124	G6
Dadong[YN]	148	F3
Dadongba[ZJ]	84	D4
Dadonggou[SX]	54	D6
Dadongliu[BJ]	36	C3
Dadongshui[GD]	118	E4
Dadu He[SC]	138	H5
Daduan[JX]	98	B3
Daduanwa[BJ]	36	E3
Daduchuan[HL]	70	F7
Dadugang[YN]	148	F8
Dadukou Qu[CQ]	132	C4
Dadukou[AH]	90	D6
Dadukou[SC]	138	K7
Daduling[JL]	66	F6
Daduma[GS]	160	E3
Daduo[JS]	80	F4
Dadushe[BJ]	36	D4
Daduzhai[HEN]	106	F3
Da'erhao[HEB]	48	D2
Dafa[GX]	124	H3
Dafa[HI]	128	C3
Dafang[GZ]	144	D3
Dafangshen[JL]	66	F3
Dafangshen[LN]	62	G4
Dafankou[TJ]	42	A3
Dafen[JX]	98	B5
Dafen[TJ]	42	B3
Dafeng[HI]	128	C2
Dafeng[JS]	80	F3
Dafengdui[TJ]	42	B4
Dafengshan[QH]	164	E2
Daftar[XJ]	172	E7
Dafu Shui[HB]	110	G3
Dafu[HN]	114	D4
Dafuying[SD]	102	C3
Dafuzhuang[SX]	54	D2
Dagain[SC]	138	F4
Dagan[FJ]	94	C3
Dagang Qu[TJ]	42	B4
Dagang[GD]	118	E3
Dagang[JL]	66	G2
Dagang[JS]	80	F3
Dagang[JX]	98	D2
Dagang[SH]	74	C2
Dagangtou[ZJ]	84	D4
Dagangzi[JL]	66	D2

Dagaocun[HEB]	48	C6
Dagaoping[HN]	114	B6
Daggyai Co[XZ]	152	D5
Daglung[XZ]	152	G5
Daglung[XZ]	152	I4
Dagmadên[XZ]	152	H5
Dagmoxar[XZ]	152	E5
Dagong Dao[SD]	102	G4
Dagong[JS]	80	F4
Dagongcha[GS]	160	C3
Dagou He[GX]	124	E2
Dagou He[GZ]	144	F5
Dagou[GD]	118	E5
Dagou[GS]	160	G5
Dagou[HB]	110	E2
Dagrag Zangbo[XZ]	152	E4
Dagsar[XZ]	152	H4
Dagtog[QH]	164	L7
Dagu He[SD]	102	G3
Dagu[TJ]	42	C4
Daguan Dao[SD]	102	G3
Daguan Hu[AH]	90	C6
Daguan[AH]	90	D5
Daguan[CQ]	132	C4
Daguan[GZ]	144	E4
Daguan[GZ]	144	E5
Daguan[SC]	138	J7
Daguan[YN]	148	I3
Daguang Dingshan[NM]	58	N3
Daguangba Shuiku[HI]	128	B3
Daguangdingzi Shan[HEB]	48	E1
Daguangdingzi Shan[NM]	58	L6
Daguanting[HEB]	48	D5
Daguantou[BJ]	36	C2
Daguben[LN]	62	F2
Dagucun[TJ]	42	C2
Dagui Shan[GX]	124	I4
Dagui[HL]	70	D5
Dagui[SN]	156	F8
Dagujia He[SD]	102	H2
Dagujiazi[LN]	62	G2
Daguokou[YN]	148	G6
Daguokui Shan[HL]	70	D6
Dagur[QH]	164	H4
Dagushan[JL]	66	F4
Daguyun[AH]	90	E6
Dagxung[XZ]	152	D4
Da'gyug Tan[GS]	160	F5
Dagzê Co[XZ]	152	E4
Dagzê[XZ]	152	F5
Dagzê[XZ]	152	G5
Dagzê[XZ]	152	H4
Dahai[YN]	148	I4
Dahaituo Shan[BJ]	36	B2
Dahaituo Shan[HEB]	48	C3
Dahaozhuang[TJ]	42	A4
Dahe[CQ]	132	F2
Dahe[FJ]	94	B4
Dahe[GZ]	144	C3
Dahe[GZ]	144	F5
Dahe[HB]	110	C5
Dahe[HEB]	48	B2
Dahe[HEN]	106	E5
Dahe[NX]	168	C3
Dahe[SC]	138	K4
Dahe[SC]	138	L3
Dahe[XJ]	172	N4
Dahe'an[HB]	110	I4
Daheba[QH]	164	L5
Dahei He[NM]	58	X11
Dahei Shan[HL]	70	D3
Dahei Shan[JL]	66	E4
Dahei Shan[XJ]	172	N4
Dahei Shan[YN]	148	J3
Daheiding Shan[HL]	70	E5
Daheifa[BJ]	36	D4
Daheignazi[LN]	62	F3
Daheishan Dao[SD]	102	G2
Daheishan[YN]	148	G8
Daheiting Shuiku[HEB]	48	F3
Dahekou[CQ]	132	E4
Dahekou[HL]	70	D4
Dahekou[YN]	148	G5
Dahenan[HEB]	48	C4

Name	Page	Grid	Name	Page	Grid	Name	Page	Grid
Dahenan[LN]	62	G3	Dajing[HN]	114	F4	Dalubeikou[TJ]	42	B4
Daheng[FJ]	94	D3	Dajing[YN]	148	I4	Dalubian[GD]	118	E1
Dahengshuihu[BJ]	36	D2	Dajing[ZJ]	84	F4	Dalugou[SN]	156	E3
Daheping[HN]	114	C4	Dajishan[JX]	98	B7	Dalukou[AH]	90	D3
Dahetun[HEN]	106	E5	Dakai Shuiku[GX]	124	G4	Daluli[HEN]	106	F4
Dahong Shan[HB]	110	F3	Dakar[QH]	164	M8	Daluo Shan[GD]	118	F3
Dahong Shan[HB]	110	F3	Dakeng[FJ]	94	E3	Daluo Shan[NX]	168	C3
Dahongcheng[NM]	58	X11	Dakeng[JX]	98	B5	Daluo[HL]	70	D5
Dahongliutan[XJ]	172	G8	Dakog[QH]	164	H7	Daluo[YN]	148	F9
Dahongluo Shan[LN]	62	D4	Dakouqin[JL]	66	G3	Daluomi[HL]	70	E6
Dahongqi[LN]	62	F3	Dakoutun[TJ]	42	B2	Dalupo[HI]	128	C2
Dahongshan[HN]	114	B5	Dakouzi[NX]	168	B2	Dalupu[HN]	114	D7
Dahu[FJ]	94	C3	Dakuang[SD]	102	G3	Dam Qu[QH]	164	F7
Dahu[FJ]	94	E3	Dakuishang[HN]	114	F7	Damaidi[YN]	148	G6
Dahu[SD]	102	D2	Dala[GS]	160	F6	Damaigu[TJ]	42	C2
Dahua Jiao[HI]	128	C3	Dala[HI]	128	B2	Damang Ding[GX]	124	I5
Dahua[GX]	124	E4	Dalad Qi[NM]	58	I7	Damanhe[TJ]	42	B2
Dahua[HN]	114	C5	Dalad Qi[NM]	58	W11	Damao Shan[JX]	98	E3
Dahuabei Shan[NM]	58	H7	Dalaga[JL]	66	D2	Damao[HI]	128	C3
Dahuabei Shan[NM]	58	V11	Dalai Nur[NM]	58	L6	Damaqun Shan[HEB]	48	C2
Dahuai Jiang[GX]	124	F2	Dalai[NM]	58	L3	Damaying[GS]	160	E3
Dahuai[GD]	118	E4	Dalama[LN]	62	G3	Dameigou[QH]	164	I3
Dahuang[GD]	118	C6	Dalan[GD]	118	G3	Damen Dao[ZJ]	84	F5
Dahuang[JX]	98	D3	Dalang[GD]	118	E2	Damen[ZJ]	84	F5
Dahuangbu[TJ]	42	B3	Dalang[GX]	124	G2	Damenshanya[HEN]	106	C4
Dahuanggou[JL]	66	I5	Dalanqi[NM]	58	X10	Damgyang[XZ]	152	H3
Dahuangji[SD]	102	B4	Daleng[GX]	124	D4	Damiao[AH]	90	D3
Dahuanglong[ZJ]	84	G2	Daleng[LN]	62	F2	Damiao[AH]	90	D4
Dahuangshan[JS]	80	C2	Dali He[SN]	156	F3	Damiao[HB]	110	C2
Dahuangwa[TJ]	42	A4	Dali[FJ]	94	D3	Damiao[HEB]	48	E2
Dahuaping[AH]	90	C5	Dali[GX]	124	H4	Damiao[LN]	62	D3
Dahulun[HEB]	48	C2	Dali[SN]	156	F6	Damiao[NM]	58	W10
Dahuo Dao[GD]	118	E5	Dali[YN]	148	F5	Damiao[SH]	74	C3
Dahuofang Shuiku[LN]	62	H3	Dalian Hu[HN]	114	E4	Damiao[SX]	54	D3
Dai Hai[NM]	58	J7	Dalian[LN]	62	E6	Damiaogou[LN]	62	F4
Dai Jiang[FJ]	94	E3	Daliang Shan[SC]	138	I7	Daming Shan[GX]	124	F4
Dai Xian[SX]	54	D2	Daliang[GX]	124	G3	Daming Shan[GX]	124	F4
Daibu[JS]	80	E5	Daliang[TJ]	42	B2	Daming[HEB]	48	C7
Daibu[NX]	168	C4	Daliangtou[NX]	168	C4	Daming[HN]	114	C3
Daicheng[HEB]	48	D5	Daliao He[LN]	62	F4	Daming[LN]	62	G2
Daicun[ZJ]	84	E2	Daligezhuang[TJ]	42	B2	Damintun[LN]	62	F3
Daidoi[SC]	138	E3	Dalihai[SD]	102	B5	Damjong[QH]	164	H7
Daigu[SD]	102	E4	Daliji[SD]	102	B4	Damkug[QH]	164	M6
Daihui[AH]	90	E6	Dalijia[LN]	62	F5	Damnyain[XZ]	152	I5
Dailing Qu[HL]	70	E5	Daling He[LN]	62	C3	Damoujia[SD]	102	F3
Dailing[ZJ]	84	E5	Daling He[LN]	62	E3	Damozhuang[BJ]	36	B4
Dailou[JS]	80	D3	Daling[BJ]	36	E3	Damqog Zangbo (Maquan He) [XZ]	152	C4
Daimao Shan[FJ]	94	B4	Daling[CQ]	132	E3			
Dainkog[XZ]	152	J3	Daling[HL]	70	D4	Damtog[QH]	164	J8
Daiqin Ju[NM]	58	T11	Daling[JL]	66	E4	Damu Yang[ZJ]	84	G3
Daiqu Yang[ZJ]	84	G2	Daling[JL]	66	E4	Damu[HI]	128	B2
Daishan Dao[ZJ]	84	G2	Dalinghe Kou[LN]	62	E4	Damxung[XZ]	152	G4
Daishan[AH]	90	D4	Dalinghou[BJ]	36	E3	Damxung[XZ]	152	I4
Daishan[ZJ]	84	G2	Dalinhe[SX]	54	E2	Dan He[SX]	54	E6
Daitou[FJ]	94	E4	Dalinzi[JL]	66	F2	Dan Jiang[SN]	156	G7
Daixi[FJ]	94	E3	Daliu[AH]	90	E4	Danagpu[XZ]	152	F5
Daixi[JX]	98	B3	Daliu[HB]	110	D1	Danan Shan[GD]	118	I3
Daixi[ZJ]	84	E2	Daliu[HEN]	106	E4	Danan[FJ]	94	B3
Daiyao[JS]	80	F4	Daliu[SD]	102	C2	Danan[JX]	98	F3
Daiyue Qu[SD]	102	D3	Daliuhang[SD]	102	H2	Dananban[FJ]	94	C5
Daiyun Shan[FJ]	94	D4	Daliuta[SN]	156	G1	Danangou[XJ]	172	M4
Daiyun Shan[FJ]	94	D4	Daliutan[TJ]	42	A3	Danba[SC]	138	G5
Daji Shan[ZJ]	84	G2	Daliutun[LN]	62	F2	Danba[SN]	156	E4
Daji Yang[ZJ]	84	G2	Daliuzi[TJ]	42	A3	Dancheng[AH]	90	C3
Daji[FJ]	94	C2	Dalizhuang[TJ]	42	C2	Dancheng[HEN]	106	G4
Daji[SD]	102	B5	Dalizi Shan[HEB]	48	E1	Dandai[JL]	66	D1
Dajiahe[HL]	70	G5	Dalizi[JL]	66	G6	Dandian[HB]	110	I4
Dajian[SX]	54	C3	Dalong[AH]	90	E5	Dandong[LN]	62	H4
Dajianchang[TJ]	42	B3	Dalong[GX]	124	I5	Dandong[SC]	138	G4
Dajiang[GX]	124	G2	Dalongdong Shuiku[GX]	124	F4	Danfeng[SN]	156	G7
Dajiang[HI]	128	B2	Dalonghua[GD]	118	I2	Dang He[GS]	160	B3
Dajiangkou[HN]	114	D6	Dalonghua[HEB]	48	C4	Dangan Dao[GD]	118	G4
Dajiawa[SD]	102	E2	Dalongwan[TJ]	42	B3	Dangan Liedao[GD]	118	G5
Dajie[GZ]	144	C3	Dalou Shan[GZ]	144	D3	Dangba[HEB]	48	F3
Dajie[YN]	148	G6	Dalt[XJ]	172	I3	Dangbizhen[HL]	70	F6
Dajin Chuan[SC]	138	G4	Dalu Dao[LN]	62	G5	Dangchang[GS]	160	G5
Dajin Dao[GD]	118	F5	Dalu Shan[ZJ]	84	F4	Dangcheng[TJ]	42	A3
Dajin Shan[SH]	74	C3	Dalu[AH]	90	D3	Dangchuan[GS]	160	H5
Dajin Shan[SH]	74	C3	Dalu[CQ]	132	C4	Danghe Nanshan[GS]	160	B3
Dajin[CQ]	132	E2	Dalu[GS]	160	G4	Dangjiaxian[GS]	160	G5
Dajin[HB]	110	I5	Dalu[HB]	110	H5	Dangjiazhuang[SD]	102	C3
Dajindian[HEN]	106	D3	Dalu[HI]	128	C2	Dangpu[HB]	110	E2
Dajing[GD]	118	C4	Dalu[NM]	58	X11	Dangshan[AH]	90	C2
Dajing[GS]	160	F4	Daluankou[ZJ]	84	C4	Dangtu[AH]	90	E5

Dangxung[QH]	164	L7
Dangyang[HB]	110	E4
Dangzhadara[QH]	164	F6
Danhua[HI]	128	C2
Danian[GS]	160	G6
Danian[GX]	124	G2
Danian[LN]	62	D3
Daning He[CQ]	132	F2
Daning He[GX]	124	I3
Daning[GX]	124	I3
Daning[SX]	54	B5
Daniudian[SX]	54	D3
Danjiang[HN]	114	D7
Danjiangkou Shuiku[HB]	110	E2
Danjiangkou Shuiku[HEN]	106	C5
Danjiangkou[HB]	110	E2
Danjinlicao He[JS]	80	E5
Dankou[HN]	114	C6
Danling[SC]	138	I5
Danlongsi[AH]	90	C5
Danshui[HEN]	106	C4
Dansi[SD]	102	E2
Dantu Qu[JS]	80	E4
Danxi[JX]	98	C7
Danxia[GD]	118	F1
Danyan[FJ]	94	C5
Danyang[AH]	90	E5
Danyang[FJ]	94	E3
Danyang[JS]	80	E5
Danyun[FJ]	94	E4
Danzhai[GZ]	144	F4
Danzhou[HI]	128	B2
Danzhu[GX]	124	H4
Dao Shui[HB]	110	H3
Dao Xian[HN]	114	D7
Daoba[GZ]	144	G2
Daocheng[SC]	138	F6
Daode[NM]	58	N6
Daodian[HI]	128	B2
Daodong Linchang[HI]	128	C2
Dao'erdeng[LN]	62	C4
Daogouzi[TJ]	42	C4
Daohugou[HEB]	48	F3
Daojiang[GX]	124	G3
Daojiao[GD]	118	F3
Daojie[YN]	148	D5
Daolang[SD]	102	C3
Daolin[HN]	114	E4
Daoping[GZ]	144	F4
Daoshi[ZJ]	84	C2
Daoshichong[AH]	90	C5
Daotai[ZJ]	84	D4
Daotaiqiao[HL]	70	E5
Daotanghe[QH]	164	M4
Daotian[SD]	102	E3
Daotiandi[HL]	70	F4
Daowu[GX]	124	E4
Daoxian[SN]	156	F6
Daoyuan[SH]	74	C3
Daozhen[GZ]	144	F2
Daozhen[SN]	156	F4
Daozi[JL]	66	D3
Dapan Shan[ZJ]	84	D3
Dapan Shan[ZJ]	84	E3
Dapan Shan[ZJ]	84	E4
Dapan Shan[ZJ]	84	G2
Dapan[SN]	156	D8
Dapan[ZJ]	84	E3
Dapeng Wan[GD]	118	G4
Dapeng Wan[HK]	176	F1
Dapeng[GX]	124	H4
Dapeng[JS]	80	C2
Daping Tianshan[GX]	124	G4
Daping[FJ]	94	D3
Daping[GD]	118	F2
Daping[GD]	118	H2
Daping[GD]	118	H3
Daping[GX]	124	I3
Daping[GZ]	144	G3
Daping[HN]	114	F7
Daping[JX]	98	B5
Daping[SN]	156	G8
Dapinggou[HL]	70	F4
Dapingshan[GX]	124	G5

Dapingtai[HL]	70	E4
Dapingxu[GX]	124	G5
Dapo[GX]	124	G2
Dapo[GX]	124	I4
Dapo[HI]	128	A3
Dapo[HI]	128	C2
Dapu[HN]	114	E5
Dapu[LN]	62	H4
Dapuchaihe[JL]	66	I5
Dapuchang[HL]	70	D4
Dapuzi[NX]	168	C4
Daqi[FJ]	94	C4
Daqiao[FJ]	94	D3
Daqiao[GD]	118	F2
Daqiao[GX]	124	F4
Daqiao[GX]	124	H5
Daqiao[HN]	114	E5
Daqiao[HN]	114	E7
Daqiao[JL]	66	I4
Daqiao[JS]	80	E4
Daqiao[JS]	80	F4
Daqiao[JX]	98	B3
Daqiao[JX]	98	C6
Daqiao[SC]	138	J3
Daqiao[SH]	74	C3
Daqiao[XJ]	172	H5
Daqiao[YN]	148	I4
Daqiao[ZJ]	84	C4
Daqin Dao[SD]	102	G1
Daqin Shan[FJ]	94	C5
Daqing He[HEB]	48	D5
Daqing He[LN]	62	F4
Daqing He[SD]	102	C3
Daqing He[TJ]	42	A3
Daqing Shan[HL]	70	D6
Daqing Shan[LN]	62	C4
Daqing Shan[LN]	62	D3
Daqing Shan[NM]	58	W11
Daqing[HL]	70	C5
Daqing[LN]	62	G2
Daqingbei[JL]	66	H4
Daqinggou[HEB]	48	B2
Daqinggou[HEN]	106	C4
Daqingshan[NM]	58	X11
Daqingzui[JL]	66	F3
Daqiu[FJ]	94	E4
Daqiutian[JX]	98	B7
Daqiuzhuang[TJ]	42	B4
Daqu Shan[ZJ]	84	G2
Daquandian[HEN]	106	G6
Daquandong[HB]	110	H5
Daquanwan[XJ]	172	N4
Daren[SN]	156	E7
Darenzhuang[TJ]	42	B3
Dargo Zangbo[XZ]	152	E4
Dargo[XZ]	152	E4
Darhan Muminggan Qi[NM]	58	I7
Darhan Ulo[NM]	58	J5
Darog[XZ]	152	E4
Darong Shan[GX]	124	H4
Darqung[XZ]	152	D5
Daru Co[XZ]	152	G4
Daryaboyi[XJ]	172	H6
Dasanhezeng[TJ]	42	A3
Dasanjia[LN]	62	D3
Dasanmen Dao[GD]	118	G4
Dasha He[HEB]	48	B5
Dasha He[HEN]	106	G3
Dasha He[SD]	102	B3
Dasha[SC]	138	M4
Dashahe Shuiku[GD]	118	E4
Dashahe[TJ]	42	A2
Dashan Dao(Danian Shan)[JS]	80	E1
Dashan Dao[SD]	102	F4
Dashan[GD]	118	I3
Dashan[GZ]	144	C5
Dashan[GZ]	144	D3
Dashan[JL]	66	E3
Dashan[SD]	102	D1
Dashan[YN]	148	F7
Dashanbao[YN]	148	I3
Dashanji[AH]	90	D3
Dasheng[HN]	114	D6
Dashengling[BJ]	36	C2

Dashennongjia[HB]	110	D3
Dashentang[TJ]	42	C3
Dashetai[NM]	58	H7
Dashetai[NM]	58	V10
Dashetou[SX]	54	C3
Dashi He[BJ]	36	B4
Dashi He[BJ]	36	C4
Dashi[AH]	90	C6
Dashi[CQ]	132	C3
Dashi[LN]	62	E3
Dashi[SC]	138	K5
Dashi[ZJ]	84	D4
Dashicun[JL]	66	J4
Dashidongzi[HEB]	48	D2
Dashimen[BJ]	36	D2
Dashiqiao[HEN]	106	C4
Dashiqiao[LN]	62	F4
Dashitou[JL]	66	I4
Dashitou[SH]	74	C3
Dashiwo[BJ]	36	B4
Dashiyao[SX]	54	B5
Dashu[AH]	90	D4
Dashu[CQ]	132	F2
Dashuang[SN]	156	F8
Dashuigou[NX]	168	C2
Dashuijing[YN]	148	I3
Dashuikeng[NX]	168	C3
Dashuitian[HN]	114	B5
Dashuiyu[BJ]	36	D3
Dashun[ZJ]	84	D4
Dasi[GX]	124	F5
Dasijiazi[LN]	62	G2
Dasiping[LN]	62	H3
Dasongfa[BJ]	36	D4
Dasuhe[LN]	62	H3
Dasuifen He[HL]	70	F7
Dasuji[HEB]	48	B2
Dasungezhuang[BJ]	36	D3
Dasunzhuang[TJ]	42	B4
Datai[BJ]	36	B4
Datai[HEB]	48	B5
Datan[AH]	90	D7
Datan[HEB]	48	D2
Datan[LN]	62	F5
Datan[SN]	156	D7
Datanchuan[NX]	168	B3
Datang[GD]	118	E3
Datang[GD]	118	F2
Datang[GX]	124	F3
Datang[GX]	124	F5
Datang[GX]	124	H5
Datang[GZ]	144	E5
Datang[HN]	114	F7
Datang[XZ]	152	H4
Datangbu[JX]	98	B6
Datangkou[HN]	114	B6
Datangzhuang[TJ]	42	B3
Datian Ding[GD]	118	D4
Datian[FJ]	94	B3
Datian[FJ]	94	C4
Datian[GD]	118	E4
Datian[GD]	118	H3
Datian[HI]	128	A2
Datian[HI]	128	A2
Datian[LN]	62	E5
Datian[TJ]	42	C3
Datian[ZJ]	84	F4
Datianba[YN]	148	E5
Datianji[SD]	102	C4
Datianwa[HEB]	48	B3
Datianzhu Shan[SN]	156	G7
Datiebang[SH]	74	C2
Datiezhuang[BJ]	36	E3
Dating[GZ]	144	E5
Dating[TJ]	42	C3
Datong[QH]	164	N4
Datong He[QH]	164	L2
Datong Hu[HN]	114	E3
Datong Jiang[SC]	138	M3
Datong Qu[AH]	90	D4
Datong Qu[HL]	70	C5
Datong Shan[QH]	164	L3
Datong[AH]	90	D6
Datong[CQ]	132	C5

Name	Page	Grid
Datong[GS]	160	F4
Datong[GZ]	144	D2
Datong[GZ]	144	H4
Datong[HB]	110	I4
Datong[HI]	128	C2
Datong[JL]	66	C2
Datong[SC]	138	K5
Datong[SX]	54	E1
Datong[SX]	54	E1
Datonghu Nongchang[HB]	110	G4
Datongqiao[HN]	114	F5
Datoushan[HEB]	48	E2
Datu Dingzi[HL]	70	E6
Datuan[SH]	74	D3
Datulong[JL]	66	E3
Datun[AH]	90	C2
Datun[HEB]	48	C6
Datun[HEB]	48	E3
Datun[LN]	62	C4
Datun[LN]	62	F4
Datuo[HN]	114	B4
Dawa Co[XZ]	152	D4
Dawa[AH]	90	C6
Dawa[JL]	66	E2
Dawa[LN]	62	F3
Dawa[LN]	62	G1
Dawan[GD]	118	D4
Dawan[GD]	118	E2
Dawan[GZ]	144	C4
Dawan[NX]	168	C5
Dawang Shan[JX]	98	D4
Dawang[SD]	102	E3
Dawang[SN]	156	E6
Dawang[SN]	156	F6
Dawangcun[TJ]	42	A3
Dawangdian[HEB]	48	C4
Dawangjia Dao[LN]	62	G5
Dawangtai[TJ]	42	B3
Dawangtan Shuiku[GX]	124	F5
Dawangzhuang[SD]	102	D3
Dawanshan Dao[GD]	118	F5
Dawatou[TJ]	42	A4
Dawe[SC]	138	H5
Daweijia[LN]	62	E5
Daweishan[HN]	114	G4
Daweixi[HN]	114	C4
Dawen He[SD]	102	C4
Dawen He[SD]	102	D3
Dawen[YN]	148	E7
Dawenkou[SD]	102	D4
Dawu Shan[HB]	110	H3
Dawu[HB]	110	H3
Dawu[SC]	138	G5
Dawu[SD]	102	C4
Dawu[SX]	54	C4
Dawudeng[TJ]	42	B2
Dawujiazi[LN]	62	E2
Dawukou[NX]	168	C1
Dawusu[HL]	70	C3
Daxi[CQ]	132	F4
Daxi[CQ]	132	F5
Daxi[FJ]	94	C5
Daxi[GD]	118	G2
Daxi[HN]	114	D8
Daxi[ZJ]	84	F4
Daxia He[GS]	160	F5
Daxian[HI]	128	A2
Daxiang Ling[SC]	138	H6
Daxiang[GX]	124	G2
Daxianguan[HN]	114	D6
Daxicha[LN]	62	I4
Daxie[CQ]	132	E3
Daxie[ZJ]	84	F3
Daxieji[SD]	102	C4
Daxigou[XJ]	172	H3
Daxihaizi Shuiku[XJ]	172	K5
Daxijiang[GX]	124	I1
Daxijiang[HL]	70	C4
Daxin[AH]	90	D3
Daxin[GX]	124	E5
Daxin[JS]	80	F5
Daxin[NX]	168	C2
Daxin[SC]	138	K4
Daxing Qu[BJ]	36	C4
Daxing Shuiku[TJ]	42	B3
Daxing[AH]	90	C4
Daxing[GX]	124	E3
Daxing[GZ]	144	H3
Daxing[HI]	128	B2
Daxing[HL]	70	B5
Daxing[JL]	66	D3
Daxing[JL]	66	F5
Daxing[JL]	66	J4
Daxing[JS]	80	D3
Daxing[LN]	62	F3
Daxing[LN]	62	H4
Daxing[YN]	148	I3
Daxingdi[YN]	148	D4
Daxinggou[JL]	66	J4
Daxingzhuang[BJ]	36	E3
Daxinjia[SD]	102	H3
Daxintun[HL]	70	D3
Daxinzhai[HEB]	48	G3
Daxinzhuang[BJ]	36	C4
Daxinzhuang[HEB]	48	F4
Daxiou Jiang[ZJ]	84	E4
Daxiwan[HEB]	48	B2
Daxizhai Dao[ZJ]	84	G2
Daxu[GX]	124	G4
Daxu[HN]	114	D8
Daxu[JS]	80	C2
Daxue Shan[GS]	160	C3
Daxue Shan[SC]	138	G4
Daxue Shan[YN]	148	E6
Daxue Shan[YN]	148	E7
Daxueguo Shan[YN]	148	G6
Daya Wan[GD]	118	G4
Daya[HI]	128	B2
Dayan[HB]	110	E4
Dayan[SX]	54	B6
Dayan[ZJ]	84	F3
Dayanbei[SX]	54	D2
Dayang He[LN]	62	G4
Dayang Shan[ZJ]	84	E4
Dayang Shan[ZJ]	84	G2
Dayang[AH]	90	B3
Dayang[AH]	90	D3
Dayang[AH]	90	D5
Dayang[FJ]	94	E4
Dayang[GX]	124	H4
Dayang[GZ]	144	F5
Dayang[HI]	128	C2
Dayang[JL]	66	F5
Dayang[SD]	102	C3
Dayang[ZJ]	84	D3
Dayang[ZJ]	84	G2
Dayanggang Kou[JS]	80	G4
Dayangji[HEN]	106	H3
Dayangqi[NX]	168	C3
Dayangzhuang[TJ]	42	B3
Dayangzhuang[TJ]	42	B3
Dayanjia[SD]	102	H3
Dayao Shan[GX]	124	H4
Dayao[HI]	128	B2
Dayao[HN]	114	F5
Dayao[YN]	148	G5
Dayaopu[TJ]	42	A4
Daye Hu[HB]	110	I4
Daye[GX]	124	I5
Daye[HB]	110	H4
Dayi[GZ]	144	E5
Dayi[HN]	114	F6
Dayi[JS]	80	E4
Dayi[SC]	138	I5
Dayi[SD]	102	C4
Dayin[GZ]	144	D3
Dayin[GZ]	144	E5
Dayin[SC]	138	L4
Dayin[ZJ]	84	F3
Dayincun[HEB]	48	C5
Daying Jiang[YN]	148	C6
Daying[AH]	90	E4
Daying[AH]	90	E4
Daying[HEB]	48	C6
Daying[JS]	80	F3
Daying[LN]	62	G5
Daying[SC]	138	K5
Daying[SH]	74	C2
Daying[SX]	54	E2
Daying[TJ]	42	A2
Daying[YN]	148	F5
Dayingpan[HEB]	48	B2
Dayingpan[SX]	54	F1
Dayingzi[LN]	62	G4
Dayishan[JL]	66	G5
Dayong[GZ]	144	D4
Dayong[HL]	70	D5
Dayou[GS]	160	F4
Dayou[JS]	80	E2
Dayou[JX]	98	D5
Dayou[LN]	62	E4
Dayu Shan[FJ]	94	F3
Dayu Shan[GD]	118	G1
Dayu Shan[ZJ]	84	F2
Dayu[BJ]	36	E3
Dayu[HEN]	106	E3
Dayu[JX]	98	B6
Dayu[SX]	54	D3
Dayu[ZJ]	84	E5
Dayuan Nongchang[HN]	114	G6
Dayuan[FJ]	94	C3
Dayuan[HB]	110	H5
Dayuan[ZJ]	84	D4
Dayuan[ZJ]	84	E2
Dayuan[ZJ]	84	E4
Dayudu[SX]	54	B7
Dayukou[GD]	118	D3
Dayukou[SN]	156	F6
Dayun[HI]	128	B2
Dayunwu Shan[GD]	118	D4
Dayushu[BJ]	36	C3
Dayuzi[BJ]	36	E3
Daze Shan[SD]	102	F3
Daze Shan[SD]	102	G3
Dazhai[HEN]	106	F2
Dazhai[SX]	54	E4
Dazhai[YN]	148	F6
Dazhai[YN]	148	F8
Dazhai[YN]	148	H3
Dazhang Xi[FJ]	94	D4
Dazhang[AH]	90	D3
Dazhang[GX]	124	G4
Dazhang[LN]	62	F3
Dazhang[SD]	102	E3
Dazhanglou[SD]	102	C4
Dazhangtun[TJ]	42	A4
Dazhangzhuang[TJ]	42	B3
Dazhaozhuang[TJ]	42	B2
Dazheng[LN]	62	F5
Dazhenzhu[SD]	102	F2
Dazhi He[SH]	74	D2
Dazhi[GX]	124	F6
Dazhiping[HB]	110	D4
Dazhipo[HI]	128	C2
Dazhongcun[SD]	102	E5
Dazhongdian[YN]	148	E3
Dazhongzhuang[TJ]	42	C2
Dazhou Dao[HI]	128	C3
Dazhou[GX]	124	H4
Dazhou[SC]	138	M4
Dazhou[TJ]	42	A2
Dazhouyi[BJ]	36	D4
Dazhu[FJ]	94	C2
Dazhu[SC]	138	M5
Dazhuang[NX]	168	C5
Dazhuang[YN]	148	G6
Dazhuang[YN]	148	I5
Dazhuangzi[GS]	160	D2
Dazhuangzi[TJ]	42	B4
Dazhubao[SC]	138	I7
Dazhushan Dao[SD]	102	G1
Dazigoumen[HEB]	48	F3
Dazongquzhoinka[QH]	164	N6
Dazou[JS]	80	E3
Dazu[CQ]	132	B4
De'an[JX]	98	C2
Debao[GX]	124	D4
Dechang[HL]	70	C6
Dechang[SC]	138	H8
Deep Water Bay[HK]	176	D4
Degan[CQ]	132	C4

Name	Page	Grid
Dêgê[SC]	138	D4
Degui[HEB]	48	D5
Dehou[YN]	148	I7
Dehua[FJ]	94	D4
Dehua[JL]	66	J5
Dehua[YN]	148	F7
Dehui Xinhe[SD]	102	C2
Dehui[JL]	66	F3
Deji[JS]	80	F4
Dejia[QH]	164	O4
Dejiang[GZ]	144	G2
Delger[NM]	58	E7
Delhi Nongchang[QH]	164	J3
Delhi[QH]	164	J3
Delingshan[NM]	58	U10
Delisi[LN]	62	F5
Delong[GX]	124	C4
Dêm[XZ]	152	H5
Dengchuan[YN]	148	F5
Dengcun[HB]	110	D4
Dengfeng[HEN]	106	D3
Denggin Nomor[QH]	164	D4
Dengjia[CQ]	132	G3
Dengjia[FJ]	94	B4
Dengjiapu[HN]	114	C6
Dengkou[NM]	58	G7
Dengkou[NM]	58	S11
Denglong[GX]	124	G3
Dêngqên[XZ]	152	I4
Dengshang[HEB]	48	F2
Dengshe[GD]	118	H3
Dengshipuzi[LN]	62	G2
Dengta[HL]	70	D5
Dengta[LN]	62	G3
Dengta[SH]	74	D1
Dengtun[LN]	62	E5
Dêngu[XZ]	152	E4
Dengyoufang[HEB]	48	B2
Dengzhen[SH]	74	D2
Dengzhou[HEN]	106	D5
Dêqên[XZ]	152	G4
Dêqên[XZ]	152	G4
Dêqên[YN]	148	D2
Deqing[GD]	118	D3
Deqing[ZJ]	84	D2
Dêr Qu[QH]	164	I6
Dêrdoin[XZ]	152	K4
Derenwu[BJ]	36	D4
Dêrnang[QH]	164	M7
Dêrong[SC]	138	E7
Deshan[HN]	114	D4
Desheng[HB]	110	C2
Desheng[LN]	62	E5
Desheng[SH]	74	C3
Desheng[YN]	148	F5
Deshengkou[BJ]	36	C3
Deshengtai[NM]	58	W11
Deshun[JL]	66	C2
Desili[YN]	148	E6
Detiangou[BJ]	36	D2
Dêwo[SC]	138	F6
Dewu[GZ]	144	C4
Dexin[GZ]	144	F4
Dexing[JX]	98	E3
Dexing[LN]	62	H2
Deyang[SC]	138	J4
Dêyü Co[XZ]	152	E2
Deyu[HL]	70	E5
Deze[YN]	148	I5
Dezhou[SD]	102	C2
Diamond Hill[HK]	176	D3
Dian He[YN]	148	I6
Dianbai[GD]	118	C5
Diancang Shan[YN]	148	E4
Diancang Shan[YN]	148	F5
Dianchang[HI]	128	C4
Dianchenyu[BJ]	36	D2
Dianchi[YN]	148	H6
Dianhutun[SD]	102	B4
Dianji[SD]	102	G3
Dianjiang[CQ]	132	D3
Dianjun Qu[HB]	110	E4
Diannan[YN]	148	E4
Dianping[HB]	110	E3
Dianping[SX]	54	C5
Dianpu He[SH]	74	C2
Dianqian[AH]	90	B6
Diansha Hu[JS]	80	F5
Dianshan Hu[SH]	74	B2
Dianshang[NM]	58	X11
Dianshang[SX]	54	E5
Dianshang[SX]	54	E6
Dianshanhu[JS]	80	G5
Dianshi[SN]	156	F3
Dianshi[SN]	156	F3
Dianta[SN]	156	G2
Diantou[FJ]	94	F2
Diantou[SD]	102	E5
Diantou[SN]	156	E6
Diantou[SN]	156	F5
Dianxia[FJ]	94	F2
Dianxia[JX]	98	C4
Dianya[HB]	110	E3
Dianzhong[YN]	148	H6
Dianzi[HB]	110	C1
Dianzi[HEN]	106	C3
Dianzi[SD]	102	B3
Dianzi[SD]	102	D4
Dianzi[SD]	102	F3
Dianzishang[SN]	156	C6
Diao He[HEN]	106	C5
Diao Jiang[GX]	124	E3
Diaobingshan[LN]	62	G2
Diaocheng[AH]	90	A3
Diao'e[HEB]	48	C3
Diaofeng[GD]	118	C6
Diaofeng[JX]	98	C5
Diaoling[HL]	70	E6
Diaolongzui[SD]	102	F2
Diaolou[HI]	128	B2
Diaoluoshan[HI]	128	B3
Diaoluoshanpai[GD]	118	H2
Diaoyu[JS]	80	E3
Diaozhen[SD]	102	D3
Dibabu[SX]	54	B3
Dibao[CQ]	132	E3
Dicun[SX]	54	C5
Didao Qu[HL]	70	F6
Didian[SN]	156	F6
Didou[GD]	118	E3
Die Shan[GS]	160	F5
Diema[YN]	148	G7
Dieshan[JX]	98	E3
Difang[SD]	102	D4
Digang[AH]	90	E5
Diliubu[TJ]	42	A3
Diliutun[HEB]	48	B3
Dimda[QH]	164	M8
Dimiao[SN]	156	E5
Ding Qu[SC]	138	E7
Ding'an[GX]	124	C3
Ding'an[HI]	128	C2
Dingba Qu[XZ]	152	I5
Dingbei[JX]	98	C5
Dingbian[SN]	156	D3
Dingbu[JS]	80	E5
Dingcheng Qu[HN]	114	D3
Dingdang[GX]	124	E4
Dingdong[GZ]	144	F4
Dingfuzhuang[BJ]	36	C4
Dinggyê[XZ]	152	E5
Dinghai Wan[FJ]	94	E3
Dinghu Qu[GD]	118	E3
Dinghu[HN]	114	F3
Dingjia[NX]	168	C3
Dingjiabu[BJ]	36	B2
Dingjiang[JX]	98	C4
Dingjiatang[NX]	168	B3
Dingjiayao[SX]	54	D2
Dingjiaying[HB]	110	E2
Dingli[AH]	90	C2
Dinglichang[SD]	102	B4
Dingluo[SD]	102	E2
Dingnan[JX]	98	C7
Dingpeng[SH]	74	C1
Dingpur[SC]	138	E6
Dingqiao[ZJ]	84	E2
Dingshan[CQ]	132	C5
Dingshan[JX]	98	D2
Dingshan[ZJ]	84	E2
Dingshi[CQ]	132	E5
Dingshu[JS]	80	E5
Dingsidang[HB]	110	I4
Dingtao[SD]	102	B4
Dingwu[SD]	102	D2
Dingxi[GS]	160	G5
Dingxiang[AH]	90	D6
Dingxiang[SX]	54	D3
Dingxianyan[SN]	156	G3
Dingxiao[GZ]	144	D5
Dingxin[GS]	160	D2
Dingxin[GZ]	144	E3
Dingxing[HEB]	48	C4
Dingyang[SX]	54	D5
Dingyuan[AH]	90	D4
Dingyuan[HEN]	106	F6
Dingzhai[HB]	110	C5
Dingzhai[ZJ]	84	E3
Dingzhou[HEB]	48	B5
Dingzhuang[SD]	102	E2
Dingzi Gang[SD]	102	H3
Dingzidi[HB]	110	G4
Dingzikou[QH]	164	F2
Diping[GZ]	144	H5
Dirangzong[XZ]	152	H6
Disanbu[HEB]	48	B3
Disanpu[GS]	160	G5
Discorery Bay[HK]	176	C3
Dishiying[HEB]	48	C7
Dishui Quan[XJ]	172	L3
Disong[GZ]	144	F4
Ditang[CQ]	132	E4
Ditang[QH]	164	M7
Ditang[ZJ]	84	F2
Ditou[HB]	110	F5
Dixiongshan[LN]	62	H4
Diyag[XZ]	152	A4
Diyu[YN]	148	J6
Dizangsi[LN]	62	D3
Dizhengdang[YN]	148	D2
Dizhou[GX]	124	D4
Do Qu[QH]	164	I6
Dobdain[QH]	164	N5
Dogai Coring[XZ]	152	F2
Dogaicoring Qangco[XZ]	152	F2
Dogarma[QH]	164	L6
Dogarmo[QH]	164	N5
Dogxung Zangbo[XZ]	152	E5
Doiba[XZ]	152	H5
Doice[QH]	164	H7
Doile[XZ]	152	B3
Doilungdêqên[XZ]	152	G5
Doincêrxü[QH]	164	I8
Dojê[XZ]	152	J5
Dojoi[QH]	164	K6
Dokog He[SC]	138	F3
Dokongma[QH]	164	M7
Dolod[NM]	58	N5
Dolon[QH]	164	N3
Domar[XZ]	152	B3
Domar[XZ]	152	E4
Domar[XZ]	152	F3
Domba[QH]	164	H8
Domkog[QH]	164	L6
Dong Chuan[SN]	156	D3
Dong Co[XZ]	152	D3
Dong Dabsan Hu[QH]	164	H3
Dong Gongin Qulu[NM]	58	W10
Dong Haxat[JL]	66	E3
Dong He[CQ]	132	E2
Dong He[SC]	138	L4
Dong Hondoi[NM]	58	X12
Dong Hu[HB]	110	H4
Dong Jiang[GD]	118	G3
Dong Jiang[HN]	114	F7
Dong Mao[HEB]	48	D3
Dong Qu[QH]	164	E7
Dong Qu[QH]	164	K5
Dong Qu[SC]	138	G9
Dong Taijnar Hu[QH]	164	F3
Dong Ujimqin Qi[NM]	58	L5
Dong Xi[FJ]	94	E2

Name	Page	Grid
Dong Xi[ZJ]	84	D5
Dong'an[BJ]	36	E2
Dong'an[CQ]	132	F2
Dong'an[HEN]	106	F4
Dong'an[HL]	70	H5
Dong'an[HN]	114	D6
Dong'anzi[TJ]	42	B3
Dong'ao[HI]	128	C3
Dongba[BJ]	36	D4
Dongba[SD]	102	E3
Dongba[XZ]	152	J5
Dongbai Shan[ZJ]	84	E3
Dongbaishan[BJ]	36	D3
Dongbaizhuang[TJ]	42	C3
Dongbanbidian[BJ]	36	C3
Dongbao[YN]	148	K7
Dongbatu[GS]	160	B2
Dongbei Pingyuan[JL]	66	D4
Dongbei Pingyuan[LN]	62	F3
Dongbeicha[JL]	66	H6
Dongbeicha[JL]	66	I4
Dongbian[JX]	98	C4
Dongbiaofa[TJ]	42	A3
Dongbo[XZ]	152	B4
Dongbo[YN]	148	K7
Dongbolhai Shan[XZ]	152	F2
Dongcang[TJ]	42	A2
Dongcha[GS]	160	H5
Dongchan[SC]	138	K5
Dongchang[GX]	124	F6
Dongchangtun[TJ]	42	A4
Dongchen[ZJ]	84	F3
Dongcheng[AH]	90	C5
Dongcheng[HI]	128	B2
Dongcheng[JL]	66	J5
Dongcheng[ZJ]	84	F4
Dongchuan Qu[YN]	148	I4
Dongchuan[SN]	156	E7
Dongco[XZ]	152	D3
Dongcun[BJ]	36	B4
Dongcun[HEN]	106	E3
Dongcun[JX]	98	B3
Dongda He[GS]	160	E4
Dongda Shan[GS]	160	E3
Dongdadi[HEB]	48	F3
Dongdalian Dao[LN]	62	F5
Dongdang[GZ]	144	E5
Dongdashankou[XJ]	172	L5
Dongdayuan[HEN]	106	C3
Dongding[NX]	168	A3
Dongditou[TJ]	42	B3
Dongdongting Shan[JS]	80	F5
Dongdongzhuang[TJ]	42	C3
Dongdu[ZJ]	84	E4
Dongduan[HEB]	48	D4
Dong'e[SD]	102	C3
Dong'erdaohe[BJ]	36	C3
Dongfang[HI]	128	A2
Dongfang[SH]	74	C1
Dongfanghong[HL]	70	B2
Dongfanghong[HL]	70	G5
Dongfeng Gang[SD]	102	D1
Dongfeng Gang[SD]	102	E1
Dongfeng Ling[GX]	124	E3
Dongfeng Qu[HL]	70	F5
Dongfeng[BJ]	36	B4
Dongfeng[FJ]	94	D2
Dongfeng[HI]	128	B2
Dongfeng[HL]	70	D5
Dongfeng[HL]	70	G6
Dongfeng[JL]	66	F5
Dongfeng[LN]	62	G3
Dongfeng[SX]	54	D6
Dongfenggang[SD]	102	E1
Dongfengquan[GS]	160	C1
Dongfu Shan[ZJ]	84	G2
Dongga[LN]	62	G2
Donggang Qu[SD]	102	F4
Donggang[GD]	118	H4
Donggang[LN]	62	E5
Donggang[LN]	62	H5
Donggang[SX]	54	F2
Dongge[HI]	128	C2
Donggi Conag[QH]	164	K5
Donggong Shan[FJ]	94	E2
Donggong Shan[ZJ]	84	D5
Donggong[FJ]	94	E2
Donggong[HB]	110	E3
Donggou[JL]	66	D2
Donggou[QH]	164	N5
Donggou[SH]	74	D2
Donggou[SN]	156	F4
Donggou[XJ]	172	L4
Donggu[JX]	98	C5
Donggu[SC]	138	G5
Dongguan[AH]	90	D5
Dongguan[GD]	118	F3
Dongguan[JX]	98	D4
Dongguan[SD]	102	E4
Dongguan[SX]	54	D4
Dongguan[ZJ]	84	E2
Dongguang[HEB]	48	D6
Dongguanying[LN]	62	D3
Dongguanzhuang[TJ]	42	B3
Donggubei[SX]	54	E4
Dongguo[LN]	62	E3
Dongguo[SD]	102	D4
Dongguo[SX]	54	C6
Donghai Dao[GD]	118	C6
Donghai[JS]	80	D2
Donghai[JS]	80	G5
Donghai[SH]	74	D2
Donghai[SH]	74	D3
Donghaihong[BJ]	36	D3
Donghe Qu[NM]	58	V11
Donghe[GX]	124	D3
Donghe[HL]	70	F5
Donghe[YN]	148	F8
Donghe[ZJ]	84	D3
Donghe[ZJ]	84	E3
Donghekou[AH]	90	C5
Donghongsheng[NM]	58	W10
Donghou Ding[HEB]	48	D2
Donghu[GS]	160	F3
Donghu[JL]	66	F4
Donghu[ZJ]	84	E3
Donghua[HI]	128	A2
Donghua[HL]	70	B5
Donghua[LN]	62	E3
Donghuangcheng[HEB]	48	C5
Donghuangshui[SX]	54	D3
Donghuangyu[HEB]	48	F3
Donghuayuan[HEB]	48	C3
Donghui[HL]	70	E5
Donghui[SX]	54	C3
Donghui[YN]	148	E8
Donghui[ZJ]	84	D3
Donghuo Shan[ZJ]	84	F2
Donghutang[HN]	114	E4
Dongji Liedao[ZJ]	84	F4
Dongji Shan[ZJ]	84	F4
Dongji[CQ]	132	D3
Dongjia[GZ]	144	E5
Dongjia[JX]	98	C3
Dongjia[TJ]	42	A4
Dongjiadian[LN]	62	D3
Dongjiaji[SD]	102	D2
Dongjiakou[TJ]	42	A4
Dongjiang Shuiku[HN]	114	F7
Dongjiang[GX]	124	F3
Dongjiang[HI]	128	B2
Dongjiao[HI]	128	C2
Dongjie[HEN]	106	D4
Dongjin Shui[JX]	98	B3
Dongjing He[HB]	110	G4
Dongjing[GX]	124	D4
Dongjing[GX]	124	H2
Dongjing[SH]	74	C2
Dongjingji[HEB]	48	B3
Dongjingling[SX]	54	E6
Dongjituo[TJ]	42	C3
Dongjiuzhai[HEB]	48	F3
Dongjug[XZ]	152	I5
Dongkeng[JX]	98	B7
Dongkeng[SN]	156	E3
Dongkeng[ZJ]	84	D5
Dongkou[HN]	114	C5
Dongkou[SD]	102	B4
Dongkuang[GX]	124	F4
Donglai[JL]	66	G6
Donglan[GX]	124	E3
Donglang[GZ]	144	G5
Donglei[SX]	54	E3
Dongli Qu[TJ]	42	B3
Dongli[GD]	118	I3
Donglian[GD]	118	I3
Dongliang[HEB]	48	B6
Dongliang[SX]	54	E3
Dongliangzhuang[TJ]	42	B3
Dongliao Dao[GD]	118	C6
Dongliao He[JL]	66	E5
Dongliao He[LN]	62	G1
Dongliao He[LN]	62	H2
Dongliao[JL]	66	E5
Donglin[JX]	98	B2
Dongling Shan[BJ]	36	A3
Dongling Shan[HEB]	48	C3
Dongling[FJ]	94	D5
Dongling[GX]	124	D4
Dongling[GZ]	144	F5
Dongling[HEB]	48	E3
Dongling[JL]	66	E3
Dongliu[AH]	90	C6
Dongliu[HI]	94	A4
Dongliuhang[TJ]	42	A3
Dongliuji[AH]	90	D3
Donglu Shuiku[HI]	128	C2
Donglu[HI]	128	C2
Dongluk[XJ]	172	L6
Dongluo Dao[HI]	128	A3
Dongluo Wan[HI]	128	A3
Dongluo[GX]	124	E5
Dongmafang[SX]	54	D3
Dongmafang[TJ]	42	A2
Dongmajuan[TJ]	42	A3
Dongmao Zhou[HI]	128	B3
Dongmen[GX]	124	E5
Dongmenying[BJ]	36	B3
Dongming[GD]	118	F3
Dongming[JL]	66	D4
Dongming[NM]	58	N6
Dongming[SD]	102	B4
Dongmingji[SD]	102	B4
Dongnanzhao[BJ]	36	C4
Dongné[SC]	138	I1
Dongnigu[TJ]	42	B3
Dongning[HL]	70	F6
Dongnong[GX]	124	D3
Dongping Hu[SD]	102	C4
Dongping[FJ]	94	D2
Dongping[FJ]	94	D4
Dongping[GD]	118	E5
Dongping[GD]	118	F2
Dongping[GX]	124	G5
Dongping[JL]	66	D1
Dongping[SD]	102	C4
Dongpo[BJ]	36	E3
Dongpo[HB]	110	C1
Dongpo[HI]	128	C1
Dongpuwa[TJ]	42	B3
Dongqian Hu[ZJ]	84	F3
Dongqianhu[ZJ]	84	F3
Dongqiao[AH]	90	C5
Dongqiao[FJ]	94	D3
Dongqiao[HB]	110	F3
Dongqiao[JX]	98	A4
Dongqiao[ZJ]	84	D2
Dongqiao[ZJ]	84	F3
Dongqilihai Shuiku[TJ]	42	C3
Dongqing[JL]	66	I5
Dongqing[SC]	138	K4
Dongquan[SX]	54	D4
Dongra[XZ]	152	G5
Dongrong[GX]	124	H4
Dongrugar[QH]	164	I9
Dongsangyuan[TJ]	42	A3
Dongsanjiazi[JL]	66	E3
Dongsha Dao[GD]	118	I6
Dongsha He[HEN]	106	G3
Dongsha Jiao[GD]	118	I6
Dongsha Qundao[GD]	118	I6

Dongsha[ZJ] 84 G2
Dongshan Dao[FJ] 94 C6
Dongshan Qu[HL] 70 F5
Dongshan[BJ] 36 C3
Dongshan[FJ] 94 C6
Dongshan[GX] 124 I2
Dongshan[HB] 110 G5
Dongshan[HI] 128 C2
Dongshan[HN] 114 E3
Dongshan[JS] 80 F5
Dongshan[SX] 54 E2
Dongshan[YN] 148 F4
Dongshan[YN] 148 F5
Dongshan[YN] 148 I6
Dongshan[YN] 148 J4
Dongshan[YN] 148 J5
Dongshan Ao[FJ] 94 C6
Dongshanba[YN] 148 H7
Dongshanbeitou[TJ] 42 B1
Dongshanpo[NX] 168 C5
Dongshanqiao[JS] 80 D5
Dongshanyangchang[NX] 168 C3
Dongshanzhuang[TJ] 42 C3
Dongshao[SD] 102 C4
Dongshe[SX] 54 E3
Dongsheng[BJ] 36 C4
Dongsheng[GS] 160 G4
Dongsheng[HL] 70 D5
Dongsheng[HL] 70 E6
Dongsheng[HL] 70 G5
Dongsheng[HL] 70 G5
Dongsheng[JL] 66 B2
Dongsheng[JL] 66 H5
Dongsheng[JX] 98 D2
Dongsheng[LN] 62 G2
Dongshengcun[TJ] 42 B2
Dongshi[FJ] 94 D5
Dongshi[GD] 118 H2
Dongshi[HB] 110 E4
Dongshi[HN] 114 D4
Dongshigou[JL] 66 I4
Dongshigu[TJ] 42 B2
Dongshiyang[SX] 54 B4
Dongshu[SD] 102 C4
Dongshuanggou[JS] 80 D3
Dongshuangtang[TJ] 42 A4
Dongshuanma[HEN] 106 E2
Dongshui[HI] 128 C2
Dongsi[SC] 138 F7
Dongsizhuang[BJ] 36 D4
Dongsuzhuang[TJ] 42 B2
Dongta[HN] 114 F3
Dongta[NX] 168 C2
Dongtai He[JS] 80 F4
Dongtai Nongchang[HI] 128 C2
Dongtai[JS] 80 F4
Dongtai[NX] 168 B3
Dongtaizi[TJ] 42 B4
Dongtang[GZ] 144 G5
Dongtang[LN] 62 H4
Dongtang[NX] 168 D3
Dongtantou[TJ] 42 A4
Dongtazhuang[TJ] 42 B2
Dongtian[FJ] 94 D5
Dongtian[HN] 114 D7
Dongting Hu[HN] 114 E3
Dongtou Dao[ZJ] 84 F5
Dongtou Liedao[ZJ] 84 F5
Dongtou Yang[ZJ] 84 F5
Dongtou[HN] 114 C6
Dongtou[JX] 98 C6
Dongtou[NX] 168 B3
Dongtou[ZJ] 84 F5
Dongtuanbu[HEB] 48 B4
Dongwan[HB] 110 F3
Dongwan[SN] 156 E6
Dongwang[HEB] 48 B5
Dongwang[HEB] 48 C6
Dongwang[YN] 148 E2
Dongwangzhuang[TJ] 42 B2
Dongwankou[HEB] 48 D3
Dongwen[SX] 54 B6
Dongwu[ZJ] 84 F3
Dongxê[XZ] 152 F5

Dongxi Liandao[JS] 80 E2
Dongxi[CQ] 132 C5
Dongxi[HN] 114 C3
Dongxi[HN] 114 C4
Dongxia[AH] 90 F5
Dongxia[NX] 168 C5
Dongxiachang[HN] 114 B5
Dongxiang Dao[FJ] 94 E4
Dongxiang[GS] 160 F5
Dongxiang[GX] 124 G4
Dongxiang[JX] 98 D3
Dongxiaocun[SX] 54 E1
Dongxihu Qu[HB] 110 H4
Dongxin[HB] 110 H3
Dongxin[JL] 66 J4
Dongxin[SH] 74 D1
Dongxing Qu[SC] 138 K6
Dongxing[GX] 124 E6
Dongxing[GX] 124 F2
Dongxing[HI] 128 C2
Dongxing[HL] 70 C5
Dongxing[HL] 70 D5
Dongxing[HL] 70 G5
Dongxinghe[HEB] 48 B4
Dongxingtun[JL] 66 H4
Dongyang He[HEB] 48 B3
Dongyang Jiang[ZJ] 84 D3
Dongyang[JX] 98 C3
Dongyang[ZJ] 84 E3
Dongyang[ZJ] 84 F4
Dongyao[SX] 54 C6
Dongye[SX] 54 E3
Dongying Qu[SD] 102 E2
Dongying[HI] 128 C1
Dongying[SD] 102 E2
Dongyou[FJ] 94 D2
Dongyu[BJ] 36 D2
Dongyu[SX] 54 D5
Dongyuan[FJ] 94 E2
Dongyuan[GD] 118 G3
Dongyuan[JS] 80 G5
Dongyuan[NM] 58 W11
Dongyuan[NX] 168 B3
Dongyuzhuang[TJ] 42 C1
Dongzhai Gang[HI] 128 C1
Dongzhai[SX] 54 D3
Dongzhai[TJ] 42 B2
Dongzhang Shuiku[FJ] 94 E4
Dongzhang[FJ] 94 E4
Dongzhang[JS] 80 F5
Dongzhang[SX] 54 B6
Dongzhaogezhuang[TJ] 42 B2
Dongzhen Shuiku[FJ] 94 D4
Dongzhen[SX] 54 C6
Dongzhi[AH] 90 D6
Dongzhibei[BJ] 36 D3
Dongzhong[GX] 124 E6
Dongzhou[GD] 118 H4
Dongzhuang[SD] 102 D4
Dongzhuang[TJ] 42 C3
Dongzhuangtou[SX] 54 E3
Dongzhujiacao[TJ] 42 B3
Doqoi[XZ] 152 G5
Doqu[XZ] 152 G5
Dora[GS] 160 F6
Doramarkog[QH] 164 I8
Dorbod[HL] 70 C5
Dorgê Co[QH] 164 E5
Dorsoidong Co[XZ] 152 F3
Dosoi Kangri[QH] 164 D6
Dosum[QH] 164 N6
Dou He[HEB] 48 F4
Douba[GS] 160 G6
Doucun[SX] 54 E3
Doudian[BJ] 36 C4
Dougezhuang[BJ] 36 D4
Dougu[GZ] 144 B4
Douhe Shuiku[HEB] 48 F4
Douhelong[QH] 164 N5
Douhong Po[GX] 124 C3
Douhutun[SD] 102 B3
Doujiang[GX] 124 G2
Doulong Gang[JS] 80 F3
Doulonggang Kou[JS] 80 F3

Douluo[SX] 54 D3
Doumen Qu[GD] 118 F4
Doumen[ZJ] 84 E4
Douqing[GZ] 144 D4
Doushui Shuiku[JX] 98 B6
Douzhangzhuang[TJ] 42 A3
Douzhuangzi[TJ] 42 B4
Douzhuangzi[TJ] 42 C2
Douziyu[HEB] 48 E3
Dowa[QH] 164 O5
Doxoggu[XZ] 152 G4
Du He[HB] 110 D2
Du'an[GX] 124 F4
Duancun[SX] 54 D4
Duanfen[GD] 118 E4
Duanji[HEN] 106 G6
Duanjiabu[HEB] 48 C3
Duanjiazhai[SX] 54 C3
Duanliu[SX] 54 D5
Duanlong[HN] 114 B4
Duanlutou[HEB] 48 C6
Duanmugou[BJ] 36 B3
Duanmuliang[BJ] 36 C2
Duanshan[GZ] 144 E5
Duanshi[SX] 54 D6
Duanxin[JX] 98 E2
Dubu[GD] 118 E2
Duchang[JX] 98 D2
Ducheng[HB] 110 H4
Ducun[AH] 90 D6
Ducun[SX] 54 D5
Dudian[BJ] 36 D4
Dudong[GX] 124 G2
Dudu[CQ] 132 E4
Duge[GZ] 144 C4
Dugezhuang[BJ] 36 D3
Duguan[HEN] 106 C3
Dugui Tal[NM] 58 U11
Duifang[JX] 98 C5
Duijiaogoumen[BJ] 36 D2
Duijiushi[BJ] 36 C3
Duiqiao[JX] 98 D3
Duiziliang[SN] 156 E3
Duji Qu[AH] 90 C3
Duji[HEN] 106 G3
Dujiacun[SX] 54 D3
Dujiang[GZ] 144 G5
Dujiangyan[SC] 138 I4
Dujiaping[HN] 114 C4
Dujiazhuang[BJ] 36 B4
Dujie[GX] 124 E4
Dukou[HN] 114 D3
Dukou[NM] 58 T11
Dulan[QH] 164 K4
Dulansi[QH] 164 K3
Duliang[HEN] 106 F3
Dulishi Hu[XZ] 152 B2
Duliu Jianhe[GZ] 144 G5
Duliu Jianhe[TJ] 42 B3
Duliu[TJ] 42 A3
Duliuke[BJ] 36 D4
Dulong Jiang[YN] 148 D3
Dulong Qianxinkuang[QH] 164 L5
Dulong[YN] 148 J8
Dumen[GD] 118 D4
Dumo[GX] 124 H3
Dumuqiao[NX] 168 C2
Duncao[GZ] 144 E5
Duncha[HI] 128 B2
Dunfangdian[HEN] 106 F2
Dung[XZ] 152 G4
Dungang[GD] 118 G2
Dunhua[JL] 66 I4
Dunhuang[GS] 160 B2
Dunkou[HB] 110 H4
Dunling[HB] 110 G3
Dunmu[HI] 128 B2
Dunshang[JS] 80 E2
Duntou Wan[HI] 128 A2
Duntou[HI] 128 A2
Duntou[ZJ] 84 D3
Dunzhai[GZ] 144 H4
Duobao[HB] 110 F4
Duobao[JX] 98 D2

Duobaoshan[HL]	70	C3
Duodao Qu[HB]	110	F4
Duofu[SC]	138	K5
Duohuo[SX]	54	E6
Duojundian[TJ]	42	C3
Duolun[NM]	58	L6
Duowen[HI]	128	B2
Duowunianzha[QH]	164	I6
Duozhu[GD]	118	G3
Duozhuang[SD]	102	D3
Duozhuang[SD]	102	E4
Dupang Ling[GX]	124	I2
Duping[GD]	118	D3
Duping[GZ]	144	G3
Duqiao[ZJ]	84	F4
Duquan[SN]	156	G5
Dure[XJ]	172	L2
Dushan Hu[SD]	102	C4
Dushan[AH]	90	C5
Dushan[GZ]	144	F5
Dushan[HB]	110	H4
Dushan[SD]	102	C4
Dushanzi Qu[XJ]	172	J3
Dushanzi[GS]	160	B3
Dusheng[HEB]	48	D5
Dushi[CQ]	132	C4
Dushikou[HEB]	48	C2
Dushu[HEN]	106	E4
Dushui He[GZ]	144	F4
Dusi[HEN]	106	D5
Dut[NM]	58	U11
Dutian[YN]	148	G6
Duwa[XJ]	172	G7
Duxiang[GD]	118	G2
Duyang Shan[GX]	124	E3
Duyang[GX]	124	E4
Duyu[SX]	54	F2
Duyun[GZ]	144	F4
Duzhenwan[HB]	110	D4
Duzhou[CQ]	132	D4
Duzhuang[SX]	54	E2

E

East China Sea[FJ]	94	E4
East China Sea[SH]	74	E3
East China Sea[ZJ]	84	G3
East Lamma Channel[HK]	176	D4
Ebian[SC]	138	I6
Ebinur Hu[XJ]	172	I3
Ebu[GD]	118	H4
Echeng[SD]	102	C3
Echi[CQ]	132	E4
Edaocun[HI]	128	B2
Egong[JX]	98	C7
Ehu[JX]	98	E2
Ehu[JX]	98	E3
Ehutan[SX]	54	C3
Ej Nur[NM]	58	L5
Ejin Horo Qi[NM]	58	H8
Ejin Qi[NM]	58	D7
Eling[AH]	90	E6
Elixku[XJ]	172	F6
Eljet Ul[XJ]	172	J4
Eman[HI]	128	B2
Emei Feng[FJ]	94	C2
Emei Shan[SC]	138	I6
Emeishan[SC]	138	I6
Emin He[XJ]	172	I2
Emin(Dorbiljin)[XJ]	172	I2
Emu[JL]	66	I4
Emur He[HL]	70	B2
Emur Shan[HL]	70	B2
En Jiang[JX]	98	C4
Encheng[SD]	102	C2
Engh Had[NM]	58	N1
Enping[GD]	118	E4
Enshi[HB]	110	C4
Enyu[JL]	66	G3
Eping[HB]	110	C2
Eqiao[AH]	90	E5
Er'an[HEN]	106	F2

Erba[HL]	70	D5
Erbeng Shan[XJ]	172	J4
Erbu[TJ]	42	A4
Erbukeng[NX]	168	D2
Ercheng[HB]	110	H3
Erdao Baihe[JL]	66	I5
Erdao He[LN]	62	H1
Erdao Jiang[JL]	66	H5
Erdao[LN]	62	F3
Erdaobaihe[JL]	66	I5
Erdaodianzi[JL]	66	H4
Erdaogou Bingzhan[QH]	164	E6
Erdaogou[BJ]	36	B4
Erdaogu[HEB]	48	C2
Erdaohe[BJ]	36	C3
Erdaohezi[HL]	70	E6
Erdaohezi[JL]	66	G3
Erdaojiang Qu[JL]	66	G6
Erdaoqiao[NM]	58	S11
Erdaowan[HL]	70	C5
Erden Balag[NM]	58	U11
Erebgei[NM]	58	D8
Eregqui[QH]	164	J4
Ereh Hasah[NM]	58	E8
Eren Gobi[NM]	58	M4
Eren Nur[NM]	58	I6
Erenhabirga Shan[XJ]	172	I4
Erenhot[NM]	58	I6
Erfenzi[NM]	58	W10
Ergongdui[HI]	128	C2
Ergu[HL]	70	E6
Ergun He[NM]	58	M2
Ergun[NM]	58	N2
Erhai[YN]	148	F5
Erhaobu[HEB]	48	B2
Erhaofangzi[HL]	70	D3
Erhaoyuan[TJ]	42	B4
Erhe[HL]	70	D6
Erhlin[TW]	186	D3
Erhshui[TW]	186	D3
Erhuangtai[BJ]	36	C3
Erjiegou[LN]	62	E4
Erjieling[ZJ]	84	D2
Erkou[JX]	98	E4
Erlang[AH]	90	B3
Erlang[GZ]	144	E2
Erlangba[SN]	156	D7
Erlangdong[QH]	164	K3
Erlangkou[AH]	90	E5
Erlangmiao[BJ]	36	E2
Erlangmiao[HEN]	106	D4
Erlangmiao[HEN]	106	E4
Erlangping[HEN]	106	C4
Erli[SN]	156	D8
Erlin[SN]	156	F2
Erlintu[SN]	156	F1
Erlong[HEN]	106	D4
Erlong[JL]	66	D2
Erlong[SC]	138	L4
Erlongshan Shuiku[JL]	66	E4
Erlongshan[HL]	70	D4
Erlongshan[HL]	70	G5
Erlongshan[JL]	66	F2
Erlongshan[JL]	66	F5
Erlongshan[NM]	58	O4
Ermizhuang[TJ]	42	C2
Ermudi[BJ]	36	E2
Erniusuokou[LN]	62	G2
Erong[CQ]	132	F5
Erpengdianzi[LN]	62	I3
Erpu[XJ]	172	L4
Erpu[XJ]	172	N4
Erquanjing[HEB]	48	B2
Errenban[HL]	70	F6
Ershidi[QH]	164	M4
Ershierzhan[HL]	70	C2
Ershijiazi[LN]	62	D3
Ershizhan[HL]	70	C2
Ertai[HEB]	48	B2
Ertaiping[SD]	102	C3
Ertan Shuiku[SC]	138	G8
Ertang[GX]	124	H3
Ertang[JX]	98	D3
Ertix He[XJ]	172	J2

Ertuanjiulian[NM]	58	T11
Erwangzhuang Shuiku[TJ]	42	B3
Erwangzhuang[TJ]	42	B3
Erwanzi[NX]	168	C4
Eryuan[YN]	148	E4
Erzhan[HL]	70	D4
Eshan[YN]	148	H6
Ewenki[NM]	58	N3
Ewenkizu Qi[NM]	58	M3
Ewu[SX]	54	E6
Exian[HI]	128	B2
Ezhou[HB]	110	H4

F

Facheng[SD]	102	G2
Fada[YN]	148	J3
Fa'er[GZ]	144	C4
Fairview Park[HK]	176	C2
Faku[LN]	62	G2
Fan Lau Kok[HK]	176	A4
Fan Lau[HK]	176	A4
Fan Tsang Chau[HK]	176	F3
Fan Xian[HEN]	106	G2
Fanchang[AH]	90	E5
Fancheng[HEN]	106	E4
Fancun[SX]	54	D4
Fancunhe[SX]	54	D6
Fandi[SX]	54	C6
Fang He[SD]	102	E4
Fang Xian[HB]	110	D2
Fangang[AH]	90	C6
Fangang[AH]	90	D4
Fangcheng Gang[GX]	124	F6
Fangcheng Qu[GX]	124	F6
Fangcheng[HEN]	106	D4
Fangcheng[SD]	102	D4
Fangchenggang[GX]	124	F6
Fangcun[JS]	80	C2
Fangdao[FJ]	94	D2
Fangdou Shan[CQ]	132	E3
Fangdou Shan[CQ]	132	E3
Fangji Dao[GD]	118	D5
Fangji[AH]	90	B4
Fangji[HB]	110	F3
Fangjiahe[NX]	168	B4
Fangjiayao[SH]	74	C2
Fangjiazhuang[TJ]	42	B2
Fangjiazui[HB]	110	I4
Fanglou[JX]	98	A4
Fangmu[LN]	62	H2
Fangping[JX]	98	E4
Fangqiang[JS]	80	F3
Fangshan Qu[BJ]	36	C4
Fangshan[GS]	160	H5
Fangshan[JS]	80	D2
Fangshan[LN]	62	F3
Fangshan[SX]	54	C4
Fangshan[TW]	186	D4
Fangtai[JX]	98	C5
Fangtai[SH]	74	C2
Fangtang[AH]	90	E6
Fangtian[FJ]	94	B3
Fangxi[ZJ]	84	E4
Fangyang[HB]	110	H4
Fangyuan[TW]	186	D3
Fangzhen[SN]	156	G5
Fangzheng[HL]	70	E6
Fangzi Qu[SD]	102	F3
Fangzi[SD]	102	C2
Fanhuxu[GD]	118	E3
Fanjia[HI]	128	B2
Fanjia[LN]	62	D4
Fanjialin[SD]	102	D2
Fanjiang[HN]	114	E5
Fanjiatun[JL]	66	F4
Fanjiawan[NX]	168	B4
Fanjiayao[NM]	58	X11
Fanjiayuan[HN]	114	F4
Fanjialin[SN]	156	D6
Fanjiazhuang[TJ]	42	B2
Fanjing Shan[GZ]	144	G3

Fanli[HEN] 106 C3
Fanling[HK] 176 D1
Fanlu[TW] 186 D3
Fanrong[HL] 70 C5
Fanshan[HEB] 48 C3
Fanshi[SX] 54 E2
Fanxiang[SH] 74 C2
Fanyang[HI] 128 B3
Fanying[HEN] 106 G4
Fanzhen[JX] 98 C2
Fanzhuang[HEB] 48 B6
Fanzhuangzi[TJ] 42 B3
Fat Tong Chau[HK] 176 E3
Fat Tong Kok[HK] 176 E4
Fat Tong Mun[HK] 176 E4
Fate[JL] 66 G3
Faxiangyan[HN] 114 C6
Fazhan[HL] 70 D5
Fazhe[YN] 148 I4
Fazhong[SX] 54 D5
Fei Ngo Shan[HK] 176 D3
Fei Xian[SD] 102 D4
Feibeihe[SN] 156 F7
Feicheng[SD] 102 C3
Feidong[AH] 90 D5
Feihe[AH] 90 B3
Feihuang He[HEN] 106 G3
Feihuang He[JS] 80 B2
Feihuang He[JS] 80 C2
Feihuang He[JS] 80 E2
Feiji[AH] 90 D4
Feijiantan Shuiku[JX] 98 B4
Feili[AH] 90 F5
Feilong[CQ] 132 D4
Feilong[GX] 124 F5
Feiluan[FJ] 94 E3
Feixi[AH] 90 D5
Feixiang[HEB] 48 B7
Feizhu[FJ] 94 E3
Fen He[HEN] 106 F4
Fen He[SX] 54 C3
Fen He[SX] 54 C5
Fendou[HL] 70 D4
Fendou[HL] 70 E5
Fendou[HL] 70 F5
Feng Xian[JS] 80 B2
Feng Xian[SN] 156 C7
Feng'an[GD] 118 G3
Fengbang[SH] 74 C2
Fengbang[SH] 74 C2
Fengbian[JX] 98 C5
Fengcheng[JX] 98 C3
Fengcheng[LN] 62 H4
Fengcheng[SC] 138 M4
Fengcheng[SD] 102 H3
Fengcheng[SH] 74 D3
Fengchuan[GD] 118 D3
Fengcun[SN] 156 F6
Fengdeng[NX] 168 C2
Fengdian[HB] 110 H3
Fengdie[GS] 160 G6
Fengdikeng[SN] 156 D3
Fengding[FJ] 94 D4
Fengdingshan[JX] 98 B3
Fengdu[CQ] 132 D4
Fengdu[FJ] 94 D3
Fengfeng Kuangqu[HEB] 48 B7
Fengfu[SN] 156 E7
Fenggang Jianhe[BJ] 36 D4
Fenggang[GD] 118 E2
Fenggang[GZ] 144 F3
Fenggeling[SN] 156 C6
Fenghe[SC] 138 M5
Fenghua[GZ] 144 F3
Fenghua[HL] 70 E4
Fenghua[JL] 66 E2
Fenghua[ZJ] 84 F3
Fenghuang Shan[GD] 118 I3
Fenghuang Shan[GX] 124 E3
Fenghuang Shan[GZ] 144 G3
Fenghuang[CQ] 132 F2
Fenghuang[GS] 160 G5
Fenghuang[GX] 124 E3
Fenghuang[GX] 124 G4

Fenghuang[HB] 110 H4
Fenghuang[HI] 128 B3
Fenghuang[HN] 114 B5
Fenghuang[HN] 114 D6
Fenghuang[JS] 80 F5
Fenghuangcheng[SX] 54 D2
Fenghuangshan[HEB] 48 G3
Fenghui[ZJ] 84 E3
Fenghuo Shankou[QH] 164 E6
Fengjia Wan[HI] 128 C2
Fengjia[HI] 128 C2
Fengjia[HN] 114 C5
Fengjia[LN] 62 F2
Fengjia[SD] 102 H2
Fengjia[SX] 54 B5
Fengjiaba[CQ] 132 E4
Fengjiaba[SN] 156 C7
Fengjiachuan[SX] 54 B3
Fengjiakou[HEB] 48 D5
Fengjiang[HB] 110 G3
Fengjiang[JX] 98 B4
Fengjiangkou Shuiku[HB] 110 G2
Fengjiashan Shuiku[SN] 156 D6
Fengjiayu[BJ] 36 D2
Fengjiazhuang[NX] 168 C5
Fengjie[CQ] 132 F2
Fengjigou[NX] 168 C3
Fengjijuan[NX] 168 D3
Fengjing[SH] 74 C3
Fengjung[TW] 186 D3
Fengkai[GD] 118 D3
Fengkang[TW] 186 D4
Fengkou[HB] 110 G4
Fengle[AH] 90 D5
Fengle[HB] 110 F3
Fengle[HL] 70 C6
Fengle[SH] 74 D2
Fengli[HL] 70 E5
Fengliang[GD] 118 I3
Fenglin[AH] 90 C6
Fenglin[FJ] 94 C2
Fenglin[HB] 110 I5
Fenglin[JX] 98 C2
Fenglin[TW] 186 E3
Fengling[HI] 128 B3
Fengling[NX] 168 C5
Fenglingdu[SX] 54 B7
Fengman Qu[JL] 66 G4
Fengman[JL] 66 G4
Fengmenkou[HEN] 106 D2
Fengmiao[AH] 90 D3
Fengming[SC] 138 K4
Fengmu[GX] 124 H2
Fengmu[HI] 128 C2
Fengmuqiao[HN] 114 E4
Fengnan Qu[HEB] 48 F4
Fengnan[HI] 128 C1
Fengnan[HN] 114 E4
Fengning[HEB] 48 D2
Fengpin[TW] 186 E3
Fengping[HN] 114 D5
Fengping[YN] 148 D6
Fengping[ZJ] 84 D4
Fengpo[HI] 128 C2
Fengpu[FJ] 94 D3
Fengqiao[CQ] 132 E3
Fengqiao[ZJ] 84 E2
Fengqiao[ZJ] 84 E3
Fengqing[YN] 148 E6
Fengqiu[HEN] 106 F2
Fengquan Qu[HEN] 106 E2
Fengrun Qu[HEB] 48 F4
Fengsan[GZ] 144 E3
Fengshan[FJ] 94 C5
Fengshan[GX] 124 E3
Fengshan[GX] 124 G3
Fengshan[GX] 124 H5
Fengshan[GZ] 144 D3
Fengshan[GZ] 144 F4
Fengshan[HEB] 48 E2
Fengshan[HL] 70 E5
Fengshan[JS] 80 D3
Fengshan[JX] 98 D5
Fengshan[YN] 148 F7

Fengshi Ling[HI] 128 B2
Fengshi[FJ] 94 B5
Fengshou[JL] 66 D2
Fengshuba Shuiku[GD] 118 H2
Fengshui[SD] 102 E3
Fengshuling[ZJ] 84 C3
Fengshun[GD] 118 I3
Fengtai Qu[BJ] 36 C4
Fengtai[AH] 90 C4
Fengtan Shuiku[HN] 114 B4
Fengtian[FJ] 94 C5
Fengtian[JX] 98 B4
Fengting[GZ] 144 E5
Fengting[GZ] 144 E5
Fengtinghe Shuiku[GX] 124 F5
Fengwan[GD] 118 F2
Fengwei[HI] 128 C2
Fengwei[YN] 148 E7
Fengwu[GX] 124 E4
Fengxi[FJ] 94 B3
Fengxi[FJ] 94 D2
Fengxi[HB] 110 C3
Fengxi[SH] 74 C2
Fengxian Qu[SH] 74 C3
Fengxiang[GX] 124 I3
Fengxiang[SN] 156 D6
Fengxiangping[HB] 110 D3
Fengxiangping[HN] 114 C4
Fengxin[JX] 98 C3
Fengxin[SH] 74 D3
Fengyang[AH] 90 D4
Fengyang[GD] 118 E1
Fengyang[JX] 98 B4
Fengyang[SD] 102 D4
Fengyangshan Shuiku[AH] 90 D4
Fengyi[CQ] 132 E3
Fengyi[SD] 102 G2
Fengyi[YN] 148 F5
Fengying[HEN] 106 G4
Fengyu[NM] 58 T11
Fengyu[SC] 138 J5
Fengyuan[ZJ] 84 D4
Fengyuandian[HEB] 48 C2
Fengze Qu[FJ] 94 D5
Fengzhen[NM] 58 J7
Fengzhou[SN] 156 C7
Fengzhuang[HEN] 106 F2
Fengzhuang[NX] 168 C4
Fenhe Shuiku[SX] 54 C3
Fenjie[GD] 118 D4
Fenjie[JS] 80 F4
Fenkeng[JX] 98 C5
Fenkou[ZJ] 84 C3
Fenqing He[HB] 110 D3
Fenshui Jiang[ZJ] 84 D3
Fenshui[CQ] 132 E3
Fenshui[HB] 110 G4
Fenshui[SC] 138 K8
Fenshui[ZJ] 84 D3
Fenshuidun[SH] 74 D3
Fenshuiling[SX] 54 D4
Fenwei[FJ] 94 E4
Fenxi[SX] 54 C5
Fenxiang[HB] 110 E4
Fenyan[HB] 110 G5
Fenyang[SX] 54 C4
Fenyi[JX] 98 B4
Fenyuan[TW] 186 D2
Fo Tan[HK] 176 D2
Fo Tau Fan Chau[HK] 176 F3
Foding[GZ] 144 F4
Foding Shan[GZ] 144 G3
Fodong[HB] 110 C2
Fogang[GD] 118 F3
Fogesi[HEN] 106 F5
Foluo[HI] 128 A3
Foping[SN] 156 D7
Foshan[YN] 148 D2
Foshan[GD] 118 F3
Fosi[LN] 62 E3
Fotan[FJ] 94 C5
Fotan[YN] 148 I2
Fotang[ZJ] 84 E3
Foyedong[LN] 62 C4

Name	Page	Grid
Foziling Shuiku[AH]	90	C5
Fozizhuang[BJ]	36	B4
Fu He[JX]	98	D3
Fu Jiang[CQ]	132	B3
Fu Jiang[SC]	138	J3
Fu Jiang[SC]	138	K5
Fu Shui[HB]	110	I5
Fu Tei Chung Tsuen[HK]	176	B2
Fu Wong Chau[HK]	176	E1
Fu Xian[SN]	156	F4
Fu'an[FJ]	94	E2
Fu'an[HI]	128	B2
Fu'an[HI]	128	C2
Fu'an[JL]	66	G3
Fubang[YN]	148	E8
Fubian[SC]	138	H4
Fubin[GD]	118	I3
Fucheng[GD]	118	H2
Fucheng[GD]	118	H3
Fucheng[GX]	124	F4
Fucheng[HEB]	48	D6
Fucheng[JX]	98	C6
Fucheng[SN]	156	D8
Fucheng[SX]	54	E6
Fuchu[GZ]	144	C3
Fuchuan Jiang[GX]	124	I3
Fuchuan[GX]	124	I3
Fuchun Jiang[ZJ]	84	D3
Fuchun[JX]	98	E2
Fuchunjiang Shuiku[ZJ]	84	D3
Fuchunjiang[ZJ]	84	D3
Fucun[TJ]	42	B3
Fucun[YN]	148	J5
Fucun[ZJ]	84	D3
Fuda[GX]	124	C3
Fude[FJ]	94	C4
Fuding[FJ]	94	F2
Fudong[JS]	80	E5
Fu'er He[JL]	66	H5
Fu'er Jiang[LN]	62	I3
Fufang[JX]	98	D5
Fufeng[AH]	90	D7
Fufeng[JL]	66	F4
Fufeng[SN]	156	D6
Fugong[YN]	148	D4
Fugou[HEN]	106	F3
Fugu[SN]	156	H1
Fuguanzhuang[SD]	102	E3
Fuhai(Burultokay)[XJ]	172	K2
Fuhai[HL]	70	C5
Fuhai[ZJ]	84	F2
Fuhe[GD]	118	D4
Fuhe[GD]	118	F3
Fuhe[HB]	110	G3
Fuhsing[TW]	186	D2
Fuhsing[TW]	186	D3
Fuhsing[TW]	186	E2
Fuhuan[CQ]	132	C5
Fujia[CQ]	132	C5
Fujia[JL]	66	H3
Fujia[LN]	62	F3
Fujia[LN]	62	G1
Fujiadian[BJ]	36	D2
Fujiang[JL]	66	F6
Fujiang[JX]	98	B6
Fujiaqiao[HN]	114	D6
Fujiatan[SX]	54	C5
Fujiayan[HB]	110	D4
Fujiazhuang[SX]	54	D3
Fujin[HL]	70	G5
Fujunmiao[TJ]	42	A4
Fukang[XJ]	172	K3
Fuke Jinkuang[HL]	70	A2
Fuke[HI]	128	B2
Fukeshan[HL]	70	B2
Fukou[HN]	114	D5
Fukuang[FJ]	94	C3
Fukuei Chiao[TW]	186	E1
Fuli[AH]	90	C3
Fuli[GX]	124	I3
Fuli[TW]	186	E3
Fuliang[JX]	98	E2
Fulin[HL]	70	C3
Fulin[JX]	98	E3
Fuling Qu[CQ]	132	D4
Fuling[AH]	90	E6
Fuling[FJ]	94	D2
Fuling[ZJ]	84	D4
Fuliu[FJ]	94	D2
Fulong[GX]	124	E5
Fulong[GX]	124	E6
Fulong[GX]	124	F3
Fulong[HI]	128	B2
Fulongquan[JL]	66	E3
Fulu[GX]	124	G2
Fulu[HL]	70	C5
Fuluo[GX]	124	I3
Fuluo[HN]	114	B5
Fumin[JL]	66	G5
Fumin[JX]	98	C4
Fumin[SH]	74	D2
Fumin[YN]	148	H5
Fumincun[TJ]	42	B4
Fun Chau[HK]	176	E1
Funan[AH]	90	B4
Fung Hang[HK]	176	D1
Fung Kong Tsuen[HK]	176	B2
Fung Wong Shan[HK]	176	B4
Fung Yuen[HK]	176	D2
Funing Wan[FJ]	94	F3
Funing[HEB]	48	G4
Funing[JS]	80	E3
Funing[YN]	148	K7
Funiu Shan[HEN]	106	C4
Fuping[CQ]	132	D3
Fuping[HEB]	48	B5
Fuping[SN]	156	F6
Fuqi[HI]	128	B2
Fuqiang[HL]	70	F5
Fuqiang[JL]	66	H4
Fuqiang[SH]	74	C2
Fuqiao[SC]	138	K5
Fuqiaohe Shuiku[HB]	110	H3
Fuqing[FJ]	94	E4
Fuquan[FJ]	94	D4
Fuquan[GZ]	144	F4
Furao[HL]	70	D5
Furong Dao[SD]	102	F2
Furong[CQ]	132	D5
Furong Jiang[GZ]	144	F2
Furong[LN]	62	F3
Furongdun[JX]	98	D2
Fushan Qu[SD]	102	H2
Fushan Shuiku[HI]	128	B2
Fushan[AH]	90	E4
Fushan[HEN]	106	G6
Fushan[HI]	128	B2
Fushan[JX]	98	C3
Fushan[SC]	138	J6
Fushan[SD]	102	C4
Fushan[SD]	102	G2
Fushan[SX]	54	C6
Fushan[ZJ]	84	E4
Fusheng[HL]	70	C4
Fushi Shuiku[ZJ]	84	D2
Fushi[FJ]	94	B5
Fushi[GX]	124	G2
Fushi[JX]	98	B6
Fushu[GX]	124	E5
Fushui Shuiku[HB]	110	H5
Fushui[HB]	110	H5
Fushui[SN]	156	F6
Fushui[SN]	156	H7
Fushun[LN]	62	G3
Fushun[SC]	138	J6
Fusong[JL]	66	H5
Fusui[GX]	124	E5
Futan[JX]	98	C4
Futang[GD]	118	E2
Futang[GX]	124	G3
Futian[CQ]	132	F2
Futian[FJ]	94	C4
Futian[GD]	118	F3
Futian[JX]	98	C5
Futianhe[HB]	110	I3
Futou Hu[HB]	110	H4
Futou Ling[HI]	128	B2
Futou Wan[FJ]	94	C6
Futu[HB]	110	I5
Futun Xi[FJ]	94	C2
Fuwan[GD]	118	E4
Fuwang[GX]	124	G5
Fuwen[HI]	128	C2
Fuxi[FJ]	94	C4
Fuxi[GD]	118	F1
Fuxi[ZJ]	84	D3
Fuxi[ZJ]	84	E4
Fuxian[JL]	66	D4
Fuxianhu[YN]	148	H6
Fuxin[GX]	124	H5
Fuxin[LN]	62	E2
Fuxin[LN]	62	E2
Fuxing[AH]	90	C7
Fuxing[BJ]	36	C4
Fuxing[GS]	160	G4
Fuxing[GZ]	144	F2
Fuxing[HL]	70	F5
Fuxing[HN]	114	B4
Fuxing[JL]	66	I4
Fuxing[JL]	66	I5
Fuxing[JL]	66	K4
Fuxing[JS]	80	E3
Fuxing[NM]	58	T11
Fuxing[SC]	138	L4
Fuxingchang[HN]	114	D3
Fuxingdi[LN]	62	E2
Fuyan[YN]	148	E8
Fuyan[GZ]	144	F2
Fuyang He[HEB]	48	B7
Fuyang He[HEB]	48	C6
Fuyang[AH]	90	B4
Fuyang[GD]	118	I3
Fuyang[GZ]	144	F2
Fuyang[ZJ]	84	D2
Fuyi Shui[HN]	114	C6
Fuyi[SC]	138	K4
Fuying Dao[FJ]	94	F3
Fuyingzi[HEB]	48	E3
Fuyu[GX]	124	H3
Fuyu[HL]	70	C5
Fuyu[JL]	66	G3
Fuyu[JL]	66	J5
Fuyu[JS]	80	F3
Fuyuan[AH]	90	D5
Fuyuan[HL]	70	F6
Fuyuan[HL]	70	H4
Fuyuan[JX]	98	B3
Fuyuan[TW]	186	E3
Fuyuan[YN]	148	J5
Fuyun(Koktokay)[XJ]	172	L2
Fuzhen[HEB]	48	D5
Fuzhou He[LN]	62	E5
Fuzhou Wan[LN]	62	E5
Fuzhou[FJ]	94	E3
Fuzhou[JX]	98	D4
Fuzhoucheng[LN]	62	E5
Fuzhouwan[LN]	62	E5
Fuzhuang[TJ]	42	C3
Fuzihe[HB]	110	I4

G

Name	Page	Grid
Ga Hai[QH]	164	J3
Ga Hai[QH]	164	M3
Gab'aluma[XZ]	152	F4
Gadê[QH]	164	L7
Gadoi[QH]	164	I7
Gahai[GS]	160	F5
Gahai[QH]	164	J3
Gahai[QH]	164	N6
Gaica[YN]	148	E2
Gain'gya[GS]	160	F5
Gaishi[CQ]	132	C5
Gaiyang[FJ]	94	C3
Gaiyang[FJ]	94	D4
Gaizhou[LN]	62	F4
Gaizhu[FJ]	94	C3
Gajê[SC]	138	E5
Gakog[QH]	164	J2
Galashan[HL]	70	D3

Gamba Goukou[QH]	164	L7
Gamba[XZ]	152	F5
Gamdokamdo[QH]	164	I7
Gan He[NM]	58	P2
Gan Jiang[JX]	98	C3
Gan Xian[JX]	98	C6
Ganchazi[HL]	70	E4
Gancheng[HI]	128	A3
Gancheng[NX]	168	C4
Ganchengzi[NX]	168	B2
Ganchong[HI]	128	B2
Gandong[GX]	124	F2
Ganduo[JS]	80	E4
Gan'en Jiao[HI]	128	A3
Ganfang[JX]	98	B3
Gangbei Gang[HI]	128	C3
Gangbei[GD]	118	H2
Gangbei[HI]	128	C3
Gangca Dasi[QH]	164	M3
Gangca[QH]	164	M3
Gangca[QH]	164	O5
Gangcheng Qu[SD]	102	D3
Gangdisê Shan[XZ]	152	B4
Gangdisê Shan[XZ]	152	D5
Gangdong[HN]	114	C5
Gangdong[JS]	80	F3
Gangdong[JX]	98	E3
Gangdu[GZ]	144	E4
Ganggar[XZ]	152	E5
Gangjia[CQ]	132	D3
Gangkou[AH]	90	E6
Gangkou[GD]	118	G4
Gangkou[HB]	110	H5
Gangkou[HN]	114	F3
Gangkou[JX]	98	B2
Gangkou[JX]	98	E3
Gangkoujie[JX]	98	C2
Gangkouwan Shuiku[AH]	90	E6
Gangli[HEN]	106	E3
Ganglidian[HEN]	106	F5
Gangmei[GD]	118	D4
Gangmen[GD]	118	B5
Gangmenkou[HI]	128	C2
Gangnan Qu[GX]	124	G4
Gangnan Shuiku[HEB]	48	A5
Gangnan[HEB]	48	B5
Gangnyi[XZ]	152	G3
Gangou[GS]	160	G5
Gangou[HEB]	48	G3
Gangou[JL]	66	F6
Gangouyi[GS]	160	G5
Gangping[GD]	118	D3
Gangqênzazong[QH]	164	C7
Gangru[XZ]	152	I3
Gangshang[JS]	80	D2
Gangtun[LN]	62	D4
Gangu[GS]	160	G5
Ganguyi[SN]	156	F4
Gangwei[FJ]	94	D5
Gangwu[GZ]	144	D5
Gangxi[TJ]	42	B4
Gangyan[SH]	74	D1
Gangyao[JL]	66	G3
Gangyaoling[LN]	62	D3
Gangzi[HEB]	48	F2
Ganhe[NM]	58	O2
Ganhekou[BJ]	36	B4
Ganheyu[BJ]	36	D3
Ganjiachang[HB]	110	F5
Ganjig[QH]	164	M3
Ganjing[SN]	156	G5
Ganjingzi Qu[LN]	62	E6
Ganken[JX]	98	C3
Ganlu[JS]	80	F5
Ganluo[JX]	98	B4
Ganluo[SC]	138	H7
Ganma[JS]	80	E2
Gannan[HL]	70	B5
Ganq Ger[JL]	66	D1
Ganq Mod[NM]	58	G6
Ganquan[SN]	156	F4
Gansha[HN]	114	F4
Ganshan[ZJ]	84	E2
Ganshui[CQ]	132	C5
Gantang[NX]	168	A3
Gantang[BJ]	36	D4
Gantang[FJ]	94	D3
Gantang[FJ]	94	E3
Gantang[GX]	124	F5
Gantang[HN]	114	D5
Gantao He[HEB]	48	B6
Gantian[HN]	114	F5
Ganting[SX]	54	C5
Ganwang[LN]	62	F4
Ganxi[CQ]	132	E5
Ganxi[CQ]	132	E5
Ganxi[GZ]	144	G3
Ganxi[HN]	114	B3
Ganxi[HN]	114	B7
Ganxi[ZJ]	84	D2
Ganxiang[SH]	74	C3
Ganxu[GX]	124	F5
Ganyan[HN]	114	C3
Ganying[BJ]	36	E3
Ganyu[JS]	80	E2
Ganzhao[LN]	62	C3
Ganzhaomiao[NM]	58	T11
Ganzhou[JX]	98	B6
Ganzhu[JX]	98	D5
Ganzhuang[SH]	74	C2
Gao Feng[AH]	90	E6
Gao Xian[SC]	138	J7
Gao'an[CQ]	132	D3
Gao'an[FJ]	94	C5
Gao'an[GX]	124	G4
Gao'an[HI]	128	B2
Gao'an[JX]	98	C3
Gaobai[SN]	156	G4
Gaobao[HEN]	106	G2
Gaobei[GD]	118	I2
Gaobeidian[HEB]	48	C4
Gaobu[GZ]	144	C3
Gaobu[GD]	118	H3
Gaochang[TJ]	42	A3
Gaoche[FJ]	94	C5
Gaocheng[HB]	110	G3
Gaocheng[HEB]	48	B5
Gaocheng[HEN]	106	E3
Gaocheng[SD]	102	D2
Gaocheng[SX]	54	D3
Gaochuan[SC]	138	J4
Gaochuan[SN]	156	E8
Gaochun[JS]	80	D5
Gaocun[JX]	98	B3
Gaocun[SD]	102	I2
Gaoda[YN]	148	H7
Gaode[GX]	124	G6
Gaodeng Shan[SC]	138	L5
Gaodian[GZ]	144	D3
Gaodian[HEN]	106	E5
Gaodingji[SD]	102	B5
Gaodong[SH]	74	D2
Gaodu[JS]	80	D3
Gaodu[SX]	54	D6
Gaofeng[CQ]	132	D3
Gaofeng[CQ]	132	E3
Gaofeng[GD]	118	E4
Gaofeng[GX]	124	G5
Gaofeng[HI]	128	B3
Gaofeng[HN]	114	C3
Gaofeng[HN]	114	C4
Gaofeng[YN]	148	G5
Gaofengdui[HI]	128	B3
Gaofu[JX]	98	E4
Gaogang Qu[JS]	80	E4
Gaogang[GD]	118	F2
Gaogongdao[JS]	80	E2
Gaogou[JS]	80	E2
Gaoguan[CQ]	132	E2
Gaoguan[LN]	62	E4
Gaohongkou[SX]	54	E3
Gaohu[JX]	98	C3
Gaojia[CQ]	132	D3
Gaojia[LN]	62	F4
Gaojia[ZJ]	84	D3
Gaojiabao[SN]	156	G2
Gaojiadian[JL]	66	F3
Gaojiadian[LN]	62	H2
Gaojiagou[SN]	156	F3
Gaojiahui[SX]	54	C3
Gaojialing[BJ]	36	D2
Gaojialing[JX]	98	D2
Gaojialing[SN]	156	D8
Gaojiashui[NX]	168	B3
Gaojiayan[HB]	110	E4
Gaojiaying[HEB]	48	B3
Gaojiazha[NX]	168	C2
Gaojiazhuang[TJ]	42	B2
Gaojiazhuang[TJ]	42	B4
Gaojiecun[SN]	156	G3
Gaojingzhuang[TJ]	42	C3
Gaokan[LN]	62	F4
Gaolan Dao[GD]	118	F5
Gaolan[GS]	160	F4
Gaoli[SD]	102	E4
Gaoliang[GD]	118	D3
Gaoliang[SC]	138	K6
Gaoliang[YN]	148	J6
Gaolifang[LN]	62	F3
Gaoligong Shan	148	D3
Gaoligong Shan[YN]	148	D5
Gaoligou[JL]	66	F7
Gaolin[AH]	90	D5
Gaoling[BJ]	36	E2
Gaoling[GX]	124	F3
Gaoling[NX]	168	C4
Gaoling[SD]	102	H2
Gaoling[SN]	156	F6
Gaolingziliang[NX]	168	B4
Gaoliu[AH]	90	C5
Gaoliu[JS]	80	D2
Gaoliu[SD]	102	E3
Gaoliying[BJ]	36	C3
Gaolong[CQ]	132	C3
Gaolong[GX]	124	C3
Gaolong[HI]	128	C3
Gaolong[HN]	114	F6
Gaolou[CQ]	132	B3
Gaolou[CQ]	132	F2
Gaolou[SD]	102	D2
Gaolou[ZJ]	84	E5
Gaoluo[HB]	110	C5
Gaoluo[SX]	54	E4
Gaomi[SD]	102	F3
Gaoming Qu[GD]	118	E4
Gaoniang[GZ]	144	H4
Gaoping Qu[SC]	138	L5
Gaoping[GZ]	144	E3
Gaoping[HB]	110	D4
Gaoping[HN]	114	B4
Gaoping[HN]	114	F4
Gaoping[JX]	98	B5
Gaoping[JX]	98	D4
Gaoping[SX]	54	D6
Gaopo[GD]	118	C4
Gaopo[GZ]	144	E4
Gaopoling Shuiku[HI]	128	A2
Gaoqiang[HEB]	48	B3
Gaoqiangkuang[SX]	54	D1
Gaoqiao[AH]	90	D5
Gaoqiao[CQ]	132	E2
Gaoqiao[FJ]	94	C2
Gaoqiao[FJ]	94	C3
Gaoqiao[GD]	118	B5
Gaoqiao[HB]	110	H3
Gaoqiao[LN]	62	E4
Gaoqiao[SD]	102	E4
Gaoqiao[SH]	74	C3
Gaoqiao[SH]	74	D2
Gaoqiao[YN]	148	H5
Gaoqiao[YN]	148	I2
Gaoqiao[ZJ]	84	E2
Gaoqiaolou[JX]	98	B4
Gaoqiu[SD]	102	D2
Gaoqiu[HEN]	106	D4
Gaoren[NX]	168	C2
Gaosha[FJ]	94	C3
Gaosha[HN]	114	C6
Gaosha[JX]	98	E2
Gaoshaling[TJ]	42	C4
Gaoshan Ling[HI]	128	B2
Gaoshan Ling[HI]	128	B2

Name	Page	Grid
Gaoshan[FJ]	94	E4
Gaoshan[GD]	118	E2
Gaoshanbu[HEB]	48	C2
Gaoshanzi[LN]	62	F3
Gaoshawo[NX]	168	D2
Gaosheng[LN]	62	F3
Gaoshi[ZJ]	84	E4
Gaoshibei[HB]	110	F4
Gaoshizhuang[SX]	54	D2
Gaositai[HEB]	48	E2
Gaotai[AH]	90	B4
Gaotai[GS]	160	D3
Gaotai[NX]	168	C4
Gaotaipu[LN]	62	D4
Gaotaisi[NX]	168	B4
Gaotaizi[LN]	62	E3
Gaotaizi[LN]	62	F2
Gaotan[SN]	156	E8
Gaotang Hu[AH]	90	D4
Gaotang[AH]	90	B4
Gaotang[AH]	90	C4
Gaotang[AH]	90	D4
Gaotang[FJ]	94	C3
Gaotang[SD]	102	C3
Gaotang[ZJ]	84	F3
Gaotian[GD]	118	F3
Gaotian[GX]	124	H3
Gaotian[JX]	98	D4
Gaotian[YN]	148	K3
Gaotong[NX]	168	B5
Gaotouyao[NM]	58	V11
Gaotun[GZ]	144	H4
Gaotuo[LN]	62	F3
Gaoxi[JX]	98	A5
Gaoxian[HEN]	106	F3
Gaoxin[HEN]	106	G3
Gaoxing[JX]	98	C5
Gaoxing[SD]	102	F4
Gaoxinzhuang[BJ]	36	D4
Gaoxu[JS]	80	E2
Gaoxu[JS]	80	E4
Gaoya[GS]	160	G5
Gaoya[NX]	168	B4
Gaoya[SN]	156	D6
Gaoyakou[BJ]	36	B3
Gaoyang[CQ]	132	E2
Gaoyang[FJ]	94	D3
Gaoyang[HB]	110	D3
Gaoyang[HB]	110	F4
Gaoyang[HEB]	48	C5
Gaoyang[SX]	54	C4
Gaoyao[GD]	118	E3
Gaoyao[SN]	156	G7
Gaoyaozhang[NX]	168	C4
Gaoyi[HEB]	48	B6
Gaoyou Hu[AH]	90	F4
Gaoyou Hu[JS]	80	E4
Gaoyou[JS]	80	E4
Gaoyu[ZJ]	84	D2
Gaoyunshan[JX]	98	C6
Gaoyupu[HEB]	48	C5
Gaoze[SD]	102	F4
Gaozhai[GZ]	144	F4
Gaozhen[GZ]	144	E4
Gaozhen[SN]	156	F3
Gaozhou Shuiku[GD]	118	D4
Gaozhou[GD]	118	C5
Gaozhu[CQ]	132	F2
Gaozhuang[HEN]	106	D4
Gaozhuang[SD]	102	B4
Gaozhuang[TJ]	42	C3
Gaozhuangzi[TJ]	42	A4
Gaozhuangzi[TJ]	42	B2
Gaozuo[JS]	80	E3
Gaqag[SC]	138	F7
Gar Qu[QH]	164	D7
Gar Zangbo[XZ]	152	B4
Gar[XZ]	152	B3
Garco[XZ]	152	F3
Gardangsumdo[QH]	164	N7
Garkung Cak[XZ]	152	E3
Garla Lhamco[QH]	164	J6
Garla[XZ]	152	B3
Garlha[QH]	164	L4
Garlung[QH]	164	H8
Garma[XZ]	152	J4
Garmoyangkyi[QH]	164	M5
Garmugkau[QH]	164	H8
Garqu Yan[QH]	164	E7
Gãrqung[XZ]	152	D5
Garwa[SC]	138	F5
Garzê[QH]	164	O5
Garzê[SC]	138	E4
Gas Hure Hu[QH]	164	C2
Gas[QH]	164	C2
Gasherbrum Shan[XJ]	172	F8
Gawupu[SC]	138	I2
Gaxun Nur[NM]	58	D6
Gaxun[QH]	164	E3
Gaxung[QH]	164	H8
Gaya He[JL]	66	J4
Gayag[QH]	164	H4
Gazëgyablung[QH]	164	J6
Gazkol[XJ]	172	F6
Ge[JS]	80	E5
Ge'ao[JX]	98	C5
Gebu[GX]	124	C3
Gechong[HN]	114	B6
Gecun[BJ]	36	C3
Gedashang[SX]	54	B3
Gêdi[XZ]	152	I5
Gêding[XZ]	152	F5
Gegang[HEN]	106	F3
Gegen Gol[NM]	58	N2
Gegen He[NM]	58	M2
Gegu[TJ]	42	C4
Gêgyai[XZ]	152	B3
Gehetou[HEB]	48	C5
Geheyan Shuiku[HB]	110	E4
Geji[AH]	90	C2
Gejia[HN]	114	F4
Gejia[LN]	62	C4
Gejia[SD]	102	H2
Gejiu[YN]	148	I7
Gêla[XZ]	152	C4
Gêladaindong Feng[QH]	164	D7
Gelan[CQ]	132	D3
Geling[FJ]	94	E4
Gelong[SH]	74	C1
Gelou[SN]	156	G4
Gemai[SX]	54	B5
Gêmang[SC]	138	D2
Gêmar[XZ]	152	D4
Gengding Shan[GZ]	144	F5
Gengji[HB]	110	F3
Gengjia[YN]	148	E6
Gengke[LN]	62	H2
Genglou[GD]	118	E4
Genglou[ZJ]	84	D3
Genglou[ZJ]	84	F4
Gengma[YN]	148	E7
Gengsha[GX]	124	D3
Gengwan[SN]	160	H4
Gengxin[GX]	124	D3
Gengxin[HI]	128	C2
Gengzhen[SX]	54	E3
Gengzhuang[LN]	62	F4
Gengzhuang[TJ]	42	A2
Gengzhuangqiao[HEB]	48	B6
Gênyên[SC]	138	E6
Gepai[SN]	156	F7
Gepaitang[QH]	164	D6
Geping[JX]	98	C4
Gepo[GX]	124	I3
Gêqên[QH]	164	I7
Geqiushan[HL]	70	D4
Gêrzê[XZ]	152	D3
Geshan[JX]	98	C4
Geshan[ZJ]	84	E3
Geshang[SX]	54	D3
Getai[SN]	156	G5
Getengping[HB]	110	D3
Getu He[GZ]	144	E5
Getuo[HEB]	48	F4
Gewu[ZJ]	84	D3
Gexiang He[YN]	148	J4
Gêxoi[SC]	138	E7
Gêxung Qu[QH]	164	H5
Geyuan[JX]	98	E3
Gezhou Ba[HB]	110	E4
Gezidong[LN]	62	D4
Gezishan[NX]	168	B2
Gobdü[XZ]	152	G5
Gobi[NM]	58	V10
Gobi[QH]	164	J3
Gogarlungring[QH]	164	G6
Gogarngü[XZ]	152	D3
Goibo[XZ]	152	K4
Goikarla Ri'gyu[XZ]	152	G5
Goilung[XZ]	152	E4
Goin'gyibug[XZ]	152	E4
Goixung[XZ]	152	H3
Gola Zêsum[XZ]	152	A3
Golag[XZ]	152	J5
Golmud He[QH]	164	G4
Golmud[QH]	164	G4
Golog Shan[QH]	164	M7
Golu Co[QH]	164	E6
Gomangxung[QH]	164	N5
Gomo Caka[XZ]	152	D3
Gong Shui[JX]	98	C6
Gong Xian[SC]	138	J7
Gong'ai Nongchang[HI]	128	A3
Gong'ai[HI]	128	A3
Gong'an[HB]	110	F4
Gongbo'gyamda[XZ]	152	H5
Gongchangling Qu[LN]	62	G3
Gongcheng He[GX]	124	H3
Gongcheng[GD]	118	E4
Gongcheng[GX]	124	H3
Gongchuan[FJ]	94	C3
Gongchuan[GX]	124	E4
Gongdi[NM]	58	S11
Gongdian[AH]	90	B3
Gongdong[GX]	124	G2
Gonggan Qu[NX]	168	C3
Gonggar[XZ]	152	G5
Gonggeng[SH]	74	D3
Gongguan[GD]	118	C5
Gongguan[GX]	124	G6
Gongguan[SN]	156	F7
Gonghe[GS]	160	I5
Gonghe[GX]	124	E4
Gonghe[HL]	70	F6
Gonghe[QH]	164	M4
Gonghui[GX]	124	I3
Gonghui[HEB]	48	B2
Gongji[JL]	66	G5
Gongjianpu[BJ]	36	B4
Gongjiaqiao[HN]	114	D4
Gongjing Qu[SC]	138	J6
Gongjing[GS]	160	G4
Gongjisi[AH]	90	C3
Gongkala Shan[SC]	138	F4
Gongli[SD]	102	D4
Gongli[SN]	156	F6
Gongliu(Tokkuztara)[XJ]	172	I4
Gongmiao[NM]	58	U11
Gongnong Qu[HL]	70	F5
Gongpengzi[JL]	66	F2
Gongping Shuiku[GD]	118	H3
Gongping[GD]	118	H3
Gongpingxu[HN]	114	E6
Gongpo[HI]	128	C2
Gongpu[XZ]	152	D5
Gongqian[HEN]	106	C3
Gongqiao[GX]	124	I3
Gongqiao[HB]	110	B5
Gongqingcheng[JX]	98	C2
Gongquan[SC]	138	J7
Gongrencun[HL]	70	C3
Gongshan[YN]	148	D3
Gongshan[YN]	148	I5
Gongshanwan[NM]	58	W11
Gongshanzui[LN]	62	C4
Gongtan[CQ]	132	E5
Gongtian[HN]	114	F3
Gongwang Shan[YN]	148	H5
Gongyi[HEN]	106	D3
Gongyi[NX]	168	B5
Gongyi[SH]	74	D1

Gongyingzi[LN]	62	C3	Guang'an[SC]	138	L5	Guanmian[CQ]	132	E2
Gongzhuang[GD]	118	G3	Guangang[AH]	90	C7	Guanmiao[AH]	90	B5
Gongzhuang[JS]	80	E2	Guangang[TJ]	42	C4	Guanmiao[AH]	90	D4
Gongzhuangzi[TJ]	42	B2	Guangao[BJ]	36	C3	Guanmiao[HB]	110	G3
Gongzhuling[JL]	66	E4	Guangba[HI]	128	A2	Guannan[JS]	80	E2
Gongzhutun[LN]	62	G2	Guangchang[JX]	98	D5	Guanniu[YN]	148	F9
Gonjo[XZ]	152	K4	Guangcun[HI]	128	B2	Guanping[CQ]	132	E2
Gopug Co[XZ]	152	C4	Guangde[AH]	90	F6	Guanping[HB]	110	D2
Goruqol[XJ]	172	H5	Guangfo[SN]	156	F8	Guanqian[FJ]	94	B4
Gosu[SC]	138	D3	Guangfu[GD]	118	I2	Guanqian[FJ]	94	C3
Gouba[SN]	156	G8	Guangfu[GX]	124	G3	Guanqiao[FJ]	94	D4
Goubangzi[LN]	62	E3	Guangfu[JX]	98	C3	Guanqiao[FJ]	94	D5
Goubei[BJ]	36	D3	Guangfu[SC]	138	J5	Guanqiao[HN]	114	F5
Gouchang[GZ]	144	E5	Guanghai Wan[GD]	118	E5	Guanqiao[NX]	168	B4
Goudun[JS]	80	E3	Guanghai[GD]	118	E5	Guanshan Dao[ZJ]	84	E5
Gouhebei[TJ]	42	B1	Guanghan[SC]	138	J5	Guanshan[HB]	110	D2
Goukou[BJ]	36	D2	Guanghe[GS]	160	F5	Guanshan[JS]	80	C3
Goukou[NX]	168	C5	Guanghua[HB]	110	F4	Guanshan[JX]	98	C4
Gouli[QH]	164	K5	Guanghua[SX]	54	C5	Guanshan[SD]	102	C3
Goulin[HEN]	106	D5	Guanghua[YN]	148	F4	Guanshang[BJ]	36	E3
Goulou Shan[GX]	124	H5	Guanghuojie[SN]	156	E7	Guanshi[CQ]	132	E2
Goulou[HN]	114	E5	Guangjin[GS]	160	H6	Guanshi[HN]	114	E6
Goumen[NM]	58	W11	Guangling[SX]	54	F2	Guanshuai[SD]	102	F4
Gounaidian[LN]	62	H2	Guanglu Dao[LN]	62	F5	Guanshui[LN]	62	H4
Gounanya[SD]	102	G4	Guanglu[LN]	62	F5	Guanshui[SD]	102	H2
Gouping[GZ]	144	G2	Guangming[FJ]	94	C3	Guantai[HEB]	48	B7
Gouqi Dao[ZJ]	84	G2	Guangming[JL]	66	E3	Guantan[JS]	80	D3
Goushi[HEN]	106	D3	Guangming[JL]	66	G3	Guantan[ZJ]	84	D4
Goutai[NX]	168	C3	Guangming[JL]	66	J4	Guantangji[AH]	90	E4
Goutang[HEN]	106	E3	Guangming[SH]	74	D3	Guantangyi[HB]	110	H5
Gouxi[NX]	168	C4	Guangmingshan[LN]	62	F5	Guantao[HEB]	48	A7
Gouyan[LN]	62	F4	Guangnan[YN]	148	K6	Guantao[HEB]	48	C7
Gouyuan[SN]	156	F8	Guangning[GD]	118	E3	Guantian[JX]	98	B4
Gouzai[HI]	128	B3	Guangning[LN]	62	E3	Guantian[JX]	98	B6
Goyagtang[SC]	138	F7	Guangping[HEB]	48	B7	Guanting Shuiku[HEB]	48	C3
Goyü[XZ]	152	J5	Guangping[HN]	114	B6	Guanting[AH]	90	C5
Gozha Co[XZ]	152	B2	Guangping[JL]	66	I5	Guanting[GD]	118	G3
Grassy Hill[HK]	176	D2	Guangping[SN]	156	B8	Guanting[GS]	160	G6
Green Island[HK]	176	C3	Guangpo[HI]	128	C3	Guanting[HEB]	48	C6
Gu Jiang[JX]	98	C5	Guangrao[SD]	102	E2	Guanting[JL]	66	F4
Gu Xian[SX]	54	C5	Guangrong[HL]	70	D5	Guanting[NX]	168	C4
Gu Xiang[XZ]	152	I5	Guangshan[HEN]	106	F5	Guantou[SX]	54	B5
Guai'er[SX]	54	E4	Guangshui[HB]	110	G3	Guantouzui[HN]	114	E3
Guaihe[HEN]	106	D4	Guangshun[GZ]	144	E4	Guantun[AH]	90	C4
Guaimozi[LN]	62	I3	Guangtang[AH]	90	C3	Guantun[SN]	156	F4
Guaiziwa[NX]	168	B4	Guangtong[YN]	148	G5	Guanwangmiao[SX]	54	C6
Gualanyu[HEB]	48	E3	Guangtou Shan[HEB]	48	F2	Guanxi[HN]	114	D3
Guali[GX]	124	H1	Guangwu Shan[SC]	138	L3	Guanxia[HN]	114	C6
Guan He[JS]	80	E2	Guangwu[AH]	90	B3	Guanxu[GD]	118	D3
Guan Jiang[GX]	124	I2	Guangwu[NX]	168	B3	Guanxun[FJ]	94	C5
Guan Xian[SD]	102	B3	Guangxing[CQ]	132	C4	Guanyang[CQ]	132	F2
Gu'an[HEB]	48	D4	Guangya[HI]	128	B2	Guanyang[FJ]	94	F2
Guan'an[HI]	128	A3	Guangyan Gai[CQ]	132	E5	Guanyang[GX]	124	I2
Guanban[FJ]	94	E3	Guangyang[CQ]	132	D4	Guanyin Feng[HI]	128	A2
Guancang[GZ]	144	E2	Guangyang[SN]	156	F5	Guanyin[HB]	110	D2
Guancen Shan[SX]	54	D2	Guangyanghu[JS]	80	E3	Guanyinge Shuiku[LN]	62	H3
Guancen Shan[SX]	54	D3	Guangyuan[SC]	138	K3	Guanyinge[GD]	118	G3
Guanchang[TJ]	42	C1	Guangyubu[SX]	54	E2	Guanyinge[GX]	124	H2
Guanchao[JX]	98	B5	Guangze[FJ]	94	C2	Guanyinge[HN]	114	C4
Guancheng[SD]	102	B4	Guangzhou[GD]	118	F3	Guanyinsi[HN]	114	D4
Guanchi[SN]	156	F6	Guangzong[HEB]	48	C6	Guanyinsi[JS]	80	D3
Guanchuan'ao[ZJ]	84	G3	Guanhe Kou[JS]	80	E2	Guanyinsi[SN]	156	C7
Guancuo[FJ]	94	D1	Guanhu[JS]	80	C2	Guanyintang[HEN]	106	C3
Guandang[HB]	110	F4	Guanji[AH]	90	B3	Guanyuan[HN]	114	E3
Guandao[SN]	156	F6	Guanjiao[QH]	164	K3	Guanyuan[SN]	156	E8
Guandaokou[HEN]	106	C3	Guanjiazui[HN]	114	D6	Guanyun Shan[HEN]	106	B3
Guandi Shan[SX]	54	C4	Guanjin[HEN]	106	F5	Guanyun[JS]	80	E2
Guandi[SN]	156	D7	Guankou[AH]	90	D6	Guanzhai[YN]	148	J6
Guandian[HB]	110	D4	Guankou[SN]	156	F8	Guanzhaung[HN]	114	C4
Guandimiao[AH]	90	C2	Guanlan[GD]	118	G4	Guanzhen[JS]	80	D3
Guandiping[HN]	114	C3	Guanlin[JS]	80	E5	Guanzhou[GZ]	144	G2
Guandu He[HB]	110	D3	Guanling[FJ]	94	F2	Guanzhu[GD]	118	D5
Guandu[CQ]	132	C3	Guanling[GZ]	144	D5	Guanzhuang[AH]	90	C5
Guandu[CQ]	132	F3	Guanling[HN]	114	E6	Guanzhuang[BJ]	36	D4
Guandu[GD]	118	C5	Guanlu[FJ]	94	D1	Guanzhuang[CQ]	132	F5
Guandu[GD]	118	F2	Guanma[JL]	66	G4	Guanzhuang[FJ]	94	B4
Guandu[GZ]	144	E2	Guanmaoshan[BJ]	36	D2	Guanzhuang[HEB]	48	E5
Guandu[HB]	110	D3	Guanmei[ZJ]	84	E5	Guanzhuang[HEN]	106	D5
Guandu[HN]	114	F4	Guanmen Shan[NX]	168	B4	Guanzhuang[HEN]	106	E5
Guandu[SC]	138	N3	Guanmenshan[NM]	58	O4	Guanzhuang[HEN]	106	F3
Guan'er[SX]	54	E2	Guanmenshan[NX]	168	B4	Guanzhuang[HN]	114	F5
Guanfang[HB]	110	C1	Guanmian Shan[CQ]	132	E2	Guanzhuang[NX]	168	B4
Guanfang[HB]	110	E2	Guanmian Shan[SC]	138	N4	Guanzhuang[SD]	102	F3
Guanfang[HEB]	48	A7				Guanzhuang[SN]	156	E6

Guanzhuang[SN]	156	E6	Guiler He[NM]	58	N4	Guocun[JS]	80	E4
Guanzhuang[SN]	156	F4	Guiler He[NM]	58	N5	Guocun[SD]	102	B5
Guanzhuang[SN]	156	G2	Guilin[FJ]	94	C2	Guocun[ZJ]	84	C3
Guanzhuang[SN]	156	G4	Guilin[GX]	124	H2	Guodao[SX]	54	D5
Guanzhuang[TJ]	42	B1	Guiling[GX]	124	I3	Guodayuan[JL]	66	F4
Guanzhuang[TJ]	42	B3	Guimeng Ding[SD]	102	D4	Guodian[SD]	102	D3
Guanzhuangba[AH]	90	C2	Guinan[QH]	164	M5	Guodian[SX]	54	D5
Guanziyao[GZ]	144	C5	Guinong Shan[GX]	124	C4	Guoduwan[HB]	110	E3
Guazhou[GS]	160	B2	Guiping[GX]	124	H4	Guofu[HL]	70	D5
Guazhou[JS]	80	E4	Guiren[JS]	80	D3	Guogou[NX]	168	B4
Gubeikou[BJ]	36	E2	Guishan[YN]	148	I6	Guohuangzhuang[TJ]	42	B3
Guben[GZ]	144	G4	Guishan[ZJ]	84	E5	Guoji[HEN]	106	E5
Gubu[JX]	98	D3	Guishi Shuiku[GX]	124	I3	Guoji[JS]	80	E4
Guchang[CQ]	132	B4	Guishui He[BJ]	36	B3	Guojia[CQ]	132	E2
Gucheng Hu[JS]	80	D5	Guisi[ZJ]	84	F3	Guojiabu[BJ]	36	B3
Gucheng[AH]	90	B3	Guitai[GX]	124	F5	Guojiacha[NX]	168	C4
Gucheng[AH]	90	D3	Guitang[HN]	114	B3	Guojiadian[JL]	66	E4
Gucheng[AH]	90	D4	Guitou[GD]	118	F2	Guojiadian[SD]	102	G2
Gucheng[BJ]	36	C2	Guiwu[JS]	80	D4	Guojiagou[SN]	156	G3
Gucheng[FJ]	94	B4	Guixi[FJ]	94	C4	Guojiahe[HEN]	106	F6
Gucheng[GS]	160	G5	Guixi[JX]	98	E3	Guojiatun[HEB]	48	E2
Gucheng[HB]	110	E2	Guixi[YN]	148	I2	Guojiatun[JL]	66	C2
Gucheng[HEB]	48	C4	Guiyang[GZ]	144	E4	Guojiawan[HEB]	48	E1
Gucheng[HEB]	48	C6	Guiyang[HN]	114	E7	Guojiayao[SX]	54	E1
Gucheng[HEB]	48	D6	Guiyi[SD]	102	E5	Guojiazhuang[HB]	110	E3
Gucheng[HEB]	48	D6	Guiyunhua[LN]	62	F5	Guojiazhuang[TJ]	42	A4
Gucheng[HEN]	106	G2	Guizhuang[JS]	80	G5	Guokui Shan[HL]	70	E6
Gucheng[HL]	70	C5	Guizhumao[JX]	98	C7	Guoli[SD]	102	E3
Gucheng[HL]	70	F6	Guji[FJ]	94	D4	Guolou[HEN]	106	F5
Gucheng[JL]	66	D2	Gujia[SH]	74	C2	Guomuyuan[BJ]	36	E2
Gucheng[NM]	58	T10	Gujia[ZJ]	84	D2	Guoqiang[FJ]	94	C5
Gucheng[NM]	58	X11	Gujiang[JX]	98	B4	Guoshu[JS]	80	E3
Gucheng[NX]	168	C5	Gujiao[GZ]	144	E4	Guoshuyuan[BJ]	36	C3
Gucheng[QH]	164	N4	Gujiao[SX]	54	D4	Guosong[JL]	66	G6
Gucheng[SD]	102	E3	Gujiao[SX]	54	E6	Guosui[GX]	124	F4
Gucheng[SN]	156	D8	Gujiazhai[SH]	74	C3	Guotaiqiao[HN]	114	C3
Gucheng[SN]	156	G1	Gujiazhai[SH]	74	D2	Guotan[HEN]	106	D5
Gucheng[SX]	54	C6	Gujiazhuang[NX]	168	C2	Guowei[JX]	98	D4
Gucheng[SX]	54	D2	Gujiazi[JL]	66	E4	Guoyang[AH]	90	C3
Gucheng[SX]	54	E1	Gukyamxung[QH]	164	I8	Guoyang[SX]	54	D5
Gucheng[YN]	148	G7	Gula[GX]	124	F4	Guoyuan[FJ]	94	C2
Guchengzi[LN]	62	F3	Gulai[ZJ]	84	E3	Guoyuan[SH]	74	C2
Guchengzi[NX]	168	B3	Gulang[GS]	160	F4	Guoyuan[SH]	74	D2
Gucun[JX]	98	D5	Gulei[FJ]	94	C6	Guozhangzi[HEB]	48	F3
Gudao[SD]	102	E2	Guleitou[FJ]	94	C6	Guozhen[HN]	114	F3
Gudeng[YN]	148	D4	Guli[SD]	102	D4	Guozhen[SN]	156	B7
Gudi[SD]	102	F3	Gulianhe[HL]	70	B2	Guozhuang[HEN]	106	F3
Gudian[JL]	66	E3	Gulin[SC]	138	K7	Guozhuang[HEN]	106	H3
Gudiancun[SD]	102	B3	Guling[CQ]	132	F3	Guozhuang[JS]	80	E5
Gudianzi[JL]	66	G4	Guling[GX]	124	F4	Guozhuang[SD]	102	G3
Gudong Shan[XJ]	172	G6	Guliu[SD]	102	G3	Gupei[HN]	114	F4
Gudong[YN]	148	D5	Guliya Shan[NM]	58	O3	Gupeng[GX]	124	F4
Gudou Shan[GD]	118	E4	Gulong[GX]	124	H4	Gupi[JS]	80	C2
Gudui[HEN]	106	G5	Gulong[GZ]	144	G4	Guqianbu[SX]	54	F1
Gufengzhuang[NX]	168	D3	Gulong[HL]	70	C6	Guqiang[HEN]	106	F4
Gufosi[TJ]	42	B3	Gulong[HL]	70	D3	Guqiao[AH]	90	C4
Gugang[HN]	114	F4	Gulou[CQ]	132	C3	Gurao[AH]	90	C3
Gugang[JX]	98	D4	Gulou[FJ]	94	D1	Gurao[GD]	118	I3
Gugang[JX]	98	E3	Gulouzi[LN]	62	H4	Gurbantunggut Shamo[XJ]	172	K3
Guhe[AH]	90	D5	Gulu[SH]	74	D2	Gurnai[NM]	58	D7
Guhe[GX]	124	E4	Gulu[XZ]	152	G4	Gurong Jiang[GX]	124	E4
Guhuai[FJ]	94	E4	Guluo[SX]	54	C5	Gurum[XZ]	152	G5
Gui Jiang[GX]	124	H3	Guluoshan[HN]	114	C3	Gusang[JS]	80	D4
Gui'an[FJ]	94	E3	Gumiaoliang[SN]	156	F2	Gushan[FJ]	94	E3
Gui'ao[ZJ]	84	E4	Gumig[XZ]	152	K5	Gushanzi[HEB]	48	E3
Guichao[YN]	148	K7	Gun He[HB]	110	F2	Gushanzi[LN]	62	D3
Guide[QH]	164	N4	Gun Qarag[NM]	58	G8	Gushao[SD]	102	D5
Guide[SD]	102	C3	Gunbei[GX]	124	F2	Gushi[GD]	118	G1
Guiding[GZ]	144	F4	Gung Lam[NM]	58	X11	Gushi[HEN]	106	G5
Guidong[GD]	118	G2	Gungrigarbo Qu[XZ]	152	J5	Gushi[SN]	156	F6
Guidong[HN]	114	F6	Gungrigarbo[XZ]	152	J5	Gushou[GX]	124	D4
Guifeng Shan[HB]	110	I3	Guniushan[HN]	114	D4	Gushu[HEB]	48	E4
Guifeng[JX]	98	E3	Gunquan[NX]	168	C3	Gushui[GD]	118	E3
Guifeng[ZJ]	84	E5	Günsa[XZ]	152	A3	Gusidian[SD]	102	G2
Guigang[GD]	118	D4	Guo He[AH]	90	C3	Gutan[GX]	124	E5
Guigang[GX]	124	G4	Guo He[HEN]	106	F3	Gütang[XZ]	152	I5
Guihu[FJ]	84	D5	Guobao[FJ]	94	D4	Gutian Shuiku[FJ]	94	D3
Guihua[HB]	110	D2	Guobei[HEN]	106	G4	Gutian[FJ]	94	B4
Guihua[HB]	110	H5	Guobu[JX]	98	B6	Gutian[FJ]	94	B4
Guihua[YN]	148	G4	Guocang[SD]	102	C4	Gutian[FJ]	94	D3
Guihuayuan[HN]	114	C5	Guochuan[JS]	80	E4	Guting[JX]	98	B6
Guijiang[JX]	98	B5	Guocun[AH]	90	D6	Guwangji[HEN]	106	G3
Guikeng[FJ]	94	A4	Guocun[CQ]	132	E3	Guxi[AH]	90	E6
Guikou[HB]	110	G5	Guocun[HEB]	48	C3	Guxi[CQ]	132	B3

Guxi[JS]	80	F4
Guxian[HEB]	48	C7
Guxian[HEB]	48	D5
Guxian[HEN]	106	B3
Guxian[HEN]	106	C3
Guxian[HEN]	106	D3
Guxian[JX]	98	C4
Guxian[SD]	102	G3
Guxian[SD]	102	H2
Guxian[SX]	54	C3
Guxian[SX]	54	C5
Guxian[SX]	54	D4
Guxian[SX]	54	D5
Guxin[HEB]	48	A7
Guyang[HEN]	106	F3
Guyang[NM]	58	I7
Guyang[NM]	58	W10
Guyang[SX]	54	D5
Guyaozi[NX]	168	C2
Guye Qu[HEB]	48	F4
Guyi[HB]	110	F2
Guyuan[HEB]	48	C2
Guyuan[NM]	58	P2
Guyuan[NX]	168	C4
Guzhang[GX]	124	B3
Guzhang[GX]	124	G4
Guzhang[HN]	114	B4
Guzhen[AH]	90	D3
Guzhou[HN]	114	D5
Guzhu[GD]	118	G3
Gyaca[XZ]	152	H5
Gyaco[XZ]	152	E5
Gyanabung[XZ]	152	B4
Gyangbê[XZ]	152	H4
Gyangbê[XZ]	152	K4
Gyangda[QH]	164	J8
Gyangnyi Cak[XZ]	152	E2
Gyangqoi[QH]	164	M6
Gyangrang[XZ]	152	D4
Gyangzê[XZ]	152	F5
Gyari[XZ]	152	J4
Gyaring Co[XZ]	152	F4
Gyaring Hu[QH]	164	J6
Gyaring[QH]	164	J5
Gyawa[SC]	138	F6
Gyêcê Caka[XZ]	152	B3
Gyedoi[QH]	164	H8
Gyêmdong[XZ]	152	H5
Gyêru[XZ]	152	F5
Gyêsar Co[XZ]	152	D4
Gyiba[XZ]	152	G6
Gyimkar[QH]	164	M8
Gyirong[XZ]	152	D5
Gyirong[XZ]	152	D5
Gyitang[XZ]	152	J4
Gyizhong[XZ]	152	J4
Gyobrag[QH]	164	I8
Gyogyunda[QH]	164	I8
Gyungcang[XZ]	152	E4

H

Ha Che[HK]	176	C2
Ha Mei Wan[HK]	176	C4
Ha Miu Tin[HK]	176	E1
Ha Pak Nai[HK]	176	B2
Ha Tam Shui Hang[HK]	176	D1
Ha Tsuen[HK]	176	B2
Ha Yeung[HK]	176	E3
Haba Xueshan[YN]	148	F3
Habahe(Kaba)[XJ]	172	K1
Habiga[HEB]	48	B2
Hada[LN]	62	H3
Hadabei[LN]	62	G4
Hadadong[XJ]	172	J5
Hadamen[JL]	66	K5
Hadan Tohoi[NM]	58	G7
Hadan Tohoi[NM]	58	S11
Hadapu[GS]	160	G5
Ha'ertao[LN]	62	F2
Hai He[TJ]	42	B3
Hai Jiao[ZJ]	84	H2

Hai'an Shan[GD]	118	G4
Haian Shan[TW]	186	E3
Hai'an[GD]	118	C6
Hai'an[JS]	80	F4
Haibei[HL]	70	D5
Haibin[LN]	62	D4
Haibin[TJ]	42	B4
Haicang Qu[FJ]	94	C5
Haichao[SH]	74	D3
Haicheng[GX]	124	E4
Haicheng[HL]	70	D5
Haicheng[LN]	62	F4
Haidian Qu[BJ]	36	C4
Haidian[BJ]	36	C4
Haiding Hu[QH]	164	F5
Haifeng[GD]	118	H4
Haifeng[TJ]	42	B3
Haigong Nongchang[TJ]	42	C3
Haiguan[SH]	74	D3
Haiguang[SH]	74	C3
Haihe Kou[TJ]	42	C4
Haihe[JS]	80	F3
Haijiawan[NX]	168	C5
Haikou Gang[HI]	128	C1
Haikou[FJ]	94	E4
Haikou[HI]	128	C1
Haikou[JX]	98	E2
Haikou[YN]	148	H6
Haikou[ZJ]	84	E4
Haila[GZ]	144	B4
Hailang[LN]	62	G3
Hailar He[NM]	58	M3
Hailin[HL]	70	E6
Hailing Dao[GD]	118	D5
Hailing Qu[JS]	80	E4
Hailing[GD]	118	D5
Hailiutu[HEB]	48	B2
Hailong[JL]	66	F5
Hails[NM]	58	M6
Hailun[HL]	70	D5
Haima Tan[HI]	128	G6
Haimaotuo[LN]	62	D6
Haimen Wan[GD]	118	I3
Haimen[JS]	80	G5
Hainan Dao[HI]	128	B2
Hainan Jiao[HI]	128	C1
Hainan Qu[NM]	58	G8
Hainan[HL]	70	D5
Haining[ZJ]	84	E2
Haiqian[SH]	74	D3
Haiqing[JL]	66	E3
Haiqing[SD]	102	F4
Hairgi[QH]	164	M3
Haishan[GD]	118	I3
Haitan Dao[FJ]	94	E4
Haitan Haixia[FJ]	94	E4
Haitan Wan[FJ]	94	E4
Haitangwan[HI]	128	B3
Haitou Gang[HI]	128	A2
Haitou[HI]	128	A2
Haitou[JS]	80	E2
Haiwan[SH]	74	D3
Haiwei[HI]	128	A2
Haixin Shan[QH]	164	M4
Haixing[HEB]	48	E5
Haixing[HL]	70	D5
Haixing[JX]	98	D2
Haixinzhuang[TJ]	42	C3
Haixiu[HI]	128	C1
Haiyan[GD]	118	E5
Haiyan[JS]	80	G4
Haiyan[QH]	164	M4
Haiyan[ZJ]	84	E2
Haiyang Dao[LN]	62	G5
Haiyang He[GX]	124	H2
Haiyang Shan[GX]	124	H2
Haiyang[CQ]	132	F5
Haiyang[SD]	102	H3
Haiyu[JS]	80	F5
Haiyuan[NX]	168	B4
Haizeletuobie[GS]	160	C3
Haizetan[SN]	156	E3
Haizhou Qu[JS]	80	E2
Haizhou Wan[JS]	80	E2

Haizhouwopu[LN]	62	G2
Haizi Shan[SC]	138	G5
Haizijie[GZ]	144	D3
Haizikou[BJ]	36	C3
Haizikou[NX]	168	C5
Haizitu[NX]	58	T10
Hak Kok Tau[HK]	176	E4
Haladaokou[LN]	62	C2
Halagoinba[XZ]	152	J5
Halahai[JL]	66	F3
Halhiyn Gol[NM]	58	M4
Haliha[HEB]	48	E1
Halik Shan[XJ]	172	H4
Ham Tin[HK]	176	B4
Hamatang[JL]	66	J4
Hami(Kumul)[XJ]	172	N4
Han Jiang[GD]	118	I3
Han Shui[HB]	110	F3
Han Shui[SN]	156	D7
Han Shui[SN]	156	F8
Han Ui[NM]	58	F7
Han Ul[NM]	58	L3
Hanbei He[HB]	110	G4
Hancang[SH]	74	C3
Hancheng[HEN]	106	C3
Hancheng[SN]	156	G5
Hanchuan[HB]	110	G4
Hanconggou[HL]	70	H5
Hancun[SD]	102	E4
Hancun[SN]	156	F6
Hancunhe[BJ]	36	B4
Handan[HEB]	48	B7
Handan[HEB]	48	B7
Handian[GS]	160	H5
Handian[HL]	70	C6
Handian[SD]	102	D3
Handong[HEN]	106	F5
Hanfang[JX]	98	C6
Hang Hau Tsuen[HK]	176	B2
Hang Hau[HK]	176	E3
Hang Mei[HK]	176	A4
Hang Tau Tai Po[HK]	176	C1
Hangangzi[NX]	168	C3
Hangbu He[AH]	90	C5
Hanggai Gobi[NM]	58	T10
Hanggai[ZJ]	84	D2
Hanggin Houqi[NM]	58	G7
Hanggin Houqi[NM]	58	T11
Hanggin Nur[NM]	58	U11
Hanggin[NM]	58	H8
Hangongdu[HN]	114	D3
Hangpi Ganqu[AH]	90	C5
Hangping[ZJ]	84	D3
Hangqian[SH]	74	D3
Hangqiao[JX]	98	D2
Hangtou[SH]	74	D2
Hangu Qu[TJ]	42	C3
Hanguguan[HEN]	106	B3
Hangzhou Wan[ZJ]	84	E2
Hangzhou[ZJ]	84	E2
Hangzhoudao[TJ]	42	C3
Hanhao[GX]	124	H4
Hanji[HB]	110	G4
Hanji[HEN]	106	F5
Hanji[SD]	102	B5
Hanjiachuan[SX]	54	C3
Hanjiadian[HEB]	48	E2
Hanjialou[SX]	54	C2
Hanjiang Qu[FJ]	94	E4
Hanjiang Qu[JS]	80	E4
Hanjiashu[TJ]	42	B3
Hanjiatai[BJ]	36	B3
Hanjiayuan[HL]	70	C2
Hanjing[SN]	156	F5
Hankou[HN]	114	G6
Hanlin[HI]	128	C2
Hanling[LN]	62	G3
Hanliu[JS]	80	E4
Hanmaying[HEB]	48	E2
Hannan Qu[HB]	110	H4
Hanniu[SC]	138	H5
Hanrui[CQ]	132	F3
Hanshan[AH]	90	E5
Hanshan[JS]	80	D2

Hanshan[JX]	98	A4	Hebian[SX]	54	E3	Heishi[JL]	66	I4
Hanshan[ZJ]	84	E2	Hechakou[XJ]	172	G8	Heishitou[GZ]	144	C4
Hanshou[HN]	114	D4	Hecheng[AH]	90	D7	Heishui He[GX]	124	D5
Hantai[HEB]	48	B5	Hecheng[GD]	118	E4	Heishui He[SC]	138	H8
Hantengri Feng[XJ]	172	H4	Hechi[GX]	124	E3	Heishui He[SC]	138	I3
Hanting Qu[SD]	102	F3	Hechi[GX]	124	F3	Heishui[JL]	66	I4
Hantun[SD]	102	C3	Hechuan Qu[CQ]	132	C4	Heishui[LN]	62	C2
Hanwang[SC]	138	J4	Hechuan[NX]	168	C5	Heishui[SC]	138	H3
Hanwang[SD]	102	E4	Hechuan[SX]	54	D5	Heisi[QH]	164	K4
Hanwang[SX]	54	E4	Hechun[GD]	118	C5	Heitai[HL]	70	F6
Hanwu[SH]	74	C3	Hecun[ZJ]	84	C4	Heitu[GZ]	144	D4
Hanyang Feng[JX]	98	C2	Hecun[ZJ]	84	D3	Heituhe[GZ]	144	B3
Hanyin[SN]	156	E8	Hedi He[YN]	148	H7	Heituo Shan[SX]	54	D2
Hanyuan[SC]	138	H6	Hedi Shuiku[GD]	118	C5	Heituya[NM]	58	W11
Hanzhong[HEN]	106	D5	Hedi[SN]	156	G3	Heixiong Shan[QH]	164	B5
Hanzhong[SN]	156	D7	Hedi[SX]	54	C6	Heiyanzi[HEB]	48	F4
Hanzhuang[HEB]	48	D6	Hedian[HB]	110	G3	Heiyukou[BJ]	36	C2
Hanzhuang[HEN]	106	F5	Hedian[YN]	148	F5	Heiyupao[JL]	66	D2
Hanzhuang[SD]	102	D5	Hedong Qu[SD]	102	E4	Heizhiguo[YN]	148	K7
Haoba[SC]	138	J8	Hedong[GD]	118	H4	Heizhuanghu[BJ]	36	D4
Haobei[SX]	54	D5	Hedong[HEB]	48	C4	Heji[AH]	90	D3
Haocheng[AH]	90	D3	Hedongdian[SN]	156	C7	Heji[GX]	124	G4
Haochuan[NX]	168	B4	He'erkou[GD]	118	D3	Heji[HEN]	106	G3
Haocun[FJ]	94	D2	Hefei[AH]	90	D5	Hejiabu[SX]	54	E2
Haode[HL]	70	C6	Hefeng[HB]	110	D5	Hejiachang[HB]	110	G4
Haodian[HB]	110	G3	Hefengqiao[HEN]	106	G6	Hejiachuan[SN]	156	G2
Haodian[NX]	168	C5	Hegang[HL]	70	F5	Hejiagou[NX]	168	C5
Haodian[SN]	156	E6	Hegeng[CQ]	132	B4	Hejiahui[SX]	54	B3
Haogezhuang[TJ]	42	B2	Hegezhuang[BJ]	36	D4	Hejiaji[SN]	156	F3
Haogou[NX]	168	B4	Hehe[HB]	110	G2	Hejiajing[GS]	160	F3
Haoguantun[LN]	62	G2	Hehe[SD]	102	C3	Hejiakouzi[NX]	168	B3
Haohuahong[GZ]	144	E4	Hehe[SH]	74	D2	Hejian[HEB]	48	D5
Haojiang Qu[GD]	118	I3	Hehekou[HEB]	48	A5	Hejian[HEN]	106	E2
Haojiaping[SN]	156	F4	Hehu[JX]	98	C4	Hejiang[GD]	118	C5
Haojiaqiao[NX]	168	C2	Hehua[HB]	110	E3	Hejiang[SC]	138	K7
Haojiatai[NX]	168	D3	Hehuashan[LN]	62	F5	Hejiaping[HN]	114	D4
Haojiaying[HEB]	48	B2	Hei Hai[QH]	164	F5	Hejiaqiao[HN]	114	F5
Haokou[CQ]	132	D4	Hei He[GS]	160	E3	Hejiazhuang[NX]	168	C4
Haokou[HB]	110	F4	Hei He[QH]	164	J6	Hejie[GX]	124	I3
Haolianghe[HL]	70	E5	Hei He[QH]	164	K2	Hejin[HEB]	48	D7
Haopo[SD]	102	I2	Hei He[SC]	138	H2	Hejin[SX]	54	B6
Haoshan[HN]	114	F6	Hei He[SN]	156	C7	Hejing[XJ]	172	K4
Haoshui[NX]	168	C5	Hei Ling Chau[HK]	176	C4	Hekou Gongduan[HL]	70	D4
Haotan[SN]	156	E3	Hei Shan[GS]	160	D3	Hekou Qu[SD]	102	E2
Haotou[HN]	114	F7	Hei Shan[HEB]	48	G3	Hekou Shuiku[SN]	156	F2
Haoyanliang[BJ]	36	C2	Hei Shan[LN]	62	C4	Hekou[AH]	90	C4
Haozhai[JS]	80	B2	Hei Shan[LN]	62	G4	Hekou[BJ]	36	C2
Haozhigang Kou[JS]	80	G4	Hei Shan[XJ]	172	J7	Hekou[GD]	118	D4
Haozhuang[HEB]	48	B6	Heibugou[NX]	168	C4	Hekou[GD]	118	D5
Haozigang[HN]	114	E3	Heicha Shan[SX]	54	C3	Hekou[GD]	118	E4
Happy Valley[HK]	176	D4	Heicheng[NM]	58	X11	Hekou[GD]	118	H3
Har Axrag[QH]	164	I5	Heicheng[NX]	168	C4	Hekou[GS]	160	F4
Har Hu[QH]	164	J2	Heidouyu[BJ]	36	E3	Hekou[HI]	128	B3
Har Nur[LN]	62	D3	Heigou[LN]	62	G4	Hekou[JS]	80	B2
Har Nur[NM]	58	N5	Heigutai[BJ]	36	C4	Hekou[JS]	80	F4
Har Orbog[NM]	58	F7	Heihe[HL]	70	D3	Hekou[SN]	156	C7
Harai Gou[NM]	58	V11	Heihe[QH]	164	K6	Hekou[SX]	54	C3
Haramgal[NM]	172	K2	Heijiabao[SN]	156	F2	Hekou[YN]	148	I8
Harat[NM]	58	L5	Heijing[YN]	148	G5	Hekui[JL]	66	K4
Harba Ling[JL]	66	J4	Heilin[JL]	66	G3	Helan Shan[NM]	58	F8
Harbin[HL]	70	D6	Heilin[JS]	80	D1	Helan Shan[NX]	168	B2
Harilongjiawa[QH]	164	K5	Heilinzi[JL]	66	E4	Helan Shan[NX]	168	B2
Harqin Qi[NM]	58	M7	Heiliushui[SX]	54	D2	Helan[NX]	168	C2
Harqin Zuoyi[LN]	62	C3	Heilizhai[SD]	102	D2	Helang[GD]	118	D4
Harqin[LN]	62	D3	Heilong Jiang[HL]	70	G5	Helanshan Linkuang[NX]	168	B2
Harul[NM]	58	X10	Heilongguan[SX]	54	C5	Hele[HI]	128	C3
Hasungdo[XZ]	152	K3	Heilongji[HB]	110	F2	Heli Shan[GS]	160	D3
Haxak[XJ]	172	G7	Heilongkou[SN]	156	F6	Heli Shan[NM]	58	C8
Haxaklik He[XJ]	172	L7	Heimahe[QH]	164	L4	Heli[CQ]	132	E4
Haxi[GS]	160	F4	Heinitang[YN]	148	D5	Heli[GX]	124	F4
He Shui[JX]	98	B5	Heiniuping[NX]	168	B4	Heli[HN]	114	F5
He Xian[AH]	90	E5	Heiquan[GS]	160	D3	Heliao[GD]	118	C5
He'an[GD]	118	C6	Heisanzao[SH]	74	D3	Helin[GD]	118	I3
Heba[GZ]	144	F3	Heishan Ling[XJ]	172	N5	Heling[FJ]	94	D2
Heba[SC]	138	I5	Heishan[GS]	160	G5	Heling[SC]	138	K4
Hebao Dao[GD]	118	F5	Heishan[HL]	70	D5	Heliu[AH]	90	C3
Hebao[CQ]	132	B4	Heishan[LN]	62	F3	Helong[FJ]	94	B3
Hebei[BJ]	36	D2	Heishanke[LN]	62	C4	Helong[JL]	66	F3
Hebei[HL]	70	F5	Heishansi[BJ]	36	D3	Helong[JL]	66	J5
Hebei[QH]	164	M6	Heishantou[NM]	58	M2	Helong[LN]	62	H2
Hebei[SN]	156	C6	Heishanxia[NX]	168	A3	Helou[SD]	102	B4
Hebei[SX]	54	D6	Heishanzui[HEB]	48	D2	Helukou[HN]	114	D8
Hebeitou[BJ]	36	C4	Heishi Beihu[XZ]	152	C2	Hema[GZ]	144	E2
Hebi[HEN]	106	F2	Heishi Feng[GS]	160	B3	Hemianshi Shuiku[GX]	124	I3

Hemu[GX]	124	G3	Heping[JL]	66	F5	Heyan[CQ]	132	E2
Henan[NM]	58	H9	Heping[JL]	66	H4	Heyang[GZ]	144	F4
Henan[QH]	164	N6	Heping[JL]	66	I5	Heyang[SD]	102	E4
Henan[SX]	54	D4	Heping[JS]	80	D3	Heyang[SN]	156	G5
Henantuan[HEB]	48	C7	Heping[QH]	164	N4	Heye Ping[SX]	54	C3
Henanzhai[BJ]	36	D3	Heping[SC]	138	F5	Heye[HN]	114	E7
Heng He[SN]	156	E7	Heping[YN]	148	I7	Heyetang[ZJ]	84	E3
Heng Jiang[YN]	148	J2	Hepu[GX]	124	G6	Heyi[BJ]	36	C4
Heng On Estate[HK]	176	D2	Hepu[JX]	98	C4	Heyou[CQ]	132	D3
Heng Shan[HN]	114	E5	Hepu[ZJ]	84	F3	Heyu[HEN]	106	C4
Heng Shan[HN]	114	E5	Heqian[CQ]	132	E2	Heyu[SX]	54	D4
Heng Shan[SN]	156	F3	Heqiao[HEB]	48	C5	Heyuan[GD]	118	G3
Heng Shan[SX]	54	E2	Heqiao[JS]	80	D4	Heyuan[JL]	66	F4
Heng Shan[SX]	54	E2	Heqiao[JS]	80	E5	Heyuan[JX]	98	B5
Heng Xian[GX]	124	G5	Heqiao[ZJ]	84	D2	Heyuan[JX]	98	D4
Hengbanqiao[HN]	114	C5	Heqing[SH]	74	D2	Heyukou[SX]	54	B3
Hengbu[AH]	90	D6	Heqing[YN]	148	F4	Heyun[GD]	118	E3
Hengche[HB]	110	I4	Hequ[HEB]	48	B6	Heze[SD]	102	B4
Hengchun[TW]	186	D4	Hequ[SX]	54	C2	Hezhang[GZ]	144	C3
Hengcun[ZJ]	84	D3	Herlen He[NM]	58	L3	Hezhang[HEB]	48	A7
Hengdai[SH]	74	C3	Herlen[NM]	58	K3	Hezhen[GZ]	144	C3
Hengdan[GS]	160	G6	Heshan Qu[HEN]	106	F2	Hezheng[GS]	160	F5
Hengdaohezi[HL]	70	E6	Heshan[FJ]	94	C3	Hezheng[HI]	128	B2
Hengdaohezi[LN]	62	G2	Heshan[GD]	118	E4	Hezhi[SX]	54	C2
Hengdian[HB]	110	H4	Heshan[GD]	118	E5	Hezhou[GX]	124	I3
Hengdian[ZJ]	84	E3	Heshan[GX]	124	F4	Hezhou[HN]	114	E6
Hengdong[HN]	114	E5	Heshan[JL]	66	E4	Hezhuang[SD]	102	D3
Hengdu[ZJ]	84	F3	Heshan[JX]	98	D3	Hezui[CQ]	132	E3
Hengduan Shan[XZ]	152	J5	Heshan[SD]	102	F4	Hezui[GS]	160	F4
Hengduan Shan[YN]	148	D1	Heshe[HI]	128	B2	Hezuo[GS]	160	F5
Hengfeng[JX]	98	E3	Hesheng[GS]	160	H5	Hezuo[JS]	80	G5
Henggouqiao[HB]	110	H5	Hesheng[HN]	128	B2	Hezuo[SH]	74	C1
Henggoushi[HB]	110	F5	Hesheng[HL]	70	C4	High Island Reservoir[HK]	176	E3
Hengji[JS]	80	E3	Hesheng[ZJ]	84	E4	Himal Ayas[XZ]	152	A4
Hengjian[HEN]	106	C4	Heshengbu[SX]	54	D2	Ho Chung[HK]	176	E3
Hengjian[JS]	80	E5	Heshengqiao[HB]	110	H4	Ho Man Tin[HK]	176	D3
Hengjiangqiao[HN]	114	B6	Heshi[FJ]	94	D4	Ho Pui Reservoir[HK]	176	C2
Hengjin Shuiku[ZJ]	84	E3	Heshi[JS]	80	G5	Hoboksar[XJ]	172	J2
Hengjing[JS]	80	E4	Heshi[JX]	98	B3	Hobq Shamo[NM]	58	G7
Hengkou[SN]	156	E8	Heshi[JX]	98	B5	Hobq Shamo[NM]	58	T11
Hengliang[GS]	160	F4	Heshi[JX]	98	D3	Hoh Baxag[NM]	58	G7
Hengliang[JS]	80	D4	Heshui[GD]	118	D4	Hoh Baxag[NM]	58	S10
Hengling Hu[HN]	114	E4	Heshui[GD]	118	D4	Hoh Ere[QH]	164	L2
Hengling[BJ]	36	B4	Heshui[GD]	118	E4	Hoh Mod[NM]	58	T11
Hengling[SX]	54	E4	Heshui[GD]	118	G2	Hoh Ondor[NM]	58	S11
Henglongqiao[HN]	114	E4	Heshui[GS]	160	H5	Hoh Qel[JL]	66	C2
Henglu[JX]	98	C2	Heshui[HN]	114	B5	Hoh Sai Hu[QH]	164	E5
Hengmian[SH]	74	D2	Heshun[GD]	118	F3	Hoh Xil Hu[QH]	164	D5
Hengnan[HN]	114	E6	Heshun[SX]	54	E4	Hoh Xil Shan[QH]	164	A5
Hengqiao[SH]	74	D2	Hesuo[SX]	54	D3	Hoh[NM]	58	S11
Hengqin[GD]	118	F4	Hetan[HN]	114	B5	Hohhot[NM]	58	I7
Hengqu[SN]	156	D6	Hetang Qu[HN]	114	F5	Hohht[NM]	58	X11
Hengsha Dao[SH]	74	D2	Hetang[FJ]	94	E3	Hohod[QH]	164	K4
Hengsha[SH]	74	D2	Hetang[GD]	118	C4	Hohxil Shan[XZ]	152	F2
Hengshan Qu[HL]	70	F6	Hetang[HN]	114	D5	Hoi Ha Wan[HK]	176	E2
Hengshan[GD]	118	C5	Hetang[JX]	98	C5	Hoi Ha[HK]	176	E2
Hengshan[HN]	114	E5	Hetao[GZ]	144	D3	Hoika[QH]	164	L5
Hengshan[SN]	156	F3	Hetian[FJ]	94	B4	Hoit Taria[QH]	164	I3
Hengshi[HN]	114	E4	Hetou[GD]	118	B5	Hoit Tohig[QH]	164	E4
Hengshi[JX]	98	B5	Hetou[GD]	118	E4	Hojen[TW]	186	E2
Hengshitang[GD]	118	F2	Hetou[SX]	54	E2	Hok Tau Wai[HK]	176	D1
Hengshui[HEB]	48	C6	Hetou[TJ]	42	C3	Hok Tsui Shan[HK]	176	E4
Hengshui[HEN]	106	E1	Hetou[ZJ]	84	F2	Holin Gol[NM]	58	M5
Hengshui[SX]	54	C6	Hetoudian[SD]	102	G2	Holin He[JL]	66	D2
Hengshui[SX]	54	D5	Hetu[AH]	90	C6	Holin He[NM]	58	N5
Hengshuihe[SX]	54	E6	Hewai[YN]	148	D7	Holoi Shan[NM]	58	X10
Hengxi[SN]	156	E8	Hexi[FJ]	94	B5	Holt Gol[NM]	58	L5
Hengxi[ZJ]	84	E4	Hexi[FJ]	94	C5	Holt[NM]	58	M5
Hengyang[HN]	114	E6	Hexi[GD]	118	I3	Hom Hanas[XJ]	172	K1
Hengyang[HN]	114	E6	Hexi[HEB]	48	C7	Hondi Yanchang[QH]	164	F2
Hepa Shan[SX]	54	E2	Hexi[HI]	128	B3	Hong He[HEN]	106	F4
Hepan[GS]	160	G4	Hexi[NX]	168	B3	Hong Hu[HB]	110	G5
Hepeng[AH]	90	C5	Hexi[SN]	156	D6	Hong Kong Island[HK]	176	D4
Heping[CQ]	132	F2	Hexi[SN]	156	D8	Hong Kong[HK]	176	D3
Heping[FJ]	94	C4	Hexi[SN]	156	E8	Hong Lok Yuen[HK]	176	D2
Heping[GD]	118	G2	Hexi[SX]	54	D6	Hong'an[HB]	110	H3
Heping[GS]	160	A3	Hexi[SX]	54	D6	Hongba[SC]	138	H6
Heping[GS]	160	E3	Hexi[YN]	148	E4	Hongbao[SC]	138	G8
Heping[GX]	124	E5	Hexigten Qi[NM]	58	L6	Hongcao[GD]	118	H4
Heping[GX]	124	G2	Hexincun[TJ]	42	A4	Hongchang[SH]	74	C1
Heping[GX]	124	H2	Hexing[GZ]	144	G2	Hongcheng[GS]	160	F4
Heping[HI]	128	C3	Hexing[SH]	74	D1	Hongchuan[SD]	102	B4
Heping[HN]	114	E7	Hexipu[GS]	160	F3	Hongchun[SN]	156	E8
Heping[JL]	66	F3	Hexiwu[TJ]	42	A2	Hongcun[JX]	98	D4

Name	Page	Grid
Hongdao[HI]	128	B2
Hongdao[SD]	102	G3
Hongdao[SX]	54	E3
Hongde[GS]	160	H4
Hongdu He[GZ]	144	F2
Hongdu[GX]	124	F4
Hongdu[GZ]	144	G2
Hongdunjie[SN]	156	E3
Hongdunzi[NX]	168	C2
Hongdunzi[NX]	168	C3
Hongfang[FJ]	94	B4
Hongfeng Hu[GZ]	144	E4
Hongfeng[NM]	58	T10
Hongfuliang[SN]	156	F5
Honggang Qu[HL]	70	C5
Honggangkou[BJ]	36	B4
Honggangzi[JL]	66	D2
Honggor Shan[NM]	58	D6
Honggor[NM]	58	J5
Honggosin Gol[XJ]	172	J4
Honggou[NX]	168	B2
Honggu Qu[GS]	160	F4
Hongguan[GD]	118	D4
Hongguang[HL]	70	F4
Hongguang[JL]	66	K4
Hongguang[NX]	168	C2
Hongguang[SC]	138	L3
Hongguang[SH]	74	C2
Hongguosi[BJ]	36	C2
Hongguozi[NX]	168	C1
Honghai Wan[GD]	118	H4
Honghai[HI]	128	D2
Honghai[SH]	74	C1
Honghe[NX]	168	C5
Honghe[SD]	102	E3
Honghe[YN]	148	H7
Hongheqiao[AH]	90	B4
Honghu[CQ]	132	C4
Honghu[HB]	110	G5
Honghua[GX]	124	I3
Honghua[HB]	110	D3
Honghua[SD]	102	E5
Honghuaji[HEN]	106	F4
Honghualing[HI]	128	C2
Honghuapu[SN]	156	C6
Honghuatao[HB]	110	E4
Honghujiang Shuiku[GX]	124	G6
Hongjian Nur[SN]	156	F1
Hongjiang[HN]	114	B5
Hongjiang[JX]	98	B4
Hongjiang[YN]	148	G8
Hongjiao[GD]	118	E4
Hongjing[NX]	168	B4
Hongjing[SX]	54	E5
Hongjingzi[NX]	168	D3
Hongjuan[NX]	168	B3
Hongjun[SN]	156	F7
Hongkan[HI]	128	A2
Hongkeli[HL]	70	E5
Hongkou[FJ]	94	E3
Hongku Shuiku[HI]	128	B2
Honglan[JS]	80	D5
Honglin[AH]	90	E6
Honglingpu[LN]	62	G3
Hongliu Gou[NX]	168	B3
Hongliugou[SN]	156	D3
Hongliuquan[QH]	164	C2
Hongliuxia[GS]	160	B3
Honglong[SC]	138	F5
Honglu[CQ]	132	B4
Honglu[FJ]	94	E4
Hongmao[HI]	128	B2
Hongmei[JL]	66	F5
Hongmen Shuiku[JX]	98	D4
Hongmen[JX]	98	D4
Hongmenhe[SN]	156	F7
Hongmiaozi[LN]	62	I3
Hongnijing[NM]	58	H7
Hongnijing[NM]	58	V10
Hongniwan[HEN]	106	D4
Hongpai[HI]	128	B2
Hongping[HB]	110	D3
Hongpodui[HI]	128	C2
Hongqi Qu[HEN]	106	E1
Hongqi[HI]	128	C2
Hongqi[HL]	70	C5
Hongqi[HL]	70	D5
Hongqi[HL]	70	D6
Hongqi[JL]	66	D4
Hongqiangzi[LN]	62	E3
Hongqiao Qu[TJ]	42	B3
Hongqiao[HN]	114	F4
Hongqiao[JS]	80	E4
Hongqiao[SH]	74	D2
Hongqiao[SH]	74	D2
Hongqiao[YN]	148	F3
Hongqiao[ZJ]	84	F4
Hongqidian[NM]	58	U10
Hongqizhuang[TJ]	42	B2
Hongqu'aikou[QH]	164	N7
Hongquan[JL]	66	E3
Hongquan[NX]	168	B3
Hongshagang[GS]	160	F3
Hongshaliang[GS]	160	F3
Hongshan Shuiku[NM]	58	M6
Hongshan Xia[GS]	160	G4
Hongshan[FJ]	94	B4
Hongshan[FJ]	94	B5
Hongshan[GD]	118	F1
Hongshan[HB]	110	F3
Hongshan[HB]	110	I4
Hongshan[HI]	128	B3
Hongshan[HN]	114	E6
Hongshan[SN]	156	E8
Hongshan[YN]	148	I3
Hongshantou[XJ]	172	G8
Hongshanyao[GS]	160	E3
Hongshanzui Kou'an[XJ]	172	L1
Hongshanzui[HB]	110	E2
Hongshi Liang[SN]	156	E5
Hongshi[HN]	114	E5
Hongshi[SN]	156	F8
Hongshikan[BJ]	36	E3
Hongshilazi[JL]	66	H5
Hongshileng[SX]	54	F2
Hongshiqiao[SN]	156	F2
Hongshishan[GS]	160	C1
Hongshiwo[GS]	160	D3
Hongshiya[SN]	156	G5
Hongshui He[GS]	160	F3
Hongshui He[GX]	124	E3
Hongshui[SN]	156	E6
Hongshui[SX]	54	E5
Hongshuihe[GZ]	144	E5
Hongshuikou[BJ]	36	A4
Hongshuizhuang[TJ]	42	B1
Hongsihu[GS]	160	E3
Hongsipu[NX]	168	C3
Hongta[FJ]	94	D4
Hongtangying[HN]	114	D7
Hongtian[FJ]	94	C4
Hongtiguan[SX]	54	E5
Hongtong[SX]	54	C5
Hongtoushan[LN]	62	H2
Hongtu Zhang[GD]	118	H3
Hongtu[CQ]	132	F2
Hongtu[HB]	110	C4
Hongtu[HL]	70	C3
Hongtu[SN]	156	F5
Hongtuliang[HEB]	48	B2
Hongtumiao[LN]	62	H2
Hongtuping[HEN]	106	C3
Hongtuya[JL]	66	G6
Hongwei He[SD]	102	B5
Hongwei Qu[LN]	62	G3
Hongwei[FJ]	94	D3
Hongwei[HL]	70	B3
Hongwei[HL]	70	F5
Hongxi[YN]	148	I6
Hongxia[JX]	98	C2
Hongxing Qu[HL]	70	E4
Hongxing[FJ]	94	C6
Hongxing[FJ]	94	D4
Hongxing[HL]	70	D4
Hongxing[JL]	66	D3
Hongxing[JL]	66	G2
Hongxing[JL]	66	H4
Hongxing[SH]	74	C2
Hongxing[SH]	74	D2
Hongya[NX]	168	B3
Hongya[SC]	138	I6
Hongyamao[SX]	54	C2
Hongyan[JX]	98	E2
Hongyan[NM]	58	P3
Hongyang[AH]	90	E5
Hongyang[GD]	118	I3
Hongyang[NX]	168	B4
Hongyansi[HB]	110	C4
Hongyansi[SN]	156	F7
Hongyao[NX]	168	B4
Hongyazi[GS]	160	B3
Hongyazi[GS]	160	D3
Hongyazi[LN]	62	D4
Hongyazi[NX]	168	C1
Hongyazi[SX]	54	C2
Hongyi[JX]	98	C2
Hongyi[SH]	74	C1
Hongyuan[SC]	138	H3
Hongze Hu[JS]	80	D3
Hongze[JS]	80	D3
Hongzhou[GZ]	144	H4
Hongzhuang[JS]	80	D2
Hongzhuang[NX]	168	C5
Hoping[TW]	186	D2
Hor[QH]	164	M5
Hor[XZ]	152	B4
Horba[XZ]	152	C4
Horbo[SC]	138	D4
Horgorgoinba[QH]	164	K6
Horgos Kou'an[XJ]	172	H3
Horinger[NM]	58	I7
Horinger[NM]	58	X11
Horo Shan[XJ]	172	J4
Horo Ul[NM]	58	N4
Horqin Shadi[NM]	58	N6
Horqin Youyi Qianqi[NM]	58	N4
Horqin Youyi Zhongqi[NM]	58	N5
Horqin Zuoyi Houqi[NM]	58	O6
Horqin Zuoyi Zhongqi[NM]	58	O5
Hos Burd[NM]	58	F8
Hotan He[XJ]	172	H6
Hotan[XJ]	172	G7
Hotan[XJ]	172	G7
Hou He[AH]	90	D6
Hou Jiang[SC]	138	M4
Hou'an[HI]	128	C3
Hou'an[LN]	62	H3
Hou'anling[BJ]	36	D2
Houba[CQ]	132	E2
Houbang[TJ]	42	C3
Houchang[GZ]	144	D4
Houchang[GZ]	144	E5
Houchangjiabu[TJ]	42	A3
Houcheng[HEB]	48	D3
Hougang[HB]	110	F4
Hougang[JX]	98	E2
Hougang[SH]	74	C3
Hougang[TJ]	42	C3
Hougu[TJ]	42	C3
Houhe[BJ]	36	B2
Houhe[CQ]	132	F2
Houhe[HEN]	106	F2
Houhebu[SX]	54	D3
Houhoushang[TJ]	42	A2
Houhu[GD]	118	C6
Houhuaitai[JL]	66	I5
Houji Dao[SD]	102	G1
Houji[HEN]	106	D5
Houji[SD]	102	B5
Houjia[FJ]	94	D3
Houjia[SD]	102	I2
Houjiagang[JX]	98	D2
Houjiaying[TJ]	42	B2
Houjituo[TJ]	42	C2
Houling[HEN]	106	H4
Houling[HI]	128	D2
Houlingou[BJ]	36	C3
Houliujiakou[TJ]	42	B2
Houlung[TW]	186	D2
Houma[SX]	54	C6
Houmeng[SD]	102	D5
Houmiao[HEN]	106	G2

Hounantai[BJ]	36	E2	Huabeitun[SX]	54	D3	Huama[GS]	160	G6
Houpi[TW]	186	D3	Huabo Shan[LN]	62	I3	Huamawan[SD]	102	D3
Houping[CQ]	132	E2	Huabu[ZJ]	84	C3	Huamen[HN]	114	E5
Houping[CQ]	132	E5	Huachang[HI]	128	B2	Huamin[HL]	70	B5
Houping[HN]	114	C3	Huachi[GS]	160	I4	Huaming[TJ]	42	B3
Houqiao[BJ]	36	D3	Huachuan[HL]	70	F5	Huamu[BJ]	36	C3
Houren[ZJ]	84	D3	Huade[NM]	58	J7	Huan Jiang[GS]	160	H4
Houshan[GZ]	144	E3	Huadian[JL]	66	F6	Huan Shui[HB]	110	G3
Houshayu[BJ]	36	D3	Huadian[JL]	66	G5	Huan Xian[GS]	160	H4
Houshayu[BJ]	36	E3	Huading Shan[ZJ]	84	F3	Huanan[HL]	70	F5
Houshi[LN]	62	H2	Huadong[GX]	124	D4	Huan'an[SH]	74	C3
Houshui Wan[HI]	128	B2	Huadu Qu[GD]	118	F3	Huancheng[SD]	102	D5
Housuo[SX]	54	D2	Hua'eryuan[GS]	160	F3	Huandun[JS]	80	D2
Housuo[YN]	148	J5	Huagang[AH]	90	D5	Huang He(Yellow R.)[GS]	160	G4
Houtaizi[TJ]	42	B3	Huagu[AH]	90	F6	Huang He(Yellow R.)[HEN]	106	D3
Houwa[NX]	168	D3	Huaguo[HB]	110	D2	Huang He(Yellow R.)[NM]	58	T11
Houwu[ZJ]	84	D3	Huahai[GS]	160	C2	Huang He(Yellow R.)[NX]	168	C2
Houxi[ZJ]	84	C4	Huahaizi[GS]	160	B3	Huang He(Yellow R.)[QH]	164	K6
Houxian Ling[HI]	128	B3	Huai He[AH]	90	D3	Huang He(Yellow R.)[SD]	102	D2
Houxiang[TJ]	42	B2	Huai He[HB]	110	G2	Huang He(Yellow R.)[SN]	156	G4
Houxiaotun[TJ]	42	B4	Huai He[HEN]	106	F5	Huang He(Yellow R.)[SX]	54	B3
Houxinqiu[LN]	62	F2	Huai'an[HEB]	48	B3	Huang He(Yellow R.)[HEN]	106	G5
Houyang[FJ]	94	D3	Huai'an[JS]	80	E3	Huang Shan[AH]	90	D6
Houying[BJ]	36	D4	Huai'ancheng[HEB]	48	B3	Huang'an[CQ]	132	F2
Houying[SX]	54	E1	Huaibai[SN]	156	F5	Huanggang[JS]	80	G4
Houyu[CQ]	132	E1	Huaibao[GX]	124	G2	Huangbai He[HB]	110	E3
Houzhai[HEN]	106	E3	Huaibei[AH]	90	C3	Huangbai[FJ]	94	E2
Houzhai[JS]	80	F5	Huaibei[BJ]	36	D3	Huangbai[HN]	114	F4
Houzhang[SN]	156	E5	Huaibin[HEN]	106	G5	Huangbai[JX]	98	E3
Houzhen[SD]	102	E3	Huaide[JL]	66	E4	Huangbai[SC]	138	H9
Houzhenzi[SN]	156	D7	Huaihe[HB]	110	G2	Huangbaiyuan[SN]	156	D7
Houzhuang[SN]	156	F5	Huaihe[JS]	80	D4	Huangban[GZ]	144	H2
Hoxud[XJ]	172	K4	Huaihua[HN]	114	B5	Huangbao[HB]	110	E3
Hoyor Hudag[NM]	58	V11	Huaiji[GD]	118	E3	Huangbayi[SN]	156	C8
Hoyor Mod[NM]	58	T11	Huaijia[JL]	66	G2	Huangbei[JX]	98	C5
Hsiafu[TW]	186	E1	Huaijiu He[BJ]	36	C3	Huangbei[JX]	98	D4
Hsialun[TW]	186	D3	Huaikan[ZJ]	84	D1	Huangbeijiao[HEN]	106	D2
Hsiangshan[TW]	186	D2	Huailai[HEB]	48	C3	Huangbeiqiao[HN]	114	D5
Hsiaokang[TW]	186	D4	Huaili[ZJ]	84	E3	Huangbi[JX]	98	E4
Hsiaolan Yu[TW]	186	E5	Huaimao[GS]	160	D3	Huangbi'ao[ZJ]	84	F3
Hsiaolin[TW]	186	D3	Huainan[AH]	90	D4	Huangbizhuang Shuiku[HEB]	48	B5
Hsichi Yu[TW]	186	C3	Huaining[AH]	90	C6	Huangbu[FJ]	94	B3
Hsichuan Tao[FJ]	94	E3	Huainingwan[SN]	156	G3	Huangcai[HN]	114	E4
Hsienhsi[TW]	186	D2	Huaiqiao[HEB]	48	C7	Huangcao[HN]	114	F7
Hsihu[TW]	186	D2	Huairen[SD]	102	D2	Huangcaoling[NX]	168	B4
Hsihu[TW]	186	D3	Huairen[SX]	54	E2	Huangcaotan[NX]	168	C2
Hsikou[TW]	186	E3	Huairou Qu[BJ]	36	D3	Huangcha[TJ]	42	A3
Hsilo[TW]	186	D3	Huairou Shuiku[BJ]	36	D3	Huangcheng[JX]	98	C3
Hsincheng[TW]	186	E2	Huaisha He[BJ]	36	C3	Huangcheng[QH]	164	N3
Hsinchu[TW]	186	D2	Huaishu He[JS]	80	D3	Huangchuan[HEN]	106	G5
Hsinchu[TW]	186	E2	Huaixiang[GD]	118	D4	Huangcun[GD]	118	H3
Hsinfeng[TW]	186	D2	Huaiyang[HEN]	106	F4	Huangcun[GX]	124	H3
Hsinhua[TW]	186	D3	Huaiyin Qu[JS]	80	E3	Huangcun[SX]	54	B6
Hsin—i[TW]	186	D3	Huaiyu Shan[JX]	98	E3	Huangda Yang[ZJ]	84	G2
Hsinkang Shan[TW]	186	E3	Huaiyuan[AH]	90	D4	Huangdao Qu[SD]	102	G4
Hsinpi[TW]	186	D4	Huaiyuan[GX]	124	F3	Huangdi[HEB]	48	E2
Hsinsheng[TW]	186	D2	Huaizhen[HEB]	48	D5	Huangdi[LN]	62	D4
Hsintien[TW]	186	E2	Huaji[AH]	90	B4	Huangdian[SD]	102	B4
Hsinwu[TW]	186	E2	Huaji[AH]	90	D5	Huangdong[GX]	124	I3
Hsinyuan[TW]	186	D4	Huajia[JL]	66	F3	Huangdu[SH]	74	C2
Hsitou[TW]	186	D3	Huajia[YN]	148	K7	Huangdun[AH]	90	C6
Hsiukuluan Hsi[TW]	186	E3	Huajian[GS]	160	E4	Huangdun[JS]	80	D2
Hsiukuluan Shan[TW]	186	E3	Huajian[HEB]	48	F3	Huangdun[SD]	102	F4
Hsiulin[TW]	186	E2	Huajian[NM]	58	V11	Huangduobu[NX]	168	C4
Hsiungkung[TW]	186	E2	Huajiang[GZ]	144	D5	Huangfu[SN]	156	H1
Hsiyin Tao[FJ]	94	F3	Huajiang[HN]	114	D7	Huanggai Hu[HN]	114	F3
Hsiyu[TW]	186	C3	Huajianzi[LN]	62	I3	Huanggainao Shuiku[HEB]	48	B2
Hsueh Shan[TW]	186	E2	Huajue[GZ]	144	E3	Huanggainao[HEB]	48	C2
Hsuehchia[TW]	186	D3	Hualan[GX]	124	E6	Huanggang Liang[NM]	58	L6
Hsuhai[TW]	186	D4	Huale[SX]	54	C5	Huanggang Shan[FJ]	94	C3
Hu Xian[SN]	156	E6	Huali[GZ]	144	F3	Huanggang Shuiku[TJ]	42	C3
Hu Zhen[CQ]	132	E3	Huali[SN]	156	F8	Huanggang[AH]	90	B4
Hu Zhen[ZJ]	84	D3	Hualiangting Shuiku[AH]	90	C6	Huanggang[AH]	90	C6
Hu Zhen[ZJ]	84	E4	Hualien Hsi[TW]	186	E3	Huanggang[HB]	110	H4
Hua Shan[SN]	156	F6	Hualien Kang[TW]	186	E3	Huanggang[HEN]	106	E5
Hua Shan[SN]	156	G6	Hualien[TW]	186	E3	Huanggang[JX]	98	B3
Hua Xian[HEN]	106	F3	Hualin[JX]	98	C2	Huanggang[JX]	98	B3
Hua Xian[SN]	156	F6	Hualinshan[JX]	98	C3	Huanggang[JX]	98	E2
Hua Yu[TW]	186	C3	Hualinsi[HB]	110	E3	Huanggang[SD]	102	C5
Hua'an[FJ]	94	C4	Hualong[GX]	124	H3	Huanggualiang[QH]	164	D2
Hua'ao Dao[ZJ]	84	F3	Hualong[QH]	164	O4	Huangguan[GX]	124	I2
Huabaoliang[NX]	168	C4	Hualongyan[HB]	110	D2	Huangguan[SN]	156	E7
Huabei Pingyuan[HEB]	48	C6	Hualou[SD]	102	D2	Huangguoshu Pubu[GZ]	144	D5
Huabei[HEN]	106	F4	Hualu[SH]	74	D2	Huangguoshu[GZ]	144	D5

Name	Page	Grid
Huanghe Kou[SD]	102	F2
Huanghe Zongqu[NM]	58	T11
Huanghe(Yellw R.)[NM]	58	G7
Huanghe[CQ]	132	E4
Huanghe[JL]	66	F5
Huanghe[QH]	164	K6
Huanghekou[SD]	102	E2
Huangheya[SD]	102	C2
Huangheying[SD]	102	G2
Huanghongjie[SN]	156	F3
Huanghu[AH]	90	E5
Huanghua[HEB]	48	E5
Huanghua[NX]	168	C5
Huanghua[SD]	102	F4
Huanghua[ZJ]	84	E5
Huanghuacheng[BJ]	36	C3
Huanghuadian[LN]	62	G4
Huanghuadian[TJ]	42	A3
Huanghuashan[NM]	58	N5
Huanghuatan[GS]	160	F4
Huanghuatang[JS]	80	D4
Huanghuawopu[NM]	58	X10
Huangji[HB]	110	F2
Huangjia[LN]	62	D4
Huangjia[ZJ]	84	C4
Huangjiaba[GZ]	144	F3
Huangjiaci[HB]	110	D3
Huangjiao Shan[ZJ]	84	F4
Huangjiao[GS]	160	G4
Huangjiazhai[GZ]	144	C4
Huangjin[GX]	124	F3
Huangjin[JL]	66	E3
Huangjin[JX]	98	C2
Huangjinbu[JX]	98	D3
Huangjindong[HN]	114	G4
Huangjinxia[SN]	156	D7
Huangkang[FJ]	94	D3
Huangkeng[FJ]	94	C2
Huangkeng[GD]	118	G1
Huangkou[AH]	90	C2
Huangla[GZ]	144	E4
Huanglang[SC]	138	I7
Huanglang[ZJ]	84	F4
Huanglaomen[JX]	98	C2
Huanglei[HN]	114	A5
Huangli[JS]	80	E5
Huanglian Shan[GX]	124	D4
Huanglian[GZ]	144	F2
Huangliang[HB]	110	D3
Huanglianguan[SC]	138	H8
Huanglianyu[FJ]	94	B4
Huangligang[NX]	168	C2
Huanglin[JX]	98	C6
Huangling[AH]	90	B3
Huangling[GX]	124	H5
Huangling[HI]	128	C2
Huangling[JX]	98	D2
Huangling[SN]	156	F5
Huangling[SX]	54	D4
Huanglishu Shuiku[AH]	90	E4
Huangliu[HI]	128	A3
Huanglong Shan[SN]	156	F4
Huanglong[SN]	156	F5
Huanglongtan Shuiku[HB]	110	D2
Huanglou[HEN]	106	F5
Huanglu[SH]	74	D2
Huangludian[HEN]	106	D4
Huangmao Hai[GD]	118	F4
Huangmao Jian[ZJ]	84	D5
Huangmao[GX]	124	G4
Huangmaoling[YN]	148	H7
Huangmaoyuan[HN]	114	C5
Huangmei[HB]	110	I4
Huangmei[HEB]	48	B3
Huangmian[GX]	124	G3
Huangmiao[AH]	90	D3
Huangnan[ZJ]	84	E4
Huangni He[GZ]	144	C5
Huangni He[YN]	148	J6
Huangni[AH]	90	C6
Huangni[HN]	114	F6
Huangnian[SX]	54	E5
Huangnibao[GS]	160	D3
Huangnihe[HL]	70	F7
Huangnihe[JL]	66	I4
Huangnihe[YN]	148	J5
Huangnitang[GZ]	144	D3
Huangniupu[SN]	156	C6
Huangniushi[GD]	118	G2
Huangniuti[SX]	54	E5
Huangpi Hu[AH]	90	D5
Huangpi Qu[HB]	110	H4
Huangping[GZ]	144	F4
Huangpo[GD]	118	C5
Huangpu Jiang[SH]	74	C3
Huangpu Qu[GD]	118	F3
Huangpu[AH]	90	C2
Huangqi[FJ]	94	E3
Huangqi[HEB]	48	D2
Huangqiao He[JS]	80	F4
Huangqiao[JS]	80	F4
Huangqiao[JX]	98	C4
Huangquqiao[NX]	168	C1
Huangsangping[HN]	114	C6
Huangsha[GD]	118	H3
Huangsha[HN]	114	E7
Huangsha[JX]	98	B3
Huangshagang[JS]	80	F3
Huangshahe[GX]	124	I1
Huangshajie[HN]	114	F3
Huangshan Qu[AH]	90	E6
Huangshan[AH]	90	E7
Huangshan[SD]	102	F3
Huangshan[ZJ]	84	E3
Huangshanguan[SD]	102	G2
Huangshankou[HEN]	106	E4
Huangshanpu[SD]	102	E4
Huangshantou[HB]	110	F5
Huangshaping[HN]	114	E7
Huangshawo[NX]	168	C3
Huangshen[SH]	74	C2
Huangshi Shuiku[HN]	114	D3
Huangshi[CQ]	132	E3
Huangshi[FJ]	94	E4
Huangshi[GD]	118	H2
Huangshi[HB]	110	I4
Huangshi[HN]	114	E6
Huangshi[JX]	98	F3
Huangshicha[BJ]	36	D2
Huangshikou[HEB]	48	B4
Huangshui[CQ]	132	E3
Huangsi[HEB]	48	B6
Huangsongdian[JL]	66	H4
Huangsongyu[BJ]	36	E3
Huangta[BJ]	36	B4
Huangtai[BJ]	36	B3
Huangtan[FJ]	94	C3
Huangtan[JX]	98	E2
Huangtan[ZJ]	84	E3
Huangtan[ZJ]	84	F3
Huangtang[HN]	114	E6
Huangtankou Shuiku[ZJ]	84	C4
Huangtian[FJ]	94	D3
Huangtian[GD]	118	G3
Huangtian[ZJ]	84	C5
Huangtianpu[HN]	114	D6
Huangtong[HI]	128	B2
Huangtu Gaoyuan[GS]	160	G4
Huangtu Gaoyuan[NX]	168	A4
Huangtu Gaoyuan[SN]	156	C4
Huangtu[CQ]	132	C3
Huangtu[GZ]	144	G2
Huangtu[HN]	114	B6
Huangtu[JS]	80	F5
Huangtu[SX]	54	C5
Huangtudian[HN]	114	D4
Huangtugang[BJ]	36	C3
Huangtukan[HEB]	48	E2
Huangtukan[LN]	62	G5
Huangtukuang[HN]	114	C6
Huangtuling[BJ]	36	E3
Huangtuliangzi[HEB]	48	F2
Huangtuling[HN]	114	F5
Huangtun[SD]	102	C4
Huangtun[TJ]	42	A2
Huangwan[AH]	90	D3
Huangwan[SN]	156	D3
Huangwan[ZJ]	84	E2
Huangwei Yu[TW]	186	G1
Huangwei[AH]	90	C5
Huangwei[JS]	80	E2
Huangwutun[GX]	124	F6
Huangxikou[HN]	114	C5
Huangxing Dao[ZJ]	84	G2
Huangxu[JS]	80	E4
Huangyaguan[TJ]	42	B1
Huangyan Dao[HI]	128	G5
Huangyan Qu[ZJ]	84	F4
Huangyang He[SN]	156	F8
Huangyang[ZJ]	84	E4
Huangyangchuan[GS]	160	F4
Huangyangsi[HN]	114	D6
Huangyao[GX]	124	I3
Huangyin[CQ]	132	C4
Huangying[JS]	80	E3
Huangyuan[QH]	164	N4
Huangyunpu[HB]	110	D1
Huangze Shan[ZJ]	84	G2
Huangze Yang[ZJ]	84	G2
Huangzhai[ZJ]	84	D3
Huangzhawan[GS]	160	C2
Huangzhen[AH]	90	C6
Huangzhen[SD]	102	B4
Huangzhong[QH]	164	N4
Huangzhou[JX]	98	C3
Huangzhu[HI]	128	C2
Huangzhuang[HEN]	106	C5
Huangzhuang[TJ]	42	C3
Huanian[YN]	148	H6
Huaniao Shan[ZJ]	84	G2
Huaning[YN]	148	H6
Huanjiang[GX]	124	F3
Huankou[JS]	80	B2
Huanren Shuiku[LN]	62	I3
Huanren[LN]	62	I3
Huanshan[TW]	186	E2
Huantai[SD]	102	E3
Huanxi[FJ]	94	E3
Huanxi[HN]	114	F6
Huapao[HL]	70	F5
Huapidianzi[JL]	66	K4
Huaping Yu[TW]	186	E1
Huaping[GX]	124	D3
Huaping[GZ]	144	F2
Huaping[HB]	110	C4
Huaping[SN]	156	F9
Huaping[YN]	148	G4
Huapingzi[SN]	156	G7
Huapiyao[HL]	70	D3
Huaqiao[FJ]	94	C2
Huaqiao[FJ]	94	D2
Huaqiao[FJ]	94	D2
Huaqiao[GZ]	144	G3
Huaqiao[HN]	114	C5
Huaqiao[JX]	98	B3
Huaqiao[SD]	102	E5
Huaqiao[ZJ]	84	F4
Huaqiu[GZ]	144	E2
Huaquan[HN]	114	E6
Huarong Qu[HB]	110	H4
Huarong[HN]	114	E3
Huashan[GX]	124	F2
Huashan[HB]	110	G3
Huashan[HL]	70	D5
Huashan[JS]	80	B2
Huashan[JX]	98	B3
Huashan[SD]	102	D3
Huashan[SD]	102	G3
Huashan[YN]	148	J3
Huashaoying[HEB]	48	B3
Huashi Shan[GD]	118	F2
Huashi[AH]	90	B5
Huashi[HEN]	106	E3
Huashixia[QH]	164	K5
Huashiya[SN]	156	G2
Huashu[JL]	66	H6
Huashulinzi[JL]	66	H4
Huatang[HN]	114	E7
Huatanshan[JX]	98	E3
Huating[GS]	160	H5
Huating[JX]	98	F3
Huating[SH]	74	C2

Huatou Jian[SC]	138	H7
Huaxi Qu[GZ]	144	E4
Huaxi[GZ]	144	E3
Huaxi[SC]	138	I6
Huaxi[YN]	148	I6
Huaxicun[JS]	80	F5
Huaxin[SH]	74	C2
Huaxin[SH]	74	C3
Huaxing[FJ]	94	C4
Huayan[CQ]	132	B3
Huayang[AH]	90	C6
Huayang[SH]	74	C2
Huayang[SN]	156	D7
Huayang[SN]	156	F6
Huayin[SN]	156	G6
Huaying Shan[SC]	138	L5
Huaying[SC]	138	L5
Huayu[SD]	102	C5
Huayu[SX]	54	B6
Huayuan He[GZ]	144	H2
Huayuan Hu[AH]	90	D4
Huayuan[AH]	90	C4
Huayuan[BJ]	36	E2
Huayuan[HB]	110	I4
Huayuan[HEN]	106	G3
Huayuan[HL]	70	C5
Huayuan[HN]	114	B4
Huayuan[HN]	114	C6
Huayuan[JX]	98	C2
Huayuan[SD]	102	E5
Huayuan[SN]	156	G6
Huayuankou[HEN]	106	E3
Huayuankou[JL]	66	H5
Huazhai[GS]	160	E3
Huazhou[GD]	118	C5
Huazhuang[HB]	110	E3
Huazhuang[HEN]	106	G5
Huazhuangzi[TJ]	42	B3
Huaziping[SN]	156	F3
Hubei[SX]	54	D3
Hubeikou[HB]	110	C1
Huchang[HB]	110	G4
Huchen[ZJ]	84	F3
Hucheng[AH]	90	D4
Hucun[FJ]	94	B3
Hucun[JX]	98	E3
Huder[NM]	58	N2
Hudi[SX]	54	D6
Hudian[HEN]	106	F5
Hudong[JS]	80	D2
Hufang[FJ]	94	C3
Hufang[JX]	98	E4
Hugang[FJ]	94	B5
Hugezhuang[HEB]	48	F4
Hugou[AH]	90	D3
Huguan[SX]	54	E5
Huguo[YN]	148	D6
Huhe[HB]	110	I4
Huhsi[TW]	186	C3
Huhu[AH]	90	C4
Hui He[AH]	90	C3
Hui He[NM]	58	M3
Hui He[SX]	54	D2
Hui Shan[JS]	80	F5
Hui Shui[AH]	90	E6
Hui Xian[GS]	160	H6
Hui'an[FJ]	94	D4
Hui'anpu[NX]	168	C3
Huibaoling Shuiku[SD]	102	D5
Huibie Yang[ZJ]	84	F2
Huibu[JX]	98	C3
Huibu[JX]	98	C3
Huibu[SD]	102	F3
Huichang[JX]	98	C6
Huicheng Qu[GD]	118	G3
Huichuan[GS]	160	F5
Huidong[GD]	118	G4
Huidong[SC]	138	H9
Huidong[SH]	74	D2
Huidun[JS]	80	E2
Huifa He[JL]	66	G5
Huifa[HL]	70	E6
Huifacheng[JL]	66	G5
Huifeng[JS]	80	G5
Huigu[AH]	90	D3
Huiji He[HEN]	106	F3
Huiji Shan[ZJ]	84	E3
Huijiao[SH]	74	D3
Huijiazhuang[SX]	54	C4
Huijiazhuang[TJ]	42	C2
Huikou[AH]	90	C7
Huilai[GD]	118	I3
Huili[SC]	138	H9
Huili[SX]	54	C4
Huilong[GD]	118	F2
Huilong[GX]	124	H3
Huilong[GX]	124	I3
Huilong[GZ]	144	D5
Huilong[SC]	138	I4
Huilong[SN]	156	F7
Huilong[SX]	54	C5
Huilongguan[BJ]	36	C3
Huilongsi[HN]	114	D6
Huilongxu[HN]	114	D7
Huimin[SD]	102	D2
Huimin[YN]	148	F8
Huimin[ZJ]	84	E2
Huiminxiang[NX]	168	C2
Huinan[JL]	66	G5
Huinan[JL]	66	G5
Huinan[SH]	74	D2
Huining[GS]	160	G5
Huining[HEB]	48	B6
Huinong Qu[NX]	168	C1
Huinong Qu[NX]	168	C2
Huiqi[HL]	70	D5
Huishan Qu[JS]	80	F5
Huishan[HI]	128	C2
Huishan[ZJ]	84	E3
Huishangang[HN]	114	E4
Huishui[GZ]	144	E4
Huishui[SN]	156	E8
Huitai[NX]	168	C5
Huitan[FJ]	94	D2
Huiten Gol[GS]	160	C3
Huiten Nur[QH]	164	D5
Huiting[HEN]	106	H3
Huitong[HN]	114	B6
Huitong[JX]	98	D5
Huiwan[HB]	110	C2
Huiwen[HI]	128	C2
Huixian[HEN]	106	E2
Huixing[CQ]	132	C4
Huiyang Qu[GD]	118	G4
Huiyao[HEB]	48	C3
Huiyu[BJ]	36	C3
Huize[YN]	148	I4
Huizhai[GD]	118	I3
Huizhou Qu[AH]	90	E7
Huizhou[GD]	118	G3
Huizhou[LN]	62	C3
Huji[AH]	90	C4
Huji[HB]	110	F3
Huji[SD]	102	C4
Huji[SD]	102	D2
Hujia[HL]	70	E4
Hujia[JL]	66	G3
Hujia[LN]	62	E3
Hujia[LN]	62	F3
Hujia[SC]	138	M4
Hujiaba[SN]	156	C8
Hujiadian[BJ]	36	E3
Hujianao[NX]	168	B4
Hujiang[JX]	98	B5
Hujianshan[SN]	156	E3
Hujiao[JX]	98	F3
Hujiaying[HB]	110	D2
Hujiayuan[SN]	156	F7
Hujiazhuang[SD]	102	F3
Hujinzhuang[TJ]	42	C3
Hujir Gu[NM]	58	W11
Hujirt[XJ]	172	I2
Hukeng[FJ]	94	B5
Hukou Pubu[SN]	156	G4
Hukou Pubu[SX]	54	B5
Hukou[HN]	114	F6
Hukou[JX]	98	D2
Hukou[SX]	54	B5
Hukou[TW]	186	E2
Hulan Erge Qu[HL]	70	B5
Hulan He[HL]	70	D5
Hulan He[JL]	66	H3
Hulan Qu[HL]	70	D6
Hulan[JL]	66	G4
Hule[AH]	90	E6
Huli Qu[FJ]	94	D5
Hulianzhuang[TJ]	42	B4
Hulin[FJ]	94	C4
Hulin[HL]	70	G6
Huliu He[HEB]	48	B4
Huliu He[SX]	54	F2
Huliuzi[TJ]	42	A3
Hulqut[NM]	58	C6
Hulstai[NM]	58	T10
Hulu He[GS]	160	G5
Hulu He[NX]	168	B5
Hulu He[SN]	156	F5
Hulu Hu[QH]	164	D6
Hulu Shan[GX]	124	E5
Hulu[HN]	114	B4
Huludao[LN]	62	D4
Hulufa[BJ]	36	C4
Hulukou[SC]	138	H9
Hulun Buir[NM]	58	M3
Hulun Nur[NM]	58	L3
Hulushan Wan[LN]	62	E5
Huma He[HL]	70	B3
Huma He[HL]	70	C2
Huma[HL]	70	D3
Humen[GD]	118	F4
Hun He[LN]	62	F3
Hun He[LN]	62	H2
Hun He[SX]	54	E2
Hun Jiang[JL]	66	F6
Hun Jiang[LN]	62	I3
Hunan[JX]	98	D4
Hunanzhen Shuiku[ZJ]	84	C4
Hunchun He[JL]	66	K5
Hunchun[JL]	66	K5
Hunei[TW]	186	D4
Hung Fa Leng[HK]	176	D1
Hung Fa Ngan[HK]	176	B3
Hung Hom[HK]	176	D3
Hung Lung Hang[HK]	176	D1
Hung Shek Mun Tsuen[HK]	176	E1
Hung Shui Kiu[HK]	176	B2
Hunjiang[LN]	62	I4
Hunyuan[SX]	54	E2
Huo Shan[AH]	90	C5
Huo Shan[SX]	54	C5
Huochangping[HN]	114	D5
Huocheng[XJ]	172	H3
Huodao[GD]	118	E4
Huodoushan[HEB]	48	E3
Huogang[BJ]	36	C3
Huogezhuang[TJ]	42	B2
Huohong[YN]	148	I4
Huojia[HEN]	106	E2
Huojialaozhuang[NX]	168	C4
Huoju[SH]	74	C2
Huokou[FJ]	94	E3
Huolianpo[HN]	114	D3
Huolong[HEN]	106	E3
Huolong[JS]	80	G4
Huolongmen[HL]	70	C4
Huolu[CQ]	132	D4
Huomachong[HN]	114	C5
Huopai[HB]	110	F2
Huoqiu[AH]	90	C4
Huoshan[AH]	90	C5
Huoshaoliao[TW]	186	E2
Huoshaoping[HB]	110	D4
Huoshi[CQ]	132	E4
Huoshiying[HEB]	48	F4
Huoshizhai[NX]	168	B4
Huoshui[HEB]	48	A7
Huotian[FJ]	94	C5
Huotong Xi[FJ]	94	E3
Huotong[FJ]	94	E3
Huoxian[BJ]	36	D4
Huoxing[SH]	74	C2
Huoyan Shan[SX]	54	B6

Huozhou[SX] 54 C5
Huozhuangzi[TJ] 42 B3
Hupei[FJ] 94 E3
Huping Shan[HN] 114 C2
Hupingshan[HN] 114 C3
Huqiao[SH] 74 C3
Huqin Ail[NM] 58 X11
Huqiu[FJ] 94 C4
Hure Bulang[NM] 58 U10
Hure Qi[NM] 58 N6
Hureng Tohoi[QH] 164 E4
Huret[JL] 66 B2
Huret[NM] 58 M3
Hurleg Hu[QH] 164 I3
Hurun[GX] 124 D5
Hushan Shuiku[HI] 128 C2
Hushan[FJ] 94 B5
Hushan[HI] 128 C2
Hushan[JX] 98 C6
Hushan[LN] 62 H4
Hushan[SD] 102 F4
Hushi[GZ] 144 D2
Hushiha[HEB] 48 D3
Hustai He[NM] 58 W11
Hutang[FJ] 94 D2
Hutiao[SC] 138 K4
Hutiaoxia[YN] 148 F3
Hutou[FJ] 94 D4
Hutou[HL] 70 G6
Hutou[SD] 102 E4
Hutubi[XJ] 172 K3
Hutun[SD] 102 C3
Hutuo He[HEB] 48 B5
Hutuo He[SX] 54 D3
Huwan[HEN] 106 F6
Huwan[JX] 98 D4
Huwei[JX] 98 D3
Huwei[TW] 186 D3
Huxi[FJ] 94 C5
Huxi[JX] 98 C4
Huxincun[HI] 128 C1
Huxingshan[HN] 114 C5
Huxingshan[JX] 98 D3
Huyang[AH] 90 E5
Huyang[FJ] 94 B4
Huyang[FJ] 94 D4
Huyang[HEN] 106 D5
Huying[HB] 110 E3
Huyuan Xi[ZJ] 84 D3
Huyuan[FJ] 94 C3
Huyuan[HL] 70 B3
Huyuan[TJ] 42 B3
Huzhai[ZJ] 84 E3
Huzhang[SX] 54 C6
Huzhong[HL] 70 B2
Huzhou[ZJ] 84 E2
Huzhu[QH] 164 N4
Huzhuang[SH] 74 C2

I

Ih Jirin Gol[NM] 58 L5
Ih Tol Gol[NM] 58 N2
Ih Ulan[QH] 164 M3
I-lan[TW] 186 E2
Ili He[XJ] 172 H4
Inder[QH] 164 M4
Inggen[NM] 58 F7
Iqe He[QH] 164 G3
Iqe[QH] 164 G3
Issikbulak[XJ] 172 E7

J

Jabhlangt[NM] 58 W11
Jagdaqi[NM] 58 P2
Jaggang[XZ] 152 F4
Jaggong[SC] 138 F5
Jaggong[XZ] 152 H4
Jagka[XZ] 152 K5

Jagritang[QH] 164 M8
Jah Namag[NM] 58 D7
Jah Us[NM] 58 T11
Jainca[QH] 164 O5
Jaincatang[QH] 164 N5
Jalaid Qi[NM] 58 O4
Jam[XJ] 172 H5
Jamda[QH] 164 M7
Jamda[XZ] 152 I4
Jangngai Shan[XZ] 152 E3
Jangngai Zangbo[XZ] 152 E3
Jarantai[NM] 58 F8
Jardine's Lookout[HK] 176 D3
Jargal Saihan[NM] 58 F9
Jargalang[XJ] 172 I4
Jargalangt[NM] 58 I6
Jargalangt[NM] 58 K5
Jargalangt[NM] 58 T10
Jarud Qi[NM] 58 N5
Jasamka[XZ] 152 J4
Jasammari[XZ] 152 B2
Jegestei[NM] 58 W11
Jeminay[XJ] 172 J2
Jenai[TW] 186 E2
Jenwu[TW] 186 D4
Ji Qu[QH] 164 H8
Ji Qu[QH] 164 L7
Ji Xian[SX] 54 B5
Ji Xian[TJ] 42 B1
Jia Xian[HEN] 106 E4
Jia Xian[SN] 156 G2
Jiabang[GZ] 144 G5
Jiabeiyan[LN] 62 C4
Jiabi[CQ] 132 E4
Jiabi[SC] 138 H4
Jiachao[HI] 128 C3
Jiache[YN] 148 H7
Jiache[YN] 148 I5
Jiacun[HEB] 48 C5
Jiading Qu[SH] 74 C2
Jiading[SH] 74 C2
Jiafang[GX] 124 F4
Jiafeng[SX] 54 D6
Jiagao[CQ] 132 F3
Jiagou[AH] 90 C4
Jiahe[GS] 160 F3
Jiahe[HB] 110 D2
Jiahe[HN] 114 E7
Jiahe[YN] 148 G8
Jiahu[JX] 98 B7
Jiajia[SH] 74 C3
Jiajiang[SC] 138 I6
Jiajiaping[SN] 156 G4
Jiajiatun[SX] 54 F1
Jiajiawa[TJ] 42 B4
Jiajiawazi[BJ] 36 D3
Jiajin Shan[SC] 138 H5
Jiajiu[GZ] 144 G5
Jiajiu[YN] 148 G6
Jiake[YN] 148 I7
Jialai[HI] 128 B2
Jiale[HI] 128 B2
Jialiang[GZ] 144 F5
Jialidui[HI] 128 B2
Jialing Jiang[CQ] 132 C3
Jialing Jiang[SC] 138 L5
Jialing Jiang[SN] 156 C7
Jialing Qu[SC] 138 L5
Jialing[GS] 160 H6
Jialou[HEN] 106 E5
Jialu[SN] 156 G6
Jiamao[HI] 128 B3
Jiameihu[QH] 164 F2
Jiamusi[HL] 70 F5
Jian He[HEN] 106 D3
Jian Jiang[GD] 118 C5
Jian Ling[HI] 128 B3
Jian Xi[FJ] 94 D3
Ji'an[CQ] 132 B4
Ji'an[FJ] 94 D4
Ji'an[JL] 66 G6
Ji'an[JX] 98 B4
Ji'an[JX] 98 B4
Ji'an[SC] 138 L5

Jian'ai[GX] 124 F3
Jianba[GZ] 144 F2
Jianbang[SH] 74 C2
Jianbi[JS] 80 E4
Jianbian Erdui[HL] 70 C4
Jiancaichang[NX] 168 B2
Jiancao[YN] 148 E4
Jiancaoping Qu[SX] 54 D4
Jiancha[GZ] 144 F2
Jianchang[LN] 62 C4
Jianchangying[HEB] 48 F3
Jiancheng[GD] 118 D3
Jiancheping[HN] 114 C4
Jianchewan[SN] 156 E7
Jianchi[SN] 156 D8
Jianchuan[YN] 148 E4
Jiandao Feng[XJ] 172 H8
Jiande[ZJ] 84 D3
Jiandou[FJ] 94 C4
Jianfang[HEB] 48 E2
Jianfeng Ling[HI] 128 A3
Jianfeng[HI] 128 A3
Jiang Xian[SX] 54 C6
Jiangan He[TJ] 42 B2
Jiang'an[SC] 138 K7
Jiangao Shan[YN] 148 D5
Jiangba[JS] 80 D3
Jiangbei Qu[CQ] 132 C4
Jiangbei[HN] 114 F4
Jiangbian[HI] 128 B3
Jiangbian[SH] 74 D1
Jiangbian[YN] 148 G5
Jiangbian[YN] 148 I6
Jiangbiancun[JX] 98 C4
Jiangcheng[GX] 124 E4
Jiangcheng[YN] 148 G8
Jiangchi[CQ] 132 E4
Jiangchuan[YN] 148 H6
Jiangcun[BJ] 36 D2
Jiangcun[HN] 114 D7
Jiangcun[JX] 98 E2
Jiangcun[SN] 156 E6
Jiangcun[SX] 54 E3
Jiangdian[AH] 90 B5
Jiangdian[JL] 66 F6
Jiangdianzi[AH] 90 C4
Jiangding[NX] 168 C2
Jiangdong[HN] 114 E7
Jiangdong[TJ] 42 B2
Jiangdu[JS] 80 E4
Jiange[SC] 138 K3
Jiangfang[FJ] 94 C2
Jianggang[JS] 80 F4
Jianggen[ZJ] 84 D5
Jianggezhuang[HEB] 48 G4
Jianggezhuang[SD] 102 H2
Jianghai[SH] 74 C3
Jianghe[QH] 164 L3
Jianghong[GD] 118 B5
Jianghua[HN] 114 D7
Jiangji[AH] 90 C3
Jiangjia[HN] 114 C5
Jiangjia[SH] 74 C2
Jiangjiadian[HEB] 48 E1
Jiangjiadian[SD] 102 C2
Jiangjiahu[AH] 90 C4
Jiangjiajie[JL] 66 F5
Jiangjiaping[SX] 54 D2
Jiangjiayan[HB] 110 C2
Jiangjiehe[GZ] 144 F3
Jiangjin Qu[CQ] 132 C4
Jiangjing[FJ] 94 E4
Jiangjunguan[BJ] 36 E3
Jiangjunmiao[XJ] 172 L3
Jiangjunmu[HEB] 48 B6
Jiangjuntou[FJ] 94 C5
Jiangkou Shuiku[JX] 98 B4
Jiangkou[AH] 90 C4
Jiangkou[AH] 90 D6
Jiangkou[CQ] 132 D4
Jiangkou[CQ] 132 E2
Jiangkou[FJ] 94 D2
Jiangkou[GS] 160 G5
Jiangkou[GZ] 144 G3

Jiangkou[HEN]	106	H3
Jiangkou[HN]	114	B6
Jiangkou[HN]	114	D6
Jiangkou[JX]	98	C6
Jiangkou[SN]	156	D7
Jiangkou[SN]	156	E7
Jiangkou[ZJ]	84	F3
Jiangkouxu[HN]	114	B5
Jiangle[FJ]	94	C3
Jiangling[HB]	110	F4
Jianglou[SD]	102	C3
Jiangluo[GS]	160	G6
Jiangmen[GD]	118	F4
Jiangmifeng[JL]	66	G4
Jiangnan[HN]	114	F3
Jiangniang Shuidianzhan[QH]	164	M6
Jiangning Qu[JS]	80	D5
Jiangou[BJ]	36	C3
Jiangqiao[HL]	70	B5
Jiangqiao[JS]	80	E4
Jiangqiao[SH]	74	C2
Jiangshan[GX]	124	F6
Jiangshan[ZJ]	84	C4
Jiangshang[JX]	98	C2
Jiangshu[JS]	80	E5
Jiangshui[HEB]	48	A6
Jiangtai[BJ]	36	C4
Jiangtai[NX]	168	B5
Jiangtang[AH]	90	C6
Jiangtang[SX]	54	E4
Jiangtian[FJ]	94	E4
Jiangtou[GD]	118	G1
Jiangtou[GX]	124	G3
Jiangtousi[HN]	114	C6
Jiangtouwei[JX]	98	C6
Jiangtun[GD]	118	E3
Jiangui[NM]	58	G8
Jiangguo[HEB]	48	C6
Jiangwakou[TJ]	42	C2
Jiangwan[GD]	118	F2
Jiangwan[HL]	70	B5
Jiangxi[GX]	124	F5
Jiangxia Qu[HB]	110	H4
Jiangxiadian[AH]	90	C5
Jiangxigou[QH]	164	M4
Jiangxin[AH]	90	E5
Jiangyan[JS]	80	F4
Jiangyin[FJ]	94	E4
Jiangyin[JS]	80	F5
Jiangying[GD]	118	E2
Jiangyong[HN]	114	D7
Jiangyou[SC]	138	J4
Jiangyu[SD]	102	E3
Jiangyuan[JL]	66	G5
Jiangyuan Qu[JL]	66	I4
Jiangzhen[SH]	74	D2
Jiangzhou[GX]	124	E5
Jiangzhou[SC]	138	H9
Jiangzhuang[HEN]	106	E4
Jiangzhuang[SH]	74	C3
Jiangzuo[HEN]	106	D3
Jianhe[GZ]	144	G4
Jianhu[JS]	80	E3
Jianhuai[JS]	80	E3
Jianjiang[FJ]	94	E3
Jiankang[SC]	138	G9
Jiankou[SD]	102	F3
Jianli[HB]	110	F5
Jianli[SD]	102	C2
Jianmin[SN]	156	E8
Jiannan[HB]	110	B4
Jianning[FJ]	94	B3
Jiannong[CQ]	132	F2
Jian'ou[FJ]	94	D2
Jianping[LN]	62	C3
Jianping[LN]	62	C3
Jianqiao[SH]	74	C2
Jianquan[NX]	168	C1
Jianquansizhan[NX]	168	C1
Jianshan[GS]	160	G6
Jianshan[HB]	110	B5
Jianshan[HI]	128	C2
Jianshan[LN]	62	F5
Jianshanzi[HL]	70	G5
Jianshe[AH]	90	C4
Jianshe[FJ]	94	C4
Jianshe[FJ]	94	C6
Jianshe[GS]	160	B3
Jianshe[HL]	70	D5
Jianshe[QH]	164	L7
Jianshe[SH]	74	C1
Jiansheying Linsuo[HL]	70	E5
Jianshi[HB]	110	C4
Jianshui[YN]	148	H7
Jiantang[HL]	70	F6
Jiantian[JX]	98	B5
Jiantianjie[JX]	98	D2
Jiantong Tag[XJ]	172	G7
Jiantou[GD]	118	G2
Jiantouji[SD]	102	D5
Jianxi[AH]	90	E4
Jianxi[FJ]	94	C3
Jianxi[FJ]	94	D3
Jianxin[SH]	74	C2
Jianxin[TJ]	42	B4
Jianxing[SC]	138	K4
Jianyang[FJ]	94	D2
Jianyang[SC]	138	J5
Jianyi[LN]	62	F4
Jianyucha[SN]	156	F3
Jianzha[SH]	74	C1
Jianzhang[SX]	54	E5
Jianzhong[GZ]	144	F3
Jianzhong[SH]	74	D1
Jiao He[SD]	102	F3
Jiao Jiang[ZJ]	84	F4
Jiao Qu[SX]	54	E4
Jiao Qu[SX]	54	E5
Jiao Xi[FJ]	94	E2
Jiaoba[GZ]	144	G2
Jiaobei[SX]	54	B6
Jiaocha[NX]	168	C4
Jiaochang[SC]	138	I3
Jiaocheng[SX]	54	D4
Jiaodao[BJ]	36	C4
Jiaodao[ZJ]	84	D3
Jiaodi[SX]	54	C6
Jiaogong[GS]	160	G6
Jiaohe[HEB]	48	D5
Jiaohe[JL]	66	H4
Jiaojiang[GX]	124	H2
Jiaojiazhuang[GS]	160	E3
Jiaokeng[JX]	98	C4
Jiaokou[SN]	156	F6
Jiaokou[SN]	156	G4
Jiaokou[SX]	54	B5
Jiaokou[SX]	54	C4
Jiaokou[SX]	54	C5
Jiaokou[SX]	54	D5
Jiaokouhe[SN]	156	F5
Jiaolai He[NM]	58	N6
Jiaolai He[SD]	102	F3
Jiaolan[FJ]	94	C2
Jiaoling[GD]	118	I2
Jiaoliu He[JL]	66	B2
Jiaoliudao[LN]	62	E5
Jiaoliuhe[JL]	66	C2
Jiaolong[SD]	102	E5
Jiaolou[SD]	102	B4
Jiaoloushen[SX]	54	C3
Jiaomiao[SD]	102	C3
Jiaonan[SD]	102	F4
Jiaopenggou[NX]	168	C4
Jiaopi[AH]	90	B4
Jiaotan[JX]	98	E2
Jiaotan[ZJ]	84	C4
Jiaotou[GS]	160	I5
Jiaotou[ZJ]	84	G3
Jiaowei[FJ]	94	D4
Jiaoxi[HN]	114	F4
Jiaoxie[JS]	80	F4
Jiaoyuan[HB]	110	C4
Jiaoyuan[SC]	138	L8
Jiaoyuan[SD]	102	A4
Jiaozhou Wan[SD]	102	G3
Jiaozhou[SD]	102	G3
Jiaozhuanghu[BJ]	36	D3
Jiaozi Ding[GZ]	144	C4
Jiaozuo[HEN]	106	E2
Jiapeng Liedao[GD]	118	G5
Jiapigou[JL]	66	H5
Jiaping[CQ]	132	C5
Jiapu[ZJ]	84	D1
Jiaqiao Ling[GX]	124	H3
Jiaqiao[JX]	98	D3
Jiardun Shan[NM]	58	O3
Jiarong[GZ]	144	E5
Jiarong[GZ]	144	G5
Jiashan[HN]	114	D3
Jiashan[JL]	66	E4
Jiashan[JL]	84	E2
Jiashi(Payzawat)[XJ]	172	F6
Jiashi[GZ]	144	G2
Jiashihe[HEB]	48	B3
Jiasi[CQ]	132	C4
Jiatan Shuiku[HI]	128	C2
Jiatang[NX]	168	B4
Jiatie[SX]	138	H8
Jiatou[FJ]	94	C3
Jiawang Qu[JS]	80	C2
Jiaxiang[SD]	102	C4
Jiaxin[HL]	70	E6
Jiaxing[ZJ]	84	E2
Jiayi[HL]	114	F4
Jiayi[YN]	148	I7
Jiayin[HL]	70	F4
Jiayou[GX]	124	D3
Jiayu[HB]	110	G5
Jiayuguan[GS]	160	D3
Jiazhuang[SX]	54	D2
Jiazhuyuan[HB]	110	F5
Jiazi Gang[GD]	118	H4
Jiazi Yu[GD]	118	I4
Jiazi[GD]	118	I4
Jiazi[HI]	128	C2
Jibki[XJ]	172	L4
Jichang[GZ]	144	D4
Jichang[GZ]	144	F5
Jichang[JL]	66	F4
Jichang[SC]	138	N4
Jichangping[GZ]	144	C5
Jicheng[GD]	118	E4
Jicheng[HN]	114	F3
Jicui[SX]	54	C4
Jicun[HEB]	48	B6
Jidar[XZ]	152	J5
Jidong[HL]	70	F6
Jidongyu[LN]	62	G4
Jieba[JX]	98	B6
Jiedi Jianhe[TJ]	42	B4
Jiedong[GD]	118	I3
Jiedu[JX]	98	E3
Jiedu[SX]	54	E4
Jiegou[HEN]	106	G3
Jieguan[HB]	110	G3
Jieguan[HEB]	48	C6
Jiehe[AH]	90	C5
Jiehe[SD]	102	D4
Jiehekou[SX]	54	C3
Jieheshi[HB]	110	E4
Jieji[HL]	70	B5
Jieji[JS]	80	D3
Jiejing[SH]	74	C2
Jiejinkou[HL]	70	G5
Jiekeng[ZJ]	84	E4
Jieling[SN]	156	E8
Jielong[CQ]	132	C4
Jielong[HN]	114	C5
Jiemian[FJ]	94	D4
Jiepai[HN]	114	D4
Jiepaiji[AH]	90	D4
Jiepao[GD]	118	B5
Jieshan[FJ]	94	D4
Jieshi Wan[GD]	118	H4
Jieshi[GD]	118	H4
Jieshipu[GS]	160	G5
Jieshou[AH]	90	B3
Jieshou[GX]	124	H2
Jieshou[JS]	80	E3
Jietian[JX]	98	E3
Jieting[GX]	124	C3
Jieting[ZJ]	84	E3

Jietou[YN]	148	D5	Jindun[YN]	148	F4	Jingtai[GS]	160	G4
Jietou[ZJ]	84	E3	Jinfeng Qu[NX]	168	C2	Jingtao[HL]	70	B2
Jietoumiao[SN]	156	F5	Jinfeng[CQ]	132	F2	Jingtie Shan[GS]	160	C3
Jietoupu[HN]	114	E4	Jinfo Shan[CQ]	132	D4	Jingtou[HN]	114	E6
Jiewen[LN]	62	G4	Jinfosi[GS]	160	D3	Jingtou[JS]	80	D3
Jiexi[GD]	118	H3	Jing He[GS]	160	H5	Jingtouxu[HN]	114	D6
Jiexiang[YN]	148	C7	Jing[SN]	156	E6	Jingui[HN]	114	F6
Jiexiu[SX]	54	C4	Jing Shan[HB]	110	E3	Jingui[NX]	168	C2
Jieyang[GD]	118	I3	Jing Xian[AH]	90	E6	Jingwai[YN]	148	I4
Jieyuanji[SD]	102	B4	Jing Xian[HEB]	48	D6	Jingwuzhou[HN]	114	B6
Jiezhi[GD]	118	G1	Jing'an[GS]	160	G4	Jingxi[GX]	124	D4
Jiezhuang[HEB]	48	C5	Jing'an[JS]	80	B2	Jingxin[JL]	66	K5
Jiezhuang[SD]	102	C4	Jing'an[JX]	98	C3	Jingxin[YN]	148	E8
Jiezishi[BJ]	36	C3	Jing'an[YN]	148	I3	Jingxing Kuangqu[HEB]	48	B5
Jigdoi[XZ]	152	J4	Jingang Tai[AH]	90	B5	Jingxing[HEB]	48	B5
Jigong Shan[HEN]	106	F6	Jingang Tai[HEN]	106	G6	Jingxing[HL]	70	B5
Jiguan[JL]	66	J4	Jingangcun[TJ]	42	B4	Jingxing[YN]	148	G7
Jiguanshan[LN]	62	G4	Jingbian[SN]	156	E3	Jingyan[SC]	138	J6
Jigzhi[QH]	164	N7	Jingchuan[GS]	160	H5	Jingyang He[SN]	156	D8
Jihe[HB]	110	F2	Jingcun[SN]	156	G6	Jingyang[FJ]	94	E4
Jihe[SN]	156	E8	Jingde[AH]	90	E6	Jingyang[HB]	110	C2
Jihong[HB]	110	E2	Jingde[GX]	124	D4	Jingyang[HB]	110	C4
Jihui[FJ]	94	C3	Jingdezhen[JX]	98	E2	Jingyang[NM]	58	T11
Jihyueh Tan[TW]	186	D3	Jingdian[HEB]	48	A7	Jingyang[QH]	164	N3
Jiji[GS]	160	D2	Jingdian[HEN]	106	F2	Jingyang[SN]	156	E6
Jijia[GD]	118	B6	Jingdong[FJ]	94	C3	Jingyou[SX]	54	C3
Jijia[NX]	168	B3	Jingdong[YN]	148	F6	Jingyu Hu[XJ]	172	L7
Jijiang[ZJ]	84	E3	Jingfeng[SX]	54	D5	Jingyu[JL]	66	G5
Jijiazhuang[HEB]	48	B3	Jingfu[YN]	148	F6	Jingyuan[GS]	160	G4
Jijiazhuang[SX]	54	E2	Jinggang Shan[JX]	98	B5	Jingyuan[NX]	168	C5
Jijie[YN]	148	I7	Jinggang[CQ]	132	E5	Jingzhi[SD]	102	F3
Jijie[YN]	148	J7	Jinggangshan[JX]	98	B5	Jingzhong[SD]	102	E3
Jijihu[XJ]	172	M3	Jinggangqiao[JX]	98	E2	Jingzhou Qu[HB]	110	F4
Jijing[CQ]	132	F2	Jinggou[NX]	168	B3	Jingzhou[AH]	90	E6
Jili Hu[XJ]	172	K2	Jinggu[GS]	160	F5	Jingzhou[HB]	110	F4
Jili Qu[HEN]	106	D3	Jinggu[YN]	148	F7	Jingzhou[HN]	114	B6
Jiliao[HEN]	106	D3	Jinggu[YN]	148	F7	Jingzhu[CQ]	132	F3
Jilin Hada Ling[JL]	66	F5	Jinghai Gang[GD]	118	I4	Jingzhu[HN]	114	D7
Jilin Hada Ling[LN]	62	I2	Jinghai Wan[SD]	102	H3	Jingzhuang[NX]	168	A3
Jilin[JL]	66	G4	Jinghai[GD]	118	I3	Jingzi[GD]	118	H3
Jiling[XZ]	152	I4	Jinghai[SD]	102	I3	Jingzi[HN]	114	E5
Jiliu He[NM]	58	N1	Jinghai[TJ]	42	A4	Jingziguan[HEN]	106	C4
Jilong Shan[GD]	118	E3	Jinghang Yunhe(Grand Canal)[HEB]	48	C6	Jingziyu[BJ]	36	D3
Jilong[GD]	118	G4	Jinhai Hu[BJ]	36	E3
Jilong[HI]	128	B2	Jinghang Yunhe(Grand Canal)[JS]	80	C2	Jinhaihu[BJ]	36	E3
Jilong[HN]	114	E6	Jinhe[HL]	70	D3
Jilong[HN]	114	F7	Jinghang Yunhe(Grand Canal)[SD]	102	B3	Jinhe[HN]	114	B5
Jimei Qu[FJ]	94	D5	Jinhe[NM]	58	N2
Jimi[SC]	138	H7	jinghang Yunhe(Grand Canal)[TJ]	42	A4	Jinhe[SC]	138	G8
Jimiao[HEN]	106	G5	Jinhu[JS]	80	E3
Jiming Dao[SD]	102	I2	Jinghang Yunhe(Grand Canal)[ZJ]	84	E2	Jinhua Jiang[ZJ]	84	D3
Jimo[SD]	102	G3	Jinhua[GZ]	144	F3
Jimsar[XJ]	172	L4	Jinghe(Jing)[XJ]	172	I3	Jinhua[JL]	66	F5
Jin Hu[FJ]	94	C3	Jinghe[JS]	80	E3	Jinhua[SC]	138	K5
Jin Jiang[FJ]	94	D5	Jinghe[SC]	138	L5	Jinhua[ZJ]	84	D3
Jin Jiang[GZ]	144	G3	Jinghe[SN]	156	E7	Jinhui Gang[SH]	74	C3
Jin Jiang[JX]	98	C3	Jinghong[YN]	148	F9	Jinhui Qu[JX]	98	C3
Jin Xi[FJ]	94	C3	Jinghua Shan[CQ]	132	D3	Jinhui[SH]	74	C3
Jinan[SD]	102	C3	Jingjiadian[HL]	70	D5	Jining[SD]	102	C4
Jinbao[GX]	124	H3	Jingjiang[JS]	80	F4	Jinji Ling[HI]	128	C2
Jinbaotang[HN]	114	E6	Jingjiao[GZ]	144	G2	Jinji[AH]	90	F4
Jinbei[JS]	80	E3	Jingjiawu[BJ]	36	C4	Jinji[GD]	118	E4
Jinbi[GZ]	144	D4	Jingkou[GD]	118	C4	Jinji[GX]	124	H4
Jinbingcun[HI]	128	B2	Jingkou[GD]	118	E3	Jinji[NX]	168	C3
Jinbo[HI]	128	B2	Jinglan[FJ]	94	D2	Jinjia[LN]	62	G2
Jinchang[GS]	160	F3	Jingle[SX]	54	C3	Jinjia[SH]	74	C3
Jinchang[YN]	148	J8	Jinglonggong[HEN]	106	F3	Jinjiahe[SN]	156	B7
Jinchanggou[JL]	66	F6	Jinglou[JX]	98	C3	Jinjiajing[HEB]	48	B4
Jincheng Jiang[GX]	124	E3	Jingmao[SX]	54	C6	Jinjiang Shuiku[GD]	118	E4
Jincheng[SC]	138	L4	Jingmen[HB]	110	F3	Jinjiang[FJ]	94	D5
Jincheng[SD]	102	G2	Jingmi Yinshuiqu[BJ]	36	C3	Jinjiang[JX]	98	B4
Jincheng[SX]	54	D6	Jingna[YN]	148	F8	Jinjiang[JX]	98	D3
Jincheng[YN]	148	H6	Jingnan[GD]	118	H2	Jinjiapu[HB]	110	I4
Jinchengshi[HN]	114	D6	Jingnan[GZ]	144	C6	Jinjiazhuang Qu[AH]	90	E5
Jinchuan[HL]	70	G4	Jingning[GS]	160	G5	Jinjiazhuang[SX]	54	B4
Jinchuan[JL]	66	G5	Jingning[ZJ]	84	D5	Jinjiazhuang[TJ]	42	B3
Jinchuan[SC]	138	H4	Jingou[HL]	70	B2	Jinjie[GX]	124	E4
Jinchuan[SN]	156	E7	Jingpo[HL]	70	E7	Jinjing[HN]	114	F4
Jinchuan[SN]	156	E8	Jingqiao[JS]	80	E5	Jinjing[SX]	54	B7
Jindai[CQ]	132	D3	Jingshan[HB]	110	G3	Jinju Ding[GD]	118	D3
Jinding[SN]	156	E4	Jingshan[JL]	66	G5	Jinkeng[FJ]	94	C2
Jindong Qu[ZJ]	84	D3	Jingshang[SX]	54	E4	Jinkeng[JX]	98	B6
Jindou[FJ]	94	D4	Jingshanwa[SD]	102	F3	Jinkou[HB]	110	H4
Jindou[GZ]	144	C4	Jingsheng[SX]	54	C5	Jinkou[JX]	98	C2

Jinkou[SD]	102	G3	Jinuoshan[YN]	148	G8	Jiucheng[YN]	148	E6
Jinkouhe Qu[SC]	138	I6	Jinwan Qu[GD]	118	F4	Jiucheng[YN]	148	K2
Jinlan[HN]	114	E5	Jinweizhou[HN]	114	E6	Jiuchong[HEN]	106	C5
Jinli[GD]	118	E3	Jinwozi[XJ]	172	O5	Jiudao[HB]	110	D3
Jinling[GX]	124	F5	Jinwutaizi[LN]	62	F3	Jiudian[HEN]	106	F5
Jinlong[GX]	124	D5	Jinwutang[HN]	114	C5	Jiudian[SD]	102	G3
Jinlong[HN]	114	B5	Jinxi Hu[JX]	98	D3	Jiudian[SN]	156	E7
Jinluo[SX]	54	C4	Jinxi[HN]	114	E5	Jiuding Shan[SC]	138	I4
Jinma[JL]	66	H3	Jinxi[JX]	98	D4	Jiudu[FJ]	94	E3
Jinma[SD]	102	C4	Jinxi[ZJ]	84	D4	Jiudu[GX]	124	F3
Jinma[YN]	148	I6	Jinxian[JX]	98	D3	Jiuduhe[BJ]	36	C3
Jinmiaopu[SX]	54	D6	Jinxiang[GD]	118	H4	Jiudun[GS]	160	F3
Jinming[SH]	74	C3	Jinxiang[SD]	102	C4	Jiufeng Shan[FJ]	94	D2
Jinmu Jiao[HI]	128	B3	Jinxin[SH]	74	C1	Jiufeng[FJ]	94	C5
Jinnan Qu[TJ]	42	B4	Jinxing[SD]	102	E4	Jiufeng[GD]	118	F1
Jinning[YN]	148	H6	Jinxiu[GX]	124	H3	Jiufenzi[NM]	58	V10
Jinniu[AH]	90	C5	Jinya[GS]	160	G4	Jiugong Shan[HB]	110	H5
Jinniu[AH]	90	D5	Jinya[GX]	124	D3	Jiugong Shan[JX]	98	B2
Jinniu[HEB]	48	E5	Jinyan[HN]	114	C3	Jiugong[BJ]	36	C4
Jinpanling[JX]	98	D2	Jinyang[SC]	138	I8	Jiugongqiao[HN]	114	D5
Jinpengwan[SN]	156	F8	Jinyao[SC]	138	J6	Jiugongshan[HB]	110	H5
Jinpenshan[JX]	98	C6	Jinyao[SH]	74	B2	Jiuhe[YN]	148	E4
Jinping Shan[SC]	138	G7	Jinyi[SX]	54	D5	Jiuheyinzi[TJ]	42	B3
Jinping Shan[SC]	138	G8	Ji'nyinsib[QH]	164	I8	Jiuhu[HB]	110	C3
Jinping[FJ]	94	E2	Jinyuan Qu[SX]	54	D4	Jiuhua Shan[AH]	90	D6
Jinping[GZ]	144	H4	Jinyuan[YN]	148	I5	Jiuhuangjiang[GD]	118	F4
Jinping[HN]	114	C3	Jinyun[ZJ]	84	E4	Jiuji[HB]	110	E3
Jinping[YN]	148	I8	Jinze[SH]	74	B2	Jiujiang[JX]	98	C2
Jinpu[HEN]	106	F4	Jinzhai[AH]	90	B5	Jiujiang[JX]	98	C2
Jinqi[NM]	58	U11	Jinzhong Shan[GX]	124	B3	Jiujie[HB]	110	H4
Jinqian He[SN]	156	F7	Jinzhong[GS]	160	G5	Jiujie[HL]	70	E6
Jinqiao[HN]	114	E6	Jinzhong[GZ]	144	C4	Jiujie[YN]	148	H6
Jinqiao[SH]	74	D2	Jinzhong[SX]	54	D4	Jiujing[YN]	148	E8
Jinqing[ZJ]	84	F4	Jinzhong[ZJ]	84	D4	Jiukeng[ZJ]	84	C3
Jinrui[JX]	98	B4	Jinzhou Qu[LN]	62	E5	Jiukou[HB]	110	F4
Jinsha Jiang[SC]	138	E5	Jinzhou Wan[LN]	62	E4	Jiukouzi[HEB]	48	B5
Jinsha Jiang[SC]	138	I8	Jinzhou Wan[LN]	62	E5	Jiulian Shan[GD]	118	G3
Jinsha Jiang[XZ]	152	K3	Jinzhou[HEB]	48	C5	Jiulian[GD]	118	G2
Jinsha Jiang[YN]	148	E2	Jinzhou[JL]	66	F4	Jiuliancheng[HEB]	48	B2
Jinsha Jiang[YN]	148	H3	Jinzhou[LN]	62	E3	Jiuling Shan[JX]	98	B3
Jinsha Xi[JX]	98	F3	Jinzhu[JX]	98	C4	Jiuling[HB]	110	G5
Jinsha[FJ]	94	B5	Jinzhuang[GD]	118	D3	Jiuling[SC]	138	M4
Jinsha[FJ]	94	D3	Jinzhuang[YN]	148	E3	Jiuliqi[JS]	80	E1
Jinsha[GZ]	144	E3	Jinzhushan[JX]	98	E2	Jiuliwan[SX]	54	C4
Jinsha[JL]	66	G4	Jinzi[CQ]	132	C3	Jiulong Jiang[FJ]	94	C5
Jinsha[NX]	168	C2	Jinziyan[HN]	114	B6	Jiulong Shan[ZJ]	84	C4
Jinshan Qu[SH]	74	C3	Jipan[SN]	156	D3	Jiulong Xi[FJ]	94	B3
Jinshan[CQ]	132	D5	Jiqi[ZJ]	84	F3	Jiulong[GD]	118	E2
Jinshan[FJ]	94	C2	Jiqing[HN]	114	D5	Jiulong[GX]	124	F5
Jinshan[FJ]	94	C5	Jiqu[QH]	164	I9	Jiulong[SC]	138	G6
Jinshan[HB]	110	H4	Jiri'gya'nyag[QH]	164	G8	Jiulong[SD]	102	F3
Jinshan[HI]	128	C2	Jirmainna[QH]	164	K5	Jiulong[YN]	148	F3
Jinshan[HL]	70	D3	Jirmeng[QH]	164	L3	Jiulong[YN]	148	H5
Jinshan[HL]	70	F5	Jisa[QH]	164	N5	Jiulong[YN]	148	J6
Jinshan[NX]	168	C2	Jishan[SX]	54	B6	Jiulongchi[HN]	114	D4
Jinshan[ZJ]	84	E2	Jishi[JS]	80	F4	Jiulongdi[LN]	62	F4
Jinshantun Qu[HL]	70	E5	Jishi[SX]	54	D5	Jiulongpo Qu[CQ]	132	C4
Jinshatan[SX]	54	D2	Jishishan[GS]	160	F5	Jiulongshan[JX]	98	B4
Jinshen[AH]	90	C6	Jishou[HN]	114	B4	Jiumen[LN]	62	D4
Jinshi[GX]	124	H2	Jishu[SD]	102	C5	Jiumiao[LN]	62	E2
Jinshi[HN]	114	D3	Jishui[JX]	98	C4	Jiumo[YN]	148	J7
Jinshi[HN]	114	E4	Jisuo[SD]	102	D4	Jiumu[FJ]	94	D1
Jinshi[JX]	98	B5	Jiti[JL]	66	E3	Jiupeng[FJ]	94	D2
Jinshidong[HB]	110	E4	Jiuba[GZ]	144	E2	Jiupu[JS]	80	D4
Jinshiqiao[HN]	114	C5	Jiuba[GZ]	144	E2	Jiuqian[GZ]	144	G5
Jinshui He[SN]	156	D7	Jiubaihu[TJ]	42	B2	Jiuqingpu[SH]	74	C2
Jinshui[HL]	70	D3	Jiubaihu[TJ]	42	C1	Jiuqu[SH]	74	C2
Jinshui[SN]	156	D7	Jiubao[JX]	98	C6	Jiuquan[GS]	160	D3
Jinshuihe[YN]	148	I8	Jiubei[GD]	118	E2	Jiuqujiang[HI]	128	C2
Jinshuitan Shuiku[ZJ]	84	D4	Jiubujiang Shuiku[HN]	114	F5	Jiushan Liedao[ZJ]	84	G3
Jinsu[SC]	138	I6	Jiubujiang[HN]	114	F5	Jiushan[HEN]	106	E3
Jinsuoguan[SN]	156	F5	Jiucai Dingzi[LN]	62	H3	Jiushi[HN]	114	F7
Jinta[GS]	160	D3	Jiucai Ling[GX]	124	I2	Jiushu[CQ]	132	F3
Jintan[GD]	118	E2	Jiucai Ling[HN]	114	D7	Jiushu[GD]	118	H3
Jintan[JS]	80	E5	Jiucai Ping[GZ]	144	C4	Jiusou Nongchang[HI]	128	B3
Jintang[HB]	110	H5	Jiucai[NX]	168	B4	Jiusuo[HI]	128	A3
Jintang[SC]	138	J5	Jiucaigou[GS]	160	D3	Jiutai[JL]	66	F3
Jintang[YN]	148	I4	Jiucaitai[LN]	62	F3	Jiutun[HEB]	48	E2
Jintang[ZJ]	84	F2	Jiucheng[AH]	90	C3	Jiuwan Dashan[GX]	124	F2
Jintangchuan[NX]	168	B5	Jiucheng[GX]	124	E4	Jiuwan Dashan[GZ]	144	G5
Jintao[FJ]	94	D4	Jiucheng[GZ]	144	F2	Jiuxian[AH]	90	B3
Jintian[GX]	124	H4	Jiucheng[HEB]	48	E5	Jiuxian[BJ]	36	C2
Jintian[JX]	98	B4	Jiucheng[SD]	102	B4	Jiuxian[CQ]	132	C4
Jintun[JX]	98	E3	Jiucheng[YN]	148	D6	Jiuxian[FJ]	94	B4

Jiuxian[FJ]	94	D2
Jiuxian[HEN]	106	C3
Jiuxian[SD]	102	C3
Jiuxian[SX]	54	C2
Jiuxian[SX]	54	C5
Jiuxiang[YN]	148	I5
Jiuxianqiao[BJ]	36	C4
Jiuxu[GX]	124	E3
Jiuyi Shan[HN]	114	D7
Jiuyi[HN]	114	D7
Jiuying[GZ]	144	C5
Jiuying[NX]	168	B5
Jiuyuan[SC]	138	N4
Jiuzhai[SD]	102	E4
Jiuzhaigou[SC]	138	J2
Jiuzhen[FJ]	94	C5
Jiuzhen[FJ]	94	D3
Jiuzhen[HB]	110	G4
Jiuzhongjin[SN]	156	C7
Jiuzhou[GX]	124	C3
Jiuzhou[GX]	124	F5
Jiuzhou[GZ]	144	F4
Jiuzhou[HEB]	48	D4
Jiuzhou[HEB]	48	E5
Jiuzhuang[YN]	148	G5
Jiuzi[AH]	90	D4
Jiwang[SH]	74	C2
Jiwei[HN]	114	B4
Jixi[AH]	90	E6
Jixi[HL]	70	F6
Jixian[GS]	160	H5
Jixian[HL]	70	F5
Jixiang[GX]	124	F2
Jixin[HN]	114	B4
Jixinggang[HL]	70	C4
Jiyang[FJ]	94	C4
Jiyang[FJ]	94	D2
Jiyang[HEN]	106	G3
Jiyang[SD]	102	D3
Jiyek[XJ]	172	I2
Jiyi[SN]	156	G5
Jiyi[YN]	148	H4
Jiyizhuang[SX]	54	E2
Jiyuan[HEN]	106	D2
Jiyuan[SN]	156	D3
Jiyun He[HEB]	48	E4
Jiyun He[TJ]	42	B2
Jiyun He[TJ]	42	C2
Jize[HEB]	48	B7
Jizhai[ZJ]	84	E4
Jizhou[HEB]	48	C6
Jizhuangzi[TJ]	42	B3
Jizu Shan[YN]	148	F5
Jomda[XZ]	152	K4
Jonê[GS]	160	F5
Jonglong[FJ]	94	D2
Jordan Valley[HK]	176	D3
Jorra[XZ]	152	H5
Ju He[HB]	110	E3
Ju He[HEB]	48	E3
Ju He[TJ]	42	B1
Ju Shui[HB]	110	H4
Ju Xian[SD]	102	E4
Juancheng[SD]	102	B4
Juandong[CQ]	132	D4
Juanqiao[AH]	90	D6
Juanyun He[SD]	102	B4
Jubao[CQ]	132	D4
Jubao[HL]	70	C5
Jubao[JL]	66	C2
Jubaoshan[JL]	66	D3
Jubaoshan[JL]	66	E3
Juexi[SC]	138	J7
Juexi[ZJ]	84	F3
Jufeng[GZ]	144	F3
Jufeng[SD]	102	F4
Jugezhuang[BJ]	36	D3
Jugezhuang[SD]	102	H2
Jugezhuang[TJ]	42	B4
Juhe[HL]	70	C4
Juhin Gol[QH]	164	G4
Juhongtu[QH]	164	I3
Juhua Dao[LN]	62	D4
Juhuadao[LN]	62	D4
Juisui[TW]	186	E3
Jukou[FJ]	94	C2
Jule[SX]	54	E1
Juling[HEN]	106	E4
Julong Shan[HB]	110	E3
Julu[HEB]	48	C6
Juma He[BJ]	36	A4
Juma He[HEB]	48	C4
Jun He[SD]	102	D4
Jun Helhe[NM]	58	E8
Jun Jahin Us[NM]	58	D6
Jun Mahai Hu[QH]	164	G2
Jun Qagan[NM]	58	O3
Junan[SD]	102	E4
Junbu[JX]	98	C5
Junchuan[HB]	110	G3
Jundu Shan[BJ]	36	C3
Junfeng Shan[JX]	98	D4
Jungar Qi[NM]	58	I8
Junggar Pendi[XJ]	172	K3
Junkou[FJ]	94	B3
Junlian[SC]	138	J7
Junliangcheng[TJ]	42	B3
Junmahe[HEN]	106	C4
Junmenling[JX]	98	C6
Junmin Shuiku[JX]	98	D2
Junshan Hu[JX]	98	D3
Junshan Qu[HN]	114	F3
Junshan[HB]	110	H4
Junshan[HN]	114	F6
Juntian[HN]	114	E7
Junul[QH]	164	I3
Junxian[HB]	110	E2
Junxiang[BJ]	36	B4
Ju'nyung[SC]	138	D2
Junzhuang[BJ]	36	C3
Jupu[ZJ]	84	E4
Juqianbu[SX]	54	E1
Jurhen Ui[QH]	164	C6
Jurong[JS]	80	E5
Juting[SN]	156	C7
Juxi[FJ]	94	B4
Juxing[AH]	90	C5
Juye[SD]	102	C4
Juyongguan[BJ]	36	C3
Juyuan[SN]	156	D7
Juzhang He[HB]	110	E4
Juzhuangzi[TJ]	42	A4

K

Ka Qu[XZ]	152	H3
Ka Qu[XZ]	152	I4
Kachang[YN]	148	C6
Kafaling Linchang[HI]	128	B3
Kafang[YN]	148	I7
Kai Chau[HK]	176	E3
Kai Ham[HK]	176	E3
Kai Kung Leng[HK]	176	C2
Kai Kung Tau[HK]	176	E1
Kai Leng[HK]	176	D1
Kai Xian[CQ]	132	E2
Kai Yet Kok[HK]	176	A4
Ka'an[JL]	66	F3
Kaiben[GZ]	144	G3
Kaibian[GS]	160	H5
Kaicheng[AH]	90	D5
Kaicheng[NX]	168	C5
Kaidu He[XJ]	172	J4
Kaifeng[HEN]	106	F3
Kaifeng[HEN]	106	F3
Kaifeng[JL]	66	H5
Kaifeng[SC]	138	K4
Kaifu[SX]	54	C3
Kaigoin[XZ]	152	C4
Kaihua[ZJ]	84	C3
Kaihuang[QH]	164	H5
Kaijiang[SC]	138	M4
Kaikukang[HL]	70	C2
Kaili[GZ]	144	F4
Kailu[NM]	58	N6
Kaintang[XZ]	152	J4
Kaiping Qu[HEB]	48	F4
Kaiping[GD]	118	E4
Kaishan[FJ]	94	C3
Kaishantun[JL]	66	J5
Kaiyang[GZ]	144	E3
Kaiyuan[LN]	62	H2
Kaiyuan[YN]	148	I7
Kaizhang[SX]	54	B7
Kaizuo[GZ]	144	E4
Kala[SC]	138	G7
Kalong[SC]	138	I3
Kalpin[XJ]	172	G5
Kalunhu[JL]	66	F3
Kaluo[GZ]	144	F5
Kam Chuk Kok[HK]	176	C3
Kam Hing Wai[HK]	176	C2
Kam Tin[HK]	176	C2
Kam Tsin Wai[HK]	176	C2
Kam Tsin[HK]	176	C1
Kamen[XZ]	152	F6
Kamen He[XZ]	152	H6
Kamisti[XJ]	172	L3
Kamra[QH]	164	N4
Kamru[XZ]	152	F5
Kan He[GZ]	144	E2
Kan Xiang[XJ]	172	H4
Kanbian[GZ]	144	E5
Kang Lau Shek[HK]	176	F1
Kang Xian[GS]	160	G6
Kangbao[HEB]	48	B2
Kangcheng[SX]	54	C5
Kangcuo[FJ]	94	E2
Kangding[SC]	138	G5
Kanggezhuang[BJ]	36	E3
Kanghe[GD]	118	H3
Kanghe[SX]	54	C5
Kangji[SD]	102	B5
Kangjiahui[SX]	54	D3
Kangjiawan[NM]	58	W11
Kangjin[HL]	70	D5
Kangkir[XJ]	172	G7
Kangle[CQ]	132	F2
Kangle[GS]	160	F5
Kangleng[HEB]	48	B2
Kangliuzhuang[TJ]	42	B2
Kanglung[QH]	164	M7
Kanglung[XZ]	152	E4
Kanglungda[QH]	164	M7
Kangmar[XZ]	152	F5
Kangmatou[NX]	168	B3
Kangmei[FJ]	94	D4
Kangning[SX]	54	C3
Kangping[LN]	62	G2
Kangqiao[SH]	74	D2
Kangqung Kangri[XZ]	152	D4
Kangrinboqê Feng[XZ]	152	B4
Kangsar[QH]	164	N7
Kangsar[SC]	138	F4
Kangshan Kenzhichang[JX]	98	D3
Kangshengzhuang[SD]	102	B3
Kangtan[NX]	168	B3
Kangtangxung[QH]	164	I6
Kangtzu[TW]	186	D4
Kangyang[QH]	164	N4
Kangyü[XJ]	152	J4
Kangzêgyai[QH]	164	J2
Kangzhag Ri[XZ]	152	F2
Kangzhuang[BJ]	36	B3
Kangzhuang[TJ]	42	B2
Kangzhuangzi[TJ]	42	B2
Kanjia[SC]	138	J6
Kanmen[ZJ]	84	F4
Kanshi[FJ]	94	B5
Kansu[XJ]	172	E6
Kantuan[AH]	90	C3
Kantuan[AH]	90	D3
Kaohsiung Kang[TW]	186	D4
Kaohsiung[TW]	186	D4
Kaolao[SX]	54	B7
Kaoping Hsi[TW]	186	D4
Kaoshan[JL]	66	F3
Kaoshan[JL]	66	F4
Kaoshan[LN]	62	H2
Kaoshu[TW]	186	D4

Name	Page	Grid
Kap Lung[HK]	176	C2
Kap shui Mun[HK]	176	C3
Kar Qu[QH]	164	I6
Karabulak[XJ]	172	F5
Karabulgin[XJ]	172	L2
Karag[XZ]	152	G5
Karajol[XJ]	172	F5
Karakax He[XJ]	172	G7
Karakazan[QH]	164	G4
Karakorum Shan[XJ]	172	E7
Karakorum Shan[XZ]	152	A2
Karakorum Shankou[XJ]	172	F8
Karamay[XJ]	172	J3
Karamiran He[XJ]	172	J7
Karaqi[XJ]	172	F5
Karasay[XJ]	172	G7
Karasu[XJ]	172	F6
Karatag Shan[XJ]	172	F7
Karateki Shan[XJ]	172	F5
Karatüngke[XJ]	172	L2
Karcang[QH]	164	L6
Kardag[XZ]	152	H5
Kardoi[XZ]	152	F5
Kargang[XZ]	152	K4
Karjaw[XJ]	172	K2
Karmar[QH]	164	K3
Karmardo[XZ]	152	J4
Karmarsumdo[QH]	164	I6
Karnag[XZ]	152	A3
Karquga[XJ]	172	J5
Karrong Chakou[QH]	164	I8
Karub[XZ]	152	J4
Karxung[QH]	164	I6
Kashi(Kaxgar)[XJ]	172	E6
Kasi[YN]	148	E6
Kaskirso[XJ]	172	L3
Kat O Hoi[HK]	176	E1
Kat O[HK]	176	E1
Kata[XZ]	152	I4
Kau Sai Chau[HK]	176	E3
Kau Sai[HK]	176	E3
Kau Yi Chau[HK]	176	C3
Kawak[XJ]	172	H7
Kax He[XJ]	172	I4
Kaxgar He[XJ]	172	G6
Kaxsay[XJ]	172	K6
Kaxtexi Shan[XJ]	172	I7
Kaxtexi[XJ]	172	G7
Kazan[XJ]	172	H3
Kecheng[SX]	54	C5
Keda[CQ]	132	F4
Kedian[HB]	110	F3
Kedong[HL]	70	D4
Kedu He[GZ]	144	C4
Kedu He[YN]	148	J4
Kedu[YN]	148	H5
Ke'er[SC]	138	F7
Kefang[FJ]	94	B3
Kêgor[SC]	138	E3
Kei Kok Tau[HK]	176	F3
Kei Ling Ha Hoi[HK]	176	E2
Kei Lun Wai[HK]	176	B2
Kejie[YN]	148	E6
Kelan[SX]	54	C3
Kele[GZ]	144	C3
Kelegou[HEB]	48	F2
Kelin[HL]	70	E4
Kelou[GZ]	144	G3
Kelu[GD]	118	B5
Keluo Gang[FJ]	94	D5
Keluo He[HL]	70	C4
Keluo[HL]	70	C4
Keming[FJ]	94	C4
Kengdi[FJ]	94	E2
Kenghsin[TW]	186	E2
Kengjiazhuang[TJ]	42	B2
Kêngko[QH]	164	I7
Kengkou[FJ]	94	D2
Kengkou[GD]	118	E3
Kengkou[ZJ]	84	C4
Kengwei[FJ]	94	D1
Kengyuan[FJ]	94	E3
Kengzhen[SN]	156	G3
Kenli[SD]	102	E2
Kennedy Town[HK]	176	D3
Keriya He[XJ]	172	H7
Keriya Shankou[XJ]	172	H8
Keriya Shankou[XZ]	152	B2
Kesha[HN]	114	B3
Keshan[HL]	70	C4
Ketian[AH]	90	D6
Keung Shan[HK]	176	A4
Keyi[XJ]	172	I4
Keyihe[NM]	58	O2
Keyin He[HL]	70	D5
Kiliyang[XJ]	172	F7
Kiu Tsui Chau[HK]	176	E3
Kiu Tsui[HK]	176	E3
Kizil[XJ]	172	F6
Kizil[XJ]	172	I5
Kizillik[XJ]	172	H6
Kizilsu[XJ]	172	F6
Kizilto[XJ]	172	F6
Ko Lau Wan[HK]	176	F2
Ko Po[HK]	176	D1
Ko Tong[HK]	176	E2
Kocê[GS]	160	F5
Kogbo[SC]	138	G3
Koguxluk[XJ]	172	E7
Koikyim Qu[QH]	164	G6
Koixün[QH]	164	N6
Kokterak[XJ]	172	H4
Kokyar[XJ]	172	F7
Kong Tau pai[HK]	176	F3
Kongdang[YN]	148	D3
Konggar Shan[SC]	138	G6
Konggar Shan[SC]	138	G6
Kongka Shankou[XJ]	172	G8
Kongkeshu[HN]	114	C3
Konglong[HB]	110	I5
Kongma[XZ]	152	F5
Kongmo[XZ]	152	D3
Kongque[SC]	138	J7
Kongtan[SC]	138	J6
Kongtian[JX]	98	C7
Kongtong Dao[SD]	102	H2
Kongur Shan[XJ]	172	E6
Kongyu[SC]	138	H5
Kongzhuangzi[TJ]	42	C1
Konqi He[XJ]	172	K5
Ko'nyai[XZ]	152	I4
Kop Tong[HK]	176	E1
Korgan[XJ]	172	I4
Korla[XJ]	172	K5
Kormar[XZ]	152	H4
Kou He[LN]	62	H2
Koudong[TJ]	42	B2
Kouhu[TW]	186	D3
Koujiang[GZ]	144	G4
Koutou[HEB]	48	B5
Kouzhen[SD]	102	D3
Kouzi[AH]	90	C4
Kouzi[SD]	102	I2
Kouzigou[NX]	168	C3
Kowloon Bay[HK]	176	D3
Kowloon City[HK]	176	D3
Kowloon[HK]	176	D3
Koxrap[XJ]	172	F7
Koxtag[XJ]	172	G7
Koyak[XJ]	172	I7
Kuai He[SX]	54	C6
Kuaize He[YN]	148	J5
Kuancheng[HEB]	48	F3
Kuanchuan[SN]	156	C8
Kuandian[LN]	62	H4
Kuang Qu[SX]	54	E1
Kuang Qu[SX]	54	E4
Kuangchang[HI]	128	C1
Kuangdonggou[LN]	62	F4
Kuangfu[TW]	186	E3
Kuangshan[HN]	114	D5
Kuanhsi[TW]	186	E2
Kuanmiao[TW]	186	D4
Kuanshan[TW]	186	E3
Kuantzuling[TW]	186	D3
Kuanyin[TW]	186	E1
Kuanzhuang[YN]	148	H5
Kueishan Tao[TW]	186	E2
Kuicheng[FJ]	94	C4
Kuidou[FJ]	94	D4
Kuihu[AH]	90	E5
Kuimeishan[JX]	98	B7
Kuishan Ding[GX]	124	G5
Kuishan[SD]	102	F4
Kuitai[SD]	102	D2
Kuixi[HN]	114	C4
Kuixiang[YN]	148	J3
Kuixu[GX]	124	D4
Kuiyang[FJ]	94	C5
Kuiyang[GX]	124	G5
Kuk Po[HK]	176	D1
Kukeng[TW]	186	D3
Kukuan[TW]	186	E2
Kulansarak[XJ]	172	G5
Kuliang[GX]	124	F5
Kulongshan[HEB]	48	D2
Kumtag Shamo[XJ]	172	L5
Kümüx[XJ]	172	L4
Kuncheng Hu[JS]	80	F5
Kung Chau[HK]	176	F2
Kunggyü Co[XZ]	152	C4
Kunggyü[XZ]	152	B4
Kunghsi[TW]	186	E2
Kungtang[XZ]	152	D5
Kunhe[HL]	70	D4
Kunjirap Daban[XJ]	172	E7
Kunjirap Kou'an[XJ]	172	E7
Kunkou[FJ]	94	D2
Kunlun Nongchang[HI]	128	B2
Kunlun Shan[QH]	164	F5
Kunlun Shan[XJ]	172	F7
Kunlun Shan[XZ]	152	D1
Kunlun Shankou[QH]	164	G5
Kunlun[GX]	124	F4
Kunlun[SD]	102	D3
Kunming Hu[BJ]	36	C4
Kunming[YN]	148	H5
Kunping[GX]	124	D4
Kunshan[JS]	80	F5
Kunyu Shan[SD]	102	H3
Kunzhai[GZ]	144	D4
Kuocang Shan[ZJ]	84	E4
Kuocang Shan[ZJ]	84	E4
Kuoda[SC]	138	J3
Kuohsing[TW]	186	D2
Küp[XJ]	172	I3
Kuqa He[XJ]	172	I4
Kuqa[XJ]	172	I5
Kuquan[SN]	156	F5
Kurqên[XZ]	152	C4
Kürti[XJ]	172	L2
Kuruk Tag[XJ]	172	K5
Kushan[SD]	102	E4
Kushui He[NX]	168	C3
Kushui[GS]	160	F4
Kushui[XJ]	172	O4
Kutengpu[HN]	114	C4
Kutzulun[TW]	186	D4
Kuye He[SN]	156	G2
Kuytun He[XJ]	172	I3
Kuytun[XJ]	172	J3
Kuzhu[HB]	118	D2
Kuzhu[JX]	98	D5
Kwai Chung[HK]	176	D3
Kwai Tau Leng[HK]	176	D1
Kwo Chau Islands[HK]	176	F4
Kwu Tung[HK]	176	C1
Kwun Tong[HK]	176	D3
Kwun Tsoi Kok[HK]	176	E2
Kwun Yam Shan[HK]	176	D3
Kyadig[QH]	164	O4
Kyag Xiang[XZ]	152	F4
Kyangmar[XZ]	152	K5
Kyêbxang Co[XZ]	152	G3
Kyêrdo[XZ]	152	E5
Kyikug[QH]	164	M4
Kyinzhi[QH]	164	M6
Kyunglung[XZ]	152	B4
Kyungzê[XZ]	152	F5

L

Labagoumen[BJ]	36	D2
Labo[YN]	148	F3
Ladoi[XZ]	152	E4
Lafa[JL]	66	H4
Lagê[XZ]	152	J5
Lagkor Co[XZ]	152	D3
Lagoqiao[XZ]	152	I5
Lagou[GX]	124	H3
Laha[HL]	70	C4
Lai Chi Chong[HK]	176	E2
Lai Chi Kok[HK]	176	D3
Lai Chi Van[MC]	182	B6
Lai'an[AH]	90	E4
Laibang[AH]	90	C6
Laibin[GX]	124	G4
Laibin[YN]	148	J4
Laicun[JX]	98	C5
Laifang[JX]	98	D5
Laifeng[CQ]	132	C4
Laifeng[HB]	110	C5
Laifu[JL]	66	D2
Lai—i[TW]	186	D4
Laishan[SD]	102	H2
Laishui[HEB]	48	C4
Laituan[GX]	124	E5
Laiwu[SD]	102	D3
Laixi[SD]	102	G3
Laiyang[SD]	102	G3
Laiyu Dao[GD]	118	H4
Laiyuan[FJ]	94	C4
Laiyuan[HEB]	48	B4
Laiyuan[SX]	54	D4
Laizhou Wan[SD]	102	F2
Laizhou[SD]	102	F2
Laji shan[QH]	164	N4
Laji Shan[QH]	164	O4
Lakou[ZJ]	84	D4
Lalang[GX]	124	F3
Lalho[XZ]	152	F5
Lali[GX]	124	F3
Lalie[GX]	124	F3
Lalin He[HL]	70	D6
Lalin He[JL]	66	F2
Lalin He[JL]	66	H3
Lalin[HL]	70	D6
Lam Tei[HK]	176	B2
Lam Tin[HK]	176	E3
Lam Tsuen Valley[HK]	176	D2
Lam Uk Wai[HK]	176	F2
Lamadian[JL]	66	E4
Lamadong[LN]	62	C4
Lamdo[SC]	138	D3
Lamin Tohoi[NM]	58	X11
Lamma Island[HK]	176	C4
Lan He[SN]	156	E8
Lan Kok Tsui[HK]	176	B2
Lan Xian[SX]	54	C3
Lan Yu[TW]	186	E4
Lancang Jiang[XZ]	152	J4
Lancang Jiang[YN]	148	D2
Lancang Jiang[YN]	148	F7
Lancang[YN]	148	E8
Lancheng[SX]	54	C3
Lancun[SD]	102	G3
Landi[SD]	102	F3
Lang Shan[NM]	58	S10
Lang Shan[NM]	58	G7
La'nga Co[XZ]	152	B4
Langan[AH]	90	D3
Lan'gang[HL]	70	E6
Langanji[AH]	90	D5
Langao[SD]	102	G2
Labagou[SN]	156	E8
Langbuzhang[NX]	168	C3
Langchuan[ZJ]	84	C3
Langdai[GZ]	144	D4
Langdong[GZ]	144	G4
Langdu[YN]	148	F2
Langfang[HEB]	48	D4
Langgangshan Liedao[ZJ]	84	G2
Langgongmiao[HEN]	106	E2
Langjiazhuang[HEB]	48	B5
Langkou[HB]	110	E2
Langmai[XZ]	152	K4
Langmusi[GS]	160	F5
Langnying[QH]	164	L4
Langping[HB]	110	D4
Langpiziliang[NX]	168	C3
Langqên Zangbo (Xiangquan He) [XZ]	152	A4
Langqi[FJ]	94	E3
Langqiao[AH]	90	E6
Langqiao[YN]	148	J7
Langshan[NM]	58	T10
Langtou[LN]	62	H4
Langu[FJ]	94	D2
Languan[AH]	90	D6
Languan[GZ]	144	F4
Langwang[GD]	118	F4
Langwo Shan[AH]	90	D4
Langxi[AH]	90	F5
Langxi[CQ]	132	E4
Langxi[HN]	114	C4
Langxi[JL]	66	K4
Langxia[SH]	74	C3
Langxiang[HL]	70	E5
Langya Shan[HEB]	48	C4
Langya[SD]	102	F4
Langyagou[SX]	54	F2
Langzhong[SC]	138	K4
Langzhuangzi[TJ]	42	B3
Lanhe[GD]	118	G1
Lanheyu[LN]	62	H3
Lanjia[JL]	66	F4
Lanjiahe[SX]	54	B5
Lanjiaoshan[HN]	114	D6
Lanjiatangzi[JL]	66	L4
Lanjiazhuang[TJ]	42	C2
Lanju[ZJ]	84	D5
Lankao[HEN]	106	F3
Lanling[HL]	70	D6
Lanling[SD]	102	D5
Lanlongkou[QH]	164	N4
Lanlu Gang[SH]	74	C2
Lanmu[GX]	124	E3
Lannihuchong[HB]	110	E4
Lanping[YN]	148	E4
Lanqi[LN]	62	G4
Lanqiao[CQ]	132	E5
Lanqiao[HN]	114	E7
Lanqiao[SN]	156	F6
Lanqikalun[HEB]	48	F2
Lanrong[HN]	114	C6
Lanshan Qu[SD]	102	F4
Lanshan[HN]	114	E7
Lanshan[JL]	66	F5
Lantang[GD]	118	G3
Lantau Island[HK]	176	B3
Lantian[CQ]	132	E2
Lantian[GD]	118	G3
Lantian[GX]	124	H2
Lantian[JX]	98	B6
Lantian[SN]	156	F6
Lanting[ZJ]	84	E3
Lanxi[FJ]	94	B5
Lanxi[HL]	70	D5
Lanxi[ZJ]	84	D3
Lanxia[FJ]	94	C3
Lanxu[GX]	124	E5
Lanxun[HI]	128	B2
Lanyang Hsi[TW]	186	E2
Lanyang[GX]	124	E3
Lanyang[HI]	128	B2
Lanyu[TW]	186	E4
Lanzhou[GS]	160	F4
Lao He[JX]	98	C3
Lao ling[JL]	66	G6
Lao Mangnai[QH]	164	D3
Lao Shan[SD]	102	G3
Lao Shan[SD]	102	G3
Lao Shan[SN]	156	F4
Lao'aoba[GZ]	144	D4
Laobagang[JS]	80	F4
Laobao[GX]	124	G2
Laobian Qu[LN]	62	F4
Laobian[LN]	62	G3
Laobie Shan[YN]	148	E7
Laochang[YN]	148	J5
Laocheng[HI]	128	C2
Laocheng[HEN]	106	C4
Laocheng[HEN]	106	G4
Laocheng[JX]	98	B7
Laocheng[LN]	62	H2
Laocheng[SD]	102	B2
Laocheng[SD]	102	C3
Laocheng[YN]	148	G5
Laocun[GZ]	144	F5
Laodao[HN]	114	F4
Laodaodian[HL]	70	D3
Laodaohe[HN]	114	F4
Laodaosi[SN]	156	C7
Laodazhangzi[LN]	62	C4
Laodongwa[NX]	168	C3
Laogang[SH]	74	D2
Laogaochuan[SN]	156	G1
Laoguan He[HEN]	106	C4
Laoguanzhai[HEB]	48	C7
Laoha He[LN]	62	C3
Laoha He[NM]	58	N6
Laoheishan[HL]	70	F7
Laohekou[HB]	110	E2
Laohetu[LN]	62	F2
Laohuanghe Kou[SD]	102	E1
Laohuanghe Kou[SD]	102	F2
Laohugang[BJ]	36	B3
Laohugang[HL]	70	C5
Laohugou[NX]	168	B3
Laohutai[XJ]	172	H5
Laoji[AH]	90	B4
Laojinchang[JL]	66	H5
Laojun Shan[HEN]	106	C4
Laojun Shan[YN]	148	E4
Laojun[GS]	160	E3
Laojundian[SN]	156	F3
Laojunmiao[GS]	160	C3
Laolai[HL]	70	C4
Laolin[SC]	138	L4
Laomei[AH]	90	C6
Laomeng[YN]	148	H8
Laomidian[TJ]	42	B3
Laonung Hsi[TW]	186	D3
Laopeng[GX]	124	E3
Laopingshi[GD]	118	E1
Laopo[SD]	102	E4
Laorite Co[QH]	164	C7
Laoshan Qu[SD]	102	G3
Laoshan Wan[SD]	102	G3
Laosiping[LN]	62	H1
Laotougou[JL]	66	J5
Laotu Dingzi[HL]	70	F5
Laowa[HEB]	48	E3
Laowo[HEN]	106	F4
Laowopu[HEB]	48	D1
Laowuji[HB]	110	B4
Laoxian[SN]	156	F8
Laoxin[HB]	110	F4
Laoyachanao[HEN]	106	B3
Laoyanchi[NX]	168	C3
Laoye[HL]	70	E7
Laoye Ling[JL]	66	H4
Laoye Ling[JL]	66	H4
Laoye Ling[JL]	66	K4
Laoyemiao[BJ]	36	D2
Laoyemiao[BJ]	36	D2
Laoyemiao[XJ]	172	O3
Laoying[SX]	54	C2
Laoying[YN]	148	E5
Laoyinggou[JL]	66	G6
Laoyingpan[JX]	98	C5
Laoyu[SN]	156	E7
Laozhong[HEN]	106	F4
Laozhou[AH]	90	D6
Laozhou[HL]	70	D6
Laozhuang[SN]	156	D7
Laozhuangzi[BJ]	36	C4
Laozhuangzi[TJ]	42	B2
Laozishan[JS]	80	D3
Larenguan[GS]	160	F5

Name	Page	Grid
Lau Fau Shan[HK]	176	B2
Lawu[YN]	148	F5
Laxong Co[XZ]	152	D2
Lazhushan[SN]	156	G7
Lazikou[GS]	160	F5
Le'an Jiang[JX]	98	E3
Le'an[HN]	114	D4
Le'an[JX]	98	C4
Le'anpu[HN]	114	B6
Leba[SC]	138	L3
Lechang[GD]	118	F1
Ledong[HI]	128	B3
Ledong[JX]	98	A6
Ledu[QH]	164	O4
Lefeng[FJ]	94	D4
Lefeng[YN]	148	J4
Legong[JX]	98	E2
Leguan[JX]	98	D2
Leguang Nongchang[HI]	128	B3
Lehua[JX]	98	C3
Lei Shui[HN]	114	E6
Lei Uk[HK]	176	D2
Lei Yue Mun[HK]	176	E3
Leiba[GS]	160	G6
Leibo[SC]	138	I7
Leibu[AH]	90	C6
Leichi[AH]	90	C6
Leichi[SN]	156	G4
Leifeng[FJ]	94	D4
Leigao[GD]	118	C6
Leigong Shan[GZ]	144	G4
Leigong Shan[GZ]	144	G4
Leigong[HB]	110	G3
Leigongjian[JX]	98	C3
Leiguan[AH]	90	E4
Leihe[HB]	110	F3
Leijiafen[NX]	168	C4
Leijiaqi[SX]	54	B3
Leijiawa[SN]	156	F5
Leiming[HI]	128	C2
Leishan[GZ]	144	G4
Leiyang[HN]	114	E6
Leiyuan[SN]	156	F5
Leizhou Bandao[GD]	118	B5
Leizhou Wan[GD]	118	C6
Leizhou[GD]	118	C6
Lejia[LN]	62	F5
Lejian[GZ]	144	F2
Lejiang[GX]	124	G2
Lelai[HI]	128	C3
Leli He[GX]	124	D3
Leli[GZ]	144	G4
Leling[SD]	102	D2
Leluo[HI]	128	A3
Lemin[GD]	118	B5
Lemin[GZ]	144	C5
Lêmon[XZ]	152	G6
Lenghu[QH]	164	F2
Lengji[HB]	110	E2
Lenglong Ling[GS]	160	E4
Lenglong Ling[GS]	160	F4
Lenglong Ling[QH]	164	M2
Lenglong Ling[QH]	164	O3
Lengqi[SC]	138	H6
Lengquan[YN]	148	I7
Lengshui He[SN]	156	C8
Lengshui[CQ]	132	E3
Lengshui[HB]	110	F3
Lengshui[HEN]	106	C4
Lengshui[JX]	98	E4
Lengshui[SN]	156	F8
Lengshuijiang[HN]	114	D5
Lengshuixi[HN]	114	B5
Leping[GZ]	144	E4
Leping[JX]	98	E3
Leqiao[AH]	90	D5
Leshan[GZ]	144	E3
Leshan[JL]	66	F4
Leshan[SC]	138	I6
Leting[HEB]	48	F4
Letu[AH]	90	C3
Leung King Estate[HK]	176	B2
Leung Shuen Wan Hoi[HK]	176	E3
Leung Shuen Wan[HK]	176	E3
Lewang[GZ]	144	E5
Leye[GX]	124	D3
Leye[HL]	70	G5
Leyuan[HB]	110	D4
Leyuan[JX]	98	C2
Lezhi[SC]	138	K5
Lhabupu[XZ]	152	F5
Lhagcang[XZ]	152	D5
Lhagoi Kangri[XZ]	152	E5
Lha'gyai[XZ]	152	K4
Lhain Xiang[XZ]	152	F5
Lhakang[XZ]	152	G5
Lhamosi[SC]	138	H1
Lhari[XZ]	152	H4
Lharilhaxing[XZ]	152	B3
Lhasa He[XZ]	152	G5
Lhasa[XZ]	152	G5
Lhato[XZ]	152	K4
Lhazê[XZ]	152	E5
Lholing[XZ]	152	H5
Lhoma[XZ]	152	G4
Lhorong[XZ]	152	I4
Lhozhag[XZ]	152	G5
Lhünzê[XZ]	152	H5
Lhünzhub[XZ]	152	G5
Li Jiang[GX]	124	D5
Li Jiang[GX]	124	H2
Li Shan[SN]	156	F6
Li Shan[SX]	54	C6
Li Shan[YN]	148	I5
Li Shui[HN]	114	C3
Li Xian[GS]	160	G5
Li Xian[HEB]	48	C5
Li Xian[HN]	114	D3
Li Xian[SC]	138	I4
Li'an Gnag[HI]	128	C3
Lian Jiang[GD]	118	E2
Lian Jiang[GX]	124	G6
Lian Jiang[GZ]	144	E4
Lian Jiang[JX]	98	C6
Lian Shui[HN]	114	E5
Li'an[HI]	128	C3
Liancai[NX]	168	B5
Liancheng[FJ]	94	B4
Liancheng[GS]	160	F4
Liancun[JX]	98	B4
Liandaowan[SN]	156	F3
Lian'er[SH]	74	C2
Lianfeng[YN]	148	I3
Liang Shan[SD]	102	C4
Liang'an[SC]	138	J5
Liangcha[CQ]	132	C4
Liangcha[JS]	80	E3
Liangcheng[NM]	58	J7
Liangcheng[SD]	102	F4
Liangchiu[TW]	186	E3
Liangcun[GZ]	144	E2
Liangcun[SD]	102	C3
Liangdang[GS]	160	H6
Liangdaohe[HB]	110	D2
Liangditou[SD]	102	B5
Liangdong[GD]	118	C5
Liangdu[SX]	54	C5
Liang'erzhuang[HEB]	48	C7
Liangfu[FJ]	94	B4
Lianggang[HEB]	48	C4
Liangguang[GD]	118	C5
Liangguoji[SD]	102	G2
Lianghe[CQ]	132	E4
Lianghe[GX]	124	G6
Lianghe[GX]	124	I2
Lianghe[GZ]	144	C5
Lianghe[HB]	110	E4
Lianghe[HL]	70	E6
Lianghe[HN]	114	B4
Lianghe[SC]	138	H4
Lianghe[SN]	156	E7
Lianghe[SN]	156	E7
Lianghe[YN]	148	D6
Lianghekou[GZ]	144	D2
Lianghekou[HB]	110	D4
Lianghekou[SN]	156	C7
Lianghekou[SX]	54	D4
Lianghui[ZJ]	84	F3
Liangji[HB]	110	F2
Liangji[JS]	80	C3
Liangjia[HEB]	48	F2
Liangjia[SD]	102	D2
Liangjiachang[SN]	156	F7
Liangjiacun[HEB]	48	C5
Liangjiadian[HEB]	48	E4
Liangjiadian[LN]	62	E5
Liangjiagu[TJ]	42	C2
Liangjianfang[BJ]	36	C4
Liangjianfang[GS]	160	D2
Liangjianfang[HEB]	48	E3
Liangjiang[GD]	118	F1
Liangjiang[GX]	124	G4
Liangjiang[GX]	124	H2
Liangjiaping[SX]	54	C3
Liangjiatan[HN]	114	C4
Liangjiazhai[SX]	54	E3
Liangjiazhuang[SX]	54	C3
Liangjiazi[JL]	66	D2
Liangma[SX]	54	D5
Liangmao Ding[GD]	118	E5
Liangmianjing[HEB]	48	B2
Liangnong[ZJ]	84	F3
Liangping[CQ]	132	D3
Liangqi[GX]	124	F5
Liangqiao[SN]	156	D8
Liangqing Qu[GX]	124	F5
Liangqiu[SD]	102	D4
Liangsan[HN]	114	A5
Liangshan[HEB]	48	G4
Liangshan[LN]	62	F2
Liangshan[SD]	102	C4
Liangshang[GZ]	144	G4
Liangshe[SN]	156	D6
Liangshi[HN]	114	E6
Liangshui He[BJ]	36	D4
Liangshui[CQ]	132	E3
Liangshui[GS]	160	G6
Liangshui[JL]	66	F7
Liangshui[JL]	66	K5
Liangshuihezi[JL]	66	G5
Liangtang[GX]	124	G4
Liangtian[AH]	90	C6
Liangtian[GZ]	144	D5
Liangtian[HN]	114	E7
Liangting[AH]	90	C6
Liangting[SN]	156	D6
Liangtingxia[NX]	168	C5
Liangtou[TJ]	42	A4
Liangtun[LN]	62	F4
Liangwan[YN]	148	J2
Liangwang Shan[YN]	148	I5
Liangwang[GZ]	144	G4
Liangwangzhuang[TJ]	42	A3
Liangxiongdi[ZJ]	84	G2
Liangya[CQ]	132	F5
Liangyaping[HN]	114	C5
Liangyong[SC]	138	L4
Liangyuan[GS]	160	H5
Liangzhai[GX]	124	G2
Liangzhai[JS]	80	B2
Liangzhongqiao[LN]	62	G2
Liangzhu[HL]	70	D6
Liangzhu[ZJ]	84	E2
Liangzhuangzi[TJ]	42	B2
Liangzi Hu[HB]	110	H4
Liangzihu Qu[HB]	110	H4
Lianhe[AH]	90	E5
Lianhe[CQ]	132	E4
Lianhe[FJ]	94	D3
Lianhe[LN]	62	D3
Lianhe[SH]	74	C2
Lianhe[ZJ]	84	D4
Lianhu[CQ]	132	E4
Lianhua Feng[AH]	90	E6
Lianhua Shan[GD]	118	H3
Lianhua Shan[GD]	118	H3
Lianhua Shan[GX]	124	G4
Lianhua Shan[JX]	98	F2
Lianhua[FJ]	94	D5
Lianhua[GS]	160	D3
Lianhua[GS]	160	G5
Lianhua[GX]	124	H3

Lianhua[HI]	128	C3	Libo[GZ]	144	F5	Liju[YN]	148	E4
Lianhua[HL]	70	E6	Libu[GX]	124	I4	Lijun[NX]	168	B4
Lianhua[HL]	70	F5	Licai Nongchang[HI]	128	B3	Lijun[NX]	168	C2
Lianhua[HN]	114	E7	Licang Qu[SD]	102	G3	Likang[TW]	186	D4
Lianhua[JX]	98	A4	Licang[AH]	90	C3	Lilancheng[HEB]	48	D4
Lianhua[LN]	62	H2	Licha[SD]	102	F3	Lilin[JX]	98	E3
Lianhua[SC]	138	K5	Lichang[HB]	110	G4	Liling[FJ]	94	B4
Lianhuachi[BJ]	36	D3	Lichangshan Haixia[LN]	62	F5	Liling[HN]	114	F5
Lianhuashan[JX]	98	D2	Licheng[SX]	54	E5	Lilou[SD]	102	B2
Lianhuatan[BJ]	36	C3	Lichuan[HB]	110	B4	Limen[FJ]	94	E2
Lianhuatan[HEB]	48	C2	Lichuan[JX]	98	D4	Limin[SH]	74	D2
Lianhuatan[YN]	148	I8	Lichuan[SX]	54	D6	Limin[SX]	54	D2
Lianjiang[FJ]	94	E3	Licun[GX]	124	H5	Liming[GX]	124	E4
Lianjiang[GD]	118	C5	Licun[JX]	98	C4	Liming[HL]	70	C5
Lianjiangkou[GD]	118	F2	Licun[JX]	98	C6	Liming[YN]	148	E3
Lianjie[SC]	138	J6	Licun[SX]	54	C6	Liming[YN]	148	G8
Lianmai[GD]	118	E2	Lidang[GX]	124	F4	Limingzhuang[TJ]	42	B3
Lianmeng[TJ]	42	B4	Lidang[HB]	110	F3	Limu Ling[HI]	128	B2
Lianmeng[TJ]	42	B4	Lidao[SD]	102	I2	Limu Ling[HI]	128	B3
Lianmin[HN]	114	C6	Lide[AH]	90	B3	Limu[GX]	124	H2
Liannan[GD]	118	E2	Lidian[HB]	110	G3	Limu[GX]	124	I5
Lianping[GD]	118	G2	Lidian[LN]	62	E5	Limu[HN]	114	E5
Lianping[HN]	114	F7	Lidong[HL]	70	D5	Limushan[HI]	128	B2
Lianpu[AH]	90	D4	Lidu[CQ]	132	D4	Lin Ma Hang[HK]	176	D1
Lianshan[GD]	118	E2	Lidu[JX]	98	D3	Lin Xian[SX]	54	B4
Lianshan[HN]	114	B6	Liebu[SX]	54	C2	Lin'an[SH]	74	D3
Lianshan[LN]	62	F5	Lieshan Qu[AH]	90	C3	Lin'an[ZJ]	84	D2
Lianshanguan[LN]	62	G4	Lieyan[ZJ]	84	E5	Lincai[HEN]	106	F4
Lianshi[ZJ]	84	E2	Lifa[BJ]	36	C4	Lincang[YN]	148	F7
Lianshui[JS]	80	E3	Lifang[FJ]	94	C2	Linchang Jiao[HI]	128	B2
Lianshui[SN]	156	C8	Lifuta[HN]	114	C3	Linchangwudui[NM]	58	S11
Liansi[HEN]	106	F4	Ligang[GD]	118	C5	Lincheng[HEB]	48	B6
Liantang[GX]	124	G5	Ligang[NX]	168	C5	Lindian[HL]	70	C5
Liantang[HN]	114	E6	Ligang[ZJ]	84	F2	Lindian[SN]	156	F6
Liantang[SH]	74	C2	Ligangzifen[NX]	168	C3	Linfen[SX]	54	C5
Liantie[YN]	148	E5	Ligao[GX]	124	G3	Linfeng[LN]	62	H2
Lianwu[SD]	102	D2	Ligen[BJ]	36	B4	Ling He[ZJ]	84	F4
Lianxi[GD]	118	F4	Ligonggang[HN]	114	D3	Ling Xian[SD]	102	C2
Lianxi[SH]	74	C2	Liguan[LN]	62	E4	Lingao[HI]	128	B2
Lianxing[HL]	70	C4	Liguo[HI]	128	A3	Lingaojiao[HI]	128	B1
Lianyuan[HN]	114	D5	Liguo[SD]	102	E2	Lingbao[HEN]	106	B3
Lianyuan[JX]	98	D4	Lihai[ZJ]	84	E2	Lingbei[GD]	118	E2
Lianyun Qu[JS]	80	E2	Lihaiwu[SD]	102	B3	Lingbei[JX]	98	C5
Lianyun Shan[HN]	114	F4	Lihe[NX]	168	C1	Lingbei[JX]	98	C7
Lianyun Shan[HN]	114	F4	Lihong[SC]	138	G9	Lingbei[LN]	62	C3
Lianyungang[JS]	80	E2	Lihu[GX]	124	E2	Lingbi[AH]	90	D3
Lianyungang[JS]	80	E2	Lihuamao[TJ]	42	C3	Lingcuan[FJ]	94	D4
Lianzhan[AH]	90	D3	Lija[XZ]	152	I5	Lingchuan[GX]	124	H2
Lianzhen[HEB]	48	D6	Liji[HEN]	106	G6	Lingchuan[SX]	54	E6
Lianzhou[AH]	90	C6	Liji[JS]	80	C3	Lingdi[JX]	98	F3
Lianzhou[GD]	118	D4	Liji[JS]	80	E2	Lingdi[ZJ]	84	E4
Lianzhou[GD]	118	E2	Liji[SD]	102	B4	Lingdian[HL]	70	D3
Lianzhou[JX]	98	B4	Lijia[FJ]	94	B4	Lingdong Qu[HL]	70	F5
Lianzhu[ZJ]	84	D4	Lijia[LN]	62	F3	Lingdong[BJ]	36	D3
Lianzhuang[TJ]	42	C3	Lijia[SC]	138	K6	Lingfeng[GX]	124	I4
Liao He[LN]	62	F3	Lijia[SC]	138	L4	Linggo Co[XZ]	152	F3
liao He[LN]	62	G2	Lijia[SD]	102	C2	Linggou[LN]	62	G4
Li'ao[ZJ]	84	E5	Lijia[SD]	102	E2	Lingguan[HN]	114	F6
Liaobin[SH]	74	D3	Lijia[SN]	156	F8	Lingguan[SC]	138	H5
Liaocheng[SD]	102	B3	Lijia[ZJ]	84	D3	Linghai[LN]	62	E3
Liaodi[HEN]	106	F3	Lijiacha[SN]	156	F3	Linghe[SD]	102	F3
Liaodong Bandao[LN]	62	E5	Lijiadian[JL]	66	E3	Linghu[HN]	114	E6
Liaodong Wan[LN]	62	E4	Lijiagou[NX]	168	C1	Lingjiao[GX]	124	G6
Liaohe Kou[LN]	62	F4	Lijiahe[HB]	110	C5	Lingjiao[GX]	124	I4
Liaohe[HEN]	106	D5	Lijiahe[TJ]	42	B3	Lingjing[GX]	124	H4
Liaohepo[HEN]	106	D4	Lijiang[FJ]	94	D2	Lingjing[SX]	54	E3
Liaojiawan[HN]	114	E7	Lijiang[YN]	148	F4	Lingjing[ZJ]	84	F3
Liaolan[SD]	102	F3	Lijiaping[HN]	114	D6	Lingjingdian[SX]	54	D3
Liaotian[HN]	114	E6	Lijiaping[SX]	54	C2	Lingka[XZ]	152	J5
Liaowa[HB]	110	D2	Lijiapu[HN]	114	D3	Lingkou[CQ]	132	E5
Liaoyan[FJ]	94	E3	Lijiaqu[SN]	156	F4	Lingkou[FJ]	94	D3
Liaoyang[LN]	62	G3	Lijiashui[NX]	168	B3	Lingkou[HI]	128	C2
Liaoyang[LN]	62	G3	Lijiata[SN]	156	G3	Lingkou[JS]	80	E5
Liaoyuan[HL]	70	C5	Lijiatai[BJ]	36	E3	Lingkou[SN]	156	G6
Liaoyuan[JL]	66	F5	Lijiatai[LN]	62	H2	Lingli[FJ]	94	E3
Liaoyuan[SN]	156	E8	Lijiatian[HN]	114	C4	Lingling Qu[HN]	114	D6
Liaozhong[LN]	62	F3	Lijiaxiang[ZJ]	84	D2	Linglong[SD]	102	G2
Liaozi[CQ]	132	E2	Lijiaxinzhuang[NX]	168	C2	Linglong[SX]	156	F7
Liazê[XZ]	152	I4	Lijiazhai[SH]	74	D2	Linglong[ZJ]	84	D2
Libang[SH]	74	C2	Lijiazhai[SX]	54	E3	Linglongta[LN]	62	C4
Libao[JS]	80	F4	Lijiazhuang[NX]	168	C4	Linglu[FJ]	94	D4
Libazhuang[SX]	54	E2	Lijiazhuang[SX]	54	E4	Lingma[GX]	124	E4
Libazhuang[TJ]	42	B4	Lijin[SD]	102	E2	Lingmen[GD]	118	D5
Libei[JX]	98	D4	Lijingzhuang[TJ]	42	A4	Lingqiao[SH]	74	D2

Lingqiu[SX]	54	F2	Linsheng[JL]	66	I4	Litou Ding[GX]	124	I4
Lingquan[SD]	102	E4	Linshi[CQ]	132	D4	Liu He[HEB]	48	E3
Lingsha[NX]	168	C2	Linshu[SD]	102	E5	Liu He[JL]	66	F5
Lingshan Dao[SD]	102	G4	Linshui[AH]	90	B4	Liu He[JS]	80	G5
Lingshan Wan[SD]	102	G4	Linshui[SC]	138	L5	Liu He[LN]	62	F2
Lingshan[GX]	124	G5	Lintan[GS]	160	F5	Liu He[SH]	74	C2
Lingshan[HEB]	48	B5	Lintan[JX]	98	B6	Liu Jiang[GX]	124	G3
Lingshan[HI]	128	C2	Lintao[GS]	160	F5	Liu'anlou[AH]	90	C2
Lingshan[SD]	102	G3	Lintian[FJ]	94	C4	Liu'ao[FJ]	94	C6
Lingshang[HI]	128	C2	Lintian[HI]	128	B3	Liu'ao[ZJ]	84	F3
Lingshanwei[SD]	102	G4	Lintong Qu[SN]	156	F6	Liuba[GS]	160	E3
Lingshi[SX]	54	C5	Lintou[GD]	118	D5	Liuba[SN]	156	C7
Lingshou[HEB]	48	B5	Linwang[HI]	128	B3	Liubao[GX]	124	I4
Lingshui He[HI]	128	B3	Linwu[HN]	114	E7	Liubao[JS]	80	E3
Lingshui Jiao[HI]	128	C3	Linxi[AH]	90	E7	Liubinbu[BJ]	36	C2
Lingshui Wan[HI]	128	B3	Linxi[GX]	124	G2	Liubing Tai[SX]	54	F1
Lingshui[HI]	128	C3	Linxi[HEB]	48	C7	Liubu[SD]	102	D3
Lingtai[GS]	160	H5	Linxi[NM]	58	M6	Liucai[BJ]	36	B4
Lingtang[JS]	80	E4	Linxia[GS]	160	F5	Liuchang[GZ]	144	E4
Lingti[XZ]	152	H4	Linxia[GS]	160	F5	Liucheng[GX]	124	G3
Lingting[TW]	186	E3	Linxiang[HN]	114	F3	Liucheng[ZJ]	84	D4
Lingtingkou[TJ]	42	C2	Linxing[HL]	70	D5	Liuchia[TW]	186	D3
Lingtou[FJ]	94	D3	Linxu[GX]	124	F4	Liuchiu Yu[TW]	186	D4
Lingtou[HEN]	106	D3	Linyi[SD]	102	C2	Liuchiu[TW]	186	D4
Lingtou[HI]	128	A3	Linyi[SD]	102	E4	Liuchong He[GZ]	144	C3
Lingtou[ZJ]	84	D5	Linyi[SX]	54	B6	Liuchuan[GS]	160	G4
Lingui[GX]	124	H2	Linying[HEN]	106	E4	Liuchuanhe[SN]	156	D6
Lingwa[SC]	138	H2	Linyou[SN]	156	D6	Liucun[BJ]	36	C3
Lingwei[HI]	128	C2	Linyuan[SN]	156	G5	Liudao[HI]	128	B3
Lingwu[NX]	168	C2	Linyuan[TW]	186	D4	Liudaogou[JL]	66	H6
Lingxi[HN]	114	D3	Linze[GS]	160	E3	Liudaohe[BJ]	36	C2
Lingxia[FJ]	94	D2	Linze[JS]	80	E3	Liudaohe[HEB]	48	E3
Lingxia[JL]	66	C2	Linzhai[GD]	118	H2	Liudaokou[TJ]	42	A3
Lingxia[ZJ]	84	D3	Linzhang[HEB]	48	B7	Liudi[JL]	66	H3
Lingxiang[HB]	110	H4	Linzhen[AH]	90	E4	Liudian[AH]	90	D5
Lingxiatun[JL]	66	G4	Linzhen[GS]	160	I4	Liudian[HB]	110	G3
Lingxiu[HN]	114	F7	Linzhen[SN]	156	F4	Liudong[AH]	90	F5
Lingyang[FJ]	94	D1	Linzhou[HEN]	106	E1	Liudou[HB]	110	D1
Lingyuan[LN]	62	C3	Linzi Qu[SD]	102	E3	Liudu[AH]	90	D6
Lingyun[GX]	124	D3	Linzi[JL]	66	E2	Liudu[BJ]	36	B4
Lingzhan[GX]	124	D3	Linzi[JS]	80	F4	Liudu[GZ]	144	F2
Linhai[HL]	70	C3	Lion Rock[HK]	176	D3	Liuduo[JS]	80	F2
Linhai[JL]	66	C2	Liping[GS]	160	G6	Liufangzi[JL]	66	E4
Linhai[JL]	66	D4	Liping[GZ]	144	H4	Liufeng[HN]	114	E7
Linhai[JS]	80	F3	Liping[SN]	156	C8	Liugang[AH]	90	C4
Linhai[ZJ]	84	F4	Lipo[HN]	114	C4	Liugangjing[NX]	168	B3
Linhe[NX]	168	C2	Lipu[GX]	124	H3	Liugangzhuang[TJ]	42	B4
Linhong Kou[JS]	80	E2	Lipu[ZJ]	84	F4	Liugezhuang[BJ]	36	D3
Linhu[JX]	98	E3	Liqian[FJ]	94	C2	Liugezhuang[TJ]	42	B2
Linhuai[JS]	80	D3	Liqiao[AH]	90	E5	Liugong Dao[SD]	102	I2
Linhuan[AH]	90	C3	Liqiao[GS]	160	E3	Liugong[HI]	128	B3
Linian[JS]	80	D2	Liqiao[GS]	160	H5	Liugongmiao[JX]	98	C3
Linji[JS]	80	E3	Liquan[SN]	156	E6	Liugou[HEB]	48	F3
Linjiang[CQ]	132	B4	Lishadi[YN]	148	D3	Liugou[SC]	138	K4
Linjiang[CQ]	132	E2	Lishan Qu[LN]	62	F3	Liugu He[LN]	62	D4
Linjiang[FJ]	94	D2	Lishan[AH]	90	D6	Liuguan[GZ]	144	C5
Linjiang[GD]	118	G3	Lishan[AH]	90	F6	Liuguanzhai[SN]	156	F2
Linjiang[HB]	110	H4	Lishan[SX]	54	C6	Liuguoju[SN]	156	G2
Linjiang[HL]	70	C4	Lishan[TW]	186	E2	Liuhan[HEB]	48	B7
Linjiang[HL]	70	G4	Lishanba[HN]	114	F5	Liuhang[SH]	74	C2
Linjiang[JL]	66	G6	Lishe Jiang[YN]	148	F6	Liuhao[TJ]	42	C3
Linjiang[JS]	80	G5	Lishi[CQ]	132	C4	Liuhe[BJ]	36	D4
Linjiang[JX]	98	C3	Lishi[GD]	118	H2	Liuhe[HB]	110	I4
Linjiaping[SX]	54	B4	Lishi[HB]	110	F4	Liuhe[HEB]	48	D5
Linjie[YN]	148	F6	Lishi[SC]	138	K6	Liuhe[HEN]	106	E3
Linjin[SX]	54	B6	Lishu Qu[HL]	70	F6	Liuhe[HEN]	106	G3
Linkou[HL]	70	F6	Lishu[FJ]	94	C3	Liuhe[JL]	66	F5
Linkou[YN]	148	K3	Lishu[JL]	66	E4	Liuhe[JS]	80	G5
Linkuang[HB]	110	F3	Lishu[YN]	148	F6	Liuhe[SD]	102	E2
Linli[HN]	114	D3	Lishuangfeng[ZJ]	84	F3	Liuhe[TJ]	42	B3
Linmu[ZJ]	84	D2	Lishugou[HL]	70	E6	Liuhegou[LN]	62	F3
Linnan[SD]	102	C2	Lishui[CQ]	132	E4	Liuheng Dao[ZJ]	84	G3
Linnancang[HEB]	48	E4	Lishui[JS]	80	E5	Liuhezi[LN]	62	G3
Linpien[TW]	186	D4	Lishui[ZJ]	84	D4	Liuhong[SC]	138	I7
Linping[SN]	156	E6	Lishuping[SX]	54	E2	Liuhou[SN]	156	C7
Linqi[ZJ]	84	D3	Lisong[GX]	124	I3	Liuhu[JX]	98	C3
Linqing[SD]	102	B3	Litan[HEB]	48	D5	Liuhuangkuang[QH]	164	J1
Linqu[SD]	102	E3	Litang He[SC]	138	F7	Liuji[HB]	110	E3
Linquan[AH]	90	B3	Litang[GX]	124	G4	Liuji[JS]	80	E4
Linquan[GZ]	144	D3	Litang[HEN]	106	G3	Liujia[GX]	124	E3
Linru[HEN]	106	D3	Litang[SC]	138	F6	Liujia[GX]	124	I3
Linshan[ZJ]	84	C3	Litian[FJ]	94	B3	Liujia[JL]	66	F3
Linshanhe[HB]	110	H4	Litian[HN]	114	F7	Liujia[SC]	138	J6
Linsheng[JL]	66	C3	Litian[JX]	98	B4	Liujiachang[HB]	110	E4

Liujiadian[BJ]	36	D2	Liutao[NX]	168	B4	Lize[SD]	102	D2
Liujiading[TJ]	42	B2	Liutiangezhuang[HEB]	48	G4	Lizhai[JX]	98	E2
Liujiafan[AH]	90	D5	Liuting[SD]	102	G3	Lizhai[SX]	54	D6
Liujiafangzi[TJ]	42	B4	Liutong[GZ]	144	E3	Lizhigou[HI]	128	B3
Liujiagou[NX]	168	C4	Liutuan[HL]	70	E6	Lizhuang[HEN]	106	F3
Liujiaguanzi[JL]	66	D4	Liutuan[SH]	74	D2	Lizhuang[SD]	102	E5
Liujiahe[LN]	62	G4	Liutun[GZ]	144	E4	Lizhuangzi[TJ]	42	B2
Liujialaozhuang[NX]	168	B4	Liuwan Dashan[GX]	124	G5	Lizifang[LN]	62	G2
Liujianfang[LN]	62	F3	Liuwang[GX]	124	H5	Lizui[GD]	118	H2
Liujiang[GX]	124	G4	Liuwang[SD]	102	F4	Lo Chau Pak Pai[HK]	176	D4
Liujiaping[GS]	160	G6	Liuwei[JS]	80	E4	Lo Chau[HK]	176	D4
Liujiaping[SX]	54	C4	Liuxi He[GD]	118	F3	Lo Chau[HK]	176	E4
Liujiaqiao[JX]	98	D4	Liuxi[HEB]	48	F2	Lo Kei Wan[HK]	176	B4
Liujiashan[SN]	156	G3	Liuxiang[AH]	90	E3	Lodo[XZ]	152	C4
Liujiatai[HEB]	48	C4	Liuxiang[GX]	124	H4	Loi Tung[HK]	176	D1
Liujiaxia Shuiku[GS]	160	F5	Liuxianping[SN]	156	G7	Loinbo Kangri[XZ]	152	D5
Liujiayao[NX]	168	B3	Liuxianzhuang[TJ]	42	C2	Loinqê[QH]	164	N5
Liujiayao[SX]	54	D2	Liuyang He[HN]	114	F4	Lok Ma Chau[HK]	176	C1
Liujiazhuang[SD]	102	G3	Liuyang[AH]	90	C6	Lomai[XZ]	152	H4
Liujiazi[JL]	66	H4	Liuyang[HN]	114	F4	Long Jiang[GD]	118	H3
Liujiazi[LN]	62	D3	Liuyangpu[NX]	168	D3	Long Jiang[GX]	124	F3
Liujie[YN]	148	H6	Liuyegua[NX]	168	C3	Long Jiang[JX]	98	C4
Liujie[YN]	148	H6	Liuyin[CQ]	132	C4	Long Ke[HK]	176	F2
Liujing[GX]	124	F5	Liuyu[SD]	102	D4	Long Shan[GS]	160	G5
Liujing[GX]	124	H5	Liuyu[SX]	54	B4	Long Shan[SN]	156	C6
Liujing[SD]	102	D4	Liuyuan[GS]	160	B2	Long Xian[SN]	156	C6
Liujing[YN]	148	J7	Liuyuan[GX]	124	H4	Long'an[CQ]	132	E3
Liujun[JS]	80	E3	Liuyuan[HEB]	48	B7	Long'an[FJ]	94	C3
Liuke[SX]	54	F2	Liuyuan[NX]	168	C5	Long'an[GX]	124	E4
Liukuaizhuang[TJ]	42	B3	Liuzan[HEB]	48	F4	Long'an[GX]	124	G2
Liukuei[TW]	186	D4	Liuzao[SH]	74	D2	Long'an[JX]	98	D4
Liulang[HB]	110	D2	Liuzhai[GX]	124	E2	Long'anqiao[HL]	70	C5
Liuli[ZJ]	84	E2	Liuzhen[HL]	70	D4	Longba[HB]	110	C2
Liulihe[BJ]	36	C4	Liuzhangzi[HEB]	48	E3	Longbang[GX]	124	D5
Liulimiao[BJ]	36	D2	Liuzhangzi[LN]	62	B4	Longbao[CQ]	132	E3
Liulin[AH]	90	C3	Liuzhao Shan[YN]	148	K7	Longbao[QH]	164	I7
Liulin[HB]	110	D3	Liuzhi Tequ[GZ]	144	D4	Longbo[HI]	128	B2
Liulin[HB]	110	G3	Liuzhong[NX]	168	C2	Longbu[JX]	98	B6
Liulin[HEN]	106	E3	Liuzhong[SD]	102	D2	Longbu[JX]	98	C6
Liulin[HEN]	106	F6	Liuzhou[GX]	124	G3	Longcaoping[SN]	156	D7
Liulin[SD]	102	B3	Liuzhuang[HEN]	106	F5	Longchang[GZ]	144	C4
Liulin[SN]	156	D7	Liuzhuang[JS]	80	F3	Longchang[GZ]	144	C4
Liulin[SN]	156	F4	Liuzhuang[SD]	102	E4	Longchang[GZ]	144	D5
Liulin[SX]	54	B4	Liuzhuang[TJ]	42	A4	Longchang[HN]	114	C5
Liulinjian Shan[SX]	54	D3	Liuzhuangzi[TJ]	42	B2	Longchang[LN]	62	G4
Liulinshui[BJ]	36	B4	Liuzhuo[HEB]	48	C4	Longchang[SC]	138	K6
Liuliping[HB]	110	D2	Liuzikou[TJ]	42	B2	Longche[GX]	124	D3
Liulizhuang[TJ]	42	B3	Liuzuo[HB]	110	J5	Longchi[CQ]	132	F5
Liulongou[LN]	62	E3	Liwai[YN]	148	F6	Longchi[SD]	102	F3
Liulongtai[LN]	62	D3	Liwan[CQ]	132	E4	Longchiwan[NX]	168	B4
Liuma[GX]	124	H5	Liwang[NX]	168	C4	Longchuan Jiang[YN]	148	D6
Liumaowan[XJ]	172	J3	Liwo[GZ]	144	E4	Longchuan Jiang[YN]	148	G5
Liunan[JL]	66	F6	Liwuguan[SD]	102	F4	Longchuan[GD]	118	H2
Liupan Shan[GS]	160	H5	Lixi[CQ]	132	E5	Longchuan[GS]	160	G5
Liupan Shan[NX]	168	C5	Lixi[GD]	118	F3	Longchuan[GX]	124	D3
Liupan Shan[NX]	168	C5	Lixi[JX]	98	D4	Longchuan[YN]	148	C6
Liupan[HI]	128	B3	Lixian Jiang[YN]	148	G8	Longchuanjiang[YN]	148	D5
Liupanshui[GZ]	144	C4	Lixian[BJ]	36	C4	Longcun[FJ]	94	D2
Liupen[HEN]	106	F4	Lixin[AH]	90	C3	Longde[NX]	168	C5
Liuping[AH]	90	B6	Lixin[FJ]	94	B3	Longdepu[NX]	168	B5
Liuqiao[GX]	124	E5	Lixin[QH]	164	I7	Longdong[CQ]	132	D4
Liuqiao[JS]	80	F4	Lixin[SD]	102	D3	Longdong[CQ]	132	F3
Liuqingdi[NX]	168	C2	Lixin[SH]	74	C2	Longdong[GX]	124	G5
Liuquan[BJ]	36	C3	Lixindian[HEN]	106	F5	Longfeng Qu[HL]	70	C5
Liuquan[HEN]	106	D3	Lixing[AH]	90	B3	Longfeng[CQ]	132	C3
Liuquan[JS]	80	C2	Lixinzhuang[BJ]	36	D4	Longfeng[HB]	110	C4
Liuquhe[GZ]	144	C3	Lixioidain Co[QH]	164	C5	Longfeng[HI]	128	C1
Liusha Gang[GD]	118	B6	Liya[SC]	138	K4	Longfeng[HN]	114	F5
Liusha[GD]	118	B6	Liyang[JS]	80	E5	Longfeng[JL]	66	D3
Liushan[SD]	102	E3	Liyang[SX]	54	E4	Longfeng[JL]	66	H4
Liushi[HEB]	48	C5	Liye[HN]	114	B4	Longfengshan[HL]	70	D6
Liushi[JX]	98	A4	Liyi[SX]	54	E6	Longfusi[TJ]	42	C1
Liushigang[HEB]	48	B7	Liying[BJ]	36	C2	Longgan Hu[AH]	90	C7
Liushipu[AH]	90	B4	Liyong[GX]	124	G3	Longgan Hu[HB]	110	J5
Liushu[HL]	70	B5	Liyuan He[GS]	160	D3	Longgang Qu[GD]	118	G4
Liushu[HL]	70	E6	Liyuan[BJ]	36	B4	Longgang Qu[LN]	62	D4
Liushuhezi[JL]	66	H5	Liyuan[HN]	114	E7	Longgang Shan[JL]	66	F5
Liushui[FJ]	94	E4	Liyuan[SX]	54	C6	Longgang Shan[LN]	62	I3
Liushukou[SX]	54	E6	Liyuan[SX]	54	D5	Longgang[AH]	90	D5
Liushuquan[HEB]	48	F4	Liyuan[TW]	186	E3	Longgang[HB]	110	H5
Liutaizhuang[HEB]	48	G4	Liyuan[YN]	148	I4	Longgang[JX]	98	C5
Liutang[CQ]	132	E4	Liyuanping[SX]	54	C3	Longgang[JX]	98	D5
Liutang[GX]	124	F3	Liyue Tan[HI]	128	G6	Longgang[ZJ]	84	D2
Liutang[SC]	138	M5	Liyutang[HN]	114	F6	Longgao[SN]	156	E6

Name	Page	Grid	Name	Page	Grid	Name	Page	Grid
Longgong[GZ]	144	D4	Longmen[HI]	128	C2	Longting[SD]	102	D4
Longgong[SX]	54	D3	Longmen[HL]	70	D4	Longtou[FJ]	94	B3
Longgong[ZJ]	84	C5	Longmen[HN]	114	G4	Longtou[GX]	124	F3
Longgu[JS]	80	B2	Longmen[QH]	164	K3	Longtou[HL]	70	G5
Longguan[HEB]	48	C3	Longmen[SN]	156	G5	Longtou[HN]	114	B4
Longguang[GX]	124	D4	Longmensuo[HEB]	48	C3	Longtoushan[HEB]	48	E2
Longguang[GZ]	144	D5	Longmentan[FJ]	94	D4	Longwan Qu[ZJ]	84	E5
Longguang[HI]	128	B3	Longmenzhuang[HEB]	48	B5	Longwan[FJ]	94	D3
Longgun[HI]	128	C2	Longmiao[JS]	80	D2	Longwan[GX]	124	F4
Longhai[FJ]	94	C5	Longming[GX]	124	E5	Longwan[HB]	110	F4
Longhai[HN]	114	F6	Longmu[GD]	118	H2	Longwan[ZJ]	84	E5
Longhai[YN]	148	J3	Longmu[JX]	98	B5	Longwang Jian[AH]	90	E4
Longhe[AH]	90	C5	Longnan[GS]	160	G6	Longwang Shan[ZJ]	84	D2
Longhe[CQ]	132	D4	Longnan[JX]	98	B7	Longwang[AH]	90	B4
Longhe[HI]	128	C2	Longnan[ZJ]	84	D5	Longwang[JL]	66	E3
Longhe[HL]	70	B2	Longpan[SC]	138	K5	Longwang[SN]	156	E7
Longhe[HL]	70	C4	Longpan[YN]	148	F3	Longwanggou[HB]	110	D1
Longhe[JS]	80	E2	Longpeng[YN]	148	H7	Longwangmiao[AH]	90	D3
Longhekou Shuiku[AH]	90	C5	Longping[GZ]	144	F3	Longwangmiao[HEB]	48	C7
Longhu[FJ]	94	C2	Longping[HB]	110	D4	Longwangmiao[HL]	70	G6
Longhu[FJ]	94	C2	Longping[HB]	110	E3	Longwangmiao[LN]	62	G4
Longhu[FJ]	94	C3	Longpu[ZJ]	84	E3	Longwangshan Shuiku[JS]	80	D4
Longhu[FJ]	94	D5	Longqiao[HI]	128	C2	Longwangtang[SX]	54	D5
Longhu[GX]	124	H2	Longqing[YN]	148	J6	Longwangtou[BJ]	36	D3
Longhu[HI]	128	C2	Longqiongjibao[QH]	164	F6	Longwangzhuang[SD]	102	G3
Longhu[JX]	98	D4	Longquan He[AH]	90	C7	Longwantun[BJ]	36	D3
Longhua[FJ]	94	D4	Longquan Xi[ZJ]	84	D4	Longwei Co[XZ]	152	F3
Longhua[HEB]	48	C5	Longquan[FJ]	94	C3	Longwen Qu[FJ]	94	C5
Longhua[HEB]	48	E2	Longquan[HL]	70	C5	Longwo[GD]	118	H3
Longhua[SX]	54	C6	Longquan[JL]	66	G5	Longwu He[QH]	164	N5
Longhui[HN]	114	D5	Longquan[SX]	54	E5	Longxi He[CQ]	132	D3
Longhuo[GX]	124	C3	Longquan[ZJ]	84	D4	Longxi Shan[FJ]	94	C3
Longhushan Shuiku[HI]	128	C2	Longquanguan[HEB]	48	A5	Longxi[GD]	118	G3
Longhushan[JX]	98	D3	Longquansi[HEB]	48	B6	Longxi[GS]	160	G5
Longji[AH]	90	F4	Longquanyi Qu[SC]	138	J5	Longxi[GZ]	144	F3
Longji[JS]	80	D2	Longsang[GX]	124	D4	Longxi[HN]	114	F7
Longji[JS]	80	D3	Longsang[QH]	164	M5	Longxi[SX]	54	E5
Longjia[GZ]	144	F3	Longsangsi[SD]	102	D2	Longxi[ZJ]	84	D5
Longjiang[GD]	118	F4	Longsha[CQ]	132	E3	Longxi[ZJ]	84	E3
Longjiang[HI]	128	C2	Longshan[FJ]	94	C5	Longxing[CQ]	132	B3
Longjiang[HL]	70	B5	Longshan[HL]	70	F5	Longxing[CQ]	132	C3
Longjiao[CQ]	132	E3	Longshan[HN]	114	B3	Longxingshi[HN]	114	F6
Longjiao[FJ]	94	D5	Longshan[SC]	138	K8	Longxipu[HN]	114	D5
Longjiao[SX]	54	B4	Longshan[ZJ]	84	E3	Longxu He[GX]	124	D4
Longjiaoshan[HB]	110	H5	Longshan[ZJ]	84	F2	Longxudao[SD]	102	I2
Longjiazhuang[SX]	54	D3	Longshandian[SD]	102	G2	Longxumen[HEB]	48	F3
Longjie[GD]	118	G2	Longshe[CQ]	132	E4	Longyan[FJ]	94	C4
Longjie[GZ]	144	C3	Longsheng[CQ]	132	C4	Longyan[GX]	124	F2
Longjie[YN]	148	E5	Longsheng[GX]	124	H2	Longyang Xia[QH]	164	M4
Longjing[CQ]	132	F2	Longsheng[SN]	156	F7	Longyangxia Shuiku[QH]	164	M5
Longjing[GD]	118	E5	Longshenghe[NM]	58	S11	Longyangxia[QH]	164	M4
Longjing[GZ]	144	E3	Longshi[CQ]	132	B4	Longyao[HEB]	48	B6
Longjing[JL]	66	J5	Longshi[CQ]	132	C3	Longyin[GX]	124	G2
Longjingtou[FJ]	94	D1	Longshi[JX]	98	A5	Longyin[GZ]	144	D4
Longju[CQ]	132	E3	Longshou Shan[GS]	160	E3	Longyou[ZJ]	84	D3
Longjuan[FJ]	94	C5	Longshou Shan[NM]	58	D8	Longyuan[HN]	114	F3
Longkeng[GZ]	144	E3	Longshui[YN]	148	I3	Longyuanba[JX]	98	B7
Longkou Gang[SD]	102	G2	Longshui[CQ]	132	B4	Longzha[HN]	114	F6
Longkou[GD]	118	E4	Longshui[GX]	124	H1	Longzhai[HN]	114	B3
Longkou[HB]	110	G5	Longshui[GX]	124	I3	Longzhao[JL]	66	D2
Longkou[JX]	98	C5	Longtai[SC]	138	J5	Longzhen[HL]	70	D4
Longkou[SD]	102	G2	Longtai[SC]	138	K5	Longzhen[SN]	156	F3
Longli[GZ]	144	E4	Longtai[SC]	138	L5	Longzhou He[HI]	128	C2
Longli[GZ]	144	H4	Longtan[AH]	90	B4	Longzhou[GX]	124	D5
Longlin[GX]	124	C3	Longtan[CQ]	132	E5	Longzhou[HI]	128	C2
Longlin[GX]	124	D4	Longtan[GX]	124	G6	Longzhou[SN]	156	E3
Longling[JX]	98	B6	Longtan[HN]	114	B4	Lop Nur[XJ]	172	M5
Longling[YN]	148	D6	Longtan[HN]	114	E7	Lop Nur[XJ]	172	M5
Longlou[HI]	128	C2	Longtan[HN]	114	F5	Lop[XJ]	172	H7
Longma[HI]	128	C2	Longtan[LN]	62	D3	Loqung[SC]	138	D3
Longma[SX]	54	C5	Longtan[LN]	62	G4	Loso Shing[HK]	176	D4
Longmatan Qu[SC]	138	K7	Longtan[YN]	148	F8	Lou Shui[HN]	114	C3
Longmen Gang[HI]	128	B2	Longtang[HN]	114	D4	Loucun[HEB]	48	C4
Longmen Shan[SC]	138	J3	Longtang[HN]	114	D5	Loude[SD]	102	D4
Longmen Shan[SX]	54	B6	Longtang[HN]	114	F6	Loudi[HN]	114	D5
Longmen Shan[ZJ]	84	D3	Longtang[JX]	98	C7	Loufan[SX]	54	C3
Longmen[CQ]	132	D3	Longtanhe[HN]	114	D3	Loufangping[SN]	156	E4
Longmen[FJ]	94	B4	Longtanping[HN]	114	C3	Lougou[SX]	54	C2
Longmen[FJ]	94	C4	Longtanqiao[HN]	114	E4	Louguan[SN]	156	E6
Longmen[FJ]	94	D5	Longtian[AH]	90	E7	Louhe[HB]	110	G4
Longmen[GD]	118	C6	Longtian[FJ]	94	E4	Loulan Site[XJ]	172	L5
Longmen[GD]	118	G3	Longtian[GZ]	144	G3	Loushanguan[GZ]	144	E3
Longmen[GX]	124	G5	Longtian[HN]	114	D4	Louta[ZJ]	84	E3
Longmen[HI]	128	B2	Longting[JX]	98	C7	Loutai[HB]	110	D2

Loutang[SH]	74	C2	Luhuitou Jiao[HI]	128	B3	Luobo[GX]	124	F4
Louziying[SX]	54	C2	Luhuitou[HI]	128	B3	Luobotou[TJ]	42	C3
Louzizhuang[BJ]	36	C3	Luhun Shuiku[HEN]	106	D3	Luobu[ZJ]	84	D3
Lower Shing Mun Reservoir[HK]	176	D3	Luhuo[SC]	138	F4	Luobugu[YN]	148	I4
Lü He[HEN]	106	G5	Luhushan[HB]	110	F5	Luobuyuan[SN]	156	D4
Lu He[SN]	156	F3	Lujia[BJ]	36	C3	Luochang[SC]	138	J7
Lu Hu[HB]	110	H4	Lüjiacun[BJ]	36	B4	Luocheng[GS]	160	D3
Lu Shan[JX]	98	C2	Lujiadaying[GZ]	144	C4	Luocheng[GX]	124	F3
Lu Shan[SD]	102	D3	Lujiang[AH]	90	D5	Luocheng[JX]	98	B3
Lu Shan[SD]	102	E3	Lujiang[YN]	148	D6	Luochuan[NX]	168	C4
Lu Shui[JX]	98	B4	Lujiao[CQ]	132	E4	Luochuang[SN]	156	F5
Lu Tao(Huoshao Tao)[TW]	186	E4	Lujiawan[SX]	54	F1	Luocun[SX]	54	B5
Lu Xian[SC]	138	K6	Lujiayao[NX]	168	C3	Luodai[HI]	128	A2
Luan He[HEB]	48	D2	Lujiaying[HEB]	48	B2	Luodian[GZ]	144	E5
Luan He[HEB]	48	F4	Lujing[BJ]	36	C4	Luodian[HB]	110	G3
Luan Xian[HEB]	48	F4	Lüjing[GS]	160	G5	Luodian[HB]	110	G3
Lu'an[AH]	90	C5	Lujing[NM]	58	C7	Luoding Jiang[GD]	118	D4
Luancheng[HEB]	48	B6	Lujing[SN]	156	G5	Luoding[GD]	118	D4
Luanchuan[HEN]	106	C4	Lujuhe[TJ]	42	C4	Luodong[GD]	118	D3
Luanhe Kou[HEB]	48	G4	Luk Chau Village[HK]	176	D4	Luodong[GX]	124	F3
Luanlong[FJ]	94	D3	Luk Chau Wan[HK]	176	D4	Luodou Sha[GD]	118	C6
Luannan[HEB]	48	F4	Luk Chau[HK]	176	D4	Luodou[HI]	128	C2
Luanping[HEB]	48	E3	Luk Keng[HK]	176	D1	Luofang[FJ]	94	C4
Luanshan[HN]	114	F5	Luk Wu[HK]	176	A4	Luofu Shan[GD]	118	G3
Luanshanzi[GS]	160	C2	Lukang[TW]	186	D2	Luofu Shan[GD]	118	G3
Luanwan[SD]	102	C3	Lukou[AH]	90	D5	Luofu[GX]	124	E3
Luanyang[HEB]	48	F3	Lukou[HB]	110	H5	Luogang[AH]	90	D5
Lubei[SH]	74	D3	Lukou[HEN]	106	F5	Luogang[GD]	118	H2
Lubu[GD]	118	E3	Lukou[HN]	114	F4	Luoguhe[HL]	70	A2
Lubuge[GZ]	144	C6	Lukou[JS]	80	D5	Luoha[SC]	138	H7
Luchaogang[SH]	74	D3	Lukou[JX]	98	B2	Luohansi[HB]	110	H4
Lucheng[GX]	124	D3	Luku[TW]	186	D3	Luohantang[QH]	164	N4
Lucheng[HN]	114	F3	Lüliang Shan[QH]	164	G3	Luohe[AH]	90	D5
Lucheng[SX]	54	E5	Lüliang Shan[SX]	54	C4	Luohe[HEN]	106	F4
Luchong[HN]	114	B6	Lüliang[JS]	80	E3	Luohe[SN]	156	F8
Luchu[TW]	186	D4	Lüliang[SX]	54	C4	Luohu[JX]	98	D3
Luchuan[GX]	124	H5	Luliang[YN]	148	I5	Luohui Qu[SN]	156	F5
Luchuan[SN]	156	G4	Lulin[HI]	128	C2	Luoji[HEN]	106	H3
Lüchun[YN]	148	H7	Luling[XZ]	152	G4	Luoji[HI]	128	B2
Luchuying[GZ]	144	D5	Lulong[HEB]	48	F4	Luojia[BJ]	36	B4
Luci Yu[FJ]	94	E4	Luluo[HEB]	48	A6	Luojia[HN]	114	D6
Luci[JX]	98	E3	Luma[HI]	128	C3	Luojiang Qu[FJ]	94	D5
Luci[ZJ]	84	D5	Lumajangdong Co[XZ]	152	B2	Luojiang[CQ]	132	E2
Lucidu[HN]	114	D4	Luming[SC]	138	M4	Luojiang[SC]	138	J4
Lücongpo[HB]	110	D4	Luna[YN]	148	I4	Luojiang[SC]	138	M4
Lucun[AH]	90	F6	Lunag Qu[QH]	164	J6	Luojiaping[SC]	138	H8
Lucun[SD]	102	E3	Lunan Qu[HEB]	48	F4	Luojiayuanzi[NX]	168	C1
Lucun[SX]	54	D5	Lunan Shan[SC]	138	H9	Luojin[GX]	124	H2
Ludian[HEN]	106	E3	Lunan Shan[SC]	138	H9	Luojing[HI]	128	C2
Lüdian[HEN]	106	D3	Lunang[XZ]	152	I5	Luojing[SH]	74	C2
Ludian[YN]	148	I3	Lung Kwu Tan[HK]	176	B2	Luojiu[HN]	114	B5
Luding[SC]	138	H6	Lung Mei Tsuen[HK]	176	B3	Luokan[YN]	148	J3
Luen Wo Hui[HK]	176	D1	Lung Yeuk Tau[HK]	176	D1	Luoke Shan[GD]	118	E3
Lüeyang[SN]	156	C7	Lungdinglê[XZ]	152	D4	Luokeng[GD]	118	D5
Lufang[JX]	98	D3	Lunggar Shan[XZ]	152	C4	Luokeng[GD]	118	F2
Lufeng[FJ]	94	B5	Lunggar[XZ]	152	D4	Luokou[JX]	98	D5
Lüfeng[FJ]	94	C4	Lungkug[XZ]	152	D4	Luokui[HI]	128	B3
Lufeng[GD]	118	H4	Lungkwu Chau[HK]	176	A3	Luoli[GZ]	144	G4
Lufeng[YN]	148	H5	Lungmar[QH]	164	H6	Luoling[HEN]	106	C3
Lugang[HEN]	106	F2	Lungmarda[QH]	164	H8	Luoling[HI]	128	C2
Lugang[HEN]	106	F2	Lungmu Co[XZ]	152	B2	Luolong Qu[HEN]	106	D3
Lugba[SC]	138	G6	Lungmugnang[QH]	164	H7	Luolong[GZ]	144	F1
Lugba[XZ]	152	A4	Lungmugda[QH]	164	I7	Luolou[GX]	124	D3
Lugba[XZ]	152	E5	Lungra'gyagoi[QH]	164	J5	Luoluopu[LN]	62	E3
Lügezhuang[SD]	102	G3	Lungring[QH]	164	M7	Luoma Hu[JS]	80	D2
Lugong[GZ]	144	D5	Lungsang Qu[XZ]	152	D2	Luoman[GX]	124	G3
Lugouhu[NX]	168	B3	Lungsangda[QH]	164	I7	Luomen[GS]	160	G5
Lugousha[QH]	164	I9	Lungtan[TW]	186	E2	Luomu[GZ]	144	E5
Lugouzi[NX]	168	C3	Lungyagda[QH]	164	I8	Luonan[SN]	156	G6
Lugu Hu[SC]	138	F8	Lunhe[HL]	70	D5	Luoning[HEN]	106	C3
Lugu Hu[YN]	148	F3	Luniao[ZJ]	84	D2	Luoping[GD]	118	D4
Lugu[SX]	54	C2	Lunnan[XJ]	172	J5	Luoping[HN]	114	C3
Lugu[XZ]	152	D3	Lunpei[TW]	186	D3	Luoping[JX]	98	C2
Luguhu[SC]	138	F8	Luntai(Bügür)[XJ]	172	J5	Luoping[YN]	148	J6
Luguo[JL]	66	J5	Luo He[GD]	118	H3	Luoqiao[HN]	114	E6
Luhe Qu[JS]	80	D4	Luo He[HEN]	106	C3	Luoqing Jiang[GX]	124	G3
Luhe[GD]	118	H3	Luo He[SN]	156	E4	Luoqiying[BJ]	36	C4
Lühe[HEN]	106	F5	Luo He[SN]	156	F5	Luoquanwan[NX]	168	B3
Luhe[HL]	70	D5	Luo He[SN]	156	G6	Luoren[HI]	128	B2
Luhe[SC]	138	H9	Luo Hu[HK]	176	C1	Luosha[GX]	124	D3
Lühe[YN]	148	G5	Luoba[GD]	118	G2	Luoshan[HB]	110	G5
Luhongshi[HN]	114	D6	Luoba[GS]	160	G5	Luoshan[HEN]	106	F5
Lühua[SH]	74	C1	Luobei[HL]	70	F5	Luoshan[JX]	98	C4
Luhui[SH]	74	D2	Luobiao[SC]	138	J7	Luoshan[JX]	98	C6

Luoshan[NX]	168	B4
Luoshanchuan[GS]	160	H4
Luoshui[YN]	148	J4
Luosu[GZ]	144	E5
Luota[HN]	114	B3
Luotang[AH]	90	D4
Luotang[GS]	160	G6
Luotian[CQ]	132	E3
Luotian[HB]	110	I4
Luotian[JX]	98	C4
Luotian[JX]	98	C4
Luoting[JX]	98	C3
Luotongshan[JL]	66	G5
Luotuo Feng[XJ]	172	L6
Luotuo Hu[XZ]	152	B2
Luotuo[GS]	160	D3
Luotuo[GZ]	144	E5
Luotuoshan[SX]	54	D2
Luowa[NX]	168	C4
Luowan[GZ]	144	C6
Luowan[JX]	98	C3
Luowang[HI]	128	A2
Luowei[JS]	80	D3
Luowen[SC]	138	M4
Luowenzao[SX]	54	E1
Luoxi[FJ]	94	D4
Luoxi[GX]	124	D2
Luoxi[JS]	80	E5
Luoxi[JX]	98	B2
Luoxi[JX]	98	B5
Luoxiang[GZ]	144	H5
Luoxiao Shan[HN]	114	F5
Luoxiao Shan[JX]	98	A4
Luoxiao Shan[JX]	98	A5
Luoxiu[GX]	124	G3
Luoxiu[GX]	124	H4
Luoxu[GX]	124	F4
Luoyan[FJ]	94	C5
Luoyang Shan[GX]	124	G5
Luoyang Shan[GX]	124	G5
Luoyang[GD]	118	F2
Luoyang[GX]	124	F3
Luoyang[HB]	110	G3
Luoyang[HEN]	106	D3
Luoyang[SN]	156	F5
Luoyixi[HN]	114	C4
Luoyuan Wan[FJ]	94	E3
Luoyuan[FJ]	94	D3
Luoyuan[FJ]	94	E3
Luoyuan[SN]	156	F6
Luoyukou[SX]	54	B3
Luoyun[SX]	54	D5
Luoze He[YN]	148	I3
Luozehe[YN]	148	I3
Luozhen[SN]	156	D8
Luozheng[HEN]	106	F3
Luozhou[FJ]	94	E4
Luozhou[GZ]	144	C3
Luozhuang Qu[SD]	102	E5
Luozhuangzi[TJ]	42	B1
Luozhuangzi[TJ]	42	B4
Luozigou[JL]	66	K4
Luozishan[SN]	156	G4
Luozuo[SC]	138	H9
Luping[GZ]	144	F4
Luping[HI]	128	C3
Lupu[JS]	80	E3
Luqiao Qu[ZJ]	84	F4
Lüqiao[HEB]	48	E5
Luqiao[JS]	80	F5
Luqiao[SH]	74	C3
Lüqiao[SH]	74	C3
Luqu[GS]	160	F5
Luquan[HEB]	48	B5
Luquan[YN]	148	H5
Luringma[QH]	164	E7
Lushan Qu[JX]	98	C2
Lushan[GZ]	144	F4
Lushan[HEN]	106	D4
Lushan[SC]	138	H5
Lushan[TW]	186	E2
Lushi[HEN]	106	C3
Lushui Shuiku[HB]	110	H5
Lüshui[HB]	110	C5

Lushui[HN]	114	F6
Lushui[JL]	66	C2
Lushui[YN]	148	D5
Lüshunkou Qu[LN]	62	E6
Lüsigang[JS]	80	G4
Lusigang[JX]	98	D3
Lutai Nongchang[TJ]	42	C3
Lutao[TW]	186	E4
Lutian[FJ]	94	C4
Lutian[GD]	118	F3
Lutian[HN]	114	F6
Lutian[JX]	98	B5
Lutian[JX]	98	D3
Lutou[HB]	110	F2
Lutou[SD]	102	G2
Lutou[ZJ]	84	E2
Lutun[LN]	62	F4
Lüwang[HB]	110	H3
Luwu[GX]	124	F5
Luxi Dao[ZJ]	84	F5
Luxi[AH]	90	D7
Luxi[FJ]	94	C5
Luxi[HB]	110	G5
Luxi[HN]	114	C4
Luxi[JX]	98	B4
Luxi[JX]	98	C2
Luxi[SC]	138	J4
Luxi[SC]	138	L5
Luxi[YN]	148	D6
Luxi[YN]	148	I6
Lüxi[ZJ]	84	E3
Luxia[FJ]	94	D3
Luxia[FJ]	94	D3
Luxia[FJ]	94	F3
Lüxiang[SH]	74	C3
Luxiangzhuang[TJ]	42	B2
Luxin[GX]	124	G4
Luxinhe[TJ]	42	B3
Luxinzhuang[TJ]	42	A4
Luxu[GX]	124	G4
Luxu[JS]	80	F5
Luya Shan[SX]	54	C3
Luyang[CQ]	132	E2
Luyeh[TW]	186	E4
Luyi[HEN]	106	G4
Luying[HEN]	106	D5
Luyuan[HL]	70	G5
Luzao[JS]	80	F4
Luzhai[GX]	124	G3
Luzhai[HI]	128	C2
Luzhang[YN]	148	D5
Luzhen[AH]	90	C5
Lüzhi Jiang[YN]	148	G6
Lüzhi[JS]	80	F5
Lüzhi[YN]	148	G6
Luzhou[SC]	138	K7
Luzhuang[JS]	80	C2
Luzhuangzi[TJ]	42	B1
Luzishui[BJ]	36	A4

M

Ma He[AH]	90	E6
Ma Lam Wat[HK]	176	E3
Ma Liu Shui[HK]	176	D2
Ma Niu[HK]	176	D2
Ma On Kong[HK]	176	C2
Ma On Shan Tsuen[HK]	176	E2
Ma On Shan[HK]	176	D2
Ma On Shan[HK]	176	E2
Ma Shi Chau[HK]	176	D2
Ma Tseuk Leng[HK]	176	D1
Ma Tso Lung[HK]	176	C1
Ma Wan Channel[HK]	176	C3
Ma Wan[HK]	176	C3
Ma Yau Tong[HK]	176	E3
Ma'an Liedao[ZJ]	84	G2
Ma'an Ling[HI]	128	B2
Ma'an[HN]	114	B5
Ma'an[SC]	138	L4
Ma'an[ZJ]	84	E2
Ma'andi[YN]	148	I8

Ma'anshan[AH]	90	E5
Ma'anshan[JL]	66	F4
Ma'anshan[YN]	148	F5
Maba[JS]	80	D4
Mabang[GX]	124	B3
Mabaoquan[BJ]	36	B3
Mabi[FJ]	94	E3
Mabi[SX]	54	D6
Mabian[SC]	138	I7
Mabie He[GZ]	144	C5
Mabja[XZ]	152	E5
Mabja[XZ]	152	H5
Mabugang[GD]	118	H2
Macau[MC]	182	A2
Macau[MC]	182	B1
Machang Chakou[QH]	164	H6
Machang Jianhe[TJ]	42	B4
Machang Shidui[QH]	164	M5
Machang[BJ]	36	E2
Machang[GZ]	144	D4
Machang[GZ]	144	D4
Machang[GZ]	144	E3
Machang[GZ]	144	E4
Machang[GZ]	144	E4
Machang[JL]	66	C3
Machang[JS]	80	E2
Machang[LN]	62	C2
Machang[QH]	164	I8
Machang[SH]	74	D3
Machanghao[NM]	58	W11
Machangpu[NX]	168	B5
Machangying[BJ]	36	D3
Mache[ZJ]	84	D3
Macheng[AH]	90	D4
Macheng[HB]	110	I3
Machikou[BJ]	36	C3
Machunbu[NX]	168	B4
Macongzhuang[TJ]	42	C3
Macun Qu[HEN]	106	E2
Macun[HEB]	48	B6
Macun[HI]	128	C2
Macun[SX]	54	D6
Madao[SN]	156	C7
Madaotou[SX]	54	D2
Madaoyu[BJ]	36	D3
Madi[BJ]	36	D4
Madian[AH]	90	B4
Madian[HEB]	48	C5
Madian[HEN]	106	C3
Madian[SD]	102	E3
Madian[SD]	102	G3
Madianji[AH]	90	C3
Madianzi[AH]	90	C3
Madoi[QH]	164	I5
Madoi[QH]	164	K6
Madong[GX]	124	H4
Maduantou[NX]	168	C3
Maduqiao[HN]	114	D6
Ma'er Dao[SD]	102	G3
Ma'erzhuang[NX]	168	C3
Mafan[HEN]	106	F6
Mafang[BJ]	36	C3
Mafang[BJ]	36	E3
Mafang[CQ]	132	C4
Mafang[NX]	168	D3
Mafang[SN]	156	E6
Mafang[SX]	54	C3
Mafang[SX]	54	D2
Mafang[SX]	54	E4
Mafeng[LN]	62	F4
Mafenggang[BJ]	36	D4
Magang[HB]	110	G5
Magazine Island[HK]	176	D4
Mageda[NX]	168	C4
Magedang[SX]	54	E6
Magezhuang[SD]	102	F3
Magou[JS]	80	F3
Magu[GZ]	144	C4
Maguan[CQ]	132	D3
Maguan[YN]	148	J7
Magui[GD]	118	D4
Magutang[JX]	98	B7
Magutian[HEN]	106	E5
Mahai[QH]	164	G2

Mahaokou[HB]	110	F5	Malipo[YN]	148	J7	Maoba[HB]	110	C4
Mahe[GS]	160	G5	Maliu[CQ]	132	E2	Maoba[SN]	156	C7
Mahe[HB]	110	E3	Maliu[SN]	156	E8	Maobahe[SN]	156	C8
Mahe[HL]	70	E6	Malong He[YN]	148	G6	Maoban[ZJ]	84	C4
Mahe[SN]	156	F2	Malong[HN]	114	B6	Maochang[GZ]	144	D4
Mahekou[AH]	90	C5	Malong[YN]	148	I5	Maochang[GZ]	144	E4
Mahekou[HN]	114	C3	Malonggang[TJ]	42	B2	Maochen[HB]	110	G4
Mahuangliang[SN]	156	F2	Malou[SD]	102	C5	Maochengzi[JL]	66	E4
Mahuangshan[NX]	168	D3	Malu[CQ]	132	E5	Maocun[JS]	80	C2
Mahuo Ling[HI]	128	B3	Malu[GS]	160	H5	Maodan[HI]	128	B3
Mai Po[HK]	176	C1	Malu[GX]	124	E6	Maodao[HI]	128	B3
Maiba[XZ]	152	F4	Malu[HN]	114	D4	Maodian[FJ]	94	B3
Maichen[GD]	118	B6	Malu[SH]	74	C2	Maodian[SH]	74	C2
Maidar Ju[NM]	58	W11	Malun[HL]	70	C2	Maodian[ZJ]	84	D3
Maihao[HI]	128	C2	Maluping[SN]	156	G7	Maodianzi[LN]	62	H4
Maiji Qu[GS]	160	G5	Malutang[YN]	148	H4	Maoding[YN]	148	E2
Maiji[GS]	160	G5	Maluzhai[YN]	148	G7	Maoduzhan[JL]	66	E2
Mailing[GX]	124	I2	Mamba[XZ]	152	H4	Mao'er Shan[GX]	124	H2
Maima[XZ]	152	G3	Mamba[XZ]	152	K5	Mao'erliang[CQ]	132	F3
Mainling[XZ]	152	I5	Mamiao[AH]	90	C6	Maogan[HI]	128	B3
Mainpu[XZ]	152	E5	Mamiao[SD]	102	C4	Maogang Qu[GD]	118	D5
Maintang[XZ]	152	F4	Mamo He[SC]	138	D2	Maogang[SH]	74	C3
Maintang[XZ]	152	G5	Mamu[HEN]	106	H3	Maogudui[HEN]	106	G3
Maishi[HB]	110	G5	Mamu[SX]	54	C5	Maohushang[HB]	110	E4
Maizhokunggar[XZ]	152	G5	Mamu[ZJ]	84	F2	Maojia[HN]	114	B6
Maji Shan[JS]	80	F5	Man Cheung Po[HK]	176	A4	Maojiadian[LN]	62	H1
Maji[HB]	110	F2	Man He[HB]	110	E3	Maojian Qu[HB]	110	D2
Maji[JS]	80	D4	Man Kok[HK]	176	C3	Maojiaping[NX]	168	B5
Maji[SD]	102	C3	Manas He[XJ]	172	J4	Maojiazao[SX]	54	E2
Maji[YN]	148	D3	Manas[XJ]	172	K3	Maojiazhaizi[NX]	168	D2
Majia He[SD]	102	B3	Mancheng[HEB]	48	C5	Maojing[GS]	160	H4
Majia He[SD]	102	C2	Manchou[TW]	186	D4	Maojing[GZ]	144	E5
Majia[FJ]	94	D4	Manchuanguan[SN]	156	G7	Maojingba[HEB]	48	F2
Majia[SN]	156	E6	Mandal[NM]	58	I6	Maolan[GZ]	144	G5
Majiabian[SN]	156	F3	Mandetang[HEB]	48	B2	Maoli[HN]	114	E7
Majiadian[LN]	62	G5	Mandong[SD]	102	C4	Maoligang[SN]	156	G7
Majiadian[TJ]	42	B2	Manduhu[LN]	62	F3	Maolin[AH]	90	E6
Majiagaozhuang[NX]	168	C4	Mangchang[GX]	124	E2	Maolin[JL]	66	D4
Majiahewan[NX]	168	B3	Mangdang Shan[HEN]	106	H3	Maoling[GX]	124	F6
Majiahu[NX]	168	C3	Mangdong[YN]	148	D6	Maomao Shan[GS]	160	F4
Majiajuan[GS]	160	F3	Manghai[YN]	148	D6	Maoming[GD]	118	C5
Majialiang[NX]	168	B3	Manghan[NM]	58	N6	Maoniu shan[QH]	164	J4
Majialong[HB]	110	I4	Manghe[SX]	54	D6	Maopai[JX]	98	D4
Majian[NX]	168	B5	Manghuai[YN]	148	F6	Maoping[HN]	114	B3
Majian[ZJ]	84	D3	Mangkam Shan[XZ]	152	J4	Maoping[HN]	114	C6
Majiang[GX]	124	I4	Mangkuan[YN]	148	D5	Maoping[SN]	156	F7
Majiang[GZ]	144	F4	Mangnai[QH]	164	C2	Maopingchang[HB]	110	E3
Majiang[HN]	114	F6	Mangniu He[LN]	62	E2	Maopitou[TW]	186	D5
Majiapuzi[NX]	168	C4	Mangra Qu[QH]	164	M5	Maopu[HB]	110	H5
Majiatai[SN]	156	D6	Mangra[QH]	164	M5	Maoshan[HEB]	48	E3
Majiatan[NX]	168	C3	Mangra[XZ]	152	F5	Maoshanling[HB]	110	D3
Majiatun[BJ]	36	C5	Mangshan[HN]	114	E8	Maoshe[ZJ]	84	F4
Majiawan[NX]	168	C1	Mangshi He[YN]	148	D6	Maoshi[HN]	114	E6
Majiawan[SN]	156	D8	Mangshikou[HEB]	48	C4	Maota[HB]	110	D2
Majiazhuang[SN]	156	G6	Mangui[NM]	58	O1	Maotai[GZ]	144	E3
Majie[YN]	148	F6	Mangxin[YN]	148	E8	Maotian[HB]	110	C4
Majie[YN]	148	H7	Mangyun[YN]	148	C6	Maotiao He[GZ]	144	E4
Majie[YN]	148	J5	Mangzhang[HEN]	106	F5	Maotou Shan[YN]	148	F6
Majie[YN]	148	K7	Mangzhang[YN]	148	D6	Maotou Yang[ZJ]	84	F4
Majin Xi[ZJ]	84	C3	Manhui[NM]	58	T10	Maoxi[JS]	80	E5
Majing'ao[HN]	114	B4	Mani[SC]	138	E4	Maoxing[HL]	70	C6
Majitang[HN]	114	D4	Maniao[HI]	128	B2	Maoya[GZ]	144	F2
Majuangou[NX]	168	B4	Manjiang[JL]	66	H6	Maoyang[HI]	128	B3
Majuanzi[HEB]	48	G3	Manjiang[JX]	98	B3	Maoyang[ZJ]	84	D5
Majuanzi[LN]	62	H3	Manjiatan[LN]	62	E5	Maoyazi[SN]	156	C7
Makaru Shan[XZ]	152	E6	Manla[YN]	148	G8	Maoying[GZ]	144	E5
Makeng[AH]	90	D7	Manma[YN]	148	F9	Maoyun[GZ]	144	F4
Makeng[FJ]	94	C5	Manshui[HB]	110	C5	Maozang[GS]	160	F4
Malan He[SN]	156	E5	Manshui[SX]	54	D5	Maozhen Shan[HEB]	48	D3
Malan[FJ]	94	D2	Manta[XZ]	152	I3	Maozhou[HEB]	48	D5
Malan[HEN]	106	F3	Mantang[LN]	62	G3	Maozhu[HN]	114	D6
Malan[SN]	156	E5	Mantanghong[LN]	62	F2	Maozhuang[BJ]	36	C3
Malê[SC]	138	G4	Mantianxing[GZ]	144	G4	Maozhuang[HEN]	106	F3
Malian He[GS]	160	H5	Mantouying[HEB]	48	B2	Mapam Yumco[XZ]	152	B4
Malian[GX]	124	H4	Manwan[YN]	148	F6	Mapaoquan[SX]	54	C3
Malian[QH]	164	N3	Manzhangzi[HEB]	48	F3	Mapeng[JS]	80	E4
Maliang[HB]	110	E3	Manzhouli[NM]	58	L3	Mapengkou[TJ]	42	C4
Maliang[HB]	110	F4	Mao Shan[JS]	80	E5	Maping[HB]	110	G3
Malianjing Daoban[GS]	160	B2	Mao Xian[SC]	138	I4	Mapo[BJ]	36	D3
Malianzhuang[SD]	102	G2	Mao Yu[TW]	186	C3	Mapo[GX]	124	H5
Malin[HL]	70	C2	Mao'an[HI]	128	B3	Mapo[SD]	102	C4
Maling[GS]	160	H4	Maoao[TW]	186	E1	Mapu[FJ]	94	C5
Maling[GX]	124	H3	Maoba Gai[CQ]	132	E5	Mapu[HEN]	106	G3
Maling[GZ]	144	C5	Maoba[CQ]	132	E4	Maqen Kangri[QH]	164	L6

Maqên[QH]	164	M6	Mayi[GZ]	144	C5	Meishan[FJ]	94	C4
Maqiao[HB]	110	I4	Mayidui[YN]	148	F6	Meishan[FJ]	94	D4
Maqiao[HEN]	106	H4	Mayihe[JL]	66	H6	Meishan[HI]	128	B3
Maqiao[SH]	74	C2	Maying[BJ]	36	D4	Meishan[SC]	138	I5
Maqiaohe[HL]	70	F6	Maying[GS]	160	E3	Meishan[TW]	186	D3
Maqu[GS]	160	F5	Maying[HEB]	48	C2	Meishan[ZJ]	84	F3
Maqu[NX]	168	C4	Maying[SX]	54	D2	Meishi[AH]	90	D4
Maquzi[NX]	168	C3	Maying[TJ]	42	A3	Meitai[HI]	128	B2
Margai Caka[XZ]	152	E2	Mayingzhuang[SX]	54	D2	Meitan[GZ]	144	F3
Margam Shan[XZ]	152	D3	Mayingzi[HEB]	48	E3	Meitan[TW]	186	E2
Margog Cak[XZ]	152	E3	Mayoin[XZ]	152	F4	Meitang[JX]	98	B4
Margyang[XZ]	152	F5	Mayouying[LN]	62	E3	Meitian[HB]	110	H5
Markam[XZ]	152	K5	Mayu[ZJ]	84	E5	Meitian[HN]	114	E7
Markit[XJ]	172	F6	Mazar Tag[XJ]	172	G6	Meiting[HI]	128	C2
Markog[QH]	164	M7	Mazar[XJ]	172	F7	Meiwen[HI]	128	B2
Marla[XZ]	152	B4	Mazha[GD]	118	G3	Meixi Qu[HL]	70	E5
Marlamco[SC]	138	G6	Mazha[GZ]	144	C4	Meixi[AH]	90	D6
Marmê[XZ]	152	C3	Mazhai[SH]	74	C2	Meixi[FJ]	94	C4
Marritang[QH]	164	H8	Mazhan[SD]	102	E3	Meixi[HN]	114	E6
Marrong[XZ]	152	G3	Mazhang Qu[GD]	118	C5	Meixi[ZJ]	84	D2
Marzhing[QH]	164	M7	Mazhen[SN]	156	H1	Meixia[HI]	128	B2
Masha[FJ]	94	C2	Mazheshao[YN]	148	I7	Meixian[FJ]	94	D3
Mashakou[TW]	186	D3	Mazhu[ZJ]	84	F2	Meixian[HN]	114	F4
Mashan Qu[HL]	70	F6	Mazhuang[GX]	124	D3	Meiyang[SX]	54	B6
Mashan[GX]	124	F4	Mazhuang[HEB]	48	D4	Meiyu Yang[ZJ]	84	G3
Mashan[GX]	124	G5	Mazhuangzi[BJ]	36	C3	Meiyu[SC]	138	G8
Mashan[GZ]	144	E5	Mazong Shan[GS]	160	C2	Meiyuan[SH]	74	C3
Mashan[GZ]	144	F2	Mazongshan[GS]	160	C2	Meizhou Dao[FJ]	94	E4
Mashan[HB]	110	F4	Mazongshan[NM]	58	C7	Meizhou Wan[FJ]	94	D4
Mashan[JS]	80	F5	Mazui Ling[HI]	128	B3	Meizhou[FJ]	94	E4
Mashan[SD]	102	C3	Mazui[CQ]	132	D4	Meizhou[GD]	118	I2
Mashan[ZJ]	84	D2	Mêdog[XZ]	152	I5	Meizhu[HI]	90	F5
Mashan[ZJ]	84	E2	Mêgor[SC]	138	G3	Meizi[YN]	148	G7
Mashankou[HEN]	106	D4	Mei Jiang[CQ]	132	F5	Melmeg[JL]	66	D2
Mashanzi[SD]	102	D1	Mei Jiang[GD]	118	I2	Mêmar Co[XZ]	152	C2
Mashi[GD]	118	G1	Mei Jiang[JX]	98	C5	Mencun[SD]	102	F3
Mashi[HN]	114	E8	Mei Jiang[JX]	98	D5	Meng Jiang[GX]	124	H4
Mashi[JX]	98	B5	Mei Xian[GD]	118	I2	Meng Jiang[GZ]	144	E5
Mashidian[SD]	102	H2	Mei Xian[SN]	156	D6	Meng Shan[SD]	102	D4
Mashiping[HEN]	106	D4	Meïan[HI]	128	C2	Menga[YN]	148	E8
Mashou[SX]	54	E4	Meichang[TJ]	42	B3	Menga[YN]	148	F8
Mashu[YN]	148	I4	Meicheng[HN]	114	D4	Mengba[GS]	160	H5
Mashuang[JX]	98	B6	Meicheng[ZJ]	84	D3	Mengban[YN]	148	F7
Mashui[GD]	118	D4	Meichi[ZJ]	84	E3	Mengban[YN]	148	G9
Mashui[HN]	114	F6	Meichuan[HB]	110	I4	Mengcheng[AH]	90	C3
Masong[SD]	102	E3	Meifeng[HL]	70	E4	Mengcheng[NX]	168	C3
Mat Chau[HK]	176	E4	Meigang[JX]	98	D3	Mengcun[GX]	124	G4
Mata[GD]	118	D5	Meigu He[SC]	138	H7	Mengcun[HEB]	48	E5
Mataigou[NX]	168	C2	Meigu[SC]	138	I7	Mengding[YN]	148	E7
Matang[YN]	148	J7	Meihe[HI]	128	B2	Mengdong[YN]	148	J8
Matangshan[HN]	114	C5	Meihekou[JL]	66	F5	Mengdui[YN]	148	D7
Matian[HN]	114	E6	Meihou[HI]	128	B2	Mengfeng[SX]	54	D4
Matian[JX]	98	B4	Meihua Ding[GX]	124	H5	Menggong[HN]	114	D5
Matian[SX]	54	E5	Meihua[FJ]	94	E3	Menggong[YN]	148	E7
Matiwan[SN]	156	C7	Meihua[GD]	118	F1	Menggu[YN]	148	I4
Matou[HEN]	106	G3	Meihua[HN]	114	D7	Menggutun[JL]	66	E2
Matou[SD]	102	E5	Meihua[JS]	80	D3	Menghai[YN]	148	F9
Matou[TW]	186	D3	Meijiang[CQ]	132	F5	Menghan[YN]	148	F9
Matouli[HEB]	48	C6	Meijiang[HN]	114	D5	Menghewusu[HEB]	48	F2
Matoushan[JX]	98	E4	Meijie[AH]	90	D6	Menghu[YN]	148	G4
Matouying[HEB]	48	F4	Meikeng[GD]	118	G2	Menghun[YN]	148	F9
Matsu Liehtao[FJ]	94	F3	Meikou[FJ]	94	C3	Mengji[AH]	90	C4
Matsu Tao[FJ]	94	E3	Meikou[FJ]	94	C3	Mengjiafangzi[TJ]	42	B4
Matun[HEN]	106	D3	Meilan[HI]	128	C2	Mengjiagang[HL]	70	F5
Mawang[CQ]	132	E5	Meili[JS]	80	F5	Mengjiajing[SX]	54	D4
Mawei Qu[FJ]	94	E3	Meiliang[HI]	128	B2	Mengjialou[TJ]	42	B2
Mawei[GZ]	144	F5	Meilin[AH]	90	F6	Mengjiang[GX]	124	H4
Mawei[JX]	98	D3	Meilin[FJ]	94	C5	Mengjiao[YN]	148	E7
Mawu[CQ]	132	D4	Meilin[GD]	118	H3	Mengjiaping[SX]	54	B3
Mawu[GS]	160	G5	Meilin[GX]	124	F2	Mengjiawan[NX]	168	A3
Maxi[GZ]	144	G3	Meilin[JX]	98	E2	Mengjiawan[SN]	156	F2
Maxia[GS]	160	H5	Meilin[ZJ]	84	F3	Mengjiaxi[HB]	110	F5
Maxiang[FJ]	94	D5	Meiling[FJ]	94	C6	Mengjiayuan[HEB]	48	F3
Maxiang[HEN]	106	F5	Meiling[GD]	118	G1	Mengjiazhuang[HEB]	48	A5
Maxing[SN]	156	F6	Meiling[JX]	98	C3	Mengjin[HEN]	106	D3
Maxipu[HN]	114	C4	Meilisi Qu[HL]	70	B5	Mengkeshan[HL]	70	C2
Maxüt[XJ]	172	H6	Meilong[GD]	118	H4	Mengla[YN]	148	G9
Mayang Xi[FJ]	94	C2	Meilong[SH]	74	C2	Mengla[YN]	148	G9
Mayang[HB]	110	G4	Meinan[GD]	118	I2	Mengla[YN]	148	I8
Mayang[HN]	114	B5	Meinung[TW]	186	D4	Menglian[YN]	148	E8
Mayang[ZJ]	84	D4	Meipu[HB]	110	E1	Menglong[YN]	148	F9
Mayanhe[GS]	160	G5	Meiqiao[AH]	90	D3	Menglou[HB]	110	E2
Mayêr Kangri[XZ]	152	E3	Meiqiao[HN]	114	E5	Menglun[YN]	148	G9
Mayi He[HL]	70	E6	Meishan Shuiku[AH]	90	B5	Mengma[YN]	148	E8

Name	Page	Grid
Mengman[YN]	148	F8
Mengman[YN]	148	G9
Mengmen[SX]	54	B4
Mengnong[YN]	148	G7
Mengnuo[YN]	148	E6
Mengpeng[YN]	148	D6
Mengpeng[YN]	148	G9
Mengqiao[YN]	148	I8
Mengquan[HN]	114	D3
Mengsa[YN]	148	E7
Mengshan[GX]	124	H3
Mengshan[SX]	54	D4
Mengsheng[YN]	148	E7
Mengsong[YN]	148	F8
Mengtong[YN]	148	E6
Mengtuan[SD]	102	F3
Mengwang[YN]	148	F8
Mengwang[YN]	148	G8
Mengxing[YN]	148	G9
Mengxingzhuang[JS]	80	E2
Mengxu[GX]	124	G4
Mengyang[YN]	148	D6
Mengyang[YN]	148	F8
Mengyin[SD]	102	D4
Mengyingzi[BJ]	36	D2
Mengyong[YN]	148	E7
Mengyuan[NX]	168	C5
Mengzhai[HEN]	106	E4
Mengzhe[YN]	148	F9
Mengzhou[HEN]	106	D3
Mengzhu Ling[GX]	124	I3
Mengzhu Ling[HN]	114	D8
Mengzhuangzi[TJ]	42	A4
Mengzhuangzi[TJ]	42	C3
Mengzi[YN]	148	I7
Mengziling[HEB]	48	F3
Mentougou Qu[BJ]	36	C4
Menxianshi[SX]	54	E3
Menyuan[QH]	164	N3
Mêqu Zangbo[XZ]	152	E4
Mêrqung Co[XZ]	152	D4
Merren[NM]	58	U10
Mi He[SD]	102	E3
Mi Shui[HN]	114	F6
Mi Zhen[SD]	102	C2
Mian Shui[JX]	98	C6
Mian Xian[SN]	156	C7
Mianchi[HEN]	106	C3
Mianchuan[JX]	98	D1
Mianda[XZ]	152	J3
Miandu[HN]	114	F6
Mianjin[JX]	98	B5
Mianmian Shan[YN]	148	F3
Mianning[SC]	138	H7
Mianyang[GD]	118	H3
Mianyang[SC]	138	J4
Mianzhu[SC]	138	J4
Miao Dao[SD]	102	G1
Miao Ling[GZ]	144	E4
Miao Shan[SN]	156	F5
Miaoba[SN]	156	C7
Miaoba[YN]	148	J3
Miaocha[AH]	90	A4
Miaocun[HI]	128	C2
Miaodao Haixia[SD]	102	G2
Miaodao Qundao[SD]	102	G2
Miao'ergou[XJ]	172	I3
Miao'ergou[XJ]	172	K4
Miaofeng Shan[BJ]	36	C3
Miaofengshan[BJ]	36	C4
Miaogang[JS]	80	F6
Miaogong Shuiku[HEB]	48	E2
Miaogou[YN]	148	J3
Miaogoumen[SN]	156	G1
Miaohang[SH]	74	C2
Miaohou[SD]	102	H2
Miaohuang[GX]	124	G4
Miaoji[AH]	90	B4
Miaokou[HEN]	106	F2
Miaoli[TW]	186	D2
Miaoliang[BJ]	36	E2
Miaoling[JX]	98	B2
Miaomiaohu[NX]	168	C2
Miaoping[HB]	110	D3

Name	Page	Grid
Miaoping[SN]	156	F7
Miaoqian[FJ]	94	B4
Miaoqian[SX]	54	C6
Miaoqiao[JS]	80	F5
Miaoquan[CQ]	132	F5
Miaoshan[AH]	90	C6
Miaoshan[SD]	102	D3
Miaoshan[SD]	102	E5
Miaoshi[HN]	114	D3
Miaotai[NX]	168	C1
Miaotai[SN]	156	G6
Miaotang[CQ]	132	G2
Miaotou[GX]	124	I1
Miaotou[HEN]	106	D3
Miaowan[CQ]	132	F3
Miaowan[HEN]	106	F4
Miaowan[SN]	156	E5
Miaowan[SX]	54	C3
Miaoxi[ZJ]	84	E2
Miaoxia[HEN]	106	D3
Miaoya[SC]	138	M4
Miaoyu[CQ]	132	F3
Miaozhen[SH]	74	C1
Miaozhuang[TJ]	42	C3
Miaozi[HEN]	106	C4
Miaozi[SD]	102	E3
Miaozigou[HEB]	48	E2
Miaozihu Dao[ZJ]	84	G2
Micang Shan[SN]	156	D8
Micang Shan[SC]	138	L3
Micheng[HEB]	48	B5
Midu[YN]	148	F5
Mienhua Yu[TW]	186	F1
Migang Shan[NX]	168	C5
Mijiang[JL]	66	K5
Mijiawu[HEB]	48	D4
Milagabma[QH]	164	J7
Mile[YN]	148	I6
Miliangsi[SN]	156	E7
Miluo Jiang[HN]	114	F4
Miluo[HN]	114	F4
Min Jiang[FJ]	94	D3
Min Jiang[SC]	138	I4
Min Jiang[SC]	138	I6
Min Shan[SC]	138	I2
Min Xian[GS]	160	G5
Min'an[GD]	118	C5
Mindong[GZ]	144	G4
Minfeng(Niya)[XJ]	172	I7
Minfengchakou[XJ]	172	I6
Ming Jiang[GX]	124	E5
Mingcheng[GD]	118	E4
Mingcheng[JL]	66	G4
Mingchien[TW]	186	D3
Mingchih[TW]	186	E2
Mingcun[SD]	102	F3
Minggan[NM]	58	V11
Minggang[HEN]	106	F5
Minggang[ZJ]	84	F3
Minggao[HEN]	106	D3
Mingguang[AH]	90	D4
Mingguang[YN]	148	D5
Minghai[GS]	160	D3
Minghua[HEB]	48	C6
Mingji[SD]	102	E2
Mingjia[CQ]	132	D4
Mingjing Hu[QH]	164	C5
Mingjing[GD]	118	E2
Mingjiu[YN]	148	I7
Mingqu[TJ]	42	B2
Mingsha Shan[GS]	160	A3
Mingsha[NX]	168	B3
Mingshan[CQ]	132	D4
Mingshan[HL]	70	F5
Mingshan[SC]	138	I5
Mingshui[GS]	160	C1
Mingshui[HL]	70	C5
Mingteke Daban[XJ]	172	E7
Mingtong[CQ]	132	E2
Mingxi[FJ]	94	C3
Mingxikou[HN]	114	C4
Mingyang Shan[SN]	156	D7
Mingyang[LN]	62	F5
Mingyihe[YN]	148	H6

Name	Page	Grid
Mingyin[YN]	148	F3
Mingyue Shan[SC]	138	M5
Mingyue Shan[CQ]	132	D3
Mingyuedian[HEB]	48	B5
Mingzhong[CQ]	132	E2
Mingzhu[SX]	54	B5
Minhang Qu[SH]	74	C2
Minhe[QH]	164	O4
Minhe[GZ]	144	G3
Minhou[FJ]	94	E3
Minjian[SH]	74	C2
Minjiang Kou[FJ]	94	E3
Minjiang[SC]	138	I3
Minle[GS]	160	E3
Minle[GX]	124	H5
Minle[HL]	70	D5
Minle[YN]	148	F7
Minning[NX]	168	C2
Minqiao[JS]	80	E4
Minqin[GS]	160	F3
Minqing[FJ]	94	D3
Minquan[HEN]	106	G3
Minshengcun[TJ]	42	B3
Mintang[QH]	164	N7
Minxiao[GZ]	144	G3
Minyang[GX]	124	E4
Minzhong[GD]	118	F4
Minzhu[FJ]	94	A4
Minzhu[GS]	160	B3
Minzhu[GZ]	144	E4
Miping[GZ]	144	F3
Miquan[XJ]	172	K4
Mishan Shuiku[SD]	102	H2
Mishan[HL]	70	F6
Mishan[SX]	54	D6
Mishazi[JL]	66	F3
Mishi[HB]	110	F4
Mishidu[SH]	74	C3
Mituo[AH]	90	B6
Mixinguan[SX]	54	F1
Miyi[SC]	138	H9
Miyu[SX]	54	C4
Miyun Shuiku[BJ]	36	D2
Miyun[BJ]	36	D3
Mizhi[SN]	156	G3
Mizidian[BJ]	36	D4
Mo Fan Heung[HK]	176	C2
Mobin[HN]	114	B5
Mochong[GZ]	144	F4
Mod[NM]	58	N5
Mo'ershui[NX]	168	B3
Mogan Shan[ZJ]	84	D2
Moganshan[ZJ]	84	D2
Mogao[GS]	160	B2
Mogoit[NM]	58	U10
Mogoukou[HEN]	106	B4
Mohan[YN]	148	G9
Mohe[YN]	70	B2
Mohe[HL]	70	B2
Mohekou[AH]	90	D4
Mohong[YN]	148	J5
Mohuan[ZJ]	84	D3
Moincêr[XZ]	152	B4
Moindawang[XZ]	152	G6
Moirig Xueshan[XZ]	152	K5
Moirigkawagarbo[YN]	148	D2
Mojiang[YN]	148	G7
Mojiehao[NM]	58	T11
Mojing[HN]	114	F6
Mola[XZ]	152	F5
Moli Feng[JS]	80	F5
Moli[SX]	54	C6
Moling[HEN]	106	F4
Moliuqiao[TJ]	42	B3
Monan[HEB]	48	C5
Monan[SX]	54	B7
Mong Hau Shek[HK]	176	B3
Mong Kok[HK]	176	D3
Mong Tung Wan[HK]	176	B4
Mong Yue Kok[HK]	176	F2
Mongdoi[XZ]	152	G4
Monggon Bulag[NM]	58	E7
Monggon Qulu[NM]	58	M3
Monggon Us[NM]	58	X10

Name	Page	Grid
Moni[SC]	138	K8
Monte de Guia[MC]	182	B2
Monte Ka Ho[MC]	182	D6
Mopan Yang[ZJ]	84	G3
Mopan[LN]	62	F5
Mopanzhang[AH]	90	D3
Moqêndo[XZ]	152	D4
Mori[XJ]	172	M4
Morihong Shan[LN]	62	H2
Morin Dawa Qi[NM]	58	P3
Moron Gol[NM]	58	D7
Moron Gol[NM]	58	U10
Moron He[NM]	58	T11
Morong[HN]	114	B4
Morri[XZ]	152	J4
Morro de Artilharia[MC]	182	B7
Mosha[YN]	148	G7
Moshi[HB]	110	E4
Moshi[HN]	114	C3
Motan[SC]	138	L3
Motan[SC]	138	L5
Motian Ling[GS]	160	G6
Motian Ling[GX]	124	F2
Motian Ling[SC]	138	J3
Motou[JS]	80	F4
Moudao[HB]	110	B4
Mouding[YN]	148	G5
Moujia[JL]	66	G4
Mount Parker[HK]	176	D3
Moxi[JX]	98	C2
Moyang Jiang[GD]	118	D4
Moyang[GZ]	144	E5
Moye Dao[SD]	102	I3
Moyu(Karakax)[XJ]	172	G7
Moyuan[FJ]	94	C3
Mozhong[QH]	164	I8
Mozhongqo[QH]	164	I8
Mozi[SC]	138	L4
Moziqiao[SN]	156	D7
Mt. Collinson[HK]	176	D4
Mu Bulag Hondoi Gou[NM]	58	U11
Mu Us Shadi[NM]	58	G8
Mu Us Shadi[SN]	156	E2
Mübaqêqên[XZ]	152	E4
Muce[HEN]	106	C3
Muchang[AH]	90	C5
Muchangling[BJ]	36	E3
Mucheng[YN]	148	D6
Muchuan[SC]	138	I7
Mudan Jiang[HL]	70	E6
Mudan Jiang[JL]	66	I4
Mudan Ling[JL]	66	I4
Mudanjiang[HL]	70	E6
Mudong[CQ]	132	C4
Mu'er[CQ]	132	C4
Mufu Shan[HB]	110	H5
Mufu Shan[HN]	114	F4
Mufu Shan[JX]	98	B2
Mufu[HB]	110	C4
Mug Qu[QH]	164	F7
Mugan[YN]	148	I2
Mugang[HB]	110	I5
Muge[GD]	118	E3
Muge[GX]	124	H4
Mugen[GX]	124	H4
Muggar Kangri[XZ]	152	E3
Muggargoibo[XZ]	152	E3
Mugqu Co[XZ]	152	F4
Muguka[QH]	164	F6
Mugua[GZ]	144	E2
Mugua[SN]	156	G1
Muguaping[SX]	54	C4
Muguashan[HN]	114	C5
Mugui[GX]	124	H4
Mugxung[QH]	164	G7
Muhuguan[SN]	156	F6
Mui Wo[HK]	176	B3
Muji[AH]	90	D5
Muji[XJ]	172	E6
Muji[XJ]	172	G7
Mujia[YN]	148	E7
Mujiao[HN]	114	B6
Mujiawan[NX]	168	C4
Mujiayu[BJ]	36	D3
Mujin[HN]	114	F4
Mulan[HL]	70	E6
Mulan[JX]	98	D5
Mule[GX]	124	H4
Muli[SC]	138	G8
Mulin[BJ]	36	D3
Muling He[HL]	70	F6
Muling He[HL]	70	G6
Muling[HL]	70	F6
Muling[HL]	70	F6
Muluhu[HN]	114	E3
Mulun[GX]	124	E2
Mumen[SC]	138	L3
Mumendian[HEB]	48	D5
Munabulak[XJ]	172	J7
Mundo[XZ]	152	G4
Muniu[LN]	62	G4
Mupai[HI]	128	B2
Muping Hu[HN]	114	E4
Muping Qu[SD]	102	H2
Muqi[LN]	62	H3
Muri[QH]	164	K3
Muri[QH]	164	M3
Murqê[GS]	160	E6
Mushan[AH]	90	D5
Mushanhu[AH]	90	E4
Mushihe[JL]	66	G3
Mushuang[GX]	124	I4
Muta[AH]	90	D7
Mutan[TW]	186	D4
Mutang[HI]	128	B2
Mutong[HEN]	106	B3
Mutouchengzi[LN]	62	D3
Mutoudeng[HEB]	48	G3
Mutouwo[TJ]	42	C3
Muwang[SN]	156	E7
Muyang[YN]	148	K7
Muyun[HN]	114	E4
Muyuzi[LN]	62	H3
Muz Shan[XJ]	172	H7
Muz Tag[XZ]	152	E1
Muzart Kou'an[XJ]	172	H4
Muzat He[XJ]	172	H5
Muzhen[AH]	90	D6
Muzhijie[HEN]	106	D4
Muzi[GX]	124	G5
Muzidian[HB]	110	I3
Muztag Feng[XJ]	172	K7
Muztagata Shan[XJ]	172	E6
Muztaw Shan[XJ]	172	J2

N

Name	Page	Grid
Nabi[GX]	124	C3
Nabi[GX]	124	D4
Nabo[SC]	138	F6
Nachen[GX]	124	F5
Nada[HI]	128	B2
Nadou[HI]	128	A2
Naduli He[NM]	58	P2
Nag Qu[XZ]	152	H4
Nagainma[QH]	164	L7
Nagarzê[XZ]	152	G5
Nagdê Kangri[XZ]	152	E3
Naggor[XZ]	152	B4
Naggorgor[XZ]	152	B3
Nagjog[XZ]	152	J4
Nagqu[XZ]	152	C5
Nagqu[XZ]	152	H4
Nai Chung[HK]	176	E2
Naij Gol[QH]	164	F5
Naij Tal[QH]	164	G5
Naijin Gu[QH]	164	G4
Nailung[XZ]	152	E5
Nailung[XZ]	152	H5
Naiman Qi[NM]	58	N6
Naimin Bulak[XJ]	172	M3
Naimona'nyi[XZ]	152	B4
Nai'nying[XZ]	152	F5
Naiqag[QH]	164	H6
Naiqu[SC]	138	G7
Naixi[XZ]	152	G5
Naji Shuiku[GX]	124	F5
Naji[GD]	118	E4
Najin[JL]	66	C2
Najiu[YN]	148	J7
Naken[FJ]	124	E4
Nakou[FJ]	94	C2
Nalai[GX]	124	E6
Nalang[GS]	160	F5
Nali[GX]	124	F6
Nalin[GX]	124	G5
Naling[GX]	124	E5
Nalong[GD]	118	E4
Nalong[GX]	124	E5
Nalou[GX]	124	F5
Nam A[HK]	176	E2
Nam Chung[HK]	176	D1
Nam Co[XZ]	152	G4
Nam Hang Tsuen[HK]	176	C2
Nam Kok Tsui[HK]	176	E5
Nam Kwo Chau[HK]	176	E4
Nam Long[HK]	176	B2
Nam Sang Wai[HK]	176	C2
Nam Shan Tung[HK]	176	E2
Nam Shan[HK]	176	B4
Nam She Tsim[HK]	176	F2
Nam Tam[HK]	176	C4
Nam Tong Mei[HK]	176	E4
Nam Tong[HK]	176	E4
Nam Wai[HK]	176	E3
Namarqê[XZ]	152	G4
Namco[XZ]	152	G4
Namco[XZ]	152	G4
Namda[SC]	138	G3
Namjagbarwa Feng[XZ]	152	I5
Namling[XZ]	152	F5
Namoqê[XZ]	152	D4
Namoro[XZ]	152	B4
Namsai[QH]	164	H8
Nan He[CQ]	132	E2
Nan He[HB]	110	E2
Nan He[NX]	168	B5
Nan Hulsan Hu[QH]	164	H4
Nan Jiang[SC]	138	L3
Nan Ling[GD]	118	D1
Nan Ling[GX]	124	I2
Nan Ling[HN]	114	D7
Nan Ling[JX]	98	A6
Nan Ling[JX]	98	B6
Nan Tuo[SX]	54	E3
Nan Wan[TW]	186	D5
Nan Xi[ZJ]	84	E4
Nan Xian[HN]	114	E3
Nan'an Jiao[HI]	128	F7
Nan'an Qu[CQ]	132	C4
Nan'an Zongganqu[NM]	58	U11
Nan'an[FJ]	94	D5
Nanan[GX]	124	E6
Nan'an[JX]	98	C4
Nan'ao Dao[GD]	118	J3
Nan'ao[GD]	118	G4
Nan'ao[GD]	118	J3
Nanao[TW]	186	E2
Nanba[SC]	138	G8
Nanbalikou[TJ]	42	B4
Nanbao[HI]	128	B2
Nanbaxian[QH]	164	G3
Nanbei[HN]	114	C3
Nanbei[SD]	102	C3
Nanbeihe[HL]	70	D4
Nanbiancun[HEB]	48	C6
Nanbianshan[GX]	124	H3
Nanbu[HEB]	48	F4
Nanbu[SC]	138	L4
Nanbuzi[SX]	54	C2
Nancaicun[TJ]	42	B3
Nancha Qu[HL]	70	E5
Nancha[GS]	160	B2
Nancha[HI]	128	B2
Nanchang[HI]	128	C2
Nanchang[JX]	98	C3
Nanchang[JX]	98	C3
Nanchang[NM]	58	U10
Nanchangshan Dao[SD]	102	G2
Nanchangtan[NX]	168	A3

Nancheng[FJ]	94	D4	Nanji Shan[ZJ]	84	F5	Nanpeng Liedao[GD]	118	E5
Nancheng[JX]	98	D4	Nanji[HI]	128	B2	Nanpi[HEB]	48	D5
Nanchengsi[HEB]	48	C4	Nanji[JX]	98	D3	Nanpiao Qu[LN]	62	D3
Nanchenji[JS]	80	D3	Nanjia[GZ]	144	G4	Nanping Liedao[GD]	118	J3
Nanchenzhuang[TJ]	42	A3	Nanjia[SX]	54	C6	Nanping[CQ]	132	C4
Nanchong[GD]	118	E3	Nanjia[SX]	54	D6	Nanping[FJ]	94	D3
Nanchong[SC]	138	L5	Nanjian[LN]	62	G5	Nanping[GX]	124	E6
Nanchuan[CQ]	132	D4	Nanjian[YN]	148	F5	Nanping[HI]	128	C3
Nancun[HEN]	106	C2	Nanjianchang[BJ]	36	D3	Nanping[YN]	148	F8
Nancun[HEN]	106	E2	Nanjiang[GX]	124	H5	Nanping[YN]	148	K7
Nancun[SD]	102	G3	Nanjiang[HN]	114	F4	Nanping[ZJ]	84	E3
Nancun[SX]	54	F2	Nanjiang[SC]	138	L3	Nanpinghe[HN]	114	C2
Nandan[GX]	124	E3	Nanjiangu[TJ]	42	C3	Nanpingzhuang[BJ]	36	C4
Nandao[HI]	128	C2	Nanjiao Qu[SX]	54	E1	Nanpu Xi[FJ]	94	D2
Nandashan[LN]	62	D4	Nanjin[HN]	114	D4	Nanpu[FJ]	94	C5
Nanding He[YN]	148	E7	Nanjin[SC]	138	J5	Nanqi[SX]	54	D4
Nandong[HN]	114	F7	Nanjing[FJ]	94	C5	Nanqiao[HI]	128	C3
Nandu Jiang[HI]	128	B2	Nanjing[HN]	114	E6	Nanqiao[HN]	114	D6
Nandu Jiang[HI]	128	C2	Nanjing[JS]	80	D4	Nanqiao[HN]	114	F5
Nandu[GX]	124	H5	Nanjing[JX]	98	B7	Nanqiao[JX]	98	C7
Nandu[JS]	80	E5	Nanjingoutun[BJ]	36	D3	Nanqiao[SD]	102	D5
Nandu[SH]	74	C2	Nanjishan Liedao[ZJ]	84	F5	Nanqinggou[TJ]	42	B2
Nandulehe[BJ]	36	E3	Nanjiu Shan[ZJ]	84	G3	Nanquan[SX]	54	D5
Naneng[YN]	148	K7	Nanjuma He[HEB]	48	C4	Nanrenfu[TJ]	42	B2
Nanfan[SX]	54	C6	Nanka Jiang[YN]	148	E8	Nanri Dao[FJ]	94	E4
Nanfang[HI]	128	B3	Nankai[HI]	128	B2	Nanri Qundao[FJ]	94	E4
Nanfen Qu[LN]	62	G3	Nankang[JX]	98	B6	Nanri[FJ]	94	E4
Nanfeng[GS]	160	E3	Nankang[TW]	186	E1	Nansan Dao[GD]	118	C5
Nanfeng[HEN]	106	G4	Nankeng[JX]	98	A4	Nansan[GD]	118	C5
Nanfeng[HI]	128	B2	Nankeng[JX]	98	C5	Nansha Qundao[HI]	128	F7
Nanfeng[JX]	98	D2	Nankou Nongchang[BJ]	36	C3	Nansha[GD]	118	F4
Nanfeng[JX]	98	D4	Nankou[BJ]	36	C3	Nansha[JS]	80	F4
Nanfengmian[HN]	114	G6	Nankou[FJ]	94	C3	Nansha[JS]	80	F5
Nanfengmian[JX]	98	B5	Nankouqian[LN]	62	H3	Nanshahe[SD]	102	D4
Nanfu Shuiku[HI]	128	C2	Nankun[HI]	128	B2	Nanshan Ding[GX]	124	H1
Nang Xian[XZ]	152	H5	Nanla He[YN]	148	G9	Nanshan Ding[HN]	114	C6
Nangang He[SX]	54	F1	Nanlan He[YN]	148	E8	Nanshan Jiao[HI]	128	B3
Nangang Ling[JL]	66	J5	Nanlao He[JX]	98	C3	Nanshan Qu[GD]	118	F4
Nangang[AH]	90	D5	Nanle[HEN]	106	G1	Nanshan Qu[HL]	70	F5
Nangang[HI]	128	A3	Nanlei He[YN]	148	E8	Nanshan[FJ]	94	B4
Nangang[JX]	98	B3	Nanli He[YN]	148	K7	Nanshan[FJ]	94	D3
Nangao[BJ]	36	D3	Nanliang[SX]	54	C6	Nanshan[HI]	128	B3
Nangao[GZ]	144	F4	Nanliji[SD]	102	B5	Nanshan[HN]	114	E3
Nangaoya[SX]	54	F1	Nanlin[HI]	128	B3	Nanshang[TJ]	42	B3
Nange[SC]	138	H9	Nanling[AH]	90	E6	Nanshangle[BJ]	36	B4
Nangezhuang[BJ]	36	C4	Nanling[BJ]	36	B4	Nanshankou[QH]	164	G4
Nangong[HEB]	48	C6	Nanling[FJ]	94	B4	Nanshanzui[HEB]	48	E2
Nangongyingzi[LN]	62	C4	Nanling[FJ]	94	E4	Nanshao[GZ]	144	G4
Nangou[BJ]	36	D2	Nanling[GD]	118	H3	Nansheng[FJ]	94	C5
Nangou[TJ]	42	B4	Nanling[HI]	128	B2	Nansheng[GD]	118	E4
Nangqên[QH]	164	I8	Nanlingzhuang[HEB]	48	B4	Nansheng[HI]	128	B3
Nanguan Dao[ZJ]	84	E5	Nanlinqiao[HB]	110	H5	Nanshenzao[JS]	80	F4
Nanguan[HEB]	48	D2	Nanliu Jiang[GX]	124	G5	Nanshenzhuang[TJ]	42	C2
Nanhai Qu[GD]	118	F3	Nanliuzhuang[HEB]	48	B4	Nanshi Dao[HI]	128	D2
Nanhai[CQ]	132	E4	Nanlizigu[TJ]	42	B3	Nanshi[HN]	114	E7
Nanhang[SH]	74	D3	Nanlong[HI]	128	A3	Nanshi[JX]	98	C2
Nanhe[BJ]	36	D3	Nanlou Shan[JL]	66	G4	Nanshi[SD]	102	D5
Nanhe[GS]	160	G5	Nanlou[SX]	54	E3	Nanshipian[BJ]	36	D2
Nanhe[HEB]	48	B6	Nanloudi[HEB]	48	C5	Nanshiqiao[ZJ]	84	D2
Nanhe[JS]	80	E2	Nanlu[HI]	128	C2	Nanshuangmiao[LN]	62	D3
Nanhe[TJ]	42	B3	Nanluji[SD]	102	B4	Nanshui Shuiku[GD]	118	F2
Nanhedian[HEN]	106	D4	Nanluo[HI]	128	A2	Nanshui[GD]	118	F4
Nanhegou[SN]	156	G4	Nanma[ZJ]	84	E3	Nansong[ZJ]	84	E5
Nanhegou[SX]	54	C3	Nanmafang[TJ]	42	A3	Nantai[JX]	98	D3
Nanheng Yinhe[SH]	74	C1	Nanmazhuang[HEB]	48	B4	Nantai[LN]	62	F4
Nanheng[JX]	98	B7	Nanmei[HI]	128	B3	Nantai[NX]	168	C5
Nanheshun[TJ]	42	B4	Nanmen[CQ]	132	E3	Nantang[GD]	118	H4
Nanhongmen[BJ]	36	C4	Nanmeng[HEB]	48	B5	Nantong[CQ]	132	C5
Nanhsi[TW]	186	D3	Nanming He[GZ]	144	E4	Nantong[FJ]	94	E4
Nanhsiao Tao[TW]	186	G1	Nanming[GZ]	144	G4	Nantong[JS]	80	F4
Nanhu Tashan[TW]	186	E2	Nanmo[JS]	80	F4	Nantou[TW]	186	D3
Nanhu[GS]	160	B3	Nanmu[GX]	124	H4	Nantoudaogou[TJ]	42	B4
Nanhu[GS]	160	F3	Nanmupu[HN]	114	C4	Nantuo[CQ]	132	D4
Nanhu[HB]	110	I3	Nanniantou[BJ]	36	E3	Nantuo[HEB]	48	A5
Nanhu[XJ]	172	N4	Nanning[GX]	124	F5	Nantzu[TW]	186	D4
Nanhu[ZJ]	84	E2	Nanniwan[SN]	156	F4	Nanwaizi[JL]	66	E4
Nanhua[GS]	160	D3	Nanpaihe[HEB]	48	E5	Nanwan He[YN]	148	C6
Nanhua[YN]	148	G5	Nanpan Jiang[GX]	124	C3	Nanwan Shuiku[HEN]	106	E5
Nanhuaidian[TJ]	42	C3	Nanpan Jiang[GZ]	144	C6	Nanwan[HI]	128	B3
Nanhuang Dao[SD]	102	H3	Nanpan Jiang[YN]	148	I5	Nanwan[HN]	114	F6
Nanhuang[SD]	102	H3	Nanpan Jiang[YN]	148	J6	Nanwang[SD]	102	E3
Nanhuangcheng Dao[SD]	102	G1	Nanpaozhuang[TJ]	42	B4	Nanwang[SX]	54	D3
Nanhuatang[HB]	110	D1	Nanpeng Dao[GD]	118	E5	Nanwangdian[SD]	102	B4
Nanhui Qu[SH]	74	D2	Nanpeng Dao[GD]	118	J3	Nanwanggang[HEN]	106	F6

Nanwangping[TJ]　42　B3
Nanwei Tan[GD]　118　H6
Nanwei Tan[HI]　128　F7
Nanweng He[NM]　58　P2
Nanwenhe[YN]　148　J8
Nanwo[TJ]　42　C3
Nanwushijiazi[HEB]　48　F3
Nanxi He[YN]　148　I7
Nanxi[AH]　90　B5
Nanxi[CQ]　132　E2
Nanxi[SC]　138　J7
Nanxi[YN]　148　I8
Nanxia[FJ]　94　C3
Nanxiang[SH]　74　C2
Nanxiangcheng[HB]　110　E3
Nanxiangdian[HEN]　106　F6
Nanxiao[GX]　124　F5
Nanxin[BJ]　36　C3
Nanxindian[SX]　54　C6
Nanxing[GD]　118　C4
Nanxing[HI]　128　C2
Nanxiong[GD]　118　G1
Nanxu[GX]　124　E4
Nanxun Qu[ZJ]　84　E2
Nanya[FJ]　94　D3
Nanyan[FJ]　94　B4
Nanyancun[HEB]　48　B7
Nanyandang Shan[ZJ]　84　E5
Nanyang He[HEB]　48　B3
Nanyang Hu[SD]　102　C4
Nanyang[FJ]　94　B4
Nanyang[FJ]　94　C3
Nanyang[FJ]　94　C4
Nanyang[FJ]　94　E2
Nanyang[HB]　110　D3
Nanyang[HEN]　106　D4
Nanyang[HI]　128　C2
Nanyang[JS]　80　G5
Nanyangqiao[HN]　114　C4
Nanyao[TJ]　42　C4
Nanye[BJ]　36　C3
Nanyi Hu[AH]　90　E5
Nanyi[GS]　160　H5
Nanyi[JX]　98　C2
Nanyi[SD]　102　D4
Nanying[HEB]　48　A5
Nanyuan[JX]　98　D4
Nanyue Qu[HN]　114　E5
Nanyue[ZJ]　84　F4
Nanyulin[SX]　54　D2
Nanzhai[GZ]　144　G4
Nanzhai[HEN]　106　E2
Nanzhan[SD]　102　C4
Nanzhang[HB]　110　E3
Nanzhang[SD]　102　C4
Nanzhangcheng[HEB]　48　B6
Nanzhangdian[SX]　54　D6
Nanzhao[AH]　90　B4
Nanzhao[HEN]　106　D4
Nanzhao[SX]　54　B6
Nanzhao[SX]　54　C6
Nanzhaofu[HEB]　48　D5
Nanzhaolou[SD]　102　B4
Nanzheng[SN]　156　C8
Nanzhiqiu[HEB]　48　C6
Nanzhuang[HEB]　48　C5
Nanzhuang[SX]　54　B5
Nanzhuang[SX]　54　E3
Nanzhuang[YN]　148　H7
Nanzhuotou[TJ]　42　A4
Nanzui[HN]　114　E3
Naodehai Shuiku[LN]　62　F2
Naoguaping[NX]　168　C4
Naoli He[HL]　70　G5
Naoli[HEN]　106　F2
Naomaohu[XJ]　172　O4
Naozhou Dao[GD]　118　C6
Naozhou[GD]　118　C6
Napeng[GX]　124　F6
Napo[GX]　124　C4
Napo[GX]　124　D4
Narat Shan[XJ]　172　I4
Narat[XJ]　172　I4
Narhong[JL]　66　G5

Narin Bulag[NM]　58　K5
Narin Gol[QH]　164　E4
Narin Gu[NM]　58　X11
Narinker[XJ]　172　K4
Nartang[XZ]　152　F5
Nasêr[XZ]　152　G3
Nashan[JX]　98　B5
Nashe[GX]　124　E3
Nasi[GX]　124　G6
Nasuo[GX]　124　F6
Natao[GX]　124　E3
Natong[GX]　124　E4
Nau Co[XZ]　152　C3
Naweng[GX]　124　F3
Nawu[GD]　118　C4
Naxi Qu[SC]　138　K7
Nayong[GZ]　144　D4
Nazhi[GX]　124　D3
Nazuo[GX]　124　C3
Nêdong[XZ]　152　G5
Nehe[HL]　70　C4
Nei Gang[MC]　182　A2
Nei Mongol Gao Yuan[NM]　58　G7
Neihuang[HEN]　106　F2
Neijiang[SC]　138　K6
Neijing He[HB]　110　G5
Neiliang[JX]　98　B6
Neilin[FJ]　94　C4
Neimen[TW]　186　D4
Neipu[TW]　186　D4
Neiqiu[HEB]　48　B6
Neixi[HN]　114　B4
Neixiang[HEN]　106　C4
Nemor He[HL]　70　C4
Nen Jiang[HL]　70　B5
Nen Jiang[HL]　70　C4
Nen Jiang[JL]　66　D1
Nen Jiang[NM]　58　P3
Nenan[HL]　70　C4
Nengyu[YN]　148　G5
Nenjiang[HL]　70　C4
Nêsü[XZ]　152　A3
New Territories[HK]　176　C2
Ng Fan Chau[HK]　176　E4
Nga He[SC]　138　G3
Nga Ying Chau[HK]　176　C3
Ngamnaxung Qu[QH]　164　G7
Ngamnaxung[QH]　164　G7
Ngamra Qu[QH]　164　H5
Ngamring[XZ]　152　E5
Ngan Chau[HK]　176　D4
Ngan Chau[HK]　176　E2
Ngangchugchu Co[XZ]　152　C3
Ngangla Ringco[XZ]　152　C4
Ngangzi Co[XZ]　152　E4
Ngangzi Shan[XZ]　152　E4
Ngarnang[XZ]　152　G4
Ngau Mei Hoi[HK]　176　E3
Ngau Chi Wan[HK]　176　D3
Ngau Hom Sha[HK]　176　B2
Ngau Kwu[HK]　176　B3
Ngau Mei Chau[HK]　176　E3
Ngau Tam Mei[HK]　176　C2
Ngau Tau Kok[HK]　176　D3
Ngo Mei Chau[HK]　176　E1
Ngola Shan[QH]　164　K4
Ngola Shankou[QH]　164　L5
Ngom Qu[XZ]　152　J4
Ngong Ping[HK]　176　B4
Ngong Shuen Au[HK]　176　C3
Ngong Shuen Chau[HK]　176　D3
Ngoqu[XZ]　152　E3
Ngoring Hu[QH]　164　J6
Ngorosumdo[XZ]　152　F4
Ngtung River[HK]　176　D1
Ngüra[GS]　160　E5
Ngüraxoima[GS]　160　E5
Ngüxoi[XZ]　152　I4
Nianbadu[ZJ]　84　C4
Niandailai[QH]　164　H7
Nianfengcun[TJ]　42　B3
Niangniangba[GS]　160　G5
Niangnianggong[LN]　62　E3
Niangniangmiao[LN]　62　D4

Niangziguan[SX]　54　E4
Niangzishen[SX]　54　D3
Niantan Shuiku[BJ]　36　C4
Niantuozi[BJ]　36　D2
Nianyushan Shuiku[HEN]　106　G6
Nianyushan[JX]　98　E2
Nianzhang[SX]　54　C6
Nianzi[BJ]　36　C2
Nianzisha Qu[HL]　70　B5
Niao Yu[TW]　186　C3
Niaohe[HL]　70　D6
Niaotsui[TW]　186　E2
Nicha[AH]　90　D5
Nicheng[SH]　74　D3
Nidang[GZ]　144　C6
Nidi[FJ]　94　C3
Niedu[JX]　98　B6
Nieguantun[TJ]　42　B3
Niejiahe[HB]　110　E4
Niezhuangzi[TJ]　42　B3
Nigou[SD]　102　D5
Nihe[AH]　90　C4
Nihe[AH]　90　D5
Nihe[SX]　54　D2
Nijiangkou[HN]　114　E4
Nijiao[YN]　148　I6
Nijing[HEB]　48　G4
Nilka[XJ]　172　I4
Nim Shue Wan Village[HK]　176　C3
Nim Wan[HK]　176　B2
Nim Yuen[HK]　176　B3
Ning Jiang[GD]　118　H2
Ning Xian[GS]　160　H5
Ning'an[HL]　70　E6
Ningbo Gang[ZJ]　84　F2
Ningbo[ZJ]　84　F3
Ningchegu[TJ]　42　C3
Ningcheng[NM]　58　M7
Ningde[FJ]　94　E3
Ningdu[JX]　98　D5
Ningdun[AH]　90　F6
Ninggan[GX]　124　E4
Ninggu[GZ]　144　D4
Ninggu[SX]　54　D4
Ningguo[AH]　90　F6
Ningguo[HEN]　106　E2
Ninghai[ZJ]　84　F3
Ninghe[TJ]　42　C3
Ninghe[TJ]　42　C3
Ninghua[FJ]　94　B3
Ningjiang Qu[JL]　66　E2
Ningjin[HEB]　48　B6
Ningjin[SD]　102　C2
Ningjin[SD]　102　I3
Ninglang[YN]　148　F3
Ningling[HEN]　106　G3
Ningming[GX]　124　E5
Ningnan[SC]　138　H8
Ningqiang[SN]　156　C8
Ningshan[SN]　156　E7
Ningtiaoliang[SN]　156　E3
Ningwang[GZ]　144　E4
Ningwu[GX]　124　F4
Ningwu[SX]　54　D2
Ningxi[SH]　74　C1
Ningxi[ZJ]　84　E4
Ningxiang[HN]　114　E4
Ningyang[SD]　102　C4
Ningyuan He[HI]　128　B3
Ningyuan[GS]　160　G5
Ningyuan[HL]　70　D6
Ningyuan[HN]　114　D7
Ningzhen Shan[JS]　80　D4
Ninlaozhuang[AH]　90　B3
Niqiu[AH]　90　B3
Nitun[SX]　54　D3
Niubaotun[BJ]　36　D4
Niubiziliang[QH]　164　E2
Niucao He[HB]　110　C5
Niuchang[GZ]　144　F4
Niudaokou[TJ]　42　B2
Niu'erhe[NM]　58　N2
Niugang[HEN]　106　G5
Niujiakouzi[NX]　168　C3

Niujialiang[SN]	156	F2
Niujiao Shan[HB]	110	D2
Niujiaodian[SD]	102	C3
Niujiapai[TJ]	42	B2
Niujiaqiao[HEB]	48	B6
Niujie[YN]	148	E4
Niujie[YN]	148	F5
Niujie[YN]	148	H7
Niujie[YN]	148	J3
Niukong[YN]	148	H7
Niulan Jiang[GZ]	144	B3
Niulan Jiang[YN]	148	I4
Niulanshan[BJ]	36	D3
Niulou[HI]	128	C3
Niululing Shuiku[HI]	128	C3
Niumaojing[NX]	168	D3
Niumaowu[LN]	62	H4
Niumasi[HN]	114	D5
Niuniuba[SC]	138	I7
Niuqi Zhou[HI]	128	B3
Niushan Dao[ZJ]	84	F4
Niushang Ling[HI]	128	C3
Niushiyao[SX]	54	D2
Niushou Shan[NX]	168	C3
Niushou[HB]	110	E2
Niuti[SN]	156	E8
Niutian[HN]	114	E4
Niutian[JX]	98	C4
Niutou Shan[ZJ]	84	G3
Niutun[HEN]	106	F2
Niuweizhuang[SX]	54	D3
Niuwu[SN]	156	F4
Niuxin Ding[HL]	70	E7
Niuxinding[JL]	66	F5
Niuyingzi[LN]	62	C3
Niuzhen[TJ]	42	A2
Niuzhuang[HB]	110	D4
Niuzhuang[LN]	62	F4
Niuzhuang[SD]	102	E2
Nixi[AH]	90	C7
Nixi[SC]	138	J6
Nixi[SC]	138	M3
Niya He[XJ]	172	I7
Niyu Shan[ZJ]	84	F5
Nomhon Burd[NM]	58	M4
Nomhon He[QH]	164	I4
Nomhon[QH]	164	I4
Nong Jiang[HL]	70	G5
Nong'an[JL]	66	F3
Nongche[HN]	114	B3
Nonghe[HL]	70	E5
Nongke[HB]	110	B5
Nongqiao[HL]	70	H4
Nongwa[GX]	124	C3
Nongwang[GX]	124	C3
Nongxing[AH]	90	D5
Nongzhan[SH]	74	D3
Noqilek[XJ]	172	J7
Norlung[GS]	160	E6
Norma Co[XZ]	152	F3
North Point[HK]	176	D3
Norzagabma[QH]	164	H5
Nu Jiang[XZ]	152	J4
Nu Jiang[XZ]	152	K5
Nu Jiang[YN]	148	D4
Nu Shan[YN]	148	E4
Nuanchitang[LN]	62	D3
Nuanmutiaozi[JL]	66	H4
Nuanquan[SX]	54	B4
Nuanshui[HN]	114	F7
Nuanya[SX]	54	D2
Nu'er He[LN]	62	D4
Nuli[SH]	74	D2
Nuluerhu Shan[LN]	62	C3
Nulu'Erhu Shan[NM]	58	M7
Numin He[HL]	70	D5
Nuodong[GX]	124	I4
Nuofu[YN]	148	E8
Nuogu[YN]	148	I4
Nuomin He[NM]	58	O3
Nuoshuihe[SC]	138	M3
Nur[XJ]	172	H7
Nurgai[NM]	58	D8
Nushan Hu[AH]	90	D4
Nyabxang Qu[XZ]	152	G6
Nyagla[QH]	164	I8
Nyainboyuzê Feng[QH]	164	N7
Nyainlung[SC]	138	F3
Nyainqêntanglha Feng[XZ]	152	G4
Nyainqêntanglha Shan[XZ]	152	G4
Nyainrong[XZ]	152	H3
Nyalam[XZ]	152	D5
Nyalung[QH]	164	N5
Nyamgyi[SC]	138	E4
Nyang Qu[XZ]	152	F5
Nyang Qu[XZ]	152	H5
Nyangbo[XZ]	152	H4
Nyanggo[XZ]	152	J5
Nyangra[XZ]	152	F4
Nyangug[SC]	138	E3
Nya'nying[QH]	164	K6
Nyaxi[QH]	164	E6
Nyêmo[XZ]	152	G5
Nyêmo[XZ]	152	I4
Nyêr Co[XZ]	152	C3
Nyêrudoi[XZ]	152	F5
Nyêwomo[XZ]	152	I5
Nyêxükongma[QH]	164	G7
Nyidog[QH]	164	J8
Nyidoi[SC]	138	E3
Nyigo[XZ]	152	E4
Nyikog Qu[SC]	138	E3
Nyikog[SC]	138	F4
Nyilung[XZ]	152	G4
Nyima[XZ]	152	E4
Nyima[XZ]	152	G4
Nyima[XZ]	152	H4
Nyimajangra[XZ]	152	G5
Nyimta[QH]	164	N6
Nyinba[GS]	160	F5
Nyingchi[XZ]	152	I5
Nyinqug[QH]	164	M5
Nyixar[YN]	148	E2
Nyogzê[XZ]	152	C4

O

Obo liang erhao[QH]	164	E2
Obo liang[QH]	164	E2
Obo[QH]	164	M3
Obon Xil[NM]	58	W12
Obot[NM]	58	F9
Odaklik[XJ]	172	F6
Ogan He[XJ]	172	I5
Ogtang[XZ]	152	K5
Oisêr[QH]	164	L7
Olji Moron He[NM]	58	M5
Olji Moron[NM]	58	N5
Olji[NM]	58	F7
Oluanpi[TW]	186	D5
Oma[XZ]	152	C3
Ombu[XZ]	152	E4
Ombudangsang[XZ]	152	C3
Omon Gol[NM]	58	D7
Ondor Hana[NM]	58	E7
Ondor[QH]	164	O5
Onggon[NM]	58	H7
Onggon[NM]	58	M5
Onggon[NM]	58	U10
Onggot[NM]	58	O3
Ongniud Qi[NM]	58	M6
Ongt Gol[NM]	58	E7
Ongt[NM]	58	L5
Onor[NM]	58	N3
Onqin Daga Shadi[NM]	58	K6
Orba Co[XZ]	152	B2
Orbog[NM]	58	F8
Ordos[NM]	58	I8
Orgon Tal[NM]	58	J6
Orgon[NM]	58	T11
Orong[XZ]	152	H5
Oroqen Qi[NM]	58	O2
Oroqen[NM]	58	O3
Orxon He[NM]	58	L3
Otog Qi[NM]	58	H8
Otog Qianqi[NM]	58	G8

Ou Shui[HN]	114	F7
Ouchi[HB]	110	F5
Oudian[HB]	110	E3
Oudong[GX]	124	F3
Ougeng[JS]	80	F3
Ouhai Qu[ZJ]	84	E5
Oujiacun[SX]	54	D1
Oule[HB]	110	F3
Oupu[HL]	70	D2
Outuan[HN]	114	B6
Ouyanghai Shuiku[HN]	114	E7
Oymak[XJ]	172	K2
Oyyaylak[XJ]	172	J7

P

Pa Tau Kwu[HK]	176	C3
Paca[XZ]	152	F4
Pafen[TW]	186	D2
Paggai[XZ]	152	I4
Paggor[XZ]	152	F5
Pagma[QH]	164	M6
Pagmar[XZ]	152	D4
Pagqu[XZ]	152	H5
Pagri[XZ]	152	F6
Paibu[JX]	98	B3
Paidoi Co[XZ]	152	E3
Paikou[HN]	114	E4
Paikü Co[XZ]	152	D5
Paila[XZ]	152	G4
Pailai[SC]	138	I8
Pailou[AH]	90	C3
Pailou[AH]	90	C6
Pailou[AH]	90	D6
Pailou[HB]	110	D2
Pailou[HEB]	48	E2
Pailou'ao[HN]	114	B5
Paingar[XZ]	152	I4
Painqi[XZ]	152	C5
Paipu[HI]	128	B2
Paisha Tao[TW]	186	C3
Paisha[TW]	186	C3
Paishang[JX]	98	A4
Paishi[HB]	110	I5
Paitou[ZJ]	84	E3
Pak A[HK]	176	E3
Pak Chau[HK]	176	A3
Pak Kok San Tsuen[HK]	176	C4
Pak Kok[HK]	176	C4
Pak Kong[HK]	176	E2
Pak Kwo Chau[HK]	176	E3
Pak Lap[HK]	176	F3
Pak Ma Tsui[HK]	176	E3
Pak Sha Chau[HK]	176	E1
Pak Sha O[HK]	176	E2
Pak Sha Tau[HK]	176	E2
Pak Sha Tsuen[HK]	176	C2
Pak Sha Wan[HK]	176	E3
Pak Shek Wo[HK]	176	E3
Pak Shing Kok[HK]	176	E3
Pak Tai To Yan[HK]	176	D2
Pak Tam Au[HK]	176	E2
Pak Tam[HK]	176	E2
Pak Tin[HK]	176	D2
Pak Wai[HK]	176	E3
Pak Wan[HK]	176	C3
Palasashe[TW]	186	E3
Pali[TW]	186	E1
Palung Co[XZ]	152	C4
Pamai[SC]	138	G5
Pan Long Wan[HK]	176	E3
Pan Shan[BJ]	36	E3
Pan Shan[TJ]	42	B1
Pan Xian[GZ]	144	C5
Pan'an[SC]	138	H5
Pan'an[ZJ]	84	E3
Pandaogou[BJ]	36	D2
Pandian[SD]	102	C3
Pandu[FJ]	94	E3
Pandu[SD]	102	B4
Panggezhuang[BJ]	36	C4
Panggezhuang[TJ]	42	B2

Pangguang[SN]	156	E6	Peijiachuankou[SX]	54	B3	Ping'an[CQ]	132	E4
Panggurtang[GS]	160	F5	Peijiaying[GS]	160	F4	Ping'an[GD]	118	G3
Panghai[GZ]	144	G4	Peikang Hsi[TW]	186	D2	Ping'an[JL]	66	C2
Panghuang[SH]	74	D1	Peikang[TW]	186	D3	Ping'an[JL]	66	H3
Pangjiabu[HEB]	48	C3	Peiliu[JS]	80	E3	Ping'an[LN]	62	F2
Pangjiazuo[HEB]	48	C5	Peimei[JX]	98	E3	Ping'an[QH]	164	O4
Pangkog Co[XZ]	152	F4	Peimen[TW]	186	D3	Ping'an[SH]	74	D3
Pangou[SN]	156	F3	Peinan Chushan[TW]	186	D3	Ping'an[SN]	156	D8
Pangqiaotou[TJ]	42	B2	Peinan Hsi[TW]	186	E4	Ping'andi[LN]	62	E2
Pangquangou[SX]	54	C4	Peinan[TW]	186	E4	Ping'anzhuang[TJ]	42	B3
Pangu He[HL]	70	C2	Peiqiao[HEN]	106	H4	Pingba[CQ]	132	E1
Pangu[FJ]	94	D4	Peishan[HEB]	48	C4	Pingba[GZ]	144	E4
Pangu[HL]	70	B2	Peitawu Shan[TW]	186	D4	Pingba[HB]	110	G3
Pangushan[JX]	98	C6	Peitou[TW]	186	D3	Pingbaying[HB]	110	B5
Pangzhuang[SD]	102	D4	Peitou[TW]	186	E1	Pingbian[YN]	148	I8
Pangzhuangzi[TJ]	42	B3	Peiying[HEN]	106	D5	Pingcha[HN]	114	B6
Panhe[NX]	168	C4	Peizhuang[SX]	54	B6	Pingchang[SC]	138	M4
Panji Qu[AH]	90	C4	Pênda[SC]	138	C3	Pingchangguan[HEN]	106	E5
Panjiabu[NX]	168	C4	Pênda[XZ]	152	J4	Pingchao[JS]	80	F4
Panjiakou Shuiku[HEB]	48	F3	Peng Chau[HK]	176	C3	Pingcheng[HEN]	106	F3
Panjiang[GZ]	144	C5	Peng'an[SC]	138	L4	Pingchuan Qu[GS]	160	G4
Panjiang[YN]	148	I5	Pengbu[NX]	168	C4	Pingchuan[GS]	160	E3
Panjiawa[TJ]	42	B4	Pengcheng[SC]	138	L3	Pingchuan[YN]	148	F4
Panjiawan[HB]	110	D4	Pengchia Yu[TW]	186	F1	Pingcun[YN]	148	F7
Panjiawan[HB]	110	H4	Pengcun[HEB]	48	D4	Pingdeng[GX]	124	G1
Panjiazhuang[GZ]	144	D5	Pengdian[HEN]	106	F3	Pingdi[SC]	138	G9
Panjin[LN]	62	F3	Pengfang[JX]	98	B4	Pingding Shan[HL]	70	E5
Panlong Jiang[YN]	148	J7	Penggong[ZJ]	84	D2	Pingding Shan[QH]	164	L7
Panlong[CQ]	132	B4	Penghu Liehtao[TW]	186	C3	Pingding[GD]	118	C4
Panlong[GZ]	144	D4	Penghu Shuitao[TW]	186	C3	Pingding[SX]	54	E4
Panlong[SH]	74	C1	Penghu Tao[TW]	186	C3	Pingdingshan[HEN]	106	E4
Panlong[SN]	156	F4	Penghu[TW]	186	C3	Pingdingshan[LN]	62	H3
Panlong[SX]	54	E5	Penghua[FJ]	94	D4	Pingdong[GX]	124	E3
Panpo[QH]	164	N3	Pengji[SD]	102	C4	Pingdong[SH]	74	D1
Panqiao Shuiku[JX]	98	C4	Pengkou[FJ]	94	B4	Pingdu[SD]	102	F3
Panshan[LN]	62	F3	Penglai[FJ]	94	D4	Pingdu[SN]	156	D7
Panshi[GZ]	144	H2	Penglai[HI]	128	C2	Pingdu[ZJ]	84	C5
Panshi[JL]	66	G5	Penglai[SD]	102	G2	Pingfang Qu[HL]	70	D6
Panshi[SH]	74	D2	Penglai[TW]	186	D2	Pingfang[BJ]	36	C3
Panshidian[SD]	102	H3	Penglong[AH]	90	D7	Pingfang[BJ]	36	D4
Panshui[GZ]	144	E3	Pengpu[YN]	148	I7	Pingfangzi[LN]	62	C4
Panshui[HI]	128	C2	Pengqiao[HEN]	106	C5	Pingfeng[GD]	118	D3
Pantang[HB]	110	H4	Pengshan[SC]	138	I5	Pingfeng[NX]	168	B5
Pantang[HN]	114	D3	Pengshui[CQ]	132	E4	Pingfu[GX]	124	E5
Pantian[GD]	118	I3	Pengta[SC]	138	H5	Pingfu[GX]	124	H4
Pantian[JX]	98	B4	Pengxi[SC]	138	K5	Pingfu[JX]	98	B6
Pantiange[YN]	148	E3	Pengxin[HEN]	106	F6	Pinggang[GD]	118	D5
Panting[FJ]	94	D1	Pengyang[NX]	168	C5	Pinggang[LN]	62	H2
Pantuo[FJ]	94	C5	Pengze[JX]	98	D2	Pinggezhuang[BJ]	36	D3
Panwan[JS]	80	F3	Pengzhai[GD]	118	H2	Pinggu Qu[BJ]	36	E3
Panxi[YN]	148	I6	Pengzhou[JX]	98	C4	Pingguo[GX]	124	E4
Panxin[GZ]	144	H2	Pengzhou[SC]	138	I5	Pinghai Wan[FJ]	94	E4
Panyu Qu[GD]	118	F4	Pi He[AH]	90	C5	Pinghai[FJ]	94	E4
Panzhihua[SC]	138	G9	Pi Xian[SC]	138	I5	Pinghai[GD]	118	G4
Panzhong[JX]	98	B5	Piancheng[NX]	168	B5	Pinghe[CQ]	132	F2
Panzhuang[TJ]	42	B3	Pianguan He[SX]	54	C2	Pinghe[FJ]	94	C5
Panzhuangzi[TJ]	42	A4	Pianguan[SX]	54	C2	Pinghe[HI]	128	C2
Pao Jiang[YN]	148	F5	Pianjiao[YN]	148	F4	Pinghe[YN]	148	H8
Pao'ai[LN]	62	E5	Piankou[SC]	138	J3	Pinghsi[TW]	186	E1
Paojun[GX]	124	D3	Pianling[LN]	62	G4	Pinghu[FJ]	94	D3
Paoli[GX]	124	E3	Pianpoying[HEB]	48	E2	Pinghu[ZJ]	84	F2
Paomaping[YN]	148	F4	Pianqiao[BJ]	36	D2	Pingji[GX]	124	F5
Paoshan[TW]	186	D2	Piaohe[JL]	66	H4	Pingjiang[HN]	114	F4
Paotai[LN]	62	E5	Piaohe[JL]	66	H4	Pingjiang[ZJ]	84	E3
Paotaibang[SH]	74	D2	Piaojing[GZ]	144	D3	Pingjin[CQ]	132	D3
Paozi[LN]	62	F2	Piaoli[GX]	124	G2	Pingkou[HN]	114	D4
Parbuglê[XZ]	152	C4	Piaomiao Feng[JS]	80	F5	Pinglang[GX]	124	F5
Parlung Zangbo[XZ]	152	I5	Picheng[JS]	80	E4	Pingle[GX]	124	H3
Parongsi[SC]	138	C2	Picun[BJ]	36	D4	Pingli[JX]	98	A4
Parque Industrial da Concórdia [MC]	182	B6	Pidian[HEN]	106	F5	Pingli[SN]	156	F8
Parxixingka Nongchang[QH]	164	L4	Pihe Zongganqu[AH]	90	C5	Pingliang[GS]	160	H5
Paryang[XZ]	152	C4	Pihe[JL]	66	H4	Pinglidian[SD]	102	G2
Pat Heung[HK]	176	C2	Pihe[YN]	148	D4	Pinglin[HB]	110	F3
Pavoação de Hác Sá[MC]	182	C7	Pikou[LN]	62	F5	Pinglin[HL]	70	E6
Paxxiyim[XJ]	172	I7	Piluo[CQ]	132	C5	Pingling[GD]	118	G3
Pearl Island[HK]	176	B3	Ping Chau[HK]	176	F1	Pinglu Qu[SX]	54	D2
Pêca[SC]	138	F5	Ping Che[HK]	176	D1	Pinglu[SX]	54	C2
Pei Xian[JS]	80	B2	Ping Dao(Pingshan Dao)[JS]	80	E1	Pinglue[GZ]	144	H4
Peicheng[HEN]	106	E4	Ping Dao(Pingshan Dao)[SD]	102	F4	Pingluo[NX]	168	C2
Peichiang Hsi[TW]	186	D3	Ping Jiang[JX]	98	C5	Pingmeng[GX]	124	C5
Peide[HL]	70	F6	Ping Long[HK]	176	D2	Pingmu[SN]	156	D7
Peigou[SX]	54	B4	Ping Min Chau[HK]	176	E3	Pingnan[FJ]	94	D3
Peihsiao Tao[TW]	186	G1	Ping Xi[HN]	114	C5	Pingnan[GX]	124	F3
			Ping'an[AH]	90	E4	Pingnan[GX]	124	H4

Pingnan[ZJ]	84	D5
Pingpo[YN]	148	F5
Pingpu[AH]	90	E5
Pingqiao Qu[HEN]	106	F5
Pingqiao[CQ]	132	D4
Pingqiao[SN]	156	F3
Pingqiao[ZJ]	84	E3
Pingqiu[GZ]	144	H4
Pingquan[HEB]	48	F2
Pingshan[AH]	90	D3
Pingshan[GD]	118	D4
Pingshan[GX]	124	E5
Pingshan[GZ]	144	C3
Pingshan[HEB]	48	B5
Pingshan[HL]	70	D5
Pingshan[HL]	70	D6
Pingshan[JX]	98	D5
Pingshan[SC]	138	J7
Pingshan[YN]	148	D6
Pingshang[GZ]	144	D4
Pingshang[SD]	102	F4
Pingshi[GD]	118	F1
Pingshi[HEN]	106	E5
Pingshi[HI]	128	D2
Pingshi[JX]	98	B6
Pingshu[SX]	54	E4
Pingshui[HB]	110	D3
Pingshui[HN]	114	F6
Pingshun[SX]	54	E5
Pingtai[GD]	118	D3
Pingtaihu[NX]	168	B3
Pingtaizi[BJ]	36	C2
Pingtan[CQ]	132	B4
Pingtan[FJ]	94	E4
Pingtang[GD]	118	D4
Pingtang[GX]	124	C3
Pingtang[GZ]	144	F5
Pingtianxu[GD]	118	G1
Pingtong[SC]	138	J3
Pingtou[SN]	156	C6
Pingtou[SX]	54	D4
Pingtou[SX]	54	E5
Pingtung[TW]	186	D4
Pingwang[JS]	80	F6
Pingwu[SC]	138	J3
Pingxi[FJ]	94	E2
Pingxi[GD]	118	I3
Pingxi[GZ]	144	F3
Pingxi[JX]	98	C4
Pingxiang[GX]	124	D5
Pingxiang[HEB]	48	B7
Pingxiang[HEB]	48	C6
Pingxiang[JX]	98	A4
Pingxing Guan[SX]	54	E2
Pingyan[GZ]	144	F5
Pingyang[GX]	124	F4
Pingyang[HEB]	48	B5
Pingyang[HL]	70	B5
Pingyang[HL]	70	C4
Pingyang[ZJ]	84	E5
Pingyao[SX]	54	D4
Pingyi[SD]	102	D4
Pingyin[SD]	102	C3
Pingyong[GZ]	144	G4
Pingyu[BJ]	36	B4
Pingyu[HEN]	106	F5
Pingyuan[GD]	118	H2
Pingyuan[SD]	102	C2
Pingyuan[YN]	148	I7
Pingyuen River[HK]	176	D1
Pingzhai[YN]	148	J6
Pingzhang Ling[XJ]	172	L7
Pingzheng[GX]	124	H5
Pingzhuang[GZ]	144	G3
Pipa Dingzi[JL]	66	I4
Pipa[GS]	160	G6
Piqan[XJ]	172	F5
Pishan Dao[ZJ]	84	F4
Pishan(Guma)[XJ]	172	G7
Piyalma[XJ]	172	G7
Pizhou[JS]	80	C2
Plover Cove Reservoir[HK]	176	E2
Po Hu[AH]	90	C6
Po Jiang[JX]	98	D2

Po Pin Chau[HK]	176	F3
Po Toi Islands[HK]	176	E4
Po Toi[HK]	176	E4
Pobeihe[HEN]	106	F6
Pocang[HEB]	48	B4
Pogang Hu[AH]	90	D6
Pohao[GX]	124	E3
Pohe[GX]	124	C4
Pohong[GX]	124	D4
Poin Qu[XZ]	152	H3
Poingya[QH]	164	M5
Pointa[XZ]	152	H3
Pojiao[GZ]	144	D6
Pojiao[YN]	148	J7
Pojie[GX]	124	E2
Pok Fu Lam[HK]	176	D3
Poliang[AH]	90	C6
Polubu[SX]	54	D1
Pomei[GZ]	144	D5
Pomenheqiao[QH]	164	H3
Pondo[XZ]	152	G4
Pongqung[QH]	164	I7
Pongyin Co[XZ]	152	F3
Porto Exterior[MC]	182	B2
Posarrong[SC]	138	G6
Potang[GX]	124	E4
Potoi O[HK]	176	E3
Potou Gang[HI]	128	C3
Potou Qu[GD]	118	C5
Potou[HEN]	106	D3
Potou[SN]	156	E6
Potou[SN]	156	F6
Potou[SX]	54	B5
Potou[YN]	148	H7
Potzu[TW]	186	D3
Povoação de Ká Hó[MC]	182	D6
Povoação de Lai Chi Van[MC]	182	B7
Poxin[HI]	128	C2
Poyang Hu[JX]	98	D2
Poyang[JX]	98	D3
Poyu[SD]	102	I2
Pozao[GX]	124	E4
Pozhai[HI]	128	C2
Pozi[SD]	102	F3
Praia de Hác—Sá[MC]	182	C6
Praia de Nossa Senhora da Esperanca[MC]	182	C5
Práia do Bom Parto[MC]	182	A3
Pu He[HEB]	48	F3
Pu Xian[SX]	54	C5
Pu'an[GZ]	144	C5
Pu'an[GZ]	144	F4
Pubei[GX]	124	G5
Puchang[GZ]	144	F3
Pucheng[FJ]	94	D2
Pucheng[HEN]	106	G2
Pucheng[SD]	102	E2
Pucheng[SN]	156	F6
Pudi[SN]	156	F4
Puding[GZ]	144	D4
Pudog Zangbo[XZ]	152	D4
Pudong Xinqu[SH]	74	D2
Pudong Yunhe[SH]	74	D2
Pudu He[YN]	148	H5
Pu'er[YN]	148	G7
Pu'er[YN]	148	J2
Puge[SC]	138	H8
Pugêntang[QH]	164	F8
Pugu[GZ]	144	C4
Puhe[GX]	124	C3
Puhe[HB]	110	F3
Puhuisi[HEN]	106	F5
Puhuy[XJ]	172	J5
Pui O Wan[HK]	176	B4
Pui O[HK]	176	B4
Puji[SD]	102	D3
Puji[SD]	102	F3
Pujiachuan[NX]	168	C4
Pujiang[SC]	138	I5
Pujiang[SH]	74	C2
Pujiang[ZJ]	84	D3
Pukou Qu[JS]	80	D4
Pukou[FJ]	94	E3
Pukou[HN]	114	B6

Pukou[HN]	114	F5
Pukou[JS]	80	D4
Puladi[YN]	148	D3
Pulandian Wan[LN]	62	E5
Pulandian[LN]	62	E5
Puli[TW]	186	D3
Pulianji[SD]	102	B5
Puliqiao[HN]	114	D6
Pulong[SC]	138	H9
Pulu[GX]	124	H3
Pulu[XJ]	172	H7
Pum Qu[XZ]	152	E5
Puma Yumco[XZ]	152	G5
Puma[GS]	160	G5
Pumaqangtang[XZ]	152	G5
Pumei[FJ]	94	C6
Pumen[GX]	124	I4
Puming[SX]	54	C3
Punan Yunhe[SH]	74	C3
Pundam[XZ]	152	F5
Pung Co[XZ]	152	G4
Pungzhang[XZ]	152	C4
Puning[GD]	118	I3
Pupai[GD]	118	D5
Pupeng[YN]	148	F5
Puping[GZ]	144	D5
Puqian Wan[HI]	128	C1
Puqian[HI]	128	C1
Puqian[JX]	98	E3
Pur Co[XZ]	152	B2
Purog Kangri[XZ]	152	F3
Purong[HN]	114	B4
Pushan[HEN]	106	D4
Pushi[HN]	114	C4
Pushun[CQ]	132	D3
Putai[QH]	164	O4
Putai[TW]	186	D3
Putang[GX]	124	G5
Putao[CQ]	132	E4
Putaojiang[HEN]	106	G4
Putian[FJ]	94	D4
Puting[ZJ]	84	E5
Putou[FJ]	94	D4
Putou[SX]	54	D6
Putuo Qu[SH]	74	C2
Putuo Qu[ZJ]	84	G3
Putuo Shan[ZJ]	84	G2
Puwa[BJ]	36	B4
Puwei[SC]	138	G8
Puwen[YN]	148	G8
Puxiong[SC]	138	H7
Puyang Jiang[ZJ]	84	E3
Puyang[HEN]	106	F2
Puyang[HEN]	106	G2
Puyi[GZ]	144	D3
Puyi[YN]	148	G7
Puyuan[FJ]	94	E2
Puyuan[ZJ]	84	E2
Puzhang[SX]	54	D6
Puzhou[SX]	54	B7
Puzhuang[JS]	80	F5
puzi[CQ]	132	D4

Q

Qab[NM]	58	G8
Qabnag[XZ]	152	I5
Qabog[GS]	160	G6
Qagan Hua[JL]	66	E3
Qagan Nur[HEB]	48	A2
Qagan Nur[JL]	66	E2
Qagan Nur[NM]	58	H8
Qagan Nur[NM]	58	K6
Qagan Nur[QH]	164	K4
Qagan Obo[NM]	58	J5
Qagan Tolgoi[NM]	58	D8
Qagan Tungge[XJ]	172	H3
Qagan Us He[QH]	164	K4
Qagan Usu[XJ]	172	H4
Qagan Usu[XJ]	172	H4
Qagan[NM]	58	M3
Qagca[SC]	138	D3

Name	Page	Grid
Qagzê[XZ]	152	H4
Qahar Tan[NM]	58	F8
Qahar Youyi Houqi[NM]	58	J7
Qahar Youyi Qianqi[NM]	58	J7
Qahar Youyi Zhongqi[NM]	58	J7
Qaidam He[QH]	164	I4
Qaidam Pendi[QH]	164	E3
Qaidam Shan[QH]	164	H3
Qakar[XJ]	172	H7
Qakyung[XZ]	152	G4
Qalarqa[XJ]	172	I4
Qamdo[XZ]	152	J4
Qamdün[XZ]	152	J4
Qamgu[QH]	164	J8
Qammê[SC]	138	H2
Qangba[XZ]	152	B3
Qanglapoila Ri[XZ]	152	F4
Qangma[XZ]	152	G4
Qangrida[QH]	164	I6
Qangringngoinza Ri[XZ]	152	F2
Qangtang[XZ]	152	G5
Qangzê[XZ]	152	A4
Qapqal[XJ]	172	H4
Qarak[XJ]	172	F6
Qarhan[QH]	164	H4
Qarlung[XJ]	172	E6
Qarqan He[XJ]	172	K6
Qarqi[XJ]	172	H5
Qarsan[NM]	58	N4
Qatkal[XJ]	172	L4
Qatog[SC]	138	C2
Qayü[XZ]	152	H5
Qêlungringbo[QH]	164	H6
Qêm Qu[QH]	164	L6
Qêqugou[QH]	164	N4
Qêqung[XZ]	152	E4
Qêra[XZ]	152	E5
Qi He[HEN]	106	F2
Qi Jiang[CQ]	132	C4
Qi Qu[XZ]	152	K5
Qi Shui[HB]	110	I4
Qi Xian[HEN]	106	F2
Qi Xian[HEN]	106	F3
Qi Xian[SX]	54	D4
Qiachuan[SN]	156	G5
Qiacun[JX]	98	D4
Qian Gorlos[JL]	66	E2
Qian He[AH]	90	C3
Qian Jiang[GX]	124	G4
Qian Jiang[SC]	138	N4
Qian Shan[LN]	62	F4
Qian Xian[SN]	156	E6
Qian'an[HEB]	48	F3
Qian'an[JL]	66	E3
Qianbeigong[BJ]	36	E3
Qiancang[ZJ]	84	E5
Qianchang[HB]	110	G4
Qianchang[JX]	98	B6
Qianchang[YN]	148	G5
Qianchuan[JL]	66	H5
Qiandao Hu[ZJ]	84	C3
Qiandengzhuang[TJ]	42	A4
Qian'er[SN]	156	F5
Qian'erdao[JL]	66	G4
Qianfang[JX]	98	D3
Qianfeng Nongchang[HL]	70	G5
Qianfeng[HL]	70	D5
Qianfoling[SX]	54	E2
Qiangbai[SN]	156	F6
Qiangfeng[JL]	66	G4
Qiangfeng[ZJ]	84	E2
Qiangji[SX]	54	E5
Qiangjiao[ZJ]	84	F3
Qiangongping[HN]	114	B4
Qiangoumen[NX]	168	C4
Qiangpan He[NM]	58	X10
Qiangxu[GX]	124	E4
Qiangzilu[BJ]	36	E3
Qianhe[AH]	90	C6
Qianhe[NM]	58	V10
Qianhuang[JS]	80	E5
Qianhuzhuang[TJ]	42	B3
Qianji[JS]	80	D3
Qianjia[HI]	128	B3
Qianjiadian[BJ]	36	C2
Qianjiadong[HN]	114	D7
Qianjiang Qu[CQ]	132	E4
Qianjiang[GX]	124	F4
Qianjiang[HB]	110	F4
Qianjiangyi[SH]	74	D1
Qianjiashan[NX]	168	C3
Qianjin Jingyingsuo[HL]	70	D4
Qianjin Nongchang[SH]	74	D1
Qianjin[HEN]	106	F6
Qianjin[HL]	70	C4
Qianjin[HL]	70	G5
Qianjin[JL]	66	E3
Qianjin[JL]	66	H4
Qianjin[LN]	62	C4
Qianjin[NX]	168	C2
Qianjin[SN]	156	F8
Qianjing[HEN]	106	E3
Qianjishan[BJ]	36	D3
Qianjuan[TJ]	42	B4
Qiankeng[FJ]	94	B4
Qiankou[AH]	90	E7
Qiankou[ZJ]	84	C4
Qiankuang[QH]	164	K3
Qiankuang[QH]	164	K4
Qianli Gang[ZJ]	84	C3
Qianli Yan[SD]	102	H3
Qianling[JX]	98	B5
Qianliu[YN]	148	F8
Qianlou[FJ]	94	C6
Qianlugu[TJ]	42	C2
Qianma[JS]	80	E5
Qianmai[YN]	148	F8
Qianmentang[SH]	74	C2
Qianmiqiao[TJ]	42	C4
Qianmotou[HEB]	48	C6
Qianpai[GD]	118	D4
Qianping[FJ]	94	C4
Qianpu[SD]	102	D2
Qianqi[FJ]	94	F2
Qianqiao[SH]	74	C2
Qianqiao[SH]	74	D3
Qianqihao[JL]	66	D3
Qianquan Shuiku[TJ]	42	B4
Qianrenqiao[AH]	90	D5
Qianshan Qu[LN]	62	F3
Qianshan[AH]	90	C6
Qianshan[GD]	118	C6
Qianshan[JX]	98	B4
Qianshan[SX]	54	B5
Qianshao[HL]	70	B2
Qiansheng[SH]	74	B2
Qianshuangjing[LN]	62	G1
Qianshui[GD]	118	C5
Qiansun[SD]	102	C2
Qiantai[TJ]	42	B3
Qiantang Jiang[ZJ]	84	E2
Qiantang[GD]	118	C5
Qianting[FJ]	94	C5
Qiantong[HEB]	48	E6
Qiantong[ZJ]	84	F3
Qianwei[HL]	70	F6
Qianwei[LN]	62	D4
Qianwei[SC]	138	I6
Qianwei[SH]	74	D2
Qianxi[FJ]	94	D4
Qianxi[GZ]	144	E3
Qianxi[HEB]	48	F3
Qianxiang[GZ]	144	D5
Qianxiaotun[TJ]	42	A4
Qianxu[SH]	74	C3
Qianyang[LN]	62	E3
Qianyang[LN]	62	H5
Qianyang[SN]	156	D6
Qianying[LN]	62	G4
Qianyou He[SN]	156	F7
Qianzhuang[SD]	102	C3
Qianzhuangzi[BJ]	36	C3
Qi'ao Dao[GD]	118	F4
Qiaoban[GX]	124	G3
Qiaobei[HEN]	106	E3
Qiaochatan[SN]	156	G2
Qiaochuan[GS]	160	H4
Qiaodi[SN]	156	E6
Qiaogang[GX]	124	G6
Qiaogouwan[SN]	156	E3
Qiaohai[HI]	128	C3
Qiaohe[GS]	160	I4
Qiaojia[YN]	148	H4
Qiaojian[GX]	124	E4
Qiaojiatun[HEB]	48	C6
Qiaojiawan[SX]	54	C5
Qiaole[JX]	98	C3
Qiaoli[GX]	124	F4
Qiaolin[JS]	80	D5
Qiaoma[GZ]	144	D6
Qiaomaiyu[BJ]	36	D3
Qiaomu[AH]	90	E6
Qiaonan[JL]	66	I4
Qiaonan[JX]	98	C4
Qiaoniao[LN]	62	E4
Qiaopo[HI]	128	C1
Qiaoqi[SC]	138	H5
Qiaoshan[GX]	124	F3
Qiaoshan[SD]	102	E4
Qiaoshang[HB]	110	D3
Qiaoshe[JX]	98	C3
Qiaoting[GX]	124	H3
Qiaotou[AH]	90	D4
Qiaotou[CQ]	132	E3
Qiaotou[FJ]	94	C2
Qiaotou[GD]	118	D3
Qiaotou[GX]	124	F3
Qiaotou[HI]	128	B2
Qiaotou[HN]	114	D7
Qiaotou[HN]	114	G6
Qiaotou[JL]	66	I3
Qiaotou[JX]	98	B5
Qiaotou[JX]	98	C3
Qiaotou[LN]	62	G3
Qiaotou[TJ]	42	B2
Qiaotou[YN]	148	J8
Qiaotou[ZJ]	84	F2
Qiaotouhe[HN]	114	D5
Qiaotouhu[ZJ]	84	F3
Qiaotoupu[HN]	114	D7
Qiaotouzhuang[TJ]	42	B2
Qiaowan[GS]	160	C2
Qiaoxi[JX]	98	B3
Qiaoxia[ZJ]	84	E4
Qiaoxian[GX]	124	F4
Qiaoye[GX]	124	D4
Qiaoyi[HN]	114	E4
Qiaoyin[GX]	124	E3
Qiaoying[ZJ]	84	F3
Qiaozhacun[TJ]	42	C3
Qiaozhen[SN]	156	E4
Qiaozi[GS]	160	C2
Qiawan[JX]	98	D4
Qibaihu[NX]	168	B4
Qibainong[GX]	124	E3
Qibao[SH]	74	C2
Qibaoshan Tiekuang[JX]	98	B3
Qibu[FJ]	94	E2
Qibu[FJ]	94	E3
Qibu[TJ]	42	A3
Qicha[HI]	128	B2
Qichang[HI]	128	A3
Qichun[HB]	110	I4
Qicun[SD]	102	D5
Qicun[SX]	54	D3
Qidaohe[HB]	110	I4
Qidaoling[LN]	62	D3
Qidong[GX]	124	G4
Qidong[HN]	114	E6
Qidong[JS]	80	G5
Qidu[FJ]	94	E3
Qidu[JS]	80	F6
Qiemo(Qarqan)[XJ]	172	J6
Qiexue[GX]	124	E3
Qiezihe Qu[HL]	70	F6
Qifang[HB]	110	F2
Qifang[HI]	128	B2
Qifengdu[HN]	114	F7
Qigou[HEB]	48	F2
Qigzhi[QH]	164	H6
Qihe[HN]	114	D3
Qihe[SD]	102	C3

Name	Page	Grid
Qihulin He[HL]	70	G6
Qiji[HEB]	48	C6
Qijia[HEB]	48	B2
Qijia[HEB]	48	F2
Qijiabu[TJ]	42	C3
Qijiahe[SX]	54	C7
Qijiang[CQ]	132	C4
Qijiang[HN]	114	C5
Qijiao[JX]	98	D2
Qijiaojing[XJ]	172	M4
Qijiawu[HEB]	48	E5
Qijiaxi[HN]	114	C4
Qijiazhuang[NX]	168	C4
Qijiazi[LN]	62	G2
Qijiazuo[HEB]	48	B5
Qijiebamei[ZJ]	84	F2
Qijingzi[JL]	66	D3
Qika[NM]	58	M2
Qikeshu[HL]	70	B5
Qikou[SX]	54	B4
Qiktim[XJ]	172	M4
Qilaotu Shan[HEB]	48	F2
Qilaotu Shan[NM]	58	L6
Qileng[SN]	156	G2
Qili Hu[AH]	90	E4
Qili[FJ]	94	D3
Qili[JL]	66	H3
Qili[ZJ]	84	C3
Qilian Shan[GS]	160	C3
Qilian Shan[GS]	160	D3
Qilian Shan[GS]	160	E3
Qilian Shan[QH]	164	J1
Qilian[GS]	160	F4
Qilian[QH]	164	M2
Qiliao[CQ]	132	E4
Qilidian[BJ]	36	C4
Qilifen[BJ]	36	B4
Qilihai[TJ]	42	C3
Qilihe[LN]	62	E3
Qilin[AH]	90	D6
Qilin[GS]	160	D3
Qilin[JS]	80	G5
Qiling[FJ]	94	C5
Qiliping[HB]	110	C4
Qiliping[HB]	110	H3
Qilushan[JX]	98	C6
Qima Tag[QH]	164	B3
Qimaba[YN]	148	H8
Qiman Tag[XJ]	172	M7
Qiman[XJ]	172	I5
Qimantag[XJ]	172	M7
Qimen[AH]	90	D7
Qimen[GX]	124	E5
Qimeng[GZ]	144	G4
Qimo[GZ]	144	D4
Qimu Zhang[GD]	118	H3
Qin He[SX]	54	D6
Qin Jiang[GD]	118	H3
Qin Jiang[GX]	124	F5
Qin Jiang[JX]	98	D5
Qin Ling[HEN]	106	B4
Qin Ling[SN]	156	F7
Qin Xian[SX]	54	D5
Qi'na[YN]	148	F4
Qin'an[GS]	160	G5
Qincheng[BJ]	36	C3
Qincheng[XJ]	172	O4
Qinchi[HEN]	106	B3
Qinchi[SX]	54	D6
Qing He[LN]	62	H2
Qing Jiang[HB]	110	D4
Qing Xian[HEB]	48	D5
Qing'an[HL]	70	D5
Qing'anping[HN]	114	C3
Qingbaijiang Qu[SC]	138	J5
Qingbaikou[BJ]	36	B3
Qingban[JX]	98	E3
Qingcao[HI]	128	C2
Qingcaotan[NX]	168	A3
Qingchang[GZ]	144	D3
Qingche Hu[XZ]	152	B2
Qingcheng Qu[GD]	118	F3
Qingcheng[GS]	160	H4
Qingcheng[SD]	102	D2
Qingcheng[SX]	54	E3
Qingcheng[SX]	54	E4
Qingcheng[SX]	54	E4
Qingchengzi[LN]	62	G4
Qingchuan Wan[FJ]	94	F2
Qingchuan[SC]	138	K3
Qingciyao[SX]	54	E2
Qingcun Gang[SH]	74	D3
Qingcun[SH]	74	D3
Qingdao[SD]	102	G3
Qingdian[TJ]	42	B2
Qingdui[LN]	62	G5
Qingduizi[LN]	62	E3
Qingfeng[HB]	110	D2
Qingfeng[HEN]	106	G2
Qingfeng[SH]	74	D3
Qingfengdian[HEB]	48	C5
Qingfengshan[LN]	62	C3
Qinggang[HEN]	106	C3
Qinggang[HL]	70	D5
Qinggangping[CQ]	132	E4
Qinggangping[SN]	156	F7
Qinggangtang[GZ]	144	F2
Qinggilik[XJ]	172	J7
Qinggouzi[JL]	66	I4
Qingguang[TJ]	42	B3
Qinggui[GD]	118	E3
Qingguji[SD]	102	B5
Qinghai Hu[QH]	164	M4
Qinghai Nanshan[QH]	164	L4
Qinghe Nongchang[TJ]	42	C3
Qinghe Qu[LN]	62	H2
Qinghe Shuiku[LN]	62	H2
Qinghe(Qinggil)[XJ]	172	M2
Qinghe[BJ]	36	C3
Qinghe[HEB]	48	C6
Qinghe[HEN]	106	D4
Qinghe[HL]	70	C4
Qinghe[HL]	70	E5
Qinghe[HB]	70	G5
Qinghe[JL]	66	F6
Qinghe[SD]	102	C4
Qinghecheng[LN]	62	H3
Qinghei Shan[HL]	70	E5
Qinghemen Qu[LN]	62	E3
Qinghu[GX]	124	H5
Qinghu[JS]	80	D2
Qinghua[HEN]	106	D5
Qinghua[JX]	98	E2
Qinghua[SC]	138	M4
Qinghuabian[SN]	156	F4
Qingji[HEN]	106	F3
Qingjian He[SN]	156	G4
Qingjian[SN]	156	G3
Qingjian[SX]	54	B6
Qingjiang[HN]	114	C6
Qingjiang[HN]	114	F7
Qingjiang[JX]	98	B2
Qingjiang[SC]	138	L4
Qingjuan[BJ]	36	B4
Qingkou[FJ]	94	E4
Qinglan Hu[JX]	98	D3
Qinglan[HN]	114	E6
Qinglang[HN]	114	C4
Qingliang Feng[AH]	90	E6
Qingliangsi[SX]	54	B4
Qinglin[HL]	70	F4
Qinglin[QH]	164	N3
Qingling[JL]	66	G4
Qingliu[FJ]	94	B3
Qinglon Shan[GX]	124	D3
Qinglong He[HEB]	48	F3
Qinglong[CQ]	132	F3
Qinglong[GZ]	144	D5
Qinglong[HEB]	48	F3
Qinglong[SD]	102	G2
Qinglong[YN]	148	I6
Qinglonghchang[YN]	148	H7
Qinglonghu[BJ]	36	C4
Qinglongji[AH]	90	C2
Qinglung[XZ]	152	G4
Qingmajuan[NX]	168	D3
Qingmuchuan[SN]	156	B8
Qingmuguan[CQ]	132	C4
Qingni[JX]	98	D4
Qingnian Nongchang[TJ]	42	C3
Qingnian[CQ]	132	C5
Qingninghou[TJ]	42	B4
Qingong[JS]	80	E3
Qingpian[SC]	138	J3
Qingping[CQ]	132	C4
Qingping[GS]	160	G5
Qingping[GZ]	144	D5
Qingping[HB]	110	C5
Qingpu Qu[SH]	74	C2
Qingqian[AH]	90	B3
Qingqiaoyi[SN]	156	C7
Qingqu[HB]	110	D2
Qingquan[CQ]	132	E5
Qingquan[GS]	160	C3
Qingquan[GS]	160	E3
Qingquan[SN]	156	G2
Qingquluchakou[QH]	164	J7
Qingsanying[HEB]	48	C2
Qingshan Shuiku[HB]	110	H5
Qingshan Shuiku[ZJ]	84	D2
Qingshan[AH]	90	C5
Qingshan[AH]	90	C7
Qingshan[GZ]	144	D5
Qingshan[HB]	110	D2
Qingshan[HB]	110	H5
Qingshan[HL]	70	E4
Qingshan[HL]	70	E5
Qingshan[JL]	66	C2
Qingshan[JL]	66	G2
Qingshan[JS]	80	E4
Qingshan[NX]	168	D3
Qingshan[SH]	74	D3
Qingshan[SN]	156	G7
Qingshan[TJ]	42	B1
Qingshanqiao[HN]	114	E5
Qingshanqiao[HN]	114	E5
Qingshen[SC]	138	I6
Qingshi[HB]	110	I4
Qingshi[ZJ]	84	C4
Qingshitan Shuiku[GX]	124	H2
Qingshui He[BJ]	36	B4
Qingshui He[BJ]	36	E2
Qingshui He[HEB]	48	C3
Qingshui He[HEN]	106	F5
Qingshui He[NX]	168	B3
Qingshui He[NX]	168	C4
Qingshui He[SX]	54	E3
Qingshui Jiang[GZ]	144	F3
Qingshui Jiang[GZ]	144	G4
Qingshui Jiang[YN]	148	J7
Qingshui[BJ]	36	B4
Qingshui[CQ]	132	E3
Qingshui[FJ]	94	C4
Qingshui[GD]	118	E2
Qingshui[GS]	160	D3
Qingshui[GS]	160	H5
Qingshui[SD]	102	B3
Qingshui[SN]	156	D8
Qingshuigou[NX]	168	C1
Qingshuihe[GZ]	144	C5
Qingshuihe[HB]	110	I4
Qingshuihe[NM]	58	I8
Qingshuihe[NM]	58	X12
Qingshuihe[QH]	164	J7
Qingshuihe[YN]	148	D7
Qingshuijian[BJ]	36	B4
Qingshuikou[GX]	124	H5
Qingshuilang Shan[YN]	148	E4
Qingshuipu[GZ]	144	D3
Qingshuiyi[GS]	160	G5
Qingshuiying[NX]	168	C2
Qingshuping[HN]	114	E5
Qingsong[HI]	128	B2
Qingsong[JL]	66	H3
Qingsong[SH]	74	C2
Qingsongling[LN]	62	C3
Qingtai[HEN]	106	D5
Qingtaiping[HB]	110	D4
Qingtan[HB]	110	F3
Qingtang[GD]	118	F2
Qingtang[JX]	98	C5
Qingtangpu[HN]	114	D4

Qingtian[ZJ]	84	E4
Qingtong[HEB]	48	B5
Qingtongguan[SN]	156	F7
Qingtongxia Shuiku[NX]	168	B3
Qingtongxia[NX]	168	B3
Qingtongxia[NX]	168	B3
Qingtongxia[NX]	168	C3
Qingtü[XZ]	152	F4
Qingtuan[AH]	90	C3
Qingtuo[SD]	102	E4
Qingwan[GX]	124	H5
Qingxi[AH]	90	D5
Qingxi[CQ]	132	D4
Qingxi[GD]	118	G3
Qingxi[GD]	118	G4
Qingxi[GD]	118	I2
Qingxi[HL]	70	D4
Qingxi[JX]	98	C6
Qingxi[SN]	156	D6
Qingxi[ZJ]	84	E4
Qingxiang[SD]	102	F2
Qingxin[GD]	118	E3
Qingxinjie Shan[QH]	164	E2
Qingxinjie Shan[XJ]	172	N6
Qingxu[SX]	54	D4
Qingyan[GZ]	144	E4
Qingyang[AH]	90	D6
Qingyang[CQ]	132	D4
Qingyang[GS]	160	H5
Qingyang[HL]	70	E6
Qingyi Jiang[AH]	90	E6
Qingyi Jiang[SC]	138	I6
Qingyishan[LN]	62	H4
Qingyu[FJ]	94	D5
Qingyuan Qu[JX]	98	C4
Qingyuan[GD]	118	F3
Qingyuan[HEB]	48	C5
Qingyuan[HL]	70	G5
Qingyuan[LN]	62	H2
Qingyuan[SN]	156	E5
Qingyuan[ZJ]	84	D5
Qingyun Shan[GD]	118	F2
Qingyun Shan[GD]	118	G2
Qingyun Shuiku[CQ]	132	B4
Qingyun[HEB]	48	E6
Qingyun[JX]	98	D3
Qingyun[SD]	102	D2
Qingyun[SH]	74	D3
Qingyundian[BJ]	36	D4
Qingyunpu Qu[JX]	98	C3
Qingzang Gaoyuan[QH]	164	B6
Qingzang Gaoyuan[XZ]	152	D3
Qingzhang He[HEB]	48	A7
Qingzhen[GZ]	144	E4
Qingzheng[SH]	74	C2
Qingzhou[FJ]	94	C3
Qingzhou[SD]	102	E3
Qingzu[HEN]	106	G2
Qinhe[SN]	156	F2
Qinhuai He[JS]	80	D5
Qinhuangdao[HEB]	48	G4
Qinji[HB]	110	E2
Qinjia[HL]	70	D5
Qinjiatun[JL]	66	E4
Qinkou He[SD]	102	D2
Qinlan[AH]	90	F4
Qinling Shandi[SN]	156	D6
Qinling[SN]	156	D7
Qinqu[NX]	168	C3
Qinquan[SX]	54	E5
Qinshan Dao[JS]	80	E2
Qinshan[ZJ]	84	E2
Qinshui[SX]	54	D6
Qintong[JS]	80	F4
Qinyang[FJ]	94	E2
Qinyang[HEN]	106	D2
Qinyu[BJ]	36	B3
Qinyu[FJ]	94	F2
Qinyuan[SX]	54	D5
Qinzhou Wan[GX]	124	F6
Qinzhou[GX]	124	F6
Qinzhougang[GX]	124	F6
Qiong Hai[SC]	138	H8
Qionghai[HI]	128	C2
Qionglai Shan[SC]	138	H3
Qionglai[SC]	138	I5
Qiongshan Qu[HI]	128	C1
Qiongzhong[HI]	128	B2
Qiongzhou Haixia[GD]	118	B6
Qiongzhou Haixia[HI]	128	C1
Qipan[JS]	80	D2
Qipan[XJ]	172	F7
Qipanshan[HEB]	48	E1
Qiping[JX]	98	B3
Qiping[SC]	138	L4
Qipu Tang[JS]	80	G5
Qiqi[CQ]	132	D3
Qiqian[NM]	58	N1
Qiqiao[HEB]	48	D5
Qiqiao[JS]	80	D5
Qiqihar[HL]	70	B5
Qiqing[GS]	160	D3
Qiqu Liedao[ZJ]	84	G2
Qiquanhu[XJ]	172	L4
Qira[XJ]	172	H7
Qishan[JS]	80	B2
Qishan[SD]	102	G2
Qishan[SN]	156	D6
Qishe[GZ]	144	C6
Qishi[GX]	124	G4
Qishui[GD]	118	B6
Qishuyan Qu[JS]	80	F5
Qitai[XJ]	172	L3
Qitaihe[HL]	70	F6
Qitamu[JL]	66	G3
Qitan[GZ]	144	G2
Qitian Ling[HN]	114	E7
Qiting[JS]	80	E5
Qitou Yang[ZJ]	84	G3
Qiu Xian[HEB]	48	C7
Qiuba[HEN]	106	C3
Qiubei[JX]	98	C4
Qiubei[YN]	148	J6
Qiucheng[HEB]	48	C7
Qiuchuan[ZJ]	84	C4
Qiucun[AH]	90	F5
Qiucun[ZJ]	84	F3
Qiuhu[JS]	80	F4
Qiuji[JS]	80	D3
Qiuji[JS]	80	D4
Qiujin[JX]	98	C2
Qiuligou[JL]	66	I4
Qiulinpu[BJ]	36	B4
Qiumianleike Tag[QH]	164	C4
Qiumianleike Tag[XJ]	172	M7
Qiushan[ZJ]	84	E4
Qiusong[JL]	66	J4
Qiuxi[JX]	98	D4
Qiuzhuang Shuiku[HEB]	48	F4
Qiuzhuangzi[TJ]	42	B4
Qiuzigou[LN]	62	C4
Qiwei[JS]	80	F4
Qixi[SH]	74	D1
Qixi[ZJ]	84	C3
Qixia Qu[JS]	80	D4
Qixia[SD]	102	G2
Qixian[SD]	102	E3
Qixianggongzhuang[TJ]	42	A2
Qixiao[SH]	74	D1
Qixing Dao[FJ]	94	F3
Qixing Dao[ZJ]	84	E5
Qixing He[HL]	70	G5
Qixing Ling[HI]	128	C1
Qixing[HN]	114	D5
Qixingyan Ding[GD]	118	D3
Qiyang[HN]	114	D6
Qiyao Shan[CQ]	132	E3
Qiyi Shuiku[JX]	98	F3
Qiyi[HEN]	106	D5
Qizhong[XZ]	152	K5
Qizhongkou[HEB]	48	C4
Qizhou Liedao[HI]	128	D2
Qizhou Yang[HI]	128	D2
Qizhou[HB]	110	I4
Qizhuang[BJ]	36	D3
Qizhuang[TJ]	42	B2
Qogir Feng[XJ]	172	F8
Qoica[QH]	164	N5
Qoidê[XZ]	152	D3
Qoidên Co[XZ]	152	E2
Qoidên[XZ]	152	K5
Qoijê[QH]	164	L4
Qoijê[SC]	138	I2
Qoijêma[SC]	138	G2
Qoijênangwa[SC]	138	I2
Qoima Co[QH]	164	D7
Qoima[XZ]	152	E5
Qol Tag[XJ]	172	L4
Qomolangma Feng[XZ]	152	E5
Qong Muztag[XJ]	172	I8
Qonggyai[XZ]	152	G5
Qongkol[XJ]	172	J6
Qongkur[XJ]	172	K1
Qongkurqak[XJ]	172	F6
Qongmazar[XJ]	172	H7
Qonj[QH]	164	L3
Qor But[NM]	58	V11
Qoren[XJ]	172	M3
Qowo[SC]	138	F5
Qowowuyag Feng[XZ]	152	E5
Qu Jiang[SC]	138	L5
Qu Jiang[YN]	148	H6
Qu Jiang[ZJ]	84	D3
Qu Shui[HN]	114	B6
Qu Xian[SC]	138	L5
Quanbao Shan[HEN]	106	C3
Quangang Qu[FJ]	94	D4
Quangang[JX]	98	C3
Qu'angayong[QH]	164	F7
Quanjiao[AH]	90	C4
Quanjuyong[LN]	62	D3
Quankong[CQ]	132	E4
Quankou[GZ]	144	G2
Quankou[JX]	98	C2
Quanlin[SD]	102	D4
Quannan[JX]	98	B7
Quannei[YN]	148	F7
Quanpu[SD]	102	C4
Quanshan[GS]	160	F3
Quanshang[FJ]	94	B3
Quanshui[GX]	124	G6
Quanshuitou[SD]	102	G3
Quantai[JL]	66	E5
Quantang[ZJ]	84	F2
Quantou[LN]	62	H2
Quanxi[HB]	110	C2
Quanyang[AH]	90	B3
Quanyang[JL]	66	H5
Quanzhai[HEN]	106	E4
Quanzhang[SX]	54	C6
Quanzhou Wan[FJ]	94	D5
Quanzhou[FJ]	94	D5
Quanzhou[GX]	124	I2
Quanzhou[JS]	80	E5
Qubai[JX]	98	B5
Qucainka[XZ]	152	K5
Quchaihe[JL]	66	G4
Quchomo[XZ]	152	G5
Qucun[HEN]	106	G2
Qudêng[XZ]	152	E5
Qudi[SD]	102	D2
Qudong[YN]	148	E5
Qu'e[SX]	54	B5
Que'er Shan[SC]	138	E4
Que'er Shan[SC]	138	E4
Que'erao[ZJ]	84	F4
Que'ergou[XJ]	172	K4
Quekou[AH]	90	D5
Queshan[HEN]	106	F5
Qufu[SD]	102	C4
Qujiadian[LN]	62	G1
Qujiadian[TJ]	42	B4
Qujiang Qu[GD]	118	F2
Qujiang Qu[ZJ]	84	C4
Qujiang[SN]	156	E6
Qujie[GD]	118	C6
Qujing[NX]	168	C2
Qujing[YN]	148	I5
Qujiu[GX]	124	E5
Qukog[QH]	164	N5
Qukou Nongchang[NX]	168	B3
Qukou[NX]	168	B3

Qukou[ZJ] 84 E4
Qulan[HN] 114 E5
Qulho[XZ] 152 D4
Quli[GX] 124 E5
Quliang[HEN] 106 E3
Qulong[CQ] 132 F2
Quma[CQ] 132 E2
Qumar He[QH] 164 G5
Qumarhe[QH] 164 G6
Qumarlêb[QH] 164 H6
Qunda[HB] 110 G2
Qundo[XZ] 152 I4
Qungag[QH] 164 L5
Qungcang[XZ] 152 D3
Qungdo'gyang[XZ] 152 H5
Qu'ngoin He[QH] 164 L5
Qu'ngoin[GS] 160 F5
Qu'ngoin[QH] 164 M5
Qunjia[QH] 164 N4
Qunling[JL] 66 G3
Qunshan[HL] 70 D4
Qu'nyido[XZ] 152 J4
Qu'og[XZ] 152 E5
Qurügagka[QH] 164 G6
Qushan[ZJ] 84 G2
Qushi[YN] 148 D5
Qushui[YN] 148 H8
Qusum[XZ] 152 A3
Qusum[XZ] 152 H5
Qusumbo[XZ] 152 F4
Qutang Xia[CQ] 132 F2
Quting[SX] 54 C5
Qutou[BJ] 36 D4
Qutun[HEN] 106 D4
Quwan[HB] 110 F2
Quwo[SX] 54 C6
Quwu Shan[GS] 160 G4
Quwu Shan[GS] 160 G4
Quxi[FJ] 94 B4
Quxi[HB] 110 D5
Quxi[ZJ] 84 E5
Qüxü[XZ] 152 G5
Quyang[GX] 124 D4
Quyang[HEB] 48 B5
Quyang[JS] 80 D2
Quyu[SX] 54 B4
Quzhang[GX] 124 G6
Quzhou[HEB] 48 B7
Quzhou[ZJ] 84 C4
Quzi[GS] 160 H4

R

Rabang[XZ] 152 B3
Rabqên[XZ] 152 J5
Ragoka[QH] 164 L5
Ra'gya[QH] 164 M6
Ramangzalê[XZ] 152 C3
Ramda[QH] 164 G7
Ranchang[SC] 138 E3
Randian[SN] 156 D5
Ranghulu Qu[HL] 70 C5
Rangjiaxi[HN] 114 C4
Rangkou[SC] 138 H3
Rangxi[JX] 98 D2
Rangzi[JL] 66 E2
Ranmiao[AH] 90 B3
Ranran Niuchang[SC] 138 F6
Rao'er[JX] 98 E3
Raofeng[JX] 98 D3
Raofeng[SN] 156 E7
Raohe Nongchang[HL] 70 G5
Raohe[HL] 70 G5
Raoliang[HEN] 106 E5
Raoling[SD] 102 G3
Raoping[GD] 118 J3
Raoxi[SN] 156 E8
Raoyang[HEB] 48 C5
Raoyanghe[LN] 62 F3
Raqung[XZ] 152 G5
Rasa[XZ] 152 F5
Rawa[XZ] 152 H4

Rawu[XZ] 152 J5
Rayü[XZ] 152 I4
Razhêng Zangbo[XZ] 152 G4
Re Qu[XZ] 152 K4
Red Hill Peninsula[HK] 176 D4
Re'erka He[SC] 138 G3
Rêjo[XZ] 152 A3
Rên Co[XZ] 152 F4
Ren He[CQ] 132 E1
Ren Xian[HEB] 48 B6
Renao[JL] 66 G6
Renchaoxi[HN] 114 C3
Rencun[GD] 118 E4
Rencun[HEN] 106 E1
Rencun[NX] 168 C2
Renda[GS] 160 G5
Renfeng[SD] 102 D2
Rengu[HEN] 106 F2
Renhe Qu[SC] 138 G9
Renhe[HEN] 106 G6
Renhe[JS] 80 D3
Renhe[SC] 138 K5
RenHe[SC] 138 N3
Renhe[SD] 102 I3
Renhe[YN] 148 E6
Renhe[YN] 148 G4
Renhe[YN] 148 K3
Renhekou[SN] 156 F7
Renheping[HB] 110 E4
Renhua[GD] 118 F1
Renhuai[GZ] 144 E3
Renji[HEN] 106 G4
Renjia[CQ] 132 D3
Renju[GD] 118 H2
Renmin[HL] 70 C5
Renmin[SH] 74 C2
Renqiu[HEB] 48 D5
Rensha[CQ] 132 D3
Renshan[GD] 118 G4
Renshi[SC] 138 M5
Renshou[FJ] 94 C2
Renshou[SC] 138 J6
Rentaihe[NM] 58 W10
Rentian[FJ] 94 B5
Rentian[JX] 98 D6
Rentou Shan[HN] 114 C4
Renxing[HI] 128 B2
Renxing[YN] 148 H5
Renyi[GX] 124 I3
Renyi[HN] 114 E6
Renyi[SX] 54 C5
Repulse Bay[HK] 176 D4
Repulse Bay[HK] 176 D4
Reservatório de Seac Pai Van [MC] 182 C6
Reshi[HN] 114 D3
Reshui[LN] 62 C2
Reshui[QH] 164 H4
Reshui[QH] 164 K4
Ridong[JX] 98 D6
Ridung[XZ] 152 J4
Rigain Pünco[XZ] 152 E3
Rigar[XZ] 152 D4
Riha[SC] 138 I8
Rinbung[XZ] 152 F5
Rindü[XZ] 152 F4
Ringgo[SC] 138 E7
Ringtor[XZ] 152 C4
Rirong[XZ] 152 H5
Risangtang[QH] 164 I7
Risum[XZ] 152 A3
Ritang[XZ] 152 H5
Riwo[XZ] 152 E5
Riwoqe[XZ] 152 J4
Riwoqê[XZ] 152 J4
Riyue Shan[QH] 164 M4
Riyue Shankou[QH] 164 N4
Riyue[QH] 164 N4
Rizhao[SD] 102 F4
Rola Co[XZ] 152 F2
Rola Kangri[XZ] 152 F2
Rong Jiang[GX] 124 G2
Rong Xian[GX] 124 H5
Rong Xian[SC] 138 J6

Rong'an[GX] 124 G2
Rongbai[HI] 128 B2
Rongbing[JS] 80 E5
Rongbo[XZ] 152 I4
Rongchang[CQ] 132 B4
Rongcheng Wan[SD] 102 I2
Rongcheng[HEB] 48 C4
Rongcheng[SD] 102 I2
Rongdoi[XZ] 152 H4
Rongdu[GZ] 144 D5
Ronghe[SX] 54 B6
Ronghua[GX] 124 D4
Ronghuashan[LN] 62 F5
Rongjiang[GX] 124 H2
Rongjiang[GZ] 144 G5
Rongkeng[FJ] 94 B4
Rongkou[AH] 90 D7
Ronglao[GX] 124 D4
Ronglong[CQ] 132 B4
Ronglu[HI] 128 B3
Rongma[XZ] 152 E3
Rongmê[XZ] 152 K5
Rongqên[XZ] 152 I3
Rongshui[GX] 124 G2
Rongtang[JX] 98 C3
Rongwam[SC] 138 G3
Rongxi[CQ] 132 E5
Rongxing[LN] 62 F4
Rouyuan[NX] 168 B3
Ru He[HEN] 106 F5
Ruanshi[ZJ] 84 E3
Ruanxiang[SH] 74 C3
Ruanxingou[SC] 138 G7
Rucheng[HN] 114 F7
Rucun[SX] 54 E3
Rudong[HN] 114 D3
Rudong[JS] 80 G4
Rugao[JS] 80 F4
Ru'gyog[XZ] 152 D5
Ruhai Yunhe[JS] 80 F4
Rui'an[ZJ] 84 E5
Ruichang[JX] 98 C2
Ruicheng[SX] 54 B7
Ruihong[JX] 98 D3
Ruijin[JX] 98 D6
Ruili[YN] 148 C6
Ruilin[JX] 98 C5
Ruitapu[HN] 114 C3
Ruixi[HI] 128 C2
Ruiyan[HL] 70 B5
Ruji[AH] 90 B3
Rujigou[NX] 168 C1
Run He[AH] 90 B4
Runan[HEN] 106 F4
Runanbu[HEN] 106 F5
Runhe[AH] 90 C4
Runjin[HL] 70 D5
Ruo He[GZ] 144 D2
Ruo Shui[GS] 160 D2
Ruoheng[ZJ] 84 F4
Ruoli[GS] 160 G4
Ruoqiang He[XJ] 172 L6
Ruoqiang (Qarkilik)[XJ] 172 L6
Ruoshui[HN] 114 B5
Rushan Kou[SD] 102 H3
Rushan[SD] 102 H3
Rushankou[SD] 102 H3
Rushanzhai[SD] 102 H3
Rutai Yunhe[JS] 80 F4
Rutog[XZ] 152 A3
Rutog[XZ] 152 H5
Ruxi[CQ] 132 E3
Ruyang[HEN] 106 D3
Ruyi[HN] 114 E5
Ruyuan[GD] 118 F2
Ruzhou[FJ] 94 C2
Ruzhou[HEN] 106 D3

S

Sadê[SC] 138 G6
Sadêng[XZ] 152 I4

Saga[XZ] 152 D5
Sagang[XZ] 152 I4
Sa'gya[XZ] 152 E5
Sahe Linchang[NM] 58 O2
Sahezhuang[BJ] 36 C3
Sai Ap Chau[HK] 176 E1
Sai Hu[JX] 98 C2
Sai Kung Hoi[HK] 176 E3
Sai Kung[HK] 176 E2
Sai O[HK] 176 E1
Sai Tso Wan[HK] 176 A3
Sai Wan Ho[HK] 176 D3
Sai Wan[HK] 176 F2
Sai Xiang[XZ] 152 F5
Sai Xiang[XZ] 152 G5
Sai Ying Pun Central District [HK] 176 D3
Saihan Olji[NM] 58 J6
Saihan Toroi[NM] 58 D7
Saima[LN] 62 H4
Sain Us[NM] 58 U11
Saincang[XZ] 152 E5
Saiqi[FJ] 94 E3
Sairam Hu[XJ] 172 H3
Sajintuo[TJ] 42 D3
Salhi[XJ] 172 J2
Sam A Tsuen[HK] 176 E1
Samada[XZ] 152 F5
Samai[NM] 58 L5
Samar[SC] 138 E5
Samca[GS] 160 F5
Samen[XZ] 152 C3
Samka[XZ] 152 J4
Samuqi[XJ] 172 F7
San Hui Village[HK] 176 B2
San Po Tsui[HK] 176 C3
San Shek Wan[HK] 176 B2
San Tin[HK] 176 C1
San Tsuen[HK] 176 B3
San Tsuen[HK] 176 C2
San Uk Ling[HK] 176 D1
San Wai Tsuen[HK] 176 C2
Sanamarzhai[QH] 164 K5
San'an[JL] 66 K4
Sanba[CQ] 132 D4
Sanba[GD] 118 F3
Sanba[YN] 148 F3
Sanbaishan[JX] 98 C7
Sanbanqiao[GZ] 144 C5
Sanbao[GX] 124 E2
Sanbao[GX] 124 H4
Sanbao[JL] 66 F3
Sanbao[JS] 80 C2
Sanbao[LN] 62 D3
Sanbaoying[LN] 62 D3
Sancai[HI] 128 C3
Sancang[JS] 80 F4
Sancha He[GZ] 144 D4
Sancha[BJ] 36 D3
Sancha[GS] 160 F5
Sancha[GS] 160 H4
Sancha[GX] 124 F3
Sancha[HB] 110 C4
Sancha[HB] 110 H4
Sancha[JL] 66 I4
Sancha[JS] 80 E5
Sancha[SD] 102 E3
Sancha[SN] 156 C7
Sancha[SX] 54 C2
Sanchagang[JX] 98 D2
Sanchahe[SC] 138 D3
Sanchakou[GS] 160 C3
Sanchakou[HB] 110 C1
Sanchakou[HEB] 48 C3
Sanchakou[TJ] 42 B2
Sanchakou[XJ] 172 G6
Sanchazi[JL] 66 G5
Sanchazi[NX] 168 C3
Sanchih[TW] 186 E1
Sanchuan He[SX] 54 B4
Sanchuan[HEN] 106 C4
Sanchung[TW] 186 E1
Sanchunji[SD] 102 A4
Sancun[SH] 74 C3

Sandao[HI] 128 B3
Sandao[JL] 66 I5
Sandaoban[GS] 160 B3
Sandaodun[NX] 168 A3
Sandaogou[JL] 66 G6
Sandaogou[LN] 62 D4
Sandaogou[NX] 168 C2
Sandaohe Shuiku[HB] 110 E3
Sandaohe[HEB] 48 F3
Sandaotong[HL] 70 E6
Sandaowan[JL] 66 J4
Sandaoying[NM] 58 X11
Sandong[SC] 138 I6
Sandouping[HB] 110 E4
Sandu Ao[FJ] 94 E3
Sandu[FJ] 94 C2
Sandu[GZ] 144 F5
Sandu[HI] 128 B2
Sandu[HN] 114 F6
Sandu[JX] 98 B3
Sandu[SX] 54 E4
Sanduandi[NM] 58 G8
Sandun[SH] 74 D3
Sandunzi[NX] 168 C3
Sanduo[SX] 54 B5
Sanfang[JX] 98 C5
Sanfangtou[HN] 114 C5
Sanfenchang[TJ] 42 B4
Sanfengsi[HN] 114 E3
Sanfucun[BJ] 36 B4
Sang Dao[SD] 102 G2
Sang Tal[QH] 164 M4
Sangbi[SX] 54 B5
Sangdo[SC] 138 E5
Sangengluo[HI] 128 C3
Sanggan He[HEB] 48 B3
Sanggan He[SX] 54 E2
Sanggin Dalai[NM] 58 K6
Sanggou Wan[SD] 102 I2
Sanggu[HEN] 106 G3
Sangjian[AH] 90 D4
Sangkog[GS] 160 F5
Sanglang[GZ] 144 E5
Sanglin[LN] 62 F3
Sangmu[GZ] 144 E2
Sangongqiao[HN] 114 B4
Sangping[CQ] 132 F2
Sangri[XZ] 152 H5
Sangruma[QH] 164 K7
Sangsang[XZ] 152 E5
Sangshuping[SN] 156 G5
Sangshutai[JL] 66 E4
Sangtian[JX] 98 D4
Sanguan Shan[AH] 90 D5
Sanguan[AH] 90 E4
Sanguandian[HB] 110 E2
Sanguandong[HB] 110 D1
Sanguansi[HN] 114 C3
Sangxi[SN] 156 E7
Sangxu[JS] 80 D2
Sangyu[BJ] 36 C4
Sangyuan Xia[GS] 160 G5
Sangyuan[BJ] 36 D4
Sangyuan[SX] 54 C5
Sangyuan[TJ] 42 B1
Sangyuanba[SN] 156 D7
Sangzhi[HN] 114 C3
Sangzhou[ZJ] 84 F3
Sangzhuang[HEN] 106 D5
Sangzi[TJ] 42 B2
Sangzidian[SD] 102 C3
Sangzizê'za'ngo Shan[XZ] 152 E3
Sanhao[HEB] 48 C2
Sanhe[GD] 118 E4
Sanhe[GD] 118 I2
Sanhe[GX] 124 D4
Sanhe[GX] 124 G5
Sanhe[GZ] 144 E2
Sanhe[GZ] 144 E3
Sanhe[HEB] 48 E4
Sanhe[HL] 70 C5
Sanhe[HN] 114 E7
Sanhe[HN] 114 F6
Sanhe[JL] 66 C2

Sanhe[JL] 66 F5
Sanhe[JL] 66 J5
Sanhe[JS] 80 G5
Sanhe[NM] 58 N2
Sanhe[NX] 168 B5
Sanhecun[TJ] 42 B4
Sanhejian[HEN] 106 G5
Sanhou[SX] 54 B5
Sanhu[HB] 110 C5
Sanhuang[GX] 124 G3
Sanhui[SC] 138 M4
Sanhuikou[CQ] 132 E2
Sanhuzhuang[TJ] 42 A4
San-I[TW] 186 D2
Sanjia Ling[HI] 128 A2
Sanjia[GD] 118 D4
Sanjia[HEB] 48 F2
Sanjia[HI] 128 A2
Sanjia[LN] 62 C3
Sanjian[CQ] 132 D4
Sanjian[HN] 114 D5
Sanjianfang[BJ] 36 C4
Sanjianfang[BJ] 36 D4
Sanjianfang[HL] 70 D3
Sanjianfang[NM] 58 W11
Sanjianfang[TJ] 42 A2
Sanjiang[CQ] 132 C5
Sanjiang[GD] 118 F3
Sanjiang[GX] 124 G2
Sanjiang[GX] 124 H3
Sanjiang[GX] 124 I3
Sanjiang[GZ] 144 F2
Sanjiang[GZ] 144 G4
Sanjiang[HI] 128 C2
Sanjiangkou[GZ] 144 C6
Sanjiangkou[HN] 114 F7
Sanjiangkou[LN] 62 G1
Sanjiao[CQ] 132 C4
Sanjiao[GX] 124 H3
Sanjiao[SC] 138 H6
Sanjiao[SX] 54 B4
Sanjiao[SX] 54 B4
Sanjiao[SX] 54 C5
Sanjiao[SX] 54 D3
Sanjiaokou[HEN] 106 E2
Sanjiaoping[HN] 114 C4
Sanjiaotu[HI] 128 B3
Sanjiashan[LN] 62 F4
Sanjiazi[LN] 62 C4
Sanjiazi[LN] 62 G4
Sanjie[AH] 90 E4
Sanjing[SX] 54 C3
Sanjingzi[JL] 66 F2
Sanjitai[HL] 70 D5
Sanjiu[HI] 128 C2
Sanjue[AH] 90 C5
Sanka[HL] 70 D3
Sankeng[GD] 118 E3
Sankeshu[GZ] 144 G4
Sankeshu[JS] 80 D3
Sankeyushu[JL] 66 F6
Sankongqiao[HEN] 106 G5
Sankou[ZJ] 84 D2
Sankouyan[HB] 110 G3
Sanletang[HI] 128 C2
Sanli[AH] 90 E6
Sanli[GX] 124 F4
Sanli[GX] 124 G4
Sanli[HB] 110 C4
Sanli[JX] 98 D3
Sanlicheng[HB] 110 H3
Sanlifan[HB] 110 I4
Sanligang[HB] 110 G3
Sanlong[JS] 80 F3
Sanlong[JX] 98 E2
Sanlou[SX] 54 F2
Sanmen Wan[ZJ] 84 F3
Sanmen[HN] 114 F5
Sanmen[SX] 54 C7
Sanmen[ZJ] 84 F3
Sanmeng[YN] 148 H8
Sanmenpo[HI] 128 C2
Sanmenxia Shuiku[HEN] 106 C3
Sanmenxia Shuiku[SX] 54 C7

Sanmenxia[HEN]	106	C3	
Sanmin[TW]	186	D3	
Sanming[FJ]	94	C3	
Sanmudong[HI]	128	B3	
Sanping[HI]	128	B3	
Sanpo[HEB]	48	C4	
Sanpu[GS]	160	E3	
Sanqiao[GZ]	144	F1	
Sanqiao[HEN]	106	F5	
Sanqiao[SH]	74	D2	
Sanqingshan[JL]	66	E3	
Sanqu[CQ]	132	B4	
Sanquan[CQ]	132	D4	
Sanqugou Shuiku[HI]	128	A3	
Sansha Wan[FJ]	94	E3	
Sansha[FJ]	94	F3	
Sanshahong[SH]	74	C1	
Sanshan Dao[LN]	62	E6	
Sanshan[FJ]	94	D3	
Sanshan[FJ]	94	E4	
Sanshan[JX]	98	C4	
Sanshan[ZJ]	84	D3	
Sanshan[ZJ]	84	F3	
Sanshandao[SD]	102	F2	
Sanshanzi Dao[SD]	102	I3	
Sanshengyu[JL]	66	E3	
Sanshi[HN]	114	F4	
Sanshihao[JL]	66	D3	
Sanshijiazi[LN]	62	C3	
Sanshilipu[AH]	90	B4	
Sanshilipu[AH]	90	C5	
Sanshilipu[SD]	102	E4	
Sanshu[JS]	80	D3	
Sanshui Qu[GD]	118	E3	
Sanshui[GD]	118	E1	
Sanshui[GD]	118	E2	
Sansui[GZ]	144	G4	
Santai Shan[YN]	148	H4	
Santai[SC]	138	K4	
Santaizi[LN]	62	E3	
Santaji[AH]	90	B4	
Santang[HN]	114	E6	
Santang[HN]	114	E6	
Santang[YN]	148	I6	
Santanghu[XJ]	172	N3	
Santangjie[HN]	114	D4	
Santi[TW]	186	D4	
Santiao Chiao[TW]	186	F1	
Santiaoling[SX]	54	E2	
Santong He[JL]	66	F5	
Santuan[JL]	66	D3	
Santun[SX]	54	D1	
Santunying[HEB]	48	F3	
Sanwan[JX]	98	A5	
Sanwan[TW]	186	D2	
Sanwang[GX]	124	E3	
Sanwu[GX]	124	G4	
Sanxi[AH]	90	E6	
Sanxi[CQ]	132	D3	
Sanxi[FJ]	94	D3	
Sanxi[JX]	98	C5	
Sanxi[JX]	98	D4	
Sanxia Daba[HB]	110	E4	
Sanxia[FJ]	94	C2	
Sanxiang[GD]	118	I2	
Sanxianhu[HN]	114	E3	
Sanxianjie[GX]	124	H3	
Sanxin[SH]	74	C3	
Sanxing Shan[ZJ]	84	G2	
Sanxing[HL]	70	C5	
Sanxing[JS]	80	F5	
Sanxing[JX]	98	B3	
Sanxing[SH]	74	C1	
Sanya Gang[HI]	128	B3	
Sanya[HI]	128	B3	
Sanya[SC]	138	G7	
Sanyang[AH]	90	E6	
Sanyang[JX]	98	B4	
Sanyang[SN]	156	F8	
Sanyanjing[NX]	168	B3	
Sanyanjingtai[NX]	168	C3	
Sanyanlong[SC]	138	G7	
Sanyanquan[SN]	156	F3	
Sanyao[SN]	156	G7	
Sanyi[AH]	90	C3	
Sanyi[JL]	66	F2	
Sanying[NX]	168	C4	
Sanyiyong[HEB]	48	E1	
Sanyu[GX]	124	H5	
Sanyu[JS]	80	G4	
Sanyu[SH]	74	D1	
Sanyuan Qu[FJ]	94	C3	
Sanyuan[AH]	90	C5	
Sanyuan[SN]	156	D8	
Sanyuan[SN]	156	E6	
Sanzao[GD]	118	F4	
Sanzao[JS]	80	F4	
Sanzao[SH]	74	D2	
Sanzhan[HL]	70	C6	
Sanzhan[HL]	70	D4	
Sanzheng[CQ]	132	E3	
Sanzhou[FJ]	94	B4	
Sanzhou[HB]	110	F5	
Sanzhou[ZJ]	84	E3	
Sanzuohulishan[NM]	58	D6	
Saoshui[HI]	128	B3	
Saqi Shan[NM]	58	O3	
Sar[XZ]	152	E5	
Sarikol Ling[XJ]	172	E6	
Sarqoka[XJ]	172	N4	
Sartai[NM]	58	E8	
Sartokay[XJ]	172	L2	
Sarzo[SC]	138	H3	
Sasêr[XZ]	152	H3	
Sashan Qu[AH]	90	E5	
Satmalanggar[XJ]	172	H7	
Sau Mau Ping[HK]	176	E3	
Sawir Shan[XJ]	172	J2	
Sayingpan[YN]	148	H4	
Sayoi[XZ]	152	J4	
Sayu[GZ]	144	D5	
Sayu[YN]	148	I3	
Sea Ranch[HK]	176	B4	
Seac Pai Van[MC]	182	B6	
Sebei[QH]	164	G3	
See Chau[HK]	176	E3	
Sehepu[SN]	156	F7	
Sênag[QH]	164	L4	
Sêngdêng[QH]	164	L5	
Sênggê Zangbo (Shiquan He)[XZ]	152	B3	
Sênggê[QH]	164	K3	
Sênggê[XZ]	152	G5	
Sênggêzong[SC]	138	H4	
Sêngli Co[XZ]	152	D4	
Sengnian[SX]	54	C5	
Sênkar[SC]	138	E4	
Sentao[TW]	186	D3	
Seqên[XZ]	152	H3	
Sêqu[QH]	164	H8	
Sêrbug Co[XZ]	152	F3	
Sêrca[XZ]	152	I4	
Sêrcham[XZ]	152	I4	
Sêrdê[SC]	138	H2	
Sereh[QH]	164	K4	
Sêrgyog[XZ]	152	C3	
Sêrlung[QH]	164	O6	
Sêrri[XZ]	152	J3	
Sêrtang[XZ]	152	K4	
Sêrtar[SC]	138	F3	
Serteng Shan[QH]	164	F2	
Sêrwolungwa[QH]	164	H6	
Sêrxü[SC]	138	D3	
Sesikyar He[XJ]	172	L7	
Sha Chau[HK]	176	B3	
Sha He[BJ]	36	C3	
Sha He[HEB]	48	B7	
Sha He[HEN]	106	E4	
Sha He[SD]	102	D2	
Sha Kiu Tsuen[HK]	176	B1	
Sha Kok Mei[HK]	176	E2	
Sha Lan[HK]	176	D2	
Sha Lo Tung[HK]	176	D2	
Sha Lo Wan[HK]	176	B3	
Sha Tau Kok Hoi[HK]	176	D1	
Sha Tau Kok River[HK]	176	D1	
Sha Tau Kok[HK]	176	D1	
Sha Tin Heights[HK]	176	D3	
Sha Tin[HK]	176	D2	
Sha Tong Hau Mei[HK]	176	E3	
Sha Tong Hau Shan[HK]	176	E3	
Sha Xi[FJ]	94	C3	
Sha Xian[FJ]	94	C3	
Shaba[GD]	118	D5	
Shaba[GZ]	144	H3	
Shaba[HN]	114	C3	
Shaba[SN]	156	E7	
Shabei[GD]	118	E2	
Shabei[SH]	74	D2	
Shabu[GX]	124	G3	
Shacha[GZ]	144	E3	
Shache(Yarkant)[XJ]	172	F6	
Shacheng Gang[FJ]	94	F2	
Shachong[SC]	138	G5	
Shacun[JX]	98	C5	
Shadaoguan[HB]	110	E4	
Shadi[HB]	110	C4	
Shadi[JX]	98	B5	
Shagang[GD]	118	G4	
Shagang[GX]	124	G6	
Shagang[HB]	110	F4	
Shagang[JX]	98	D4	
Shagou[JS]	80	E3	
Shagou[NX]	168	B4	
Shagou[NX]	168	C2	
Shagou[QH]	164	M5	
Shagouhe[NX]	168	B4	
Shagouliang[NX]	168	B3	
Shahai[LN]	62	C3	
Shahai[NM]	58	S11	
Shahe Shuiku[BJ]	36	C3	
Shahe Shuiku[HI]	128	B2	
Shahe Zongganqu[HEB]	48	B5	
Shahe[AH]	90	E4	
Shahe[BJ]	36	C3	
Shahe[HB]	110	E2	
Shahe[HEB]	48	B7	
Shahe[HEN]	106	B3	
Shahe[SC]	138	L3	
Shahe[SN]	156	D8	
Shahe[SX]	54	E2	
Shahedian[HEN]	106	E5	
Shaheji Shuiku[AH]	90	E4	
Shahepu[LN]	62	G3	
Shahezi[HL]	70	D6	
Shahezi[SN]	156	G7	
Shahu[LN]	62	G3	
Shahukou[SX]	54	D1	
Shaigentan[GS]	160	F5	
Shaikou[FJ]	94	C2	
Shaji[AH]	90	D6	
Shaji[JS]	80	D3	
Shajian[FJ]	94	C5	
Shajiang[FJ]	94	E3	
Shajianzi[LN]	62	I3	
Shajing[GD]	118	F4	
Shajing[GD]	118	G3	
Shajingou[JL]	66	I5	
Shajingzi Shuiku[TJ]	42	B4	
Shajingzi[TJ]	42	B4	
Shakou[HB]	110	G5	
Shalan[HL]	70	E6	
Shalang[YN]	148	H5	
Shalenghe[SX]	54	D2	
Shali[GX]	124	C3	
Shali[GX]	124	D3	
Shaling[BJ]	36	C3	
Shaling[BJ]	36	D3	
Shaling[LN]	62	G5	
Shaliu He[QH]	164	L3	
Shalizhai[LN]	62	G4	
Shaluli Shan[SC]	138	E4	
Sham Chung[HK]	176	E2	
Sham Shek Tsuen[HK]	176	A3	
Sham Shui Kok[HK]	176	B3	
Sham Shui Kok[HK]	176	D4	
Sham Tseng[HK]	176	C3	
Sham Wan[HK]	176	D4	
Shamao[SN]	156	G2	
Shamen[ZJ]	84	F4	
Shaming[HN]	114	F6	
Shan Ling[FJ]	94	C2	

Name	Page	Grid	Name	Page	Grid	Name	Page	Grid
Shan Liu[HK]	176	D2	Shangjiahe[LN]	62	H3	Shangyou[JX]	98	B6
Shan Mei[HK]	176	D2	Shangjiang[YN]	148	D5	Shangyu[SX]	54	C2
Shan Xian[HEN]	106	C3	Shangjiang[YN]	148	E3	Shangyu[ZJ]	84	C4
Shan Xian[SD]	102	C5	Shangjie Qu[HEN]	106	E3	Shangyu[ZJ]	84	E2
Shanalongren[QH]	164	D7	Shangjin[HB]	110	D1	Shangyuan[BJ]	36	C3
Shancha[SN]	156	F5	Shangjing[FJ]	94	C4	Shangyuan[LN]	62	D3
Shanchahe[NX]	168	C3	Shangjing[FJ]	94	E4	Shangyuanguan[SN]	156	D7
Shanchakou[XJ]	172	N3	Shangkan[HB]	110	D3	Shangyun[YN]	148	E7
Shancheng Qu[HEN]	106	F2	Shangkou[BJ]	36	C3	Shangzhai[GZ]	144	G3
Shancheng[GS]	160	H4	Shanglan[SX]	54	D3	Shangzhang[ZJ]	84	E4
Shancheng[JL]	66	F5	Shanglan[YN]	148	E4	Shangzheng[ZJ]	84	E4
Shancheng[JX]	98	D4	Shanglaozhuang[SD]	102	C4	Shangzhi[HL]	70	D6
Shanchong[FJ]	94	C5	Shanglaxiu[QH]	164	I8	Shangzhi[LN]	62	D3
Shandan[GS]	160	E3	Shangli[FJ]	94	C3	Shangzhong[GZ]	144	G4
Shandao[HI]	128	A3	Shangli[JX]	98	A4	Shangzhou[SC]	138	J7
Shandian He[HEB]	48	C2	Shanglian[FJ]	94	D3	Shangzhuang[HEB]	48	B4
Shandong Bandao[SD]	102	F3	Shangliang[NX]	168	C5	Shangzhuang[JX]	98	C3
Shanfangbu[HEB]	48	B3	Shanglin[GX]	124	F4	Shangzhuang[SD]	102	I2
Shang Boingor[QH]	164	L8	Shanglin[HEB]	48	D5	Shanhaiguan Qu[HEB]	48	G3
Shang Dokog[SC]	138	F3	Shangling[GD]	118	G2	Shanhe[HL]	70	D6
Shang kongma[QH]	164	L7	Shanglong[GX]	124	D5	Shanhe[NX]	168	C5
Shang Tohoi[NM]	58	X10	Shanglou[HB]	110	H3	Shanhejie[JL]	66	F4
Shang Zamtang[SC]	138	G3	Shanglu[JX]	98	E3	Shanhou He[JS]	80	E2
Shang Zayü[XZ]	152	J5	Shangluo[SC]	138	J7	Shanhou[AH]	90	E5
Shang'an[HI]	128	B3	Shangluo[SN]	156	F7	Shanhu Tan[TW]	186	D3
Shangba[GS]	160	D3	Shangma Shuiku[SX]	54	B6	Shanhu[FJ]	94	B4
Shangbai[ZJ]	84	D2	Shangma[SX]	54	D5	Shanhua[SN]	156	F5
Shangbaishi[FJ]	94	E2	Shangmachang[HL]	70	D3	Shanhua[TW]	186	D3
Shangbaiyun[SN]	156	D7	Shangmahuanggou[NX]	168	B3	Shanji[JS]	80	C2
Shangbali[HEN]	106	E2	Shangmatai Shuiku[TJ]	42	B3	Shankeng[ZJ]	84	E4
Shangbao[JX]	98	B6	Shangmatou[TJ]	42	B4	Shankou[GX]	124	G6
Shangbaqing[NX]	168	C2	Shangmeng[SC]	138	I4	Shankou[HI]	128	B2
Shangcai[FJ]	94	C5	Shangmo[JX]	98	B5	Shankou[SX]	54	C5
Shangcai[HEN]	106	F4	Shangmofang[SX]	54	E2	Shanlin[TW]	186	D4
Shangcang[TJ]	42	B2	Shangnan[GX]	124	F3	Shanlingzi[TJ]	42	B3
Shangcao[GD]	118	D2	Shangnan[SN]	156	G7	Shanlixinzhuang[BJ]	36	D3
Shangchao[GX]	124	F2	Shangping[GD]	118	G2	Shanlu[FJ]	94	D2
Shangcheng[HEN]	106	G6	Shangping[GD]	118	H2	Shanmacha[NX]	168	B4
Shangchewan[HB]	110	G5	Shangpu[ZJ]	84	E3	Shanmatang Ding[GX]	124	I3
Shangchuan Dao[GD]	118	E5	Shangqian[FJ]	94	D2	Shanmatang Ding[HN]	114	D8
Shangchuan[GD]	118	E5	Shangqing[FJ]	94	C2	Shanmei Shuiku[FJ]	94	D4
Shangchuan[GS]	160	F4	Shangqing[FJ]	94	C4	Shanmen[JL]	66	E4
Shangcun[SX]	54	D5	Shangqing[JX]	98	E3	Shanmen[ZJ]	84	E5
Shangdachen Dao[ZJ]	84	F4	Shangqingshizui[NX]	168	C5	Shannan[AH]	90	C5
Shangdayan[HB]	110	F3	Shangqiu[HEN]	106	G3	Shanping[GD]	118	D4
Shangdazhuang[NX]	168	C5	Shangrao[JX]	98	E3	Shanqi[AH]	90	C5
Shangdian[HEN]	106	E4	Shangrao[JX]	98	E3	Shanqian[SH]	74	C2
Shangdian[SD]	102	D2	Shangrenli[HN]	114	D7	Shanqiao[HN]	114	E5
Shangdian[SN]	156	D6	Shangsanglin[SX]	54	D6	Shanrong[HI]	128	B3
Shangdong[GD]	118	E2	Shangsha[GD]	118	H3	Shanshan(Piqan)[XJ]	172	M4
Shangdu[NM]	58	J7	Shangshan[GD]	118	I2	Shanshanzhan[XJ]	172	M4
Shangdun[FJ]	94	C3	Shangshawo[GS]	160	G4	Shanshenmiao[LN]	62	D4
Shangen[HI]	128	C3	Shangshe[SX]	54	E3	Shanshi[JX]	98	B4
Shangfan[JX]	98	E3	Shangshi[GX]	124	D5	Shansonggang[JL]	66	G5
Shangfang[FJ]	94	D3	Shangshiqiao[HEN]	106	G6	Shantang[SH]	74	C3
Shangfang[HEB]	48	B5	Shangshui[HEN]	106	F4	Shanting Qu[SD]	102	D4
Shangfang[ZJ]	84	C3	Shangsi[GX]	124	E5	Shantou Gang[GD]	118	I3
Shangfang[ZJ]	84	C3	Shangsi[GZ]	144	F5	Shantou[AH]	90	E3
Shangfeidi[LN]	62	H2	Shangsidian[SN]	156	G6	Shantou[GD]	118	I3
Shangfeng[JX]	98	B3	Shangsiyuan[HN]	114	E6	Shantou[SX]	54	C5
Shangfu[JX]	98	C3	Shangtang[JS]	80	D3	Shantuo[CQ]	132	D4
Shanggang[JS]	80	F3	Shangtang[JX]	98	B2	Shanwan[HEB]	48	E2
Shangganling Qu[HL]	70	E5	Shangtang[JX]	98	C3	Shanwanzi[HEB]	48	E1
Shanggao[JX]	98	B3	Shangtang[JX]	98	D4	Shanwei[GD]	118	H4
Shanggaopu[BJ]	36	B4	Shangtun[HEN]	106	D5	Shanwo[CQ]	132	D4
Shanggaoqiao[YN]	148	I3	Shangwang[ZJ]	84	E5	Shanxi[FJ]	94	B3
Shanggu[HEB]	48	F3	Shangweidian[BJ]	36	B3	Shanxi[ZJ]	84	E5
Shanggu[JX]	98	C5	Shangwujiang[HN]	114	D7	Shanxia[FJ]	94	D2
Shangguan[HEN]	106	F2	Shangxi[JX]	98	C5	Shanxie[JX]	98	C4
Shangguan[HN]	114	D7	Shangxingjie[JS]	80	E5	Shanxin[GX]	124	G5
Shangguo[SX]	54	B6	Shangxu[ZJ]	84	E4	Shanxu[GX]	124	E5
Shanghai[SH]	74	C2	Shangyang[GD]	118	D5	Shanyang[FJ]	94	D3
Shanghang[FJ]	94	B4	Shangyangwu[SX]	54	D3	Shanyang[FJ]	94	E3
Shanghe[SD]	102	D2	Shangyanjiayao[NX]	168	B4	Shanyang[SH]	74	C3
Shanghetou[TJ]	42	B3	Shangyanwan[SN]	156	F3	Shanyang[SN]	156	F7
Shanghexi[HN]	114	B3	Shangyao[AH]	90	D4	Shanyin[SX]	54	C2
Shanghu[GD]	118	H3	Shangyao[SX]	54	E5	Shanzao[HN]	114	C4
Shanghu[SX]	54	E4	Shangye[SD]	102	D4	Shanzao[HN]	114	E5
Shanghu[XJ]	172	I2	Shangyi[HEB]	48	A2	Shanzhai[SX]	54	C2
Shanghua[GS]	160	G4	Shangying[GX]	124	D4	Shanzhuang[JX]	98	B4
Shanghuang[CQ]	132	F2	Shangying[JL]	66	H3	Shaobo Hu[JS]	80	E4
Shanghulin[NM]	58	N2	Shangyong[FJ]	94	D4	Shaobo[JS]	80	E4
Shangji[GZ]	144	E3	Shangyou Jiang[JX]	98	B6	Shaodian[HEN]	106	F4
Shangji[HL]	70	D5	Shangyou Shuiku[JX]	98	C3	Shaodian[JS]	80	D2

Name	Page	Grid
Shaodong[HN]	114	D5
Shaoguan[GD]	118	F2
Shaoguoyingzi[LN]	62	C2
Shaoha[HN]	114	B3
Shaojiao[TJ]	42	B2
Shaojiazhuang[SX]	54	F2
Shaomi[GZ]	144	C4
Shaoshan[HN]	114	E5
Shaosuo[NM]	58	H6
Shaowu[FJ]	94	C2
Shaoxing[ZJ]	84	E2
Shaoxing[ZJ]	84	E2
Shaoyang[HN]	114	D5
Shaoyang[HN]	114	D6
Shaoyun[CQ]	132	B4
Shaozhuang[SD]	102	B5
Shaozi He[LN]	62	G4
Shaozihe[LN]	62	G4
Shap Pat Heung[HK]	176	C2
Shap Sze Heung[HK]	176	E2
Shapang[GD]	118	D3
Shaping[CQ]	132	D3
Shaping[GX]	124	F5
Shaping[HN]	114	E7
Shaping[SN]	156	E7
Shapingba Qu[CQ]	132	C4
Shapingzhen[HN]	114	D4
Shapotou Qu[NX]	168	A3
Shaquan[NX]	168	C3
Shaquan[SX]	54	C2
Shashi[JX]	98	B4
Shatang[GX]	124	G3
Shatang[NX]	168	B5
Shatangchuan[QH]	164	N4
Shatanggou[BJ]	36	C3
Shataping[HN]	114	C3
Shatian[GX]	124	G6
Shatian[GX]	124	H5
Shatian[GX]	124	I3
Shatian[GX]	124	I4
Shatian[HN]	114	E4
Shatian[HN]	114	F7
Shatou[GX]	124	I4
Shatu[AH]	90	B3
Shatuozi[HEB]	48	F2
Shau Kei Wan[HK]	176	D3
Shaunghe[JL]	66	G4
Shawan Qu[SC]	138	I6
Shawan[XJ]	172	J3
Shawo[HEN]	106	G6
Shawo[SD]	102	B4
Shawojing[NX]	168	C3
Shawu[FJ]	94	B3
Shaxi[FJ]	94	C3
Shaxi[FJ]	94	C6
Shaxi[GD]	118	F2
Shaxi[GZ]	144	F2
Shaxi[HB]	110	B5
Shaxi[HN]	114	B6
Shaxi[JX]	98	C5
Shaxi[JX]	98	F3
Shaxi[YN]	148	E4
Shaxi[ZJ]	84	F3
Shayan[HEN]	106	D5
Shayang[HB]	110	F4
Shayu[CQ]	132	C3
Shazaoyuan[GS]	160	B3
Shazhen[SD]	102	B3
Shazhenxi[HB]	110	D4
Shazhou[SC]	138	K3
Shazhouba[JX]	98	C6
Shazhuyu He[QH]	164	L4
Shazi[CQ]	132	E3
Shazi[GX]	124	H3
Shazi[GZ]	144	D5
Shazi[GZ]	144	D5
Shazikou[SD]	102	G3
Shazipo[GZ]	144	G2
Shaziying[BJ]	36	D3
She Dao[LN]	62	D6
She Shan[SH]	74	C2
She Shan[SH]	74	E2
She Shui[HB]	110	H3
She Xian[AH]	90	E7
She Xian[HEB]	48	A7
Shebu[HN]	114	E5
Shechang[GX]	124	C3
Shecheng[SX]	54	D4
Shecun[HEN]	106	E3
Shegang[HN]	114	F4
Shehong[SC]	138	K5
Shehou[JX]	98	F3
Shejiang[GD]	118	H2
Shejiaping[HN]	114	D4
Shejing[JX]	98	B6
Shek Hang[HK]	176	E2
Shek Kip Mei[HK]	176	D3
Shek Kok Tsui[HK]	176	C4
Shek Kong[HK]	176	C2
Shek Kwu Chau[HK]	176	B4
Shek Lung Tsai[HK]	176	E2
Shek Ngau Chau[HK]	176	F2
Shek O[HK]	176	E4
Shek Pik Reservoir[HK]	176	B4
Shek Pik[HK]	176	A4
Shek Uk Shan[HK]	176	E2
Shek Wu Hui[HK]	176	D1
Shek Wu Wai[HK]	176	C1
Sheke[SX]	54	C3
Shekou[FJ]	94	E2
Shekou[HB]	110	H4
Sheli[JL]	66	D2
Shen Xian[SD]	102	B3
Shen'ao[GD]	118	J3
Shenba[SN]	156	E8
Shenbei Xin Qu[LN]	62	G2
Shenchi[SX]	54	D2
Shenchong[AH]	90	C6
Shending Shan[HL]	70	G5
Shendu[AH]	90	E7
Shendu[GS]	160	G5
Shendushui[GD]	118	G2
Shengang[JS]	80	F5
Shengang[JX]	98	D4
Shengdengshan[CQ]	132	C4
Shengfangqiang Nongchang[JS]	80	F3
Shengfeng[NM]	58	U10
Shenghuang[FJ]	94	D4
Shengjiaba[HB]	110	C5
Shengjing Hu[AH]	90	D6
Shengjing Guan[GZ]	144	C5
Shengli[HB]	110	I3
Shengli[HL]	70	B5
Shengli[HL]	70	D4
Shengli[HL]	70	E5
Shengli[HL]	70	E6
Shengli[JL]	66	D2
Shengli[JL]	66	E4
Shengli[SD]	102	E2
Shengli[TJ]	42	B4
Shenglikou[QH]	164	H3
Shengliying[NM]	58	X11
Shengmi[JX]	98	C3
Shengping[GX]	124	H2
Shengping[HL]	70	C5
Shengpu[CQ]	132	E2
Shengqiao[AH]	90	D5
Shengqiao[SH]	74	C2
Shengquan[AH]	90	C2
Shengshan Yang[ZJ]	84	G2
Shengshan[ZJ]	84	G2
Shengshuiyu[BJ]	36	B4
Shengshuiyu[SD]	102	D4
Shengsi Liedao[ZJ]	84	G2
Shengsi[ZJ]	84	G2
Shengtang Shan[GX]	124	H4
Shengtang[GD]	118	E4
Shengwan[HEN]	106	C5
Shengwang[SX]	54	C5
Shengze[JS]	80	F6
Shengzhong Shuiku[SC]	138	K4
Shengzhou[ZJ]	84	E3
Shenhe[HB]	110	D2
Shenhe[SN]	156	F8
Shenhu Wan[FJ]	94	D5
Shenhu[FJ]	94	D5
Shenji[HB]	110	F4
Shenjia[HL]	70	D5
Shenjia[SH]	74	C2
Shenjiawan[SH]	74	C1
Shenjiaying[BJ]	36	C3
Shenjing[GD]	118	E5
Shenjing[HEB]	48	B3
Shenjing[NX]	168	A3
Shenjing[NX]	168	C3
Shenjingzi[JL]	66	E3
Shenkou[FJ]	94	C3
Shenlian[SH]	74	C3
Shenlin[NX]	168	B5
Shenmu[SN]	156	G2
Shennong Ding[HB]	110	D3
Shennong[SN]	156	D6
Shennong[SX]	54	D6
Shennongjia Linqu[HB]	110	D3
Shenqingzhuang[TJ]	42	B4
Shenqiu[HEN]	106	G4
Shenquan Gang[GD]	118	I4
Shenquan[GD]	118	I4
Shenshan[JX]	98	E2
Shenshu[HL]	70	E5
Shentang[GD]	118	C5
Shentangbu[SX]	54	E2
Shenting[SD]	102	B3
Shentong[CQ]	132	C4
Shentou[SX]	54	D2
Shentu[FJ]	94	C5
Shenwan[GD]	118	F4
Shenxiang[SH]	74	C2
Shenxianwan[XJ]	172	F8
Shenxikou[HN]	114	C4
Shenyang[LN]	62	G3
Shenyugou[SX]	54	C3
Shenzao[JS]	80	F4
Shenze[HEB]	48	C5
Shenzhen He[HK]	176	C1
Shenzhen Wan(Deep Bay)[HK]	176	B2
Shenzhen[GD]	118	G4
Shenzhengqiao[JX]	98	C4
Shenzhou[HEB]	48	C5
Shenzhuang[SH]	74	C2
Shenzhuang[SH]	74	D2
Sheping[JX]	98	D4
Shepo[GX]	124	H4
Sheqi[HEN]	106	D4
Sheshan[SH]	74	C2
Sheshang Shuiku[JX]	98	B4
Shetan[CQ]	132	D4
Shetianqiao[HN]	114	D5
Shetun[HEN]	106	F5
Sheung Fa Shan[HK]	176	C2
Sheung Kwai Chung[HK]	176	D2
Sheung Pak Nai[HK]	176	B2
Sheung Shui Wa Shan[HK]	176	D1
Sheung Shui[HK]	176	C1
Sheung Sze Mun[HK]	176	E4
Shewan[HEN]	106	E5
Shewopo[SD]	102	G2
Shexing[FJ]	94	D4
Sheyang He[JS]	80	E3
Sheyang[JS]	80	F3
Sheyanghe Kou[JS]	80	F3
Shezhu[JS]	80	E5
Shi He[HEN]	106	F5
Shi He[HEN]	106	G5
Shi'an[HEN]	106	D5
Shi'ao[JX]	98	B3
Shiba[GD]	118	G3
Shiba[GX]	124	E5
Shibahujia[JL]	66	E2
Shibali[AH]	90	B3
Shibalidian[BJ]	36	C4
Shibalihe[HEN]	106	E3
Shiban[CQ]	132	C4
Shiban[GD]	118	C4
Shiban[SC]	138	M4
Shibandun[GS]	160	C2
Shibanjing[NM]	58	C7
Shibao[CQ]	132	E3
Shibao[HN]	114	C5
Shibaocheng[GS]	160	C3
Shibapan[HEN]	106	D3
Shibayong[TJ]	42	C3
Shibazhan[HL]	70	C2

Name	Page	Grid	Name	Page	Grid	Name	Page	Grid
Shibei[CQ]	132	F3	Shigui[HI]	128	B3	Shiling[GX]	124	F4
Shibei[FJ]	94	D2	Shiguipo[GD]	118	B5	Shiling[HI]	128	B3
Shibei[SX]	54	D5	Shigunhe[HEN]	106	E5	Shilingzi[JL]	66	E4
Shibi[HI]	128	C2	Shigutang[GD]	118	F2	Shiliping[JL]	66	K4
Shibi[HN]	114	C5	Shihai[QH]	164	L4	Shilipu[BJ]	36	C5
Shibianyu[SN]	156	E6	Shihao[CQ]	132	C5	Shilipu[HB]	110	F4
Shibie[GX]	124	F3	Shihe Shuiku[HI]	128	C2	Shilipu[SD]	102	C2
Shibikeng Shuiku[JX]	98	C6	Shihe[AH]	90	B3	Shilipu[SN]	156	G3
Shibing[GZ]	144	G3	Shihe[JL]	66	F4	Shiliting[HEB]	48	B7
Shibu[SD]	102	F3	Shihe[LN]	62	E5	Shiliu[FJ]	94	C5
Shibuzi[SD]	102	F3	Shihe[NX]	168	C3	Shiliulihe[SD]	102	C3
Shicang[FJ]	94	D4	Shihegang[HEN]	106	E5	Shiliwang[SD]	102	C3
Shicao[HEN]	106	G4	Shihemu[SX]	54	E6	Shilong Qu[HEN]	106	D4
Shicao[SD]	102	B3	Shiheng[SD]	102	C3	Shilong[GD]	118	D4
Shicaohe[SN]	156	D7	Shihetou[SD]	102	F4	Shilong[GX]	124	G4
Shicha[NX]	168	C4	Shihezi[XJ]	172	K3	Shilong[GZ]	144	F4
Shichang[GZ]	144	E3	Shihmen Shuiku[TW]	186	E2	Shilong[HB]	110	F4
Shichang[SD]	102	F4	Shihmen[TW]	186	E1	Shilou[BJ]	36	B4
Shicheng Dao[LN]	62	G5	Shihti[TW]	186	E3	Shilou[SX]	54	B5
Shicheng[BJ]	36	D2	Shihting[TW]	186	E2	Shilu Shuiku[HI]	128	B2
Shicheng[FJ]	94	E4	Shihtsao[TW]	186	E2	Shiluo[GD]	118	E2
Shicheng[JX]	98	D5	Shihtzu[TW]	186	D4	Shiluo[HI]	128	B3
Shicheng[LN]	62	F5	Shihu[AH]	90	D3	Shima[CQ]	132	B4
Shicheng[LN]	62	H4	Shihu[JL]	66	G6	Shima[JX]	98	C5
Shicheng[SX]	54	E5	Shihu[JS]	80	D2	Shima[SN]	156	G7
Shichuan[CQ]	132	C4	Shihua Dingzi[LN]	62	H3	Shimei[HI]	128	B3
Shichuang[GX]	124	H4	Shihua[SH]	74	C3	Shimei[SD]	102	F4
Shicongwan[NX]	168	C3	Shihuadao[JL]	66	D3	Shimeitang[HN]	114	E3
Shicun[AH]	90	D3	Shihuang[ZJ]	84	E3	Shimen[AH]	90	E7
Shicun[SD]	102	E2	Shihudang[SH]	74	C3	Shimen[GS]	160	G4
Shidao Wan[SD]	102	I3	Shihui[CQ]	132	E4	Shimen[GZ]	144	B3
Shidao[SD]	102	I3	Shihuiqiao[HB]	110	F4	Shimen[HEB]	48	B5
Shidaohe[JL]	66	G5	Shihuiqiao[JL]	66	C2	Shimen[HEB]	48	E3
Shide[SN]	156	E6	Shihuiyao[LN]	62	G4	Shimen[HN]	114	D3
Shideng[YN]	148	E4	Shiji[AH]	90	C4	Shimen[JL]	66	J4
Shidi[HN]	114	C3	Shijia[CQ]	132	E4	Shimen[JX]	98	D4
Shidian[NX]	168	B4	Shijiadian[JL]	66	F5	Shimen[SN]	156	C7
Shidian[YN]	148	E6	Shijian[GD]	118	E3	Shimen[SN]	156	F4
Shidong[GD]	118	E3	Shijian[ZJ]	84	E4	Shimen[SN]	156	G6
Shidong[GZ]	144	G4	Shijianfang[LN]	62	G2	Shimen[SX]	54	C6
Shidong[GZ]	144	H4	Shijiao[GD]	118	C5	Shimenjie[JX]	98	D2
Shidong[HEB]	48	A7	Shijiao[GD]	118	E3	Shimenkou[SX]	54	E4
Shidonggou[SN]	156	E3	Shijiao[GD]	118	G2	Shimenlou[JX]	98	B3
Shidongzi[BJ]	36	D1	Shijiapu[JL]	66	E4	Shimenshan[AH]	90	D4
Shidu[BJ]	36	B4	Shijiashui[NX]	168	B3	Shimenshui[NX]	168	A3
Shidu[JX]	98	B2	Shijiatian[SX]	54	F2	Shimenying[BJ]	36	C4
Shidu[JX]	98	F3	Shijiatun[SX]	54	D2	Shimenzhai[HEB]	48	G3
Shi'e[BJ]	36	D3	Shijiawan[SN]	156	F3	Shimenzi[JL]	66	H4
Shi'ertai[LN]	62	D3	Shijiaying[BJ]	36	B4	Shimian[SC]	138	H6
Shi'erzhan[HL]	70	C3	Shijiazhuang[HEB]	48	B5	Shimiaozi[LN]	62	G4
Shifang[CQ]	132	E2	Shijiazi[LN]	62	F2	Shimudi[SN]	156	E7
Shifang[FJ]	94	B4	Shijie[HI]	128	B3	Shimuzui[GD]	118	E5
Shifang[SC]	138	J4	Shijie[YN]	148	H6	Shinan[SH]	74	D3
Shifeng Qu[HN]	114	F5	Shijiehe[HEN]	106	C4	Shinao[JX]	98	C3
Shifeng Xi[ZJ]	84	E3	Shijing[HEB]	48	C5	Shing Mun Reservoir[HK]	176	D2
Shifo[BJ]	36	D2	Shijingshan Qu[BJ]	36	C4	Shing Mun River Channel[HK]	176	D2
Shifo[LN]	62	F4	Shijiu Hu[AH]	90	E5	Shinian[BJ]	36	C2
Shifo[SD]	102	B3	Shijiu Hu[JS]	80	D5	Shiniu Shan[FJ]	94	E5
Shifodian[HEN]	106	G5	Shijiu[TJ]	42	B2	Shiniu[HN]	114	E5
Shifosi[BJ]	36	C4	Shijiuli[AH]	90	B3	Shipai[AH]	90	C6
Shifosi[BJ]	36	C5	Shijiutuo[HEB]	48	F4	Shipai[FJ]	94	C4
Shifosi[LN]	62	G2	Shijiuwo[HEB]	48	E4	Shipai[HB]	110	F4
Shifu[HI]	128	C2	Shijiuzhan[HL]	70	C2	Shipai[HN]	114	B3
Shifu[HI]	128	C3	Shikan[GD]	118	E3	Shipaifang[BJ]	36	C3
Shigang[HEN]	106	C5	Shikan[YN]	148	K3	Shipan[SC]	138	J6
Shigang[JS]	80	F4	Shikang[GX]	124	G6	Shipan[SX]	54	D4
Shigang[JX]	98	C3	Shike[FJ]	94	C3	Shiping[YN]	148	H7
Shigangmen[SH]	74	C2	Shikengkong[GD]	118	E2	Shipodian[AH]	90	C5
Shigeta[SX]	54	D4	Shikengkong[HN]	114	E8	Shipu[JS]	80	G5
Shigezhuang[TJ]	42	A3	Shikong[NX]	168	B3	Shipu[ZJ]	84	F3
Shigezhuang[TJ]	42	B2	Shikou[JX]	98	D3	Shiqian[GZ]	144	G3
Shigezhuang[TJ]	42	B2	Shikou[SD]	102	E2	Shiqiang[CQ]	132	D4
Shigong[AH]	90	C3	Shikou[SX]	54	C5	Shiqiang[SD]	102	C4
Shigou[GD]	118	E3	Shilaba[NX]	168	C1	Shiqiao[AH]	90	E5
Shigouyi[NX]	168	C3	Shilai[SD]	102	D4	Shiqiao[AH]	90	F6
Shigu[GD]	118	C5	Shiliang Ling[GX]	124	E6	Shiqiao[HB]	110	E2
Shigu[GZ]	144	G3	Shiliang[GZ]	144	G2	Shiqiao[HN]	114	E7
Shigu[HB]	110	E2	Shiliang[ZJ]	84	C3	Shiqiao[JL]	66	F2
Shigu[SN]	156	D6	Shilianghe Shuiku[JS]	80	D2	Shiqiao[JS]	80	E1
Shigu[YN]	148	E4	Shilianzi[SD]	102	E4	Shiqiao[SC]	138	M4
Shiguai Qu[NM]	58	I7	Shilibu[TJ]	42	A4	Shiqiao[SH]	74	D3
Shiguai Qu[NM]	58	W11	Shilin[SX]	54	C5	Shiqiao[SN]	156	E6
Shiguan[AH]	90	C6	Shilin[YN]	148	I6	Shiqiao[SX]	54	D6
Shiguan[AH]	90	E4	Shiling[GD]	118	C5	Shiqiao[TJ]	42	E5

Shiqiao[XJ]	172	J3		Shizhai[HEN]	106	E2		Shuanggang[JL]	66	C2
Shiqiao[ZJ]	84	F2		Shizhe[SX]	54	D5		Shuanggang[JX]	98	D2
Shiqiaopu[SC]	138	M5		Shizhen[FJ]	94	B4		Shuanggang[TJ]	42	B3
Shiqiaozi[LN]	62	G3		Shizhen[JX]	98	D3		Shuanggou[AH]	90	B3
Shiqiaozi[SD]	102	F3		Shizheng[GD]	118	H2		Shuanggou[HB]	110	F2
Shiqishi[HN]	114	D6		Shizhi[CQ]	132	D3		Shuanggou[JS]	80	C2
Shiqiu[HI]	128	B2		Shizhong Qu[SD]	102	D5		Shuanggou[JS]	80	D3
Shiqizhan[HL]	70	C2		Shizhong[FJ]	94	C5		Shuanghe[AH]	90	C5
Shiquan Shuiku[SN]	156	E7		Shizhou[HN]	114	F6		Shuanghe[CQ]	132	B4
Shiquan[SN]	156	E7		Shizhu[CQ]	132	E4		Shuanghe[CQ]	132	D4
Shiran[ZJ]	84	E4		Shizhu[HN]	114	C5		Shuanghe[HB]	110	C4
Shiren Shan[HEN]	106	D4		Shizhu[ZJ]	84	E4		Shuanghe[HB]	110	F3
Shiren[HL]	70	D5		Shizhuang[JS]	80	E3		Shuanghe[HB]	110	F3
Shiren[JL]	66	G6		Shizhuang[JS]	80	F4		Shuanghe[HL]	70	C5
Shirengou[HEB]	48	E2		Shizhuang[SX]	54	C4		Shuanghe[HL]	70	D4
Shirong[HI]	128	B2		Shizhuang[SX]	54	D6		Shuanghe[NX]	168	B4
Shisandaogou[JL]	66	H6		Shizhuang[SX]	54	F2		Shuanghe[SC]	138	M4
Shisanling Shuiku[BJ]	36	C3		Shizhuangjing[HEB]	48	B2		Shuanghe[SN]	156	E4
Shisanling[BJ]	36	C3		Shizhuozi[HEB]	48	E2		Shuanghe[SN]	156	F8
Shishan[FJ]	94	D4		Shizhuqiao[HN]	114	D6		Shuanghui[YN]	148	J4
Shishan[HI]	128	C2		Shizi[AH]	90	F6		Shuanghekou[CQ]	132	C4
Shishan[JX]	98	B5		Shizi[NX]	168	C5		Shuanghekou[SN]	156	E7
Shishan[LN]	62	E3		Shizi[SC]	138	K6		Shuanghsi[TW]	186	E1
Shishang[JX]	98	D5		Shizi[YN]	148	J3		Shuanghu[XZ]	152	F3
Shishankou Shuiku[HEN]	106	F6		Shizigou[HEB]	48	C2		Shuanghua[GD]	118	H3
Shishi[FJ]	94	D5		Shizijie[LN]	62	H5		Shuanghua[YN]	148	H4
Shishi[JX]	98	B3		Shizilu[HI]	128	C2		Shuanghui[SC]	138	L3
Shishou[HB]	110	F5		Shizilu[NX]	168	C5		Shuangji He[HEN]	106	E3
Shisi[HEN]	106	D3		Shiziping[HEN]	106	B4		Shuangjian[AH]	90	C3
Shisihao[TJ]	42	C4		Shizishan Qu[AH]	90	D6		Shuangjian[YN]	148	E5
Shisizhan[HL]	70	C3		Shizong[YN]	148	I6		Shuangjiang[CQ]	132	B3
Shisun[HN]	114	E4		Shizui[GD]	118	E3		Shuangjiang[YN]	148	E7
Shitai[AH]	90	D6		Shizui[SX]	54	E3		Shuangjiang[GD]	118	D4
Shitan[SN]	156	E6		Shizuishan[NX]	168	C1		Shuangjie[GD]	118	D5
Shitang[GX]	124	G5		Shizuiyi[SN]	156	G3		Shuangjie[TJ]	42	B3
Shitang[GX]	124	G5		Shizuizi[HEB]	48	B3		Shuangjing[HEB]	48	B7
Shitang[GX]	124	I2		Shou Xian[AH]	90	C4		Shuangjingzi[XJ]	172	O4
Shitang[JX]	98	E3		Shou'an[JX]	98	E2		Shuangkou[TJ]	42	B3
Shitang[ZJ]	84	D4		Shoubaozhuang[BJ]	36	C4		Shuanglian[GX]	124	E4
Shitang[ZJ]	84	F4		Shouchang[ZJ]	84	D3		Shuangliao[JL]	66	D4
Shitanjing[NX]	168	C1		Shoufeng[SN]	156	G5		Shuanglienpi[TW]	186	E2
Shiti[SN]	156	F8		Shoufeng[TW]	186	E3		Shuanglin[JX]	98	B4
Shiting[HEB]	48	C4		Shouguang[SD]	102	E3		Shuanglin[ZJ]	84	E2
Shitou Shan[NM]	58	P2		Shoujiang[ZJ]	84	D2		Shuangliu[SC]	138	I5
Shitoubu[GX]	124	G6		Shouning[FJ]	94	E2		Shuangliu[SC]	138	L4
Shitoukoumen Shuiku[JL]	66	F4		Shoushan[FJ]	94	E3		Shuanglong[CQ]	132	F2
Shitoutian[GD]	118	D5		Shoushan[FJ]	94	E3		Shuanglong[GS]	160	G4
Shitouwozi[NX]	168	C4		Shoushan[YN]	148	I3		Shuanglong[JL]	66	E4
Shitouzui[HB]	110	I4		Shouson Hill[HK]	176	D4		Shuanglong[SN]	156	E5
Shituan[SC]	138	K5		Shouxian[JS]	80	B2		Shuanglongying[YN]	148	J6
Shitun[FJ]	94	D2		Shouyang[SX]	54	E4		Shuanglou[HEN]	106	G4
Shitun[GZ]	144	D5		Shouzhang[SD]	102	B3		Shuanglou[TJ]	42	A4
Shituo[CQ]	132	D4		Shu He[JS]	80	D2		Shuanglu[SX]	54	D3
Shiwan Dashan[GX]	124	E6		Shu He[SD]	102	E4		Shuangluan Qu[HEB]	48	E3
Shiwan[GX]	124	G6		Shu Shui[JX]	98	B5		Shuangmiao[SD]	102	B3
Shiwan[SN]	156	F3		Shu Xi[AH]	90	E6		Shuangmiao[SH]	74	C3
Shiwang Feng[AH]	90	D6		Shuajingsi[SC]	138	H3		Shuangmiao[TJ]	42	B3
Shiwei[NM]	58	M2		Shuang Zhou[HI]	128	A2		Shuangmiaozi[LN]	62	H2
Shiwen[LN]	62	G3		Shuang'an[TJ]	42	B1		Shuangnian[SX]	54	D2
Shiweng[SN]	156	F7		Shuang'antun[JL]	66	G6		Shuangpai Shuiku[HN]	114	D7
Shiwulidun[NX]	168	C3		Shuangbai[YN]	148	G6		Shuangpai[HN]	114	C5
Shiwulihe[HL]	70	C3		Shuangbaiyang[SN]	156	C6		Shuangpai[HN]	114	D7
Shixi[CQ]	132	D4		Shuangbao[GZ]	144	E4		Shuangping[HB]	110	E3
Shixi[GZ]	144	F2		Shuangche[FJ]	94	B4		Shuangping[SN]	156	E8
Shixi[SX]	54	B4		Shuangchenghl[HL]	70	D6		Shuangqiao Qu[CQ]	132	B4
Shixia[GS]	160	G6		Shuangchengpu[JL]	66	E3		Shuangqiao[AH]	90	C4
Shixia[JX]	98	D4		Shuangchi[SX]	54	C5		Shuangqiao[BJ]	36	D4
Shixia[SX]	54	E4		Shuangcun[JX]	98	C4		Shuangqiao[CQ]	132	E5
Shixin[LN]	62	E3		Shuangdian[JS]	80	D2		Shuangqiao[HB]	110	C3
Shixing[GD]	118	G2		Shuangdian[JS]	80	F4		Shuangqiao[HN]	114	E6
Shiya[GX]	124	G4		Shuangding[GX]	124	F5		Shuangqiao[JX]	98	B3
Shiyan[CQ]	132	D3		Shuangduiji[AH]	90	C3		Shuangqiao[JX]	98	B5
Shiyan[HB]	110	D2		Shuangdun[AH]	90	D4		Shuangqiao[SD]	102	B4
Shiyan[JL]	66	J4		Shuangfan[HI]	128	D2		Shuangqiao[SH]	74	C3
Shiyang He[GS]	160	F3		Shuangfeng[GX]	124	G5		Shuangqiao[ZJ]	84	C3
Shiyang[AH]	90	E5		Shuangfeng[HL]	70	D5		Shuangqiaohe[TJ]	42	B4
Shiyang[HN]	114	E7		Shuangfeng[HL]	70	D6		Shuangqiaomen[BJ]	36	D4
Shiyaogou[SN]	156	F3		Shuangfeng[HN]	114	D5		Shuangqiaoping[HN]	114	D3
Shiyaozi[HEB]	48	C2		Shuangfeng[HN]	114	E3		Shuangqiaozi[HL]	70	D3
Shiye[CQ]	132	F5		Shuangfeng[HN]	114	E5		Shuangqiaozi[TJ]	42	C3
Shiyibu[TJ]	42	A3		Shuangfeng[JL]	66	I3		Shuangquan[SN]	156	G6
Shiyuetian[HI]	128	A2		Shuangfeng[JS]	80	F5		Shuangsha[SC]	138	K8
Shiyun[HI]	128	B3		Shuangfu[AH]	90	B3		Shuangshan[GZ]	144	D3
Shizhai[GX]	124	I4		Shuanggang[AH]	90	C6		Shuangshan[HL]	70	C4

Shuangshan[JL]	66	D4	Shuikou[GD]	118	E4	Shuntian[GD]	118	G2
Shuangshan[JL]	66	H4	Shuikou[GD]	118	H3	Shunxi[ZJ]	84	C2
Shuangshao[YN]	148	H5	Shuikou[GX]	124	D5	Shunxi[ZJ]	84	E5
Shuangshu[TJ]	42	B2	Shuikou[GX]	124	I4	Shunyang[FJ]	94	D2
Shuangta[HEN]	106	F3	Shuikou[GZ]	144	H5	Shunyi Qu[BJ]	36	D3
Shuangta[LN]	62	F5	Shuikou[HN]	114	D8	Shunzhou[YN]	148	F4
Shuangtai[HB]	110	D2	Shuikou[HN]	114	F6	Shuo Qu[YN]	148	E2
Shuangtai[LN]	62	F4	Shuikou[ZJ]	84	D1	Shuoli[AH]	90	C2
Shuangtaizi He[LN]	62	E3	Shuikoushan[HN]	114	D6	Shuoliang[GX]	124	E4
Shuangtaizihe Kou[LN]	62	E4	Shuiku Shuifeng[LN]	62	I4	Shuolong[GX]	124	D5
Shuangtang[JS]	80	D2	Shuili[TW]	186	D3	Shuozhou[SX]	54	D2
Shuangtang[JX]	98	D3	Shuilien[TW]	186	E3	Shupi[YN]	148	J7
Shuangtangjian[BJ]	36	A4	Shuiliuzhuang[TJ]	42	C3	Shuping[SN]	156	F9
Shuangtou[GD]	118	H2	Shuiluo He[SC]	138	F7	Shuqishan[SD]	102	F4
Shuangtu[CQ]	132	E2	Shuiman[HI]	128	B3	Shuren[CQ]	132	D4
Shuangwan[GS]	160	F3	Shuimen[FJ]	94	F3	Shushan Hu[AH]	90	D5
Shuangwang[GX]	124	G6	Shuimiao[HN]	114	C6	Shutai[NX]	168	B4
Shuangxi[FJ]	94	E2	Shuimowan[NX]	168	B4	Shuxin[SH]	74	D1
Shuangxi[SN]	156	D7	Shuinan[FJ]	94	C3	Shuyang[FJ]	94	C5
Shuangxi[ZJ]	84	D4	Shuinan[GD]	118	E3	Shuyang[JS]	80	D2
Shuangxikou[FJ]	94	C2	Shuinanwei[JX]	98	D5	Shuyuan[SH]	74	D3
Shuangxikou[HN]	114	D3	Shuiping[HB]	110	C2	Shuzai[GD]	118	D5
Shuangyan[JX]	98	C6	Shuiqian Xi[FJ]	94	B3	Shuzhang[SX]	54	E6
Shuangyang Qu[JL]	66	F4	Shuiqian[FJ]	94	B3	Shuzhong[SH]	74	C1
Shuangyang[CQ]	132	F2	Shuiqing[GZ]	144	D3	Shuzi[JL]	66	D2
Shuangyang[FJ]	94	C4	Shuiquan[GS]	160	G4	Si He[SD]	102	C4
Shuangyang[HL]	70	D5	Shuiquan[SD]	102	D4	Si Xian[AH]	90	D3
Shuangyang[SD]	102	F3	Shuiquan[SX]	54	C2	Si'an[ZJ]	84	D2
Shuangyang[ZJ]	84	E4	Shuiquangou[BJ]	36	C3	Siba[GX]	124	F3
Shuangyao[TJ]	42	B4	Shuiquliu[JL]	66	H3	Sibnagqêqu'ngo[XZ]	152	G3
Shuangyashan[HL]	70	F5	Shuishi[HN]	114	D7	Sicha Xuefeng[XJ]	172	J7
Shuangyingzi[JL]	66	F4	Shuisi[JS]	80	E3	Sichakou[HEB]	48	D2
Shuangyushu[HL]	70	C5	Shuitang[GZ]	144	C5	Sichuan Pendi[SC]	138	I5
Shuangzha[TJ]	42	B4	Shuitang[GZ]	144	E5	Sicun[GX]	124	G4
Shuangzhen[JX]	98	E4	Shuitang[YN]	148	G6	Sicundian[TJ]	42	A3
Shuanmazhuang[BJ]	36	B4	Shuitangbao[GZ]	144	C3	Sidaoban[GS]	160	B3
Shuchang[GZ]	144	F5	Shuitao[NX]	168	C3	Sidaogou[HEB]	48	E2
Shucheng[AH]	90	C5	Shuitian[GZ]	144	E4	Sidaogou[JL]	66	H4
Shucheng[HEB]	48	D5	Shuitian[HN]	114	C4	Sidaogou[JL]	66	H6
Shuen Wan[HK]	176	D2	Shuitian[JX]	98	C4	Sidaoxue[BJ]	36	D2
Shufang[FJ]	94	C2	Shuitianba[HB]	110	D3	Sidaozhangfang[NM]	58	M6
Shufu[XJ]	172	E6	Shuitianba[HN]	114	B3	Sidazhai[GZ]	144	E5
Shuguang[JL]	66	K5	Shuitou[BJ]	36	B4	Siding[GX]	124	G2
Shuguang[YN]	148	K7	Shuitou[FJ]	94	D5	Sidu[FJ]	94	C6
Shuhe[SH]	74	D1	Shuitou[SX]	54	C6	Sidu[GZ]	144	E3
Shuhe[SN]	156	F8	Shuitou[ZJ]	84	E5	Sidu[SN]	156	D8
Shuhong[ZJ]	84	E4	Shuitu[CQ]	132	C4	Sidu[ZJ]	84	E4
Shui Hau[HK]	176	B4	Shuiwei[HI]	128	B2	Sidunzi[NX]	168	D3
Shui Tseng Wan[HK]	176	B4	Shuiwen[GX]	124	H5	Siduping[HN]	114	C4
Shui Xi[ZJ]	84	E4	Shuixie[YN]	148	E5	Si'erpu[LN]	62	D4
Shui'ai[HN]	114	C4	Shuiyan[GZ]	144	F5	Sifang Ling[GX]	124	E5
Shuibatang[GZ]	144	F2	Shuiyang Jiang[AH]	90	E6	Sifang Shan[JL]	66	G6
Shuibei[JS]	80	E5	Shuiyang[AH]	90	E5	Sifang Shan[SN]	156	F7
Shuibei[JX]	98	C3	Shuiyang[ZJ]	84	F4	Sifangdingzi[LN]	62	H4
Shuibeijie[FJ]	94	D2	Shuiyazidun[QH]	164	F2	Sifangtai Qu[HL]	70	F5
Shuibian[GD]	118	F2	Shuiye[HEN]	106	F1	Sifangtai[LN]	62	G3
Shuibu[GD]	118	E4	Shuiyu[BJ]	36	C4	Sifen[HN]	114	F5
Shuibuya[HB]	110	D4	Shuiyuan[FJ]	94	D2	Sifenchang[TJ]	42	B4
Shuicha[JX]	98	C5	Shuiyuesi[HB]	110	E3	Sigaozhuang[TJ]	42	B3
Shuiche[HN]	114	C5	Shuiyuguan[SX]	54	C4	Sige[GZ]	144	C4
Shuicheng[GZ]	144	C4	Shuizhai[SD]	102	D3	Sigengsha Jiao[HI]	128	A2
Shuidao[SD]	102	H2	Shuizhan[QH]	164	D3	Sigezhuang[BJ]	36	C4
Shuidi[SX]	54	B5	Shuizhuping[AH]	90	B5	Sigezhuang[HEB]	48	F4
Shuidong[HN]	114	E7	Shuizi[JL]	66	D2	Siguanyingzi[LN]	62	C3
Shuifu[YN]	148	J2	Shujiawan[HB]	110	D2	Siguniang Shan[SC]	138	H4
Shuifumiao Shuiku[HN]	114	E5	Shujie[YN]	148	F5	Sihai[BJ]	36	C2
Shuige[ZJ]	84	D4	Shujie[YN]	148	G5	Sihai[JL]	66	G5
Shuigou[SN]	156	G7	Shulan[JL]	66	G3	Sihaidian[HL]	70	D5
Shuihou[AH]	90	C6	Shule He[GS]	160	B2	Sihe[AH]	90	F6
Shuihuopu[TJ]	42	A2	Shule He[QH]	164	J2	Sihe[JL]	66	G3
Shuiji[FJ]	94	D2	Shule Nanshan[QH]	164	J2	Sihe[LN]	62	H1
Shuijiang[CQ]	132	D4	Shule[XJ]	172	F6	Sihe[SC]	138	I6
Shuijiang[JX]	98	A4	Shuliqiao[SH]	74	C2	Sihecheng[LN]	62	F2
Shuijing[GD]	118	E4	Shunchang[FJ]	94	C3	Sihetun[JL]	66	C3
Shuijing[GX]	124	G3	Shunde Qu[GD]	118	F4	Sihezhuang[BJ]	36	C4
Shuijing[HB]	110	C4	Shunde[JX]	98	D2	Sihong[JS]	80	D3
Shuijingkuang[QH]	164	D7	Shunhe[HB]	110	H3	Sihui[GD]	118	E3
Shuijinping[HN]	114	C6	Shunhe[HEN]	106	F4	Sihushan[HN]	114	E4
Shuikou He[GX]	124	D5	Shunhui[SX]	54	C3	Siji[HL]	70	D4
Shuikou[AH]	90	E4	Shunlihe[HL]	70	E5	Sijia[JS]	80	G4
Shuikou[FJ]	94	D3	Shunmintun[TJ]	42	B4	Sijiachang[HB]	110	E4
Shuikou[FJ]	94	D4	Shunning[SN]	156	E4	Sijiao[SX]	54	C6
Shuikou[GD]	118	C4	Shunping[HEB]	48	C5	Sijiazi[LN]	62	F3
Shuikou[GD]	118	E2	Shunshan[AH]	90	E4	Sijiazi[LN]	62	G2

Name	Page	Grid
Sijiemei Dao[ZJ]	84	G2
Sijihong[HN]	114	E3
Sijing[SH]	74	C2
Sijingshui[HB]	110	D4
Sijingzi[JL]	66	C3
Sikeshu[HEN]	106	D4
Sikeshu[XJ]	172	J3
Sikou[SD]	102	E2
Sikou[SD]	102	G2
Sili[JX]	98	E3
Sili[SC]	138	G4
Silian[GX]	124	F3
Siligang[TJ]	42	B2
Silihe[HN]	114	D4
Silin[GX]	124	E4
Siling Co[XZ]	152	F4
Silun[GD]	118	D4
Silver Mine Bay[HK]	176	C4
Sima[SC]	138	M4
Sima[SD]	102	C5
Sima[SX]	54	E5
Simao[YN]	148	F8
Simaqiao[HN]	114	D7
Simen[GS]	160	G5
Simen[ZJ]	84	F2
Simenzi[LN]	62	G4
Simian[GX]	124	H4
Simiancheng[LN]	62	G2
Simianshan[CQ]	132	C5
Siming Hu[ZJ]	84	F3
Siming Shan[ZJ]	84	E3
Siming Shan[ZJ]	84	F3
Siming[JS]	80	F3
Simingshan[HN]	114	D6
Simola[XJ]	172	M6
Sinan[GZ]	144	G3
Sinanjiang[YN]	148	G7
Sinda[XZ]	152	J4
Sinya[XZ]	152	E4
Sipai[GX]	124	G3
Sipeng[JL]	66	F6
Siping[JL]	66	E4
Siping[LN]	62	F5
Siping[LN]	62	I3
Siping[SX]	54	D3
Siping[ZJ]	84	G2
Sipu[AH]	90	C3
Sipu[JX]	98	E3
Siqian[FJ]	94	C2
Siqian[GD]	118	G2
Siqiao[FJ]	94	E2
Siqu[GZ]	144	G2
Siquanpu[JX]	98	B3
Sishang[BJ]	36	C3
Sishilidian[NX]	168	C2
Sishilipu[SD]	102	E4
Sishui[GD]	118	I2
Sishui[GS]	160	F4
Sishui[GX]	124	H2
Sishui[JS]	80	E3
Sishui[SD]	102	D4
Sishun[JX]	98	B6
Sitaizui[HEB]	48	C3
Sitang[GX]	124	D4
Sitang[GX]	124	E4
Sitang[GX]	124	F5
Sitang[QH]	164	N3
Sitangxu[HN]	114	E7
Sitong[HEN]	106	G4
Sitou[SD]	102	E3
Situ[JS]	80	E4
Situan[SH]	74	D3
Siu A Chau[HK]	176	B4
Siu Kau Yi Chau[HK]	176	C3
Siu Lam[HK]	176	C3
Siu Lek Yuen[HK]	176	D2
Siu Mo To[HK]	176	B3
Siwa[SC]	138	F7
Siwang[GX]	124	H4
Sixi[JX]	98	C3
Sixi[ZJ]	84	E5
Sixia[JX]	98	B6
Sixian[SN]	156	F5
Sixiaotun[TJ]	42	A3
Sixin[SN]	156	F8
Sixingang[HN]	114	D3
Siyang[JS]	80	D3
Siyingzi[BJ]	36	D2
Sizhai[GZ]	144	F5
Sizhai[SC]	138	H3
Sizhan[HL]	70	C6
Sizhilan[HEB]	48	C6
Sizhou Shan[HN]	114	E6
Sizhou[JX]	98	E2
Sizhoutou[ZJ]	84	F3
Sizhuang[HEB]	48	D4
Sizhuang[SX]	54	D6
Siziwang Qi[NM]	58	I7
Siziwang Qi[NM]	58	X10
Sizu[GS]	160	G5
So Kwun Wat[HK]	176	B2
So Lo Pun[HK]	176	E1
So Uk[HK]	176	D3
Sog Qu[XZ]	152	H3
Sog[XZ]	152	H4
Sogat[XJ]	172	F6
Sogbodo[QH]	164	L6
Sogdoi[XZ]	152	B4
Sogdoi[XZ]	152	I4
Sogruma[QH]	164	M7
Sogxung[XZ]	152	H3
So'gya[QH]	164	F7
Sok Kwu Wan[HK]	176	D4
Sokai[XZ]	152	G5
Soko Islands[HK]	176	B4
Solam Tag[XJ]	172	K7
Solon[NM]	58	N4
Song Cun[SD]	102	I2
Song Ling[LN]	62	D3
Song Shan[HEN]	106	D3
Song Shan[HEN]	106	E3
Song Xi[FJ]	94	D2
Song Xian[HEN]	106	D3
Song'acha He[HL]	70	G6
Songbai[SD]	102	F4
Songbaitan[HN]	114	B4
Songcao[HEB]	48	B6
Songcun[ZJ]	84	C3
Songdian[AH]	90	C4
Songfan[ZJ]	84	C4
Songgang[GD]	118	F3
Songgang[GD]	118	F4
Songgui[YN]	148	F4
Songhe[HB]	110	G3
Songhu[JX]	98	D4
Songhu[SH]	74	C2
Songhua Hu[JL]	66	G4
Songhua Jiang[HL]	70	F5
Songhua Jiang[JL]	66	F3
Songhua Jiang[JL]	66	G4
Songji[AH]	90	B4
Songji[HEN]	106	G3
Songjia[SN]	156	F8
Songjiagou[SX]	54	C3
Songjiang Qu[SH]	74	C2
Songjiang[HN]	114	E6
Songjiang[JL]	66	H4
Songjiang[JL]	66	H5
Songjiang[JL]	66	I5
Songjianghe[JL]	66	H5
Songjiapu[NX]	168	D3
Songjiayao[JL]	66	D3
Songjiazhuang[HEB]	48	B4
Songjiazhuang[HEB]	48	B6
Songkan[GZ]	144	E2
Songkeng[GD]	118	G3
Songkou[FJ]	94	B3
Songkou[FJ]	94	D4
Songkou[GD]	118	I2
Songlin[GZ]	144	E3
Songlin[HI]	128	B2
Songlingmen[LN]	62	D3
Songlingzi[LN]	62	C4
Songlinpo[GZ]	144	C4
Songliu[HI]	128	C2
Songluo[FJ]	94	E3
Songluo[HB]	110	D3
Songmen[ZJ]	84	F4
Songming[HI]	128	B2
Songming[YN]	148	I5
Songmuping[HB]	110	E4
Songmutang[HN]	114	E4
Songnan[SH]	74	C2
Songpan[SC]	138	I3
Songping[GS]	160	G6
Songpinggou[SC]	138	I3
Songqiao[JS]	80	E4
Songquansi[HEN]	106	C3
Songshan[GX]	124	H5
Songshan[JL]	66	G5
Songshan[JX]	98	B4
Songshan[SD]	102	E3
Songshan[SD]	102	G2
Songshan[SH]	74	C2
Songshanpu[LN]	62	H2
Songshu[JL]	66	H5
Songshugou[HL]	70	E4
Songshulin[SN]	156	F4
Songshutou[XJ]	172	H3
Songshuwan[HB]	110	D1
Songshuyu[BJ]	36	E2
Songta[SX]	54	E4
Songtao Ganqu[HI]	128	B2
Songtao Shuiku[HI]	128	B2
Songtao[GZ]	144	H2
Songtao[HI]	128	B2
Songting[JL]	66	K5
Songwang[GX]	124	G6
Songxi[FJ]	94	B3
Songxi[FJ]	94	D2
Songxinzhuang[NX]	168	C3
Songyan[GZ]	144	F3
Songyan[SX]	54	E4
Songyang[ZJ]	84	D4
Songyin Xi[ZJ]	84	D4
Songyuan[GD]	118	I2
Songyuan[JL]	66	E2
Songzhan[HL]	70	C5
Songzhuang[BJ]	36	D4
Songzhuang[SD]	102	F3
Songzi[HB]	110	E4
Songziyuan[GD]	118	F2
Sonid Youqi[NM]	58	J6
Sonid Zuoqi[NM]	58	J6
Soudengzhan[JL]	66	G4
South China Sea[GD]	118	E6
South China Sea[HI]	128	C3
Ssuchi[TW]	186	E2
Ssuhu[TW]	186	D3
Stanley Bay[HK]	176	D4
Stanley[HK]	176	D4
Su'an[SD]	102	C2
Suao Kang[TW]	186	E2
Su'ao[FJ]	94	E4
Suao[TW]	186	E2
Sub Nur[NM]	58	D6
Suban[FJ]	94	C4
Subao Ding[HN]	114	C5
Subei Guangai Zongqu[JS]	80	E3
Subei[GS]	160	B3
Subu[NX]	168	B5
Subujing[NX]	168	D2
Sucheng[SX]	54	E5
Sucun[SD]	102	E4
Sudal Nongchang[NM]	58	U10
Sudian[YN]	148	C5
Suge[SD]	102	B4
Sugongtuo[JL]	66	D3
Suhai Hu[GS]	160	A3
Suhai Hu[QH]	164	F2
Suhai[NM]	58	U11
Suhain Bom[QH]	164	J4
Suhait[NM]	58	W11
Suhong[AH]	90	E6
Suhunt[NM]	58	F7
Sui He[AH]	90	D3
Sui Xian[HEN]	106	G3
Su'an[HL]	70	C2
Suibin[HL]	70	F5
Suichang[ZJ]	84	D4
Suichuan Jiang[JX]	98	B5

Suichuan[JX]	98	B5
Suide[SN]	156	G3
Suidong[HL]	70	G5
Suifen He[HL]	70	F6
Suifen He[JL]	66	K4
Suifenhe[HL]	70	F6
Suiguantun[SD]	102	C4
Suihua[HL]	70	D5
SuiJiang[GD]	118	E3
Suijiang[YN]	148	I2
Suijiazhuang[TJ]	42	B3
Suileng[HL]	70	D5
Suining[HN]	114	C6
Suining[JS]	80	C3
Suining[SC]	138	K5
Suiping[HEN]	106	E4
Suixi[AH]	90	C3
Suixi[GD]	118	C5
Suiyang Qu[HEN]	106	G3
Suiyang[GZ]	144	F2
Suiyang[GZ]	144	F3
Suiyang[HL]	70	F6
Suiyi[GX]	124	F4
Suizhong[LN]	62	D4
Suizhou[HB]	110	G3
Suj[QH]	164	J3
Suji[AH]	90	B3
Sujia[YN]	148	I3
Sujiadian[HEB]	48	D2
Sujiagou[HB]	110	E4
Sujiaidan[HL]	70	F5
Sujiatun Qu[LN]	62	G3
Sujiatuo[BJ]	36	C3
Sujiazhuang[HEB]	48	A5
Sujitan[QH]	164	N3
Sukeng[FJ]	94	D4
Suli Hu[QH]	164	G3
Sulin Col[QH]	164	I4
Sulongkou[SX]	54	D3
Sulphur Channel[HK]	176	C3
Suluo[SC]	138	H7
Sumber[NM]	58	E7
Sumdo[QH]	164	M5
Sumdo[SC]	138	F6
Sumdoling[XZ]	152	A3
Sumigou[JL]	66	G5
Sumzom[XZ]	152	J5
Sun Chui Estate[HK]	176	D3
Sunan[GS]	160	D3
Sunbu[AH]	90	E6
Sundian[HEN]	106	F4
Sung Kong[HK]	176	E4
Sungang[AH]	90	C5
Sungezhuang[TJ]	42	B2
Sungezhuang[TJ]	42	C1
Suning[HEB]	48	C5
Sunji[SX]	54	B6
Sunjiaba[GZ]	144	G3
Sunjiacha[SN]	156	G1
Sunjiadian[SX]	54	E1
Sunjiagou[NX]	168	A3
Sunjiaqiao[SX]	54	C3
Sunjiaji[SD]	102	E3
Sunjiapo[BJ]	36	D4
Sunjiatan[NX]	168	C3
Sunjiazhuang[NX]	168	C5
Sunjiazhuang[TJ]	42	C1
Sunjiazhuang[TJ]	42	C2
Sunliu[SD]	102	C5
Sunlou[JS]	80	B2
Sunqiao[HB]	110	G3
Sunshi[HEB]	48	D5
Suntuan[AH]	90	C3
Sunwu[HL]	70	D4
Sunyangjia[NX]	168	C5
Sunying[HEN]	106	F3
Sunzhaike[NX]	168	B3
Sunzhen[SN]	156	F6
Sunzhuang[HEB]	48	C5
Sunzhuangzi[HEB]	48	C3
Suochi[GS]	160	G6
Suojiang[SC]	138	J3
Suojie[HN]	114	C3
Suolagongma[QH]	164	F8
Suomo He[SC]	138	H4
Suopo[SX]	54	D3
Suoqian[ZJ]	84	E2
Suozi[JL]	66	D3
Suqian[JS]	80	D3
Suqu[GD]	118	H3
Sur[QH]	164	K2
Surco[XZ]	152	E5
Surdêxoi[XZ]	152	K5
Surug[QH]	164	H8
Sushan Dao[SD]	102	I3
Sushui He[SX]	54	B6
Susong[AH]	90	C6
Suuxqi[XJ]	172	L6
Suwan[AH]	90	D5
Suxian Qu[HN]	114	F7
Suxiang[AH]	90	E4
Suxianshi[HEN]	106	G6
Suxu[GX]	124	F5
Suyahu Shuiku[HEN]	106	F4
Suyangshan[JS]	80	C2
Suyu Qu[JS]	80	D3
Suyukou[NX]	168	B2
Suzhou[AH]	90	C3
Suzhou[JS]	80	F5
Suzhuang[SX]	54	D6
Suzhuang[ZJ]	84	C3
Suzi He[LN]	62	H3
Suzigou[LN]	62	G4
Suzui[JS]	80	E3

T

Ta He[HL]	70	C3
Ta Ho Tun[HK]	176	E3
Ta Kwu Ling[HK]	176	D1
Ta Shek Wu[HK]	176	C2
Ta Tit Yan[HK]	176	D2
Taan Hsi[TW]	186	D2
Taan[TW]	186	D2
Taban Han Gol[NM]	58	X10
Taban Obo[NM]	58	P3
Tabu He[NM]	58	I7
Tachagpu Shan[XZ]	152	C3
Tachakou[XJ]	172	J3
Tacheng(Qoqek)[XJ]	172	I2
Tacheng[TW]	186	D3
Tacheng[YN]	148	E3
Tachia Hsi[TW]	186	E2
Tachia[TW]	186	D2
Tachien[TW]	186	E2
Tachoshui[TW]	186	E2
Tachu[TW]	186	D4
Ta'ercun[HEB]	48	B3
Ta'ergen[HL]	70	C2
Ta'erwan[NX]	168	C4
Tafang[AH]	90	D7
Tafeng[TW]	186	E3
Tagarma[XJ]	172	E7
Ta'gya[QH]	164	O5
Taha[HL]	70	C5
Tahan Hsi[TW]	186	E2
Tahe[HL]	70	C2
Tahsi[TW]	186	E2
Tahu[TW]	186	D2
Tai A Chau[HK]	176	B4
Tai Au Mun[HK]	176	E3
Tai Chau[HK]	176	F2
Tai Chek Mun[HK]	176	E1
Tai Chik Sha[HK]	176	E3
Tai Hang[HK]	176	D3
Tai Hom Sham[HK]	176	A4
Tai Hu[JS]	80	F5
Tai Kok Tau[HK]	176	E4
Tai Kok Tsui[HK]	176	D3
Tai Kok[HK]	176	D4
Tai Kong Po[HK]	176	C2
Tai Lak Lei[HK]	176	E3
Tai Lam Chung Reservoir[HK]	176	C2
Tai Lam Chung[HK]	176	C3
Tai Lam Kok[HK]	176	C3
Tai Lam Liu[HK]	176	D2
Tai Lam Wu[HK]	176	E3
Tai Lang Shui[HK]	176	B2
Tai Lei[HK]	176	C3
Tai Long Tsui[HK]	176	F2
Tai Long Wan[HK]	176	A4
Tai Long Wan[HK]	176	B4
Tai Long Wan[HK]	176	F2
Tai Long[HK]	176	B4
Tai Long[HK]	176	F2
Tai Mei Tuk[HK]	176	D2
Tai Miu Wan[HK]	176	E4
Tai Mo Shan[HK]	176	D2
Tai Mo To[HK]	176	B3
Tai Nim Chau[HK]	176	E1
Tai O[HK]	176	A4
Tai Om Shan[HK]	176	D2
Tai Pak Wan[HK]	176	C3
Tai Po Kau[HK]	176	D2
Tai Po Market[HK]	176	D2
Tai Po Tau[HK]	176	D2
Tai Po[HK]	176	D2
Tai Shan[SD]	102	D3
Tai Shui Hang[HK]	176	C3
Tai Shui Hang[HK]	176	D2
Tai Tam Bay[HK]	176	D4
Tai Tam Reservoirs[HK]	176	D4
Tai Tan Hoi[HK]	176	E2
Tai Tan[HK]	176	E2
Tai Tau Chau[HK]	176	E3
Tai Tau Chau[HK]	176	E4
Tai Tong Tsuen[HK]	176	C2
Tai Tung Shan[HK]	176	B4
Tai Van[MC]	182	B6
Tai Wan San Tsuen[HK]	176	C4
Tai Wan[HK]	176	E4
Tai Wan[HK]	176	F2
Tai Wo[HK]	176	C2
Tai'an[CQ]	132	B3
Tai'an[CQ]	132	E3
Tai'an[JL]	66	G2
Tai'an[JL]	66	G6
Tai'an[LN]	62	F3
Tai'an[SD]	102	D3
Tai'anyi[SX]	54	D3
Taibai Ding[HB]	110	G2
Taibai Ding[HEN]	106	E5
Taibai Shan[SN]	156	D7
Taibai Shan[SX]	54	F2
Taibai[GS]	160	H5
Taibai[GS]	160	I4
Taibai[GZ]	144	F2
Taibai[SN]	156	D6
Taibaihe[SN]	156	D7
Taibaozhuang[BJ]	36	D3
Taibo Ding[SD]	102	H2
Taibus Qi[NM]	58	K7
Taicang[JS]	80	G5
Taichung kang[TW]	186	D2
Taichung[TW]	186	D2
Taichung[TW]	186	D2
Taicun[SN]	156	E5
Taide[SX]	54	B5
Tai'e[GS]	160	I5
Tai'erzhuang Qu[SD]	102	D5
Taigu[SX]	54	B5
Taigu[SX]	54	D4
Taihang Shan[HEB]	48	A5
Taihang Shan[HEN]	106	E2
Taihang Shan[SX]	54	E6
Taihe Shuiku[SD]	102	D3
Taihe[AH]	90	B3
Taihe[CQ]	132	C3
Taihe[CQ]	132	F3
Taihe[GD]	118	F3
Taihe[JX]	98	B5
Taihe[JX]	98	D4
Taihe[SD]	102	E3
Taihetang[HN]	114	D6
Taihexu[HN]	114	E6
Taihezhai[SN]	156	G2
Taihsi[TW]	186	D3
Taihu[AH]	90	C6
Taihu[ZJ]	84	E2
Taihua[FJ]	94	C4

Name	Page	Grid
Taihua[JS]	80	E5
Taihuai[SX]	54	E2
Taiji[CQ]	132	E4
Taijiang[GZ]	144	G4
Taijiying[LN]	62	D2
Taijnar He[QH]	164	E3
Taikang[HEN]	106	F3
Tailai[CQ]	132	D3
Tailai[HL]	70	B5
Tailao Shan[FJ]	94	E3
Tailiang[NM]	58	V11
Tailin[SX]	54	C5
Tailing[BJ]	36	C3
Tailong[CQ]	132	E3
Tailugou[HEB]	48	B2
Taimali[TW]	186	D4
Taimei[GD]	118	G3
Taimen[ZJ]	84	G3
Tainan[JS]	80	F4
Tainan[TW]	186	D3
Tainan[TW]	186	D4
Taining[FJ]	94	C3
Taipa Grande[MC]	182	C4
Taipa Pequena[MC]	182	B4
Taipa[MC]	182	B4
Taipan[GZ]	144	G4
Taipei[TW]	186	E1
Taiping Ding[SD]	102	D3
Taiping Hu[AH]	90	E6
Taiping Ling[NM]	58	N4
Taiping[CQ]	132	C4
Taiping[FJ]	94	C6
Taiping[FJ]	94	D3
Taiping[GD]	118	E2
Taiping[GD]	118	F2
Taiping[GD]	118	F3
Taiping[GS]	160	G6
Taiping[GS]	160	H5
Taiping[GX]	124	E4
Taiping[GX]	124	F4
Taiping[GX]	124	F5
Taiping[GX]	124	F5
Taiping[GX]	124	G3
Taiping[GX]	124	H4
Taiping[GZ]	144	G3
Taiping[HB]	110	C5
Taiping[HB]	110	F2
Taiping[HI]	128	B2
Taiping[HN]	114	D3
Taiping[HN]	114	E7
Taiping[JL]	66	G4
Taiping[JL]	66	G6
Taiping[JS]	80	D3
Taiping[JS]	80	F5
Taiping[SC]	138	L7
Taiping[SD]	102	C4
Taiping[TJ]	42	B4
Taiping[TW]	186	D2
Taiping[ZJ]	84	D4
Taipingchuan[JL]	66	D3
Taipingcun[TJ]	42	B4
Taipingdian[GS]	160	G5
Taipingli[HN]	114	F7
Taipingling[LN]	62	F5
Taipingshan[JL]	66	E3
Taipingshao[LN]	62	I4
Taipingtun[NM]	58	N2
Taipingxi[HB]	110	D4
Taipingying[GZ]	144	H2
Taipingzhuang[BJ]	36	C3
Taipingzhuang[HEB]	48	E2
Taipingzhuang[HL]	70	C5
Taipingzhuang[LN]	62	C3
Taipo[HI]	128	B2
Taiqian[HEN]	106	G2
Taiqing[HN]	114	D3
Taiqiu[HEN]	106	H3
Tairi[SH]	74	D3
Tairu[FJ]	94	C4
Taishan Liedao[FJ]	94	F3
Taishan[FJ]	94	C3
Taishan[HB]	118	E4
Taishan[HI]	128	C2
Taishanmiao[SN]	156	E7
Taishitun[BJ]	36	E2
Taishun[ZJ]	84	D5
Taitou[SD]	102	E2
Taitou[SX]	54	C5
Taitou[TJ]	42	A2
Taitou[TJ]	42	A3
Taitoushan[HEB]	48	G2
Taitung Kang[TW]	186	E4
Taitung[TW]	186	E4
Taiwan Haixia[FJ]	94	D6
Taiwan Haixia[TW]	186	C2
Taiwan Reefs[TW]	186	B4
Taiwan Tao[TW]	186	D3
Taiwu[TW]	186	D4
Taixi[FJ]	94	D3
Taixi[NX]	168	C2
Taixing[JS]	80	F4
Taiyang He[HI]	128	C3
Taiyang Hu[QH]	164	C5
Taiyang[AH]	90	C5
Taiyang[GS]	160	H5
Taiyang[SX]	54	B6
Taiyanghe[HB]	110	C4
Taiyangling[SN]	156	B7
Taiyangmiao[NM]	58	S11
Taiyangping[HN]	114	B6
Taiyangshan[NX]	168	C3
Taiyangsheng[HL]	70	C6
Taiyangwei[JX]	98	C3
Taiyu[HEB]	48	B5
Taiyu[SN]	156	E6
Taiyuan[CQ]	132	E4
Taiyuan[HN]	114	E5
Taiyuan[JX]	98	E3
Taiyuan[SX]	54	D4
Taiyue Shan[SX]	54	C5
Taizhi[SD]	102	G3
Taizhimiao[HN]	114	D5
Taizhong[YN]	148	F6
Taizhou Liedao[ZJ]	84	F4
Taizhou Wan[ZJ]	84	F4
Taizhou[JS]	80	E4
Taizhou[ZJ]	84	F4
Taizi He[LN]	62	G3
Taizi[HB]	110	I4
Taizi[SD]	102	D2
Taiziwu[BJ]	36	D3
Taiziwu[TJ]	42	A3
Tajen[TW]	186	D4
Taklimakan Shamo[XJ]	172	I6
Talin[TW]	186	D3
Taling[LN]	62	G4
Talkiydi Shankou[XJ]	172	E5
Tama Daoban[SC]	138	I2
Taman Shan[TW]	186	E2
Tan Chuk Hang[HK]	176	D1
Tan Jiang[GD]	118	E4
Tan Ka Wan[HK]	176	F2
Tan Kwai Tsuen[HK]	176	B2
Tanba[SN]	156	E8
Tanbin[GD]	118	D4
Tanbu[JX]	98	B3
Tanbu[SD]	102	E4
Tanchang[GZ]	144	E3
Tancheng[JX]	98	C4
Tancheng[SD]	102	E5
Tandü[XZ]	152	H3
Tanei[TW]	186	D3
Tanfang[SD]	102	E3
Tanfu[HN]	114	D5
Tang He[AH]	90	C4
Tang He[BJ]	36	D2
Tang He[HEB]	48	B4
Tang He[HEN]	106	D5
Tang Lung Chau[HK]	176	C3
Tang Xian[HEB]	48	B5
Tangang[JX]	98	C4
Ta'ngar[QH]	164	N8
Tangba[CQ]	132	B3
Tangbei[HL]	70	E4
Tangcheng[SX]	54	D5
Tangchi[HB]	110	G4
Tangchi[LN]	62	F4
Tangchuan[FJ]	94	D3
Tangcun[JX]	98	C6
Tangdan[YN]	148	I4
Tangdaohe[HEB]	48	F3
Tangdêng[YN]	148	E3
Tangdian[JS]	80	D2
Tangdian[YN]	148	H5
Tangdian[YN]	148	I7
Tangdian[ZJ]	84	E2
Tangfang[CQ]	132	F2
Tangfang[HL]	70	D6
Tangfang[JX]	98	D5
Tangfang[SD]	102	D2
Tangfeng[HEB]	48	C5
Tanggain[QH]	164	M5
Tanggar[XZ]	152	J4
Tanggarmu Nongchang[QH]	164	M4
Tanggarnang[GS]	160	F5
Tanggo[SC]	138	G6
Tanggou[LN]	62	G4
Tanggu Nongchang[TJ]	42	C3
Tanggu Qu[TJ]	42	C3
Tanggu[XZ]	152	G4
Tangguantun[TJ]	42	A4
Tanggula Bingzhan[QH]	164	D7
Tanggula Shan[QH]	164	D7
Tanggula Shankou[QH]	164	D8
Tanggula Shankou[XZ]	152	G3
Tanggula(Dangla) Shan[QH]	164	B7
Tanggula(Dangla) Shan[XZ]	152	F3
Tanggulashan[QH]	164	E6
Tanghai[HEB]	48	F4
Tanghang[SH]	74	C2
Tanghe Shuiku[LN]	62	G3
Tanghe[CQ]	132	C5
Tanghe[HEB]	48	D2
Tanghe[HEN]	106	D5
Tanghekou[BJ]	36	D2
Tanghua[HN]	114	D3
Tangji[AH]	90	C4
Tangji[JS]	80	E3
Tangjia[GD]	118	B6
Tangjia[GD]	118	F4
Tangjiafang[HN]	114	C6
Tangjiahe[HEB]	48	G4
Tangjiahe[TJ]	42	C4
Tangjiahui[AH]	90	B5
Tangjiang[JX]	98	B6
Tangkou[AH]	90	E6
Tangkou[FJ]	94	E3
Tangkou[GD]	118	D5
Tangkou[GD]	118	E4
Tangkou[SH]	74	C2
Tanglag[QH]	164	L7
Tanglai Qu[NX]	168	C2
Tanglang[YN]	148	H4
Tangmai[XZ]	152	I4
Tangmiao[SD]	102	B4
Tangnag[QH]	164	M5
Tangong Shuiku[HI]	128	A2
Tangping[GD]	118	D4
Tangpu[JX]	98	B3
Tangpu[XZ]	152	K4
Tangpu[ZJ]	84	E3
Tangqi[FJ]	94	B4
Tangqian[FJ]	94	E4
Tangqiao[SH]	74	C2
Tangra Yumco[XZ]	152	E4
Tangsanying[HEB]	48	E2
Tangshan Gang[HEB]	48	G4
Tangshan[HEB]	48	F4
Tangshan[JS]	80	E4
Tangshan[JX]	98	C3
Tangshancheng[LN]	62	H4
Tangshi[HN]	114	F6
Tangtang[GD]	118	F3
Tangtang[YN]	148	J4
Tangtou[FJ]	94	D4
Tangtou[GZ]	144	G3
Tangtou[SD]	102	E4
Tangtougou[HEB]	48	E2
Tangwai[SH]	74	D3
Tangwan[HN]	114	C5
Tangwan[JX]	98	E3
Tangwan[SH]	74	C2

Tangwang[SD]	102	D3	Taohe[JL]	66	D2	Tashan[LN]	62	D4
Tangwanghe Qu[HL]	70	E4	Taohe[SN]	156	E8	Tashan[SC]	138	K4
Tangwu[FJ]	94	B4	Taohongpo[SX]	54	C4	Tashantun[LN]	62	D4
Tangxi[AH]	90	D6	Taohua Dao[ZJ]	84	G3	Tashi[GS]	160	B2
Tangxi[ZJ]	84	D3	Taohua[HB]	110	H3	Tashi[GZ]	144	G4
Tangxi[ZJ]	84	E2	Taohua[HEB]	48	B3	Tashi[ZJ]	84	D4
Tangxi[ZJ]	84	E4	Taohua[NM]	58	X11	Tashiyi[HN]	114	E3
Tangxi[ZJ]	84	F3	Taohua[ZJ]	84	G3	Tatalin He[QH]	164	I3
Tangxian[HB]	110	G3	Taohuatan[AH]	90	E6	Tathong Channel[HK]	176	E4
Tangxian[ZJ]	84	E3	Taohuayuan[HN]	114	D4	Tatrang[XJ]	172	J6
Tangxing[GX]	124	D3	Taojiang[GZ]	144	G4	Tatru Gou[XJ]	172	F7
Tangyang[JS]	80	F4	Taojiang[HN]	114	E4	Tatung[TW]	186	E2
Tangyang[SC]	138	F7	Taokeng[HN]	114	F6	Tau Lo Chau[HK]	176	B5
Tangyin[HEN]	106	F2	Taolaizhao[JL]	66	F3	Tawakkul[XJ]	172	H7
Tangyin[JX]	98	D4	Taolin[HN]	114	F3	Tawan[SN]	156	F3
Tangyu[SH]	74	C2	Taolin[SD]	102	F4	Tawu[TW]	186	D4
Tangyu[SN]	156	D6	Taolin[TW]	186	D4	Taxi[HL]	70	D4
Tangyuan[HL]	70	E5	Taolizhuang[HEB]	48	B2	Taxkorgan[XJ]	172	E7
Tangyuan[SD]	102	B3	Taoluo[SD]	102	F4	Tayang[HL]	128	C2
Tangzhai[AH]	90	C2	Taomiao[AH]	90	B3	Tayayi[HEB]	48	B4
Tangzhishan[BJ]	36	D3	Taonan[JL]	66	C2	Tayingzi[LN]	62	F2
Tangzhuang[HEN]	106	F4	Taoping[SN]	156	G7	Tayuan[HL]	70	C3
Tanhong[ZJ]	84	D4	Taopu[SH]	74	C2	Tayuling[TW]	186	E2
Tanhu Shan[ZJ]	84	F2	Taoran[LN]	62	H2	Tazhong[XJ]	172	I6
Tanhua[YN]	148	G5	Taosha[JX]	98	D3	Tazhuang[FJ]	94	D3
Tani[HN]	114	B3	Taoshan[NX]	168	B3	Tazicheng[HL]	70	B5
Tanintaweng Shan[XZ]	152	J4	Taoshan[NX]	168	C5	Taziling[LN]	62	G4
Tanjiahe[HEN]	106	E6	Taotiaogou[BJ]	36	C2	Têbo[XZ]	152	G4
Tanjiaqiao[AH]	90	E6	Taotun[LN]	62	G2	Tei Tong Tsai[HK]	176	B4
Tanjiashan[HN]	114	E5	Taowu[JS]	80	D5	Tekes He[XJ]	172	H4
Tanjiaying[SN]	156	F4	Taoxi[FJ]	94	B4	Tekes(Torkuztar)[XJ]	172	H4
Tanjiazhuang[TJ]	42	B2	Taoxi[HN]	114	D4	Telashi Hu[QH]	164	E6
Tanlang[GX]	124	G5	Taoxi[JX]	98	C4	Têli[XZ]	152	G5
Tanli[HEB]	48	D5	Taoxu[HN]	114	D8	Temeke[XJ]	172	L2
Tanlin[HB]	110	I4	Taoying[HEN]	106	C5	Têmpung[QH]	164	L3
Tanling[ZJ]	84	F3	Taoyu[CQ]	132	E5	Têmtog[XZ]	152	J5
Tanmen Gang[HI]	128	C2	Taoyuan[AH]	90	D6	Teng Xian[GX]	124	H4
Tanmen[HI]	128	C2	Taoyuan[CQ]	132	E2	Tengchong[YN]	148	D5
Tanniu[HI]	128	C2	Taoyuan[FJ]	94	C4	Tengger Feng[XJ]	172	K4
Tanpan[CQ]	132	C4	Taoyuan[GZ]	144	F2	Tengger Shamo[NM]	58	F8
Tanping[SX]	54	B6	Taoyuan[HB]	110	C3	Tengjia[SD]	102	I2
Tanqiu[JX]	98	C4	Taoyuan[HEB]	48	C6	Tengjiao[ZJ]	84	E5
Tanshan[GD]	118	I2	Taoyuan[HN]	114	D4	Tengke[NM]	58	P3
Tanshan[NX]	168	C4	Taoyuan[JS]	80	C3	Tengqiao Donghe[HI]	128	B3
Tanshanling[GS]	160	F4	Taoyuan[NX]	168	B5	Tengqiao[JX]	98	D4
Tanshi[ZJ]	84	C4	Taoyuan[SD]	102	F4	Tengtiao Jiang[YN]	148	H7
Tanshui Kang[TW]	186	E1	Taoyuan[TW]	186	D3	Tengzhai[HI]	128	B2
Tanshui[GD]	118	D4	Taoyuan[TW]	186	E2	Tengzhou[SD]	102	D4
Tanshui[TW]	186	E1	Taoyuan[YN]	148	F4	Tengzhuang[SD]	102	C2
Tantang Qu[GX]	124	G4	Taozhen[SN]	156	G3	Tengzhuangzi[HEB]	48	E5
Tantou Shan[ZJ]	84	G3	Taozhou[HN]	114	C4	Terak[XJ]	172	E5
Tantou[FJ]	94	E2	Taozhu[ZJ]	84	F4	Terak[XJ]	172	H5
Tantou[GD]	118	C4	Taozhuang[NX]	168	C3	Terekti[XJ]	172	I3
Tantou[HEN]	106	C3	Taozhuangzi[TJ]	42	B3	Tergun Daba Shan[GS]	160	B3
Tantou[HN]	114	D5	Tap Mun[HK]	176	F2	Terminal Maritimo[MC]	182	C2
Tantou[YN]	148	J2	Tap Shek Kok[HK]	176	B2	Tetima Hu[XJ]	172	L6
Tantu[JL]	66	D1	Tapu[HEN]	106	F2	Têwo[GS]	160	F5
Tantzu[TW]	186	D2	Tapu[TW]	186	D3	Teyong[JS]	80	F3
Tanwen[HI]	128	C2	Taqian[FJ]	94	D3	The Brothers[HK]	176	B3
Tanxi[HN]	114	D5	Taqian[JX]	98	E2	Tian He[HB]	110	D1
Tanxi[JX]	98	C3	Taqiao[JX]	98	E3	Tian Shan[XJ]	172	K4
Tanxi[ZJ]	84	D3	Taqu[YN]	148	E3	Tianba[CQ]	132	E2
Tanxia[GX]	124	H2	Tarbagatai Shan[XJ]	172	H2	Tianba[SC]	138	H6
Tanxu[GX]	124	G5	Tarêjong[XZ]	152	A4	Tianba[SN]	156	F8
Tanyi[SD]	102	E4	Targan Obo[NM]	58	L4	Tianba[YN]	148	F7
Tanying[GX]	124	F6	Targyailing[XZ]	152	D5	Tianbao[FJ]	94	C5
Tanzhesi[BJ]	36	C4	Tarian Gol[NM]	58	V11	Tianbao[HB]	110	C3
Tanzhi[SH]	74	D2	Tarim He[XJ]	172	I5	Tianbao[JX]	98	B3
Tanzishan[HN]	114	E6	Tarim Pendi[XJ]	172	I5	Tianbao[JX]	98	E2
Tao He[GS]	160	F5	Tarim[XJ]	172	I5	Tianbei[JL]	66	G3
Tao He[GS]	160	F5	Tarim[XJ]	172	I5	Tiancang[GS]	160	D2
Tao He[HB]	110	D1	Tarim[XJ]	172	K5	Tianchang[AH]	90	E4
Tao Jiang[JX]	98	B6	Tarlag[QH]	164	L7	Tianchang[JS]	80	E3
Taobei[JX]	98	D4	Tarlagjimdo[QH]	164	L7	Tiancheng[CQ]	132	E3
Taochang[AH]	90	E5	Tarlak[XJ]	172	J4	Tiancheng[SN]	156	C6
Taocheng[GX]	124	G3	Tarma[XZ]	152	F4	Tianchi Linchang[HI]	128	A3
Taocheng[HEN]	106	F4	Taro Co[XZ]	152	D4	Tianchi[HEN]	106	C3
Taochong[AH]	90	C6	Tarqi[NM]	58	N4	Tianchi[NX]	168	D3
Taochuan[HN]	114	D7	Tart[QH]	164	E3	Tianchidian[SX]	54	C4
Taochuan[SN]	156	D6	Tarungha[XZ]	152	D4	Tianci[CQ]	132	C4
Taocun[SD]	102	H2	Tarxiu[QH]	164	M5	Tianciwan[SN]	156	E3
Taocun[SX]	54	C6	Tarxü[QH]	164	L4	Tiancun[BJ]	36	D4
Taodong[JL]	66	C2	Tashan[HN]	114	E6	Tiancun[JX]	98	C5
Taoer He[JL]	66	C2	Tashan[JS]	80	C2	Tiande[LN]	62	H1

Name	Page	Grid
Tiandeng[GX]	124	E4
Tiandian[HB]	110	G3
Tiandong[GX]	124	E4
Tiandubang[SH]	74	C3
Tian'e[GX]	124	E2
Tian'e[HB]	110	G4
Tian'erhe[HB]	110	G4
Tianfanjie[JX]	98	D2
Tianfushan[SD]	102	I2
Tiangang Hu[JS]	80	C3
Tiangang[JL]	66	G4
Tianganghu[JS]	80	C3
Tiangong[FJ]	94	C5
Tianguan[CQ]	132	E5
Tianguan[HEN]	106	C4
Tiangutun[TJ]	42	A2
Tianhe[CQ]	132	E2
Tianhe[GX]	124	F3
Tianheng Dao[SD]	102	G3
Tianheng[SD]	102	G3
Tianhong[JX]	98	D2
Tianhu[HEN]	106	D3
Tianhuang[SD]	102	D4
Tianhuangping[ZJ]	84	D2
Tianjialaozhuang[NX]	168	C3
Tianjiashan[NX]	168	B2
Tianjiayao[HEB]	48	C3
Tianjiayu[TJ]	42	B1
Tianjin Xingang[TJ]	42	C4
Tianjin[TJ]	42	B3
Tianjun[QH]	164	L3
Tianlin[FJ]	94	B4
Tianlin[GX]	124	D3
Tianlong[GZ]	144	E4
Tianlu Shan[GD]	118	E4
Tianlu Shan[GD]	118	E4
Tianma Shan[SH]	74	C2
Tianma[SD]	102	E3
Tianmen He[HB]	110	F4
Tianmen Shan[HN]	114	C3
Tianmen[HB]	110	G4
Tianmen[HN]	114	D5
Tianmu Shan[AH]	90	F6
Tianmu Shan[ZJ]	84	D2
Tianmu Xi[ZJ]	84	D2
Tianmuhu[JS]	80	E5
Tianning[YN]	148	D6
Tianpeng[YN]	148	K7
Tianping Shan[GX]	124	G2
Tianping[GX]	124	H4
Tianping[GZ]	144	H3
Tianping[HN]	114	D5
Tianping[NX]	168	B5
Tianping[SH]	74	C2
Tianpu[HEN]	106	F6
Tianqiao[GZ]	144	F3
Tianqiao[GZ]	144	G3
Tianqiao[HEB]	48	D3
Tianqiao[LN]	62	E4
Tianqiaoling[JL]	66	J4
Tianqiaozi[BJ]	36	C2
Tianquan[SC]	138	H5
Tianshan Nanmai[XJ]	172	F5
Tianshan[JS]	80	E4
Tianshan[XJ]	172	N4
Tianshi[ZJ]	84	E4
Tianshifu[LN]	62	H3
Tianshui He[NX]	168	C3
Tianshui[GS]	160	G5
Tianshui[GS]	160	H4
Tianshui[LN]	62	E3
Tianshuihe[NX]	168	C2
Tianshuijing[TJ]	42	B4
Tiantai Shan[ZJ]	84	F3
Tiantai[GZ]	144	D2
Tiantai[JL]	66	F3
Tiantai[ZJ]	84	F3
Tiantang Ding[GD]	118	F3
Tiantang[GZ]	144	G2
Tiantang[HN]	114	D7
Tiantang[SN]	156	D6
Tiantangba[SC]	138	L7
Tiantangshan Shuiku[GD]	118	G3
Tiantangzhai[AH]	90	B5
Tiantangzhai[AH]	90	B5
Tiantangzhai[HB]	110	I3
Tianwan[GZ]	144	D5
Tianwan[HN]	114	C4
Tianwang[HB]	110	G3
Tianwang[JS]	80	E5
Tianwang[SN]	156	D6
Tianwei[SN]	128	C2
Tianxin[HN]	114	D5
Tianxin[JX]	98	C6
Tianxing[GZ]	144	G3
Tianxing[YN]	148	J7
Tianxingsi[CQ]	132	C4
Tianya Haijiao[HI]	128	B3
Tianya[HI]	128	B3
Tianyang[GX]	124	D4
Tianying[BJ]	36	D2
Tianyu[JX]	98	C4
Tianyuan[CQ]	132	F2
Tianyuan[FJ]	94	B3
Tianzai[HI]	128	B3
Tianzhe Shan[NX]	168	B4
Tianzhen[SX]	54	F1
Tianzhu Shan[AH]	90	C6
Tianzhu[BJ]	36	D3
Tianzhu[GS]	160	F4
Tianzhu[GZ]	144	H4
Tianzhuang[HN]	114	D4
Tianzhuang[SN]	156	F5
Tianzhuang[SN]	156	G3
Tianzhushan[JX]	98	E4
Tianzijing[JL]	66	E2
Tiaoguan[HB]	110	F5
Tiaoliangwu[TJ]	42	B2
Tiaoma[HN]	114	F4
Tiaoyu Tao[TW]	186	G1
Ticun[HEB]	48	C6
Tiechang[GD]	118	H2
Tiechang[SN]	156	F7
Tiechang[YN]	148	K7
Tiechanggou[XJ]	172	J2
Tiecheng[HEB]	48	D6
Tiefo[AH]	90	C3
Tiefo[JS]	80	D3
Tiefo[SC]	138	M4
Tiefu[JS]	80	D2
Tiegai[QH]	164	M4
Tiegai[QH]	164	M5
Tiehe[JX]	98	C2
Tiejiang[GZ]	144	C3
Tiekou[SD]	102	H2
Tieli[HL]	70	E5
Tieling[LN]	62	G2
Tielongtan[XJ]	172	G8
Tielu[HB]	110	D5
Tielu[HI]	128	B3
Tielu[JX]	98	C4
Tielu[SN]	156	E8
Tienchih[TW]	186	D3
Tienchung[TW]	186	D3
Tienhsiang[TW]	186	E2
Tieshan Gang[GX]	124	G6
Tieshan Qu[HB]	110	H4
Tieshan[CQ]	132	B2
Tieshan[FJ]	94	D2
Tieshan[JX]	98	F3
Tieshan[LN]	62	E6
Tieshangang Qu[GX]	124	G6
Tieshi[GZ]	144	E4
Tiesuo[YN]	148	F4
Tiesuoguan[SN]	156	C8
Tieta[SH]	74	D2
Tiewang[SN]	156	E6
Tiexi[SC]	138	M3
Tiezhuquan[NX]	168	C3
Tihujie[SN]	156	F5
Timen[SD]	102	C3
Timeng[HI]	128	C3
Tin Fu Tsai[HK]	176	C2
Tin Liu Tsuen[HK]	176	C2
Tin Shui Wai[HK]	176	B2
Ting Jiang[FJ]	94	B4
Ting Kau[HK]	176	C3
Ting Kok[HK]	176	D2
Tingdong[GZ]	144	G5
Tingdong[SH]	74	C3
Tingjiang[FJ]	94	E3
Tingkou[SN]	156	D5
Tingliang[GX]	124	E5
Tinglin[SH]	74	C3
Tingliuhe[HEB]	48	F4
Tingnan[GZ]	144	C3
Tingnan[SH]	74	C3
Tingpai Ling[HI]	128	B2
Tingping[FJ]	94	E3
Tingping[HN]	114	C6
Tingqian[HB]	110	I4
Tingri[XZ]	152	E5
Tingxi[FJ]	94	D5
Tingziba[GZ]	144	F3
Tingzijing[JL]	66	E3
Tiqiao[SH]	74	D2
Titch Am Chau[HK]	176	E4
Tiu Chung Chau[HK]	176	E3
Tiu Keng Leng[HK]	176	E3
Tiu Yue Yung[HK]	176	E3
Tiuri[XZ]	152	C4
Tiznap He[XJ]	172	F7
Toba[XZ]	152	J4
Todog[XJ]	172	I3
Tog Co[QH]	164	L5
Togco[QH]	164	M6
Togkuzdaban Shan[XJ]	172	J7
Togrog[NM]	58	L5
Togrog[NM]	58	U11
Togton[NM]	58	I7
Togton[NM]	58	X11
Togtun He[QH]	164	D6
Tohig Gol[QH]	164	E4
Tohoit[LN]	62	D3
Toinbo Shan[QH]	164	M4
Toinbo[QH]	164	K3
Toiroh[NM]	58	T10
Toksun[XJ]	172	L4
Tokum[XJ]	172	L6
Toli[QH]	164	M3
Toli[XJ]	172	I3
Toli[XJ]	172	I3
Toli[XJ]	172	K4
Tolo Harbour[HK]	176	D2
Tomort[XJ]	172	O4
Tomür Feng[XJ]	172	H4
Tong Fuk Miu Wan[HK]	176	B4
Tong Fuk[HK]	176	B4
Tong Po Chau[HK]	176	D4
Tong To[HK]	176	D1
Tong Yan[HK]	176	C2
Tong'an Qu[FJ]	94	D5
Tong'an[GX]	124	H3
Tong'an[JX]	98	B3
Tong'an[SC]	138	H9
Tongbai Shan[HB]	110	G2
Tongbai Shan[HEN]	106	E5
Tongbai[HEN]	106	E5
Tongbiguan[YN]	148	C6
Tongbu[AH]	90	D6
Tongbu[NM]	58	L6
Tongcheng[AH]	90	C5
Tongcheng[AH]	90	E4
Tongcheng[GS]	160	H5
Tongcheng[HB]	110	G5
Tongchuan[GS]	160	H4
Tongchuan[SN]	156	E6
Tongchun[FJ]	94	C4
Tongcun[ZJ]	84	C3
Tongda[HL]	70	C5
Tongdao[HN]	114	B6
Tongde[GX]	124	F3
Tongde[QH]	164	M5
Tongdian[YN]	148	E4
Tong'erpu[LN]	62	G3
Tongfang[FJ]	94	B4
Tongfang[JX]	98	E3
Tongfu[NX]	168	C2
Tonggor[SC]	138	H2
Tonggou[LN]	62	G3
Tonggu Zhang[GD]	118	I2
Tonggu Zui[HI]	128	D2

Tonggu[CQ]	132	F3
Tonggu[JX]	98	B3
Tongguan Shan[AH]	90	D6
Tongguan[SN]	156	G6
Tongguanyi[CQ]	132	C4
Tonggui[NX]	168	C2
Tonghai[YN]	148	H6
Tonghaikou[HB]	110	G4
Tonghe[GX]	124	H4
Tonghe[HL]	70	E6
Tonghe[SD]	102	F3
Tonghe[SD]	102	F3
Tonghua[JL]	66	F6
Tonghua[JL]	66	F6
Tonghua[SX]	54	B6
Tonghui He[BJ]	36	D4
Tonghuo Dashan[GX]	124	I4
Tongjia[JL]	66	F4
Tongjia[ZJ]	84	D3
Tongjiachong[HB]	110	F3
Tongjiadian[JL]	66	D3
Tongjiang[HL]	70	G5
Tongjiang[SC]	138	M4
Tongjiangkou[LN]	62	G2
Tongjijuan[NX]	168	D3
Tongjing[CQ]	132	C4
Tongjing[JS]	80	D5
Tongjinpu[HN]	114	C3
Tongjunzhuang[BJ]	36	D3
Tongken He[HL]	70	D5
Tonglao[GX]	124	E4
Tongli[JS]	80	F5
Tongliang[CQ]	132	C4
Tongliao[NM]	58	O6
Tonglin[GZ]	144	G4
Tonglin[JX]	98	C4
Tonglincun[TJ]	42	A2
Tongling[AH]	90	D6
Tongling[AH]	90	D6
Tongling[GX]	124	G4
Tonglu Yunhe[JS]	80	G4
Tonglu[ZJ]	84	D3
Tongmen[GD]	118	D4
Tongmian[GX]	124	E6
Tongmu[GX]	124	G3
Tongmu[JX]	98	A4
Tongmuluo[HN]	114	D7
Tongmuxi[HN]	114	C5
Tongnan[CQ]	132	B3
Tongnan[HL]	70	C4
Tongpan Shan[ZJ]	84	E5
Tongping[JX]	98	B4
Tongpu[ZJ]	84	E5
Tongqi Yunhe[JS]	80	G5
Tongqian[SN]	156	E7
Tongqiangou[SX]	54	E3
Tongqianguan[SN]	156	F8
Tongqiao[NX]	168	C2
Tongqiao[SH]	74	D3
Tongqin[ZJ]	84	D4
Tongqing[GD]	118	C5
Tongren[GZ]	144	H3
Tongren[HI]	128	C2
Tongren[QH]	164	O5
Tongshan[HB]	110	H5
Tongshan[JS]	80	C2
Tongshan[JX]	98	D3
Tongshan[SX]	54	C6
Tongshang[JS]	80	F3
Tongshankou[HB]	110	H4
Tongsheng[HB]	110	D2
Tongshi He[HI]	128	B3
Tongshi[SD]	102	D4
Tongtian Gang[HI]	128	A3
Tongtian He[QH]	164	F6
Tongtian He[QH]	164	H6
Tongwan[GX]	124	G4
Tongwan[HN]	114	C5
Tongwei[GS]	160	G5
Tongxi[CQ]	132	C4
Tongxi[CQ]	132	E5
Tongxiang[ZJ]	84	E2
Tongxin[NX]	168	B4
Tongxin[YN]	148	G8
Tongxing[JS]	80	E2
Tongxu[HEN]	106	F3
Tongyang Yunhe[JS]	80	F4
Tongyang[JS]	80	D2
Tongyi[HN]	114	E7
Tongyi[LN]	62	F5
Tongyu Shan[GX]	124	F5
Tongyu Yunhe[JS]	80	F3
Tongyu[JL]	66	D3
Tongyu[SX]	54	E5
Tongyu[ZJ]	84	F4
Tongyuan[GS]	160	F4
Tongyuan[JX]	98	D3
Tongyuanpu[LN]	62	G4
Tongzha[AH]	90	E5
Tongzhaipu[HEN]	106	D5
Tongzhen[SN]	156	G2
Tongzhou Qu[BJ]	36	D4
Tongzhou[GZ]	144	E5
Tongzhou[JS]	80	G4
Tongzi[CQ]	132	D4
Tongzi[GZ]	144	E2
Toroi[QH]	164	G4
Toson Hu[QH]	164	I3
Tost He[NM]	58	G8
Tost[NM]	58	S11
Tost[XJ]	172	K2
Toubaihu[TJ]	42	C2
Toubei[JX]	98	D5
Toucheng[TW]	186	E2
Toudao Chuan[SN]	156	D3
Toudao Jiang[JL]	66	H5
Toudao[JL]	66	J5
Toudaodun[NX]	168	C2
Toudaogou[TJ]	42	C3
Toudaohezi[JL]	66	K4
Toudaoshui[YN]	148	F6
Toudaoxue[BJ]	36	D2
Toudaoyingzi[LN]	62	C4
Toudu[CQ]	132	D5
Toufang[GS]	160	G6
Toufen[TW]	186	D2
Touguan[NX]	168	B2
Touguo[HI]	128	B2
Toulin[HL]	70	G5
Toumen Shan[ZJ]	84	F4
Tounan[TW]	186	D3
Toupai[GX]	124	H3
Toupo[HI]	128	B3
Touqiao[SH]	74	D3
Toutai[XJ]	172	J3
Toutuo[ZJ]	84	F4
Touying[NX]	168	C4
Touyuan[HI]	128	C2
Touzeng[JS]	80	F2
Touzha[NX]	168	C2
Touzhan[HL]	70	B5
Toxkan He[XJ]	172	F5
Toyun[XJ]	172	E5
Tozê Kangri[XZ]	152	C2
Tra Qu[QH]	164	L7
Tsak Yue Wu[HK]	176	E2
Tsaotun[TW]	186	D3
Tseng Lan Shue[HK]	176	E3
Tseng Tau[HK]	176	E2
Tsengwen Hsi[TW]	186	D3
Tsengwen Shuiku[TW]	186	D3
Tseung Kwan O[HK]	176	E3
Tsim Bei Tsui[HK]	176	C1
Tsim Chau[HK]	176	F2
Tsim Sha Tsui[HK]	176	D3
Tsin Yue Wan[HK]	176	A4
Tsing Fai Tong[HK]	176	C2
Tsing Lung Tau[HK]	176	C3
Tsing Shan Wan[HK]	176	B3
Tsing Yi[HK]	176	C3
Tsiu Keng San Wat[HK]	176	C2
Tso Kung Tam[HK]	176	C2
Tso Wan[HK]	176	C3
Tso Wo Hang[HK]	176	E2
Tsochen[TW]	186	D3
Tsuen Kam Au[HK]	176	C2
Tsuen Wan[HK]	176	C3
Tsuifeng[TW]	186	E2
Tsung Yuen Ha[HK]	176	D1
Tsz Wan Shan[HK]	176	D3
Tuan He[HEN]	106	C4
Tuanba[CQ]	132	F2
Tuanbao[HB]	110	C4
Tuanbo[TJ]	42	B4
Tuanbowa Shuiku[TJ]	42	B4
Tuanfeng[HB]	110	H4
Tuanhe[HN]	114	B6
Tuanjie Feng[XJ]	172	G8
Tuanjie[GS]	160	B3
Tuanjie[HL]	70	E4
Tuanjie[JL]	66	C3
Tuanjie[NM]	58	T10
Tuanjie[YN]	148	E5
Tuanjiecun[XJ]	172	L5
Tuanpi[HB]	110	I4
Tuanshan[LN]	62	F4
Tuanshansi[HB]	110	F5
Tuanshuitou[SX]	54	C4
Tuantian[YN]	148	G7
Tuanwa[TJ]	42	B4
Tuanwang[SD]	102	G3
Tuanxi[GZ]	144	F3
Tuanyuan[HN]	114	G4
Tuanzhou[HN]	114	E3
Tuban[SX]	54	B3
Tubo[GX]	124	G3
Tubu Dao[SD]	102	H3
Tuchang[GZ]	144	F5
Tucheng[GZ]	144	D2
Tucheng[HB]	110	D2
Tucheng[HEB]	48	D2
Tuchengzi[HL]	70	E5
Tuci[ZJ]	84	F3
Tudi[CQ]	132	D4
Tudiao[GZ]	144	G2
Tuding[JL]	66	F4
Tudingzi[JL]	66	I4
Tu'e[YN]	148	E4
Tuen Mun[HK]	176	B2
Tuen Tsui[HK]	176	F2
Tuen Tsz Wai[HK]	176	B2
Tufang[FJ]	94	B4
Tugang[SN]	156	G4
Tuguanya[HB]	110	E2
Tuhai He[SD]	102	D2
Tuhe[TJ]	42	B4
Tuhuang[SC]	138	N4
Tuji[SN]	156	F5
Tukan[CQ]	132	D4
Tukouzi[LN]	62	I2
Tuku[TW]	186	D3
Tulag Ar Gol[QH]	164	D4
Tulai He[QH]	164	K2
Tulai Nanshan[GS]	160	C3
Tulai Nanshan[QH]	164	J1
Tulai Nanshan[QH]	164	K2
Tulai Shan[QH]	164	K2
Tulan[TW]	186	E4
Tule Mod[NM]	58	N5
Tuling[SX]	54	E4
Tulongshan[HL]	70	F5
Tümantal[XJ]	172	F6
Tumba[QH]	164	M4
Tumd Youqi[NM]	58	I7
Tumd Youqi[NM]	58	W11
Tumd Zuoqi[NM]	58	I7
Tumd Zuoqi[NM]	58	X11
Tumen Jiang[JL]	66	I5
Tumen Shuiku[LN]	62	G4
Tumen Us[NM]	58	T11
Tumen[GS]	160	G5
Tumen[HB]	110	D1
Tumen[JL]	66	J5
Tumen[SX]	54	C5
Tumenzi[HEB]	48	G3
Tumxuk[XJ]	172	G5
Tumxuk[XJ]	172	G6
Tüna[XZ]	152	F6
Tunbao[HB]	110	C4
Tunchang[HI]	128	C2
Tung A[HK]	176	F3
Tung Chung[HK]	176	B3

Tung Kwo Chau[HK]	176	F4
Tung Lung Chau[HK]	176	E4
Tung O[HK]	176	D4
Tung Wan Mei[HK]	176	B4
Tung Wan[HK]	176	C4
Tungchi Yu[TW]	186	C3
Tungchuan Tao[FJ]	94	F4
Tungho[TW]	186	E4
Tunghsiao[TW]	186	D2
Tungkang[TW]	186	D4
Tunglo[TW]	186	D2
Tungo Wan[HK]	176	D4
Tungru[XZ]	152	B2
Tungsha Tao[FJ]	94	F3
Tungshan[TW]	186	E2
Tungshih[TW]	186	D3
Tungyin LieTao[FJ]	94	F3
Tunjiao[HI]	128	C2
Tunli[SX]	54	B5
Tunliu[SX]	54	D5
Tunqiu[GX]	124	G3
Tunsheng[GS]	160	D3
Tuo He[AH]	90	D3
Tuo Hu[AH]	90	D3
Tuo Jiang[SC]	138	J6
Tuo Shui[HN]	114	D7
Tuo'an[YN]	148	G5
Tuochangbu[NX]	168	B4
Tuocheng[GD]	118	H2
Tuochuan[JX]	98	C3
Tuochuan[JX]	98	E2
Tuo'erxiang[SN]	156	F3
Tuoheping Co[XZ]	152	C2
Tuoji Dao[SD]	102	G1
Tuojue[SC]	138	H8
Tuokou[HN]	114	B5
Tuolai Nanshan[GS]	160	D3
Tuoli[BJ]	36	C4
Tuolin[SH]	74	C3
Tuolong[GX]	124	E5
Tuolu[GX]	124	E5
Tuonan[HEB]	48	C4
Tuoniang Jiang[GX]	124	C3
Tuoning Liedao[GD]	118	G4
Tuoshan[LN]	62	E5
Tuoshi[SN]	156	C6
Tuowu[SC]	138	H7
Tuoxi[FJ]	94	E2
Tuoxing Shuiku[HI]	128	A3
Tuoyaoling[JL]	66	F5
Tuoyaozi[HL]	70	F5
Tuozhamin[NM]	58	O2
Tupan[GX]	124	D4
Tuping[CQ]	132	F4
Tuping[GZ]	144	F2
Tupo[NX]	168	B3
Tuqiang[HL]	70	B2
Tuqiao[AH]	90	D5
Tuqiao[JL]	66	G3
Tuqiao[JS]	80	E5
Tuqiao[SN]	156	E5
Tuqiaozi[NX]	168	C4
Tuquan[NM]	58	N5
Turgen[XJ]	172	I4
Turpan Pendi[XJ]	172	L4
Turpan[XJ]	172	L4
Turugart Kou'an[XJ]	172	E5
Tushan[JL]	66	J5
Tushan[JS]	80	C2
Tushan[SD]	102	F2
Tutai[HB]	110	E2
Tutan'gou[NX]	168	C3
Tuwei He[SN]	156	G2
Tuwei[TW]	186	E3
Tuwo[SX]	54	D6
Tuxi[GZ]	144	F2
Tuxiang[CQ]	132	F3
Tuzhai[FJ]	94	D5
Tuzhuang[SD]	102	F3

U

U Qagan[QH]	164	K5
Ud Qu[NM]	58	G8
Udoima[SC]	138	C2
Ugan Gol[NM]	58	T10
Uher Hudag[NM]	58	W10
Ujur Gol[NM]	58	G7
Ujur Gol[NM]	58	T10
Ujur Gol[NM]	58	U10
Ul Shan[NM]	58	V11
Ulan Buh Shamo[NM]	58	F8
Ulan Buh Shamo[NM]	58	S11
Ulan Hua[JL]	66	C3
Ulan Hudag[NM]	58	W10
Ulan Od[JL]	66	D3
Ulan Qab[NM]	58	J7
Ulan Tug[JL]	66	E3
Ulan Ul Hu[QH]	164	C6
Ulan Ul Shan[QH]	164	D6
Ulan[NM]	58	V11
Ulan[QH]	164	K4
Ulanhot[NM]	58	O4
Ulansuhai Nur[NM]	58	H7
Ulansuhai Nur[NM]	58	U11
Ulastai Kou'an[XJ]	172	M3
Ulastai[XJ]	172	I4
Ulastai[XJ]	172	K4
Ulgai[NM]	58	M5
Ulgain Gobi[NM]	58	L5
Ulgain Gol[NM]	58	M5
Ulugqat[XJ]	172	E6
Ulugsu He[XJ]	172	K7
Ulungur He[XJ]	172	L2
Ulungur Hu[XJ]	172	K2
Undralt[NM]	58	F9
Urad Houqi[NM]	58	G7
Urad Houqi[NM]	58	T10
Urad Qianqi[NM]	58	H7
Urad Qianqi[NM]	58	U11
Urad Zhongqi[NM]	58	H7
Uragxan[NM]	58	N3
Urdoi[XZ]	152	E4
Urho Qu[XJ]	172	J2
Urmston Road[HK]	176	B2
Urru Co[XZ]	152	E4
Urt Moron[QH]	164	F3
Urt Moron[QH]	164	F4
Urt Tal[NM]	58	L6
Ürümqi[XJ]	172	K4
Ustun Tag[XJ]	172	H8
Üstün Tag[XZ]	152	B2
Usu[XJ]	172	J3
Uxin Ju[NM]	58	H8
Uxin Qi[NM]	58	H8
Uxin[NM]	58	X11
Uxxarbax[XJ]	172	F7
Uyerin Gol[HL]	70	C5
Uzbel Shankou[XJ]	172	D6

V

Victoria Harbour[HK]	176	D3
Victoria Peak[HK]	176	D3

W

Wabu Hu[AH]	90	C4
Wabu[AH]	90	C4
Wacanghe[HB]	110	C3
Wachai[SC]	138	G5
Wachang[YN]	148	E5
Wadian[HEN]	106	F1
Wado[XZ]	152	J4
Wadu[YN]	148	E5
Wafang[JL]	66	C2
Wafang[YN]	148	E5
Wafangba[SN]	156	C7

Wafangdian[LN]	62	C3
Wafangdian[LN]	62	E5
Wafangzi[LN]	62	D3
Wagang[HEN]	106	F2
Waglan Island[HK]	176	E4
Wah Fu[HK]	176	D4
Wai Tau Tsuen[HK]	176	D2
Wai'an[TW]	186	C3
Waichangshan Dao[LN]	62	F5
Waichangshan Haixia[LN]	62	F5
Waifang Shan[HEN]	106	D4
Waigang[SH]	74	C2
Waigoumen[HEB]	48	D2
Wailuo[GD]	118	C6
Waipu[TW]	186	D2
Waishan[FJ]	94	D4
Waishantingchou[TW]	186	D3
Waitoushan[LN]	62	G3
Waitun[FJ]	94	D2
Waizi[HEN]	106	D5
Walagan[HL]	70	C2
Wali[BJ]	36	C3
Walong[AH]	90	C6
Walung[XZ]	152	J5
Waluo[SN]	156	G2
Wama[YN]	148	D5
Wamiao[SN]	156	E8
Wamo Zangbo[XZ]	152	C4
Wan He[AH]	90	C6
Wan Tsai[HK]	176	E4
Wan'an Tan[HI]	128	E7
Wan'an Xi[FJ]	94	B4
Wan'an[FJ]	94	B4
Wan'an[FJ]	94	C3
Wan'an[FJ]	94	C4
Wan'an[JX]	98	B5
Wan'an[SH]	74	C1
Wanbao[HL]	70	D6
Wanbao[HN]	114	D5
Wanbao[JL]	66	B2
Wanbao[JL]	66	I5
Wanbi[YN]	148	G4
Wancang[ZJ]	84	E3
Wanchang[JL]	66	F4
Wanchong[HI]	128	B3
Wanchong[JX]	98	C4
Wancun[JX]	98	E3
Wanda Shan[HL]	70	G5
Wande[SD]	102	C3
Wande[YN]	148	H4
Wandi[HEB]	48	C7
Wandian[HB]	110	G3
Wandianzi[LN]	62	I3
Wanding[YN]	148	D6
Wanfeng[SD]	102	B4
Wanfenghu[GZ]	144	D6
Wanfu He[SD]	102	B4
Wanfu[AH]	90	C4
Wanfu[JX]	98	B4
Wang Tau Hom[HK]	176	D3
Wang Chau[HK]	176	C2
Wang Chau[HK]	176	F3
Wang Gaxun Meikuang[QH]	164	J4
Wang Hu[HB]	110	I5
Wang Leng Tau[HK]	176	E1
Wang Toi Shan[HK]	176	C2
Wang Tong[HK]	176	B3
Wang Tong[HK]	176	B4
Wangan Tao(Pachao Tao)[TW]	186	C3
Wang'an[TW]	186	C3
Wangbaoyingzi[LN]	62	C4
Wangbei[TJ]	42	C3
Wangben[JL]	66	D4
Wangbi[SX]	54	D6
Wangbin[LN]	62	G3
Wangbu[GD]	118	F2
Wangcang[SC]	138	L3
Wangcao[GZ]	144	F2
Wangchang[HEB]	48	C6
Wangcheng[HB]	110	F3
Wangcheng[HN]	114	E4
Wangchenggu[HEN]	106	G2
Wangchengzhuang[SX]	54	F2
Wangchu[BJ]	36	C4

Wangchuan[SN] 156 F6
Wangcun[AH] 90 D7
Wangcun[HEB] 48 D5
Wangcun[SD] 102 D3
Wangcun[SD] 102 G3
Wangcun[SX] 54 D5
Wangcun[SX] 54 D5
Wangcundian[SD] 102 C2
Wangcunkou[ZJ] 84 C4
Wangdain[XZ] 152 F5
Wangdian[GX] 124 D3
Wangdian[HB] 110 E4
Wangdian[HEN] 106 E5
Wangdian[HEN] 106 G5
Wangdian[JS] 80 D4
Wangdian[ZJ] 84 E2
Wangdianzi[HEB] 48 F4
Wangdong[GX] 124 F2
Wangdong[GZ] 144 G5
Wangdu[HEB] 48 C5
Wangduzhuang[TJ] 42 B3
Wang'erding[TJ] 42 A3
Wangfen[SD] 102 E3
Wangfengtai[LN] 62 C4
Wangfu[GD] 118 D5
Wangfu[GX] 124 I4
Wangfu[LN] 62 E2
Wangfu[ZJ] 84 C3
Wangfuzhan[JL] 66 F3
Wanggang[HEN] 106 E5
Wanggang[JS] 80 F3
Wanggang[SH] 74 D2
Wanggao[GX] 124 I3
Wanggou[JS] 80 B2
Wanggou[SD] 102 E4
Wangguan[GS] 160 G6
Wangguantun[SX] 54 E1
Wangguiyao[NM] 58 X11
Wanghai[LN] 62 D4
Wanghai[SH] 74 C2
Wanghe[HB] 110 F2
Wanghe[SX] 54 D5
Wanghu[LN] 62 D4
Wanghu[SX] 54 E2
Wanghutun[HEB] 48 B3
Wangji[AH] 90 D3
Wangji[HB] 110 F3
Wangji[HEN] 106 F3
Wangji[JS] 80 C3
Wangji[JS] 80 D3
Wangji[SD] 102 D2
Wangjia[CQ] 132 E3
Wangjia[SC] 138 L4
Wangjia[ZJ] 84 G3
Wangjiaba[AH] 90 B4
Wangjiabian[SN] 156 G2
Wangjiachang Shuiku[HN] 114 D3
Wangjiachang[HN] 114 D3
Wangjiadao[LN] 62 G5
Wangjiadian[TJ] 42 B1
Wangjiafan[HB] 110 E4
Wangjiagou[NX] 168 C1
Wangjiahe[SN] 156 E7
Wangjiajing[HEB] 48 C6
Wangjiajuan[NX] 168 C3
Wangjialeng[SN] 156 G2
Wangjiang[AH] 90 C6
Wangjiangjing[ZJ] 84 E2
Wangjiaping[HN] 114 C3
Wangjiashan[GS] 160 G4
Wangjiataozhuang[NX] 168 C4
Wangjiawan[NX] 168 B5
Wangjiawan[SN] 156 F3
Wangjiayuan[NX] 168 C4
Wangjiayuanzi[NX] 168 B3
Wangjiazhai[GZ] 144 C4
Wangjiazhuang[SX] 54 D3
Wangjing[NX] 168 B4
Wangjun Ding[GX] 124 H5
Wangkar[XZ] 152 J4
Wangkou[HEB] 48 C6
Wangkou[TJ] 42 A4
Wangkuai Shuiku[HEB] 48 B5
Wangkuangcun[TJ] 42 A4

Wangkui[HL] 70 D5
Wanglang[SH] 74 C2
Wanglanzhuang[HEB] 48 F4
Wanglao[SD] 102 C3
Wanglaopu[BJ] 36 B4
Wanglejing[NX] 168 D3
Wangli[GX] 124 E6
Wangling[HN] 114 F5
Wanglinkou[HEB] 48 B5
Wangliu[HEN] 106 G5
Wangliu[SD] 102 F3
Wanglou Gang[HI] 128 A3
Wanglou He[HI] 128 B3
Wanglou[JS] 80 D2
Wangluo[HEN] 106 E4
Wangmao[GX] 124 G5
Wangmao[SX] 54 C6
Wangmin[NX] 168 B5
Wangmo[GZ] 144 E5
Wangmudu[JX] 98 B6
Wangmuzhuang[TJ] 42 C2
Wangou[JL] 66 G5
Wangoumen[HEB] 48 E2
Wangpan Shan[ZJ] 84 F2
Wangpanshan[SN] 156 D3
Wangpeng[HEN] 106 G5
Wangping[HEN] 106 D4
Wangpu[GS] 160 G5
Wangqi[JL] 66 G4
Wangqiao[HB] 110 F5
Wangqiao[HEB] 48 C7
Wangqing[JL] 66 J4
Wangqingmen[LN] 62 I3
Wangqingtuo[TJ] 42 A3
Wangqinzhuang[TJ] 42 B3
Wangren[AH] 90 B3
Wangsang[GS] 160 F6
Wangsha[GD] 118 D4
Wangshi[HB] 110 G4
Wangshi[SX] 54 C3
Wangshiwan[HN] 114 F5
Wangshu[HEB] 48 E6
Wangsiying[BJ] 36 D4
Wangtai[FJ] 94 C3
Wangtai[GS] 160 F5
Wangtai[SD] 102 F3
Wangtan[HEB] 48 F4
Wangtao[SX] 54 D5
Wangtian[HEN] 106 F4
Wangtian'e[JL] 66 H6
Wangting[JS] 80 F5
Wangting[SH] 74 D3
Wangtong[HEB] 48 D6
Wangtuan[AH] 90 C3
Wangtuan[NX] 168 C4
Wangtuan[SD] 102 H2
Wangtuanzhuang[NX] 168 B4
Wangu[CQ] 132 B4
Wangu[CQ] 132 F2
Wangu[HEN] 106 F2
Wangwa[NX] 168 C4
Wangwenzhuang[TJ] 42 B4
Wangwu Shan[HEN] 106 D2
Wangwu Shan[SX] 54 D6
Wangwu[HI] 128 B2
Wangwu[SD] 102 F3
Wangwuqiao[HEN] 106 F5
Wangxia[HI] 128 B2
Wangxian[JX] 98 C4
Wangxian[SX] 54 C6
Wangxing[GS] 160 H5
Wangxing[JS] 80 E3
Wangyan[SN] 156 G7
Wangyang[SC] 138 J6
Wangyao Shuiku[SN] 156 F4
Wangyao[SN] 156 F4
Wangyaoxian[NX] 168 C4
Wangyi Qu[SN] 156 F5
Wangying Shuiku[HB] 110 H5
Wangying[HB] 110 B4
Wangying[HEB] 48 E2
Wangyuan[NX] 168 C2
Wangzandarma[QH] 164 J6
Wangzhai[AH] 90 C2

Wangzhai[FJ] 94 D3
Wangzhai[SX] 54 F4
Wangzhai[ZJ] 84 D4
Wangzhuang[BJ] 36 D4
Wangzhuang[HEN] 106 F2
Wangzhuang[JS] 80 D2
Wangzhuang[SD] 102 C3
Wangzhuang[SN] 156 F5
Wangzhuang[SN] 156 G7
Wangzhuang[SX] 54 C6
Wangzhuang[TJ] 42 B1
Wangzhuang[TJ] 42 B2
Wangzhuangbu[SX] 54 E2
Wangzuo[BJ] 36 C4
Wanhe[HB] 110 G2
Wanhe[JX] 98 C5
Wanjia[AH] 90 F6
Wanjia[HB] 110 H5
Wanjia[LN] 62 C4
Wanjialing[LN] 62 F5
Wanjiazhai[SX] 54 C2
Wanjin[HEN] 106 F4
Wanjung[TW] 186 E3
Wanli Qu[JX] 98 C3
Wanli[AH] 90 E5
Wanli[TW] 186 E1
Wanling[HI] 128 B2
Wanlong[HL] 70 C6
Wanlong[JX] 98 B6
Wanma[YN] 148 G4
Wanmao[GS] 160 F5
Wanmin[HN] 114 B3
Wannian[JX] 98 E3
Wanning Shuiku[HI] 128 C3
Wanning[HI] 128 C3
Wanping[JS] 80 F5
Wanquan He[HI] 128 C2
Wanquan Hu[XZ] 152 C2
Wanquan[FJ] 94 C3
Wanquan[HEB] 48 B3
Wanquan[HEB] 48 B3
Wanquan[HI] 128 C2
Wanquan[SX] 54 B6
Wanrong[SX] 54 B6
Wanshan Qundao[GD] 118 F4
Wanshan Tequ[GZ] 144 H3
Wanshan[SC] 138 L5
Wanshan[ZJ] 84 E4
Wansheng Qu[CQ] 132 C5
Wanshengyong[HEB] 48 D2
Wanshi[SH] 74 C2
Wanshiping[HB] 110 D5
Wanshou[AH] 90 F4
Wanshun[JL] 66 E3
Wantan[HB] 110 D4
Wantan[HEN] 106 E3
Wantang[HN] 114 C6
Wantang[YN] 148 I7
Wantian[GX] 124 H2
Wantian[JX] 98 C6
Wantouqiao[HN] 114 C6
Wantun[GZ] 144 D5
Wanwu[FJ] 94 E3
Wanxiang[SH] 74 D3
Wanyang Shan[HN] 114 F6
Wanyang Shan[JX] 98 A5
Wanyang Shan[JX] 98 B5
Wanyuan[SC] 138 N3
Wanzai[GD] 118 F4
Wanzai[JX] 98 B3
Wanzhai[HB] 110 C4
Wanzhen[SN] 156 G2
Wanzhou Qu[CQ] 132 E3
Wanzi Hu[HN] 114 E4
Wanzu[CQ] 132 E4
Waqên[SC] 138 H2
Wase[YN] 148 F5
Washi[SC] 138 M3
Watang[SX] 54 C3
Wating[NX] 168 C5
Watuan[AH] 90 D3
Wawo[LN] 62 F5
Wawu[HEN] 106 D4
Waxi[GD] 118 H3

Name	Page	Grid
Waxie[SH]	74	D2
Waxü[SC]	138	D3
Waxxari[XJ]	172	K6
Wayao[NM]	58	V11
Wayaogou[HEN]	106	C4
Wazijie[SN]	156	G5
Wei He[GS]	160	G5
Wei He[HEB]	48	C7
Wei He[HEN]	106	F2
Wei He[SD]	102	B3
Wei He[SD]	102	F3
Wei He[SN]	156	F6
Wei Shui[HN]	114	E4
Wei Xian[HEB]	48	B7
Wei Xian[HEB]	48	C7
Weibao[SH]	74	D2
Weichang[HEB]	48	E2
Weichang[HL]	70	F5
Weichang[TJ]	42	C4
Weicheng[GZ]	144	E4
Weicheng[SC]	138	I4
Weideng[YN]	148	E3
Weidong[HL]	70	E5
Weifang[SD]	102	F3
Weihai Gang[SD]	102	I2
Weihai[SD]	102	I2
Weihe[GS]	160	G5
Weihu Ling[JL]	66	H4
Weihui[HEN]	106	F2
Weiji[AH]	90	D3
Weijiahe[BJ]	36	E3
Weijiang[GX]	124	H2
Weijiaqiao[HEB]	48	C6
Weijiaqiao[SN]	156	C8
Weijiatai[BJ]	36	E3
Weijiatai[SN]	156	G7
Weijiawan[SX]	54	B4
Weijing[NM]	58	I6
Weilijie[GX]	124	G4
Weima[SX]	54	E4
Weimin[FJ]	94	C2
Weimo[YN]	148	J7
Weinan[SN]	156	F6
Weining[GZ]	144	C4
Weiping[ZJ]	84	C3
Weiqiao[SD]	102	D2
Weiqing Ling[GX]	124	G2
Weiqiu[HEN]	106	F2
Weirong[GS]	160	G5
Weishahe[JL]	66	G6
Weishan Hu[SD]	102	D5
Weishan[HL]	70	D4
Weishan[HN]	114	D4
Weishan[SD]	102	D5
Weishan[YN]	148	F5
Weishanhu Shuiku[GZ]	144	D5
Weishe[GZ]	144	C5
Weishi[HEN]	106	F3
Weitang[JS]	80	E5
Weitian[FJ]	94	D2
Weitou Wan[FJ]	94	D5
Weitou[FJ]	94	D5
Weiwan[SD]	102	B5
Weixi[HN]	114	C4
Weixi[YN]	148	E3
Weixin[GX]	124	E5
Weixin[GZ]	144	D3
Weixin[HN]	114	D3
Weixin[YN]	148	K3
Weiyuan[GS]	160	G5
Weiyuan[SC]	138	J6
Weiyuan[SX]	54	D2
Weiyuanpu[LN]	62	H2
Weizha[NX]	168	C1
Weizhou Dao[GX]	124	G6
Weizhou[GX]	124	G6
Weizhou[NX]	168	C3
Weizhuang[SD]	102	B3
Weizhuang[SX]	54	B6
Weizhuang[SX]	54	C6
Weizhuangzi[NX]	168	C3
Weizigou[JL]	66	F3
Weizigou[LN]	62	F2
Weiziping[SN]	156	E7
Weiziyu[LN]	62	H3
Wen He[SD]	102	E3
Wen He[SD]	102	E4
Wen Xian[HEN]	106	E3
Wen'an[HB]	110	E4
Wen'an[HEB]	48	D5
Wenbei[JX]	98	C5
Wenbu[NX]	168	B5
Wenchang[HI]	128	C2
Wenchang[ZJ]	84	D3
Wencheng[HEN]	106	E4
Wencheng[HI]	128	C2
Wencheng[JX]	98	F3
Wencheng[SX]	54	B5
Wencheng[ZJ]	84	E5
Wenchuan Xi[FJ]	94	C4
Wenchuan[SC]	138	I4
Wencun[GD]	118	E5
Wendeng[SD]	102	I2
Wendi[GX]	124	H6
Wendou[HB]	110	B5
Wenfang[FJ]	94	B4
Wenfeng[CQ]	132	D4
Wenfeng[CQ]	132	F2
Wenfeng[FJ]	94	C5
Wenfeng[HI]	128	C2
Wenfenglu[SD]	102	F2
Weng Jiang[GD]	118	F2
Weng'an[GZ]	144	F3
Weng'ang[GZ]	144	F5
Wengcheng[GD]	118	F2
Wengda[SC]	138	F4
Wengdong[GZ]	144	H3
Wengjiang[HN]	114	F4
Wengong[SC]	138	J5
Wengshui[YN]	148	E2
Wengtai[GZ]	144	F5
Wengtian[HI]	128	C2
Wengui[HI]	128	B2
Wengxi[GZ]	144	F3
Wengxiang[GZ]	144	F4
Wengyang[ZJ]	84	E4
Wengyuan[GD]	118	G2
Wenheng[FJ]	94	B4
Wenhua[SH]	74	C3
Wenji[AH]	90	B3
Wenjia[FJ]	94	E4
Wenjia[HN]	114	D3
Wenjiafangzi[TJ]	42	B3
Wenjiang Qu[SC]	138	I5
Wenjiang[FJ]	94	C4
Wenjiang[FJ]	94	D3
Wenjiangsi[SN]	156	C7
Wenjiao[FJ]	94	C3
Wenjiashi[HN]	114	F4
Wenjiazhuang[SX]	54	E4
Wenjing[YN]	148	F6
Wenlan He[HI]	128	B2
Wenlan[TW]	186	E3
Wenlang[GD]	118	E2
Wenli[GX]	124	G5
Wenlian[HI]	128	B2
Wenlin[HI]	128	C2
Wenling[ZJ]	84	F4
Wenlong[JX]	98	B7
Wenlong[YN]	148	F6
Wenluo[HI]	128	B3
Wenming[HN]	114	D6
Wenming[HN]	114	F7
Wenping[HN]	114	C6
Wenqiao[JX]	98	D2
Wenqing[HI]	128	B2
Wenqu[HEN]	106	C5
Wenquan (Arixang)[XJ]	172	H3
Wenquan[BJ]	36	C3
Wenquan[CQ]	132	E2
Wenquan[GD]	118	F3
Wenquan[HB]	110	I4
Wenquan[HI]	128	C2
Wenquan[JL]	66	H5
Wenquan[JX]	98	D3
Wenquan[QH]	164	D7
Wenquan[QH]	164	L5
Wenquan[QH]	164	L5
Wenquan[SC]	138	G8
Wenquan[SD]	102	E3
Wenquan[SD]	102	G3
Wenquan[SX]	54	C3
Wenquan[YN]	148	G4
Wenru[HI]	128	C2
Wenshan[YN]	148	J7
Wenshang[SD]	102	C4
Wenshi[HI]	128	C2
Wenshui[GZ]	144	E2
Wenshui[SN]	156	C6
Wenshui[SX]	54	D4
Wensu[XJ]	172	H5
Wentai[SD]	160	H4
Wentang[JX]	98	B4
Wentian[HN]	114	D5
Wentuan[SD]	102	F4
Wenwu[YN]	148	G7
Wenxi[SX]	54	C6
Wenxiakou Shuiku[HB]	110	F3
WenXian[GS]	160	G6
Wenxing[FJ]	94	C4
Wenxing[YN]	148	J4
Wenyu He[BJ]	36	D3
Wenyu He[SX]	54	C4
Wenyu[HEN]	106	C3
Wenzhou Wan[ZJ]	84	E5
Wenzhou[ZJ]	84	E4
Wenzhu[JX]	98	A4
Wenzhuang[AH]	90	C2
Wenzhuang[SX]	54	E2
Wenzu[SD]	102	D3
West Lamma Channel[HK]	176	C4
Wo Che[HK]	176	D2
Wo Hop Shek[HK]	176	D1
Wo Shang Wai[HK]	176	C1
Wo Yi Hop[HK]	176	D2
Woduhe[HL]	70	C3
Wofo[CQ]	132	B4
Wofosi[HEB]	48	C3
Wohu[JL]	66	D4
Woinbodoi[SC]	138	D4
Woinbodoi[XZ]	152	K4
Wointog[SC]	138	E3
Wojiang[JX]	98	B4
Woken He[HL]	70	F5
Woken[HL]	70	F6
Wolong Gang[XJ]	172	I8
Wolong Hu[LN]	62	G2
Wolong[HL]	70	E6
Wolong[JL]	66	I5
Wolongquan[LN]	62	F4
Wong Chuk Hang[HK]	176	D4
Wong Chuk Kok Hoi[HK]	176	E1
Wong Chuk Kok Tsui[HK]	176	E1
Wong Chuk Wan[HK]	176	E2
Wong Chuk Yuen[HK]	176	C2
Wong Leng	176	D1
Wong Ma Kok[HK]	176	D4
Wong Mau Chau[HK]	176	F2
Wong Nai Chau[HK]	176	F3
Wong Tai Sin[HK]	176	D3
Wong Uk Tsuen[HK]	176	C2
Wong Wan Chau[HK]	176	E1
Wong Yi Chau[HK]	176	E2
Woniuhe[HL]	70	D4
Woniushi[LN]	62	G2
Wopu[SD]	102	E2
Woshao[HN]	114	B4
Wozhang Shan[YN]	148	H5
Wu Chau[HK]	176	E2
Wu Jiang[CQ]	132	E4
Wu Jiang[GZ]	144	F3
Wu Jiang[GZ]	144	G1
Wu Kai Sha[HK]	176	E2
Wu Kau Tang[HK]	176	E1
Wu Kwai Sha Tsui[HK]	176	E2
Wu Lei Tau[HK]	176	E2
Wu Shan[CQ]	132	F3
Wu Shui[GD]	118	F1
Wu Shui[HN]	114	B5
Wu Shui[HN]	114	C4
Wu Xia[HB]	110	D3
Wu Xian[CQ]	132	G3

Name	Page	Grid
Wu'ai[GX]	124	E3
Wu'an[HB]	110	F3
Wu'an[HEB]	48	B7
Wuba[HEN]	106	H1
Wubaihu[HEB]	48	E4
Wubaihu[TJ]	42	C2
Wubang[SH]	74	C3
Wubao[JS]	80	E4
Wubao[SN]	156	E4
Wubu[CQ]	132	C4
Wubu[FJ]	94	E4
Wubu[GZ]	144	G4
Wubu[HEB]	48	C3
Wubu[SN]	156	G3
Wubu[TJ]	42	A3
Wucangbao[SN]	156	E3
Wuchang Hu[AH]	90	C6
Wuchang[HL]	70	D6
Wuchangwa[HB]	110	D3
Wucheng[AH]	90	E7
Wucheng[HEN]	106	E5
Wucheng[JX]	98	C2
Wucheng[SD]	102	C2
Wucheng[SX]	54	B5
Wucheng[SX]	54	C4
Wucheng[SX]	54	E2
Wuchi[TW]	186	D2
Wuchieh[TW]	186	E2
Wuchuan[GD]	118	C5
Wuchuan[GS]	160	G4
Wuchuan[GZ]	144	F2
Wuchuan[NM]	58	I7
Wuchuan[NM]	58	X10
Wuci[FJ]	94	C4
Wucun[SD]	102	C4
Wucun[SX]	54	C5
Wuda Lianchi[HL]	70	D4
Wudabao[ZJ]	84	D5
Wudalianchi[HL]	70	D4
Wudang Qu[GZ]	144	E4
Wudang Shan[HB]	110	D2
Wudang Shan[HB]	110	E2
Wudangshan[HB]	110	E2
Wudaogou[JL]	66	K4
Wudaogou[NM]	58	X10
Wudaohe[HEB]	48	F2
Wudaohe[HL]	70	E6
Wudaoliang[BJ]	36	D2
Wudaoliang[QH]	164	F5
Wudaolin[HL]	70	E4
Wudaolingzi[NX]	168	C3
Wudaoshui[HN]	114	B3
Wudaoying[HEB]	48	D2
Wudi[FJ]	94	C4
Wudi[SD]	102	D2
Wudian[HB]	110	G3
Wuding He[SN]	156	G3
Wuding[YN]	148	H5
Wudong[FJ]	94	B4
Wudoujiang[JX]	98	B5
Wudu[SN]	156	D7
Wuduan[JS]	80	C2
Wuduhe[HB]	110	E3
Wudui[JS]	80	E2
Wuduizi[NX]	168	C2
Wudun[JS]	80	D3
Wufang[FJ]	94	C3
Wufemgyang[ZJ]	84	E4
Wufeng[HB]	110	D4
Wufeng[LN]	62	F2
Wufeng[QH]	164	N4
Wufeng[TW]	186	D2
Wufeng[TW]	186	D3
Wufeng[TW]	186	E2
Wufengpu[HN]	114	D6
Wufu[FJ]	94	D2
Wugailing Po[HI]	128	C2
Wugang[AH]	90	E4
Wugang[HEN]	106	E4
Wugang[HN]	114	C6
Wugen[ZJ]	84	F4
Wugong Shan[HN]	114	F5
Wugong Shan[JX]	98	A4
Wugong Shan[JX]	98	B4
Wugong[HEB]	48	C5
Wugong[HEN]	106	E4
Wugong[SN]	156	E6
Wugongli[HI]	128	B2
Wugou[AH]	90	C3
Wuguan[GZ]	144	E5
Wuguan[SN]	156	G7
Wuguanyi[SN]	156	C7
Wuguanzhai[HEB]	48	C6
Wugucheng[SN]	156	E3
Wugui[CQ]	132	B4
Wuguishan[GD]	118	F4
Wugujian[JX]	98	E2
Wuhai[NM]	58	G8
Wuhan[HB]	110	H4
Wuhang[ZJ]	84	E2
Wuhe[AH]	90	D3
Wuhe[GS]	160	G4
Wuhe[YN]	148	D6
Wuhu[AH]	90	E5
Wuhu[AH]	90	E5
Wuhua[GD]	118	H3
Wuhuanchi[LN]	62	E2
Wuji[HEB]	48	B5
Wuji[JS]	80	E2
Wujia[CQ]	132	B4
Wujia[GX]	124	G6
Wujia[LN]	62	E3
Wujiabao[SD]	102	C3
Wujiadian[AH]	90	B5
Wujiagang Qu[HB]	110	E4
Wujiahewan[NX]	168	B3
Wujiajing[GS]	160	F4
Wujialou[SD]	102	F3
Wujiamao[SX]	54	C4
Wujianfang[BJ]	36	B2
Wujianfang[JL]	66	H5
Wujiang[AH]	90	E5
Wujiang[GS]	160	E3
Wujiang[GX]	124	H3
Wujiang[GZ]	144	E3
Wujiang[JS]	80	D5
Wujiang[JS]	80	F5
Wujiang[JX]	98	C4
Wujiangdu Shuiku[GZ]	144	E3
Wujiao[SC]	138	F8
Wujiaqu[XJ]	172	K3
Wujiawa[SD]	102	E4
Wujiawan[HN]	114	C4
Wujiayao[SX]	54	D2
Wujiazhan[JL]	66	F3
Wujiazhuang[NX]	168	C4
Wujiazhuang[SN]	156	G2
Wujin Qu[JS]	80	E5
Wujing[SH]	74	C2
Wujingfu[GD]	118	I3
Wuke[TJ]	42	C3
Wukeshu[JL]	66	D1
Wukeshu[JL]	66	G3
Wukou[HN]	114	F4
Wuku[FJ]	94	C2
Wulai[TW]	186	E2
Wulangxi[HN]	114	B5
Wulei[JX]	98	D3
Wuli He[JL]	66	G4
Wuli[CQ]	132	E4
Wuli[GX]	124	G5
Wuli[GX]	124	G5
Wuli[JS]	80	D3
Wuli[QH]	164	E6
Wuli[SN]	156	F5
Wulian Feng[YN]	148	I3
Wulian Shan[SD]	102	F4
Wulian Shan[SD]	102	F4
Wulian Shan[YN]	148	I3
Wulian[GX]	124	E3
Wulian[SC]	138	K4
Wulian[SD]	102	F4
Wuliang Shan[YN]	148	F6
Wuliang[YN]	148	F6
Wuliangdian[LN]	62	F3
Wuliba[SN]	156	E8
Wulichuan[HEN]	106	C4
Wulie He[HEB]	48	F2
Wulijie[FJ]	94	D4
Wulin[SD]	102	D5
Wulindong[HL]	70	G5
Wuling Shan[GZ]	144	G3
Wuling Shan[GZ]	144	H2
Wuling Shan[HEB]	48	E3
Wuling Shan[HN]	114	B4
Wuling Shan[HN]	114	C4
Wuling Yan[JX]	98	C2
Wuling[FJ]	94	C4
Wulingyuan Qu[HN]	114	C3
Wulipai[HN]	114	F3
Wulipo[BJ]	36	B2
Wulipo[NX]	168	C3
Wulipu[HB]	110	F4
Wulituo[BJ]	36	C4
Wulong He[SD]	102	G3
Wulong[AH]	90	C4
Wulong[CQ]	132	D4
Wulong[HEN]	106	E2
Wulong[SH]	74	C3
Wulong[YN]	148	J6
Wulongbei[LN]	62	H4
Wulongchuan[SX]	54	D5
Wulonggou[HEB]	48	B4
Wulongquan[HB]	110	H4
Wulu[LN]	62	G5
Wulubutie[NM]	58	P3
Wuluo[GZ]	144	G2
Wuma[AH]	90	B3
Wuma[CQ]	132	F3
Wuma[GZ]	144	E3
Wumahe Qu[HL]	70	E5
Wumang Dao[LN]	62	F5
Wumatang[XZ]	152	G4
Wumaying[HEB]	48	D6
Wumeng Shan[YN]	148	I4
Wuming[GX]	124	F4
Wumu[HEN]	106	B3
Wumulong[YN]	148	E6
Wunan[GS]	160	F4
Wuning Shui[JX]	98	B3
Wuning[JX]	98	C2
Wunudian[HEN]	106	F3
Wuping[CQ]	132	E4
Wuping[FJ]	94	B4
Wupo[HI]	128	C2
Wupu[XJ]	172	N4
Wuqi[FJ]	94	D2
Wuqi[SN]	156	E4
Wuqia[XJ]	172	E6
Wuqiang[HEB]	48	C5
Wuqiangxi[HN]	114	D4
Wuqiao Ling[GS]	160	F4
Wuqiao[AH]	90	D3
Wuqiao[HEB]	48	D6
Wuqiao[JX]	98	C3
Wuqiao[SH]	74	C3
Wuqing Nongchang[TJ]	42	B3
Wuqing Qu[TJ]	42	B3
Wuqu[FJ]	94	E2
Wusha[AH]	90	D6
Wushan[AH]	90	D4
Wushan[CQ]	132	F2
Wushan[FJ]	94	C4
Wushan[GS]	160	G5
Wushan[HB]	110	E2
Wushan[HB]	110	G2
Wushan[NX]	168	C3
Wusheng[SC]	138	L5
Wushenggong[HN]	114	E3
Wushengtang[JL]	66	D2
Wushengyi[GS]	160	F4
Wushi Gang[GD]	118	B6
Wushi[GD]	118	B6
Wushi[GX]	124	H5
Wushi[HN]	114	F4
Wushi[JX]	98	D4
Wushi[QH]	164	O4
Wushi[SN]	156	F5
Wushi[XJ]	172	G5
Wushih Pi[TW]	186	E2
Wushui[HN]	114	E7
Wusi Jiang[GX]	124	G5

Wusong Jiang(Suzhou He)[SH]	74	C2
Wusong Jiang[JS]	80	G5
Wusong Kou[SH]	74	D2
Wusong[SH]	74	C2
Wusu[HL]	70	H4
Wusu[HN]	114	C4
Wusuli Jiang[HL]	70	H5
Wutai Shan[SX]	54	E3
Wutai[JL]	66	G3
Wutai[SD]	102	D4
Wutai[SX]	54	E3
Wutai[TJ]	42	B3
Wutai[TW]	186	D4
Wutai[XJ]	172	I3
Wutan[CQ]	132	C4
Wutan[HN]	114	D4
Wutang[FJ]	94	E4
Wutang[GD]	118	C5
Wutang[GX]	124	F5
Wutangmen[JS]	80	F5
Wutong[FJ]	94	D4
Wutong[GX]	124	H2
Wutong[JX]	98	E3
Wutong[QH]	164	N6
Wutong[SC]	138	K7
Wutong[ZJ]	84	D5
Wutongdaquan[XJ]	172	O4
Wutonggou[GS]	160	A3
Wutonghao[BJ]	36	D2
Wutonghua[NM]	58	M6
Wutongqiao Qu[SC]	138	I6
Wutongshu[NX]	168	C2
Wutongshugou[BJ]	36	E2
Wutun[FJ]	94	D2
Wuwangkou[HEB]	48	B4
Wuwei[AH]	90	D5
Wuwei[GS]	160	F4
Wuxi[AH]	90	D6
Wuxi[AH]	90	E5
Wuxi[CQ]	132	F2
Wuxi[JS]	80	F5
Wuxian[AH]	90	C5
Wuxiang[NX]	168	C2
Wuxiang[SX]	54	D5
Wuxiang[ZJ]	84	F3
Wuxin[HI]	128	B2
Wuxing Hu[SX]	54	B7
Wuxing[FJ]	94	D4
Wuxing[HEN]	106	D5
Wuxing[LN]	62	F3
Wuxing[YN]	148	I4
Wuxinzhuang[TJ]	42	B3
Wuxu[AH]	90	D4
Wuxu[GX]	124	E3
Wuxu[GX]	124	F5
Wuxuan[GX]	124	G4
Wuxue[HB]	110	I5
Wuya[HN]	114	B3
Wuyang He[GZ]	144	G3
Wuyang[HB]	110	D4
Wuyang[HEN]	106	E4
Wuyang[HN]	114	C6
Wuyang[JX]	98	C6
Wuyao[SH]	74	D3
Wuyi Jiang[ZJ]	84	D4
Wuyi Shan[FJ]	94	B4
Wuyi Shan[JX]	98	D5
Wuyi Yunhe[JS]	80	E5
Wuyi[AH]	90	E4
Wuyi[FJ]	94	C2
Wuyi[HEB]	48	C6
Wuyi[ZJ]	84	D4
Wuyiling Qu[HL]	70	E4
Wuying Qu[HL]	70	E4
Wuyishan[FJ]	94	D2
Wuyishan[JX]	98	E3
Wuyuan[HN]	114	E7
Wuyuan[JX]	98	E2
Wuyuan[NM]	58	H7
Wuyuan[NM]	58	U10
Wuyun Ding[HB]	110	D3
Wuyun[GD]	118	H3
Wuyun[HL]	70	E4
Wuyun[JX]	98	B6
Wuzhai[FJ]	94	C5
Wuzhai[SX]	54	C3
Wuzhan[HL]	70	D6
Wuzhen[SN]	156	F3
Wuzhi Feng[HN]	114	F7
Wuzhi Shan[HI]	128	B3
Wuzhi Shan[HI]	128	B3
Wuzhi[HEN]	106	E2
Wuzhifeng[JX]	98	B6
Wuzhishan[HI]	128	B3
Wuzhong Qu[JS]	80	F5
Wuzhong[NX]	168	C3
Wuzhou[GX]	124	I4
Wuzhu Zhou[GD]	118	E5
Wuzhu[GS]	160	G5
Wuzhu[GX]	124	F3

X

Xabar Hure[NM]	58	W10
Xago[XZ]	152	F4
Xagqu[XZ]	152	H3
Xagzi[XZ]	152	D4
Xainza[XZ]	152	F4
Xaitongmoin[XZ]	152	F5
Xamgyi'nyilha[YN]	148	E3
Xamqu[XZ]	152	H4
Xang[QH]	164	J5
Xangd[NM]	58	X11
Xanggin Dalai[NM]	58	F8
Xar Ail[NM]	58	X11
Xar Gol[QH]	164	I5
Xar Gut[NM]	58	M4
Xar Hamar Shan[XJ]	172	K1
Xar Moron He[NM]	58	M6
Xar Moron[NM]	58	M6
Xar Moron[NM]	58	X10
Xar Teg[NM]	58	W11
Xar Tolgoi Baixing[QH]	164	J5
Xarag[QH]	164	K4
Xaralj[NM]	58	G7
Xaralj[NM]	58	T11
Xarba La[XZ]	152	D5
Xarhu[XJ]	172	N4
Xarlag[NM]	58	H8
Xarma[XZ]	152	H4
Xarqu[XZ]	152	H4
Xarru[XZ]	152	E5
Xayar[XJ]	172	I5
Xazgat[XJ]	172	K2
Xeilapu Kangri[XZ]	152	F5
Xekarkol[XJ]	172	F6
Xênkyêr[XZ]	152	F4
Xêxung[XZ]	152	I4
Xi Ail[JL]	66	C3
Xi Amqin[NM]	58	U11
Xi Chuan[HEN]	106	C4
Xi He[LN]	62	E3
Xi He[LN]	62	G4
Xi He[SC]	138	K4
Xi Jiang[GD]	118	D3
Xi Jiang[GD]	118	F4
Xi Jiang[JX]	98	D2
Xi Qu[SC]	138	G9
Xi Shan[BJ]	36	B4
Xi Shui[HB]	110	I4
Xi Taijnar Hu[QH]	164	F3
Xi Ujimqin Qi[NM]	58	L5
Xi Ulan Bulag[NM]	58	W10
Xi Xi[FJ]	94	C2
Xi Xian[HEN]	106	F5
Xi Xian[SX]	54	B5
Xia Boingor[QH]	164	L8
Xia Dawo[QH]	164	L5
Xia kongma[QH]	164	M7
Xia Xian[SX]	54	C6
Xia Zayü[XZ]	152	J5
Xia'ao[GX]	124	E3
Xiaba[JX]	98	C5
Xiabaoping[HB]	110	E3
Xiabazhai[SC]	138	I3
Xiacang[AH]	90	C6
Xiacang[TJ]	42	B2
Xiacengpu[HN]	114	D7
Xiǎchao[HEB]	48	E2
Xiachayuan[HB]	110	D4
Xiache[GD]	118	H2
Xiache[JS]	80	E2
Xiachen[ZJ]	84	D3
Xiachengzi[HL]	70	F6
Xiachuan Dao[GD]	118	E5
Xiachuan[GD]	118	E5
Xiacun[HN]	114	F6
Xiacun[JX]	98	B4
Xiacun[SX]	54	D6
Xiadachen Dao[ZJ]	84	F4
Xiadahe[LN]	62	G3
Xiadaliushu[NX]	168	A3
Xiadang[FJ]	94	E2
Xiadao[FJ]	94	D3
Xiadi[FJ]	94	D3
Xiadian[HB]	110	H3
Xiadingjia[SD]	102	G2
Xiadong[GX]	124	D5
Xiadu[FJ]	94	B5
Xiaduopu[HN]	114	E4
Xiafang[FJ]	94	B3
Xiafang[FJ]	94	D2
Xiafuqiao[AH]	90	C5
Xiage[FJ]	94	C6
Xiagezhuang[SD]	102	G3
Xiagongcun[HEB]	48	B4
Xiaguan[HEN]	106	C4
Xiaguan[SX]	54	F2
Xiaguan[ZJ]	84	E5
Xiahan[SX]	54	E2
Xiahe[FJ]	94	C5
Xiahe[GS]	160	F5
Xiahe[LN]	62	G3
Xiahe[SD]	102	E2
Xiaheqing[GS]	160	D3
Xiahong[ZJ]	84	D5
Xiahu[FJ]	94	E3
Xiahua[SX]	54	B6
Xiahuang[HB]	110	H5
Xiahuayuan Qu[HEB]	48	C3
Xiahuofang[HEB]	48	E2
Xiaji[HEN]	106	D5
Xiajiang[JX]	98	C4
Xiajin[SD]	102	B3
Xiakou[GS]	160	G5
Xiakou[HB]	110	D3
Xiakou[HEB]	48	A5
Xiakou[SN]	156	D8
Xiakou[ZJ]	84	C4
Xialao[GX]	124	D2
Xialaoba[XJ]	172	M4
Xialaxiu[QH]	164	I8
Xiali[HEN]	106	E4
Xiali[SX]	54	C5
Xialiang[SC]	138	L3
Xialiang[SN]	156	F7
Xialihuaping[NX]	168	B4
Xialiu[GD]	118	B5
Xialiu[HN]	114	E5
Xialiushui[NX]	168	B3
Xialong[GX]	124	H3
Xialu Qu[HB]	110	H4
Xialu[CQ]	132	E4
Xialuhe[LN]	62	I4
Xialujiao[SX]	54	C2
Xiamaguan[NX]	168	C3
Xiamajuan[HEB]	48	B3
Xiamalugou[BJ]	36	C2
Xiamao[FJ]	94	C3
Xiamao[GD]	118	E3
Xiamaoshan[BJ]	36	D1
Xiamatou[TJ]	42	B4
Xiamaya[XJ]	172	O4
Xiamayu[SX]	54	E2
Xiamei[FJ]	94	C6
Xiamen Gang[FJ]	94	D5
Xiamen[FJ]	94	D5
Xiamen[FJ]	94	F2
Xiamen[NX]	168	A3
Xiamiangao[SX]	54	D2

Xiamiao[NX]	168	C2
Xiamiao[NX]	168	C2
Xiamujiao[SX]	54	D2
Xi'an Qu[JL]	66	F5
Xian Xian[HEB]	48	D5
Xi'an[GD]	118	E2
Xi'an[GX]	124	G3
Xi'an[HN]	114	D4
Xi'an[LN]	62	F4
Xi'an[NX]	168	B4
Xi'an[SN]	156	E6
Xian'an Qu[HB]	110	H5
Xian'an[GD]	118	I3
Xianan[GX]	124	E3
Xianbin Jiao[HI]	128	G7
Xianbo[HB]	110	G4
Xianchang[GZ]	144	F4
Xiancun[FJ]	94	E3
Xiandi[GX]	124	H5
Xiandu[FJ]	94	C4
Xianfeng[CQ]	132	C4
Xianfeng[HB]	110	C5
Xianfeng[HI]	128	A2
Xi'anfeng[JS]	80	E3
Xianfengcun[SN]	156	D3
Xiang Jiang[GX]	124	H2
Xiang Jiang[GZ]	144	F3
Xiang Jiang[HN]	114	D6
Xiang Jiang[HN]	114	E5
Xiang Shan[NX]	168	B3
Xiang Shui[JX]	98	C6
Xiang'an Qu[FJ]	94	D5
Xiang'an[AH]	90	D5
Xiangba[HB]	110	C3
Xiangbei[GX]	124	F3
Xiangcheng Qu[JS]	80	F5
Xiangcheng[HEN]	106	E4
Xiangcheng[HEN]	106	F4
Xiangcheng[SC]	138	E7
Xiangcheng[SD]	102	D4
Xiangcheng[SD]	102	D5
Xiangdao[AH]	90	D4
Xiangdian[FJ]	94	B4
Xiangdong Qu[JX]	98	A4
Xiangdong[FJ]	94	B5
Xiangdu[GX]	124	D4
Xiangfan[HB]	110	F2
Xiangfen[SX]	54	C6
Xiangfu[JX]	98	C3
Xianghai[JL]	66	C2
Xianghe[HEB]	48	E4
Xianghe[HL]	70	D4
Xianghe[SN]	156	G7
Xianghongdian Shuiku[AH]	90	C5
Xianghongqi[BJ]	36	C4
Xianghu[FJ]	94	C4
Xianghua Ling[HN]	114	E7
Xianghua[FJ]	94	C4
Xianghua[HEN]	106	C5
Xianghua[QH]	164	N3
Xianghuang(Hobot Xar)Qi[NM]	58	J6
Xianghuaqiao[SH]	74	C2
Xiangjiang[HN]	114	D7
Xianglan[HL]	70	E5
Xianglinpu[HN]	114	D7
Xianglutai[SX]	54	F2
Xiangning[SX]	54	B6
Xiangong[SN]	156	D6
Xiangou[HI]	128	C2
Xiangpi Shan[QH]	164	L4
Xiangquan[GS]	160	G5
Xiangquan[SN]	156	C6
Xiangride He[QH]	164	J5
Xiangride Nongchang[QH]	164	J4
Xiangride[QH]	164	J5
Xiangshan Gang[ZJ]	84	F3
Xiangshan[BJ]	36	C4
Xiangshan[JX]	98	C3
Xiangshan[JX]	98	D4
Xiangshan[SC]	138	K5
Xiangshan[ZJ]	84	F3
Xiangshanzeng[JX]	98	C7
Xiangshi[HN]	114	C3
Xiangshui[GD]	118	G3
Xiangshui[GX]	124	E5
Xiangshui[GZ]	144	C5
Xiangshui[HI]	128	B3
Xiangshui[JL]	66	F4
Xiangshui[JS]	80	E2
Xiangshui[SN]	156	F2
Xiangshuihe[LN]	62	I3
Xiangshuihe[SX]	54	C6
Xiangshuitan[JX]	98	D2
Xiangtan[HN]	114	E5
Xiangtan[HN]	114	E5
Xiangtang[CQ]	132	C4
Xiangtang[HN]	114	E5
Xiangtang[JX]	98	C3
Xiangtang[SH]	74	C3
Xiangwu[SH]	74	B2
Xiangxi He[HB]	110	D3
Xiangxian[GX]	124	F4
Xiangxiang[HN]	114	E5
Xiangxing[JX]	98	B4
Xiangyang Hu[XZ]	152	F2
Xiangyang Qu[HB]	110	F2
Xiangyang[AH]	90	D3
Xiangyang[BJ]	36	D3
Xiangyang[CQ]	132	E2
Xiangyang[GX]	124	D2
Xiangyang[HL]	70	D6
Xiangyang[HL]	70	E4
Xiangyang[HN]	114	E6
Xiangyang[JL]	66	D4
Xiangyang[JL]	66	F5
Xiangyang[JL]	66	G3
Xiangyang[SN]	156	E8
Xiangyang[TJ]	42	C3
Xiangyanghu[HB]	110	H5
Xiangyin[HN]	114	E4
Xiangyindu[HN]	114	F6
Xiangying[BJ]	36	C2
Xiangying[LN]	62	E5
Xiangyu[AH]	90	C6
Xiangyuan[SX]	54	D4
Xiangyuan[SX]	54	E5
Xiangyun[FJ]	94	D5
Xiangyun[YN]	148	F5
Xiangzhi[FJ]	94	D5
Xiangzhou[GX]	124	E4
Xiangzhou[GX]	124	G4
Xiangzhou[SD]	102	F3
Xiangzikou[HN]	114	D4
Xianhe[SD]	102	E2
Xianhu Shuiku[GX]	124	F4
Xianhu[GX]	124	F4
Xianhui[GX]	124	H3
Xianjiaoshui[NX]	168	B3
Xianjin[SH]	74	D2
Xianju[HB]	110	F3
Xianju[HEN]	106	F5
Xianju[ZJ]	84	E4
Xianlai[HI]	128	C2
Xianmi[QH]	164	O3
Xianning[HB]	110	H5
Xianpu[FJ]	94	E2
Xianqian[XZ]	152	C3
Xianren[ZJ]	84	D5
Xianrendong[BJ]	36	B3
Xianrendu[HB]	110	E2
Xianrenwan[HN]	114	C5
Xianrenzhuang[HEN]	106	F3
Xianru[JL]	66	I4
Xianshan[HN]	114	E6
Xianshui He[SC]	138	G5
Xianshui[GX]	124	H2
Xiantai[HEN]	106	E4
Xiantang Gang[SH]	74	D2
Xiantang[GZ]	144	E5
Xiantao[HB]	110	G4
Xiantuoshi[NX]	168	B3
Xianxi[HN]	114	D4
Xianxia Ling[ZJ]	84	C4
Xianxia[JX]	98	C5
Xianyang[FJ]	94	D1
Xianyang[SN]	156	E6
Xianyi[CQ]	132	E2
Xianyou[FJ]	94	D4
Xianyuan[GZ]	144	E2
Xianyuan[JX]	98	B3
Xianyuwan[LN]	62	E5
Xianzi[JL]	66	D3
Xianzijiao[HN]	114	D7
Xianzong[AH]	90	E5
Xiao Hai[HI]	128	C3
Xiao Haltang He[GS]	160	B3
Xiao He[HEB]	48	B6
Xiao He[SX]	54	D4
Xiao Hinggan Ling[HL]	70	D4
Xiao Jiang[CQ]	132	E2
Xiao Onggon[NM]	58	X10
Xiao Qaidam Hu[QH]	164	H3
Xiao Qaidam[QH]	164	H3
Xiao Shan[HEN]	106	C3
Xiao Shui[HN]	114	D6
Xiao Xi[ZJ]	84	D4
Xiao Xian[AH]	90	C2
Xi'ao[GD]	118	H2
Xiaoba[GZ]	144	D3
Xiaoba[NX]	168	C2
Xiaoba[SN]	156	C8
Xiaobaiyu[SX]	54	E2
Xiaoban[HB]	110	G4
Xiaobeihe[LN]	62	F3
Xiaobianhe[SN]	156	C7
Xiaobu[JX]	98	C5
Xiaocang[FJ]	94	E3
Xiaocha[NX]	168	C4
Xiaochang[GX]	124	E2
Xiaochang[HB]	110	G3
Xiaochang[HEB]	48	C2
Xiaochang[SH]	74	C2
Xiaochangshan[LN]	62	F5
Xiaocheng[JL]	66	H3
Xiaochengzi[JL]	66	E4
Xiaochengzi[JL]	66	F3
Xiaochengzi[LN]	62	C3
Xiaochengzi[LN]	62	G2
Xiaochi[FJ]	94	B4
Xiaochi[HB]	110	I5
Xiaochuan[AH]	90	E7
Xiaocun[HB]	110	B5
Xiaocuo[HI]	94	D4
Xiaodeyingzi[LN]	62	D4
Xiaodian Qu[SX]	54	D4
Xiaodian[AH]	90	C4
Xiaodian[AH]	90	D6
Xiaodian[SD]	102	C2
Xiaodian[TJ]	42	B3
Xiaodong[GX]	124	F5
Xiaodong[LN]	62	F2
Xiaodong[LN]	62	G3
Xiaodongzhuang[BJ]	36	D3
Xiaodu[CQ]	132	B4
Xiaodu[GD]	118	H3
Xiao'ertai[HEB]	48	B2
Xiao'ertun[JL]	66	D2
Xiaofangshen[JL]	66	F3
Xiaogan[HB]	110	G4
Xiaogang[HB]	110	G3
Xiaogang[JX]	98	C3
Xiaogang[TJ]	42	C1
Xiaogaokou[TJ]	42	B3
Xiaogu[HI]	128	B2
Xiaoguan[GZ]	144	F3
Xiaoguan[SD]	102	H3
Xiaogushan[JL]	66	E4
Xiaohai[JS]	80	F3
Xiaohaizi Shuiku[XJ]	172	G6
Xiaohanzhuang[TJ]	42	B4
Xiaohanzhuang[TJ]	42	C3
Xiaohaotu[SN]	156	F2
Xiaohaozhuang[TJ]	42	B4
Xiaohe Qu[GZ]	144	E4
Xiaohe[CQ]	132	E5
Xiaohe[HB]	110	B4
Xiaohe[HB]	110	F3
Xiaohe[HB]	110	H3
Xiaohe[HEN]	106	B3
Xiaohe[HEN]	106	F2
Xiaohe[HN]	114	G4
Xiaohe[JS]	80	E4

Name	Page	Grid	Name	Page	Grid	Name	Page	Grid
Xiaohe[SN]	156	D7	Xiaosanjiang[GD]	118	E2	Xiaqiu[SD]	102	F2
Xiaohe[SN]	156	F3	Xiaoshahe[JL]	66	I5	Xiaqu[FJ]	94	C3
Xiaohe[SN]	156	F7	Xiaoshan Qu[ZJ]	84	E2	Xiasan[HI]	128	C3
Xiaohe[YN]	148	I3	Xiaoshan[GX]	124	E5	Xiasanxing[SH]	74	C1
Xiaoheihe[NM]	58	X11	Xiaoshan[HEB]	48	E5	Xiasha[FJ]	94	C2
Xiaohekou[HB]	110	F5	Xiaoshanzi[HL]	70	D6	Xiasha[SH]	74	D2
Xiaohekou[SN]	156	F7	Xiaoshazigou[QH]	164	F5	Xiashan Qu[GD]	118	C5
Xiaohenghe[SH]	74	C1	Xiaosheng[GD]	118	I2	Xiashan Shuiku[SD]	102	F3
Xiaohetou[SX]	54	C2	Xiaoshentang[TJ]	42	C3	Xiashan[GZ]	144	D5
Xiaohezhuang[TJ]	42	B3	Xiaoshentou[SX]	54	C4	Xiashan[SX]	54	B5
Xiaohezi[HEB]	48	C2	Xiaoshidian[HEN]	106	E4	Xiashan[ZJ]	84	C3
Xiaohonggou[NX]	168	B3	Xiaoshikou[SD]	102	H3	Xiashe[FJ]	94	C2
Xiaohuan Jiang[GX]	124	F3	Xiaoshitou[NX]	168	B2	Xiashe[SX]	54	E2
Xiaohuang[JX]	98	D3	Xiaoshui[HN]	114	E6	Xiashe[SX]	54	E3
Xiaohuangzhuang[TJ]	42	B4	Xiaosigou[HEB]	48	F3	Xiashenjing[SX]	54	E1
Xiaoji[HEB]	48	F4	Xiaosiping[JL]	66	F5	Xiashibu[BJ]	36	B4
Xiaoji[SD]	102	G3	Xiaosizhuang[SN]	156	F5	Xiashihao[NM]	58	W11
Xiaojia[JL]	66	F2	Xiaosong[FJ]	94	D2	Xiashu[JS]	80	E4
Xiaojiacun[HN]	114	E6	Xiaosuan[SX]	54	B4	Xiashuai[GD]	118	E2
Xiaojiahe[HL]	70	G5	Xiaosuangou[HEB]	48	B3	Xiashuitou[SX]	54	D2
Xiaojiahui[SX]	54	E3	Xiaosungezhuang[TJ]	42	B1	Xiasi[AH]	90	F5
Xiaojialing[JX]	98	D2	Xiaosunzhuang[TJ]	42	B4	Xiasi[GZ]	144	F5
Xiaojian[AH]	90	C3	Xiaotang[LN]	62	C3	Xiataizi[HEB]	48	E3
Xiaojian[JS]	80	E2	Xiaotangshan[BJ]	36	C3	Xiatang[AH]	90	D4
Xiaojiang Shuiku[GX]	124	G5	Xiaotao[FJ]	94	C4	Xiatang[CQ]	132	E4
Xiaojiang[JX]	98	B6	Xiaotashan Shuiku[JS]	80	D2	Xiataoshu[BJ]	36	D2
Xiaojiaqiao[HN]	114	C4	Xiaotazi[LN]	62	E3	Xiatuo[SC]	138	F5
Xiaojiawan[NX]	168	B4	Xiaotianba[HB]	110	C2	Xiawa[SD]	102	D2
Xiaojie[HEN]	106	C3	Xiaotianlong[ZJ]	84	C3	Xiawanzi[BJ]	36	E2
Xiaojie[YN]	148	F9	Xiaoting Qu[HB]	110	E4	Xiawuqi[TJ]	42	B2
Xiaojin Chuan[SC]	138	H4	Xiaotun[HEN]	106	D3	Xiaxi[AH]	90	E6
Xiaojin He[SC]	138	G8	Xiaotun[TJ]	42	A3	Xiaxi[JX]	98	F3
Xiaojin Shan[SH]	74	C3	Xiaowang[HEN]	106	F5	Xiaxiang[HN]	114	B6
Xiaojin[GS]	160	H5	Xiaowangcun[TJ]	42	A3	Xiaxindian[HB]	110	G4
Xiaojin[SC]	138	H5	Xiaowangzhuang[TJ]	42	A2	Xiayang[FJ]	94	B5
Xiaojingzi[NX]	168	B2	Xiaowangzhuang[TJ]	42	B4	Xiayang[FJ]	94	C3
Xiaojinwan[GS]	160	C2	Xiaowu[HB]	110	H3	Xiayang[FJ]	94	D4
Xiaojinzhuang[TJ]	42	B4	Xiaowutai Shan[HEB]	48	C4	Xiayanxi[CQ]	132	E4
Xiaojue[AH]	48	A5	Xiaoxi[AH]	90	D3	Xiaye[SX]	54	C5
Xiaokeng[GD]	118	F2	Xiaoxi[FJ]	94	C4	Xiayi[GX]	124	H3
Xiaokouzi[NX]	168	B2	Xiaoxi[HB]	110	B5	Xiayi[HEN]	106	H3
Xiaokunshan[SH]	74	C2	Xiaoxi[JX]	98	C6	Xiaying[GX]	124	I4
Xiaolan[GD]	118	F4	Xiaoxiang Ling[SC]	138	H7	Xiaying[SD]	102	F2
Xiaolangdi Shuiku[HEN]	106	D3	Xiaoxiang[GD]	118	E3	Xiaying[TJ]	42	B1
Xiaoliang[AH]	90	E3	Xiaoxiang[YN]	148	I5	Xiayu[FJ]	94	C4
Xiaolin[HB]	110	G2	Xiaoxi'nancha[JL]	66	K4	Xiayu[HEN]	106	C3
Xiaoling He[LN]	62	D3	Xiaoxingkai Hu[HL]	70	G6	Xiayuan[JS]	80	F4
Xiaoling[HB]	110	H4	Xiaoxingshan Dao[GD]	118	G4	Xiayunling[BJ]	36	B4
Xiaoling[SN]	156	F7	Xiaoxinji[AH]	90	C3	Xiazao[JX]	98	B5
Xiaoliu[SD]	102	B4	Xiaoxinjie[YN]	148	I5	Xiazhai[FJ]	94	C5
Xiaoliuzhuang[TJ]	42	B4	Xiaoxinmatou[TJ]	42	B2	Xiazhai[NX]	168	B5
Xiaolong[JX]	98	C5	Xiaoxinzhuang[TJ]	42	C1	Xiazhuang[SD]	102	C3
Xiaolong[JX]	98	C6	Xiaoxu[HN]	114	D8	Xiazhen[JX]	98	F3
Xiaolongmen[HN]	114	C5	Xiaoxue[SD]	102	C4	Xiazhen[SD]	102	E2
Xiaolongtan[BJ]	36	D2	Xiaoyan[HB]	110	E3	Xiazhi Dao[ZJ]	84	G3
Xiaolu Dao[LN]	62	G5	Xiaoyang Shan[ZJ]	84	G2	Xiazhongtuo[BJ]	36	B4
Xiaoluan He[HEB]	48	D2	Xiaoyang[FJ]	94	E2	Xiazhu[FJ]	94	D3
Xiaolüdian[HEN]	106	G5	Xiaoyang[SN]	156	D8	Xiazhuang[BJ]	36	B4
Xiaomei Shuiku[HI]	128	B3	Xiaoyanqu[NX]	168	C2	Xiazhuang[BJ]	36	C3
Xiaomei[ZJ]	84	C5	Xiaoyao[HEN]	106	F4	Xiazhuang[FJ]	94	B4
Xiaomengzhuang[TJ]	42	A2	Xiaoyi[GX]	124	G5	Xiazhuang[HEB]	48	A5
Xiaomenjia[SD]	102	G2	Xiaoyi[JS]	80	E2	Xiazhuang[HEN]	106	G5
Xiaomiao[AH]	90	D5	Xiaoyi[SX]	54	C4	Xiazhuang[SD]	102	E4
Xiaomuhe[HL]	70	G5	Xiaoyi[SX]	54	C4	Xiazhuang[SD]	102	F3
Xiaonanchong[HB]	110	G2	Xiaoying[SD]	102	E2	Xiazhuang[SX]	54	E4
Xiaonan'gou[GS]	160	H4	Xiaoyingzi[HEB]	48	F3	Xiazhuang[YN]	148	F5
Xiaonanhe[TJ]	42	B3	Xiaoyuanzi[NX]	168	C4	Xiazhuzhuang[TJ]	42	B3
Xiaonianzhuang[TJ]	42	B4	Xiaoyuehe[TJ]	42	C2	Xiazi[GZ]	144	F3
Xiaoping[HN]	114	B5	Xiaozhai[SD]	102	B3	Xiba[GS]	160	D2
Xiaoping[JX]	98	C6	Xiaozhan[TJ]	42	B4	Xibagou[TJ]	42	B2
Xiaopingshan[GX]	124	G5	Xiaozhao[HEN]	106	E3	Xibaifa[BJ]	36	B4
Xiaopingyang[GX]	124	G4	Xiaozhao[NM]	58	T11	Xibaita[BJ]	36	C4
Xiaopingyi[SX]	54	D2	Xiaozhi[SD]	102	C3	Xibaxa Qu[XZ]	152	I5
Xiaopu[BJ]	36	C2	Xiaozhongdian[YN]	148	E3	Xibian[FJ]	94	D2
Xiaopu[ZJ]	84	D1	Xiaozhou[CQ]	132	E3	Xibian[FJ]	94	D5
Xiaoqiao[FJ]	94	D3	Xiaozhuanghugou[BJ]	36	D2	Xibin[FJ]	94	D3
Xiaoqing[QH]	164	H4	Xiaozuo[FJ]	94	D5	Xibin[LN]	62	F3
Xiaoqing He[BJ]	36	C4	Xiaping[SX]	54	C7	Xibuhe[YN]	148	F3
Xiaoqing He[SD]	102	D2	Xiapu[CQ]	132	F2	Xicen[SH]	74	B2
Xiaoqing[GZ]	144	E4	Xiapu[FJ]	94	E3	Xicetian[SX]	54	E2
Xiaoqiuzhuang[TJ]	42	B2	Xiapu[HB]	110	H5	Xichahe[SN]	156	D7
Xiaoqu Shan[ZJ]	84	G2	Xiapu[NX]	168	B4	Xichang[GD]	118	G3
Xiaoruo[FJ]	94	D3	Xiaqiao[AH]	90	C4	Xichang[GX]	124	F6
Xiaosalong[QH]	164	K2	Xiaqiao[GD]	118	C6	Xichang[HI]	128	C2

Xichang[SC]	138	H8
Xichangfa[HL]	70	D5
Xiche He[HN]	114	B3
Xicheng Shan[SX]	54	D6
Xicheng Yunhe[JS]	80	F5
Xicheng[FJ]	94	D3
Xicheng[HEB]	48	C5
Xicheng[HEN]	106	G2
Xicheng[HL]	70	C4
Xicheng[JL]	66	J5
Xicheng[JX]	98	D4
Xicheng[SD]	102	G2
Xichong[SC]	138	K5
Xichou[YN]	148	J7
Xichuan[HEN]	106	C4
Xichuan[YN]	148	F3
Xicun[HEN]	106	C3
Xicun[SX]	54	E1
Xida He[GS]	160	E3
Xidagu[TJ]	42	C4
Xidaming Shan[GX]	124	E5
Xidaming Shan[GX]	124	E5
Xidatan[NX]	168	C2
Xidawa[JL]	66	E2
Xidayang Shuiku[HEB]	48	B5
Xidaying[BJ]	36	C4
Xidazhuangke[BJ]	36	B2
Xide[SC]	138	H7
Xidi[HEB]	48	E3
Xidianzi[LN]	62	C4
Xiding[YN]	148	F9
Xiditou[TJ]	42	B3
Xidong[FJ]	94	D2
Xidong[GS]	160	D3
Xidong[GS]	160	E3
Xidongting Shan[JS]	80	F5
Xidongzhuang[TJ]	42	C3
Xidoupu[NM]	58	V10
Xidu[SH]	74	C3
Xiduzhuang[TJ]	42	B3
Xie Chi[SX]	54	B7
Xie Shui[HN]	114	C3
Xiecheng[NM]	58	T11
Xiede[XZ]	152	F3
Xie'erqu[NX]	168	D3
Xiehe[GS]	160	F4
Xieji[HEN]	106	G3
Xieji[JS]	80	E4
Xiejiabao[SN]	156	G2
Xiejiabu[HEB]	48	C4
Xiejiagou[SN]	156	G3
Xiejiaji Qu[AH]	90	C4
Xiejiapu[HN]	114	D4
Xiejiashan[BJ]	36	D3
Xiejiatan[JX]	98	D2
Xielai Shui[HN]	114	F6
Xiema[HB]	110	E3
Xieqiao[AH]	90	C4
Xieqiao[ZJ]	84	F3
Xi'er[YN]	148	I6
Xi'erdaohe[BJ]	36	C3
Xi'erpu[AH]	90	C3
Xietai[TJ]	42	B2
Xietan[FJ]	94	E2
Xietang[ZJ]	84	E2
Xietun[LN]	62	E5
Xiexingxu[SH]	74	D2
Xieyang Dao[GX]	124	G7
Xiezhou[SX]	54	B7
Xifang[SN]	156	D6
Xifangcheng[SX]	54	E2
Xifangzi[TJ]	42	A3
Xifei He[AH]	90	B3
Xifeng[AH]	90	D5
Xifeng[GZ]	144	E3
Xifeng[LN]	62	H2
Xifengku[JL]	66	D3
Xifengshan[BJ]	36	C3
Xifo[LN]	62	F3
Xifuji[HEB]	48	C7
Xigan Qu[NX]	168	C2
Xigang[JL]	66	H5
Xigang[SD]	102	D5
Xigangcun[TJ]	42	A4
Xigangzi[HL]	70	D4
Xigaze[XZ]	152	F5
Xigongyi[GS]	160	G5
Xigou[HEB]	48	E2
Xigou[HEN]	106	D4
Xigou[SN]	156	F7
Xigou[SN]	156	G2
Xigou[TJ]	42	B4
Xigouyan[NX]	168	B4
Xigu Dao[HI]	128	A3
Xiguan[TJ]	42	C3
Xiguantun[LN]	62	G2
Xiguanying[HEB]	48	D2
Xiha Gol[NM]	58	V10
Xiha He[NM]	58	V10
Xihai[LN]	62	F4
Xihan Shui[SN]	156	B8
Xihe[AH]	90	E6
Xihe[GD]	118	I2
Xihe[GS]	160	F4
Xihe[GS]	160	G5
Xihe[GZ]	144	F2
Xihe[HB]	110	G3
Xihe[HB]	110	H3
Xihe[JL]	66	G3
Xihe[SN]	156	D8
Xihe[SN]	156	E8
Xihedi[SX]	54	E6
Xihekou[SN]	156	F4
Xiheying[HEB]	48	B4
Xihongmen[BJ]	36	C4
Xihongshanzi[NM]	58	W10
Xihongsi[BJ]	36	B3
Xihu[AH]	90	B4
Xihu[CQ]	132	C4
Xihu[GS]	160	B2
Xihu[HN]	114	B3
Xihu[JX]	98	E2
Xihua[HEN]	106	F4
Xihuaigu[TJ]	42	C2
Xihuang[HEN]	106	C4
Xihuangcun[HEB]	48	B6
Xihuanghulu[NX]	168	C3
Xihuangliang[BJ]	36	D2
Xihuaying[HEN]	106	F4
Xihuo Shan[ZJ]	84	F2
Xihuoshichong[NX]	168	C3
Xihxu[XJ]	172	F7
Xiji[BJ]	36	D4
Xiji[FJ]	94	C2
Xiji[NX]	168	B5
Xijia[SX]	54	D5
Xijiadian[HB]	110	E2
Xijiang[GD]	118	E2
Xijiang[GZ]	144	G4
Xijiangzhai[HEN]	106	F3
Xijiao[SX]	54	E2
Xijing Shuiku[GX]	124	G5
Xijing[SN]	156	F6
Xijing[SX]	54	E5
Xijingyu[TJ]	42	C1
Xijir Ulan Hu[QH]	164	C5
Xijir[XJ]	172	M4
Xijiu[GZ]	144	E2
Xikeng[GD]	118	H3
Xikou[AH]	90	D7
Xikou[FJ]	94	B4
Xikou[FJ]	94	C2
Xikou[HN]	114	B6
Xikou[JX]	98	B2
Xikou[SN]	156	F7
Xikou[ZJ]	84	D4
Xikou[ZJ]	84	E4
Xikou[ZJ]	84	F3
Xil Sum[NM]	58	I6
Xilai[JS]	80	F4
Xilan[FJ]	94	E3
Xilangdonggou[NX]	168	C3
Xilaotou Shan[NM]	58	N5
Xilian[GD]	118	B6
Xilian[HN]	114	C3
Xiliang Hu[HB]	110	H5
Xiliang[GZ]	144	F5
Xiliao He[NM]	58	O6
Xilijin[BJ]	36	E3
Xilin Gol[NM]	58	F8
Xilin Gol[NM]	58	L6
Xilin Qu[HL]	70	E5
Xilin[GX]	124	C3
Xiling Xia[HB]	110	D4
Xiling[FJ]	94	E3
Xiling[HN]	114	E6
Xilingjing[SX]	54	D3
Xilinhe[JL]	66	H5
Xilinhot[NM]	58	L6
Xilinzi[HL]	70	G5
Xiliu[HEB]	48	C6
Xiliu[LN]	62	F4
Xiliu[SD]	102	G2
Xiliucheng[TJ]	42	B3
Xiliujiazi[LN]	62	F2
Xiliumu[TJ]	42	A4
Xiliuyuan[SX]	54	E3
Xiliuzhai[SX]	54	D5
Xilong Shan[YN]	148	H8
Xilonghuyu[TJ]	42	C1
Xilongtou[HEB]	48	D2
Xilt[JL]	66	D2
Xiluo[HN]	114	B3
Xiluo[SX]	54	D4
Xima[GZ]	144	F4
Xima[HB]	110	I4
Xima[HN]	114	C5
Ximafeng[LN]	62	G3
Ximalin[HEB]	48	B3
Ximao Zhou[HI]	128	B3
Ximatou[ZJ]	84	G2
Ximawan[SN]	156	E3
Ximayi Dao[LN]	62	E5
Ximazhuang[HB]	110	I3
Ximeng[YN]	148	E8
Ximeng[YN]	148	E8
Ximu[LN]	62	F4
Ximu[ZJ]	84	D2
Xin Barag Youqi[NM]	58	L3
Xin Barag Zuoqi[NM]	58	M3
Xin Bulag Jun[NM]	58	M3
Xin Hu[XZ]	152	D2
Xin Jiang[JX]	98	D3
Xin Ju[NM]	58	G8
Xin kai He[NM]	58	O5
Xin Xian[HEN]	106	F6
Xin'aili[JL]	66	C2
Xin'an Jiang[AH]	90	E7
Xin'an[AH]	90	D7
Xinan[FJ]	94	C4
Xinan[FJ]	94	E3
Xin'an[GX]	124	E4
Xin'an[HEN]	106	D3
Xin'an[HN]	114	D3
Xin'an[JL]	66	D3
Xin'an[JX]	98	D5
Xin'an[NM]	58	U11
Xin'an[SD]	102	G3
Xin'an[SX]	54	C6
Xin'an[TJ]	42	C2
Xin'anbian[SN]	156	E3
Xin'nancha[JL]	66	G5
Xin'ansuo[YN]	148	I7
Xin'anzhuang[BJ]	36	C5
Xinba[HEB]	48	E1
Xinbang[SH]	74	C3
Xinbao[GD]	118	D4
Xinbei[NX]	168	B3
Xinbi[ZJ]	84	E4
Xinbian He[AH]	90	D3
Xinbin[GX]	124	F4
Xinbin[LN]	62	I3
Xinbu[HI]	128	C1
Xinbuhai[HI]	128	C1
Xincai[HEN]	106	F5
Xincang[AH]	90	C6
Xincang[ZJ]	84	E2
Xinchang[GZ]	144	D4
Xinchang[HB]	110	F5
Xinchang[SC]	138	M3
Xinchang[SN]	156	E3
Xinchang[YN]	148	E8

Xinchang, ZJ	84	C3	Xingdong[HN]	114	F6	Xingren[HL]	70	D5
Xinchang[ZJ]	84	E3	Xingdongkou[GX]	124	F2	Xingren[NX]	168	B4
Xincheng[GS]	160	F5	Xingfa[GZ]	144	C4	Xingrong[XZ]	152	I4
Xincheng[GS]	160	H5	Xingfeng[CQ]	132	D3	Xingshan[HB]	110	D3
Xincheng[GX]	124	F3	Xingfu Qu[SD]	102	D2	Xingshan[LN]	62	E4
Xincheng[HEB]	48	D4	Xingfu[JL]	66	C2	Xingsheng[NX]	168	C5
Xincheng[HL]	70	F5	Xingfu[SD]	102	E2	Xingsheng[SH]	74	D2
Xincheng[NM]	58	V11	Xingfulukou[XJ]	172	L3	Xingshunxi[NM]	58	V10
Xincheng[SD]	102	D3	Xingga[XZ]	152	J4	Xingshutun[LN]	62	F5
Xincheng[TJ]	42	C4	Xingge[HL]	70	C4	Xingshuwan[BJ]	36	E3
Xincheng[YN]	148	F8	Xingguo[JX]	98	C5	Xingshuwan[NX]	168	D3
Xincheng[ZJ]	84	E2	Xinghai[QH]	164	L5	Xingsi[SH]	74	D3
Xinchengju[JL]	66	G3	Xinghe[NM]	58	J7	Xingta[SH]	74	C3
Xinchengzi[BJ]	36	E2	Xinghe[SN]	156	E4	Xingtai[HEB]	48	B6
Xinchengzi[GS]	160	E3	Xinghua Wan[FJ]	94	E4	Xingtai[LN]	62	F5
Xinchengzi[NM]	58	M6	Xinghua[GS]	160	G5	Xingtang[HEB]	48	B5
Xinchi[JX]	98	D2	Xinghua[GZ]	144	G5	Xingtian[FJ]	94	D2
Xinchi[SH]	74	B2	Xinghua[HL]	70	D2	Xingtian[JX]	98	E2
Xinci[FJ]	94	C5	Xinghua[JL]	66	F5	Xinguan[HN]	114	D3
Xincun Gang[HI]	128	B3	Xinghua[JS]	80	E4	Xinguang[SH]	74	C1
Xincun[HEB]	48	E5	Xinghuacun[SX]	54	C4	Xinguo[SH]	74	C1
Xincun[HI]	128	A2	Xinghuo[HL]	70	C3	Xingwang[GX]	124	D4
Xincun[HI]	128	B3	Xinghuo[SC]	138	L5	Xingwen[SC]	138	K7
Xincun[NM]	58	V10	Xinghuo[XJ]	172	L4	Xingxiang[JS]	80	E5
Xincun[SH]	74	C1	Xingji[HEB]	48	D5	Xingxingshao Shuiku[JL]	66	G4
Xincun[TJ]	42	B3	Xingjiang[JX]	98	C5	Xingxingxia[XJ]	172	O5
Xincun[TJ]	42	C3	Xingjiashe[SX]	54	D4	Xingxiong[HB]	110	G3
Xincun[TJ]	42	C3	Xingjiawan[HEB]	48	B6	Xingyang[HEN]	106	E3
Xincun[YN]	148	G6	Xingjie[YN]	148	J7	Xingye[GX]	124	G5
Xindai[ZJ]	84	F2	Xingjing[NX]	168	C2	Xingyi[CQ]	132	D4
Xindeng[ZJ]	84	D3	Xingkai Hu[HL]	70	G6	Xingyi[GZ]	144	C5
Xindi[GX]	124	I4	Xingkai[HL]	70	G6	Xingyi[HEB]	48	C5
Xindi[HEB]	48	F2	Xingkaihu Nongchang[HL]	70	G6	Xingyuan[GS]	160	G5
Xindian[AH]	90	C4	Xingkou[HEN]	106	F3	Xingzhai[SX]	54	E2
Xindian[BJ]	36	E3	Xinglian[JX]	98	C5	Xingzhuang[HEN]	106	F3
Xindian[GZ]	144	E4	Xinglingzi[SX]	54	C3	Xingzi[GD]	118	E2
Xindian[HB]	110	G5	Xinglong Nongchang[HI]	128	C3	Xingzi[JX]	98	D2
Xindian[HEB]	48	B6	Xinglong[CQ]	132	C4	Xinhai[HI]	128	C1
Xindian[HEB]	48	E5	Xinglong[CQ]	132	F3	Xinhai[SH]	74	C1
Xindian[YN]	148	I3	Xinglong[GZ]	144	D3	Xinhe(Toksu)[XJ]	172	I5
Xindianping[HN]	114	B5	Xinglong[GZ]	144	F3	Xinhe[GS]	36	D4
Xindianzi[HEB]	48	F3	Xinglong[HB]	110	F2	Xinhe[GS]	160	G6
Xindiaopu[HEN]	106	D5	Xinglong[HEB]	48	E3	Xinhe[GX]	124	E5
Xindihe Shuiku[TJ]	42	B3	Xinglong[HL]	70	B4	Xinhe[HEB]	48	C6
Xindong[GD]	118	D5	Xinglong[HL]	70	C3	Xinhe[JL]	66	I5
Xindu Qu[SC]	138	J5	Xinglong[HL]	70	D4	Xinhe[JS]	80	C2
Xindu[AH]	90	C6	Xinglong[HL]	70	D5	Xinhe[SH]	74	D1
Xin'e[HL]	70	D4	Xinglong[JL]	66	D4	Xinhekou[HEB]	48	B3
Xinfa[HL]	70	C5	Xinglong[JL]	66	F3	Xinhouzhuang[TJ]	42	B3
Xinfa[JL]	66	C3	Xinglong[LN]	62	G5	Xinhu[SD]	102	E2
Xinfan[ZJ]	84	D4	Xinglong[NX]	168	B4	Xinhua[GX]	124	D3
Xinfang[GZ]	144	D4	Xinglong[NX]	168	B5	Xinhua[HB]	110	D3
Xinfang[HI]	128	B2	Xinglong[SC]	138	K6	Xinhua[HN]	114	D5
Xinfang[JX]	98	B4	Xinglongbu[TJ]	42	B1	Xinhua[JL]	66	C3
Xinfangzi[TJ]	42	B1	Xinglongchang[HN]	114	B4	Xinhua[NM]	58	T10
Xinfeng Jiang[GD]	118	G2	Xinglongchuan[JL]	66	D2	Xinhua[SC]	138	N4
Xinfeng[AH]	90	E5	Xinglonggang[HL]	70	G5	Xinhuacun[HL]	70	D4
Xinfeng[GD]	118	G2	Xinglonggong[HEB]	48	D5	Xinhuang[HN]	114	B5
Xinfeng[GD]	118	I2	Xinglongjie[HN]	114	D4	Xinhuaqiao[NX]	168	C2
Xinfeng[GX]	124	H5	Xinglongpu[LN]	62	G3	Xinhuaying[BJ]	36	C2
Xinfeng[JS]	80	F3	Xinglongquan[HL]	70	C5	Xinhui Qu[GD]	118	F4
Xinfeng[JX]	98	B6	Xinglongshan[JL]	66	C3	Xiniantou[SX]	54	D2
Xinfeng[JX]	98	D4	Xinglongshan[LN]	62	F2	Xinigi[XJ]	172	K5
Xinfeng[SH]	74	C2	Xinglongsi[SN]	156	G2	Xining[QH]	164	N4
Xinfengjiang Shuiku[GD]	118	G3	Xinglongzhuang[BJ]	36	C4	Xiningpu[NX]	168	C3
Xinfu[HL]	70	C6	Xinglongzhuang[LN]	62	C3	Xiniqi[NM]	58	N2
Xinfu[YN]	148	G7	Xinglongzhuang[SD]	102	C4	Xiniu[GD]	118	F2
Xing Xian[SX]	54	C3	Xingmiao[SH]	74	D3	Xiniu[JX]	98	B6
Xing'an Qu[HL]	70	F5	Xingning[GD]	118	H2	Xiniu'erhe[NM]	58	N2
Xing'an[GX]	124	H2	Xingning[HN]	114	F7	Xiniujiao[GX]	124	F6
Xing'an[HL]	70	B2	Xingnong[HL]	70	F6	Xinji[AH]	90	C4
Xing'an[HL]	70	D4	Xingnongcun[TJ]	42	B3	Xinji[GS]	160	H5
Xingan[JX]	98	C4	Xingou[HB]	110	F4	Xinji[HB]	110	E3
Xingang[GD]	118	G3	Xingou[HB]	110	G4	Xinji[HEB]	48	C6
Xingang[LN]	62	E6	Xingou[JS]	80	E3	Xinji[HEB]	48	E5
Xingang[SD]	102	G2	Xingping[GX]	124	H3	Xinji[HEN]	106	G4
Xingang[SH]	74	D2	Xingping[NX]	168	B5	Xinji[JS]	80	D4
Xingao[SX]	54	D2	Xingping[SN]	156	E6	Xinji[JS]	80	E2
Xingcheng[HL]	70	C6	Xingping[SN]	156	F7	Xinji[NX]	168	C5
Xingcheng[LN]	62	D4	Xingqiao[FJ]	94	C3	Xinji[SD]	102	C3
Xingcun[FJ]	94	C2	Xingqiao[JS]	80	F3	Xinji[SN]	156	C7
Xingdaohu[GX]	124	G6	Xingquan[HL]	70	C5	Xinjian[HI]	128	A3
Xingdian[JS]	80	D4	Xingren[GZ]	144	D5	Xinjian[HI]	128	B2
			Xingren[GZ]	144	F4	Xinjian[JX]	98	C3

Xinjian[JX]	98	E2	Xinping[YN]	148	G6	Xinxiang[HEN]	106	E2		
Xinjian[NM]	58	W11	Xinping'an[JL]	66	D2	Xinxing Qu[HL]	70	F6		
Xinjian[SH]	74	D1	Xinpingbu[SX]	54	F1	Xinxing[AH]	90	C3		
Xinjian[TJ]	42	B3	Xinpo[HI]	128	C2	Xinxing[GD]	118	E4		
Xinjian[ZJ]	84	E4	Xinpu[GS]	160	F4	Xinxing[HI]	128	C2		
Xinjiang[GD]	118	F2	Xinpu[GZ]	144	D5	Xinxing[HL]	70	C5		
Xinjiang[GX]	124	F5	Xinpu[GZ]	144	F3	Xinxing[HL]	70	E4		
Xinjiang[JX]	98	B5	Xinpuzi[NX]	168	B4	Xinxing[JL]	66	H5		
Xinjiang[SX]	54	C6	Xinqiang He[HN]	114	F3	Xinxing[JL]	66	J4		
Xinjiayuan[SX]	54	D2	Xinqiao He[FJ]	94	C4	Xinxing[JS]	80	F3		
Xinjichuan[SN]	156	C5	Xinqiao[AH]	90	E5	Xinxing[LN]	62	E3		
Xinjie[HB]	110	G3	Xinqiao[FJ]	94	B4	Xinxing[LN]	62	F3		
Xinjie[HB]	110	H4	Xinqiao[FJ]	94	C2	Xinxing[SC]	138	H6		
Xinjie[HI]	128	A2	Xinqiao[FJ]	94	C4	Xinxing[SD]	102	F3		
Xinjie[JS]	80	F4	Xinqiao[GX]	124	H5	Xinxingdong[JL]	66	J5		
Xinjie[JX]	98	C3	Xinqiao[HI]	128	C2	Xinxu[GX]	124	F4		
Xinjie[NM]	58	H8	Xinqiao[HN]	114	E5	Xinxu[GX]	124	H3		
Xinjie[QH]	164	N5	Xinqiao[SC]	138	J6	Xinxu[GX]	124	I2		
Xinjie[YN]	148	E5	Xinqiao[SH]	74	C2	Xinxu[HN]	114	E7		
Xinjie[YN]	148	G5	Xinqiao[SH]	74	D2	Xinxu[HN]	114	E7		
Xinjie[YN]	148	H7	Xinqiao[SH]	74	D2	Xinxujiang[HN]	114	D6		
Xinjiebu[JX]	98	C3	Xinqiao[ZJ]	84	C2	Xinyang[FJ]	94	C3		
Xinjin[SC]	138	I5	Xinqiao[ZJ]	84	C3	Xinyang[HEN]	106	F5		
Xinjing[GS]	160	F4	Xinqiao[ZJ]	84	F3	Xinyang[SD]	102	D2		
Xinjing[SH]	74	C2	Xinqing Qu[HL]	70	E4	Xinyang[SD]	102	F4		
Xinkai Ling[SN]	156	G7	Xinqiu Qu[LN]	62	E2	Xinyang[SH]	74	C2		
Xinkai[BJ]	36	B3	Xinquan[FJ]	94	B4	Xinyanggang Kou[JS]	80	F3		
Xinkai[HN]	114	F3	Xinquanjing[NX]	168	C3	Xinye[HEN]	106	D5		
Xinkai[LN]	62	F3	Xinrong Qu[SX]	54	E1	Xinyi He[JS]	80	E2		
Xinkaikou[TJ]	42	B2	Xinruandian[HEN]	106	F5	Xinyi[GD]	118	C4		
Xinkeng[FJ]	94	D3	Xinshao[HN]	114	D5	Xinyi[JS]	80	D2		
Xinkou[FJ]	94	D2	Xinshao[YN]	148	I6	Xinyi[SD]	102	C4		
Xinkou[TJ]	42	A3	Xinsheng[CQ]	132	C4	Xinyi[SX]	54	C4		
Xinle[CQ]	132	E4	Xinsheng[CQ]	132	D3	Xinying[HI]	128	B2		
Xinle[HEB]	48	B5	Xinsheng[HL]	70	D3	Xinying[HI]	128	B2		
Xinli[GX]	124	D4	Xinsheng[HL]	70	D5	Xinying[HL]	70	D4		
Xinli[JL]	66	E2	Xinsheng[HL]	70	D5	Xinying[JX]	98	E3		
Xinli[JL]	66	F4	Xinsheng[SC]	138	K5	Xinying[NX]	168	B4		
Xinli[JL]	66	G3	Xinshengdian[SD]	102	C2	Xinyingpan[YN]	148	F3		
Xinli[JL]	66	H4	Xinshi[CQ]	132	D4	Xinyu[FJ]	94	D5		
Xinli[TJ]	42	B3	Xinshi[HB]	110	F2	Xinyu[JX]	98	B4		
Xinlian[YN]	148	E2	Xinshi[HI]	128	C2	Xinyuan (Kunes)[XJ]	172	I4		
Xinliao Dao[GD]	118	C6	Xinshi[HN]	114	E6	Xinyuan[GS]	160	G4		
Xinlicheng Shuiku[JL]	66	F4	Xinshi[SC]	138	I7	Xinyuan[JL]	66	F3		
Xinlin[HL]	70	C3	Xinshi[SN]	156	F6	Xinyuan[JS]	80	D3		
Xinlin[NM]	58	O4	Xinshi[ZJ]	84	E2	Xinzai[HI]	128	B2		
Xinlitun[HL]	70	D3	Xinshu He[JS]	80	D2	Xinzha[ZJ]	84	F2		
Xinlitun[JL]	66	F4	Xinshu[JL]	66	K4	Xinzhai[QH]	164	J7		
Xinlitun[LN]	62	F2	Xinshu[SD]	102	E5	Xinzhai[SD]	102	D3		
Xinlizhuang[HEB]	48	D4	Xinshuguang[HL]	70	D4	Xinzhai[SN]	156	D4		
Xinlong[HI]	128	A3	Xinshui He[SX]	54	B5	Xinzhai[YN]	148	K7		
Xinlong[SC]	138	F5	Xinshunxi[NM]	58	I7	Xinzhai[ZJ]	84	D4		
Xinlong[SH]	74	D2	Xinsui He[AH]	90	D3	Xinzhaidian[HEB]	48	B6		
Xinmachang[GZ]	144	D5	Xintai[SD]	102	D4	Xinzhan[GZ]	144	E2		
Xinmapengkou[TJ]	42	C4	Xintaimen[LN]	62	D4	Xinzhan[JL]	66	F3		
Xinmei[HI]	128	C3	Xintaizi[LN]	62	G2	Xinzhan[JL]	66	H4		
Xinmi[HEN]	106	E3	Xintan[HB]	110	G4	Xinzhangfang[NM]	58	N2		
Xinmiao[CQ]	132	D4	Xintang[GX]	124	F5	Xinzhangzi[HEB]	48	E2		
Xinmiao[SH]	74	C2	Xintang[GZ]	144	E5	Xinzhen[BJ]	36	C4		
Xinmiao[SH]	74	C2	Xintang[JS]	80	D2	Xinzheng[HEN]	106	E3		
Xinmin[CQ]	132	D3	Xintian[AH]	90	E6	Xinzheng[HI]	128	B3		
Xinmin[CQ]	132	F3	Xintian[CQ]	132	E4	Xinzhi[JX]	98	B4		
Xinmin[GX]	124	D4	Xintian[GD]	118	H2	Xinzhi[SX]	54	C5		
Xinmin[GZ]	144	C5	Xintian[GD]	118	H3	Xinzhongyi[HEB]	48	D5		
Xinmin[HI]	128	A3	Xintian[HN]	114	E7	Xinzhou Qu[HB]	110	H4		
Xinmin[HI]	128	C2	Xintian[NM]	58	P2	Xinzhou[GD]	118	E2		
Xinmin[HI]	128	C3	Xintian[SC]	138	H9	Xinzhou[GD]	118	E5		
Xinmin[HL]	70	D4	Xintian[YN]	148	I5	Xinzhou[GZ]	144	F2		
Xinmin[JX]	98	C3	Xintianpu[HN]	114	D5	Xinzhou[HB]	110	C2		
Xinmin[LN]	62	E3	Xintongyang Yunhe[JS]	80	E4	Xinzhou[HI]	128	B2		
Xinmin[LN]	62	F3	Xintun[GZ]	144	E5	Xinzhou[HN]	114	D3		
Xinmin[NM]	58	J7	Xintun[HEB]	48	C6	Xinzhou[SX]	54	D3		
Xinmin[NX]	168	C5	Xintun[YN]	148	F4	Xinzhu[HI]	128	C2		
Xinmin[SC]	138	H6	Xintunzi[JL]	66	H5	Xinzhuang[BJ]	36	C4		
Xinmin[SH]	74	D1	Xinwan[HN]	114	E4	Xinzhuang[GS]	160	G4		
Xinmin[SN]	156	E5	Xinwan[JX]	98	B2	Xinzhuang[HEB]	48	D6		
Xinmin[YN]	148	F6	Xinwanfa[JL]	66	F2	Xinzhuang[SD]	102	D3		
Xinminbu[NM]	58	W11	Xinwei[FJ]	94	C5	Xinzhuang[SD]	102	D4		
Xinnan[GZ]	144	F3	Xinwei[SH]	74	C1	Xinzhuang[SD]	102	G2		
Xinning[HN]	114	C6	Xinwen[SD]	102	D4	Xinzhuang[TJ]	42	B3		
Xinningpo[HI]	128	A2	Xinwu[HI]	128	C2	Xinzhuangcha[NX]	168	C5		
Xinnong[JL]	66	F3	Xinxi[JX]	98	C4	Xinzhuangji[NX]	168	C3		
Xinnong[LN]	62	G5	Xinxian[YN]	148	I7	Xinzhuangzi[HEB]	48	F3		
Xinnong[SH]	74	C3	Xinxiang[HEN]	106	E2	Xinzipu[HN]	114	E5		

Xiong Xian[HEB]	48	D5
Xiongbei[HEN]	106	D4
Xiongdi Yu[FJ]	94	C6
Xiongdonggou[BJ]	36	C2
Xionger Shan[HEN]	106	C3
Xionger Shan[SX]	54	F2
Xiongerzhai[BJ]	36	E3
Xiongguan[HL]	70	B3
Xiongguantun[LN]	62	G2
Xionghe Shuiku[HB]	110	F3
Xionghe[HB]	110	F4
Xiongjiang[FJ]	94	D3
Xiongjiatang[NX]	168	C3
Xiongkou[HB]	110	F4
Xiongyue[LN]	62	F4
Xiongzhai[HEN]	106	F5
Xipan[SX]	54	E3
Xipanlou[AH]	90	C3
Xipanzhuang[TJ]	42	B2
Xiping[GX]	124	C3
Xiping[HEN]	106	C4
Xiping[HEN]	106	F4
Xipingle[HEB]	48	B5
Xipingpo[LN]	62	D4
Xipo[SX]	54	B6
Xiqên[XZ]	152	E5
Xiqianpu[SH]	74	C2
Xiqin[FJ]	94	D3
Xiqing Qu[TJ]	42	B3
Xiqiuwan[HB]	110	D3
Xiquan[AH]	90	D4
Xiquan[CQ]	132	C4
Xiquan[GS]	160	G4
Xisaishan Qu[HB]	110	I4
Xisan[YN]	148	I6
Xisha Qundao[HI]	128	F5
Xishacheng[HEB]	48	B3
Xishan Qu[JS]	80	F5
Xishan Qu[YN]	148	H5
Xishan[GD]	118	G2
Xishan[GX]	124	H2
Xishan[GZ]	144	G5
Xishan[JS]	80	F5
Xishan[JX]	98	C3
Xishan[XJ]	172	N4
Xishan[YN]	148	D6
Xishancun[HL]	70	D5
Xishandi[HEN]	106	C3
Xishanyi[AH]	90	D5
Xishaoqu[BJ]	36	D3
Xishatun[BJ]	36	C3
Xishawo[BJ]	36	C4
Xishe[SX]	54	C4
Xishelu[YN]	148	G6
Xishenba[SN]	156	C8
Xishu[HEB]	48	A7
Xishuangzhuang[TJ]	42	C3
Xishuba[SX]	54	C4
Xishui[GS]	160	E3
Xishui[GZ]	144	E2
Xishui[HB]	110	I4
Xishui[HI]	128	B2
Xishuidao[NM]	58	V10
Xishuijie[SX]	54	D2
Xisipo[AH]	90	D3
Xisizhuang[TJ]	42	B2
Xisong[SD]	102	E2
Xitai[BJ]	36	D2
Xitaizi[BJ]	36	D2
Xitan[FJ]	94	E2
Xitang[ZJ]	84	E2
Xitao[HEN]	106	E2
Xitian[GD]	118	H3
Xitiangezhuang[BJ]	36	D3
Xitiao Xi[ZJ]	84	D2
Xitie Shan[QH]	164	H3
Xitie Shan[QH]	164	H3
Xitieshan[QH]	164	H3
Xitou[GD]	118	D5
Xitou[JX]	98	F2
Xituan[JS]	80	F3
Xitushan[HEB]	48	B7
Xiu Shui[JX]	98	B2
Xiu Shui[JX]	98	C2
Xiufeng[HL]	70	C2
Xiujing[SH]	74	C3
Xiuning[AH]	90	E7
Xiuren[GX]	124	H3
Xiushan[CQ]	132	E5
Xiushan Dao[ZJ]	84	G2
Xiushan[HL]	70	C2
Xiushan[HN]	114	E4
Xiushan[ZJ]	84	G2
Xiushi[JX]	98	C3
Xiushui[GZ]	144	B4
Xiushui[JL]	66	G3
Xiushui[JX]	98	B2
Xiushuihezi[LN]	62	G2
Xiuwen[GZ]	144	E4
Xiuwen[SX]	54	D4
Xiuwu[HEN]	106	E2
Xiuyan[LN]	62	G4
Xiuyu Qu[FJ]	94	E4
Xiuzhuan[FJ]	94	B5
Xiwaizi[JL]	66	J4
Xiwan[HEN]	106	D2
Xiwan[ZJ]	84	E5
Xiwanbu[HEB]	48	B3
Xiwang[AH]	90	D4
Xiwanhe[TJ]	42	B4
Xiwei[FJ]	94	D3
Xiwei[FJ]	94	E3
Xiwei[JL]	66	F4
Xiwei[JS]	80	E2
Xiweidian[TJ]	42	C2
Xiwen[HEB]	48	B7
Xiwengzhuang[BJ]	36	D3
Xiwol[XJ]	172	H7
Xiwu[QH]	164	J7
Xiwu[ZJ]	84	F3
Xixabangma Feng[XZ]	152	D5
Xixi He[SC]	138	H8
Xixi[FJ]	94	C2
Xixi[FJ]	94	E2
Xixi[GD]	118	I4
Xixi[HN]	114	C4
Xixi[JX]	98	D4
Xixia Qu[NX]	168	C2
Xixia[HEN]	106	C4
Xixiang[JX]	98	B3
Xixiang[SN]	156	D8
Xixiangdapu[LN]	62	H3
Xixiaoliang[TJ]	42	B2
Xixiaowang[SD]	102	D2
Xixiaozhao[NM]	58	U11
Xixiating[HEN]	106	F4
Xixikou[FJ]	94	C3
Xixinying[HEB]	48	C2
Xixinzhuang[TJ]	42	A3
Xixinzhuang[TJ]	42	B2
Xiyan[GX]	124	F4
Xiyan[HEB]	48	C5
Xiyan[HEN]	106	B3
Xiyan[HN]	114	C6
Xiyan[SX]	54	C6
Xiyan[SX]	54	E3
Xiyang Dao[FJ]	94	E3
Xiyang Jiang[GX]	124	C3
Xiyang Jiang[YN]	148	K6
Xiyang[AH]	90	C3
Xiyang[FJ]	94	C4
Xiyang[GD]	118	I2
Xiyang[HEN]	106	C3
Xiyang[HN]	114	E5
Xiyang[JL]	66	G4
Xiyang[SN]	156	F6
Xiyang[SX]	54	E4
Xiyanggao[HEB]	48	B7
Xiyganjiyde[XJ]	172	K2
Xiyi[YN]	148	E6
Xiying He[GS]	160	E4
Xiying[BJ]	36	C4
Xiying[GS]	160	F4
Xiying[SD]	102	D3
Xiying[SN]	156	F8
Xiyingcheng[JL]	66	F3
Xiyuan[FJ]	94	D4
Xiyuan[JX]	98	D2
Xiyuan[ZJ]	84	E4
Xize[YN]	148	I4
Xizebu[ZJ]	84	F3
Xizha[TJ]	42	C4
Xizhai[SN]	156	G6
Xizhai[SX]	54	E4
Xizhangcun[HEN]	106	C3
Xizhangdian[HB]	110	H3
Xizhi Jiang[GD]	118	G3
Xizhong Dao[LN]	62	E5
Xizhou Shan[SX]	54	D3
Xizhou[YN]	148	F5
Xizhou[ZJ]	84	F3
Xizhuang[BJ]	36	D3
Xizhuang[SN]	156	F3
Xizhuang[SN]	156	G5
Xizhuang[SX]	54	B5
Xizhuang[YN]	148	H7
Xizhuangtuo[TJ]	42	C3
Xizuoling[SX]	54	C5
Xo Qu[SC]	138	E7
Xobo[XZ]	152	H5
Xogba[QH]	164	I7
Xoima[QH]	164	M5
Xoisar[XZ]	152	H5
Xomong[XZ]	152	G4
Xorēg[SC]	138	F4
Xorkol[XJ]	172	L6
Xorkol[XJ]	172	M6
Xu Jiang[JX]	98	D5
Xu Shui[HN]	114	C5
Xuancheng[AH]	90	E6
Xuancheng[FJ]	94	B4
Xuan'en[HB]	110	C4
Xuanfeng[JX]	98	B4
Xuanhan[SC]	138	M4
Xuanhe[NX]	168	B3
Xuanhua Qu[HEB]	48	C3
Xuanhua[HEB]	48	C3
Xuanhua[HL]	70	C5
Xuanhuadian[HB]	110	H3
Xuanjiangying[HEB]	48	D2
Xuanping Xi[ZJ]	84	D4
Xuanqiao[SH]	74	D2
Xuanwei[YN]	148	J4
Xuanwo[SN]	156	E8
Xuba[AH]	90	D5
Xubao[HEN]	106	E2
Xubu[FJ]	94	D2
Xubu[JX]	98	D2
Xubu[SX]	54	E1
Xuchang[HB]	110	F4
Xuchang[HEN]	106	E3
Xuchang[HEN]	106	E4
Xucun[JX]	98	E2
Xudao[SN]	156	F5
Xudun[FJ]	94	D2
Xue Shan[YN]	148	E3
Xuebai[GS]	160	F3
Xueban Shan[YN]	148	E4
Xuebao Ding[SC]	138	I3
Xuecha[SN]	156	E4
Xuecheng Qu[SD]	102	D5
Xuecheng[SC]	138	I4
Xuedian[HEN]	106	E3
Xuefang[SD]	102	G3
Xuefeng Shan[HN]	114	C5
Xuefeng[FJ]	94	E3
Xuefeng[HN]	114	C5
Xuegezhuang[BJ]	36	D3
Xueguan[SX]	54	B5
Xuehu[HEN]	106	H3
Xuehua Shan[SX]	54	B7
Xuehuan Hu[XZ]	152	F2
Xuejiadao[SD]	102	G4
Xuejiahe[SN]	156	G3
Xuejiawa[SX]	54	D2
Xuejiaying[BJ]	36	C4
Xuejing Hu[XZ]	152	E2
Xuejingzi[NX]	168	C2
Xuelian Hu[QH]	164	C6
Xuepan Shan[YN]	148	E4
Xueshan Zhang[GD]	118	F2
Xueshan[GZ]	144	C3

Name	Page	Grid
Xueshan[QH]	164	L6
Xueshan[YN]	148	E6
Xueshan[YN]	148	H4
Xuetian[HL]	70	C4
Xueweitai[TJ]	42	B4
Xuexin[JL]	66	D2
Xueyan[JS]	80	F5
Xueye Shuiku[SD]	102	D3
Xueye[SD]	102	D3
Xuezhuang[SD]	102	D4
Xuezhuang[TJ]	42	B3
Xuezhulin Dashan[YN]	148	E7
Xugba[XZ]	152	D3
Xugin Gol[QH]	164	H5
Xugou[SX]	54	D4
Xuhang[SH]	74	C2
Xuhe[HEN]	106	G3
Xuhui Qu[SH]	74	C2
Xuji[AH]	90	C5
Xuji[HEN]	106	G5
Xuji[JS]	80	E3
Xujia[SD]	102	H3
Xujiaba[GZ]	144	G3
Xujiadian[SD]	102	G2
Xujiadun[JS]	80	F4
Xujiahe Shuiku[HB]	110	G3
Xujiatai[TJ]	42	B1
Xujiawan[HEN]	106	B4
Xujiaya Shuiku[SD]	102	D4
Xujiaya[SD]	102	D4
Xujiazhuang[NX]	168	B4
Xujing[SH]	74	C2
Xukou[JS]	80	F5
Xukou[ZJ]	84	D3
Xuling[AH]	90	C6
Xuling[LN]	62	F5
Xuliu[JS]	80	D3
Xumeng[SD]	102	F4
Xumingsi[CQ]	132	D3
Xun He[HL]	70	D4
Xun He[SN]	156	F7
Xun Jiang[GX]	124	G2
Xun Jiang[GX]	124	H4
Xun Xian[HEN]	106	F2
Xuncun[AH]	90	E7
Xundian[HB]	110	G3
Xundian[YN]	148	I5
Xungba[XZ]	152	B3
Xungba[XZ]	152	E5
Xungmai[XZ]	152	F4
Xunhe[HL]	70	E4
Xunhua[QH]	164	O5
Xunjian[HB]	110	E3
Xunjiansi[YN]	148	I7
Xunke[HL]	70	E4
Xunle[GX]	124	F2
Xunwu Shui[GD]	118	H2
Xunwu Shui[JX]	98	C7
Xunwu[JX]	98	C7
Xunxi[JX]	98	D4
Xunyang Qu[JX]	98	C2
Xunyang[SN]	156	F8
Xunyangba[SN]	156	E7
Xunyi[SN]	156	E5
Xunzhen[SX]	54	C2
Xupei Yunhe[JS]	80	B2
Xupu[HN]	114	C5
Xuru Co[XZ]	152	E4
Xushe[JS]	80	E5
Xushi[FJ]	94	D2
Xushui He[SN]	156	D7
Xushui[HEB]	48	C4
Xutang[SC]	138	J3
Xutang[SH]	74	C2
Xutao[NX]	168	B4
Xuting[HEB]	48	B6
Xutuan[AH]	90	C3
Xutun[LN]	62	F4
Xutun[LN]	62	F4
Xuwei[JS]	80	E2
Xuwen[GD]	118	C6
Xuxinzhuang[BJ]	36	D4
Xuxur[SC]	138	G4
Xuyi[JS]	80	D3
Xuying[HEN]	106	E2
Xuyong[SC]	138	K7
Xuyuan[ZJ]	84	C3
Xuzhou[JS]	80	C2
Xuzhuangzi[TJ]	42	A4
Xuzhuangzi[TJ]	42	B4

Y

Name	Page	Grid
Ya He[HEN]	106	D4
Ya'an[SC]	138	H6
Yabai[SN]	156	E6
Yabral Shan[NM]	58	E8
Yabuli[HL]	70	E6
Yacha[GX]	124	C3
Yachang[GX]	124	D3
Yacheng[FJ]	94	F3
Yacheng[GS]	160	G5
Yacheng[HI]	128	B3
Yachi He[GZ]	144	E3
Yachuan[GZ]	144	F3
Yadian Shuiku[TJ]	42	B4
Yadingchuankou[NX]	168	B4
Yadong[XZ]	152	F6
Ya'ergenchu[NM]	58	O4
Ya'ergou[NX]	168	C3
Ya'ergou[NX]	168	C3
Ya'erma[NX]	168	C4
Yag Qu[QH]	164	G6
Yagan[NM]	58	E6
Yaggain Canco[XZ]	152	F3
Yagkêng Qu[QH]	164	K3
Yagkeng[QH]	164	K3
Yagmo[XZ]	152	E5
Yagra[XZ]	152	C4
Yagra[XZ]	152	D5
Yagra[YN]	148	E2
Yagradagzê Feng[QH]	164	H5
Yahe[LN]	62	I3
Yahekou Shuiku[HEN]	106	D4
Yahongqiao[HEB]	48	E4
Yahuai[HI]	128	C2
Yahui[GZ]	144	G4
Yaigêndo[QH]	164	I7
Yaji Shan[JS]	80	E5
Yajiang[CQ]	132	D4
Yajiang[CQ]	132	F5
Yajiang[SC]	138	G5
Yajiangqiao[HN]	114	F5
Yajing[GX]	124	F2
Yaka[XJ]	172	I5
Yake Shan[NM]	58	N3
Yakeshi[NM]	58	N3
Yalaoba[NM]	58	W11
Yalian[YN]	148	E6
Yaliang[HI]	128	B3
Yalihe[HL]	70	B3
Yalin[XZ]	152	F4
Yalong Jiang[SC]	138	E3
Yalong Jiang[SC]	138	G6
Yalong Jiao[HI]	128	B3
Yalong Wan[HI]	128	B3
Yalong[HI]	128	B3
Yalu He[NM]	58	O4
Yalu Jiang[JL]	66	G6
Yalu Jiang[LN]	62	I4
Yaluhe[HL]	70	B5
Yalujiang Kou[LN]	62	H5
Yalungsêlung Ri[XZ]	152	B4
Yam O[HK]	176	C3
Yaman Gol[NM]	58	N1
Yamansu[XJ]	172	N5
Yamat[LN]	62	E3
Yamen[GD]	118	F4
Yamzho Yumco[XZ]	152	G5
Yan Chau Tong[HK]	176	E1
Yan He[JS]	80	E3
Yan He[SN]	156	F4
Yan Shan[BJ]	36	E2
Yan Shan[HEB]	48	D2
Yan'an[SN]	156	F4
Yanbei[HN]	114	E5
Yanbei[JX]	98	C4
Yanbian[SC]	138	G9
Yancang[GZ]	144	C4
Yancang[SH]	74	D2
Yanchang[SN]	156	D8
Yanchang[SN]	156	G4
Yanchangbu[SN]	156	D3
Yanchasi[SN]	156	G4
Yancheng Qu[HEN]	106	E4
Yancheng[JS]	80	F3
Yanchi[BJ]	36	B3
Yanchi[GS]	160	D3
Yanchi[HB]	110	F3
Yanchi[NX]	168	B4
Yanchi[NX]	168	D3
Yanchi[XJ]	172	K5
Yanchi[ZJ]	84	F4
Yanchihe[HB]	110	E2
Yanchihe[SN]	156	F7
Yanchiwan[GS]	160	C3
Yanchuan[SN]	156	G4
Yancun[BJ]	36	C4
Yancun[HN]	114	C6
Yandang Shan[ZJ]	84	E5
Yandian[AH]	90	D5
Yandian[HB]	110	G3
Yandian[LN]	62	E5
Yandian[NM]	58	W11
Yandian[SD]	102	B3
Yandian[SD]	102	C4
Yandong[GX]	124	E3
Yandong[GZ]	144	G4
Yandou Qu[JS]	80	F3
Yanduhe[HB]	110	D3
Yandun[AH]	90	E6
Yandun[SH]	74	C3
Yandun[XJ]	172	O4
Yandunxu[HI]	128	C2
Yanfang[YN]	148	J5
Yanfeng[HL]	70	D4
Yang He[HEB]	48	B3
Yang He[SN]	156	D8
Yang Hu[XZ]	152	D2
Yang Xian[SN]	156	D7
Ya'ngamdo[XZ]	152	I4
Yang'an[SD]	102	D2
Yang'an[SX]	54	D5
Yangang[HEN]	106	G5
Yangba[GZ]	144	D6
Yangba[XZ]	152	J4
Yangbai[SX]	54	D6
Yangbai[SX]	54	E3
Yangbajain[XZ]	152	G4
Yangbei[SH]	74	D1
Yangbi Jiang[YN]	148	E5
Yangbi[YN]	148	E5
Yangbin[SH]	74	D1
Yangbu[JX]	98	B6
Yangcen[YN]	148	E4
Yangchang[GZ]	144	D3
Yangchang[GZ]	144	D4
Yangchang[GZ]	144	E4
Yangchang[GZ]	144	G3
Yangchang[YN]	148	J4
Yangchangzigou[QH]	164	I3
Yangcheng Hu[JS]	80	F5
Yangcheng[HEB]	48	C5
Yangcheng[SX]	54	D6
Yangchengzhuang[TJ]	42	B4
Yangchu[SD]	102	G2
Yangchun[GD]	118	D4
Yangcun[AH]	90	C4
Yangcun[AH]	90	E4
Yangcun[AH]	90	E7
Yangcun[GD]	118	G3
Yangcun[HN]	114	C5
Yangcun[JX]	98	B7
Yangcun[SX]	54	E6
Yangcunqiao[ZJ]	84	D3
Yangdang[HB]	110	F2
Yangdi[GX]	124	H2
Yangdi[JX]	98	D5
Yangdi[SN]	156	F7
Yangdian[HEN]	106	B3

Name	Page	Grid
Yangdong[GD]	118	E5
Yangdong[SH]	74	C2
Yangdu[CQ]	132	D3
Yangdun[FJ]	94	C2
Yange[JX]	98	B5
Yang'erzhuang[HEB]	48	E5
Yangfang[BJ]	36	C3
Yangfang[BJ]	36	C4
Yangfangkou[SX]	54	D2
Yangfeng[HN]	114	C4
Yangfu[SH]	74	C1
Yanggang[HB]	110	I5
Yanggang[HL]	70	G6
Yanggangzhuang[TJ]	42	C2
Yanggao[SX]	54	E1
Yangge[GS]	160	D3
Yanggong[GZ]	144	G5
Yanggou[NX]	168	C5
Yanggu[FJ]	94	B4
Yanggu[HEN]	106	F3
Yanggu[SD]	102	B3
Yangguangzhan[SX]	54	E4
Yangguo[SN]	156	F6
Yanghang[SH]	74	C2
Yanghe Shuiku[HEB]	48	G4
Yanghe[LN]	62	G4
Yanghe[NX]	168	C5
Yanghenan[HEB]	48	C3
Yanghou[FJ]	94	D3
Yanghu[AH]	90	D6
Yanghukou[HEN]	106	G4
Yangji[HB]	110	F3
Yangji[HEN]	106	G4
Yangji[HEN]	106	G5
Yangji[JS]	80	E2
Yangji[JS]	80	E3
Yangji[SD]	102	E5
Yangjia[HL]	70	D5
Yangjiaba[SC]	138	H9
Yangjiaba[SN]	156	C7
Yangjiabanqiao[HEB]	48	E4
Yangjiabo[TJ]	42	C3
Yangjiabu[BJ]	36	E2
Yangjiachang[TJ]	42	B2
Yangjiafang[HN]	114	D3
Yangjiafeng[HB]	110	F4
Yangjiahe[SN]	156	D8
Yangjiakou[TJ]	42	B2
Yangjialing[HB]	110	G5
Yangjiang[GD]	118	D5
Yangjiang[HI]	128	C2
Yangjiang[JS]	80	D5
Yangjiao[SX]	54	E5
Yangjiaogou[LN]	62	C3
Yangjiaotang[HN]	114	D4
Yangjiaotang[HN]	114	E6
Yangjiapu[LN]	62	G4
Yangjiatai[SN]	156	E5
Yangjiatan[NX]	168	B3
Yangjiawan[HB]	110	F5
Yangjiawan[HEB]	48	F1
Yangjiaxinzhuang[NX]	168	C4
Yangjiazhuang[HEB]	48	B4
Yangjiazhuang[SN]	156	G5
Yangjiazhuang[SX]	54	C4
Yangjiazui[NX]	168	B5
Yangjie[YN]	148	H7
Yangjie[YN]	148	I5
Yangjie[YN]	148	J6
Yangjing[SN]	156	D3
Yangjinzhuang[TJ]	42	B2
Yangjizigou[NX]	168	B4
Yangjuan[HEB]	48	B4
Yangjuan[HN]	114	D8
Yangjuanshan[NX]	168	D3
Yangjuantou[BJ]	36	C4
Yangjuanzi[LN]	62	E3
Yangjun[SD]	102	G3
Yangkou[SD]	102	E2
Yangkou[ZJ]	84	C4
Yanglang[NX]	168	C4
Yanglin[HN]	114	F3
Yanglin[HN]	114	F6
Yanglin[ZJ]	84	C3
Yangling Qu[SN]	156	E6
Yanglinzhai[HN]	114	E4
Yangliu[AH]	90	E6
Yangliu[SD]	102	D4
Yangliu[SD]	102	D4
Yangliu[YN]	148	E5
Yangliu[YN]	148	J4
Yangliuchi[HB]	110	D4
Yangliujing[YN]	148	K7
Yangliuqing[TJ]	42	B3
Yangliutang[GZ]	144	G4
Yanglong[FJ]	94	C3
Yanglou[SD]	102	C5
Yanglousi[HB]	110	G5
Yanglu[NX]	168	C4
Yangluchang[HN]	114	C6
Yangma[JS]	80	F3
Yangmadao[SD]	102	H2
Yangmahu[NX]	168	C3
Yangmanshao[GZ]	144	G4
Yangmei[FJ]	94	D4
Yangmei[GD]	118	E2
Yangmei[GX]	124	H5
Yangmei[HI]	128	C3
Yangmei[TW]	186	E2
Yangmei'ao[HN]	114	C6
Yangmeishan[HN]	114	F7
Yangmiao[AH]	90	D4
Yangmijian[SN]	156	E3
Yangming Shan[HN]	114	D6
Yangming Shan[HN]	114	D7
Yangming[NX]	168	B4
Yangmingbu[SX]	54	D2
Yangmingshan[TW]	186	E1
Yangmu[HL]	70	G6
Yangmu[JL]	66	G3
Yangmuchuan[LN]	62	H4
Yangmugou[JL]	66	I3
Yangmulin[JL]	66	F5
Yangmuzhazi[HEB]	48	D3
Yangou[SX]	54	D3
Yangping[GS]	160	I4
Yangping[HB]	110	H3
Yangping[SX]	54	C3
Yangpingguan[SN]	156	C8
Yangpo[BJ]	36	C2
Yangpo[BJ]	36	D2
Yangpo[HEN]	106	C3
Yangpotai[NX]	168	B5
Yangpu Qu[SH]	74	D2
Yangpu Wan[HI]	128	B2
Yangpu[HI]	128	B2
Yangqianhe[SX]	54	D1
Yangqiao[AH]	90	B3
Yangqiao[AH]	90	D6
Yangqiao[JX]	98	B4
Yangqiaodian[JX]	98	D3
Yangqiaopan[SN]	156	F3
Yangqing[GD]	118	C5
Yangqu Shan[SX]	54	E4
Yangqu[SX]	54	D3
Yangqu[SX]	54	D4
Yangquan[SX]	54	C4
Yangquan[SX]	54	E4
Yangquanqu[SX]	54	C4
Yangqungou[NM]	58	X11
Yangri[HB]	110	D3
Yangsha Pao[JL]	66	D1
Yangsha[GS]	160	F5
Yangshan[GD]	118	E2
Yangshan[JX]	98	C3
Yangshan[LN]	62	D3
Yangshan[SD]	102	C4
Yangshi[CQ]	132	B5
Yangshi[CQ]	132	F3
Yangshi[HN]	114	E7
Yangshu[BJ]	36	B3
Yangshufang[LN]	62	F5
Yangshulin[JL]	66	E3
Yangshuling[HEB]	48	F2
Yangshuo[GX]	124	H3
Yangshuwai[LN]	62	I2
Yangshuwan[LN]	62	D3
Yangshuwan[LN]	62	D4
Yangsi[SH]	74	C2
Yangsi[SN]	156	E7
Yangsong[BJ]	36	D3
Yangtan[AH]	90	F6
Yangtian[AH]	90	D6
Yangtian[GS]	160	G6
Yangtian[HEB]	48	C3
Yangtian[SN]	156	D7
Yangting[SD]	102	I2
Yangtou[GX]	124	I3
Yangtou[GZ]	144	H3
Yangtun[AH]	90	D3
Yangtun[LN]	62	F5
Yanguan[GS]	160	G5
Yanguoxia Shuiku[GS]	160	F5
Yangwan[GX]	124	E4
Yangwang[SX]	54	C6
Yangwei[HB]	110	D2
Yangwei[JX]	98	C3
Yangwu[GZ]	144	E4
Yangwu[YN]	148	H7
Yangxi[FJ]	94	C3
Yangxi[GD]	118	D5
Yangxi[GD]	118	F1
Yangxi[GX]	124	G2
Yangxi[GZ]	144	F1
Yangxi[HB]	110	E4
Yangxi[JX]	98	D5
Yangxi[SN]	156	E6
Yangxiang[GS]	160	E3
Yangxie[SN]	156	F7
Yangximu He[LN]	62	F2
Yangxin[HB]	110	I5
Yangxin[SD]	102	D2
Yangxing[SX]	54	D3
Yangxoi[XZ]	152	H4
Yangxu[GX]	124	D4
Yangyi[HEN]	106	G3
Yangyi[SX]	54	D4
Yangying[AH]	90	E4
Yangyuan[FJ]	94	B3
Yangyuan[FJ]	94	E2
Yangyuan[HEB]	48	B3
Yangyuan[SH]	74	D2
Yangyun[LN]	62	F4
Yangzha[TJ]	42	B4
Yangzhen[BJ]	36	D3
Yangzhong[FJ]	94	D3
Yangzhong[FJ]	94	E3
Yangzhong[JS]	80	E4
Yangzhou[JS]	80	E4
Yangzhou[ZJ]	84	D3
Yangzhuang[FJ]	94	C2
Yangzhuang[HEN]	106	E4
Yangzhuang[SD]	102	D5
Yangzhuang[SD]	102	E2
Yangzhuang[SX]	54	E2
Yangzhuangpu[SD]	102	D2
Yangzhuangzi[TJ]	42	C3
Yangzi[HB]	110	F3
Yangzi[SD]	102	F2
Yangzishao[JL]	66	G5
Yanhai[HI]	128	C2
Yanhe[CQ]	132	E1
Yanhe[GZ]	144	G2
Yanhe[HL]	70	E6
Yanhe[JS]	80	E3
Yanhecheng[BJ]	36	B3
Yanhewan[SN]	156	F4
Yanheying[HEB]	48	G3
Yanhui[SX]	54	E4
Yanji[AH]	90	B3
Yanji[HB]	110	I4
Yanji[JL]	66	J5
Yanji[JS]	80	D2
Yanjia[GZ]	144	D5
Yanjia[LN]	62	E3
Yanjia[ZJ]	84	C3
Yanjiahe[SN]	156	C6
Yanjiang[FJ]	94	B5
Yanjiang[HL]	70	C2
Yanjiang[JL]	66	D2
Yanjiang[JL]	66	H5

Yanjiao[GZ]	144	D4	Yanyuan[SC]	138	G8	Yaozhen[SN]	156	G2
Yanjiatai[BJ]	36	B3	Yanyuan[YN]	148	J3	Yaozhuangzi[TJ]	42	B4
Yanjiayu[SD]	102	D3	Yanzao[GD]	118	G4	Yaozitou[SX]	54	D2
Yanjiazhong[TJ]	42	B4	Yanzhang[ZJ]	84	D4	Yaozitou[SX]	54	D4
Yanjin[HEN]	106	F2	Yanzhen[GD]	118	H2	Yapo[HI]	128	B3
Yanjin[YN]	148	J2	Yanzhou[SD]	102	C4	Yapu[NX]	168	C4
Yanjing[CQ]	132	C4	Yanzhuang[HEN]	106	D3	Yaqian[JX]	98	D3
Yanjing[HN]	114	B3	Yanzhuang[SD]	102	B3	Yardoi[XZ]	152	G5
Yanjing[HN]	114	C6	Yanzhuang[SD]	102	D3	Yarkant He[XJ]	172	F7
Yanjing[HN]	114	D3	Yanzhuang[SX]	54	D3	Yarkant He[XJ]	172	G6
Yankou[HN]	114	D5	Yanzhuang[TJ]	42	A4	Yarlêb[XZ]	152	E5
Yankou[ZJ]	84	D2	Yanzi He[AH]	90	B5	Yarlung Zangbo Daxiagu[XZ]	152	I5
Yankoushan[QH]	164	J7	Yanzi[HB]	110	D5	Yarlung Zangbo Jiang[XZ]	152	D5
Yanlai[GX]	124	D2	Yanzi[JL]	66	D3	Yarrigang[SC]	138	E6
Yanliang Qu[SN]	156	F6	Yanzibian[SN]	156	B8	Yarri'gyü[GS]	160	F5
Yanling[GD]	118	F2	Yanzidun[NX]	168	C1	Yartang[QH]	164	M8
Yanling[HEN]	106	F3	Yanzigang[HB]	110	H3	Yashan[AH]	90	E6
Yanling[HN]	114	F6	Yanzihe[AH]	90	B5	Yashui[GZ]	144	E5
Yanling[JS]	80	E5	Yanzihe[HB]	110	G3	Yatang[GZ]	144	F4
Yanling[JX]	98	D5	Yanzikou[GZ]	144	D3	Yatian[HN]	114	D5
Yanliu[AH]	90	C4	Yao Shan[GD]	118	F1	Yatou[HN]	114	C4
Yanlou[SD]	102	B3	Yao'an[GD]	118	E1	Yau Ma Tei[HK]	176	D3
Yanma[SN]	156	G7	Yaoan[YN]	148	G5	Yau Tong[HK]	176	E3
Yanmai[CQ]	132	E2	Yaobao[LN]	62	G2	Yaxi[GZ]	144	E3
Yanmeidong[HEB]	48	B4	Yaobei[HN]	114	F6	Yaxi[JS]	80	E5
Yanmen[YN]	148	D2	Yaochuan[ZJ]	84	E3	Yaxi[SD]	102	I2
Yanmen[HN]	114	B5	Yaocun[AH]	90	F6	Yaxia[SX]	54	C6
Yanmenguan[SX]	54	D2	Yaodian[NM]	58	N1	Yaxing[HI]	128	B2
Yanmenkou[HB]	110	F4	Yaodian[SN]	156	D5	Yayang[ZJ]	84	E5
Yanminghu[JL]	66	I4	Yaodian[SN]	156	F4	Yayao[GX]	124	G2
Yanping[HB]	110	E3	Yaodianzi[SD]	102	E4	Yayou[HN]	114	B4
Yanpizhuang[TJ]	42	B3	Yaofu[NX]	168	C2	Yayuan[JL]	66	G6
Yanqi[XJ]	172	K4	Yaogou[JS]	80	D3	Yazhou Wan[HI]	128	B3
Yanqian[FJ]	94	B5	Yaogu[GD]	118	E4	Yazhou[JS]	80	F4
Yanqian[FJ]	94	C3	Yaoguan[YN]	148	E6	Ye He[HEB]	48	B5
Yanqiao[AH]	90	D5	Yaoguantun[HEB]	48	D5	Ye Xian[HEN]	106	E4
Yanqing Nongchang[BJ]	36	B3	Yaohe[AH]	90	C5	Yecheng(Kargilik)[XJ]	172	F7
Yanqing[BJ]	36	B3	Yaohe[SN]	156	F5	Yedian[SD]	102	E4
Yanshan Qu[GX]	124	H2	Yaohua[HB]	110	E4	Yefang[FJ]	94	C2
Yanshan[BJ]	36	B4	Yaohuai[HB]	110	D2	Yehe[JL]	66	E5
Yanshan[FJ]	94	C2	Yaoji[JS]	80	C2	Yeji[AH]	90	B5
Yanshan[FJ]	94	C4	Yaojiaba[HN]	114	F5	Yejia[ZJ]	84	C3
Yanshan[GZ]	144	F4	Yaojie[YN]	148	F6	Yejituo[HEB]	48	F4
Yanshan[HEB]	48	E5	Yaokou[AH]	90	C4	Yeli[SX]	54	F2
Yanshan[HN]	114	C5	Yaoli[AH]	90	C5	Yellow Sea[JS]	80	H3
Yanshan[JX]	98	E3	Yaolin[ZJ]	84	D3	Yellow Sea[LN]	62	F6
Yanshan[YN]	148	J7	Yaoling[BJ]	36	D2	Yellow Sea[SD]	102	H5
Yanshanying[NM]	58	X11	Yaolong Shuiku[HI]	128	B2	Yema Nanshan[GS]	160	B3
Yanshi Xi[FJ]	94	C4	Yaolongbang[SH]	74	C3	Yema Shan[GS]	160	B3
Yanshi[FJ]	94	C4	Yaolugou[LN]	62	C4	Yemaotai[LN]	62	F2
Yanshi[HEN]	106	D3	Yaomo Shan[GS]	160	C3	Yenchao[TW]	186	D4
Yanshi[SD]	102	B4	Yaomuyuan[SN]	156	B7	Yengibag[XJ]	172	H7
Yanshiping[QH]	164	E7	Yaoping[HB]	110	D2	Yengisar[XJ]	172	F6
Yanshou[HL]	70	E6	Yaoping[SN]	156	D7	Yengisar[XJ]	172	J5
Yanshou[HN]	114	F7	Yaoping[SN]	156	E5	Yengisu[XJ]	172	K5
Yantai Gang[SD]	102	H2	Yaopu[AH]	90	E4	Yeniugou Shisuzhan[QH]	164	J6
Yantai[SD]	102	H2	Yaopu[GZ]	144	D4	Yeniugou[QH]	164	L2
Yantan Qu[SC]	138	J6	Yaopu[LN]	62	F2	Yenshui[TW]	186	D3
Yantan[GX]	124	E3	Yaoqu[SN]	156	E5	Yeren[SH]	74	C3
Yantang[HI]	128	C2	Yaoqu[SX]	54	B5	Yesanguan[HB]	110	D4
Yantang[HN]	114	D5	Yaoqu[YN]	148	G9	Yesheng[NX]	168	C2
Yantang[HN]	114	F6	Yaoshan[NX]	168	C3	Yetan[HB]	110	D2
Yantangping[HB]	110	C5	Yaoshan[SN]	148	I8	Yetang[GD]	118	H2
Yantian Qu[GD]	118	G4	Yaoshang[BJ]	36	C4	Yetimbulak[XJ]	172	M6
Yantian[FJ]	94	E3	Yaoshang[BJ]	36	D3	Yetou[SX]	54	E4
Yantian[JX]	98	B4	Yaoshi[HN]	114	B5	Yetou[SX]	54	E6
Yanting[SC]	138	K4	Yaoshi[JX]	98	B4	Yeung Chau[HK]	176	D2
Yanting[ZJ]	84	E5	Yaotian[GD]	118	F3	Yeung Chau[HK]	176	E1
Yantongshan[JL]	66	G4	Yaotian[JX]	98	C4	Yeung Chau[HK]	176	E2
Yantongtun[HL]	70	C5	Yaoting[BJ]	36	E2	Yeung Ka Tsuen[HK]	176	C2
Yantou[ZJ]	84	E4	Yaotou[JX]	98	B5	Yeung Siu Hang[HK]	176	B2
Yanwan[SN]	156	C6	Yaotou[SX]	54	C3	Yexie[SH]	74	C3
Yanweigang[JS]	80	E2	Yaotou[SX]	54	D6	Yexing[SH]	74	C3
Yanwo[SD]	102	E2	Yaotun[HL]	70	F5	Yexu[GX]	124	E4
Yanwu[GS]	160	H4	Yaotuo[HEB]	48	F4	Yeyik[XJ]	172	I7
Yanxi[FJ]	94	C5	Yaowa[SX]	54	C3	Yeyuan[SD]	102	E3
Yanxi[HN]	114	C4	Yaowan[SX]	54	E5	Yeyungou[XJ]	172	J5
Yanxi[HN]	114	C5	Yaowei[JX]	98	D3	Yezhi[YN]	148	E3
Yanxi[JX]	98	C4	Yaoxian[NX]	168	C5	Yezhong[GZ]	144	C4
Yanxi[ZJ]	84	D5	Yaoxian[SN]	156	F5	Yezhu[HN]	114	C4
Yanxianfa[BJ]	36	C4	Yaoxianzigou[NX]	168	B3	Yezhugou[LN]	62	I3
Yanyang[JX]	98	C2	Yaoxin[HL]	70	C6	Yi He[HEB]	48	F4
Yanyoufang[HEB]	48	B2	Yaozhai[SD]	102	C3	Yi He[HEN]	106	D3
Yanyuan[HI]	128	C2	Yaozhan[SD]	102	C2	Yi He[SD]	102	E4

Yi He[SD]　102　E5
Yi O[HK]　176　A4
Yi Pak Au[HK]　176　B3
Yi Shan[SD]　102　E3
Yi Shan[SD]　102　E3
Yi Shui[HEB]　48　C4
Yi Xian[AH]　90　D7
Yi Xian[HEB]　48　C4
Yi'an[HL]　70　C5
Yibei[JS]　80　E2
Yibin[SC]　138　J7
Yibin[SC]　138　J7
Yibug Caka[XZ]　152　E3
Yichang[HB]　110　E4
Yiche[YN]　148　I4
Yicheng Qu[SD]　102　D5
Yicheng[HB]　110　F3
Yicheng[SX]　54　C6
Yichenggong[LN]　62　C2
Yichongqiao[HN]　114　C3
Yichuan[HEN]　106　D3
Yichuan[SN]　156　G4
Yichun[HL]　70　E5
Yichun[JX]　98　B4
Yici[YN]　148　G6
Yidao[SD]　102　G2
Yidouquan[SX]　54　F2
Yidu[FJ]　94　C4
Yidu[HB]　110　E4
Yiduhe[BJ]　36　D3
Yidushui[HN]　114　D6
Yifeng[JX]　98　B3
Yigou[HEN]　106　F2
Yiguojue[SC]　138　I7
Yigxung[QH]　164　L6
Yihe[HB]　110　G4
Yihe[SD]　102　E2
Yihe[SN]　156　G3
Yihuang Shui[JX]　98　D4
Yihuang[JX]　98　D4
Yihuqiao[GS]　160　G5
Yijiang Qu[AH]　90　E5
Yijiang[HN]　114　F7
Yijiang[JX]　98　C4
Yijiangshan Dao[ZJ]　84　F4
Yijigu Shan[ZJ]　84　F4
Yijin[AH]　90　D6
Yijing[SN]　156　E6
Yijing[SX]　54　C2
Yijing[SX]　54　E2
Yijun[SN]　156　F5
Yilan[HL]　70　E5
Yilan[JL]　66　J4
Yilaxi[JL]　66　G4
Yile[YN]　148　K3
Yilehuli Shan[HL]　70　C3
Yilehuli Shan[NM]　58　O2
Yilhung[SC]　138　E4
Yili He[YN]　148　I4
Yiliang[YN]　148　I6
Yiliang[YN]　148　J3
Yiligou[QH]　164　E2
Yilin[JS]　80　E3
Yiling Qu[HB]　110　E4
Yiling[JS]　80　E4
Yiliping[QH]　164　F3
Yiliu[HN]　114　E7
Yilong[HL]　70　C5
Yilong[SC]　138　L4
Yilunbu[HEB]　48　D5
Yiluo He[HEN]　106　D3
Yim Tin Tsai[HK]　176　D2
Yim Tin Tsai[HK]　176　E2
Yima[GS]　160　H5
Yima[HEN]　106　C3
Yima[JL]　66　G4
Yima[SX]　54　C4
Yimatu[HEB]　48　C2
Yimen[YN]　148　H6
Yimianpo[HL]　70　E6
Yimin He[NM]　58　M3
Yimin[NM]　58　M3
Yimin[SH]　74　C3
Yin Shan[NM]　58　H7

Yin Shan[NM]　58　V10
Yin Tsz Ngam[HK]　176　F2
Yina[GZ]　144　B3
Yina[GZ]　144　D4
Yinan[SD]　102　E4
Yi'nanhe[HL]　70　E4
Yin'aoxia[GS]　160　C2
Yincha[GX]　124　E4
Yinchuan[NX]　168　C2
Yincun[SH]　74　D2
Yindi[GZ]　144　D3
Yindian[HB]　110　G2
Yindian[HEN]　106　D4
Yinding Shan[GX]　124　I3
Yindou[SN]　156　G3
Yinfang[HEB]　48　B4
Ying He[AH]　90　C4
Ying He[HEN]　106　E3
Ying He[HEN]　106　F4
Ying Pun[HK]　176　C2
Ying Xian[SX]　54　E2
Yingbei[SH]　74　D1
Yingchang[LN]　62　H2
Yingcheng[BJ]　36　C3
Yingcheng[HB]　110　G4
Yingcheng[TJ]　42　C3
Yingchengzi[JL]　66　F4
Yingchun[HL]　70　C5
Yingchun[HL]　70　G5
Yingcun[ZJ]　84　D4
Yingde[GD]　118　F2
Yingdianjie[ZJ]　84　E3
Ying'emen[LN]　62　I2
Yingge Ling[HI]　128　B2
Yingge Zui[HI]　128　A3
Yingge[SN]　156　D6
Yinggehai[HI]　128　A3
Yinggezhuang[BJ]　36　D3
Yingguang[HN]　114　D5
Yingguantun[TJ]　42　B4
Yinghai[BJ]　36　C4
Yinghe[AH]　90　C4
Yinghua[JL]　66　D2
Yingiawat[XJ]　172　G5
Yingjia[HN]　114　D4
Yingjiang[YN]　148　C6
Yingjing[SC]　138　H6
Yingju[HEN]　106　F2
Yingko[TW]　186　E2
Yingkou[LN]　62　F4
Yinglan[HL]　70　E5
Yingli[GD]　118　C6
Yingli[HEB]　48　A5
Yingli[SD]　102　E2
Yingluo[LN]　62　F4
Yingna He[LN]　62　F4
Yingoi[SC]　138　G4
Yingpan Shan[YN]　148　J5
Yingpan[BJ]　36　C2
Yingpan[GX]　124　G6
Yingpan[SN]　156　F7
Yingpan[SN]　156　F9
Yingpan[YN]　148　E4
Yingpan[YN]　148　E6
Yingpanshui[NX]　168　A3
Yingpantai[NX]　168　D3
Yingpanwei[JX]　98　B5
Yingshan[HB]　110　I4
Yingshan[SC]　138　L4
Yingshang[AH]　90　C4
Yingshouyingzi Kuangqu[HEB]　48　E3
Yingsi[BJ]　36　D4
Yingtan[JX]　98　E3
Yingtaogou[BJ]　36　C3
Yingtaoyuan[SD]　102　B4
Yingtou[SN]　156　D6
Yingwang[SN]　156　F4
Yingwu[SH]　74　C2
Yingxian[AH]　90　B4
Yingxian[HI]　128　A2
Yingzhou[HI]　128　B3
Yingzi[SD]　102　E3
Yingzui Shan[GS]　160　B3
Yingzui Shan[GS]　160　C3

Yinhao[NM]　58　W10
Yinhua[SN]　156　G7
Yinhui[AH]　90　D6
Yining(Gulja)[XJ]　172　H4
Yining(Gulja)[XJ]　172　H4
Yinji Tan[HI]　128　F5
Yinji[AH]　90　D3
Yinji[JS]　80　E3
Yinjia[LN]　62　G2
Yinjiafu[BJ]　36　D3
Yinjiang[GD]　118　I2
Yinjiang[GZ]　144　G2
Yinjiaping[HB]　110　E3
Yinkeng[JX]　98　C5
Yinlingzhi[SX]　54　E4
Yinliu[TJ]　42　B2
Yinlong[SN]　156　E7
Yinma He[JL]　66　F3
Yinma Hu[QH]　164　C5
Yinmahe[JL]　66　F3
Yinong[ZJ]　84　E2
Yinping Shan[AH]　90　D5
Yinqiao[SN]　156　E7
Yinqiao[YN]　148　F5
Yinqing Qunjiao[HI]　128　F7
Yinshan[SD]　102　C3
Yintai Qu[SN]　156　F5
Yintian[QH]　164　N3
Yintun[SD]　102　C2
Yinxian[AH]　90　C4
Yinxiang[SD]　102　D2
Yinyang[JS]　80　G5
Yinzhu[ZJ]　84　D3
Yi'ong Zangbo[XZ]　152　I4
Yi'ong[XZ]　152　I4
Yipin[CQ]　132　C4
Yipingyuan[SX]　54　C5
Yiqên[XZ]　152　J4
Yiqian[JX]　98　D5
Yiqing[SH]　74　C1
Yirong[GD]　118　G3
Yirshi[NM]　58　M4
Yirtkuq Bulag[XJ]　172　L5
Yishan[AH]　90　D6
Yishan[AH]　90　E6
Yishan[JX]　98　C4
Yishan[SD]　102　C4
Yishan[SD]　102　E3
Yishanzi Dao[SD]　102　I3
Yishui[HB]　110　D2
Yishui[SD]　102　E4
Yishui[SN]　156　D7
Yishun[HL]　70　C6
Yitang[SD]　102　E4
Yitang[SX]　54　C5
Yitao[JS]　80　E2
Yitong He[JL]　66　F3
Yitong[JL]　66　F4
Yiwanquan[XJ]　172　N4
Yiwen[SD]　102　E4
Yiwu(Aratürük)[XJ]　172　O4
Yiwu[YN]　148　G9
Yiwu[ZJ]　84　E3
Yiwulü Shan[LN]　62　E3
Yixi[CQ]　132　F2
Yixian[LN]　62　E3
Yixiang[YN]　148　G8
Yixiken[HL]　70　C2
Yixing[JS]　80　E5
Yixingbu[TJ]　42　B3
Yixiu Qu[AH]　90　C6
Yixu[GX]　124　E4
Yixun He[HEB]　48　E2
Yiyajialake Shan[XJ]　172　M6
Yiyang[HEN]　106　D3
Yiyang[HN]　114　E4
Yiyang[JX]　98　E3
Yiyuan[SD]　102　E3
Yizhang[HN]　114　E7
Yizheng[JS]　80　E4
Yizhi[YN]　148　F7
Yizhou[GX]　124　F3
Yizhuang[BJ]　36　C4
Yizhuang[JS]　80　C2

Name	Page	Grid	Name	Page	Grid	Name	Page	Grid
Yizuoying[JL]	66	F5	Yongning[NX]	168	C2	Youshi[JX]	98	B6
Yoigilanglêb Qu[QH]	164	I5	Yongning[SC]	138	K3	Youshui He[SN]	156	D7
Yomqu[XZ]	152	H3	Yongning[SN]	156	E4	Youshui[JX]	98	C6
Yong Jiang[GX]	124	F5	Yongning[YN]	148	F3	Youtingxu[HN]	114	D6
Yong Jiang[ZJ]	84	F3	Yongning[YN]	148	I6	Youwei[SX]	54	D1
Yong'an Xi[ZJ]	84	E4	Yongping YN	148	E5	Youxi[CQ]	132	C4
Yong'an[AH]	90	D3	Yongping[FJ]	94	B4	Youxi[FJ]	94	D3
Yong'an[CQ]	132	D3	Yongping[HN]	114	C4	Youxian Qu[SC]	138	J4
Yong'an[FJ]	94	C4	Yongping[JX]	98	E3	Youxikou[FJ]	94	D3
Yong'an[GX]	124	G3	Yongping[SN]	156	E6	Youyang[CQ]	132	E5
Yong'an[GX]	124	G5	Yongping[SN]	156	F3	Youyang[FJ]	94	D4
Yong'an[NM]	58	N5	Yongping[YN]	148	F7	Youyi Feng[XJ]	172	K1
Yong'an[SD]	102	E2	Yongqing[HEB]	48	D4	Youyi[HL]	70	C5
Yong'anbu[BJ]	36	C3	Yongqing[HL]	70	C2	Youyi[HL]	70	E4
Yong'anpu[LN]	62	C4	Yongqing[JL]	66	I5	Youyi[HL]	70	F5
Yongbao[YN]	148	F6	Yongquan[HL]	70	C4	Youyi[SC]	138	E5
Yongbei[SH]	74	D1	Yongquan[SX]	54	D5	Youyiguan[GX]	124	D6
Yongchang[GS]	160	E3	Yongren[YN]	148	G4	Youyu[SX]	54	D2
Yongchang[ZJ]	84	D2	Yongshan[JX]	98	E2	Youzhen[JX]	98	B5
Yongcheng[HEN]	106	H4	Yongshan[YN]	148	I2	Youzixu[SH]	74	D2
Yongchuan Qu[CQ]	132	B4	Yongsheng[NM]	58	U11	Yu He[SX]	54	E1
Yongchun[FJ]	94	D4	Yongsheng[YN]	148	F4	Yu Jiang[CQ]	132	E4
Yongcong[GZ]	144	H4	Yongshengyu[NM]	58	X11	Yu Jiang[GX]	124	G5
Yongde[YN]	148	E6	Yongshou[SN]	156	E6	Yu Ling[AH]	90	E6
Yongdeng[GS]	160	F4	Yongshun[HN]	114	B3	Yu Ling[ZJ]	84	C3
Yongding He[BJ]	36	B3	Yongtai[FJ]	94	D4	Yu Shan[JS]	80	F5
Yongding He[HEB]	48	D4	Yongtai[JL]	66	H3	Yu Shan[JX]	98	C5
Yongding Xinhe[TJ]	42	B3	Yongtai[JX]	98	C4	Yu Shan[TW]	186	D3
Yongding[BJ]	36	C4	Yongtaizhuang[BJ]	36	C3	Yu Xian[HEB]	48	B4
Yongding[FJ]	94	B5	Yongwan[SX]	54	E6	Yu Xian[SX]	54	E3
Yongdinghe Guanqu[BJ]	36	C4	Yongwen[GZ]	144	E3	Yuan Dao[LN]	62	F6
Yongfa[HI]	128	C2	Yongxi[CQ]	132	B4	Yuan Jiang[HN]	114	C5
Yongfeng[BJ]	36	C3	Yongxi[FJ]	94	D4	Yuan Jiang[YN]	148	H7
Yongfeng[CQ]	132	D3	Yongxiang[SN]	156	F5	Yuan Shui[JX]	98	B4
Yongfeng[GD]	118	E3	Yongxin[GS]	160	G4	Yuan Shui[JX]	98	C4
Yongfeng[GS]	160	F4	Yongxin[JX]	98	B5	Yuan'an[HB]	110	E3
Yongfeng[HEN]	106	F4	Yongxin[SH]	74	C2	Yuanba Qu[SC]	138	K3
Yongfeng[HI]	128	C2	Yongxin[YN]	148	E6	Yuanbao Shan[GX]	124	G2
Yongfeng[HL]	70	D5	Yongxing Dao[HI]	128	F5	Yuanbao[HB]	110	C4
Yongfeng[JX]	98	C4	Yongxing[FJ]	94	D2	Yuanbaoshan Qu[NM]	58	M6
Yongfeng[JX]	98	C5	Yongxing[HB]	110	G4	Yuanbuzi[SX]	54	D2
Yongfeng[SN]	156	G6	Yongxing[HI]	128	C2	Yuanchang[TW]	186	D3
Yongfeng[XJ]	172	K4	Yongxing[HN]	114	F6	Yuancun[GZ]	144	E3
Yongfu[FJ]	94	C4	Yongxing[SC]	138	J6	Yuancun[HEN]	106	G1
Yongfu[GX]	124	G3	Yongxing[SC]	138	M4	Yuandongtou[SD]	102	E4
Yonggu[NX]	168	C2	Yongxing[YN]	148	G4	Yuandu[JX]	98	D3
Yonghan[GD]	118	F3	Yongxing[YN]	148	G4	Yuandun[SN]	156	C7
Yonghe[GS]	160	I5	Yongxiu[JX]	98	C2	Yuangezhuang[SD]	102	F3
Yonghe[GZ]	144	F3	Yongxiu[YN]	148	F6	Yuangezhuang[SD]	102	H2
Yonghe[HN]	114	F4	Yongxu[HL]	70	E5	Yuanguping[HN]	114	C3
Yonghe[SX]	54	B5	Yongzhou[HN]	114	D6	Yuanhongqiao[TJ]	42	C3
Yongheng[HL]	70	F5	Yopurga[XJ]	172	F6	Yuanji[AH]	90	D3
Yongji[GS]	160	G5	Yoqag Co[XZ]	152	F4	Yuanjiang[HN]	114	E4
Yongji[JL]	66	G4	Yorba[XZ]	152	J4	Yuanjiang[YN]	148	H7
Yongji[SX]	54	B7	You Jiang[GX]	124	E4	Yuankang[HEN]	106	E2
Yongjia[ZJ]	84	E4	You Shan[GD]	118	G1	Yuankeng[FJ]	94	B4
Yongjicheng[NM]	58	V10	You Shan[JX]	98	B6	Yuankou[HN]	114	D7
Yongjing[GS]	160	F5	You Shui[CQ]	132	F5	Yuankou[SD]	102	C4
Yongjiu[JL]	66	E3	You Shui[HN]	114	C4	Yuanli[TW]	186	D2
Yongkang[AH]	90	D4	You Xi[FJ]	94	D3	Yuanlin[TW]	186	D3
Yongkang[GZ]	144	F5	You Xi[JX]	98	B5	Yuanlinchang[NX]	168	C2
Yongkang[NX]	168	B3	You Xian[HN]	114	F5	Yuanling[HN]	114	C4
Yongkang[YN]	148	E6	Youcheng[JX]	98	D2	Yuanmen[GS]	160	G5
Yongkang[ZJ]	84	E4	Youchou[CQ]	132	F5	Yuanmen[HI]	128	B2
Yongle Jiang[HN]	114	F6	Youdunjie[JX]	98	D2	Yuanmengkou[TJ]	42	A4
Yongle[CQ]	132	F3	Youfangdian[AH]	90	B5	Yuanmou[YN]	148	G5
Yongle[GX]	124	D4	Youfangwan[HB]	110	F3	Yuanping[SX]	54	D3
Yongle[HL]	70	C6	Youguzhuang[TJ]	42	B2	Yuanqian[FJ]	94	C6
Yongle[SX]	54	B7	Youhao Qu[HL]	70	E5	Yuanqiang[AH]	90	B3
Yongle[SX]	54	D5	Youhe[HEN]	106	E5	Yuanqu[SX]	54	C6
Yongledian[BJ]	36	D4	Youji[AH]	90	D3	Yuanquan[SD]	102	E3
Yongli[GZ]	144	G5	Youjingzi[NX]	168	B3	Yuanren[SN]	156	F6
Yongli[NM]	58	U10	Youju[JX]	98	B3	Yuansha[SH]	74	D2
Yongling[LN]	62	H3	Youkou[JX]	98	D3	Yuanshan[SC]	138	K4
Yonglong[JX]	98	C6	Youlougou[HEB]	48	B2	Yuanshan[TW]	186	E2
Yonglong[SH]	74	D1	Youlun[HI]	128	B2	Yuanshi[HEB]	48	B6
Yongmao[JL]	66	C2	Youma[GX]	124	H4	Yuantai[LN]	62	F5
Yongming He[HN]	114	D7	Youmu[GX]	124	I2	Yuantan[AH]	90	C6
Yongnian[HEB]	48	B7	Younan[SH]	74	D1	Yuantan[GD]	118	F3
Yongning He[SC]	138	K7	Youquanzi[QH]	164	D2	Yuantan[HN]	114	F3
Yongning Qu[GX]	124	F5	Youshan[JX]	98	B6	Yuantaozi[NX]	168	B4
Yongning[BJ]	36	C2	Youshashan[QH]	164	C2	Yuantou[GX]	124	H3
Yongning[GD]	118	D4	Yousheng[GD]	118	H2	Yuantuan[AH]	90	D4
Yongning[LN]	62	E5	Youshi[HN]	114	E6	Yuanwu[HEN]	106	E3

Yuanxiang[HEN]	106	G3
Yuanxiang[SX]	54	D4
Yuanxinzhuang[TJ]	42	A3
Yuanyang[HEN]	106	E2
Yuanyang[YN]	148	H7
Yuanyi[CQ]	132	D3
Yuanyi[NX]	168	C1
Yuanzhu[JS]	80	F4
Yuanzhuang[CQ]	132	E3
Yuanzhuang[FJ]	94	D4
Yuanzi He[SX]	54	D2
Yuanzi[NX]	168	C5
Yuanzijie[SN]	156	F7
Yubei Qu[CQ]	132	C4
Yucha Zangbo[XZ]	152	D4
Yucha[SN]	156	F4
Yucheng[HEN]	106	G3
Yucheng[SD]	102	C3
Yucheng[SD]	102	C5
Yucheng[ZJ]	84	E2
Yuchi[CQ]	132	E3
Yuchi[HL]	70	E6
Yuchih[TW]	186	D3
Yuching[TW]	186	D3
Yuchuan[HB]	110	I4
Yuchuan[SN]	156	F7
Yucun[AH]	90	E6
Yucun[TJ]	42	C3
Yudai He[SN]	156	C8
Yudao[HI]	128	A3
Yudaokou[HEB]	48	D1
Yudi Shan[HL]	70	A2
Yudian[HB]	110	G3
Yuding[NX]	168	B3
Yudou[FJ]	94	D4
Yudu[GS]	160	H5
Yudu[JX]	98	C6
Yudu[SN]	156	D8
Yueba[SN]	156	D7
Yuecheng Ling[GX]	124	H2
Yuecheng Shuiku[HEB]	48	B7
Yuecheng[HEB]	48	B7
Yuechi[SC]	138	L5
Yuedong[GX]	124	H5
Yuegezhuang[BJ]	36	B4
Yuegong[SH]	74	C1
Yuehe[HEN]	106	E5
Yuehmei[TW]	186	E3
Yuehu Qu[JX]	98	E3
Yuehu[ZJ]	84	E5
Yuejia[SC]	138	M4
Yuejiazhuang[SD]	102	D4
Yuejin Nongchang[SH]	74	C1
Yuejin[BJ]	36	B3
Yuekou[HB]	110	G4
Yuekou[JX]	98	D4
Yuelai[CQ]	132	E3
Yuelai[JS]	80	D2
Yuele[GS]	160	H4
Yueli[GX]	124	E2
Yueliang Pao[JL]	66	D2
Yueliangpao[JL]	66	D2
Yuelu Shan[HN]	114	E4
Yuen Chau Kok[HK]	176	D2
Yuen Chau Tsai[HK]	176	D2
Yuen Chau[HK]	176	B4
Yuen Kong Chau[HK]	176	B4
Yuen Leng[HK]	176	D2
Yuen Long[HK]	176	C2
Yuen Ng Fan[HK]	176	E2
Yuepu[SH]	74	C2
Yueqing Wan[ZJ]	84	F4
Yueqing[ZJ]	84	E4
Yu'erhong[GS]	160	C3
Yu'ershan[HEB]	48	D2
Yu'erya[HEB]	48	F3
Yueshan[HN]	114	E5
Yuetang Qu[HN]	114	E5
Yuetian[HN]	114	F3
Yuetuo[HEB]	48	G4
Yuexi[AH]	90	C6
Yuexi[CQ]	132	E3
Yuexi[HN]	114	C5
Yuexi[SC]	138	H7
Yueyahu[NX]	168	C2
Yueyang[HN]	114	F3
Yueyang[HN]	114	F3
Yueyawan[NX]	168	B3
Yuezhangji[AH]	90	C4
Yuezhe[YN]	148	I6
Yuezhou[YN]	148	I5
Yuezhuang[SD]	102	E3
Yufa[BJ]	36	C4
Yufeng[GX]	124	E4
Yugan[JX]	98	D3
Yugê[QH]	164	H6
Yugêzib[QH]	164	G5
Yugong[HB]	110	F5
Yugong[HL]	70	F5
Yugou[AH]	90	D3
Yuhang Qu[ZJ]	84	E2
Yuhe[GS]	160	G6
Yuhe[HEN]	106	E2
Yuhe[SN]	156	F3
Yuhe[YN]	148	J3
Yuhong Qu[LN]	62	G3
Yuhong[GX]	124	D3
Yuhua[JS]	80	F3
Yuhua[SH]	74	C2
Yuhua[SN]	156	E5
Yuhuan Dao[ZJ]	84	F4
Yuhuan[ZJ]	84	F4
Yuhuang Ding[SD]	102	D3
Yuhuang Shan[SN]	156	D6
Yuhuangmiao[BJ]	36	B4
Yuhuangmiao[HEN]	106	F4
Yuhui[SH]	74	C3
Yuhuzhai[HEB]	48	F3
Yuji[HEN]	106	G6
Yuji[LN]	62	E3
Yujia[CQ]	132	D3
Yujia[JL]	66	G3
Yujia[TJ]	42	A4
Yujiafang[LN]	62	F3
Yujiahu[HB]	110	F3
Yujialingxicun[TJ]	42	C3
Yujiang[JX]	98	D3
Yujiaping[SN]	156	F3
Yujiawopu[LN]	62	F2
Yujiawu[BJ]	36	D4
Yujiayuan[NX]	168	C3
Yujiazhuang[TJ]	42	A4
Yujing Feng[JX]	98	F3
Yujing[AH]	90	C6
Yujing[SX]	54	D2
Yuju[SN]	156	F4
Yukeding[SD]	102	G2
Yukou[BJ]	36	E3
Yukou[HB]	110	D2
Yukou[SX]	54	D4
Yulan[HN]	114	C5
Yulan[SN]	156	E8
Yulao[GD]	118	D3
Yuli(Lopnur)[XJ]	172	K5
Yuli[HEN]	106	C2
Yuli[SD]	102	E4
Yuli[SD]	102	H2
Yuli[SX]	54	C5
Yuli[TW]	186	E3
Yulian[HI]	128	A2
Yuliangpu[NM]	58	N6
Yulin Gang[HI]	128	B3
Yulin He[SN]	156	F2
Yulin Jiao[HI]	128	A2
Yulin[GX]	124	H5
Yulin[HEN]	106	E4
Yulin[HL]	70	E6
Yulin[JL]	66	E4
Yulin[NM]	58	Y11
Yulin[SN]	156	F2
Yuling[SN]	156	G7
Yuling[SX]	54	D2
Yulinkou[BJ]	36	B3
Yulinzi[GS]	160	I5
Yulong Shan[YN]	148	F3
Yulong Xueshan[YN]	148	F3
Yulong[CQ]	132	B4
Yulong[GZ]	144	B3
Yulong[LN]	62	H4
Yulong[YN]	148	F4
Yulong[YN]	148	G6
Yulu[YN]	148	I4
Yümai[XZ]	152	H5
Yumen[GS]	160	C2
Yumin[TJ]	42	C4
Yumin[XJ]	172	I2
Yumingzhuang[TJ]	42	B3
Yumo[GZ]	144	E3
Yumuqiaozi[JL]	66	G4
Yun Ling[YN]	148	E3
Yun Shui[HB]	110	G3
Yun Xian[YN]	148	F6
Yun'an[CQ]	132	E3
Yunan[GD]	118	D3
Yun'an[GD]	118	D3
Yun'an[GD]	118	E3
Yunbiao[GX]	124	G5
Yunchao[ZJ]	84	E2
Yuncheng[SD]	102	B4
Yuncheng[SX]	54	B6
Yunfeng Shuiku[JL]	66	G6
Yunfeng[CQ]	132	E3
Yunfu[GD]	118	E4
Yung Shue Au[HK]	176	E1
Yung Shue Wan[HK]	176	C4
Yungaisi[SN]	156	F7
Yungan[TW]	186	D4
Yungang[BJ]	36	C4
Yungang[SX]	54	E1
Yungbo Co[XZ]	152	E2
Yungui[GZ]	144	C3
Yunhe[ZJ]	84	D4
Yunhuqiao[HN]	114	E5
Yunji[CQ]	132	D4
Yunjiang[GX]	124	G3
Yunkai Dashan[GX]	124	H5
Yunkai Dashan[GX]	124	H5
Yunlin[TW]	186	D3
Yunling[YN]	148	D2
Yunlong[CQ]	132	D3
Yunlong[HI]	128	C2
Yunlong[YN]	148	E5
Yunlong[YN]	148	H5
Yunluo[GD]	118	I3
Yunmeng Shan[BJ]	36	D2
Yunmeng[HB]	110	G3
Yunping[GS]	160	H6
Yunshan[JX]	98	D3
Yunshan[SC]	138	L4
Yunshu[TJ]	42	B4
Yuntai Shan[JS]	80	E2
Yuntai[GS]	160	G6
Yuntan[GD]	118	D5
Yuntian[GS]	160	G5
Yunwu Shan[GD]	118	D4
Yunwu Shan[HEB]	48	D2
Yunwu[GZ]	144	F4
Yunxi Qu[HN]	114	F3
Yunxi[HB]	110	D2
Yunxi[SN]	156	E8
Yunxi[ZJ]	84	C3
Yunxian[HB]	110	D2
Yunxian[YN]	148	F8
Yunxiao[FJ]	94	C6
Yunyan[SN]	156	G4
Yunyang[CQ]	132	E3
Yunyang[CQ]	132	E3
Yunyang[HEN]	106	D4
Yunyang[SN]	156	E6
Yunzhong Shan[SX]	54	D3
Yunzhou[HEB]	48	C2
Yunzhu[SX]	54	D4
Yupeng[FJ]	94	C3
Yuping[GZ]	144	G3
Yupug[XZ]	152	J5
Yuqag[XZ]	152	J5
Yuqian[ZJ]	84	D2
Yuqiao Shuiku[TJ]	42	C1
Yuqiao[NX]	168	B5
Yuqing[GZ]	144	F3
Yuqingtun[JL]	66	G4
Yuquan[CQ]	132	D4

Yuquan[CQ]	132	E2
Yuquan[HB]	110	E4
Yuquanying Nongchang[NX]	168	C2
Yuquanyingzhan[NX]	168	B2
Yuri[XZ]	152	I4
Yurungkax He[XJ]	172	H8
Yusha[CQ]	132	E2
Yushan Liedao[ZJ]	84	G4
Yushan[CQ]	132	E4
Yushan[FJ]	94	D3
Yushan[GZ]	144	F3
Yushan[HB]	110	F3
Yushan[HEN]	106	E4
Yushan[JX]	98	F3
Yushan[SN]	156	F6
Yushe[SX]	54	D4
Yushu[JL]	66	G3
Yushu[JL]	66	H5
Yushu[LN]	62	H3
Yushu[QH]	164	J7
Yushudian[NM]	58	W11
Yushugou[JL]	66	H3
Yushugou[NX]	168	C5
Yushulinzi[HEB]	48	G2
Yushulinzi[LN]	62	C3
Yushutai[JL]	66	E4
Yusi[LN]	62	E2
Yutai[SD]	102	C5
Yutai[TJ]	42	C3
Yutang[HN]	114	E5
Yutang[YN]	148	G7
Yutian(Keriya)[XJ]	172	H7
Yutian[FJ]	94	E4
Yutian[HEB]	48	E4
Yutian[HN]	114	E7
Yuting[AH]	90	D7
Yutou[ZJ]	84	C4
Yutun[SD]	102	C4
Yuwan[YN]	148	I3
Yuwang[NX]	168	C4
Yuwang[SX]	54	C6
Yuwang[YN]	148	J5
Yuweng Tao[TW]	186	C3
Yuxi[CQ]	132	B3
Yuxi[FJ]	94	E4
Yuxi[HB]	110	E4
Yuxi[JX]	98	F3
Yuxi[YN]	148	H6
Yuxiaguan[SX]	54	E5
Yuxiakou[HB]	110	D4
Yuxian[HB]	110	G4
Yuxiang[SX]	54	B7
Yuxikou[AH]	90	E5
Yuxin[HB]	110	F4
Yuxingzhuang[SN]	156	F2
Yuyan He[SN]	156	F4
Yuyangbang[SH]	74	C2
Yuyangguan[HB]	110	E4
Yuyao Jiang[ZJ]	84	F3
Yuyao[ZJ]	84	F2
Yuye Hu[XZ]	152	F1
Yuyi[JX]	98	D3
Yuying[HI]	128	C2
Yuying[HL]	70	B2
Yuyingwa[TJ]	42	C1
Yuyuan[ZJ]	84	D4
Yuyuancun[HEN]	106	B3
Yuza[SC]	138	H9
Yuzhong[GS]	160	G5
Yuzhou[HEN]	106	E3
Yuzhuang[SX]	54	D3
Yŭzhu'oma[XZ]	152	F4
Yuzi[JL]	66	E2

Z

Za Qu[QH]	164	G7
Za Qu[QH]	164	J7
Zadoi[QH]	164	H8
Zadoi[QH]	164	I7
Za'gya Zangbo[XZ]	152	F3
Zaibian[GZ]	144	G5

Zaima[GZ]	144	G4
Zaima[GZ]	144	G4
Zaimiao[GX]	124	E5
Zainmo Qu[QH]	164	D6
Zainmo[QH]	164	N5
Zalantun[NM]	58	O3
Zamashi[QH]	164	M2
Zamtang[SC]	138	F3
Zamu He[GS]	160	F4
Zanda[XZ]	152	A4
Zangbawa[GS]	160	F5
Zangmai[SC]	138	F4
Zangnan[SD]	102	F4
Zangqênrong[SC]	138	E6
Zangsêr Kangri[XZ]	152	D2
Zanguo[HN]	114	B3
Zangwan[JX]	98	E2
Zangxoi[XZ]	152	K5
Zangzhai[SX]	54	E2
Zanhuang[HEB]	48	B6
Zanzi[JL]	66	E3
Zaogoutou[SD]	102	E4
Zaohe[JS]	80	D2
Zaojia[AH]	90	D4
Zaojiacheng[TJ]	42	B3
Zaojiao[GS]	160	G5
Zaolin[BJ]	36	D4
Zaolin[SX]	54	E2
Zaoqiang[HEB]	48	C6
Zaoshi[HN]	114	F6
Zaoxi[JX]	98	B3
Zaoxi[ZJ]	84	D2
Zaoyang[HB]	110	F2
Zaoyuan[NX]	168	B3
Zaoyuan[SD]	102	D3
Zaoyuan[SN]	156	D5
Zaozhuang[SD]	102	D5
Zaqên[QH]	164	H7
Zaqungngomar[XZ]	152	F3
Zara[XZ]	152	H5
Zari[XZ]	152	G5
Zarikando[QH]	164	G8
Zaring[XZ]	152	G4
Zasib[XZ]	152	H3
Zawa[QH]	164	N4
Zaxoi[XZ]	152	G4
Zayu Qu[XZ]	152	J5
Zayü[XZ]	152	J5
Zeguo[ZJ]	84	F4
Zejia[HN]	114	B4
Zêkog[QH]	164	N5
Zekou[HB]	110	F4
Zeku[SD]	102	I3
Zênda[SC]	138	C3
Zeng Jiang[GD]	118	F3
Zengbutou[HB]	110	F4
Zengcheng[GD]	118	F3
Zengfeng Shan[JL]	66	I5
Zengfu[CQ]	132	C4
Zenggang[NX]	168	C2
Zengjiapan[NX]	168	D3
Zengmu Ansha[HI]	128	F8
Zengsheng[JL]	66	F3
Zengtian[GD]	118	G2
Zengtian[JX]	98	C4
Zepu(Poskam)[XJ]	172	F6
Zesui[ZJ]	84	D3
Zetou[SD]	102	H2
Zezhang[SX]	54	C6
Zezhou[SX]	54	D6
Zha He[YN]	148	F6
Zhabei Qu[SH]	74	C2
Zhacangsi[QH]	164	N5
Zhaga Shan[SC]	138	F6
Zhag'yab[XZ]	152	J4
Zhai'an[GX]	124	E5
Zhaigang[GD]	118	E2
Zhaigeda[SX]	54	D6
Zhaigen[HEN]	106	C4
Zhaihao[GZ]	144	G4
Zhaihao[SD]	102	E2
Zhaihe[HEN]	106	F5
Zhaiji[GZ]	144	F3
Zhaike[NX]	168	C4

Zhaikou[BJ]	36	C3
Zhaikou[ZJ]	84	E3
Zhaili[FJ]	94	C2
Zhaili[SD]	102	D3
Zhaili[SD]	102	E3
Zhaili[SD]	102	G2
Zhailong[GX]	124	G3
Zhaiqiao[JS]	80	E5
Zhaisha[GX]	124	G3
Zhaishang[SX]	54	D4
Zhaitang[BJ]	36	B4
Zhaitou[HEB]	48	B5
Zhaiwang[SD]	102	D2
Zhaiwu[GD]	118	E4
Zhaixi[ZJ]	84	D3
Zhaixia[JX]	98	B3
Zhaixia[JX]	98	B7
Zhaixinzhuang[TJ]	42	B2
Zhaixiu[GX]	124	G5
Zhaiying[GZ]	144	G3
Zhaizhen[SD]	102	D4
Zhaizhong[FJ]	94	E2
Zhaizhuang[TJ]	42	B1
Zhaizhuangzi[TJ]	42	B4
Zhaizi[HEB]	48	D6
Zhaizi[SX]	54	B5
Zhajiang[HN]	114	E5
Zhakeqi Shan[NM]	58	O2
Zhakou[GX]	124	G6
Zhamla[SC]	138	E6
Zhan He[HL]	70	D4
Zhanan[HI]	128	B3
Zhanang[XZ]	152	G5
Zhanbing[FJ]	94	D4
Zhancheng[JS]	80	C2
Zhandian[HEN]	106	E2
Zhang He[HB]	110	E3
Zhang He[HEB]	48	B7
Zhang Shui[JX]	98	B6
Zhang Xian[GS]	160	G5
Zhangba Ling[AH]	90	E4
Zhangba[SN]	156	D6
Zhangbaling[AH]	90	E4
Zhangbei[HEB]	48	B2
Zhangbu[GZ]	144	F4
Zhangcheng[NX]	168	B5
Zhangchong[AH]	90	C5
Zhangcun[AH]	90	B3
Zhangcun[FJ]	94	D1
Zhangcun[HEN]	106	C5
Zhangcun[SX]	54	C6
Zhangcun[ZJ]	84	C4
Zhangcun[ZJ]	84	D4
Zhangcun[ZJ]	84	D5
Zhangcunji[HEB]	48	B7
Zhangcunping[HB]	110	E3
Zhangcunyi[SN]	156	F5
Zhangcuo[FJ]	94	C2
Zhangdatun[SD]	102	C3
Zhangdazhuang[SD]	102	C2
Zhangde[HEN]	106	E3
Zhangdeng[HEB]	48	C5
Zhangdian[HEN]	106	D5
Zhangdian[JS]	80	F4
Zhangdian[SX]	54	C7
Zhangdian[SX]	54	D5
Zhangdo[XZ]	152	G5
Zhangdu Hu[HB]	110	H4
Zhangdu[AH]	90	E6
Zhang'erzhuang[HEB]	48	B7
Zhangfang[BJ]	36	B4
Zhangfang[HN]	114	G4
Zhangfeng[SD]	102	C4
Zhanggang[HB]	110	F4
Zhanggangpu[TJ]	42	B2
Zhanggongmiao[HN]	114	D3
Zhanggou[HB]	110	G4
Zhangguan[AH]	90	B4
Zhangguangcai Ling[HL]	70	D6
Zhangguanghe[HB]	110	I3
Zhangguanmiao[HEN]	106	G5
Zhangguo[JS]	80	F4
Zhanggutai[LN]	62	F2
Zhangguying[HN]	114	F3

Zhangguzhuang[HEB]	48	C5
Zhanghe Shuiku[HB]	110	E3
Zhanghe Shuiku[SX]	54	D5
Zhanghe[HB]	110	F4
Zhangheping[SN]	156	E8
Zhanghong[SN]	156	E5
Zhanghu[AH]	90	C6
Zhanghu[FJ]	94	D3
Zhanghua[SD]	102	C2
Zhanghuang[GX]	124	G5
Zhangji[AH]	90	B3
Zhangji[AH]	90	D4
Zhangji[HB]	110	F3
Zhangji[HEB]	48	B2
Zhangji[JS]	80	C2
Zhangji[JS]	80	C2
Zhangjia[GS]	160	H5
Zhangjia[GX]	124	H3
Zhangjia[JX]	98	E3
Zhangjia[SN]	156	F6
Zhangjiabao[HB]	110	D3
Zhangjiabu[HEB]	48	C3
Zhangjiabu[NX]	168	C4
Zhangjiachuan[GS]	160	H5
Zhangjiadian[JL]	66	E2
Zhangjiafen[BJ]	36	D2
Zhangjiagang[JS]	80	F5
Zhangjiahe[SN]	156	C7
Zhangjiajie[HN]	114	C3
Zhangjiakou[HEB]	48	B3
Zhangjialou[SD]	102	F4
Zhangjiang[SH]	74	D2
Zhangjiapo[SD]	102	E3
Zhangjiapu[LN]	62	E3
Zhangjiasai[HN]	114	E4
Zhangjiashe[TJ]	42	B2
Zhangjiashu[NX]	168	B4
Zhangjiawan[GZ]	144	D4
Zhangjiawan[HEB]	48	E1
Zhangjiawan[SN]	156	E4
Zhangjiawo[TJ]	42	B3
Zhangjiayan[NX]	168	C4
Zhangjiayingzi[LN]	62	C3
Zhangjiayuan[NX]	168	C4
Zhangjiazhai[GZ]	144	G3
Zhangjiazhuang[BJ]	36	D3
Zhangjiazhuang[HEB]	48	C4
Zhangjiazhuang[SX]	54	D2
Zhangjin[HB]	110	F4
Zhangjing[JS]	80	F5
Zhanglan[SX]	54	D4
Zhanglao[GX]	124	E3
Zhangliang[HEN]	106	E4
Zhanglin[HEN]	106	D5
Zhangling[HL]	70	B2
Zhangling[SD]	102	F3
Zhanglou[HEN]	106	D5
Zhangming[HEN]	106	F4
Zhangmu[JX]	98	C5
Zhangmulin[GX]	124	I3
Zhangou[AH]	90	C4
Zhangping[FJ]	94	C4
Zhangpu[FJ]	94	C5
Zhangpu[JS]	80	F5
Zhangpu[SH]	74	C2
Zhangqiang[LN]	62	F2
Zhangqiao[AH]	90	D4
Zhangqiao[HB]	110	E3
Zhangqiao[HEN]	106	F4
Zhangqiao[JS]	80	F4
Zhangqiao[SH]	74	D2
Zhangqiu[SD]	102	D3
Zhangqu[SN]	156	E3
Zhangsanying[HEB]	48	E2
Zhangshanying[BJ]	36	B3
Zhangshe[SD]	102	F3
Zhangshi[GD]	118	F2
Zhangshi[HN]	114	E7
Zhangshifu[SD]	102	C2
Zhangshiyan[HEB]	48	B6
Zhangshu[HN]	114	E4
Zhangshu[JX]	98	C3
Zhangtai[HEB]	48	C6
Zhangtai[TJ]	42	B2
Zhangtang[JX]	98	C5
Zhangtao[HEN]	106	F5
Zhangtiansi[HB]	110	F5
Zhangtieji[HEB]	48	C7
Zhangting[ZJ]	84	F2
Zhangtouwo[TJ]	42	C2
Zhangwan[FJ]	94	E3
Zhangwan[JS]	80	E2
Zhangwan[NX]	168	B5
Zhangwanji[HEN]	106	G4
Zhangwei Xinhe[HEB]	48	D6
Zhangwei Xinhe[SD]	102	C2
Zhangwei[HL]	70	D5
Zhangwengmiao[SH]	74	C3
Zhangwu[HEN]	106	C3
Zhangwu[LN]	62	F2
Zhangwu[SX]	54	B6
Zhangwu[ZJ]	84	D2
Zhangwudian[TJ]	42	C2
Zhangxi[AH]	90	D6
Zhangxi[GD]	118	G2
Zhangxi[JX]	98	D4
Zhangxi[ZJ]	84	F3
Zhangxia[SD]	102	C3
Zhangxiang[JX]	98	C3
Zhangxibu[HEB]	48	B7
Zhangxihe[SX]	54	F1
Zhangxinzhuang[TJ]	42	B2
Zhangyan[SH]	74	C2
Zhangyan[SH]	74	C3
Zhangyaoxian[SN]	156	D4
Zhangye[GS]	160	E3
Zhangyi[NX]	168	C5
Zhangyuan[SX]	54	D5
Zhangzhai[HEN]	106	F2
Zhangzhai[JS]	80	B2
Zhangzhai[SD]	102	B3
Zhangzhen[BJ]	36	D3
Zhangzheng[NX]	168	C2
Zhangzhishan[JS]	80	G5
Zhangzhou[FJ]	94	C5
Zhangzhu[JS]	80	E5
Zhangzhuang[HEN]	106	G5
Zhangzhuang[SD]	102	C2
Zhangzhuang[SD]	102	D4
Zhangzhuang[SD]	102	E4
Zhangzhuang[SH]	74	C3
Zhangzhuangpu[HB]	110	E5
Zhangzi Dao[LN]	62	F5
Zhangzi[SX]	54	D5
Zhangzipu[TJ]	42	C3
Zhangziying[BJ]	36	D4
Zhanhe[YN]	148	F4
Zhanhua[SD]	102	E2
Zhanjia[SD]	102	D2
Zhanjiang Gang[GD]	118	C5
Zhanjiang[GD]	118	C5
Zhanjiang[GX]	124	G5
Zhanmao[ZJ]	84	G2
Zhanpu[CQ]	132	D4
Zhanqi[ZJ]	84	F3
Zhanqiao[HN]	114	F3
Zhanshang[SX]	54	E4
Zhanwei[JX]	98	D3
Zhanxi[JX]	98	C3
Zhanyi[YN]	148	I5
Zhanyu[JL]	66	C3
Zhao He[AH]	90	D5
Zhao Xian[HEB]	48	B6
Zhao'an Wan[FJ]	94	C6
Zhao'an[FJ]	94	C6
Zhaobai[SX]	54	F2
Zhaobei[SX]	54	F2
Zhaobenzhuang[TJ]	42	C3
Zhaobi[SX]	54	E4
Zhaobishan[NX]	168	B3
Zhaobu[JX]	98	D3
Zhaochuan[HEB]	48	C3
Zhaochuan[SN]	156	G7
Zhaodi[HEN]	106	F2
Zhaodian[HEN]	106	C4
Zhaodong[HL]	70	C5
Zhaodun[JS]	80	C2
Zhaogang[HEN]	106	G6
Zhaoge[SD]	102	F3
Zhaogezhuang[HEB]	48	C4
Zhaogezhuang[TJ]	42	B2
Zhaohang[SH]	74	D2
Zhaohe[AH]	90	C6
Zhaohe[HEN]	106	D4
Zhaoji[AH]	90	B4
Zhaoji[JS]	80	D3
Zhaoji[CQ]	132	E2
Zhaojia[SC]	138	M5
Zhaojiadouwan[NX]	168	C3
Zhaojiagang[HN]	114	C3
Zhaojiagou[SX]	54	C3
Zhaojiahe[NX]	168	C5
Zhaojiahe[SN]	156	G4
Zhaojiapu[TJ]	42	B2
Zhaojiaquan[HEB]	48	C6
Zhaojue[SC]	138	H7
Zhaojunfen[NM]	58	V11
Zhaokua[YN]	148	I6
Zhaoliqiao[HB]	110	G5
Zhaoluzhuang[TJ]	42	C3
Zhaomaotao[HEB]	48	E5
Zhaomiao[AH]	90	B3
Zhaomin[JS]	80	G4
Zhaoniu He[SD]	102	C3
Zhaopeng[HB]	110	G3
Zhaoping[GX]	124	H3
Zhaopingtai Shuiku[HEN]	106	D4
Zhaopu[HEN]	106	D3
Zhaoqiao[AH]	90	E5
Zhaoqing[GD]	118	E3
Zhaoqizhuang[TJ]	42	B4
Zhaoquanhe[LN]	62	E4
Zhaoquanying[BJ]	36	D3
Zhaoshan[HB]	110	H4
Zhaoshi[HN]	114	B3
Zhaoshipan[SN]	156	F3
Zhaoshugou[LN]	62	F2
Zhaosu(Mongolkire)[XJ]	172	H4
Zhaosutai He[LN]	62	G1
Zhaotan[AH]	90	C7
Zhaoting[SH]	74	C2
Zhaotong[YN]	148	I3
Zhaowan[HB]	110	E3
Zhaowan[SN]	156	F8
Zhaowang[HEB]	48	D6
Zhaowang[SH]	74	C3
Zhaoxian[SD]	102	E4
Zhaoxian[SN]	156	D6
Zhaoxiang[SH]	74	C2
Zhaoxin[AH]	90	E4
Zhaoxing[HL]	70	F5
Zhaoyang Hu[SD]	102	C5
Zhaoyanghe[HEB]	48	B1
Zhaoyangwan[HEB]	48	E1
Zhaoyuan[HEN]	106	D2
Zhaoyuan[HL]	70	C6
Zhaoyuan[SD]	102	G2
Zhaozhaizi[SD]	102	C3
Zhaozhou[HL]	70	C6
Zhaozhuang[HEB]	48	B6
Zhaozhuang[JS]	80	B2
Zhaozhugou[SN]	156	F5
Zhapo Gang[GD]	118	D5
Zhapo[GD]	118	D5
Zhapu[ZJ]	84	F2
Zhari Namco[XZ]	152	D4
Zhashui[SN]	156	F7
Zhaxi[SH]	74	D1
Zhaxia[JS]	80	D2
Zhaxigang[XZ]	152	A3
Zhaxigang[XZ]	152	F5
Zhaxigang[XZ]	152	G5
Zhaxizom[XZ]	152	E5
Zhayang[FJ]	94	E2
Zhaye[HI]	128	B3
Zhazuo[GZ]	144	E4
Zhe'ai[GX]	124	C3
Zhêba[XZ]	152	D5
Zhecheng[HEN]	106	G3
Zhedaikou[ZJ]	84	C4
Zheduo Shan[SC]	138	G5
Zhefang[YN]	148	D6

Zhehai[YN]	148	I4	Zhenping[SC]	138	I3	Zhixin[SH]	74	D2
Zhehang[GX]	124	B3	Zhenping[SN]	156	F9	Zhiyan[ZJ]	84	D3
Zhehou[YN]	148	G6	Zhenqian[FJ]	94	E2	Zhiyang[JX]	98	B5
Zhejue[GZ]	144	B4	Zhentai[YN]	148	F7	Zhiyi[HL]	70	F6
Zhelang[GD]	118	H4	Zhentou[HN]	114	F4	Zhizhong[HI]	128	B3
Zhelang[GX]	124	C3	Zhenwen[GD]	118	C5	Zhizhushan[LN]	62	E3
Zhelin Hu[JX]	98	C2	Zhenwu[JS]	80	E4	Zhogxog[QH]	164	H8
Zhelin[GD]	118	J3	Zhenxi[CQ]	132	D4	Zhoinda[QH]	164	J7
Zhemiao[GX]	124	C3	Zhenxiang[HL]	70	C5	Zhong Lingka[XZ]	152	J5
Zhen Shui[GD]	118	F2	Zhenxin[TJ]	42	C3	Zhong Shui[HN]	114	E7
Zhen'an[CQ]	132	E2	Zhenxing[HL]	70	F5	Zhong Xian[CQ]	132	E3
Zhen'an[SN]	156	F7	Zhenxing[LN]	62	H2	Zhong Zakog[SC]	138	E3
Zhen'an[YN]	148	D6	Zhenxiong[YN]	148	J3	Zhong'an[LN]	62	E3
Zhenba[SN]	156	D8	Zhenyuan[GS]	160	H5	Zhong'an[SH]	74	D2
Zhenbao Ding[GX]	124	H1	Zhenyuan[GZ]	144	G3	Zhong'ao[CQ]	132	B4
Zhenbei[SH]	74	C1	Zhenyuan[SN]	156	E6	Zhongba[GD]	118	H3
Zhenbeipu[NX]	168	C2	Zhenyuan[YN]	148	G6	Zhongba[GZ]	144	E5
Zhenchengdi[SX]	54	D4	Zhenzhudong[GD]	118	D5	Zhongba[GZ]	144	G2
Zhenchuan[SN]	156	G3	Zhenzi[HB]	110	D3	Zhongba[HB]	110	D2
Zhendong[JS]	80	F2	Zhenzi[SC]	138	K6	Zhongba[XZ]	152	D5
Zhendong[YN]	148	F8	Zhenzijie[CQ]	132	C5	Zhongbao[FJ]	94	B4
Zhenfeng[GZ]	144	D5	Zhenziling Shuiku[LN]	62	H2	Zhongbao[HB]	110	C5
Zheng'an[GZ]	144	F2	Zherong[FJ]	94	E2	Zhongbao[SN]	156	F9
Zheng'an[HEN]	106	E3	Zhesang[YN]	148	K7	Zhongbaoping[ZJ]	84	D3
Zhengang[JX]	98	C7	Zheshan[SD]	102	E3	Zhongbei[TJ]	42	B3
Zhengba[CQ]	132	E2	Zhesi Gou[NX]	168	C4	Zhongbu[SD]	102	E3
Zhengchang[GZ]	144	F3	Zhetai[YN]	148	J6	Zhongcang[XZ]	152	D3
Zhengcheng[SD]	102	D4	Zhetian[JX]	98	B4	Zhongchao[GZ]	144	H4
Zhengcun[AH]	90	E5	Zhetu[YN]	148	J6	Zhongcheng[HL]	70	G6
Zhengda[GZ]	144	H3	Zhexi Shuiku[HN]	114	D4	Zhongchi[FJ]	94	B5
Zhengdi[FJ]	94	C4	Zhexi[HN]	114	D4	Zhongchuan[GS]	160	F4
Zhengdian[SH]	74	C3	Zhexiang[GZ]	144	D5	Zhongcun[JX]	98	C5
Zhengding[HEB]	48	B5	Zhexiang[GZ]	144	E6	Zhongcun[SD]	102	D4
Zhengdong[YN]	148	G8	Zhi'an[NM]	58	N6	Zhongcun[SN]	156	G7
Zhengdun[FJ]	94	D2	Zhibao[HI]	128	B2	Zhongcun[SX]	54	C6
Zhengfang[FJ]	94	C3	Zhibu[ZJ]	84	E3	Zhongcun[SX]	54	D5
Zhengguo[GD]	118	F3	Zhichanghe[HB]	110	C4	Zhongdai[ZJ]	84	E2
Zhenghe[FJ]	94	D2	Zhicheng[HB]	110	E4	Zhongdam[SC]	138	E6
Zhenghong[JS]	80	E3	Zhicheng[HEN]	106	D2	Zhongdian[AH]	90	C5
Zhenghuangqi[BJ]	36	C3	Zhichu[SD]	102	H2	Zhongding[SD]	102	D2
Zhengji[JS]	80	C2	Zhichuan[SN]	156	G5	Zhongdong[GD]	118	C5
Zhengjia[SD]	102	B3	Zhicun[YN]	148	I7	Zhongdong[GX]	124	E5
Zhengjiatai[BJ]	36	B4	Zhidan[SN]	156	E4	Zhongdong[HN]	114	F4
Zhengjiawu[ZJ]	84	E3	Zhidian[HEN]	106	G4	Zhongdu[FJ]	94	B5
Zhengjiazhai[SD]	102	C2	Zhidoi[QH]	164	H7	Zhongdu[GX]	124	G3
Zhengjiazhazi[BJ]	36	C2	Zhifang[GZ]	144	F3	Zhongfan[JX]	98	E3
Zhengjipu[NX]	168	D3	Zhifang[HEN]	106	D3	Zhongfang[HN]	114	B5
Zhenglan(Xulun Hoh)Qi[NM]	58	L6	Zhifang[SD]	102	C4	Zhonggang[JX]	98	D4
Zhengmu[SD]	102	E3	Zhifang[XJ]	172	M3	Zhonggong[SD]	102	D3
Zhengning[GS]	160	I5	Zhifeng[AH]	90	C6	Zhonggu[LN]	62	H2
Zhengping[JX]	98	B6	Zhifu Dao[SD]	102	H2	Zhonggu[SC]	138	G5
Zhengqi[NX]	168	B4	Zhifu Qu[SD]	102	H2	Zhonggu[SH]	74	C2
Zhengshan[SD]	102	E5	Zhig[XZ]	152	F5	Zhongguan[JX]	98	D2
Zhengxiangbai(Xulun Hobot Qa-gan)Qi[NM]	58	K6	Zhigao[AH]	90	D5	Zhongguanyi[HB]	110	H3
			Zhigoikongma[QH]	164	G6	Zhonghe[GS]	160	F4
Zhengxing[YN]	148	F7	Zhigou[SD]	102	F4	Zhonghe[GX]	124	H5
Zhengyang[AH]	90	C4	Zhihe[AH]	90	D3	Zhonghe[HI]	128	B2
Zhengyang[HEN]	106	F5	Zhijiang[HB]	110	E4	Zhonghe[HL]	70	C5
Zhengyang[SN]	156	E6	Zhijiang[HN]	114	B5	Zhonghe[HL]	70	E6
Zhengyang[SN]	156	F8	Zhijichang Shan[NM]	58	O1	Zhonghe[HN]	114	D7
Zhengyangshan[HL]	70	D4	Zhijin[GZ]	144	D4	Zhonghe[NX]	168	C4
Zhengyi[JS]	80	F5	Zhike[SX]	54	C4	Zhonghe[YN]	148	D5
Zhengzhi[SC]	138	L4	Zhilan[HB]	110	D4	Zhonghexu[GD]	118	E4
Zhengzhou[HEN]	106	E3	Zhilang[GX]	124	E6	Zhongheying[YN]	148	I7
Zhengzhuang[SN]	156	F4	Zhile[HEN]	106	F4	Zhongji[SN]	156	G1
Zhengzhuang[SX]	54	D6	Zhiluo[SN]	156	F5	Zhongjiagou[SN]	156	D8
Zhenhai Qu[ZJ]	84	F3	Zhima[FJ]	94	C2	Zhongjian Dao[HI]	128	F5
Zhenhai Wan[GD]	118	E5	Zhima[GZ]	144	E3	Zhongjian Nongchang[HI]	128	C2
Zhenhu[JS]	80	F5	Zhimadun[SD]	102	E4	Zhongjiang[SC]	138	J4
Zhenjiang[GD]	118	C5	Zhimugkamdo[QH]	164	L7	Zhongjiang[YN]	148	F4
Zhenjiang[JS]	80	E4	Zhina[YN]	148	D5	Zhongjianhe[HB]	110	C4
Zhenjiang[LN]	62	I4	Zhingwazalung[QH]	164	I5	Zhongjiao[SN]	156	G3
Zhenkang[YN]	148	D7	Zhipao[HI]	128	B3	Zhongjiapu[HN]	114	D3
Zhenkou[JX]	98	D4	Zhiping[FJ]	94	B3	Zhongjiaqiao[HN]	114	F5
Zhenlai[JL]	66	D2	Zhiping[ZJ]	84	D3	Zhongjieshan Liedao[ZJ]	84	G2
Zhenlong Shan[GX]	124	G4	Zhiqu[QH]	164	H6	Zhongke[GX]	124	F4
Zhenlong[GX]	124	G4	Zhiqutong[QH]	164	F6	Zhongke[YN]	148	E8
Zhenluo[NX]	168	B3	Zhiren[ZJ]	84	F4	Zhonglian[SH]	74	C2
Zhenluoying[BJ]	36	E3	Zhishan[GD]	118	E4	Zhongliang[CQ]	132	F2
Zhennan[GZ]	144	F2	Zhitan[JX]	98	E2	Zhongliao[HI]	128	B3
Zhennan[JL]	66	D2	Zhitang[JS]	80	F5	Zhongling[CQ]	132	E5
Zhenning[GZ]	144	D4	Zhixi[JS]	80	E5	Zhongling[CQ]	132	E5
Zhenningbu[HEB]	48	C3	Zhixia[JX]	98	C5	Zhongling[JX]	98	D3
Zhenping[HEN]	106	D4	Zhixin[JL]	66	J5	Zhonglou[SD]	102	E4

Zhonglu[HB]	110	B4
Zhonglupu[HN]	114	E5
Zhongmen[FJ]	94	E4
Zhongmiao[AH]	90	D5
Zhongmiao[GS]	160	G6
Zhongming[AH]	90	E6
Zhongmou[HEN]	106	F3
Zhongnan Shan[SN]	156	F7
Zhongnan[SN]	156	E6
Zhongning[NX]	168	B3
Zhongpai[YN]	148	E4
Zhongping[HI]	128	C2
Zhongping[YN]	148	H5
Zhongpu[GS]	160	F4
Zhongpu[GS]	160	F5
Zhongqiao[BJ]	36	E3
Zhongquan[GS]	160	G4
Zhongrui Nongchang[HI]	128	C2
Zhongsanjia[LN]	62	C3
Zhongsha Qundao[HI]	128	F5
Zhongsha[HI]	128	A3
Zhongsha[HN]	114	E5
Zhongshan He[JS]	80	E2
Zhongshan[CQ]	132	C5
Zhongshan[FJ]	94	B4
Zhongshan[FJ]	94	D4
Zhongshan[GD]	118	F4
Zhongshan[GX]	124	E3
Zhongshan[GX]	124	I3
Zhongshan[GZ]	144	E4
Zhongshan[YN]	148	D6
Zhongshanhe Kou[JS]	80	F2
Zhongshanjian[SN]	156	E3
Zhongshui[GZ]	144	B3
Zhongtai[TJ]	42	B3
Zhongtang[GD]	118	F3
Zhongtiao Shan[SX]	54	B7
Zhongting[GX]	124	D3
Zhongtun[YN]	148	J3
Zhongwang[TJ]	42	B4
Zhongwei[NX]	168	B3
Zhongxia[HN]	114	C5
Zhongxian[FJ]	94	D4
Zhongxiang[HB]	110	F3
Zhongxin[FJ]	94	D1
Zhongxin[GD]	118	G2
Zhongxin[SH]	74	C2
Zhongxincun[BJ]	36	E3
Zhongxing[AH]	90	C4
Zhongxing[AH]	90	D3
Zhongxing[CQ]	132	E3
Zhongxing[HI]	128	B2
Zhongxing[HL]	70	B5
Zhongxing[SH]	74	D1
Zhongxinzhuang[TJ]	42	C3
Zhongyang[SX]	54	C4
Zhongyang[SX]	54	D3
Zhongyangfang[BJ]	36	B2
Zhongye Qunjiao[HI]	128	F6
Zhongying[TJ]	42	B1
Zhongying[YN]	148	F4
Zhongyong[GX]	124	H2
Zhongyuan[HI]	128	C2
Zhongyukou[HN]	114	E3
Zhongyun[JX]	98	E2
Zhongyushudian[BJ]	36	D2
Zhongzhai[GS]	160	G6
Zhongzhai[GZ]	144	D4
Zhongzhai[HN]	114	B5
Zhongzhao[HEN]	106	F2
Zhongzhou[GD]	118	E2
Zhongzhuang[JS]	80	E3
Zhongzhuang[SD]	102	E3
Zhongzhuang[SD]	102	F3
Zhongzhuang[SX]	54	C4
Zhongzhuang[SX]	54	D3
Zhou He[SC]	138	M4
Zhou He[SN]	156	E4
Zhou He[TJ]	42	B2
Zhoubang[SH]	74	C2
Zhoucheng[NX]	168	C2
Zhoucheng[SD]	102	C4
Zhoucheng[YN]	148	F5
Zhoucun Qu[SD]	102	D3
Zhoucun[HEB]	48	C6
Zhoudang[HEN]	106	F6
Zhoufang[JX]	98	E3
Zhoufen[JS]	80	E3
Zhougang[AH]	90	E4
Zhougou[HB]	110	F5
Zhouhe[HB]	110	G5
Zhouhe[HEN]	106	G6
Zhouhe[SN]	156	E3
Zhouhu[JX]	98	B4
Zhouhuaban[SX]	54	D2
Zhouji[HB]	110	F4
Zhoujia[LN]	62	F4
Zhoujiabang[SH]	74	D2
Zhoujiacun[AH]	90	E7
Zhoujiadian[HN]	114	D3
Zhoujiagang[SH]	74	C2
Zhoujiang[GD]	118	H3
Zhoujiaping[SC]	138	G7
Zhoujiazhuang[NX]	168	C5
Zhoukou[HEN]	106	F4
Zhoukoudian[BJ]	36	B4
Zhoulangzui[HB]	110	G5
Zhoulaozui[HB]	110	F4
Zhouli[SC]	138	K6
Zhouliangzhuang[TJ]	42	B2
Zhouling[ZJ]	84	D5
Zhoumensi[HN]	114	F6
Zhouning[FJ]	94	E2
Zhouping[HB]	110	D4
Zhouqin[GZ]	144	F5
Zhoushan Dao[ZJ]	84	G2
Zhoushan Qundao[ZJ]	84	G2
Zhoushan[ZJ]	84	E4
Zhoushan[ZJ]	84	G2
Zhoushizhuang[SX]	54	E1
Zhoutaizi[SN]	156	D3
Zhoutan[AH]	90	D6
Zhoutian[JX]	98	C6
Zhoutie[JS]	80	E2
Zhoutuozi[LN]	62	F2
Zhouwangmiao[ZJ]	84	E2
Zhouwangpu[HN]	114	D5
Zhouxi[GZ]	144	F4
Zhouxi[JX]	98	D2
Zhouxiang[HB]	110	H3
Zhouxu[GX]	124	E4
Zhouying[HEN]	106	G4
Zhouying[SD]	102	D5
Zhouzai Dao[HI]	128	C3
Zhouzhai[AH]	90	C2
Zhouzhi[SN]	156	E6
Zhouzhuang[JS]	80	E4
Zhouzhuang[JS]	80	F5
Zhu Dao[LN]	62	E5
Zhu Jiang[GD]	118	F4
Zhuanchang[BJ]	36	D4
Zhuanduo[TJ]	42	B4
Zhuangbian[FJ]	94	E4
Zhuangbu[JX]	98	C6
Zhuangdingtun[BJ]	36	D4
Zhuang'ershang[SX]	54	D5
Zhuanggang[SD]	102	F4
Zhuangguoyu[TJ]	42	B1
Zhuanghe[LN]	62	F5
Zhuangkou[JX]	98	C6
Zhuanglang He[GS]	160	F4
Zhuanglang[GS]	160	H5
Zhuangmo[SX]	54	D3
Zhuangmu[AH]	90	D4
Zhuangwang[SX]	54	E2
Zhuangyuan'ao[ZJ]	84	F5
Zhuangzhai[SD]	102	B4
Zhuanjing[SN]	156	D3
Zhuanmiaoliang[SN]	156	G5
Zhuanqiao[AH]	90	D5
Zhuanqiao[HN]	114	F5
Zhuanqiao[SH]	74	D2
Zhuanshui[GD]	118	H3
Zhuantang[CQ]	132	C5
Zhuantang[ZJ]	84	E2
Zhuanyao[NX]	168	C4
Zhu'ao[ZJ]	84	F3
Zhuba[JS]	80	D3
Zhubahe[SN]	156	C8
Zhubi Jiang[HI]	128	B2
Zhubian[SD]	102	E4
Zhubo[GX]	124	D5
Zhucang[GZ]	144	D4
Zhucaoying[HEB]	48	G3
Zhuchang[GX]	124	C3
Zhuchang[GZ]	144	D3
Zhucheng[SD]	102	F4
Zhuchengzi[JL]	66	F3
Zhudong[GZ]	144	C5
Zhudu[JS]	80	E2
Zhu'erduohe[JL]	66	I4
Zhufeng[AH]	90	E6
Zhufo[CQ]	132	E4
Zhufo'an[AH]	90	C5
Zhugan He[HEN]	106	F6
Zhuge[SD]	102	E4
Zhuge[ZJ]	84	D3
Zhugkyung[QH]	164	L3
Zhugou[HEN]	106	E5
Zhugou[SD]	102	F3
Zhugou[SD]	102	G3
Zhugqu[GS]	160	G6
Zhugu[QH]	164	O3
Zhuguang Shan[HN]	114	F7
Zhuguang Shan[JX]	98	A6
Zhuguanlong[FJ]	94	E2
Zhuhai[GD]	118	F4
Zhuhe[HB]	110	G5
Zhuhong[JS]	80	E4
Zhuhu[JS]	80	D3
Zhuilijie[YN]	148	J7
Zhuji[HB]	110	F2
Zhuji[YN]	148	J6
Zhuji[ZJ]	84	E3
Zhujia Jian[ZJ]	84	G3
Zhujia[SH]	74	C2
Zhujia[SH]	74	C3
Zhujia[ZJ]	84	D3
Zhujiachang[GZ]	144	G3
Zhujiacun[TJ]	42	A4
Zhujiafang[LN]	62	F3
Zhujiajian[ZJ]	84	G3
Zhujiajiao[SH]	74	C2
Zhujiang Kou[GD]	118	F4
Zhujiaqiao[SH]	74	C2
Zhujiating[HN]	114	D5
Zhujiawo[TJ]	42	B2
Zhujiazhai[SH]	74	C2
Zhujiazhuang[SN]	156	D6
Zhujie[YN]	148	J7
Zhujing[SH]	74	C3
Zhuke[ZJ]	84	D4
Zhukou[AH]	90	D7
Zhukou[FJ]	94	C3
Zhukou[HEN]	106	G3
Zhula[XZ]	152	H4
Zhuli He[JS]	80	E3
Zhuli[HEN]	106	F4
Zhulian[HN]	114	E4
Zhuliang[JX]	98	D4
Zhuliangqiao[HN]	114	E4
Zhulin[JS]	80	E5
Zhulin[YN]	148	J7
Zhulinguan[SN]	156	G7
Zhulong[ZJ]	84	C4
Zhulou[AH]	90	C2
Zhulu[SD]	102	F4
Zhuluke[LN]	62	C3
Zhuma[JS]	80	E3
Zhumadian[AH]	90	C4
Zhumadian[HEN]	106	F5
Zhumushan[HN]	114	D4
Zhungda[XZ]	152	H5
Zhungyai[XZ]	152	I4
Zhuo He[CQ]	132	E4
Zhuogang[HB]	110	I4
Zhuolu[HEB]	48	C3
Zhuoshui[CQ]	132	E4
Zhuoshui[GZ]	144	F2
Zhuotian[FJ]	94	B4
Zhuoyang[FJ]	94	E3
Zhuozhang He[SX]	54	E5

Name	Page	Grid
Zhuozhou[HEB]	48	C4
Zhuozi Shan[NM]	58	G8
Zhuozi[NM]	58	J7
Zhuping[JX]	98	B2
Zhupo[HB]	110	E2
Zhuqiang[NX]	168	C2
Zhuqiao[AH]	90	E5
Zhuqiao[SH]	74	D2
Zhuqiao[SH]	74	D3
Zhusha[CQ]	132	E4
Zhusha[GD]	118	C4
Zhushan[HB]	110	D2
Zhushan[HN]	114	D6
Zhushan[HN]	114	F6
Zhushan[YN]	148	I6
Zhushanqiao[HN]	114	D6
Zhushui He[SD]	102	B4
Zhutai[SD]	102	E3
Zhutan[JX]	98	B3
Zhutang[HEN]	106	F6
Zhuwa[HB]	110	I4
Zhuwangpu[GS]	160	F3
Zhuwo[BJ]	36	B3
Zhuwu[SD]	102	H3
Zhuxi[GZ]	144	G3
Zhuxi[GZ]	144	H3
Zhuxi[HB]	110	C2
Zhuxi[ZJ]	84	E3
Zhuxi[ZJ]	84	E4
Zhuxiang[AH]	90	D4
Zhuxianzhuang[AH]	90	D3
Zhuyang[CQ]	132	B4
Zhuyang[HEN]	106	B3
Zhuyou[SD]	102	F2
Zhuyu[SC]	138	M3
Zhuyuan[CQ]	132	F2
Zhuyuan[FJ]	94	D3
Zhuyuan[SD]	102	E4
Zhuyuan[YN]	148	I6
Zhuzaiyuan[GD]	118	C6
Zhuzang[GZ]	144	F3
Zhuze[JS]	80	E5
Zhuzhai[JS]	80	B2
Zhuzhai[SH]	74	C2
Zhuzhen[JS]	80	D4
Zhuzhou[HN]	114	F5
Zhuzhou[HN]	114	F5
Zhuzhu[XZ]	152	C5
Zhuzhuang Shuiku[HEB]	48	B6
Zhuzhuang[HEN]	106	E5
Zhuzikou[HN]	114	E3
Zi Shui[HN]	114	C6
Zi Zhen[SD]	102	C2
Zibo[SD]	102	E3
Zichang[SN]	156	F3
Zichuan Qu[SD]	102	D3
Zidutai[LN]	62	E2
Zi'er[SC]	138	G7
Zifu[HN]	114	E4
Zigan[SX]	54	D3
Zigar[XZ]	152	J4
Zigê Tangco[XZ]	152	G3
Zigezhuang[BJ]	36	C4
Zigong[SC]	138	J6
Zigui[HB]	110	D4
Zijiao[SD]	102	D2
Zijin Shan[JS]	80	D4
Zijin[GD]	118	H3
Zijin[HB]	110	E2
Zijing Shan[SX]	54	C5
Zijing[GX]	124	H4
Zijingguan[HEB]	48	C4
Zijingling[HB]	110	E4
Zilaiqiao[AH]	90	E4
Zili[JL]	66	C3
Ziliang[HN]	114	D2
Ziliang[HN]	114	E7
Zilijia[YN]	148	D4
Ziling[HEN]	106	D2
Zilingpu[HB]	110	F3
Ziliujing[QH]	164	D3
Ziluo[HI]	128	C2
Ziluo[SX]	54	E4
Zimenqiao[HN]	114	E5
Zin Qu[SC]	138	E4
Zingqi[XZ]	152	H5
Zinkog[SC]	138	E4
Ziqiang[HL]	70	C5
Ziqiu[HB]	110	D4
Zirun[SX]	54	D2
Zishan[HB]	110	F3
Zishi[SC]	138	H5
Zitong He[SC]	138	K4
Zitong[SC]	138	K4
Ziwu He[SN]	156	E7
Ziwu Ling[GS]	160	I4
Ziwu Ling[GS]	160	I5
Ziwu Ling[SN]	156	E5
Ziwu[YN]	148	G6
Zixi[JX]	98	E4
Zixing[HN]	114	F7
Ziya He[HEB]	48	D5
Ziya He[HEB]	42	A4
Ziya Xinhe[HEB]	48	D5
Ziya[TJ]	42	A4
Ziyang Qu[HN]	114	E4
Ziyang[AH]	90	E3
Ziyang[SC]	138	J5
Ziyang[SN]	156	E8
Ziyu[SN]	156	G7
Ziyuan[GX]	124	H1
Ziyun[GZ]	144	E5
Ziyundong Shan[FJ]	94	C4
Ziyunshan Shuiku[JX]	98	C4
Zizhong[SC]	138	J6
Zizhou[SN]	156	G3
Zoco[XZ]	152	B3
Zogang[XZ]	152	J5
Zoigê[SC]	138	H2
Zomdo[SC]	138	E4
Zongbur[SC]	138	G3
Zongda[SC]	138	G3
Zongdian[HEN]	106	F3
Zongjia[QH]	164	J4
Zongluzui[HB]	110	I4
Zongmu[SN]	156	F5
Zongshizhuang[HEB]	48	C6
Zongyang[AH]	90	D6
Zongza[SC]	138	E6
Zoucheng[SD]	102	C4
Zoulang Nanshan[QH]	164	K2
Zouma[CQ]	132	E3
Zouma[CQ]	132	E4
Zouma[HB]	110	D5
Zoumajie[HN]	114	E5
Zoumayi[HEB]	48	B4
Zouping[SD]	102	D3
Zouqiao[JX]	98	C2
Zouxu[GX]	124	F4
Zouzhuang[JS]	80	D2
Zubie[GX]	124	C3
Zudun[FJ]	94	D2
Zuimatan[QH]	164	L5
Zuli He[GS]	160	G4
Zumin[JL]	66	F4
Zunhua[HEB]	48	E3
Zuntan[HI]	128	C2
Zunyi[GZ]	144	E3
Zunyi[GZ]	144	E3
Zuo Jiang[GX]	124	E5
Zuo Xi[JX]	98	B5
Zuo'an[JX]	98	B5
Zuoba[AH]	90	C6
Zuoba[AH]	98	B6
Zuocheng[HEN]	106	F2
Zuodeng[GX]	124	E4
Zuodian[AH]	90	D4
Zuofang[JX]	98	D4
Zuohutan[HL]	70	C4
Zuojia[JL]	66	G3
Zuoli[JX]	98	D2
Zuolong[SN]	156	E8
Zuomu[SX]	54	C5
Zuoquan[SX]	54	E4
Zuowei[HEB]	48	B3
Zuoxi[SN]	156	D8
Zuoxi[ZJ]	84	D5
Zuoyun[SX]	54	D1
Zuozhou[GX]	124	E5
Zurong[GX]	124	D4
Zushan[HEB]	48	G3
Zushimiao[HEN]	106	G6
Zuyan Shan[XJ]	172	J7

Ürümqi
174-175

Yinch
170-1

Xining
166-167

Lanzhou
162-163

Yarlung

Zangbo

Jiang

Lhasa
154-155

Jinsha Jiang

Yalong Jiang

Lancang Jiang

Chengdu
140-141

Kunming
150-151